The Knights of England. A Complete Record From the Earliest Time to the Present Day of the Knights of All the Orders of Chivalry in England, Scotland, and Ireland, and of Knights Bachelors, Incorporating a Complete List of Knights Bachelors Dubbed In...

The Knights
of England

The Knights
of England

A Complete Record from the Earliest Time to the
Present Day of the Knights of all the Orders of
Chivalry in England, Scotland, and Ireland, and
of Knights Bachelors

BY

WM. A. SHAW, Litt.D.

Editor of the Calendar of Treasury Papers at H.M. Record Office ;
Author of the History of the English Church under the
Commonwealth ; Author of the History of Currency ; etc.

INCORPORATING

A Complete List of Knights Bachelors dubbed in Ireland

Compiled by

G. D. BURTCHAELL, M.A., M.R.I.A.

Barrister-at-Law, Office of Arms, Ireland
Author of Genealogical Memoirs of the Members of Parliament
for Kilkenny

Vol. I.

Printed and Published for the

CENTRAL CHANCERY OF THE ORDERS OF KNIGHTHOOD,
Lord Chamberlain's Office, St. James's Palace

SHERRATT and HUGHES

LONDON 1906

CONTENTS

Vol. I.

Vol. II.

Preface.

Preface.

In the compilation of this book the following sources have been used :—

(1) For the ORDER OF THE GARTER the earlier portions of the list are based upon Beltz, Ashmole, Anstis, and Nicolas, primarily of course upon Beltz. But as Beltz includes King Edward III. among the original knights founders, and as I exclude him from their number (on the principle that the Sovereign stands outside the fraternity of knights proper), there is a difference between my enumeration and that of Beltz. I have also adopted a different method of expressing the succession. Where these authorities cease, I have relied entirely on the original records of the Order, viz., the Register of the Garter; Young's MS. Register, and the other collections, volumes, and loose papers of Garter King of Arms. For the very freest access to these records and kindest assistance throughout I am indebted to the courtesy of Sir Alfred Scott Scott-Gatty, Garter King of Arms, and of the Very Reverend Philip P. Eliot, D.D., Dean of Windsor.

(2) The lists of the ORDER OF THE THISTLE are based entirely on the original records of the Order. These records consist of two volumes of registers and a mass of papers. The registers were carefully kept, and the entries fully recorded in them until the year 1830. From that date no further entry was made in them, and it is quite clear that these volumes dropped out of sight until they were re-discovered in the present year. The loose papers consisted of the usual official papers relating to knighthoods, ceremonial, and the statutes of the Order. To facilitate reference to all this material Sir Duncan A. D. Campbell, Bart., Usher of the Green Rod, and Secretary of the Order of the Thistle, most considerately had it all removed from the Heralds' College to the Record Office, and there we have together gone through the whole, sorted, classified and arranged it chronologically, and prepared the whole mass of it for the binder. As so arranged the knighthood papers extend to ten volumes, the official and ceremonial

B

papers to two more volumes, and the statutes fill a final volume. The whole thirteen volumes are now being bound at Sir Duncan's private expense. In giving me access to the papers and his most ungrudging co-operation throughout Sir Duncan has laid me under the greatest obligation.

(3) The lists of the ORDER OF ST. PATRICK were taken directly in the first place from those published by G. E. Cockayne, Esq., Clarenceux in the *Genealogist* in 1888, with MS. additions from that date down to 1902, most kindly furnished to me by Clarenceux himself. This list was then submitted to Sir Arthur E. Vicars, K.C.V.O., Ulster King of Arms, and by him most carefully collated with the original records of the Order, and amended, annotated, and amplified. The kindness of Sir Arthur Vicars in this is enhanced by the fact that he had himself intended to print and prepare for the press just such a list. It is impossible to express sufficient appreciation of such courtesy

(4) For the records of the ORDER OF THE BATH the most diverse and varied sources have been used. For the very earlier periods the ultimate records are the Close Rolls and Wardrobe Accounts, preserved in the Public Record Office. Early in the eighteenth century Anstis surveyed this untravelled ocean of material with a zeal that would put to the blush any modern scholar. The results he published in the appendix to his "Essay upon the Knighthood of the Bath" (1725). This appendix has been the fountain head from which all later writers have drawn their information as to the early Knights of the Bath, and in the main in the present volume I have followed it and the appendix in Vol. III. of Nicolas. Here and there, however, I have gone behind Anstis to the original rolls and wardrobe accounts, with results that convince me that there is a rich harvest awaiting the man who will dare to do over again the work which Anstis did nearly two centuries since. In addition, I have printed from Ashmole the list of Knights of the Bath, made in 34 Edw. I., a list which Anstis, consciously, and Nicolas, unconsciously, omitted to print.

After the wardrobe accounts I have used the better known Heraldic MSS. from the date that these latter commence, viz., the early part of the fifteenth century.

These comprise the following:—

> Harl. MS. 2165, fo. 134 (Bath Knights in 1603).
> Lansdowne MS. 865, fo. 153–7 (Bath Knights temp. James I.
> and Charles I).

Lansdowne MS, 261, fo. 140^b (Bath Knights temp. James I.).

Lansdowne MS. 94, p. 137 (Bath Knights in 1603).

Lansdowne MS. 269, fo. 241 (Bath Knights temp. Charles I.).

Harl. MS. 1462 (Bath Knights in 1603).

Addit. MS. 34217 (Bath Knights in 1625).

Addit. MS. 33053 (Newcastle Papers. Bath Knights about 1752).

Addit. 6303, fo. 38 (Bath Knights in 1661).

Stowe MS. 731 (Bath Knights in 1725).

Addit. 34721 c. (Bath Knights from 1725).

Harl. MS. 41, fos. i., 18, 25 (roughly Bath Knights temp. Edward IV.).

Stowe MS. 1047, fo. 225 (same).

Harl. MS. 1386, fos. 16, 18 (Bath Knights temp. Richard III., Henry IV.).

Lansdowne MS. 255, fo. 450 (Bath Knights temp. Henry VII.).

Harl. 1951 (Bath Knights temp. James I. and Charles I.).

Harl. 6341 and addit. MSS. 6324 to 6328 (Bath Knights from 1725).

Harl. MS. 6166, fo. 130–2 (Bath Knights temp. Queen Mary).

And in addition the following MSS. which will be found more fully described (*infra* pp. viii.—ix.).

Harl. 5177; Harl. 6063; Cotton Claud C. III.; Harl. 1156; Harl. 293; Harl. 1959; Harl. 6069.

The above sources extend from the earliest beginnings of Knighthood by the Bath to the definitive erection of the Order of the Bath by George I. in 1725. From this latter date I have used several parallel sources, viz.: (1) the Gazette; (2) the records of the Home Office as printed in the Calendar of Home Office papers; (3) the appendix to vol. iii. of Nicolas; (4) the records of the Bath as preserved in 12 folio MS. volumes at the War Office which I have collated from their commencement in 1827 to the present day; (5) the MS. records of the Order itself. These records were until his death in the keeping of Sir Albert Woods at the College of Arms. After his death they were, on the formation of the Central Chancery of Knighthood, transferred by Sir Albert's literary executors to the custody of the Central Chancery in the Lord Chamberlain's department at St. James's Palace. I must defer any full statement on them to another occasion. For access to them I am indebted first and foremost to the courtesy of Sir Arthur E. A. Ellis, G.C.V.O.,

Comptroller in the Lord Chamberlain's department and Secretary and Registrar of the Central Chancery of Knighthood. For every assistance in handling them and also in connexion with many other parts of my book I am indebted to the officials of the Lord Chamberlain's department. Similarly for access to the records at the War Office, and for assistance in working them I am indebted to Mr. Leland L. Duncan, M.V.O., of the War Office.

(5) The Lists of the ORDER OF THE STAR OF INDIA are based almost entirely on the *Gazette*, collated with the lists which appeared annually in Burke, Dod, and the Imperial Calendar, and collated also with a list of present living knights, which has been compiled in the Central Chancery of the Orders of Knighthood. The India Office in London does not possess the original register of the Order. If that register exists at all (which I cannot ascertain) it is in the keeping of the Secretary of the Order at Calcutta, and is quite inaccessible to me. Accordingly, I view this list of the Knights of the Star of India with dissatisfaction. Exactly the same sources have been used in compiling, and exactly the same remark applies to, the list of the Knights of the Order of the Indian Empire. In the indexing of the Indian names I have received very kind help from Mr S. G. Smith, of the India Office. With regard to the spelling of Indian names it may be explained that there is as yet no normal standard or uniform spelling agreed upon as a convention. Accordingly the spelling followed throughout the text has been that of the *Gazette*—regardless of the fact that the *Gazette* is often inconsistent with itself. When a convention has been established it will be easy to remedy this blemish. But in the index the spelling of the place names has been made to conform to that fixed in the last edition of the India Office List.

(6) The lists of the ORDER OF ST. MICHAEL AND ST GEORGE are based upon the original records of the Order, in the main upon the Register. This beautifully kept record is preserved at the Colonial Office, and for access to it, as well as for the kindest assistance in handling it, I am indebted to Mr. C. H. Niblett, of the Colonial Office. Occasionally I have taken a brief statement of 'services' from the periodical lists of knights which the Colonial Office has printed. But otherwise, the statements of services contained in the following lists are drawn from the express words of the warrant of appointment, as contained in the Register, or from the *London Gazette* My collation of the register of this Order has destroyed the superstitious reverence which I once felt for the *London Gazette*.

All Englishmen have been bred in the belief that questions of promotion and of precedence are decided entirely by the date of gazetting. It was a rude shock to this belief to find that for more than 50 years of the history of the Order of St. Michael and St. George the dates of the warrants of appointment, as contained in the Register, never agree with the dates of gazetting. In some cases there is a difference even of months. There can surely be no doubt that if the *Gazette* does not agree with the warrant of appointment, then the *Gazette* is wrong. The warrant of appointment is the decisive and final authority. So far as I have been able to trace this matter the superstition with regard to the *London Gazette* has originated in the War Office. As army promotions and decorations are so closely connected, it is very convenient to have a single rule applicable to both, and to count both the one and the other from the date of gazetting. But it is illogical and historically very confusing and deplorable that this rule which has been adopted by the War Office as a mere matter of convenience should, by implication, have been extended to other Orders quite differently circumstanced.

There are two alternative methods which are possible in gazetting. The first is to gazette only the date of appointment—that is, to give to the *Gazette* notice the precise date of the warrant of appointment. The objection to this method is that it leaves undefined the status of the individual for the interim period between the time of his appointment and the time of his investiture. If a man is gazetted as a knight bachelor on the 9th November and is actually dubbed by the King on the 21st December what is his status during the period Nov. 9—Dec. 21? He is certainly not a knight bachelor. He is certainly only an esquire until the very moment that he is dubbed. Then how can he possibly rank for precedence as a knight bachelor from a date at which he is still only an esquire? Or again, take the case of a C. B. who is appointed a K.C.B. on the 24th June and is invested six months later. What is his status during those interim six months. The difficulty may be got over by a royal warrant (bearing even date with the warrant of appointment) containing a grant of the dignity and another royal warrant of same date granting him permission to wear the insignia and to enjoy the precedence of his new rank and the style and title of a knight bachelor of England. But this is a very cumbersome and clumsy way of getting round a perfectly simple difficulty, and it is only excusable if it is applied indifferently to every individual—a supposition which is not true in fact.

The second alternative method is to gazette only the date of investiture (using that term for the moment as inclusive of the ceremony of dubbing) and to reckon all precedence from that date. This would be very precise, and would conform to the common sense conclusion that a man is not a knight till he is dubbed, and that a man cannot be a knight of an order until he has been first dubbed and then invested

There is only one forcible objection to this second method, and that is, that if the mere investiture were gazetted the outside world would miss the historical cause or reason for the conferring of the dignity. But this could be easily overcome by a note of the date of appointment accompanied by a brief description of occasion, or statement of services, to be placed in brackets after the name of each person invested or dubbed.

On these lines a *Gazette* notice of investiture would run thus:—

> 1910, Jan. 20. At St. James's Palace. A.B. invested K.C.B. (having been appointed by warrant dated 1909, Dec. 11, in recognition of services for so and so, or on the occasion of the King's visit to so and so).

In the same classes and on the same day the names would be arranged alphabetically, and there would be no distinction between those who being present were invested or dubbed personally and those who being absent in the colonies or India were invested or knighted by letters patent. This could be secured easily by making the letters patent bear the same date as the particular investiture. I can see no possible objection to making this method a rigorous rule for gazetting all and every species of preferment of honour. It could be open to absolutely no species of question or dispute as regards precedence, and would be an inestimable boon to the historical student. In compiling this book I have been confronted hundreds of times with three conflicting and different dates for one and the same preferment, viz., (1) the date of the warrant of appointment; (2) the date of the gazetting, being subsequent to No. 1; and (3) the date of investiture, being again subsequent to No. 2. This is simply deplorable from the point of view of exact historical science.

(7) The lists of the ORDER OF THE INDIAN EMPIRE have been compiled in exactly the same manner as those of the Star of India

(*supra*, p. iv.), and exactly the same remark applies as to their unsatisfactory nature.

(8) The lists of the ROYAL VICTORIAN ORDER are based upon the original records of the Order as preserved in the Privy Purse Office at Buckingham Palace. For access to these records I am indebted to the courtesy of the Rt. Hon. Sir Dighton Macnaghten Probyn, P.C., G.C.B., G.C.V.O.

(9) The lists of the ROYAL HANOVERIAN GUELPHIC ORDER are the most unsatisfactory in the whole book, for the simple reason that I have been quite unable to find the whereabouts of the original records of that Order. As the Order was a Hanoverian one the presumption was that on the separation of the kingdoms the records would be removed from the old German Chancery at St. James's to Hanover. But Dr. Doebner, Staatsarchivar at Hanover, has kindly informed me that the records which are at present preserved among the archives of the Hanoverian Ministry for Foreign Affairs concern only the German and not the English Knights of that Order. All my enquiries after the records relating to the English Knights of the Order have been fruitless. It is quite clear that Sir Harris Nicolas never saw the original records, so presumably they had vanished even as early as 1842. As a result the lists contained in the following pages have been drawn entirely from the annual "Königlich grossbritannisch-hannoverscher Staatskalendar" known later as the "Hof- und Staats Handbuch für das Königreich Hannover."

These lists have been collated with those given by Nicolas, and with the imperfect lists given in John Frost's "Translation of the Statutes of the Royal Hanoverian Guelphic Order, with a list of Grand Crosses, Commanders and Knights" London, 1831.

None of these authorities give the exact date (year, month, and day) of appointment of the various knights, so that for the present the reader will have to be content with the simple record of the year only and with the general statement that the appointments to the Order were usually made early in the year.

(10) Finally, as to the KNIGHTS BACHELORS. The reader will gather from the introduction (*infra*, p. xlix.), the enormous difficulty attending the compilation of a list of knights bachelors from the earliest times. There has never existed a register of knights bachelors from the earliest times. Reasons are given below p. xlix—li. for the opinion that the register which James I. instituted in 1622 has not been properly kept. In the absence of such a record for the

earlier period I have fallen back upon certain heraldic MSS.   For
the seventeenth century onwards I have relied upon the register at
the Heralds' College, some of the MSS. mentioned below, the *London
Gazette,* and general historical sources.

The heraldic MSS. so employed for the earlier period have been
as follow : —

Harl MS. 5177.   Gives from fo. 102 onwards a note of
knights made in the reigns of Henry VI , Edward IV.,
Richard III., Henry VII., Henry VIII , Edward VI.,
Queen Mary, and Queen Elizabeth, unto the year 1584.
This MS. includes both Knights Bachelors, and Knights
of the Bath.

Harl. MS. 6063   'List of Knights from Edward III. to 1624.'
This MS. also gives both Knights of the Bath and Knights
Bachelors.

Harl. MS. 6062.   Knights made 1603—1636, with an alpha-
betical index, by Sir Rich. St. George.

Cotton MS   Claudius C. III , the well known MS. which
formed the main basis of a great part of Metcalfe's
Book of Knights.   This MS. begins in 1426 and ends on
the 24th July, 1624.   It gives both Knights of the Bath
and Knights Bachelors.

Lansdowne MS 678   A catalogue of all the Knights dubbed
in the reigns of Elizabeth and James I., drawn into an
alphabet.

Harl. MS 6141.   Containing Knights made in 1536, and from
1592 to 1607, March 29th.

Harl. MS. 1156, p. 82.   Knights made at the Siege of Calais
by Edward III.; p. 71-3   Knights of the Bath and
Bachelors temp. Edward VI.; p. 102, Knights temp.
Elizabeth, arranged alphabetically.

Harl. MS. 3320.   Contains Bath Knights temp. James I.,
and from pp 405-56, "a general catalogue of all Bachelor
Knights made by King James, with the place of their
knighthood, the day of the month and year . . . from the
first year of His Majesty's reign to the 2nd day of March,
1616-7, drawn up alphabetically.

Addit. MS. 5482.   Dubbings from 36 Henry VIII. onwards.

Lansd. MS. 870.   Alphabetical catalogue of knights 1625-1646
and a similar but mutilated alphabetical catalogue of
knights 1660-1686.

Addit. MS. 32102.   Knights from 1558-1752.

Harl 983. Alphabetical catalogue of knights temp. Eliz ; knights made by James I.; knights made by Charles I. to 1633.

Harl. MS. 1441. Knights by King James.

Harl. MS. 293. Knights made (roughly) temp. Edward IV. and Richard III , and Knights temp. James I.

Addit. MS. 34766. "Anthony Dering's Alphabet of English Knights, 1550–1660." This British Museum MS. is a copy. The original MS. is preserved in the Office of Arms, at Dublin Castle, and has been kindly collated for this book by Mr. G. D. Burtchaell, of that office. From folio 89 of the British Museum copy I have taken the List of Knights made by Oliver Cromwell.

Harl. 1959. Bath Knights and Knights Bachelors made temp. James I.

Addit. MS. 4784. Knights made in Ireland from 1599 to 1639.

Addit. 4763, pp. 12, 13. Knights made in Ireland temp. Elizabeth.

Harl. MS. 35. Knights by Essex in Ireland.

Addit. 5482. Bath Knights, Henry IV.—Henry VII , and Bachelor Knights, Henry VIII.—Elizabeth.

Harl. 1925 and Lansdowne 94. Knights Bachelors and Bath Knights made in 1603.

Harl. 1408, fo. 58b. Knights made 19 October, 1553, "out of a book in the Office of Arms marked with a letter K, intituled burials in several churches, &c."

Harl 6069, fos 107–12. Knights Bachelors temp. Henry VIII. and Bath Knights temp. Queen Mary.

Harl. MSS. 5801, 5802 (Le Neve's "Pedigrees of Knights") have been printed by the Harleian Society.

Harl. 304, fo. 140b. Knights of the Carpet temp. Henry VII.

Cotton MS. Titus B. VIII. Knights Bachelors temp Eliz.

Cotton MS. Titus B. XI , fo. 21. Knights in 1449.

Ashmolean MS. 1121, fo. 431–67 and fo. 468. Knights Bachelors temp. Henry VII. and Henry VIII.

Ashmolean 805, fo. 1–9. Knights Bachelors temp. Henry VIII.

Ashmolean 840 Knights Bachelors temp. Elizabeth.

Ashmolean 219, p. 133. Names of 58 Knights made in Ireland by the Earl of Essex.

No words of mine can convey an adequate idea of the welter, chaos, confusion and contradictions of these manuscripts The names of Knights are given with every possible variation, the lists disagree perpetually amongst themselves in the order of the names, and the dates assigned to the battles or other occasions on which knighthoods occur, are in the majority of cases totally incorrect. In the attempt to collate these manuscripts and to verify them from extraneous sources, I have spent four painful years, and I regard the outcome as the most distressingly unsatisfactory piece of historical work I have ever set my hand to. I freely invite from everyone who uses the book, corrections, additions, or the indication of fresh sources.

Leaving this region of Cimmerian darkness, the records of dubbings of Knights Bachelors in modern times is almost as distressing in its incompleteness. In the main I have relied on the Register, and the *Gazette* from the year 1667 onwards, employing alongside that work the printed sources which are described *infra*, p. xlix, and the Annual Lists of Knights Bachelors, from the middle of the 19th century, when these appear in the Royal Calendar, the Imperial Calendar, and the Annual Peerages, such as Burke and Dod. For access to the Register of Knights Bachelors which is preserved at the Heralds' College, and which I have collated exhaustively from its first page to the present day, I am indebted to the Chapter of the College. I have also received much help from Chas H Athill, Esq., *Richmond Herald*. For Knighthoods conferred by Letters patent three parallel sources exist—(1) Docquet book of the Crown Office preserved at the House of Lords. This record commences with the close of the sixteenth century, and is in perfect state and practically unbroken in continuity. I have collated it up to the time (1833) when it meets the parallel record at the Home Office. For access to it I am indebted to the courtesy of J. W. Lisle, Esq., of the Crown Office (2) From 1833 onwards the Home Office kept a separate record of all creations conferred by Letters patent. This is styled the Creation Book, and I have carefully collated the record throughout. It is to be understood as representing the initial step in the process of the issue of Letters patent to a grantee. The concluding steps are contained in the Crown Office Docquet Book, so that from the moment that the two series travel together they are to be regarded as duplicate, save for the important fact that the date of entries in the Home Office Creation Book is always that of the Secretary of State's letter setting a grant on foot, whilst the date in the Crown Office record is that of the

Letters patent itself, and is therefore bound to be some days later. For access to the Home Office Creation Book, and for the very kindest help in using it, I am indebted to Mr. A. H. Eggett, of the Home Office. (3) The *Gazette*. As a rule the *Gazette* gives the date, not of the Secretary of State's Letter, but of the Letters patent themselves.

The main drawback to the *Gazette* as an authority for dubbings of Knights Bachelors is that until within the last few months it has never noticed casual dubbings; and failing the *Gazette* I know of no source from which such dubbings can be gathered together except the daily papers—a source which no human being could ever work.

The list of Knights dubbed in Ireland whose names are incorporated seriatim among the Knights Bachelors in this book has been compiled by Mr. G. D. Burtchaell, of the Office of Arms, Ireland. The task of compiling this list has covered several years of exacting toil on Mr. Burtchaell's part, such as can only be properly appreciated by those who have any idea of the intricacy of the subject and of the unsatisfactory nature of all previous compilations of Irish Knights. Mr. Burtchaell's list was intended for separate publication, but on hearing of my book he freely offered to me the result of these years' toil, a generosity of which I have made all too insufficient acknowledgement by putting Mr. Burtchaell's name on the title page of the book. His separate introduction dealing with the sources he has used and the several historical problems connected with the subject will be found on page lv. *infra.*

The two introductions to the Order of the Bath and to Knights Bachelors (*infra* pp. x and xxxvii.) raise questions which will provoke discussion and probably dissent. The theories advanced are put forward without the slightest wilfulness or desire of contentiousness on my part. They are simply offered to scholars for their examination, as suggestions towards the explanation of a really difficult subject. On this subject I have had the benefit of kindliest criticism and assistance from Mr. C. Johnson, of the Public Record Office.

Before concluding, I would fain express my indebtedness to Sir Henry Maxwell-Lyte, Deputy Keeper of the Records, for advice and help in the preparation of this book. I first projected the work as a book of Knights Bachelors merely, and it is entirely due to Sir Henry's advice that I subsequently extended the scope of the book, and included the Orders. In addition, Sir Henry has made many valuable suggestions. But neither he nor Mr. Johnson are in any way responsible for anything put forward in this work.

As to my indebtedness to my wife that is beyond expression. Without her help I could not have accomplished such a task. She has turned over the *Gazette*, page by page, from the very earliest issue to the present day, taking out every knighthood, and has further assisted me in the transcription and indexing of the book, as well as in the stupefying work of collating with the annual publications, such as the Imperial Calendar, Burke and Dod.

WM. A. SHAW.

Introduction.

Introduction.

The Knights of the Garter.

THE Order of the Garter dates from 1348. The opinion that the Order was founded in 1344 is demonstrably incorrect. What happened in 1344 was that Edward III., stirred to emulation by the formation at Lincoln of a voluntary association of knights, determined to found an Order himself. A great tournament was held at Windsor, and at its close, after a stately service in Windsor Chapel, Edward swore a solemn oath that he *would at the expiry of a certain time found a Round Table like King Arthur's Table of 300 knights*.

The account of Adam Murimuth (pp. 231-2) of which the above paragraph is a condensation is indubitably that of an eye witness, and completely disposes of all subsequent accounts like that of Froissart, etc. The outbreak of the French war prevented Edward from immediately carrying out his purpose, but in October, 1347, the king returned to England and at once set about fulfilling his oath. In the joustings which took place between October, 1347, and January, 1348, at Bury, Eltham, and Windsor, certain knights (possibly 12 in number) were chosen on the king's side and received garters and robes from the king's wardrobe. Certain other knights received similar gifts from the Black Prince and may therefore be presumed to have been chosen on his side for the jousting.

At the same time the king was engaged in extending the ecclesiastical foundation of Windsor Chapel. By letters patent of August, 1348, it was erected into a College consisting of a Warden, 23 Canons, and 24 Poor Knights. Whether the first feast of the Order had already taken place at the preceding Easter of 1348 or was deferred until the completion of the ecclesiastical foundation we cannot say. The earliest feast of which we have authentic record is that of Easter, 1350, of which the chronicle of Geoffrey Le Baker (p. 109) gives us so circumstancial an account.

Even in the days of Charles II. the original statutes of the order were no longer extant, and no transcript of them exists of an earlier date than the reign of Henry V. In his appendix to his "Institution, laws and ceremonies of the most noble order of the Garter" Ashmole has printed the earliest known form of these statutes. His text probably represents the ordinances observed by the Order with little change from the days of its institution to the time of Henry VIII. According to these ordinances there were to be 25 original knights together with the Sovereign who was to be the King of England for the time being. The knights were to wear the Garter and the mantle when in the Chapel of St. George, at Chapters, in processions and at feasts of the order. There were to be in addition 26 priests and 26 poor knights. The remaining ordinances concerned the election and installation of the knights, their succession in their stalls, the affixing their escutcheons to their stalls and the ensigns and habits of the Order, viz., the Garter, mantle, surcoat and hood.

To these ensigns was added in the reign of Henry VII. the collar of the order with the image of St. George pendant therefrom. A further addition was made in 1626 when it was ordained at a Chapter at Westminster that the knights should on ordinary occasions wear on the left side of their cloaks, coats and riding cassocks an escutcheon of the cross of St. George within the Garter. This badge was shortly after, in 1629, converted into a star by the addition of a glory or radii issuant from and surrounding the cross.

Additional statutes concerning election of knights, ceremonial, dress, etc., etc., were enacted in the reigns of Henry V. (1418), Henry VI. (1423) and Edward IV. (1477). In the ordinance made at a Chapter held at Windsor during the feast of 1488 it was prescribed that the annals of each Sovereign should be regularly kept and the elections and deaths of the knights duly registered. The reformation of the statutes of the order which was promulgated by Henry VIII. on the 29th May, 1519, was intended for the removal of all ambiguities and doubts touching certain of the ancient statutes. Among other fresh provisions contained in this reformation were one concerning precedence (which was ordered to be according to the companions' seniority in their stalls and not according to their several ranks) and another prescribing the holding of a Chapter for the purpose of filling a vacancy within six weeks of the notification of the death of a knight. The 38th Article of these statutes of Henry VIII. contains a clear prescription as to the weight and fashion of the collar, which is to be of 30 oz. troy weight, and composed of pieces of the fashion of Garters with a double rose between alternately, the one red the other within white. A further reformation of the statutes projected and promulgated by Edward VI. in 1553 was not carried into effect owing to the king's death. Under Elizabeth no material change was made in the Order save for the discontinuance of the annual St. George's feast at Windsor. The subsequent reformations under Charles I. (1636) and Charles II. (1669) are of less importance, but the ordinance of November 19, 1682, concerning the wearing-of-the-riband-is worthy of note. This ordinance decreed 'that whereas King Charles I. had ordained that every knight companion not wearing the mantle should nevertheless wear upon the left side of his under habit or cassock the cross of St. George encompassed with the Garter; and whereas it had also been customary to wear the George in a blue riband over the habit it was now agreed that the riband with the George should be worn over the upper habit beltways over the left shoulder and under the right arm in such a manner as that it might be best seen.'

With the exception of the appointment in 1704, December 20, of a 'formulary of ceremonies to be used at elections of knights' no further change of importance was made in the statutes of the Order until the close of the 18th century. Ever since the year 1567 the annual solemn convention of the knights on the 23rd April, the feast of St. George, had been discontinued. In addition to this Charles II. had obtained in August, 1680, an admission from the Chapter that the will of the Sovereign was the law of the Order—an admission which ran counter to all the past history of the Order. The drastic changes which were made in the Order in 1786 were based upon these revolutionary ideas. George III. wished to accelerate the reception of his four younger sons into the Order and to bestow three other garters which happened not to be vacant. He therefore in a chapter held at St. James's 2nd June, 1786, promulgated a new statute dated 1786, May 31, decreeing that the sons of the Sovereign should be excepted from (and therefore should be additional to) the original number of 25 knights as decreed by the ancient statutes. The creation of these supernumerary knights necessitated an alteration in the arrangement of the stalls in St. George's Chapel. Nineteen years later a further enlargement of the Order took place. By a new statute dated 1805, January 10, and promulgated at a chapter held at St. James's 1805, January 17, it was decreed that the Order should consist of the

Sovereign and 25 knights companions, together with such lineal descendants of George II. as had been elected or thereafter might be elected; the Prince of Wales always excepted as 'a constituent part of the original constitution, he having been included in the extending statute of 1786, May 31. This precedent was again followed in 1831 when a new statute dated 1831, June 28, and promulgated at a Chapter at Windsor on the 20th of August still further enlarged the Order by including in it as extra or supernumerary to the original 25 knights companions such lineal descendants of George I. as had been or might thereafter be elected into the order. In the following pages the extra knights created under these statutes will be found marked as supernumerary. Where any of the supernumerary knights were subsequently absorbed into the original number of 25 knights companions as any of the stalls of these latter fell vacant, the proper succession is stated in the list below. With regard to the marginal dates given in the following list they are to be understood as the date of election up to the middle of the 19th century and, unless otherwise stated, from the middle of the 19th century the dates are those of the letters patent dispensing with all ceremonies of installation. If the date of investiture and installation is identical with that of election it is in some cases not separately mentioned—otherwise the separate dates are given. As there is no record of the precise date of election existing prior to the reign of Henry VI. the dates prior to that reign are mostly based upon deduction and are not to be taken as precise. They represent the date of the ascertained death or the last historic mention of the predecessor in the stall of the elected knight. Theoretically, according to the 20th statute of the order, an election in the room of a deceased knight should take place within six weeks of the notification of such decease. The inference therefore would be that where the marginal date gives the time of decease of a predecessor knight, the actual election should be dated only a few weeks later. But this inference is by no means a safe one to follow as there are many recorded instances of stalls being kept vacant for a much longer period. Such doubtful dates will be found marked in the following list by the use of the word 'after' in the margin. Theoretically the decisive or distinctive date should be, throughout, the date of installation [or of letters patent dispensing with installation] not that of election [nomination] or investiture. The 13th statute of the Order prescribes that stranger [or foreign] knights shall within seven months of the reception of the insignia send a sufficient deputy to be installed as their proxy. If they send not such proxy and send no sufficient excuse the election then to be void. If they send sufficient excuse then a further four months' time is granted, and if the proxy be not sent within those four months then the election to be wholly void. In the case of knights not foreigners installation was according to the 21st statute to take place 'in all good diligence' after the reception of the Garter, and if it did not take place within 12 months thereafter, then the election was to be void.

But as it is not possible in the earlier centuries of the history of the Order to state the dates of installation systematically I have of necessity followed the dates as printed by Beltz. From the point where Beltz's lists cease I have adhered rigorously to the date of installation [or of the letters patent dispensing with installation]. In another matter I have ventured to vary from Beltz. He includes Edward III. among the original number of knights and numbers the original or founder knights 1—26 accordingly, I exclude the Sovereign from the number of knights and accordingly number the original or founder knights 1—25. There will therefore be found a difference of one unit all the way through between my enumeration and that of Beltz. With this exception I have preserved Beltz's order throughout because of the authority attaching to his book. But for this I should have been strongly tempted to alter the relative precedence or enumeration of two or three of the knights where important corrections of date have been made by later research (*See* numbers 258-9). The only remaining point to notice (and it is a most important one) is that from the early part of the 19th century all foreign members of the Order are regarded as supernumerary or extra; whereas previously they had been regarded as ordinary knights or constituent members within the limits of the original number of 25.

The recognition of foreign potentates as supernumerary knights seems to have been of gradual growth. In the case of Alexander I. of Russia in 1813 he was elected a supernumerary knight by special statute. This election 'formed a precedent for subsequent similar [supernumerary] nominations of foreign potentates who previously had been elected only when a vacancy occurred. . . . After this period the missions [for conferring investiture on foreign potentates] appear to have been conducted with greater ceremony and the foreigners thus admitted into the order were for the first time reckoned as supernumerary knights.'

With regard to regulation of stalls, it is clear that up to the close of the 18th century the knights succeeded to their stalls according to seniority within the Order and without regard to their rank outside the Order. For instance, a knight, a subject of the Sovereign, might succeed to the Prince's stall. But when, from about the commencement of the 19th century, foreign royalties began to be looked upon as extra knights outside the original number of 25, it became necessary to revise the old customary regulation of the stalls. Accordingly a statute dealing with this subject and dated 1805, Feb. 2, was read and promulgated in a chapter of the Order on St. George's Day, 1805. This statute provided that the stalls of princes of the blood should be placed according to their rank nearest that of the Sovereign; that [foreign] emperors and kings should have their stalls next to those of the blood royal according to their elections and installations; [foreign] sovereigns and princes similarly immediately next to emperors and kings, "and that all other Knights Companions subjects and strangers not of the dignity abovementioned shall be installed in the lowest stalls so that they may be translated to the higher [as vacated by death] according to their seniority in the Order and the ancient practice of the same."

This statute had the effect of introducing the arrangement of the stalls which exists at the present day, viz., that of devoting the stalls to the east of the chapel (to the left of the Sovereign's stall) to the royalties, and those to the west of the chapel (the right-hand side of the Sovereign's stall) to the 25 Knights Companions.

The Most Ancient and Most Noble Order of the Thistle.

THE legendary antiquity generally ascribed by perfervid Scotsmen to the Order of the Thistle is unsupported by any historical evidence. The adoption of the Thistle as a royal badge does not appear to date much earlier than the reign of James III. of Scotland, and no collar, either of knighthood or even of the royal livery existed in Scotland before 1539 in the reign of James V. The mere fact that this king himself wore a collar composed partly of thistles and that such a collar with the cross or effigy of St. Andrew attached was placed round his achievement does not prove the existence of an Order composed of knights on whom the ensign had been bestowed by the sovereign. There is no evidence that any person received the ensign from the sovereign until the reign of James VII., or that any person prior to that date was styled a knight of the Order of St. Andrew or of the Thistle.

The warrant of James II. of date 1687, May 29, though it purports only the revival of the Order, should be regarded as having in reality *instituted* the Order as such. The patent which was prepared in pursuance of this warrant never passed the Great Seal, and the statutes which were annexed to it have only the authority of the king's signet. According to these statutes the Order was to consist of 12 knights with the sovereign. The Chapel of the Order was to be the Royal Chapel of Holyrood House.

On the 6th June of the same year King James nominated 8 knights, of whom 4 were invested at Windsor Castle on that day. The others being in Scotland, took the oath, were knighted and received the ensigns at Edinburgh shortly after. All the knights received letters of dispensation from instalment. The Order remained in abeyance during the reign of William and Mary, but was revived by queen Anne by letters patent under the great Seal of Scotland dated 1703, Dec. 31. On the same day she also ordained the statutes of the Order which, with slight alterations, still obtain. The only material alteration in these statutes was that of 1827, May 8, when the number of knights was permanently increased from 12 to 16. By the statutes of queen Anne it was provided that before any one can be admitted into the Order of the Thistle he must be a knight bachelor. Strangely enough there is no provision in the statutes for the precedency of the knights, either collectively or individually.

George III   1783.

The Most Illustrious Order of St. Patrick.

THE Most Illustrious Order of St. Patrick was instituted by king George III. by warrant dated 1783, Feb. 5. The statutes of the order were signed on the 28th Feb. and the first investiture held on the 11th March following. As originally constituted the order consisted of the Sovereign, the Grand Master (the Lord Lieutenant for the time being), and fifteen knights.

At the Coronation of George IV., 1821, July, six extra knights were nominated with the intention that they should be gradually absorbed into the ordinary knights in the ordinary way of succession. Similarly at the Coronation of William IV. in November, 1831, four extra knights were nominated.

The ceremonial of installation was abrogated by royal warrant of 1871, July 14. The ceremonial of investiture was formerly performed in the Cathedral Church at Dublin, and the old banners still hang there. Afterwards it was performed in St. Patrick's Hall, Dublin Castle, or in the Council Chamber, Dublin Castle, or at Windsor, or even occasionally dispensed with.

On the 24th January, 1833, it was enacted that the number of knights should be fixed at 22, the five extraordinary knights then existing forming part of that number.

Since the royal warrant of 1833, Jan. 30, the installation of all knights in ordinary has been dispensed with.

In 1839 queen Victoria authorised each successive Grand Master to retain and wear the Star, Riband, and Badge of the order after he had ceased to be Chief Governor of Ireland.

The Most Honourable Order of the Bath.

THE Order of the Bath as a distinct Order—that is, as composed of a certain and particular brotherhood of knights with statutes, insignia and ceremonies peculiar to them, and with a proper succession of knights within the fraternity by means of election—dates only from the reign of George I. It was erected by that sovereign in 1725. Between this Order of the Bath as so erected by George I. and the older ceremony or formality of creating knights by the process of bathing and investing there is no genuine historical connexion whatever. The preamble to the letters patent of George I., dated 1725, May 18, which erected the Order recites as follows : " Whereas our royal predecessors upon divers wise and honourable considerations have on occasion of certain august solemnities conferred with great state upon their royal issue male, the princes of the blood royal, several of their nobility, principal officers and other persons distinguished by their birth, quality and personal merit, that degree of knighthood which hath been denominated the knighthood of the Bath : we being moved by the same considerations do hereby declare our royal intention not only to *re-establish and support the said honour of knighthood in its former lustre and dignity, but to erect the same into a regular military order.*"

The terms used in the concluding sentence, which I have italicised, aptly describe the difference existing between the properly constituted order existing from 1725 onward and the mere form of ceremonial knighthood which had been practised or had been in use prior to that date.

As to this latter its origin is lost in immemorial obscurity. Some highly elaborate form of knighthood or of knightly investiture, probably at first purely secular but afterwards partly secular, partly religious in its ceremonial, existed among the Franks, and as derived from them was in use among the Anglo Saxons as early at least as the reign of Alfred, if we may trust the testimony of William of Malmesbury. This author's description of king Alfred's knighting of his grandson Athelstan mentions only the bestowal of a scarlet

mantle, a jewelled girdle and a Saxon sword. There is no word of
any vigils or bathing. The importation of the idea of these latter
ceremonies must be due to the church. Prior to the Norman conquest
ecclesiastics had been accustomed to make knights on their own
account and had elaborated a ceremonial purely in the interests of
the church. The knight who was made by this religious ceremonial
solemnly entered the church, offered his sword on the altar and took
it up again from the altar with a vow to devote himself and it to
God and the church. There can be no doubt that in such a
transaction the motive of the church was a worldly one. It was the
commencement of the process of subinfeudation of knightly
retainers by the church. And it was this which was forbidden by
the 17th of Anselm's Canons at Westminster in 1102 "That abbots
do not make soldiers." For the purpose which the church had in
mind in such a transaction the mere ceremonial of knighthood was
itself simply an added incident. But it is this ceremonial which
forms the only conceivable source or origin of the later secular
investiture of the Bath. It was doubtless to the interests of the
church to increase the solemnity of the ceremonial and it is possible
to conjecture the lines on which development would take place.
Firstly, there would be added to the ceremony of the devotion of the
sword on the altar the further ceremony of fasting and vigils with
the object of deepening the religious impression in the mind of the
aspirant for knighthood; and secondly, there would be added the
further step or ceremony of washing or purifying the body or person
itself as a further preparation for knighthood. Reconstructing
conjecturally the routine of the fully-developed ecclesiastical
ceremony of knighthood it would commence with the purification of
the knight's person by bathing and then would follow the purification
of his soul by fasting and vigils and the solemn offering of his sword
on the altar. I offer this as pure conjecture, for there is no record of
any such complete ecclesiastical ceremonial of knighthood, and it is
open to one very damaging objection, viz., that such an ecclesiastical
ceremonial must have developed itself very early, at any rate before
1102, when abbots were forbidden to make knights,* and between this
date and the first specific mention of bathing in the account of
secular knightings there is a gap of two centuries or more. But the

---

* The prohibition is contained in the 17th of Anselm's Canons issued in 1102 at Westminster. It has
been assumed by all editors of these Canons and by Ashmole and other heraldic authorities that the term
'facere milites' here employed means to dub soldiers. Might it not refer, as I have suggested in the text
to the creation of knightly tenures by sub-infeudation?

general drift of the conjecture, viz., that the idea of the ceremonials of vigils and washing was derived from the church is, I think, irresistible. There is no other source from which such an idea could be derived. I take it therefore as possible that such portions of the above ecclesiastical ceremonial as the secular power found suitable to itself it adopted from the church, and these portions are vigils and bathing. In this way, probably before the 12th century the old purely secular Frankish form of knighthood by investiture with spurs, girdle, mantle and sword, had become a partly religious, partly secular form in which the secular investiture with the sword and spurs was preceded by the religious ceremonials of bathing and vigils. Putting aside the often quoted passage from Ingulphus as quite anachronistic and untrustworthy, the first recorded instance of such a ceremonial is the knighthood, in 1127, by king Henry I. of England, of his prospective son-in-law Geoffrey, son of Fulk, count of Anjou.

> "Tota dies illa in gaudio et exultatione expenditur. Illucescente die altera *balneorum usus uti tyrocinii suscipiendi consuetudo expostulat* paratus est. Post corporis ablutionem ascendens de balneorum lavacro, bysso retorta ad carnem induitur, cyclade auro texta supervestitur (hereupon follows a long description of his clothing and of his investing with spurs, shield, spear and sword).

This account, if trustworthy, makes clear that the process of bathing was in use by the beginning of the 12th century. Like the equally specific account in Ingulphus it seems to me suspicious partly because it is, if anything, too specific, and partly because it stands so entirely alone. Although there are so many references in English official records to the issue of robes and bed furniture for the divers ceremonial knighthoods, the actual use of the bath itself in so many words is not specified until the 1st year of the reign of Edward III. The earliest existing rolls of the pipe and wardrobe accounts contain quite sufficient references to the issue of robes for these ceremonial knighthoods, but it is very noticeable how the type of the entry or reference in these records gradually expands as if the ceremonial itself was gradually expending or developing. For instance, in the earliest existing Pipe Roll that of 2 Henry II., the type of entry is as follows :—

> et Ade de la Mare £13. 6s. 8d. ad faciendum se militem; per breve Regis.

et Will: de Doura £13. 6s. 8d. per breve Regis ad faciendum se
militem.

et pro armis et apparatu ad duos milites faciend.

. In each of these cases the sheriff deducts the money item in
question from his charge as so much paid by him by command of the
king. The royal writs commanding the sheriff to make such
provision were entered on the Close Rolls.

> Johannes Rex, etc. Vicecomiti Southampton salutem. Praecipi-
> mus tibi quod facias habere Thomae Sturmy valletto nostro
> unam robam de' scarletto cum quadam penula de byssis et
> aliam robam de viridi vel burnetta, et unam sellam, et unum
> par loranorum et capam ad pluvium et unam culcitram et
> unum par lintheorum quando ipse fiet miles. Et quod in his
> posueris computabitur tibi ad scaccarium. (18 July, 1204.)

Anstis in the appendix to his "Observations Introductory to an
Historical Essay upon the Knighthood of the Bath" gives many in-
stances of such briefs extracted from the Close Rolls.

By the time of John the entries in the Pipe Roll had similarly
become more specific than the brief entries quoted above from the
Pipe Roll of Henry II.

> Et pro tribus robis de scarletto et tribus de viridi et duobus balde-
> kinis et una culcitra et aliis necessariis ad faciendum unum
> militem. xxxiii¹.

Later entries mention the bed (lectum militarem), the bed-
coverings (lectum cum matricio co-opertorio et culcitra), the capa
mentioned in 6 John as *ad pluvium* but not definitely stated to be
pro vigilia sua until 19 Edward II., and finally the bath itself (tria
linthementa pro iisdem balneis, 1 Ed. III.).

It is by no means to be inferred that the bath was not in use
before the date of this last entry. Nothing is more perilous than the
argument from silence in the matter of such details or items. But I
conceive it possible that the scattered data given above may furnish
in rough outline a sketch of the growth of the ceremonial form of
knighthood, viz., from an investiture preceded by vigils (in use say
in the time of John) to an investiture preceded by bathing as well as
vigils (in full use by the time of Edward III.). It may be some

slight confirmation of this view that in the account of the creation of knights in 1306 (Flores Historiarum iii. p. 131) mention is only made of the vigils and investiture. The account is so circumstancial that it is hardly credible the chronicler could have omitted so striking an item as the bathing had that been in use.

> . . . Rex fecit proclamari ut quotquot tenerentur fieri milites . . . adessent apud Westmonasterium . . . admissuri singuli omnem ornatum militarem praeter equitaturam, de regia Garderoba. Confluentibus itaque ccc. juventibus . . . distribuebantur purpura, byssus, syndones, cyclades auro textae . . . Ipsa quoque nocte in Templo praedicti tyrones . . . suas vigilias faciebant . . . Die autem crastino cinxit Rex filium suum baltheo militari in palatio suo . . . Princeps autem . . . super magnum altare . . . socios suos cinxit.

Whatever opinion is formed as to the above conjecture it is clear that if not by the reign of Henry I. or of John, at any rate by that of Edward III. the full ceremonial of knighthood by the bath was in use. The only noticeable change which the institution underwent from this date onwards was that it became gradually confined more and more to great and splendid occasions such as coronations, royal marriages, etc.; whilst the mere knighthood of individual persons was left to a simpler ceremony which was coming into vogue, viz., that of dubbing merely. The difference between these two forms or ceremonies of knighthood is so characteristic as to be instantly recognisable in the official records. In the first place no preparation whatever was needed for the knighting by the sword or by dubbing simply, so that where the records state that such and such knights were summoned to prepare themselves for knighthood and to receive from the Great Wardrobe such and such robes in order thereto, it is at once conclusive proof that the form of knighthood here intended was the highly dignified ceremonial of the Bath. Any formal notification by royal brief directing the recipient to prepare himself for knighthood, or any references whatever to the bestowal of robes from the Great Wardrobe are to be taken as signifying this form of ceremonial. In the second place in cases where the king determined to summon any large body of his tenants in chief to assume knighthood, he caused the summons to be made by proclamation through the sheriffs of the counties. The meaning of this summons will be treated of below in the introduction to the list of knights bachelors. The point to notice is that it was an entirely different procedure which was adopted when the King determined to call on any person or persons to undergo the ceremony of knighthood by the Bath. In this latter case the King sent his royal brief direct to the person in question, or in case that person was a minor then the writ was addressed to his father or guardian. A good instance of an order for such briefs is given in Rymer x., p. 256. With regard to this particular instance it may be at once premised that it was the custom at coronations to create knights by both ceremonies, viz., knights of the Bath by the elaborate ceremonial of the Bath, and knights bachelors by the mere instantaneous ceremony of dubbing. It sometimes happens that the list of such creations at a particular coronation does not distinguish the two species of knighthood. In such a case the occurrence of any royal brief of summons to a recipient or his guardian is a sufficient guide to enable us to determine that such a knight was made by the Bath. The absence of such a writ would, on the face of it, point to the conclusion that the knight in question was simply dubbed a knight bachelor.

The instance referred to in Rymer, above, is a very apt one in point. In 1426 Henry VI. was himself dubbed a knight by his uncle the Regent, John duke of Bedford. On this occasion some 44 persons received the honour of knighthood, but of these only 25 received royal briefs summoning them to prepare themselves for the ceremony. Only these 25, therefore, whose names are given by Rymer are to be considered knights of the Bath, the remaining 19 are knights bachelors (*see infra*, pp. 130–2).

The various high occasions on which knights of the Bath were created will be found stated in the lists *infra*. From this it will be seen that the last occasion on which the ceremonial was employed was after the Restoration, when Charles II. created 66 knights of the Bath prior to his coronation. No such creation or ceremony has ever since been used in England.

From this brief resumé it will have been gathered (1) that all through the middle ages the knighthood of the Bath was simply a form of ceremony of knighthood; (2) that as a consequence there was no Order of the Bath: there was simply a ceremony of bathing which was applicable to any number of individuals and at any time without regard to such rules of election and succession as would have governed the creations if there had been a properly constituted Order of the Bath; (3) that the highly dignified and completed form of ceremonial of the Bath was only gradually elaborated and was possibly not complete until the reign of Edward III; (4) that from the earliest times to the reign of Henry III. the only form of knighthood in use was that ceremonial form which in its fullest development was the ceremony of the Bath, but that from the 13th or 14th century at least a simpler form of creation by dubbing was adopted for less dignified occasions; and (5) that from the moment this new and simpler form of knighthood was evolved the older and more ceremonial form was reserved for occasions and events of great state and dignity, such as coronations, etc. As has been already stated between this form of ceremonial merely and the Order of the Bath as established by George I. in 1725, the only historical connexion existing is that of the conscious or deliberate imitation by George I. of an extinct ceremonial.

An objection may be made to the above exposition of the early status of the form of knighthood of the Bath. On the 4th Feb., 1625–6, the earl of Arundel and Surrey, earl marshal of England, issued an order by command of the King requiring all knights of the Bath to "continually wear the ensign of that Order about their necks as a mark of honour, and that they may not want any due unto them I am to publish that knights of the Bath and their wives are of right without question to have precedency before all knights bachelors and their wives." (Anstis, "Essay," appendix p. 79).

So far as I know this regulation stands alone, and beyond the fact that it instituted the wearing of a badge it affords no proof whatever of the existence of an Order in the proper and sole sense of the term. It simply marks the superior dignity attributed to knighthood by the Bath over mere knighthood by dubbing.

The royal letters patent erecting the military Order of the Bath were dated 1725, May 18, and the statutes of the Order were issued from the court of George I., at Hanover, on the 16th November (O.S.) of the same year.

Under those statutes the Order was to consist of the Sovereign, a Prince of the royal blood, a Great Master, and 35 other companions, "and this number shall never be augmented." The king's grandson, prince William, was nominated first and principal companion.

The seventh statute enjoins that the Prince's Chamber in the palace of Westminster should be the chapter room of the order, and that elected knights should spend the evening of their first entry there and observe the full ritual of the Bath, viz., as follows:—

"His Esquires shall not permit the elected to be seen abroad [*i.e.*, out of the Prince's Chamber] during the evening of his first entry, but shall send to the proper barber to make ready a bathing vessel handsomely lined on the inside and outside with linen, having cross hoops over it, covered with tapestry for defence against the cold air of the night; and a blanket shall be spread on the floor by the side of the bathing vessel. Then the beard of the elected being shaven and his hair cut, the Esquires shall acquaint the Sovereign or Great Master that it being the time of even-song the elected is prepared for the bath; whereupon some of the most sage and experienced knights shall be sent to inform the elected and to counsel and direct him in the order and feats of chivalry: which knights being preceded by several Esquires of the king's household making all the usual signs of rejoicing and having the minstrels playing on several instruments before them shall forthwith repair to the door of the Prince's Chamber while the Esquires Governors [*i.e.*, the squires of the knight-elect] upon hearing the music shall undress the elected and put him into the bath: and the musical instruments then ceasing to play these grave knights entering into the chamber without any noise shall severally one after the other kneeling near the bathing vessel with a soft voice instruct the elected in the nature and course of the Bath, and put him in mind that for ever hereafter he ought to keep his body and mind pure and undefiled: and thereupon the knights shall each of them cast some of the water of the bath upon the shoulders of the elected and then retire, while the Esquires Governors shall take the elected out of the bath and conduct him to his pallet bed which is to be plain and without curtains; and as soon as his body is dry they shall clothe him very warm in consideration that he is to watch that whole night: and therefore they shall then array him in a robe of russet having long sleeves reaching down to the ground and tied about the middle with a cordon of ash-coloured and russet silk, with a russet hood like to an hermit, having a white napkin hanging to the cordon or girdle; and the barber having removed the bathing vessel the experienced knights shall again enter and from thence conduct the elected to the chapel of king Henry VII. (where it is our pleasure that the religious ceremonies

relating to the Order shall for the future be constantly per-
formed), and they being there entered preceded by all the
Esquires making rejoicings and the minstrels playing before
them, during which time wine and spices shall be laid ready
for these knights, the Elected and Esquires Governors,
and the elected having returned thanks to these knights for
the great favour of their assistance, the Esquires Governors
shall shut the chapel door permitting none to stay therein save
the elected, one of the prebendaries of the church of West-
minster to officiate, two chandlers to take care of the lights
and the verger of the church : where the elected shall perform
his vigils during the whole night in orisons and prayers to
Almighty God, having a taper burning before him held by one
of his Esquires Governors who at the reading of the Gospel
shall deliver it into the hands of the elected. Which being
read he shall deliver it to one of his Esquires Governors, who
shall hold it before him during the residue of divine service ;
and when the day breaks and the elected hath heard matins
or morning prayer the Esquires Governors shall reconduct
him to the Prince's Chamber and lay him in bed and cast over
him a coverlet of gold lined with corde."

The remainder of these statutes prescribes in equal detail the
ceremony of awakening and clothing the knight-elect and of con-
ducting him to the sovereign to be dubbed and invested.

The eighth statute prescribed the details of the ceremony of
installation at the chapel of Henry VII. at Westminster. The tenth
prescribed that an annual convention of the Order should be held on
the 20th of October. The twelfth prescribed the badge or ensign
(three imperial crowns or, within the ancient motto *tria juncta in
uno* pendant to a red ribbon placed obliquely over the right shoulder
to the left side), and article seven prescribed the robes—surcoat of
red tartarin lined and edged with white sarsenet, white girdle with-
out ornament, coif or bonnet, and mantle of the same silk and colour
as the surcoat and so lined, fastened about the neck with a lace of
white silk having a pair of white gloves hanging at the end thereof
and on the left shoulder the ensign of the Order.

By sign manuals of date 1725, June 1, and November 16 George I.
prescribed the details of the collar and banner of the Order and by
sign manual of 1727, April 20, he further prescribed that in case of

invasion or rebellion the knights should maintain four men at arms for a period not exceeding 42 days.

These statutes of George I. remained practically unaltered until the reign of George III. On the 8th May, 1812, a royal warrant was issued providing that the number of knights should remain as fixed by George I., but that extra knights could be created without limitation of number, the said extra knights to succeed the knights companions on decease and by seniority. This measure was taken in order to meet the merits of officers engaged in the Napoleonic war, but at the conclusion of the war this measure was considered insufficient and the alternative step was taken of enlarging the order itself.

By royal warrant under the sign manual dated 1815, Jan. 2, the order was reconstituted and made to consist of three classes.

(1) Knights Grand Cross, who were divided into "military" and "civil," the whole number never to exceed 72, and of these the "civil" class limited to 12.

(2) Knights Commanders: confined in number to 180 exclusive of foreign officers holding British Commissions, of whom 10 might be appointed.

(3) Companions.

Four days later, Jan. 6, it was provided that fifteen knights commanders chosen from the officers in the service of the East India Company might be appointed in addition to the above specified number of knights commanders.

No further alteration of moment was made in the order until the reign of Victoria, when the last great change or remodelling was made. By new statutes dated 1847, May 15, the Order was thrown open as a reward for civil as well as military or naval services. All the three classes of the Order were sub-divided into two divisions, viz., military and civil. These statutes are embodied in letters patent dated 1847, April 14. The letters patent themselves are published in the "Gazette" of date 25th May, 1847, and the new statutes (37 in all) are subjoined in detail. Statute No. 5 fixed the membership as follows:—

1st class G.C.B.	......	military 50	...	civil	25	...	total	75
,,	K.C.B.	,, 102	..	,,	50	...	,,	152
,,	C.B.	,, 525	...	,,	200	...	,,	725

Total		952

D

These numbers to be exclusive of the Royal family, distinguished foreigners and foreign officers. In addition the power was reserved of increasing the number on special occasions. Statute No. 16 provided that on the occasion of investiture each individual of the 1st or 2nd class should first be knighted if he were not previously a knight.

By a new statute dated 1850, July 11, the membership was increased as follows (in order to admit officers of the commissariat and medical branches of the army and navy, and those of the East India Company into the military divisions of the 2nd and 3rd classes):— viz.: ordinary military members of the 2nd and 3rd classes increased from 627 to 660, thus increasing the total membership to 985.

By new general statutes dated Windsor, 1859, Jan. 31 the membership was fixed as follows:—

1st class	G.C.B.	......	military	50	...	civil	25	...	total 75
2nd „	K.C.B.	......	„	110	...	„	50	...	„ 160
3rd „	C.B.	....	„	550	...	„	200	...	„ 750

Total 985

Besides honorary members (foreigners), the number of these latter being unlimited. By the 4th of these statutes the Prince Consort was appointed Great Master and 1st or principal G.C.B.

By supplementary statutes dated 1861, June 24, the membership was fixed as follows:—

1st class	G.C.B.	......	military	50	...	civil	25	...	total 75
2nd „	K.C.B.	......	„	123	...	„	60	...	„ 183
3rd „	C.B.	....	„	690	...	„	200	...	„ 890

Total ... ..., 1148

By supplementary statute dated 1877, June 19, the membership was fixed as follows:—

1st class	G.C.B.	......	military	50	...	civil	25	...	total 75
2nd „	K.C.B.	......	„	123	...	„	80	...	„ 203
3rd „	C.B.	....	„	690	...	„	250	...	„ 940

Total 1218

By supplementary statute dated 1881, May 10, the membership was fixed as follows :—

1st class G.C.B.	military	50	... civil	25	... total	75
2nd „ K.C.B.	„	125	... „	80	... „	205
3rd „ C.B.	„	705	... „	250	... „	955

Total 1235

By supplementary statute dated 1886, May 19, the membership was fixed as follows :—

1st class G.C.B.	military	55	... civil	25	... total	80
2nd „ K.C.B.	„	145	... „	80	... „	225
3rd „ C.B.	„	705	... „	250	... „	955

Total 1260

By supplementary statute dated 1887, June 20, the membership was fixed as follows :—

1st class G.C.B.	military	55	... civil	27	... total	82
2nd „ K.C.B.	„	145	... „	86	... „	231
3rd „ C.B.	„	705	... „	264	... „	969

Total 1282

By supplementary statute dated 1890, Nov. 26, the membership was fixed as follows :—

1st class G.C.B.	military	55	... civil	27	... total	82
2nd „ K.C.B.	„	145	... „	90	... „	235
3rd „ C.B.	„	705	... „	270	... „	975

Total 1292

By supplementary statute dated 1892, Mar. 29, the membership was fixed as follows :—

1st class G.C.B.	military	55	... civil	27	... total	82
2nd „ K.C.B.	„	145	... „	93	... „	238
3rd „ C.B.	„	705	... „	273	... „	978

Total 1298

By supplementary statute dated 1895, May 18, the membership
was fixed as follows : —

1st class G.C.B.	military	55	. .	civil	27	...	total	82
2nd „ K.C.B.	„	145	...	„	100	...	„	245
3rd „ C.B.	„	705	...	„	283	...	„	988

Total 1315

By supplementary statute dated 1896, Apr. 10, the membership
was fixed as follows : —

1st class G C.B.	military	55	...	civil	27	...	total	82
2nd „ K.C.B. ...	„	145	...	„	105	..	„	250
3rd „ C B	„	705	...	„	283	...	„	988

Total 1320

By supplementary statute dated 1897, June 19, it was provided that
members admitted into the Order in commemoration of the Jubilee
of the 60th year of Queen Victoria's reign should be additional
members "and shall not now or hereafter be included within the
number of the ordinary members" of each respective class, but to
have rank and precedence in each respective class according to the
dates of their respective appointments.

By supplementary statute dated 1897, June 22, it was ordered that
a general officer of the Royal Marines should be an additional G.C.B.
military

By supplementary statute dated 1897, June 22, H.R.H. the prince
of Wales was appointed Great Master of the Order.

By supplementary statute dated 1900, July 21, it was ordered that
members admitted into the Order in connexion with the war in
South Africa shall be additional members within the respective
classes with rank and precedence according to the dates of their
respective appointments.

By supplementary statute dated 1901, Feb. 26, H.R.H. Arthur
William Patrick Albert, duke of Connaught, was appointed Great
Master of the Order.

By supplementary statute dated 1901, July 17, the membership was fixed as follows:—

1st class G.C.B.	...	military 55	..	civil 27	...	total 82
2nd „ K.C.B.	....	„ 145	...	„ 108	..	„ 253
3rd „ C.B.	....	„ 705	..	„ 298	...	„ 1003

Total *1338

By supplementary statute dated 1902, Apr. 26, it was ordained that members admitted into the civil division of the 1st, 2nd and 3rd classes of the Order in commemoration of the coronation of king Edward VII. should be additional and should not now or hereafter be included in the number of the ordinary members of each class, but have rank and precedence according to the dates of their respective appointments.

The enormous extension in the numbers of the Order, which has been sketched in the above brief resumé of the statutes has of necessity gone hand in hand with similar extending changes in the matter of qualification of membership. The qualification for a G.C.B. (military) at the present moment is the actual holding of a commission in the army of, or above, the rank of Major General, or in the navy of, or above, the rank of Rear Admiral. For a G C.B. (civil) it is the performance of such personal services to the Crown or of such public duties as shall merit the Royal favour.

For a K.C.B. (military) the qualification consists in the actual holding of a commission in the army, or marines, or Indian military forces of, or above, the rank of Colonel, and in the navy of, or above, the rank of Captain, or Inspector of Machinery, or Paymaster-in-chief, or a commission of equivalent or higher rank in the medical service of the army or navy, or in the departments of the army or Indian military forces, distinguished service in the presence of the enemy, or efficient service as Flag Officer or General Officer, or meritorious service in actual war in providing for the wants of the army or navy, or in the care of sick and wounded.

For a K.C.B. (civil) the qualifications are the same as for a G.C.B. (civil), or the performance of such lengthened service in the command of a regiment of auxiliary forces, or of a brigade of Naval artillery volunteers, or as an officer of the Royal Naval Reserve, or

---

* This statute fixes the total numbers at 1,338. But this is surely an error, as by the Statute of 1897 June 22, the 1st Class G C B had been increased by one, thus making it 83, not 82, and the total membership 1,339, not 1,338.

such as shall have contributed in a marked degree to the efficiency of such regiment, brigade or reserve; or exceptional service to the Crown in connexion with the Department of the Secretary of State for War otherwise than on active service in the field.

The present state of membership of the order is as follows :—

1st class Knights Grand Cross: 55 (? 56) military and 27 civil (exclusive of the sovereign and princes of the blood).

2nd class Knights Commanders: 145 military and 108 civil (exclusive of foreign officers who may be admitted as honorary Knights Commanders.

3rd class Companions: military 705; civil 298.

In accordance with this sub-division of the first two classes the following list of Knights of the Bath is arranged as follows :—

(1) Knights of the Bath from the earliest times to Charles II., and Knights Companions of the Bath from 1725 to 1815.

(2) Knights Grand Cross (military) from 1815 to the present time.

(3) Knights Grand Cross (civil) from 1815 to the present time.

(4) Knights Commanders (military) from 1815 to the present time.

(5) Knights Commanders (civil) from 1847 (when they were first instituted) to the present time.

With regard to installation it may be noted that the arrangement of the 36 stalls in Henry VII.'s Chapel in Westminster Abbey remained as prescribed in the statutes of George I. until 1812, when, under the Regent, they were re-arranged and extended. The drastic re-modelling of the Order in 1815, and the enormous increase in the number of knights rendered installation impossible, and with it all the archaic ceremonies of bathing and vigils. They accordingly disappear from at least the statutes of May, 1847. The process of investiture at the present moment consists only in (1) knighting in case the knight elect is not already a knight; (2) putting on the insignia.

The Most Exalted Order of the Star of India.

THIS Order was instituted by the late Queen Victoria on the 23rd Feb., 1861, by letters patent of that date (gazetted 1861, June 25). The original statutes were issued on the 7th of March following. It was not until 5 years after its original institution that the Order was divided into classes. As originally constituted it was to consist of only one class of knights (25 in number) together with the Sovereign, the Grand Master (who was to be *ex officio* the Viceroy and Governor General of India), and such extra and honorary knights as the Sovereign should from time to time appoint. In 1866, however, the Order was completely remodelled by letters patent dated March 28 (gazetted May 25), followed by statutes dated April 19 of the same year. In its re-organised form the Order was made to consist of the Sovereign, the Grand Master, 25 Knights Grand Commanders (G.C.S I.), 50 Knights Commanders (K.C.S I), and 100 Companions (C.S.I.) with power reserved to the Sovereign, as before, to appoint extra and honorary members. By No. 4 of these statutes of 1866, April 19, the Viceroy of India, by virtue of being Grand Master of the Order was to be First and Principal Knight [Grand Cross] thereof and was to remain a G.C S.I. after his term of office as viceroy had expired, either as an ordinary G.C S.I or in case of their being no vacancy as an extra G.C.S.I., to be absorbed into the number of the ordinary knights as a vacancy should arise, and with rank and precedence according to the date of his having been sworn in as viceroy.

At the time of the re-organisation of 1866 the existing K. S. I. were made G.C.S.I.

Of the 25 Knights Grand Commanders 15 were to be such native princes and chiefs of India as shall have entitled themselves to Royal favour; the remaining 10 to be such British subjects as have merited favour by important and loyal services to the Empire in India For the second and third classes the qualification was the meriting Royal favour by conduct or services in the Indian Empire.

Finally the members of the Order were to have precedence rank for rank next after those of the Bath and immediately before those of St. Michael and St. George.

In 1875 the membership of the Order was again extended. By statute dated Aug. 30 of that year the total number of the members was increased to 205, viz. 25 G.C.S.I., 60 K.C.S.I. and 120 C S.I. By separate statute of 1876, Dec. 20, these numbers were again increased, viz., to 246 in all, *i.e.*, 30 G.C.S.I. (eighteen thereof to be native princes), 72 K.C.S.I. and 144 C.S.I. By this statute of 1876 the qualification for the 2nd and 3rd classes of the Order was thus restated. "No person shall be nominated to either of these classes who shall not by their conduct and services in our Indian Empire, or after not less than 30 years service in the department of our Secretary of State for India, have merited our royal favour."

By the statute of 1897, June 10, the Order was again enlarged to a total membership of 276, viz , 36 G C.S I. (18 thereof to be native princes), 80 K.C.S.I , and 160 C.S I. At the same time the rule regarding the Grand Masters was re-stated as follows: the Viceroy and Governor General of India to be *pro temp* Grand Master and by virtue thereof First and Principal G.C.S.I. On the termination of his office he is to be an additional G C.S.I. with rank and precedence among the ordinary G C S.I. according to the date of his having been sworn in as viceroy.

The last extension of the Order was made by statute of date 1902, Oct. 21 (gazetted 1903, Jan. 1), when the total membership was increased from 276 to 291, viz., 36 G.C.S.I. as before, with ex-viceroys as additional; 85 K.C.S.I. and 170 C.S.I.

The Most Distinguished Order of St. Michael and St. George.

AT the peace in 1814 the island of Malta was ceded to England, and the seven Ionian Islands were formed into an independent State under the exclusive protection of the king of England. With the object of recognising and rewarding the loyalty of the natives of these islands the Order of St. Michael and St. George was erected in 1818. The letters patent erecting the Order were dated 1818, Apr. 27, and the statutes on the 12th Aug. following. As at first constituted the Order was confined to natives of the Ionian Islands or of Malta or to subjects of the king of England holding office in those parts. The lord commissioner of the Ionian Islands was to be Grand Master of the Order, and the Commander-in-chief of His Majesty's ships and vessels in the Mediterranean was to be *pro tempore*, *i.e.*, during the period of his command first and principal Knight Grand Cross. The Order was arranged as follows:—

First class or Knights Grand Cross, 8 in number exclusive of the Grand Master.

Second class or Knights Commanders -   -   -   12 in number.

Third class or Knights or Cavalieri -   -   -   24 in number.

Within the Ionian Islands and Malta all these three classes were to have precedence of knights bachelors, but no definite pronouncement was made in the statutes of 1818 as to whether knighthood of a non-knightly person was essential prior to investiture. This led to an anomalous state of the Order, and with the object of remedying the confusion fresh statutes were signed 1832, Aug. 16. These statutes specifically prescribed that persons of the first and second class must be knighted prior to investiture.

At the same time the numbers were increased as follows:—

Knights Grand Cross increased to 15.

Knights Commanders increased to 20.

Cavalieri or Companions increased to 25.

The most noticeable feature in these changes is the revolution in the status of the members of the third class. From 1818 to 1832 these latter had been styled knights (if of English birth) or cavalieri (if of Ionian or Maltese birth). They had been entitled to be styled Sir and had precedence over knights bachelors. It may be as well to give here the names of these cavalieri who between 1818 and 1832 were entitled to be styled Sir, with the date of their appointment :—

1820, Feb. 2. GIOVANNI MELISSINO, of Zante.
1820, Feb. 2. GIULIO DOMENICHINI, of Zante.
1820, Feb. 2. PIETRO PETRIZZOPULO, sometime Regent of Santa Maura.
1820, Feb 2. PAOLO CAPPADOCA, of Corfu
1820, Feb. 2. DEMETRIO VALSAMACHI, of Cephalonia, sometime secretary to the Legislative Assembly of the Ionian Islands.
1820, Feb 2. ANDREA MUSTOXIDI, of Corfu, sometime a senator of the Ionian Islands.
1820, Feb. 2. PAOLO PROSSALENDI, of Corfu.
1821, Mar. 22 PANDASIN CARIDI, sometime Regent of Cephalonia.
1821, Mar. 22. MARCO CARAZIA, of Corfu.
1822, Jan. 31. VINCENZO CASOLANI, of Malta
1822, Jan 31. GIUSEPPE MARQUIS TESTAFERRATA, of Malta.
1822, June 15. SPIRIDION GIALLINA, of Corfu, sometime member of the Legislative Assembly of the Ionian Islands.
1822, June 15. ANGIOLO CONDARI, of Santa Maura.
1822, June 15. GIOVANNI MORICHI, of Paxò.

From the statutes of 1832 onward, however, the members of the third class were relegated to a lower precedence. Instead of being styled "knights or cavalieri" they were to be in future styled cavalieri (if of foreign birth) or companions (if of English birth), and the knightly rank was confined to the first two classes.

Under letters patent of 1850, Dec. 31, followed by the statutes of 1851, Jan. 31, the constitution of the Order was further modified. The membership of the Order was increased to 65, viz. :—

First class G.C.M.G.   -   -   -   -   -   -   20
Second class K.C.M.G.   -   -   :   -   -   -   20
Third class Cavalieri or Companions C.M.G.   -   -   25

and a prince of the blood royal was to be Grand Master and first and principal Knight Grand Cross. Further, the lord high commissioner to the United States of the Ionian Islands, the governor of Malta and the commander-in-chief in the Mediterranean were to be extra G.C.M.G., to be absorbed into the number of ordinary G.C.M.G. as vacancies fell. But the Order still remained confined, as before, to the Ionian Islands and Malta or to English officials serving there. By the treaty of 1864, Mar. 29, however, the Ionian Islands were ceded to Greece, and it became necessary to entirely re-model the Order. By statutes of 1868, Dec. 4, and 1869, Apr. 3, the Order was extended in its scope to the British Colonies; the persons admissible were to be natural British subjects, who had held office in or performed services in the said colonies. At the same time the numbers were again increased as follows :—

Knights Grand Cross	-	-	-	25 in number.
Knights Commanders	-	-	-	60 „ „
Companions •-	-	-	-	100 „ „

and power was given to the sovereign to appoint extra numbers of the first and second classes and to increase the numbers of each class. It was at the same time ordained that the Order should have precedence after the Order of the Star of India. These numbers have been since increased on four successive occasions as follows :—

By the statutes of 1877, May 30, to

Knights Grand Cross	-	-	-	-	35
Knights Commanders	-	-	-	-	120
Companions	-	-	-	-	200

By a statute of 1879, May 6, to

Knights Grand Cross	-	-	-	-	50
Knight Commanders	-	-	-	-	150
Companions	-	-	-	-	260

By these last-named statutes the Order was made to extend to services rendered to the Crown in relation to foreign affairs.

By statute of 1886, June 28, eight knights commanders and nine companions were added as additional members for services in connection with the Colonial and Indian Exhibition, and by the statute of Mar. 19 in the succeeding year these members became ordinary members of the Order. At the same time, by this statute of 1887, Mar. 19, the total membership of the Order was increased to 607.

By statutes of 1891, Nov. 24, the membership was fixed as follows :—

First class G.C.M.G. -	-	-	-	-	65
Second class K.C M.G	-	-	-	-	200
Third class C.M.G. -	-	-	-	-	342

with princes of the blood as extra and with foreign princes and persons as honorary.

Further provision was made for the temporary increase of the membership by statutes of 1897, May 4, 1901, Apr 19 and Sept. 27, and 1902, June 26.

Finally, by fresh statutes of 1902, Oct. 30 (gazetted 1903, Mar. 13), the greatest extension of all was made. Under these statutes the Order now consists of :—

Not more than 100 Knights Grand Cross, exclusive of princes of the blood royal, extra and honorary members.

Not more than 300 Knights Commanders.

Not more than 600 Companions.

Of these numbers the Foreign Office may designate 30 of the first class, 90 of the second, and 180 of the third.

The qualification of membership is the holding by natural born or naturalised subjects of high and confidential office or the rendering of extraordinary and important services to the king and Empire in any of the dominions beyond the seas; or important and loyal services in relation to the foreign affairs of the Empire.

The Most Eminent Order of the Indian Empire.

THE most eminent Order of the Indian Empire was instituted by the late Queen Victoria on the 1st Jan., 1878 (by royal warrant dated 31st Dec., 1877) to reward services rendered to the said Queen and her Indian Empire, and to commemorate the proclamation of Her Majesty's style and title of Empress of India. As at first constituted the Order was to consist only of the Sovereign, the Grand Master and one class, viz , companions. The Viceroy of India *pro temp* was to be *ex officio* Grand Master, and the members of the Council of India were to be *ex officio* and for life Companions of the Order   The total number of companions (exclusive of *ex officio* members) was not to exceed 50, and the total number of nominations in any consecutive years was not to exceed 20

Within a few years, however, the composition of the Order was drastically altered. By letters patent of date 1886, August 2 (gazetted on the 15th Feb , 1887), the Order was divided into two classes and was to consist of the Sovereign, the Grand Master, 50 Knights Commanders as the first class, and of Companions as the second class, not limited in number. Power was at the same time given to appoint descendants of George I. as extra knights commanders. The knights commanders who were constituted on the date of the gazetting of these letters patent appear in the following list at the head of the K.C.I.E. Some few months after this alteration a further considerable change was made in the constitution of the Order. By letters patent dated 1887, June 1 (gazetted June 27), it was made to consist of the Sovereign, the Grand Master, 25 Knights Grand Commanders (G.C.I.E), 50 Knights Commanders (K.C I.E.), and companions not limited in number, with similar power as before to the Sovereign to appoint any prince of the blood royal, being descendants of George I. as extra Knights Grand Commanders.

On the 10th June, 1897, new statutes for the Order were issued by the Sovereign. These provided that the Grand Master of the Order should by virtue thereof be First and Principal Knight Grand Commander during his term of office as Viceroy, and that after the termination of his said office he should remain an additional Knight Grand Commander with rank among the ordinary Knights Grand Commanders according to the date of his being sworn in as Viceroy. Further, the Governors of Madras and Bombay Presidencies were to be additional Knights Grand Commanders with rank among the Ordinary Knights Grand Commanders according to [the date of] their respective appointments as Knights Grand Commanders of this Order.

At the same time the numbers were increased as follows :—

1st class G.C.I.E , 32 in number.
2nd class K.C.I.E. 82 in number.
3rd class C.I.E. nominations not to exceed 20 in each successive year exclusive of promotions.

The members of the Order are such persons as have merited the royal favour by their services to the Empire of India, and such distinguished representatives of Eastern potentates as the Sovereign may think fit and such honorary members also as the Sovereign may think fit.

The members of the several grades of the Order have place and precedence next to and immediately after the corresponding classes of the Order of St. Michael and St. George, and rank among themselves according to date of nomination as in the 'Gazette.'

By a fresh statute of 1901, July 22, temporary provision was made for the admission into all three classes of the Order, of persons to be named in consideration of services rendered during the South African War and in China. Similarly by statute of 1902, Oct. 22 (gazetted 1903, Jan. 1) temporary provision was made for the admission into the 3rd class, and for the year 1903 only, of 40 members as companions. At the same time the membership of the 2nd class (K.C.I.E.) was increased from 82 to 92.

The Royal Victorian Order.

THE Royal Victorian Order was instituted by Queen Victoria by letters patent dated Westminster, 1896, Apr. 21. On the 20th Dec., 1898, by further letters patent dated from Westminster, certain alterations were made in the precedency of the several classes of the Order. The statutes of the Order are dated Windsor, 1899, Dec. 30, and are 23 in number. By Statute II. the Order is to consist of the sovereign and five several classes, viz., Knights Grand Cross, Knights Commanders, Commanders, members of the fourth class and members of the fifth class. By Statute IV. the members are to be "such persons, being subjects of our Crown, as may have rendered or shall hereafter render extraordinary or important or personal services to Us, our heirs and successors, who have merited or may hereafter merit our royal favour, or any persons who may hereafter be appointed officers of this Royal Order." By Statute V. the honorary members of the several classes are to consist of such foreign princes and persons as should have the honour of an Order conferred upon them. The mode of appointment is by warrant under the royal sign manual sealed with the seal of the Order. The precedency of the various classes is, in accordance with Statute VII., as follows:—

G.C.V.O. next to and immediately after G.C.I.E.
K.C.V.O. next to and immediately after K.C.I.E.
C.V.O. next to and immediately after Knights Bachelors of England.
M.V.O. (fourth class) next to and immediately after C.I.E.
M.V.O. (fifth class) next to and immediately after eldest sons of
        Knights Bachelors of England.

Statute XIV. regulates the method of investiture, and prescribes that the sovereign will, prior to the investiture, confer the honour of knighthood upon the person nominated to be a G.C.V.O. or K.C.V.O. if that person "have not previously received the said honour" of knighthood. Further, the ceremony of investiture may by warrant under the sign manual be dispensed with, with the proviso that in the case of G.C.V.O. and K.C.V.O. this dispensing with investiture shall not entitle the person in question to the style of a knight bachelor of England "without having been duly authorised," *i.e.,* without [presumably] the said person having been knighted either by dubbing or by letters patent (Statute XVII.). The anniversary of the Order is fixed for the 20th of June, the day of the accession of Queen Victoria to the Throne.

Since the decease of Queen Victoria the already wide scope of the Order has been further enlarged. It is frequently conferred when the king is abroad on purely ceremonial occasions, and without any necessary regard to the central idea of personal service rendered to the sovereign. This is entirely in keeping, however, with the fundamental principle of the Order, viz., that it is the sovereign's *private* order.

As to the Royal Victorian Chain, *see infra,* p. 415.

Royal Hanoverian Guelphic Order.

THE Order of the Guelphs was instituted by the Prince Regent on the 12th of August, 1815. The preamble to the statutes of the Order, as issued on that date explain that King George III. had long entertained an intention of instituting an Order for Hanover, and that this intention was now carried out by the prince Regent to mark the occasion of the erection of Hanover into a kingdom, and at the same time to signalise the bravery of the Hanoverian troops in the battle of Waterloo.

By the statutes which, though issued from Carlton House, were only published in German, the Grand-Mastership of the Order was to be for ever annexed to the crown of Hanover. The members were to consist of three classes, Knights Grand Cross (G.C.H.), Knights Commanders (K.C.H.), and Knights (K.H.), none below the rank of Lieutenant General being eligible for the first class, and none below that of Major General for the second. The arms and names of the knights of all three classes were to be affixed in the church of the Palace at Hanover and in the ancient Hall of Knights in the said palace.But this portion of the statutes was not carried into effect. The Order was destined for the civil as well as the military service, the qualification being the performance of some achievement worthy of the Order. The fact that there was no restriction of number, and that it was for civil as well as military merit, at a time when the Order of the Bath had neither of these characteristics, led to an extensive use of it under king William IV. That monarch, regardless of the object for which the Order had been established, bestowed it with profusion on his British subjects, although it had presumably been created as a means of rewarding Hanoverian and not British subjects.

On the death of King William IV. on the 20th June, 1837, the Crown of Hanover devolved on his brother and heir male the duke of Cumberland, and so became separate from the British Crown. From this moment the Order became a purely Hanoverian one, and therefore in strictest parlance a foreign one.

E

The question as to whether membership of this Order entitled the holder thereof to the title of " Sir " and to the rank of a knight bachelor of Great Britain is concisely stated by Nicolas in his general remarks on the Order.   Neither George IV. nor William IV. supposed that such title or precedence would attach to the members. Regarding the Order as strictly a foreign one, both those kings always knighted those members of the Order whom they meant to make knights bachelors of Great Britain.   Further than this, William IV. expressly intimated his opinion to that effect after having taken the advice of the lord chancellor on the subject. A paper having been laid before the king in Oct. 1831, containing reasons for the contention that all the knights of the Order of the Guelphs became *ipso facto* knights bachelors, the king saw so much objection to the principle (that the acceptance of any foreign Order should confer on the individual the honour of knighthood without his being knighted by the Sovereign) that he asked it to be referred to the lord chancellor.   The lord chancellor's opinion was understood to be decidedly against any such right, and the king afterwards appointed several hundred British subjects to the Order, being assured that they would not thereby become knights bachelors of England.

Knights Bachelors of England.

ANCIENT authors have derived the antiquity of knighthood from St. Michael the Archangel, whom they term their *premier Chevalier,* Whilst not agreeing with this, other writers assert that it is as ancient as valour itself, and derived its original from Troy, which bred many in the heroic paths of virtue and arms, who were deservedly esteemed knights—such as Hector, etc.

Such ancient conceits apart, it may be at once asserted that the mediæval institution of knighthood, of which the modern institution is a derivative, is of Frankish origin. There are two streams or lines of derivation which can be, if not traced, at least conjectured.

1. The direct or immediate derivation from the ceremonial or ritual of knighthood in use in the Frankish Empire of Charlemagne.

2. The indirect or immediate derivation from that form of military organisation which, in its fullest growth, we call the feudal system.

As to the first of these it is probable that the highly ceremonial form of knighthood which was used by Charlemagne was derived by him from the Eastern Empire, and that in its origin it represents a strange admixture of the ideas or institutions of ancient Rome and of the invading Barbarians. Ancient Rome furnished the idea of a knightly Order, as a separate class; the invading barbarians changed the idea of the institution; made it wholly military in purpose, and adorned it with their own forms of ceremonial. Not that the institution of the Equestrian Order of ancient Rome was the parent of the mediæval institution of knighthood. The distinguishing feature of the Ordo Equestris of Rome was the census equestris and the censor's choice or allowance of the individual census. Both these characteristics are absent from the mediæval conception of knighthood. But the Roman institution furnished the idea of a separate Order or status, Between this idea and the barbarian idea of distinction arising only by valour in arms there is a possible connecting link, viz., the institution or custom of adoption *per arma,* which becomes a marked feature of the Roman Empire at the time of the invasions of the barbarians. It was such an adoption that Justinian used with the king of the

Ostro Goths, and that Theodoric, the king of the Ostro Goths, used with the king of the Heruli.

In his charter on this occasion Theodoric speaks of the custom as common and acknowledged :—

> "Per arma fieri posse filium grande inter gentes constat esse praeconium. . . . Et ideo more gentium et conditione virili filium te praesenti munere procreamus ut competenter per arma nascaris qui bellicosus esse dignosceris. Damus quidem tibi equos, enses, clypeos et reliqua instrumenta bellorum."

This adoption of a son by arms *per arma* was not intended as such an adoption as would convey rights of succession, but as a publication of the Prince's judgment touching the person so adopted and his solemn confirmation of him under the name of his son thus to bear and use arms.

Such an institution would inevitably tend to be regarded as the seal or mark of admission to a separate and select status.

But whilst it seems clear that this idea of knighthood as the qualification for entering a distinct status was derived by the Frankish Empire from the decaying Roman Empire it would seem also clear that in its origin the actual form which was given to the ceremony itself was of native or barbarian or Teutonic origin. Speaking of the formal assumption of arms by the young warrior in the public assembly Tacitus says :—

> Arma sumere non ante cuiquam moris quam civitas suffecturum probaverit. Tum in ipso concilio vel principum aliquis, vel pater, vel propinqui scuto frameaque juvenem ornant. Haec apud illos toga, hic primus juventae honos.

From this source have been derived and developed the various ceremonies, the investiture or girding with a sword, the putting on of spurs, the blow on the neck or cheek, etc., etc., which characterise the solemn form of knighthood in use in the Frankish Empire. In his constitutions for the Frisones Charlemagne ordains that the governor there should create knights sicut consuetudinis est by girding with a sword and striking the person created on the ear ut deinceps more militum Sacri Imperii aut Regni Franciae armati incedant.

Such was the institution—of mingled and Teutonic origin as I think—which Charlemagne adopted or revived, and which by his example and influence was spread among the surrounding nationalities.

Confining our attention to England the influence of the Frankish example or institution is traceable in the story of Alfred the Great's investiture of Athelstan.

> quem etiam premature militem fecerat, donatum chlamyde coccinea, gemmato balteo, ense Saxonico cum vagina aurea.

I take it as self-evident that this highly ceremonial form of knighthood is, as far as England is concerned, the direct and only origin of the form of knighthood by bathing or by the Bath. The introduction of the religious rites of confession, absolution, vigils, etc., is possibly attributable to the fact that in Anglo-Saxon times (and up to 1102) the bishops and abbots had the right of creating knights.

To this subject sufficient reference has been made already (*see* introduction to the Order of the Bath *supra* x.—xv). It is only necessary to state briefly that religious rites had begun to enter into the ceremony of knighthood before the Norman Conquest. The knighting of the Conqueror and his sons had the character of a religious as well as a legal rite.

Both John of Salisbury and Peter of Blois mention the knight's offering of his sword on the altar as a part of the accustomed solemnity of knighthood in the middle of the 12th century.

In the account of the knighthood at Rouen in 1127 by Henry I. of England of Geoffrey of Anjou as prior to his marriage to the empress Maud, Henry's daughter, the full and precise ritual of the Bath is detailed.

Whatever authority may or may not attach to this description, it is certain that by the time of king John the ritual of the Bath was complete, for from his reign onwards we have a series of royal Orders addressed to the Wardrobe or to particular sheriffs, etc., commanding the delivery of robes and bedding to candidates for knighthood as preliminary or preparatory to the ceremony of bathing.

Such official notices as we possess of scattered ceremonial knightings by the King during the century 1250 to 1350 almost invariably use one phrase to describe it, viz., cingulo militari accingere, cingulo militiae decorare, and so on, implying a ceremonial investiture and girding of the sword, etc. (See Rymer Foedera, i., 531, 586, 698; ii., 1062.)

I am of the opinion that throughout the late Saxon and early Norman times in England this ceremonial form of knighthood (which was later known distinctly as knighthood by the bath) was the only form of knighthood proper. If so, it would follow as a consequence that the ordinarily accepted opinion that Knights Bachelors represent an earlier institution than Knights of the Bath is entirely incorrect. Knights Bachelors are the later institution, and were practically unknown during the period in question.

2. What I have termed the second line or stream of influence in the institution of knights is derived entirely from the characteristic feature of the feudal system. Intentionally using non-technical terms for the moment, I may express my view as follows:—The feudal system centred round the idea of a military force settled on the land in a certain way or by a certain tenure. All the constituent members of that military force were milites in the sense of being warriors or horse soldiers, but they were not originally milites in the sense of being knights as being admitted by a certain ceremony into a certain dignity. They were horse soldiers merely, and their tenure of their lands was a soldier's tenure. Throughout the 11th and 12th centuries, therefore, I would not translate the generic term miles as knight but as horse soldier. This would apply equally to Anglo-Saxon times. The thegn* of the Anglo-Saxon period was a miles in the sense of being a soldier possessing such and such a qualification in the way of land, but not a knight in the sense of being a member of a certain Order or in the sense of being possessed of a dignity inseparable from himself, or inseparable from his name. From the 9th to the 12th century I take it there was only one species of, or means of approach to, knightly honour, viz., that which arose by creation by means of those solemn ceremonial rites which, as I have said, were subsequently elaborated into the ceremonial of the Bath. Outside this restricted class the large body of thegns or milites were soldier tenants simply. But from the 12th century a change takes place. The institution or idea of knighthood is itself developed or expanded in such a way as to potentially comprehend this large body of the King's soldier tenants. The limits, in point of time, of this change are possibly marked for us by the introduction of the term knight itself. Originally the Anglo-Saxon "cniht" was a boy, a servant or a military follower; then the term gathered dignity and in

* The earliest mention of a Saxon mile occurs under the year 709 A.D. (Cartalarium Saxonicum I. 184). It is to my mind a suspicious case. But from the commencement of the 10th century Saxon milites (=thegns) occur frequently among the witnesses to charters.

the latter half of the 11th century it designated a military rank next beneath that of the thegns, and, finally, from the commencement of the 13th century it assumes (though by no means uniformly) the full meaning of the name of a distinct dignity attaching to the profession of arms and to military tenure.

Hitherto the King's tenants in chief had been milites, soldier tenants, battalere, or battaliers,* or fighting tenants simply. Henceforth they, or a certain portion of them, were to constitute a distinct rank possessed of a distinct dignity, which, whilst being less in esteem than the ancient ceremonial dignity of knighthood, was to be derived from it or partially assimilated to it in matter of form and approximated to it in substance. The entry to this dignity was given by a simpler form, only one of the several ceremonies which characterised the older ceremonial knighting being used, viz., that of the mere striking by the sword, but alongside of this there had to be in the grantee the necessary qualification of a tenure in chivalry from the Crown. Whilst it is possible to lay one's finger on the approximate time of the introduction of knighthood by simple dubbing (viz., the middle of the 13th century), it is not possible to define sharply and clearly the steps in the process of evolution by which the military tenant became differentiated from the dubbed knight. That evolution implies (what the slightly earlier introduction of scutage also implies) that the feudal system was breaking down, that the military tenant was ceasing to be a professional warrior and was coming more and more to be a landed man. It was as a

---

* I suggest as a mere conjecture that the Norman French word battalere became confused with the base Latin word baccalaurii. Ultimately the form baccalaurii entirely ousted the form battelier, and occupied the field alone, either in its original form as baccalaurii or in its Anglicised form as bachelors. In this way may have been evolved the term knights bachelors, one which has been a moot point of discussion among antiquaries for generations. The idea that the term bachelor is derived from bas chevalier as representing a low or base species of knighthood is self-evidently untenable, for knighthood is a dignity and the first law of chivalry is that no dignity can be at once a source of honour and of dishonour.

I can see no difficulty in the accepted usage or meaning of it in the middle of the 13th century. It is in the middle of the 14th century that the first extant list of knight bachelors occurs. I take it, therefore, that it was about that time, say during the 13th or 14th century, that some members of the main body of tenants in chivalry began to be distinguished by the ceremonial of dubbing. Although this was a simpler form of ceremonial, and one carrying less weight with it than the older ceremony of knighting by the Bath, yet it brought with it distinction enough to make it coveted and to mark off the holders of it from the main body of the King's tenants in chivalry. The words of Matthew Paris, therefore "multi de militibus universitatis regni qui se volunt bachelarios appellari," seem to me perfectly clear and consonant. They mark the time when both the new name and the new dignity were coming into use. I see no difficulty whatever in the phrase. It means not the young knights as against the old knights, but the dubbed knights as against the undubbed main body of tenants in chivalry. The term communitas bacheleriae Angliae is to my mind not so much a collective term for the whole body of such dubbed knights (which would suggest that knights bachelors were connected by some organisation or bond more or less loose), but a pure abstraction vague and hardly translatable. But does it not stand to sense that the dubbed knights would represent the chief and most influential of the body of tenants in chivalry, and that in any agitation they would lead the rest of the King's tenants as a small but representative community or body? Finally, as to the passage in Wyke's Annales Monastici, in which the term Bachelor is applied to the London apprentices, "innumera multitudo ribaldorum quos bachelarios vocitabant," it seems to me merely to prove how general the use of the term had become, how quickly it had caught the popular fancy.

For the whole of this subject, see Professor Tout's article in the *English Historical Review*, xvii, p. 89, January, 1902.

stimulus to this decaying military professionalism that the new dignity was introduced. Whilst in matter of theory all the military tenants holding by a knight's fee were capable of this new dignity, they did not as a matter of fact assume it except when called upon to do so by the Sovereign or his deputy. Roughly speaking, therefore, we may say that through the earlier mediæval period up to the middle of the 13th century the idea of military tenure as constituting knighthood predominated over that of ceremonial admission by dubbing, whilst in the later middle ages the idea of ceremonial admission by dubbing prevailed over that of military tenure. In modern times the conception of knighthood is purely ceremonial. Is is conferred by a mere ceremony, and has no relation whatever to military tenure of land from the Crown.

Let me recapitulate and so render clear the point which I wish to make.

1. From 880 to 1250 approximately the only form of knighthood was the highly ceremonial investiture which subsequently developed into the ritual of the Bath. The honour was a peculiar and great one, and the actual number of knights was small. The main body of military followers or tenants-in-chief of the Crown were milites or soldiers simply.

2. From 1250 onwards the dignity of knighthood by dubbing is introduced. The whole body of properly qualified military tenants-in-chief is theoretically entitled to this dignity. When he assumes that dignity or submits to accept it the miles or battelier holding by military service becomes a knight battelier or knight bachelor, and henceforth miles is the accepted term for a knight bachelor, and when once the term miles has obtained this hard and fast meaning it ceases to be applied to the wider generic body of military tenants. Finally, whilst the whole body of tenants holding by knight's service was theoretically entitled to assume knighthood it came to be more and more a distinct act depending on the will of the Sovereign, Whilst some few accepted the honour eagerly at his hands the main body of military tenants remained indisposed to assume it— doubtless because they regarded it as a form of emphasising or re-enacting the military character and burden of the tenure. Periodically, therefore, we find the Crown calling upon the tenants to assume knighthood and fining them for not obeying. At first the idea was doubtless that of registering afresh or keeping actively alive the feudal obligation of military service attaching to the

military tenure, but it was quickly found that the fines levied for non-assumption of knighthood afforded a profitable source of income. It became, therefore, quite an established practice on the part of the Crown to issue proclamations calling on the tenants-in-chief to assume knighthood and then to levy fines upon or to accept compositions from those who refused to obey. This practice was observed by the Sovereigns of England down to the days of Charles I.

It is a very curious fact that, as far as the lists of Knights Bachelors are concerned, the effect of these proclamations from the king is only traceable in a single instance. Soon after his accession James I. issued orders requiring the sheriffs, etc., to summon all persons possessed of 40*l*. a year to come in and receive the dignity of knighthood. These orders were followed on the 17th July, 1603, by the issue of the usual commission for compounding with all persons who should neglect to comply with the summons. Six days afterwards more than 500 of the persons so summoned attended the King at Whitehall, and there, in the royal garden, were dubbed knights by him. See their names in the text, pp. 113—127). James's motive on the occasion was to add grace to the ceremony of his coronation, and this was also the reason of the unusually large response. But the singularity of this instance will probably serve to illustrate clearly the nature of the process which had been going on under the surface. In the first stage of that process the Crown had attempted to arrest the decay into which the feudal tenures were falling. This it attempted to do by, let us say, periodically renewing, or keeping up-to-date the registration of the tenants in chivalry. As it was the object of the tenants to evade such registration, they shirked the assumption of knighthood. But when the tenures had hopelessly decayed, when parliamentary grants had superseded the mediæval scutage and tallage, etc., and when the Crown's feudal privileges had sunk to such items as wardship, relief, etc., then the qualification of the 40*l*. per annum on lands had come to be a social qualification carrying very little of the old feudal obligations. The distinction of knighthood was therefore no longer attended with the feudal obligations which made the mediæval tenant shun it.

The abolition of the feudal-tenures in the middle of the 17th century swept away at the same time this feudal privilege of a right to knighthood hitherto existing in the 40*l*. per annum tenant. Accordingly from the days of the Restoration there has remained only the sole and simple conception of knighthood as a personal dignity conferred by the ceremony of dubbing by the Sovereign or his deputy. When this change had been effected it became an easy and not incongruous act to confer upon civilians what was originally a purely military dignity. To-day the dignity of knight bachelor is in great measure civilian in character.

The whole of the above attempted explanation of this very obscure and difficult subject is advanced tentatively, and I offer it to the consideration of scholars in the simple hope that the discussion of it may lead to the establishment of some truer theory if mine is wrong. As growing out of it there is a precedent question which will require solution at the hands of mediævalists. That question is this: What is the exact meaning of the conventional phrase used in the writs of summons to knighthood, *arma militaria suscipere?* Does it mean that the tenant should present himself to the King to receive from him in a ceremonial way the arms proper to the degree of knighthood? If so, that would be an investiture, or, let us say, at the least dubbing. Or as an alternative view does it mean that the tenant was called upon by such words to attend at some appointed time and place in order to acknowledge his liability to such and such military service? In other words, does it mean that the tenant was to attend, not to be dubbed a knight, but simply to have his name entered in a census, or register, or roll, or schedule. I incline to the latter view for the following reasons:—

1. As already stated above, the records of dubbings in the Middle Ages never correspond with the writs for the assumption of knighthood. I do not know of any record which would show that a writ of summons to knighthood was ever followed by the dubbing of a single individual, much less by the dubbing of hundreds, for undoubtedly hundreds or even thousands of persons presented themselves in obedience to the writ.

2. The earliest surviving writ for the assumption of knighthood, so far as I know, is entered on the Close Roll 16 Hen. III. A typical entry of later date may be quoted from the Close Roll of 6 Edw. I. The wording of the entry is as follows:—

Rex vicecomiti Glouc. Praecipimus tibi . . . quod omnes illos de balliva tua qui habent viginti libratas terrae vel feodum unius militis integri de nobis tenent et milites esse debent et non sunt, sine dilatione distringas *ad arma militaria . . . a nobis suscipienda.*

This is the stereotyped form, and it is not specific. It can be read both ways.

But four years later there is an entry on the Welsh roll of 10, Edw. I., which is very specific and which, to my mind, throws a reflex light on the earlier entry just quoted. The words on the Welsh roll are as follows:—

> Rex vicecomiti Glouc. . . . Statuimus quod quicunque de regno nostro qui triginta libratas terrae habuerit sibi *provideat quod promptum habeat unum equum fortem et competentem ad arma una cum armaturis competentibus ad eundem* quo in casibus emergentibus sibi servire possit quoties est necesse.

Now what is the difference between these two entries just quoted? Technically, the first is described as a writ for the assumption of knighthood; the second is described as a writ of military summons. But surely there is an intimate connection between the two entries. The first writ has the effect of putting a particular number of tenants on to the census or schedule of soldiers (milites) liable to military duty. Then, four years later, when there is occasion for the services of these men the second writ, addressed to the same county calls them to the performance of that duty. In accordance with this, I argue that the writ for the assumption of knighthood simply established a census or roll or register of persons liable to military duty. It did not affect the status, the social dignity of the soldier (miles). His social status was only enhanced when, later, the added ceremony of dubbing was applied to him.

3. The final reason for my opinion is a very curious one. Among the Miscellanea of the Receipt, vol. 223, there are still preserved the names of all the individuals, arranged county by county, who compounded for not taking knighthood at the coronation of Charles I. The record covers the years 1630—2. and amongst the persons who so compounded are at least five baronets (pp. 5, 32, 38, 52b, 155) and four knights (pp. 5, 113, 135, 155).

If the writ for the assumption of knighthood called the holder of a knight's fee or a 40l. holder to attend to be dubbed, how should knights come to be included? It is surely out of the question. The only conclusion in my mind is that the summons to knighthood was not a summons to a ceremony to a dubbing, but only a summons to the rendering of a military or feudal duty.

If I have made my main point clear the reader will easily understand the list of Knights Bachelors in the following pages. If the whole body of the feudal military tenants of the Crown were ipso facto knights then a list of the mediæval Knights Bachelors of England would be a list, generation after generation, of all the tenants-in-chief of the Crown holding by military service But if this whole body was not so much composed of knights in esse as of soldiers (milites) or knights in posse then the list of Knights Bachelors of England will be confined to the list of actually dubbed knights. And no more than this is really what all the existing MS. lists give us. The only existing records of the mediæval Knights Bachelors of England consist of lists of actual dubbings.

I have already in the preface described the M.S. sources from which the list of mediæval knights has been drawn. Owing to the fact that the public is not allowed to make search in the College of Arms it is impossible to say what is the ultimate origin of these MSS. thus described. But it is quite clear that they represent more or less direct transcripts from entries, kept of old at the College of Arms, probably some document containing miscellaneous entries of ceremonies, creations, and dubbings. That this record (whatever it was) was not on the lines of the later register of knights is shown by the fact that it frequently comprised knights who had not paid their fees to the College. (See note, Vol. II., p. 26, *infra*.) Although an official document in the sense of being compiled by some member of the College, it is plain that it was not regarded as an official register of knighthood to which reference could be had as a final authority for settling questions of right or precedency, and so forth. Until the days of James I. no such register existed, and it is to this fact that must be attributed the chaotic and imperfect nature of the lists of knights up to the 17th century.

The register of knights at the College of Arms was instituted in 1622 by a signet letter of King James couched in the following terms : —

> *James I.'s order for Knights directed to [Thomas Howard, earl of Arundel and Surrey], the Earl Marshall of England, May 15, anno 20 [appointing a register to be kept wherein the names of all knights should for the future be enrolled, and that all knights should have precedency according to such enrollment].**

By the King.

> Right trusty and well-beloved cousin and councillor, we greet you well. Whereas there is daily found great inconvenience and many differences arise about the precedence of knights

* Harl. MS. 983, f 100.

in respect that so exact a roll is not kept of them as ought to be in the Office of Arms, the partyes on whom we have bestowed that honour not resorting to that office, as they ought, to give notice thereof in due time, by reason of which neglect much inconvenience hath grown (as we are informed), some pretending to that honour who never received it from us, others losing their right of precedency, there being no record extant whereby to rectify such differences when they happen (all which we chiefly impute to the want of an Earl Marshal heretofore). We therefore, minding to redress these inconveniences, do straightly charge and command all such persons on whom we shall hereafter confer that honour that within one month at the furthest they bring unto you, our Earl Marshal, or your deputy, sufficiently authorised by you, a sufficient certificate as well of the time and place as of their priority, and that you thereupon, or your deputy, give particular warrant under your or his hand for the entry of them accordingly in the Office of Arms, to the end that according to such warrantable entry everyone may know his due precedency as well in all commissions as in other public employments and places whatsoever. And if any, having received that honour at our hands, shall not within one month bring such a certificate unto you or your deputy for such entry to be thereupon made, our pleasure is that he shall forfeit the benefit of his due precedency from that time forward until his enrolment; neither shall he pretend to any place by virtue of his knighthood until he have been so enrolled, and then shall take his place no otherwise but from the time of his enrollment. Given under our Signet at our Palace of Westminster, the 15th day of May, in the twentieth year of our reign.

Some months later the signet letter was re-enforced by James, by the following proclamation (Rymer xvii., 488) :—

"Whereas wee have taken knowledge of many and great inconveniences daily ariseing for want of an exact Roll kept in the Office of Armes of such as have received from us the *Order of Knighthood*, whereby some have presumed to challendge that dignitie, uppon whom the same was never conferred; and, amongst them that were indeed knighted, often questions arise for precedencie; which cannot be decided for want of a Record kept thereof: for redress whereof we directed our Letters dated the *fifteenth Day of May last* to our right trusty and right welbeloved Cosen and Councellor, *Thomas Earle of Arrundell and Surrey*, our Earl Marshall of England, that, according as apperteineth to that his office, he should take order therein: nevertheles, by reason of the slacknes and negligence of such as have been by us advanced unto that degree, in not giving notice thereof to the said *Earle Marshall* or his deputie, our said Letters have not taken effect according to our intent.

We do therefore hereby publish and declare our Royal Pleasure, and doe streightly charge and command, that all such persons as sithence the said *fifteenth day of May last past*, have received that dignitie; shall, within *three moneths* after the publishing of this our Proclamation and others that shall hereafter receave the like dignitie from us or any our Lieve-tenaunts, shall within *one month* after they have received the same within this our Realme of England, or within *one moneth* next after their coming into this Realme, if they receive the same out of the Realme, bring or cause to be brought a sufficient Certificate thereof, and of the time thereof, to our *Earle Marshall of England* for the tyme being, or to such other person or persons as he shall appoint, to the end the same may be Registered in a Roll to be therefore kept in the Office of Armes, uppon pain that everie person neglecting to bring such Certificate shall lose the benefit of his due precedencie, and in all commissions, employments and places shall be ranked after such as uppon the certificat brought shall be registered before them:

And wee doe likewise signifie and declare our pleasure. to be, that all such, as at any tyme before the said *fifeteenth day of May last past* did receave the said *Order of Knighthood att* our hands, shall at any tyme hereafter bring such Certificat as aforesaid, and shall have the same registered as aforesaid, for clearing all controversies and questions that may arise touching their precedencie.

Given at our Court of Windsor the seaven and twentith Day of April, in the one and twentith yeare of our Raigne of Great Brittaine, France and Ireland, 1623."

The reception of this royal letter and proclamation by the officials of the College of Arms is noted on II. p. 179 infra. It is not to be supposed, however, that even after the institution of such a register the College of Arms possessed a complete and trustworthy account of the dubbings of the Knights Bachelors of England. It did not, for the simple reason that it did not profess to do. The College would only register a knighthood when the knight paid his fees (which amounted to 108*l.*), and even then it could only register such knighthoods as were transmitted to it by certificate from the Lord Chamberlain's office. As many knights absolutely refused to pay the fees, and as the Lord Chamberlain's office may easily have omitted to transmit such certificates, it is self-evident that the register of knights at the Heralds College is an imperfect record at best. In addition a further element of confusion is introduced by means of the register. For it would appear that sometimes the date of registration is the date of payment of the fees to the College, and this may be much posterior to the date of actual dubbing. This is the only explanation that I can offer as to the singular discrepancy or variety of dates so frequently noticeable in the lists in the following pages.

As a result all the lists of Knights Bachelors which have emanated from members of the College of Arms have been characterised by incompleteness or untrustworthiness. A brief survey of these publications will serve to bring out this fact:—

1. John Philipot was successively Rouge Dragon and Somerset Herald, the latter from 1624. His "*perfect collection or catalogue of all Knights Batchelors made by king James since his coming to the Crown of England*" was not published till 1660, a matter of fifteen years after Philipot's death. This book is probably the most painstaking and reliable of all the lists which have emanated from officials of the College of Arms. But a careful collation of it with Nichols' '*progresses of King James*' and with the general authorities for the period, especially the State Papers Domestic, reveals many errors and discrepancies of date and name

2. The next list in point of time is " A Catalogue of the nobility of England and Ireland, etc " This book generally passes under the name of T[homas] W[alkley]. Walkley, however, was only the publisher, and the actual authorship has not transpired. But it must have emanated from an official of the College of Arms. The first edition appeared in 1630, and the book ran through at least eight other editions up to 1658. The last edition, that of 1658, contained

not only the Knight Bachelors of Charles I. up to his flight from
Oxford in 1646, but also the subsequent dubbings by the Protectors
Oliver and Richard Cromwell. It is from this list that I have copied
in the following pages; but again here, as in the case of Philipot,
there are noticeable errors and omissions.

3 (4). The third and fourth of these lists were the work of
Francis Townsend, Pursuivant of Arms, a son of that Francis
Townsend who was Windsor Herald from 1784. He produced

(3) *A calendar of Knights . . . from 1760 to 1828* (London, 1828).

(4) *A catalogue of Knights from 1660 to 1760* (London, 1833).
Both these lists are execrable in every way, incomplete, chaotic and
swarming with errors of name, place and date. I have derived
literally countless corrections of him from the London Gazette,
the State Papers Domestic, Le Neve, Luttrell's Diary and other
general sources.

Finally there is the work of Le Neve. His *Pedigrees of Knights
from Charles II. to Queen Anne* has been published from Harl MSS.,
5801-2, by the Harleian Society.

It is impossible to speak of Le Neve's work save with the greatest
reverence and respect, but it will be plain to anyone looking into
it that Le Neve must have been hampered by the imperfect nature
of the official record on which he based his notes. This is especially
apparent in the notes of the knights made by Charles II. immediately
before and after the Restoration—a portion which has cost me more
labour probably than any other part of this work.

All this is said not in a spirit of carping criticism but simply to
emphasise the point which I wish to make, viz., that from its very
nature the register of knights at the College of Arms must be and
surely is a most imperfect record.

The great source of correction on which I have relied is, of course,
the *London Gazette*. But the *London Gazette* only began to appear
in 1665, and for long after the appearance of the first number its
notices of ceremonials such as dubbings or creations are disappoint-
ingly casual. Such as they are, however, I trust and claim that the
reader will find every such notice entered in the present volume.
Every page and volume of the *Gazette* has been turned over from its
commencement to the present day.

One might naturally suppose that, however imperfect the register
at the College of Arms is, the record of the *London Gazette* would be
complete and unimpeachable. Why it should not be so I cannot say,

unless it is due to the extraordinary and unsystematic way in which that periodical has been edited in the past. Certain it is that many knighthoods never were gazetted at all (probably in consequence of non-payment of fees, or again by reason of the casual nature of the particular knighthood). Under the circumstances I have done the best I can by means of a collation of all the above-named sources together with others.

In conclusion, reference must be made to one or two questions touching the dignity of a Knight Bachelor. Although not an Order, the honour of Knight Bachelor is a dignity or degree, and as such inseparable from the holder. He must be named by both his Christian name and his surname as Sir A. B , knight, and his wife is to be styled Lady or Dame. If an esquire be made a knight he loses his name of esquire, but though a knight be made a nobleman or of any higher degree he still retains the name of knight and so ought to be styled in all writs In the ancient books of law the dignity of knighthood was held to be universal, so that even if a knight received his dignity of a foreign prince he was still to be styled and accounted a knight in all legal proceedings within England. Some few such knights will be found in the earlier pages of the present volume. This usage is, however, no longer accepted in England. It is now necessary in order to the recognition of such dignities that a British subject who has been honoured by a foreign Sovereign should obtain royal letters patent of the Crown of England enabling him to have that honour. Further, such permission or recognition does not carry with it the slightest title to the rank or style of a Knight Bachelor of England.

But one branch of this law of the universality of the dignity of knighthood still maintains. Within the ranks of Knights Bachelors there is no distinction or priority save that of date of creation. There is no distinction whatever of class according as the dubbing is performed by the Sovereign himself or by his deputy The ancient laws of chivalry maintained that the process of knighting could be performed by anyone who was himself of the degree of a knight. Certainly the commanders of the King's armies possessed and used the authority of creating knights as will be found in many places in the present volume. The power which still remains in the lord lieutenant of Ireland of creating knights is a survival of this ancient law of chivalry. This power was called in question by the Admiralty in 1821, but it was decided in 1823 by the

F

judges that the lord lieutenant does possess since the union of
Great Britain and Ireland the same power of conferring the honour
of knighthood which he did [as the King's deputy] whilst Ireland
was a separate kingdom. Irish knights, therefore, rank for precedence
with English knights simply according to seniority of creation.

In a similar manner the power of knighting was held to be
inherent in the warden of the Marches in the 16th century.

Again, the Crown may delegate its power of creating knights by
a specific commission. Numerous instances of this occurred under
Queen Mary and Queen Elizabeth [see Rymer, xv., p. 350].

A similar precedent was followed by James II. in 1686 (when the
duke of Albemarle as lieutenant general and general governor of
Jamaica was empowered to confer knighthood on such persons, not
exceeding six, as he should think deserving), and by his present
Majesty in the commission empowering H.R.H. the duke of York to
create knights on his colonial tour. On the other hand, the practice
of making knights by letters patent is a distinct departure from
ancient practice "He that receives the dignity of a knight kneels
down and then the King slightly touches him on the shoulder with
a sword and says in French *sois chevaler au nome de dieu;* and after-
wards *avance chivaler,* for a knight is not made by letters patent or
by the King's writ as those of high dignity be, but by the sword, for
this honour is supposed to be given on the sudden."

The adoption of the innovation of making knights by letters
patent has been caused by the growing size of the British Empire, and
by the necessity of creating knights in absentia to meet such typical
cases as those of colonial officials who could not visit England to
receive the honour at the hand of the sovereign. The first instance
of such a creation by letters patent is that of Robert Chambers, a
judge in Bengal, in 1777 (see, however, the curious cases *infra*
pp. 181 and 250 under dates 1622–3, Feb. 1, and 1674–5, Feb. 22).
Many other instances of later date will be found in the present
volume. These letters patent are invariably dated from Whitehall.

Finally, there remains for discussion the curious subject of
the privilege supposed to pertain to eldest sons of baronets of
claiming knighthood on arriving at the age of 21. This privilege
appears to me to have been an afterthought in the creation of the
dignity of baronets. In fact I am not sure that the whole privilege
deos not rest on a complete misconception.

James I's original letters patent of 1611 for the creation of baronets contains no reference to the knighting either of the baronets themselves or of their eldest sons.* But after the dignity of baronets was erected there arose a dispute as to precedence between the younger sons of viscounts and barons on the one hand and the baronets [notice, the baronets themselves, not their sons] on the other. This dispute was settled by James by fresh letters patent dated 13th March, 14 James I. These letters patent contain the following clause :—" First His Majesty is pleased to knight the present baronets that are no knights, and doth also by these presents of his mere motion and favour promise and grant for him and his successors that such baronets *and the heirs male of their bodies* as hereafter shall be no knights when they shall attain or be of the age of 21 years, upon knowledge thereof given to the Lord Chamberlain of the Household or Vice-Chamberlain for the time being, or in their abence to any other officer attending upon His Majesty's person, shall be knighted by His Majesty his heirs and successors." It has been taken for granted for two centuries and more that by this clause James I. promised to knight the eldest sons of baronets *during the life of their father.* I offer it as a more probable interpretation that James only meant that all baronets should be knights or should be knighted, not merely the first created baronets but their successors *after they succeeded to the baronetcy.* He simply meant to provide that the dignity of knighthood and the style of " Sir " should be hereditary, *i.e.,* in the baronet and his heirs male, so that the son on succeeding to the baronetcy should be either *ipso facto* knight or should have the right of claiming knighthood if of 21 years of age; but not that he should be able to claim knighthood during the life of his father. I take it that it was an entire misconception and quite unjustifiable, when at a subsequent period the letters patent of creation of this or that particular baronetcy contained a clause covenanting for the knighthood of the son of the baronet " although in the lifetime of his father or grandfather."

---

* The terms used by James I. in the commission which he issued prior to the institution of the dignity of baronets are as follows :—

Concedimus quod stilus et additio baronetti apponatur in fine nominis ejusdem et heredum suorum masculorum . . . . volumus etiam et per praesentes ordinamus quod nomini dicti A B et heredum suorum masculorum praedictorum in sermone Anglicano et in omnibus scriptis Anglicanis praeponatur haec additio videlicet Anglice Sir et similiter quod uxores ejusdem A B et heredum suorum masculorum habeant et gaudeant hac appellatione videlicet Anglice Lady, Madame et Dame respective secundum usum loquendi . . . . quod praedictus A B et heredes sui masculi praedicti nomen, stilus etc., etc., cum omnibus privilegis, etc., eic., *successive* gerant et habeant . . . . In the first patent itself the words are et praedicti baronetti et eorum heredes masculi praedicti *respective et de tempore in tempus,* etc., etc. I consider these words *successive* and *respective et de tempore in tempus* to be quite decisive as to James's meaning. Each successive holder of the baronetcy shall on succeeding to the baronetcy be entitled to the style of *Sir* as part of his name. So much and absolutely nothing more. There is not a word as to any knighting or any claim to knighthood.

Although thus without justification, this privilege claimed by eldest sons of baronets remained in force until 1827, Dec. 19. By letters patent of that date George IV. was pleased to revoke and annul the letters patent of James I. so far as the said privilege is concerned, and to declare that in future the patents of baronetages should not contain the covenant which entitled eldest sons of baronets to claim knighthood. It is clear, however, that this revocation cannot have had a retrospective force, as there is at least one instance of the privilege being claimed and allowed at a date subsequent to that letter patent of George IV. At the levee on the 21st Feb., 1865, the lord lieutenant of Ireland, in accordance with the ancient privilege, conferred knighthood on Mr. George G. O'Donnell, eldest son of Sir Richard O'Donnell, bart., of Newport, County Mayo, in compliance with a clause in the patent of baronetcy granted in 1780 to Neale O'Donnell, Esq., grandfather of the said Sir Richard Annesley O'Donnell, bart. See the note of this knighthood *infra*, Vol. II., p. 357.

WM. A. SHAW.

The Knights dubbed in Ireland.

INTRODUCTION BY G D. BURTCHAELL.

ALTHOUGH the Sovereign may authorise any of his subjects to confer the honour of knighthood, the Lord Lieutenant General and General Governor of Ireland alone in right of his office possesses at the present day the Royal prerogative of dubbing Knights Bachelors.

In Ireland, as elsewhere, in the earliest times, after the introduction of chivalry into that country by the Anglo-Norman conquerors, every Knight possessed the power of transmitting the honour he had himself received to others. Several instances of this occur in the Anglo-Irish Annals. The exact period at which the privilege became restricted to the Chief Governors is uncertain.

During the fifteenth century the authority of the Chief Governor for the time being known as Lieutenant, Deputy, or Justice, was confined to the part of the country only which became known as the Pale; outside of which the great Anglo-Irish Magnates did that which was right in their own eyes. But soon after the accession of Henry VIII. to the throne plans began to be formed for the reduction of Ireland to the English rule

In the tract entitled *State of Ireland and plan for its reformation* (circa 1515), after recommending "that of the said Irish great land-lords and chief of every great nation that shall dispend by the King's grant 1,000 marks yearly, by estimation, be create and made Lord of the King's Parliament." It is recommended "also, that the chief of every petty nation of every Irish country, that shall dispend by the King's grant the sum of 500 marks, to him and his heirs for ever, be, at the will and discretion of the Deputy and the said captain (*i.e.*, chief), made Knight and shall enjoy the honour and worship of the order of Knighthood as other English Knights doth." The King writing to the Earl of Surrey, Lord Lieutenant in 1520, says:—"And whereas ye write it hath been accustomed heretofore that our Lieutenants General of that land, have not only had full and ample commission to proceed and execute our authority Royal against criminous persons, but also to give the Order of Knighthood to such noble men from time to time as should deserve the same; ye make instance to have such commission and authority to Us; We in consideration of your laudable and right agreeable service, and having full trust and confidence in your wisdom, soberness, and circumspection, and that ye will not proceed to the condemnation or executing of any noble person of name, till ye be advertised of our pleasure, and not to advance any manner of personage to the order of Knighthood but such as shall merit the same; We according to your desire, send unto you our ample commission and authority for that purpose accordingly; and can be agreeable that ye not only make O'Nele and such other Lords of the Irishry, as ye shall think good, Knights, but also to give unto the said O'Nele a collar of gold of our livery, which we also send unto you at this time by our servant Sir John Walop."

In August, 1541, Henry VIII. was proclaimed "King of Ireland." Sir Anthony St. Leger, K.G., then Lord Deputy, thus became the first "Viceroy," and from that date onwards the power of conferring Knighthood was certainly confined to the Chief Governors. With this date then a Roll of Knights dubbed in Ireland may be commenced.

No official record of Knights was, however, kept in Ireland before the time of Daniel Molyneux, an eminent antiquary, herald and genealogist, who was appointed Ulster King of Arms, 28th June, 1597. There was indeed no person to keep any such record before the institution of the office of Ulster King of Arms in 1552. But Molyneux did not start with his own accession to office. He commenced his list from the return to Ireland of Sir Henry Sidney, K.G., as Lord Deputy for the fourth time in January 1565-6. His original idea seems to have been to begin with the accession of the reigning Sovereign, Queen Elizabeth, to the throne, commencing with a list of the Knights who then existed. Several tentative lists for the purpose of this register are among the MS. collections of Ulster's Office, Molyneux's MS. now in the Library of Trinity College, Dublin, and in the British Museum. One of the last has been printed in Mr. Metcalfe's *Book of Knights*, headed by Thomas Earl of Ormond, who was, in fact, knighted in England in 1546. The materials Molyneux had to work upon were probably what accounts he could

find of fees received by his predecessors in office. This would, to a
certain extent, explain the imperfections and inaccuracies in the
first twenty years of his register. But from the appointment of his
uncle and immediate predecessor, Christopher Ussher, as Ulster
King of Arms, 30th June, 1588, until his own death in 1632, the list
appears to be complete, with the exception of two or three names,
perhaps omitted for the non-payment of fees. His successor, Thomas
Preston, 1633—1642, continued the record. Dr. William Roberts,
who succeeded, entered upon his office within a year after the great
Civil war had broken out, and made no attempt to keep a list of
Knights. To Richard Carney, who became Principal Herald of all
Ireland under the Commonwealth, is due the credit of returning to
Molyneux's practice by recording the names and arms of the Knights
dubbed by "Lord" Henry Cromwell. At the Restoration, Carney
was made Athlone Pursuivant, and Richard St. George, Ulster King
of Arms. The latter took no notice of Knights, but we are indebted
to Carney for keeping a list of those dubbed during St. George's reign
with, however, a sad gap of nine years, 1664 to 1674. He became
Ulster on the resignation of St. George in 1683, and thenceforward
noted the conferring of Knighthood as did also his son and successor,
Richard Carney II., 1692—1698, William Hawkins, 1698—1736, and
John Hawkins, 1736—1759. No list was kept by James MacCulloch,
1759—1765, Sir William Hawkins, 1765—1787, or Gerald Fortescue,
April to October, 1787. Sir Chichester Fortescue, the next Ulster,
noted a few Knights, but when Sir William Betham became Deputy
Ulster in 1809, he resumed the practice of keeping an official Register.
Betham succeeded Fortescue as Ulster in 1821, and was succeeded at
his death in 1853 by Sir J. Bernard Burke. By him and by the
present Ulster, Sir Arthur Vicars, who, on the death of Burke, was
appointed in 1893, the Register has been regularly kept.

While therefore in such circumstances it is impossible to compile
a complete Roll of Knights dubbed in Ireland, nevertheless the
Calendars of State Papers (Ireland) and more especially the Calendar
of Fiants of Henry VIII., Edward VI., Mary and Elizabeth published
in the Reports of the Deputy Keeper of the Public Records in Ireland
supply almost complete information as to the names of persons
Knighted during the period which they cover. The subsequent gaps
in the lists in Ulster's office can to a great extent be filled from other
sources, the most difficult period to deal with being the fifty years
from 1759 to 1809. Newspapers afford a certain amount of informa-

tion, but the names of Knights were not officially gazetted unless when the fees were paid.

The Chief Governors of Ireland were known by the different titles of Lord Lieutenant, Lord Deputy, Lord Justice and Lord Justices. One Lord Justice, and sometimes two, were appointed to carry on the Government during the absence from Ireland of the Lord Lieutenant, or Lord Deputy for the time being, or during the vacancy of those offices, but since the commencement of the reign of James I. they have always been two or three in number. The last instance of Knighthood being conferred by the Lords Justices was in 1765, when their Excellencies John Lord Bowes, Lord Chancellor, and John Ponsonby, Speaker of the House of Commons, Knighted the Lord Mayor of Dublin, Sir James Taylor. Here we have an instance of the strange anomaly that Knighthood can be conferred by the Chief Governors of Ireland although they have not themselves received it, and in modern times this has frequently been the case.

Whenever the Sovereign sets foot in Ireland the functions of the Chief Governors cease, and Knights have been dubbed there by Richard II., James II., William III., George IV., Victoria and Edward VII.

The greatest number of Knights made by any Chief Governor was 83, dubbed by Henry Viscount Falkland, who was Lord Deputy for seven years from September, 1622, to October, 1629. This record was very nearly surpassed by Robert Earl of Essex, Lord Lieutenant, who in little more than four months, 5th May to 24th Sept., 1599, made 81 Knights. This drew forth the ire of Queen Elizabeth, who in October issued a Proclamation declaring the titles of 38 of those Knighted in August and September null and void. Knights, however, cannot be unmade in this manner, and the Proclamation was without effect.

From the Annals of Clyn, Grace, Ware and the Book of Howth are gathered the following early instances of Knights being made in Ireland.

1284. William Waspayl.

1308. Richard, Earl of Ulster, at Trim, at Pentecost, made Walter de Lacy and Hugh de Lacy Knights.

1312. At Christmas, Lord John Fitzthomas (Fitz-Gerald), at Adayr, made Nicholas fitz-Maurice of Kerry, and Robert de Clahull Knights. Some say two others.

1313. Lord Edmund Butler (Lord Justice) at Dublin at Michaelmas made thirty Knights.

1313. Christmas following, at the marriage of Maurice fitz-Thomas (Fitz-Gerald) with Katherine, daughter of Richard, Earl of Ulster, Edmund le Botiller made two Knights.

1316. Richard de Bermingham, Lord of Athenry, at Athenry, on St. Lawrence's day, knighted John Hussee, a butcher of Athenry for his bravery in the victory gained over the Irish.

1317. At Easter, at Loddyn, near Limerick, six Knights were made.

1317. Roger de Mortimer, Lord Justice, on landing at Youghal made two Knights.

1317. He also at Dublin, on Sunday, the day after St. Valentine's day, made John Bermingham, John Mortimer, and two or three others Knights.

1330. On Wednesday, the eve of St. Margaret the Virgin, in the Camp near Moyalby, the Earl of Ulster made Walter de Bermingham and another of his family Knights, Sir Walter made Sir Richard de la Rokel and Sir Gilbert de Bermingham; and the Earl of Ormond made Sir Edmund le Boteller, Robert and Patrick Travers Knights; and Sir William de Bermingham made Sir John de St. Aubyn and John Monsell Knights, at the same time and place.

1333. On Friday following the Saturday on the morrow of St. Remigius Thomas Cantwell was made Knight at Thurles by James le Botiller.

1335. On Wednesday, in the octaves of St. Francis, Lord James, Earl of Ormond, entered the lands of the O'Byrns, of Duffyr, spoiled and burned them, and made there Fulk de la Frene, Knight : and Sir Fulk made Sir Gregory de la Launde and Matthew fitz-Oliver (de la Frene) Knights the same day and place.

1335. On Wednesday, in the octaves of St. John the Apostle, Lord Maurice fitz-Thomas, Earl of Desmond, made seven Knights near Greyn (i.e, Pallasgrean, Co. Limerick), on the expedition against Brien O'Brien

1336. On Monday, on the feast of Fabian and Sebastian, James le Botiller, at Roscrea, made John de Rochfort and Geoffrey Schorthalis Knights

1337. On Monday, on the morrow of St. Lawrence, Henry de Valle was made Knight by the Butler on the expedition against the O'Byrnes at Arklow.

1338. On the last day of August the Earl of Desmond made fourteen Knights at Rathymegan.

1342. On the 16th day of March Richard fitz-Redmund le Ercedekne was made Knight in Desmond by Maurice fitz-Thomas Earl of Desmond, and the said Richard made three Knights the same day, and William Grant at that time made John le Ercedekne Knight.

1361. Lionel, Earl of Ulster, Justiciary, in the war with O'Byrne, made Knights—Robert Preston, Robert Holywood, Thomas Talbot, Walter Cusack, James de la Hide, John de la Freigne, Patrick and Robert de la Freigne, and many others.

1394. On Lady day, in March, King Richard II. Knighted the four Kings of Ireland—O'Neill, King of Ulster; O'Brien, King of Munster; MacMurrogh, King of Leinster; and O'Conor, King of Connaught—together with Sir Thomas Owghrem, Sir Jonathas Pado, and Sir John Pado.

1397. Edmund, Earl of March, Lord Lieutenant, wasted O'Brien's country, and at the winning of the chief house, made the following Knights—Sir Christopher Preston, Sir John Bedlow, Sir Edmund Loundres, Sir John Loundres, Sir William Nugent, Sir Walter de la Hyde, and Robert Caddell.

1399. In June in the County Kildare, King Richard II. made several Knights, among them Prince Henry of Lancaster, afterwards King Henry V. He was the only Sovereign of England who received the honour of Knighthood in Ireland.

1419. The 4th of the Ides of May MacMorthe (i.e., MacMurrogh), Chief Captain of his Nation and of all the Irish in Leinster, was taken prisoner and the same day was Sir Hugh Cokesy made Knight.

Knighthood was conferred upon the following Mayors of Dublin, in some cases probably for their Military rather than their Municipal Services:—

1428. Sir Walter Tyrrell, then being Mayor for the third time.

1450. Sir Robert Burnell. He was again Mayor in 1454, 1458 and 1461.

1453. Sir Nicholas Woder, then Mayor for the ninth time.

1464. Sir Thomas Newbury, then Mayor for the ninth time. He served a tenth time in 1467.

1468. Sir William Grampe, or Grampy, who had previously been
    Mayor in 1466.

In 1474 the Fraternity of Arms of St. George was established
by Parliament for the defence of the Pale, and has sometimes been
regarded as an Order of Knighthood. Lodge refers to it as the
Order of the Garter in Ireland. But the members of the fraternity
were not required to be Knights or to receive Knighthood upon their
admission, and the Mayors of Dublin and Drogheda for the time
being were always to be members. It was abolished by Parliament
in 1494.

The names of a vast number of Irish Knights, who flourished
prior to the middle of the sixteenth century, can be gathered from
the Patent and Close Rolls, Pipe Rolls, and Plea Rolls of Ireland,
and other sources, but the time, place and circumstances of their
Knighting it would now be impossible to determine and no attempt
has been made to collect them here. The Knights dubbed in Ireland
in the following list commence with those who, as far as can be
ascertained, exclusive of Peers, were living when Ireland was erected
into a Kingdom in 1541. Not only has free access to the entire
Records of the Office of Arms being accorded to me by Sir Arthur
Vicars, K.C.V.O., Ulster, but also to his own extensive MS. collections,
and his valuable suggestions and assistance I most gratefully
acknowledge.

                              G. D. BURTCHAELL.

Addenda of
Scotch Knights dubbed by Charles I.

Knights dubbed by Charles I. during his abode in Scotland from the 13th of June to the 16th of July, 1633. Printed from Sir James Balfour's "Historical Works," iv., pp. 364—7: "From his Majesty's coming to Scotland to his returne for England he dubbed 54 knights at severall tymes, in diversse places." (*Ibid* 1, p 202.)

These names are not recorded in the Register of Knights at the Heralds' College in London, the reason being doubtless that the fees arising therefrom were payable to Lyon King of Arms and that as a consequence the English Heralds had no interest in making the entries of the names. The proper place for these knights is, of course, their strict chronological place among the Knights Bachelors. They are entered because they were discovered after the volume was in print and it was impossible for the moment to upset the text by so large an insertion. They will be printed in their proper place in a subsequent edition.

1633, June 14. JA HACKETT, junior, of Pitfirrin (at Dalkeith).

1633, June 15. ALEX. CLERK, provost of Edinburgh (at Edinburgh, at his Majesty's entry)

1633, June 17. ARTHUR DOUGLAS, of Whittinghem (in the Withdrawing Chamber at Holyrood House, on the occasion of the creation of the Marquess of Douglas).

1633, June 17. VILL CARMICHELL, of that ilk (*ibid*, same occasion).

1633, June 17. VILL AUTHENLECK, of Balmano (*ibid*, same occasion).

1633, June 17. VILL ROBINSONE, of Neubie (*ibid*, same occasion).

1633, June 17. Jo DOUGLAS, of Barras (*ibid*, same occasion).

1633, June 17. JA NICOLESONE, of Coberspeth (*ibid*, same occasion).

1633, June 17. THO BLARE, of Balthaiocke (*ibid*, in the afternoon on the occasion of the creation of the earl of Kinnoul).

1633, June 17. PEITER HAY, of Meginche (*ibid*, same occasion).

1633, June 17. PAT OGILVEY, junior, of Inchemartyne (*ibid*, same occasion).

1633, June 17. THO STEUARTE, junior, of Gairntilley, (*ibid*, same occasion).

1633, June 17. PATRICK HAY, of Pitfoure (*ibid*, same occasion).

1633, June 18. GEO. COCKBURNE, of Ormestoune (at Holyrood House).

1633, June 20. Jo. SETTONE, of St. German's (at Holyrood).

1633, June 22. Jo. VATCHOUPE, of Nidrie (at Holyrood House).

1633, June 22. PATR. HAMILTONE, of Litlepreston (*ibid*).

1633, June 22. DAVID SYBALD, of Rankeilor (*ibid*).

1633, June 22. ALEX. CARNAGY, of Balnamoune (in the privy gallery at Holyrood, about 6 o'clock at night).

1633, June 22. JA. STEUARTE, of Butte (*ibid et tunc*).

1633, June 23. PAULE MENZIES, of Kinmundie, provost of Aberdeen (*ibid*, at 7 o'clock at night).

1633, June 23. LUDOUICK STEUARTE, junior, of Minto (*ibid et tunc*).

1633, June 28. VILL DOUGLAS, of Cavers, sheriff of Teifidale (at Edinburgh, at the Parliament House).

1633, July 5. ALEXANDER SUYNTONE, of that ilk (at Dumfermline, on the occasion of the creation of the earl of Ancrum).

1633, July 5. JA. MONEPENEY, junior, of Pitmilley (*ibid*, same occasion).

1633, July 5. Jo. DUNDAS, of Fingaslie (*ibid*, same occasion).

1633, July 5. THO. KER, of Kedden (*ibid*, same occasion).

1633, July 12. EDMOND BOYER, (Bowyer), of Camberwell, an English gentleman (*ibid*, same occasion). [As Bowyer was an English subject, his fees were due to the English Heralds. We should therefore expect that his name would be recorded by them. And this is what we do find; for in the Register at the Heralds' College there is entered the original certificate of Sir James Balfour, Lyon King of Arms, of Bowyer's knighthood. He, accordingly, appears in his proper place in the list of Knights Bachelors, *infra*, 11, p. 201. He is, of course, the only one in the present list of knights who does so appear in the English records].

1633, July 12   Archibald Douglas, junior, of Maines (at Dalkeith).

1633, July 12.   Tho. Ruthven, of Freeland (*ibid*).

1633, July 12.   Vill. Rosse, of Murrestone (at Holyrood).

1633, July 12.   Merke Ker, of Manldsley (*ibid*).

1633, July 12   Jo. Haldane, of Gleneggies (ibid).

1633, July 12.   Alex. Kennedy, of Collen (ibid).

1633, July 12.   Geo. Halibruntone, of Fodrens (*ibid*, in the morning about 10 o'clock, being Friday).

1633, July 12.   Ja. Banantyne, of Neuhall (*ibid*).

1633, July 12.   Alex. Settone, of Getlereuche (*ibid*).

1633, July 12   Three senators of the College of Justice (*ibid*).

1633, July 12.   Leufs Steuarte, advocate (*ibid*, a little after the three senators).

1633, July 14.   Ja. Murray, senior, son to the sheriff of Forrest (at Seton, being Sunday).

1633, July 14.   Ja Hamiltone, senior, of Bromehill (*ibid*)

1633, July 14.   Ja. Murray, of Baberton, master of [the] Works (*ibid*).

1633, July 14.   Ro Grahame, junior, of Morpsie (*ibid*).

1633, July 14.   David Crightone, of Lugtoune (*ibid*).

1633, July 15.   Duncane Campell, junior, of Achinbu (*ibid*, in the morning)

1633, July 15.   Will. Simple (Sempill), brother to the lord Sempill (*ibid*, after dinner)

1633, July 15.   Alex. Settone (Seton), second son of G. earl of Wintoun, and himself afterwards viscount of Kingston (*ibid et tunc*).

1633, July 15.   Tho. Settone, brother to the said earl of Wintoun (*ibid et tunc*)

1633, July 15.   Andrew Murray, of Balvaird (*ibid et tunc*).

1633, July 15   Andr. Hay, junior, of Keilor (*ibid et tunc*).

1633, July 16.   Tho Hope, junior, advocate (at Innerwicke).

1633, July 16   Bryce Blare, of that ilk (*ibid*)

1633, July 16.   Villiam Blare, of Balgillo (*ibid*).

1633, July 16   Patrick Douglas, of Kilspindey (*ibid*).

1633, July 16   Alex. Shaw, of Sauchie (*ibid*).

1633, July 16   Alex. Hamiltone, brother to the earl of Abercorn (*ibid*).

1633, July 16.   Patrick Abercrombay, a gentleman pensioner (*ibid*).

1633, July 16.   Ja Auchmutey, a gentleman pensioner (*ibid*).

The Most Noble Order of the Garter.

The Most Noble Order of the Garter.

KING EDWARD III., the first Sovereign.

Died 1377, June 21.

KNIGHTS FOUNDERS.

1348, Apr. 23. EDWARD (PLANTAGENET), prince of Wales. Died 1376, June 8. (1)

1348, Apr. 23. HENRY (PLANTAGENET), earl of Derby, afterwards duke of Lancaster. Died 1360–1, March 24. (2)

1348, Apr. 23. THOMAS (BEAUCHAMP), 11th earl of Warwick. Died 1369, Nov. 13. (3)

1348, Apr. 23. JOHN DE GRAILLY, vicomte de Benanges et Castillon, Captal de Buch. Died before April 4, 1377. (4)

1348, Apr. 23. RALPH (STAFFORD), lord, afterwards earl of, Stafford. Died 1372, Aug. 31. (5)

1348, Apr. 23. WILLIAM (DE MONTACUTE), 5th earl of Salisbury. Died 1397, June 3. (6)

1348, Apr. 23. Sir ROGER (DE MORTIMER), 4th lord Mortimer de Wigmore, afterwards 2nd earl of March. Died 1359–60, Feb. 26. (7)

1348, Apr. 23. JOHN (DE LISLE), 2nd lord Lisle de Rougemont. Died 1356, Oct. 14. (8)

1348, Apr. 23. Sir BARTHOLOMEW BURGHERSH, afterwards 3rd lord Burghersh. Died 1369, April 5. (9)

1348, Apr. 23. Sir JOHN BEAUCHAMP, afterwards lord Beauchamp de Warwick. Died 1360, Dec. 2. (10)

1348, Apr. 23. JOHN (MOHUN), 2nd lord Mohun de Dunster. Died 1376, Sept. 14. (11)

1348, Apr. 23. Sir HUGH COURTENAY, son and heir apparent of Hugh, earl of Devon. Died before 1349, Sept. 2. (12)

1348, Apr. 23. Sir THOMAS HOLAND, afterwards 7th earl of Kent. Died 1360, Dec. 28. (13)

1348, Apr. 23. JOHN (GREY), 1st lord Grey de Rotherfield. Died 1359, Sept. 1. (14)

1348, Apr. 23. Sir RICHARD FITZ-SIMON of Simons Hide, Herts. Latest notice of him 1347–8. (15)

1348, Apr. 23. Sir MILES STAPLETON of Bedale, Co. Yorks, and of Ingham, Norfolk. Died 1364, Dec. 4. (16)

1348, Apr. 23. Sir THOMAS WALE of Wedon, Pinkeney, Co. Northampton. Died 1352, Oct. 26. (17)

1348, Apr. 23. Sir HUGH WROTTESLEY of Wrottesley, Co. Stafford. Died 1380–1, Jan. 23. (18)

1348, Apr. 23. Sir NELE LORYNG of Chalgrave, Co. Bedford. Died 1385–6, March 18. (19)

1348, Apr. 23. Sir JOHN CHANDOS. Died 1369, Dec. 31. (20)

1348, Apr. 23. Sir JAMES AUDLEY of Stratton Audley, Co. Oxford. Died 1369. (21)

1348, Apr. 23. Sir OTHO HOLAND, brother of No. 13. Died 1359, Sept. 3. (22)

1348, Apr. 23. Sir HENRY EAM. Latest notice of him 1358, May 15. Died before 1360. (23)

1348, Apr. 23. Sir SANCHET D'ABRICHECOURT. Latest notice of him 1345, Oct. 20. (24)

1348, Apr. 23. Sir WALTER PAVELY of Boughton Aluph, Kent. Died 1375, June 28. (25)

---

after 1348. Sir WILLIAM FITZWARYNE. Died 1361, Oct. 28. In place of No. 24. (26)

after 1348. ROBERT (DE UFFORD), 1st earl of Suffolk. Died 1369, Nov. 4. In place of No. 15. (27)

after 1349, Sept. 2. WILLIAM (DE BOHUN), 5th earl of Northampton. Died 1360, Sept. 6. In place of No. 12. (28)

after 1352, Oct. 26. REGINALD (DE COBHAM), 1st lord Cobham of Sterborough. Died 1361, Oct. 5. In place of No. 17. (29)

after 1356, Oct. 14. Sir RICHARD DE LA VACHE. Died about 1365–6, Jan. 29. In place of No. 8. (30)

after 1358, May 15. THOMAS (UGHTRED), lord Ughtred. Died shortly before 1365, May 28. In place of No. 23. (31)

after 1359, Sept. 1. Sir WALTER (MANNY), 1st lord Manny. Died 1371-2, Jan. 13. In place of No. 14. (32)

after 1359, Sept. 3. Sir FRANK VAN HALE. Died before 1376, Apr. 4. In place of No. 22. (33)

after 1359-60, Feb. 26 Sir THOMAS UFFORD. Died before 1368, Nov. 18. In place of No. 7. (34)

after 1360, Dec. 2. LIONEL (PLANTAGENET), "of Antwerp," earl of Ulster, afterwards duke of Clarence, 3rd son of Edward III. Died 1368, Oct. 17. In place of No. 10. (35)

after 1360, Dec. 28. JOHN (PLANTAGENET), "of Gaunt," afterwards duke of Lancaster and king of Castile and Leon, 4th son of Edward III. Died 1398-9, Feb. 3. In place of No. 13. (36)

after 1360, Sept. 16. EDMUND (PLANTAGENET), "of Langley," afterwards earl of Cambridge and Duke of York, 5th son of Edward III. Died 1402, Aug. 1. In place of No. 28. (37)

after 1360-1, Mar. 24. EDWARD (LE DESPENCER), 5th lord le Despencer. Died 1375, Nov. 11. In place of No. 2. (38)

after 1361, Oct. 5. Sir JOHN SULLY. Died about 1388. In place of No. 29. (39)

after 1361, Oct. 28. WILLIAM (LATIMER), 4th lord Latimer. Died 1381, May 28. In place of No. 26. (40)

after 1364, Dec. 4. HUMPHREY (DE BOHUN), 12th earl of Hereford, etc. Died 1372-3, Jan. 16. In place of No. 16. (41)

after 1365, May 28. INGELRAM DE COUCI, sire de Couci, etc , afterwards 2nd earl of Bedford, husband of Isabella daughter of Edward III. Died 1396-7, Feb. 18. In place of No. 31. (42)

after 1365-6, Jan. Sir HENRY PERCY, afterwards 1st earl of Northumberland, attainted in 1406. Died 1407-8, Feb. 19 In place of No. 30. (43)

after 1368, Oct. 17. RALPH (BASSET), 4th lord Basset of Drayton. Died 1390, May 10. In place of No. 35. (44)

after 1368, Nov. 18. Sir RICHARD PEMBRUGGE. Died 1375, July 26. In place of No. 34. (45)

after 1369, April 5. JOHN (DE NEVILL), 3rd lord Nevill de Raby.
Died 1388, Oct. 17. In place of No. 9.   (46)

after 1369, Nov. 4. Sir ROBERT DE NAMUR. Died 1392, Aug. 18.
In place of No. 27.   (47)

after 1369, Nov. 13. JOHN (HASTINGS), 12th earl of Pembroke.
Died 1375 or 1376, Apr. 16. In place of No. 3.   (48)

? 1369. Sir THOMAS DE GRANSON. Died between April 14, 1375,
and April 4, 1376. In place of No. 21.   (49)

after 1369, Dec. 31. GUY (BRYAN), lord Bryan. Died 1390, Aug.
17. In place of No. 20.   (50)

after 1371-2, Jan. 13. Sir GUICHARD D'ANGLE, afterwards 12th earl
of Huntingdon. Died 1380, between March 25 and April
4. In place of No. 32.   (51)

after 1372, Aug. 31. Sir ALAN BUXHULL. Died 1381, Nov. 2. In
place of No. 5.   (52)

after 1372-3, Jan. 16. THOMAS (BEAUCHAMP), 12th earl of Warwick.
Died 1401, April 8. In place of No. 41.   (53)

after 1375, Apr. 16. JOHN (DE MONTFORT *otherwise* DE BRETAGNE),
duke of Brittany and count of Montfort and earl of Rich-
mond; husband of Mary, 4th daughter of Edward III.
Died 1399, Nov. 1 or 2. In place of No. 48.   (54)

after 1375, June 28. Sir THOMAS BANASTRE. Died 1379, Dec. 16.
In place of No. 25.   (55)

after 1375, July 26. WILLIAM (DE UFFORD), 2nd earl of Suffolk.
Died 1381-2, Feb. 13. In place of No. 45.   (56)

after 1375, Nov. 11. HUGH (STAFFORD), 2nd earl of Stafford. Died
1386, Sept. 26 or Oct. 2. In place of No. 38.   (57)

after 1376, Sept. 14. THOMAS (DE HOLAND), 8th earl of Kent. Died
1397, April 25. In place of No. 11.   (58)

after 1376, Apr. 4. Sir THOMAS PERCY, afterwards 2nd earl of
Worcester. Beheaded 1403, July 23. In place of No. 49. (59)

after 1376, Apr. 4. Sir WILLIAM BEAUCHAMP, afterwards 18th lord
Bergavenny. Died 1411, May 8. In place of No. 33. (60)

1377, Apr. 23. RICHARD (PLANTAGENET), prince of Wales, afterwards King Richard II. Died 1400, Feb. 10. In place of No. 1. (61)

1377, Apr. 23. HENRY (PLANTAGENET), 9th earl of Derby, afterwards duke of Lancaster and King Henry IV. Died 1412–3, March 20. In place of No. 4. (62)

RICHARD II., the second Sovereign (1377, June 21).

after 1377, June 21. Sir JOHN BURLEY Died 1383, between June and October. In place of No. 36, who was translated to the prince's stall on the accession of the Sovereign. (63)

after 1377, Aug. 26. Sir LEWIS CLIFFORD. Died between Sept. 19 and Dec. 5, 1404. In place of No. 42, who surrendered the order 1377, Aug. 26. (64)

after 1379, Dec. 16. BERMOND ARNAUD DE PREISSAC, Soudan de la Trau. Latest notice of him 1384, July 26. In place of No. 55. (65)

after 1380, Apr. 4. THOMAS (PLANTAGENET), "of Woodstock," 6th son of Edward III., earl of Buckingham, afterwards duke of Gloucester. Murdered 1397, Sept. (?) 8. In place of No 51. (66)

after 1380–1, Jan. 23. Sir THOMAS FELTON. Died 1381, Apr 26. In place of No 18. (67)

after 1381, Apr. 26. Sir JOHN HOLAND, afterwards earl of Huntingdon and 1st duke of Exeter, half-brother to Richard II. Beheaded 1399–1400, Jan. 15. In place of No 67 (68)

after 1381, May 28. Sir SIMON BURLEY. Beheaded 1388, May 15. In place of No. 40. (69)

after 1381, Nov. 2. Sir BRYAN STAPLETON. Died 1394, July 25. In place of No. 52. (70)

after 1381–2, Feb. 13. Sir RICHARD BURLEY. Died 1387, May 23 In place of No. 56. (71)

after 1383, June–Oct. THOMAS (MOWBRAY), earl of Nottingham, afterwards 2nd duke of Norfolk. Died 1400 (? 1399), Sept. 22 or 27. In place of No. 63. (72)

after 1384, July 26. ROBERT (DE VERE), 9th earl of Oxford, afterwards Duke of Ireland. Attainted 1387-8, Feb. 13. Died 1392, Nov. 22. In place of 65. (73)

after 1385-6, Mar. 18. RICHARD (FITZ-ALAN), 15th earl Arundell. Beheaded 1397, Sept. 21. In place of No. 19. (74)

after 1386, Oct. 2. Sir NICHOLAS SARNESFELD. Died 1394-5. In place of No. 57. (75)

after 1387, May 23. EDWARD (PLANTAGENET), afterwards 2nd duke of York and duke of Albemarle. Died 1415, Oct. 25. In place of No. 71. (76)

after 1387-8, Feb. 13. Sir HENRY PERCY, called Hotspur, son of the 1st earl of Northumberland. Died 1403, July 21. In place of and on the attainder of No. 73. (77)

after 1388, May 15. JOHN (DEVEREUX), 2nd lord Devereux. Died 1392-3, Feb. 22. In place of No. 69. (78)

after 1388, Oct. 17. Sir PETER COURTENAY. Died 1404-5, Feb. 2. In place of No. 46. (79)

? 1388 (or 1386). THOMAS (LE DESPENCER), 6th lord le Despencer, afterwards earl of Gloucester. Beheaded 1399-1400, Jan. 17. In place of No 39. (80)

after 1390, May 10. WILLIAM I., duke of Guelders and Juliers. Died 1401-2, Feb. 16. In place of 44. (81)

after 1390, Aug. 17. WILLIAM VI., count of Holland, duke of Bavaria and count of Hennegau, Holland and Zealand. Died 1417, May 31. In place of No. 50. (82)

after 1392, Aug. 18. JOHN (BOURCHIER), 2nd lord Bourchier. Died 1400, May 21. In place of No. 47. (83)

after 1392-3, Feb. 22. JOHN (BEAUMONT), 4th lord Beaumont. Died 1396, Sept. 9. In place of No. 78. (84)

after 1394, July 25. Sir WILLIAM LE SCROPE, afterwards 1st earl of Wiltshire. Beheaded 1399, July 30. In place of No. 70. (85)

? 1394-5. Sir WILLIAM ARUNDEL. Died 1400, Aug. In place of No. 75. (86)

after 1396, Sept. 9. Sir JOHN BEAUFORT, afterwards earl of Somerset and marquess of Dorset. Died 1410, April 21. (87)

after 1397, Apr. 25., THOMAS (DE HOLAND), 9th earl of Kent, afterwards duke of Surrey. Beheaded 1399–1400, Jan. 7. In place of No. 58. (88)

after 1397, June 3. JOHN (DE MONTACUTE), 6th earl of Salisbury. Beheaded 1399–1400, Jan. 7. In place of No. 6. (89)

after 1397, Sept. 8. ALBERT COUNT PALATINE, duke of Bavaria, count of Holland. Died 1404, Dec. 13. In place of No. 66. (90)

after 1397, Sept. 21. Sir SIMON FELBRIGGE. Died 1442, Dec. 3. In place of No. 74. (91)

after 1398–9, Feb. 3. Sir PHILIP DE LA VACHE. Died between April 25, 1407 and June 22, 1408. In place of No. 36. (92)

HENRY IV., the third Sovereign (1399, Sept. 29).

after 1399, Sept. 29. HENRY (PLANTAGENET), prince of Wales, afterwards Henry V. Upon the accession of the Sovereign. Died 1422, Aug. 31. (93)

after 1399, July 30. THOMAS (PLANTAGENET), "of Lancaster," afterwards 2nd Duke of Clarence, 2nd son of Henry IV. Died 1420–1, March 22. In place of No. 85. (94)

after 1400 (? 1399), Sept. 2. JOHN (PLANTAGENET), "of Lancaster," afterwards duke of Bedford and Regent of France, 3rd son of Henry IV. Died 1435, Sept. 14. In place of No. 72. (95)

after 1399, Nov. 1. HUMPHREY (PLANTAGENET), "of Lancaster," afterwards duke of Gloucester, 4th son of Henry IV. Died 1446–7, Feb. 28. In place of No. 54. (96)

after 1399–1400, Jan. 7. THOMAS (FITZ ALAN), 17th earl of Arundel. Died 1415, Oct. 13. In place of No. 89. (97)

after 1399–1400, Jan. 7. Sir THOMAS BEAUFORT, afterwards 2nd duke of Exeter. Died 1426, Dec. 30. In place of No. 88. (98)

1403, July 22. RICHARD (BEAUCHAMP), 13th earl of Warwick. Died 1439, Apr. 30. In place of No. 80. (99)

after 1399–1400, Jan. 15. WILLIAM (WILLOUGHBY), 5th lord Willoughby de Eresby. Died 1409, Nov. 30. In place of No. 68. (100)

after 1400, May 21. Sir THOMAS REMPSTON. Died 1406, Oct. 31.
In place of No. 83. (101)

after 1400, Aug. JOHN I., king of Portugal, brother-in-law of
Henry IV. Died 1433, Aug. 14. In place of No. 86. (102)

after 1401, Apr. 8. Sir THOMAS ERPYNGHAM. Slain 1428, July 4.
In place of No. 53. (103)

1402, April. EDMUND (STAFFORD), 5th earl of Stafford. Died 1403,
July 21. In place of No. 81. (104)

after 1402, Aug. 1. RALPH (DE NEVIL), lord Nevil de Raby, after-
wards 1st earl of Westmorland. Died 1425, Oct. 21. In
place of No 37. (105)

after 1403, July 21. EDMOND (DE HOLAND), 10th earl of Kent. Died
1408, Sept. 18. In place of No. 104. (106)

after 1403, July 21. RICHARD (GREY), 4th lord Grey de Codnor.
Died 1418, Aug. 1. In place of No. 77. (107)

after 1403, July 23. WILLIAM (DE ROS), 7th lord Ros of Hamlake.
Died 1414, Sept. 1. In place of No. 59. (108)

after 1404, Dec. 5 Sir JOHN STANLEY. Died 1413–4, Jan. 8. In
place of No. 64. (109)

after 1404, Dec 13. ERIC IX., king of Denmark, Sweden and
Norway, son-in-law to Henry IV. Died 1459. In place
of No. 90. (110)

after 1404–5, Feb. 2. JOHN (LOVEL), 5th lord Lovel of Titchmersh.
Died between July 26 and Sept. 12, 1408. In place of
No. 79. (111)

after 1406, Oct. 31 HUGH (BURNELL), 3rd lord Burnell. Died 1420,
Nov. 27. In place of No. 101. (112)

? after 1407–8, Feb. 19. EDWARD (CHERLETON), 5th lord Cherleton
de Powys. Died 1420–1, March 14. In place of No. 43.
(113)

? after 1408, June 22. GILBERT (TALBOT), 5th lord Talbot. Died
1419, Oct. 19. In place of No 92. (114)

? after 1408, Sept. 12. HENRY (FITZ-HUGH), 3rd lord Fitz-Hugh.
Died 1424–5, Jan. 11. In place of No. 111. (115)

after 1408, Sept. 18. Sir ROBERT UMFRAVILLE. Died 1436, Dec. 27.
In place of No. 106.   (116)

after 1410, Apr. 21. Sir JOHN CORNWALL, afterwards lord Fanhope.
Died 1443, Dec. 1. In place of No. 87.   (117)

after 1409, Nov. 30. HENRY (LE SCROPE), 3rd lord Scrope de
Masham. Beheaded 1415, Aug. 5. In place of No. 100. (118)

after 1411, May 8. THOMAS (DE MORLEY), 4th lord Morley. Died
1416, Sept. 24. In place of No. 60.   (119)

HENRY V., the fourth Sovereign.

Succeeded 1412–13, March 20.

after 1412–3, Mar. 20. Sir JOHN D'ABRICHECOURT. Died between
July 26 and Oct. 1, 1415. Upon accession of the Sovereign.
(120)

after 1413–4, Jan. 8. THOMAS (DE MONTACUTE), 7th earl of Salisbury.
Died 1428, Nov. 3. In place of No. 109.   (121)

after 1414, Sept. 1. THOMAS (DE CAMOYS), lord Camoys. Died 1419,
March 28. In place of No. 108.   (122)

after 1415, Aug. 5. Sir WILLIAM HARYNGTON. Died before 1439–40,
March 12. In place of No. 118.   (123)

? after 1415, Oct. 1. WILLIAM (LA ZOUCHE), 4th lord Zouche de
Haryngworth. Died 1415, Nov. 3. In place of No. 120. (124)

after 1415, Oct. 13. Sir JOHN HOLAND, afterwards earl of Hunting-
don and 3rd duke of Exeter. Died 1447, Aug. 5. In place
of No. 97.   (125)

after 1415, Oct. 25. RICHARD (DE VERE), 11th earl of Oxford. Died
1416–7, Feb. 15. In place of No. 76.   (126)

after 1415, Nov. 3. SIGISMUND, Emperor of Germany. Installed
1416, May. Died 1437, Dec. 9. In place of No. 124.   (127)

after 1416, Sept. 24. ROBERT (WILLOUGHBY), 6th lord Willoughby
de Eresby. Died 1452, July 25. In place of No. 119   (128)

after 1416–7, Feb. 15. Sir JOHN BLOUNT. Died before 1418, Nov.
11. In place of No. 126.   (129)

after 1417, May 31. Sir JOHN ROBESSART. Elected by the Sovereign
  whilst serving with him in Normandy. Died 1450, Dec. 24.
  In place of No. 82.   (130)

after 1418, Aug. 1. HUGH (STAFFORD), lord Stafford or 4th lord
  Bourchier. Elected *ut supra*. Died 1420, Oct. 25. In
  place of No. 107.   (131)

? after 1418, Nov. 11. Sir WILLIAM PHELIPP, afterwards 6th lord
  Bardolf. Elected *ut supra*. Died 1441, June 6. In place
  of No. 129.   (132)

after 1419, Oct. 19. Sir JOHN (GREY), earl of Tankerville in Nor-
  mandy. Slain 1420–1, March 22. Elected *ut supra*. In
  place of No. 114.   (133)

after 1420, Oct. 25. Sir WALTER HUNGERFORD, afterwards 1st lord
  Hungerford. Installed 1421, May 3. Died 1449, Aug. 9.
  In place of No. 131.   (134)

1421, May 3. Sir LEWIS ROBESSART, afterwards lord Robessart or
  lord Bourchier. Died 1431, Nov. 26. In place of No. 112.
                                                         (135)
1421, May 3. Sir HERTONG VON CLUX. Died about 1445–6. In
  place of No. 113.   (136)

1421, May 3. JOHN (DE CLIFFORD), 7th lord de Clifford. Slain
  1421–2, March 13. In place of No. 122.   (137)

1421, May 3. JOHN (DE MOWBRAY), earl Marshal, afterwards 4th
  duke of Norfolk. Died 1432, Oct. 19. In place of No. 133.
                                                         (138)
1421, May 3. WILLIAM (DE LA POLE), 6th earl, afterwards 1st duke
  of Suffolk. Killed 1450, May 2. In place of No. 94. (139)

1422, April 25. PHILIP II., Duke of Burgundy. Declined to accept
  the order.   (140)

HENRY VI., the fifth Sovereign.

Succeeded 1422, Aug. 31.

1424, May 6. JOHN (TALBOT), 7th lord Talbot, afterwards 4th earl
  of Shrewsbury. Slain 1453, July 17. In place of No. 140.
                                                         (141)
1425, Apr. 22. Sir THOMAS (DE SCALES), 7th lord Scales. Died 1460,
  July 25. In place of No. 115.   (142)

1426, Apr. 22. Sir JOHN FASTOLF. Died 1460, Nov. 5. In place of No. 105. (143)

1427, Apr. 22. PETER, duke of Coimbra, 3rd son of John I. of Portugal and of Philippa of Lancaster, sister of Henry IV. Ensigns sent to him 1427, May 22. Installed by proxy 1428, Apr. 22. Slain at Alfato Robero 1449, May 20. In place of No. 98. (144)

1429, Apr. 22. HUMPHREY (STAFFORD), 6th earl of Stafford, after-wards duke of Buckingham. Slain 1460, July 10. In place of No. 103. (145)

1429, Apr. 22. Sir JOHN RADCLIFFE. Died 1440-1, Feb. 26. In place of No. 121. (146)

1432, Apr. 22. JOHN (FITZ-ALAN, *alias* DE ARUNDELL), 19th earl of Arundel. Died 1435, June 12. In place of No. 135. (147)

1433, Apr. 22. RICHARD (PLANTAGENET), 3rd duke of York. Slain 1460, Dec. 30. In place of No. 138. (148)

1435, May 8. EDWARD, king of Portugal, nephew of Henry IV. of England. Died 1438, Sept. 18. In place of No. 102. (149)

before 1436, May. EDMUND (BEAUFORT), count of Morteign in Normandy, afterwards 2nd duke of Somerset. Slain 1455, May 22 or 23. In place of No. 147. (150)

before 1436, May. Sir JOHN GREY (DE RUTHYN). Died 1439, Aug. 27. In place of No. 95. (151)

before 1438, Apr. 22. Sir RICHARD (NEVILL), 8th earl of Salisbury. Beheaded 1460, Dec. 31. In place of No. 116. (152)

1438, Apr. 22. ALBERT, duke of Austria, afterwards emperor Albert II. Not installed. Died 1439, Oct. 27. In place of No. 127. (153)

after 1438, Sept. 18. GASTON DE FOIX, count of Longueville, Captal de Buch. Died about 1458. In place of No. 149. (154)

after 1439, Apr. 30. WILLIAM (NEVILL), lord Fauconberge or lord Nevill de Fauconberge, afterwards 11th earl of Kent. Died 1462-3, Jan. 9. In place of No. 99. (155)

after 1439, Aug. 27. JOHN (BEAUFORT), 3rd earl, afterwards 1st duke of Somerset. Died 1444, May 27. In place of No. 151. (156)

after 1439–40, May 12. Sir RALPH BOTELER, afterwards 6th baron Sudeley. Died 1473, May 2. In place of No. 123.   (157)

after 1440–1, Feb. 26. JOHN (BEAUMONT), 1st viscount Beaumont. Slain 1460, July 10. In place of No. 146.   (158)

after 1441, June 6. Sir JOHN BEAUCHAMP, afterwards 1st lord Beauchamp of Powyk. Installed 1445, Aug. 16. Died April, 1475. In place of No. 132.   (159)

after 1442, Dec. 3. HENRY, duke of Viseu, 4th son of John I. of Portugal by Philippa of Lancaster, sister of Henry IV. Died 1461, Nov. 13. In place of No. 91.   (160)

1445, July 11. Sir THOMAS HOO, afterwards baron of Hoo and of Hastings. Installed Aug. 16. Died 1454–5, Feb. 13. In place of No. 117.   (161)

1445, July 11. ALVARO VASQUEZ D'ALMADA, count d'Avranches. Installed Aug. 16. Slain at Alfato Robero 1449, May 20. In place of No. 156.   (162)

1446, May 12. JOHN DE FOIX, vicomte de Chastillion, Captal de Buch, &c., in France and earl of Kendal in England. Surrendered the Garter about 1462. Died about 1485. In place of No. 136.   (163)

1447, April 22. ALPHONSUS V., king of Portugal. Died 1481, Aug. 24. In place of No. 96.   (164)

1447, Nov. 27. Sir FRANCIS SURRIENNE, sire de Lunee, called " the Arragonese." Installed Dec. 8. Resigned after 1450, April 23. In place of No. 125.   (165)

1450, Aug. 4. ALPHONSUS V., king of Arragon and Naples. Died 1458, June 28. In place of No. 162.   (166)

1450, Aug. 4. WILLIAM, duke of Brunswick. Not installed, and election therefore void. In place of No. 144.   (167)

1450, Aug. 4. CASIMIR IV., king of Poland. Not installed and election thereby vacated. In place of No. 139.   (168)

1450, Aug. 4. RICHARD (WYDVILLE), baron, afterwards 1st earl Rivers. Beheaded 1469, Aug. 12. In place of No. 134. (169)

1451, May 28. JOHN (DE MOWBRAY), 5th duke of Norfolk. Installed by proxy. 1452, Apr. 22. Died 1461, Nov. 6. In place of No. 165.   (170)

after 1450, Dec 24. HENRY (BOURCHIER), lord Bourchier, count of Eu, afterwards 14th earl of Essex. Died 1483, Apr. 4. Installed 1452, Apr. 22. In place of No. 130. (171)

1453, May 7. Sir EDWARD HULL. Not installed. Slain 1453, July 18. In place of No. 128. (172)

before 1457, May 13. JOHN (TALBOT), 5th earl of Shrewsbury. Installed May 14. Slain 1460, July 10. In place of No. 141. (173)

before 1457, May 13. THOMAS (STANLEY), 1st lord Stanley. Installed May 14. Died 1458-9, Feb. 20. In place of No. 161. (174)

before 1457, May 13. LEO or LIONEL (DE WELLES), 6th lord Welles Installed May 14. Slain 1461, March 29. In place of No. 172. (175)

1457, May 14. FREDERICK III., emperor of Germany. Not installed, and election therefore void. In place of No. 150. (176)

before 1459, Apr 23. JAMES (BUTLER *otherwise* ORMOND), 2nd earl of Wiltshire, 5th earl of Ormond. Attainted 1461, Nov. 4. Died (?) after 1475. In place of No. 174. (177)

before 1459, Apr. 23 JOHN (SUTTON *alias* DUDLEY), 5th lord Dudley. Died 1487, Sept. 30. In place of No. 154. (178)

before 1459, Apr. 23. JOHN (BOURCHIER), 1st lord Berners. Died 1474, May 16 In place of No. 167. (179)

before 1459, Apr. 23. JASPER (TUDOR), 16th earl of Pembroke, afterwards 3rd duke of Bedford, uterine brother to king Henry VI. Deposed from the Order in 1461 but restored by Henry VII. Died 1495, Dec. 21. In place of No. 166. (180)

1460-1, Feb. 8. RICHARD (NEVILL), 16th earl of Warwick. Deposed about 1468. Slain 1471, April 14. In place of No. 145. (181)

1460-1, Feb. 8. WILLIAM (BONVILLE), 1st lord Bonville. Beheaded 1460-1, Feb. 18. In place of No. 142 (182)

1460-1, Feb. 8. Sir THOMAS KIRIELL. Beheaded 1460-1, Feb 18. In place of No. 173. (183)

1460-1, Feb. 8 Sir JOHN WENLOCK, afterwards 1st lord Wenlock. Slain 1471, May 4. In place of No. 158. (184)

EDWARD IV., the sixth Sovereign.

Succeeded 1460–1, Mar. 4.

? 1461. GEORGE (PLANTAGENET), 3rd duke of Clarence, brother of the sovereign. Attainted 1477–8, Jan. 15. Executed Feb. 18. In place of No. 180 on the latter's deposition in 1461.   (185)

? 1461. Sir WILLIAM CHAMBERLAINE. Died between 1461–2, March 3 and 1462, April 21. In place of No. 175.   (186)

? 1461. JOHN (DE TIPTOFT), 4th earl of Worcester. Royal warrant dated 1461–2, March 21 ordaining his installation by proxy. Beheaded 1470, Oct. 18. In place of No 170.   (187)

? 1461. WILLIAM (HASTINGS), 1st lord Hastings de Hastings. Installed *ut supra*. Beheaded 1483, June 13. In place of No. 182.   (188)

? 1461. JOHN (NEVILL), lord Nevill de Montagu or lord Montagu, afterwards marquess of Montagu. Installed *ut supra*. Slain 1471, Apr. 14. In place of No. 152.   (189)

? 1461. WILLIAM (HERBERT), lord Herbert, afterwards 17th earl of Pembroke. Installed *ut supra*. Beheaded 1469, July 27 or 28. In place of No 176.   (190)

? 1461. Sir JOHN ASTLEY. Installed *ut supra*. Died about 1488. In place of No. 177.   (191)

? 1462–3. FERDINAND I, king of Naples. Ensigns sent to him 1463, July 18: not installed before 1465. Died 1493–4, Jan. 25. In place of No. 143.   (192)

? 1462–3. GALEARD DE DUREFORT, seigneur de Duras. Surrendered the order after 1475, Aug. 29. In place of No. 160.   (193)

? 1462–3. JOHN (LE SCROPE), 5th lord Scrope de Bolton. Died 1498, July 12 or August 17 or 27. In place of No. 148.   (194)

? 1462–3. FRANCIS SFORZA, duke of Milan. Died 1465–6, March 8. In place of No. 110.   (195)

? 1462–3. JAMES (DOUGLAS), 9th earl of Douglas. Died 1488 (?), Apr. 15. In place of No. 155.   (196)

? 1462–3. Sir ROBERT HARCOURT. Slain 1470, Nov. 14. In place of No. 183.   (197)

before 1465–6, Feb. 4. RICHARD (PLANTAGENET), 3rd duke of
Gloucester, afterwards Richard III. Died 1485, Aug. 22.
In place of No. 163. (198)

? 1466, Apr. 27. ANTHONY (WYDVILLE), lord Scales, afterwards
2nd earl Rivers. Beheaded 1483, June 25. In place of
No. 195. (199)

? 1467, Apr. 22. INIGO D'AVALOS, count de Monte Odorisio. Election
vacated probably by neglect of installation. In place of
No. 186. (200)

? 1468. CHARLES THE BOLD, duke of Burgundy. Slain 1476–7,
Jan. 5. In place of No. 181. (201)

? 1471. WILLIAM (FITZ-ALAN), 21st earl of Arundel. Died 1488.
In place of No. 189. (202)

1472, Apr. 24. JOHN (DE MOWBRAY), 6th duke of Norfolk. Died
1475–6, Jan. 17. In place of No. 187. (203)

1472, Apr. 24. JOHN (STAFFORD), 3rd earl of Wiltshire. Died 1473,
May 8. In place of No. 190. (204)

1472, Apr. 24. WALTER (DEVEREUX), 7th lord Ferrers. Slain 1485,
Aug. 22. In place of No. 197. (205)

1472, Apr. 24. WALTER (BLOUNT), 1st lord Mountjoy. Died 1474,
Aug. 1. In place of No. 200. (206)

1472, Apr. 24. JOHN (HOWARD), lord Howard, afterwards 8th duke
of Norfolk. On the accession of Richard III. he removed
to the stall vacated by that sovereign. Slain 1485, Aug. 22.
In place of No. 169. (207)

? 1472–3. JOHN (DE LA POLE), 2nd duke of Suffolk. Died 1491. In
place of No. 168. (208)

1473–4, Feb. 26. THOMAS (FITZ-ALAN *alias* ARUNDELL), lord Mal-
travers, afterwards 22nd earl of Arundel. Died 1524, Oct. 25.
In place of No. 157. (209)

1473–4, Feb. 26. Sir WILLIAM PARRE. Died about 1483. In place
of No. 184. (210)

after 1474, May 16. HENRY (STAFFORD), 2nd duke of Buckingham.
Beheaded 1483, Nov. 2. In place of No. 179. (211)

1474, Aug. 18. FREDERICK UBALDI, duke of Urbino. Died 1482,
Sept. 10. In place of No. 206.   (212)

1474, Aug. 18. HENRY (PERCY), 5th earl of Northumberland.
Killed 1489, April 28. In place of No. 204.   (213)

1475, May 15 EDWARD (PLANTAGENET), prince of Wales, after-
wards king Edward V. Died 1483, June 25. Elected to
the prince's stall vacant since the death of No. 127, owing to
the fact that No. 153 died without installation.   (214)

1475, May 15. RICHARD (PLANTAGENET), 5th duke of York, second
son of the sovereign. Died 1483, June 25. In place of
No. 159.   (215)

after 1475-6, Jan. 10. THOMAS (GREY), 4th marquess of Dorset Died
1501, Sept. 20. In place of No. 203.   (216)

1476, Nov. 4. Sir THOMAS MONTGOMERY. Died 1494-5, Jan. 11.
In place of No 193.   (217)

1479-80, Feb. 10 FERDINAND V., king of Castile and Arragon.
Election voided by non-acceptance or by neglect of installa-
tion. In place of No. 185.   (218)

1479-80, Feb. 10. HERCULES D'ESTE, duke of Modena and Ferrara.
Installed 1480, Oct. 26. Died 1504-5, Jan. 25. In place of
No. 201.   (219)

1482, Sept. 15. JOHN II, king of Portugal. In place of No. 164.
Election vacated by neglect of installation and No. 222
elected in his place. Re-elected in 1488 in place of No. 202.
Died 1495, Oct. 25.   (220)

EDWARD V., the seventh Sovereign.

Succeeded 1483, April 9.

RICHARD III., the eight Sovereign.

Succeeded 1483, June 25.

? 1483. FRANCIS (LOVEL), viscount Lovel. Attainted and degraded
1485, Nov. Died 1487, June 16. In place of No. 218.   (221)

? 1483 THOMAS (HOWARD), 13th earl of Surrey. In place of No.
220. Attainted and degraded 1485, Nov. 7. Restored 1488-9,
Jan 15, and reinstated in place of No. 227 after the latter's
death in 1490. Died 1524, May 21.   (222)

? 1483. Sir RICHARD RADCLIFFE. Slain 1485, Aug. 22. In place of No. 212. (223)

? 1483. THOMAS (STANLEY), lord Stanley, afterwards 10th earl of Derby. Died 1504, July 29 (? 9). In place of No. 188. (224)

? 1483. Sir THOMAS BURGH, afterwards 1st lord Burgh. Died 1495–6, Feb. 18. In place of No. 207 on the latter's removal to the sovereign's stall. (225)

? 1483. Sir RICHARD TUNSTALL. Died 1491 or 1492. In place of No. 210. (226)

? 1483. Sir JOHN CONYERS. Died 1490. In place of No. 199. (227)

HENRY VII., the ninth Sovereign.

Succeeded 1485, Aug. 22.

before 1486, Apr. 22. JOHN (DE VERE), 13th earl of Oxford. Died 1512–3, Mar. 10. In place of No. 207. (228)

before 1486, Apr. 22. Sir JOHN (CHEYNE, CHEYNEY or CHENEY), lord Cheyne. Died 1489, July 14 (? 1495–6 ? 1499, May 30). In place of No. 205. (229)

before 1487, May 14. JOHN (DINHAM), 8th lord Dinham. Died 1500–1, Jan. 28 (? 1508–9, Jan. 28). Elected on the degradation of No. 222. (230)

before 1487, May 27. GILES (DAUBENEY), 1st lord Daubeney. Died 1508, May 28 (? 23). In place of No. 223. (231)

before 1487, May 27. Sir WILLIAM STANLEY. Beheaded 1494–5, Feb. 15. In place of No. 215. (232)

before 1487, May 27. GEORGE (STANLEY), 9th lord Strange. Died 1497, Dec. 5 (? 1503, Dec. 4). In place of No. 211. (233)

after 1487, Sept. 30. GEORGE (TALBOT), 7th earl of Shrewsbury. Installed 1488, April 27. Died 1538, July 26. In place of No. 178. (234)

after 1487, Sept. 30. Sir EDWARD WIDVILE, called lord Widvile. Installed ut supra. Slain 1488, July 27. In place of No. 221. (235)

2

before 1488, Sept. 29. JOHN (WELLES), VISCOUNT Welles. Installed 1489, July 19. Died 1498-9, Feb. 9. In place of No. 235. (236)

1488, Nov. 16. SIR JOHN SAVAGE. Installed 1489, July 19. Slain 1491, Oct. In place of No. 191. (237)

? 1488. Sir ROBERT WILLOUGHBY, afterwards 1st lord Willoughby de Broke. Died 1502, Aug. 23. In place of No. 196. (238)

? 1489, Oct. 16. MAXIMILIAN I., king of the Romans, afterwards emperor of Germany. Invested by commission dated 1490, Sept. 12, but there is a doubt as to his installation. Died 1518-9, Jan 12. In place of No. 213. (239)

? 1491. ARTHUR (TUDOR), prince of Wales. Installed 1491, May 8, in the stall vacant since the accession of No. 214 as king Edward V. Died 1502, Apr. 2 (240)

? 1491. EDWARD (COURTENAY), 18th earl of Devon. Died 1509, May 28. In place of No. 229. (241)

? 1493. ALPHONSUS, duke of Calabria, afterwards Alphonsus II., king of Naples. Invested at Suessa, 1493, May 19, installed 1494, May. Died 1495, Nov. 19. In place of No. 237. (242)

? 1493. Sir EDWARD POYNINGS Died between July 27 and Dec 19, 1521. In place of No. 208 (243)

? 1493. JOHN, king of Denmark, Sweden and Norway. Election probably vacated by neglect of installation. In place of No. 226. (244)

after 1494-5, Jan. 11. Sir GILBERT TALBOT. Died 1517, Aug. 17. In place of No. 217. (245)

? 1495. HENRY (TUDOR), duke of York, afterwards Henry VIII. Installed 1495, May 17. Died 1546-7, Jan. 28. In place of No. 192 (246)

? 1495. HENRY ALGERNON (PERCY), 6th earl of Northumberland. Died 1527, May 19 (? June 29). In place of No. 232. (247)

? 1496. EDWARD (STAFFORD), 3rd duke of Buckingham. Degraded 1521, Apr. 23. Executed 1521, May 17. In place of No 220. (248)

? 1496. Sir CHARLES SOMERSET, afterwards 6th earl of Worcester. Died 1526, Apr. 15 In place of No. 242. (249)

? 1496. EDMUND (DE LA POLE), 8th earl of Suffolk. Degraded 1500. Beheaded 1513, Apr. 5. In place of No. 180 (250)

? 1496. HENRY (BOURCHIER), 15th earl of Essex. Died 1539–40, Mar. 13 or 14. In place of No. 225. (251)

after 1498, Aug. 17. SIR THOMAS LOVELL. Died 1524, May 25 In place of No. 194. (252)

1499, Apr. 23 Sir RICHARD POLE. Died 1504, Nov. In place of No. 236. (253)

? 1500. Sir RICHARD GUILDFORD. Died 1506, Sept. 28, In place of No. 250, on the latter's degradation. (254)

after 1500–1, Jan. 28. Sir REGINALD BRAY. Died 1503, Aug. 4. In place of No. 230 (255)

after 1501, Sept. 20. THOMAS (GREY), 5th marquess of Dorset. Died 1530, Oct. 10. In place of No. 216. (256)

before 1503, May 7. PHILIP, archduke of Austria, duke of Burgundy, afterwards Philip I., king of Castile. Installed in person 1504–5, Feb. 9. Died 1506, Sept. 25. In place of No. 240. (257)

? after 1504, Aug. 19. GERALD (FITZ-GERALD), 8th earl of Kildare. Installed by proxy 1505, May 4 Died 1513. Sept. 3. In place of No. 238. (258)

before 1503–4, Feb. 22. GUIDO UBALDI DE MONTEFELTRE, duke of Urbino. Died 1507, Apr. 11. In place of No. 255. (259)

1505, April 22. RICHARD (GREY), 14th earl of Kent. Died 1524, May 3 (? April 3). In place of No. 233. (260)

before 1505, May 4. SIR HENRY STAFFORD, afterwards 5th earl of Wiltshire. Died 1523, Apr. 6 (? 1522–3, Mar. 6). In place of No. 224. (261)

before 1506, May 23. Sir RHYS ap Thomas Fitz-Urian. Died after 1524–5, Feb 2. In place of No. 253. (262)

? 1506–7. Sir THOMAS BRANDON. Installed 1507, May 10. Died 1509–10, Jan. 29. In place of No. 219. (263)

1508, Dec. 20. CHARLES, archduke of Austria, afterwards emperor Charles V. Died 1558, Sept. 21. In place of No. 257. (264)

HENRY VIII., the tenth Sovereign.
Succeeded 1509, Apr. 21.

1509, May 18   Sir THOMAS DARCY, afterwards 1st lord Darcy de
Darcy. Installed May 21. Degraded on or before Apr. 23.
Executed 1537, June 20. In place of No. 254.   (265)

1509, May 18. EDWARD (SUTTON *alias* DUDLEY), 6th lord Dudley.
Installed May 21.   Died 1531-2, Jan. 31.   In place of
No. 259.   (266)

1510, Apr. 23. EMANUEL, king of Portugal. Elected to the stall
vacant on the accession of the sovereign. Election probably
vacated by neglect of installation. Died 1521, Sept. 13.
(267)

1510, Apr. 23. Sir THOMAS HOWARD, afterwards earl of Surrey and
10th duke of Norfolk. Installed Apr. 27. In place of
No. 231. Degraded 1546-7. Restored to the Order in 1553
in place of No. 330. Died 1554, Aug. 25.   (268)

1510, Apr. 23. Sir HENRY MARNY, afterwards 1st lord Marny.
Installed Apr. 27.   Died 1523, May 24.   In place of
No. 241.   (269)

1510, Apr. 23. THOMAS (WEST), 8th lord de la Warr. Installed
May 11. Died 1525, Oct. 11. In place of No. 263.   (270)

1513, Apr. 23. GEORGE (NEVILL), 5th lord Bergavenny. Installed
May 7. Died 1535, June 14   In place of No 267.   (271)

1513, Apr. 23. Sir EDWARD HOWARD   Not installed. Slain 1513,
Apr. 25. In place of No. 244.   (272)

1513, Apr. 23. Sir CHARLES (BRANDON), 4th duke of Suffolk. In-
stalled May 7. Died 1545, Aug. 14 or 24 or 21. In place
of No. 228.   (273)

1514, Apr. 23. JULIAN DE MEDICIS, duke of Nemours, brother of
Pope Leo X. Not installed. Died 1516-7, Mar. 17. In
place of No. 258.   (274)

1514, Apr. 23. Sir EDWARD STANLEY, afterwards 1st lord Mont-
eagle. Installed May 8. Died 1523, Apr. 6. (? 1524, Apr.
7). In place of No 272.   (275)

1518, Apr. 24. THOMAS (DACRE), 3rd lord Dacre of Gillesland. In-
stalled May 16. Died 1525, Oct. 24. In place of No. 274.
(276)

1518, Apr. 24. Sir WILLIAM SANDYS, afterwards 1st lord Sandys de Vyne. Installed May 16. Died 1542. In place of No. 245.
(277)

1521, Apr. 24 HENRY (COURTENAY), 20th earl of Devon, afterwards marquess of Exeter. Installed June 9. Beheaded 1538-9, Jan. 9. In place of No 248. (278)

1522, Apr. 23. FERDINAND, archduke of Austria, afterwards emperor of Germany. Invested at Nuremberg 1523, Dec. 8. Installed by proxy 1524, July 17. Died 1564, July 25. In place of No. 239. (279)

1522, Apr. 23. Sir RICHARD WINGFIELD. Installed May 11. Died 1525, July 22 In place of No. 243. (280)

1523, Apr. 23. Sir THOMAS BOLEYN, afterwards earl of Wiltshire and earl of Ormond. Installed Aug. 15. Died 1538-9, March 13 In place of No 261. (281)

1523, July 13. WALTER (DEVEREUX), 9th lord Ferrers, afterwards 1st viscount Hereford. Installed Aug. 13. Died 1558, Sept. 27 or 17. In place of No. 269. (282)

1524, Apr. 23. ARTHUR (PLANTAGENET), natural son of king Edward IV, 6th viscount Lisle. Installed May 7. Died 1541-2, March 3. In place of No. 260. (283)

1524, Apr. 23. ROBERT (RADCLYFFE), 10th lord Fitzwalter, afterwards 8th earl of Sussex. Installed May 7. Died 1542, Nov. 27. In place of No. 275. (284)

1525, Apr. 23. WILLIAM (FITZ-ALAN), 23rd earl of Arundel. Installed June 25. Died 1543-4, Jan. 23 (? 20). In place of No. 222. (285)

1525, Apr. 24. THOMAS (MANNERS), 13th lord Ros, afterwards 2nd earl of Rutland. Installed June 25. Died 1543, Sept. 20. In place of No. 252. (286)

1525, June 7. Sir HENRY FITZROY, afterwards duke of Richmond and Somerset, natural son of Henry VIII. Installed June 25. Died 1536, July 22. In place of No 209. (287)

1525, June 7. RALPH (NEVILL), 4th earl of Westmorland. Installed June 25. Died 1549, Apr. 24. In place of No. 262. (288)

1526, Apr. 24. WILLIAM (BLOUNT), 4th lord Mountjoy. Installed May 6. Died 1534, Nov. 8. In place of No. 280. (289)

1526, Apr. 24. Sir WILLIAM FITZWILLIAM, afterwards 1st earl of Southampton. Installed May 6. Died 1542, Oct. In place of No. 276. (290)

1526, Apr. 24. Sir HENRY GUILDFORD. Installed May 6. Died between 1532, May 18, and 1532–3, Feb 10. In place of No 270. (291)

1527, Oct 21. FRANCIS I., king of France Invested Nov 10. Installed by proxy 1527–8, Jan. 26. Died 1547, Mar. 31. In place of No. 249. (292)

1527, Oct. 21. JOHN (DE VERE), 15th earl of Oxford. Installed 1527–8, Jan. 26. Died 1539–40, Mar 21. In place of No. 247. (293)

1531, Apr. 23. HENRY (PERCY), 7th earl of Northumberland. Installed May 6. Died 1537, June 30. In place of No. 256 (294)

1532, Oct. 27. ANNE DE MONTMORENCY, comte de Beaumont, duc de Montmorency. Elected and invested at Calais: installed by proxy 1533, May 18. Died 1567, Nov. 12 In place of No. 266. (295)

1532, Oct. 27. PHILIP DE CHABOT, comte de Neublanche. Elected, etc., *ut supra*. Died 1543, June 1. In place of No. 291. (296)

1534–5, Jan 20. JAMES V., king of Scotland. Invested at Edinburgh Feb. 21. Installed by proxy 1535, Aug. 22 Died 1542, Dec. 14. In place of No. 289. (297)

1536, Apr 23 Sir NICHOLAS CAREW. Installed May 21. Beheaded 1538–9, Mar. 3. In place of No. 271 (298)

1537, Apr. 23. HENRY (CLIFFORD), 1st earl of Cumberland. Installed May 13. Died 1542, Sept (or Apr.), 22. In place of No. 265. (299)

1537, Aug. 5. THOMAS (CROMWELL), 1st lord Cromwell, afterwards 16th earl of Essex. Installed Aug. 26. Executed 1540, July 28 In place of No. 294. (300)

1539, Apr 24. JOHN (RUSSELL), lord Russell, afterwards 3rd earl of Bedford Installed May 18. Died 1554–5, Mar. 14. In place of No. 281. (301)

1539, Apr. 24. Sir THOMAS CHENEY. Installed May 18. Died 1558, Dec. 15. In place of No. 278 (302)

1539, Apr. 24. Sir WILLIAM KINGSTON. Installed May 18. Died 1540, May 13. In place of No. 298. (303)

1540, Apr. 23. THOMAS (AUDLEY), lord Audley of Walden. Installed May 19. Died 1544, Apr. 30. In place of No. 251. (304)

1540, Apr. 23. Sir ANTHONY BROWNE. Installed May 19. Died 1548, May 6. In place of No. 293. (305)

1540–1, Jan. 9. EDWARD (SEYMOUR), 8th earl of Hertford, afterwards duke of Somerset. Installed 1541, May 22. Beheaded 1551–2, Jan. 22. In place of No. 303. (306)

1541, Apr. 23. Sir HENRY HOWARD, commonly called earl of Surrey, son and heir apparent of Thomas, 10th duke of Norfolk. Installed May 22. Executed 1546–7, Jan. 21. In place of No. 300. (307)

1541, Apr. 23. Sir JOHN GAGE. Installed May 22. Died 1556, Apr. 18. In place of No. 234. (308)

1541, Apr. 23. Sir ANTHONY WINGFIELD. Installed May 22. Died 1552, Aug. 20. In place of No. 277. (309)

1543, Apr. 23. JOHN (DUDLEY), 7th viscount Lisle, afterwards earl of Warwick and duke of Northumberland. Installed May 6. Beheaded 1553, Aug. 22. In place of No. 283. (310)

1543, Apr. 23. WILLIAM (PAULET), lord Saint John, afterwards 1st marquess of Winchester. Installed May 6. Died 1571–2, March 10. In place of No. 299. (311)

1543, Apr. 23. WILLIAM (PARR), lord Parr, afterwards earl of Essex and 1st Marquess of Northampton. Elected in place of No. 290. Installed Apr. 27. Degraded and attainted in 1553 : restored in blood Jan. 1558–9 : re-elected into the Order 1559, Apr. 24, and installed June 3 in place of No. 264. Died 1571, Oct. 28. (312)

1543, Dec. 24. Sir JOHN WALLOP. Installed 1544, May 18. Died 1551, July 7. In place of No. 284. (313)

1544, Apr. 24. HENRY (FITZ-ALAN), 24th earl of Arundel. Installed May 18. Died 1579–80, Feb. 24 or 25. In place of No. 297. (314)

1544, Apr. 24. Sir ANTHONY ST. LEGER. Installed May 18. Died 1558–9, Mar. 16. In place of No. 296. (315)

1545, Apr. 23. FRANCIS (TALBOT), 8th earl of Shrewsbury. Installed May 17. Died 1560, Sept. 21. In place of No. 286. (316)

1545, Apr. 23. THOMAS (WRIOTHESLEY), lord Wriothesley, afterwards 2nd earl of Southampton. Installed May 17. Died 1550, July 30. In place of No. 285. (317)

EDWARD VI, the eleventh Sovereign.
Succeeded 1546-7, Jan. 28.

1546-7, Feb. 17. HENRY (GREY), 6th marquess of Dorset, afterwards 7th duke of Suffolk. Installed May 23. Beheaded 1553-4, Feb. 23. In place of No. 287. (318)

1546-7, Feb 17. EDWARD (STANLEY), 12th earl of Derby. Installed May 23. Died 1572, Oct. 24 In place of No. 304. (319)

1546-7, Feb. 17. THOMAS (SEYMOUR), lord Seymour of Sudeley. Installed May 23. Executed 1548-9, Mar. 20. In place of No. 273 (320)

1546-7, Feb. 17. Sir WILLIAM PAGET, afterwards 1st lord Paget de Beaudesert. Installed May 23. In place of No. 307. Degraded 1552, Sept 28. Restored 1553, Sept. 27, in place of 312. Died 1563, June 9. (321)

1549, Apr. 24. FRANCIS (HASTINGS), 19th earl of Huntingdon. Installed Dec. 13. Died 1561, June 20. In place of No. 268. (322)

1549, Apr. 24. GEORGE (BROOKE), 9th lord Cobham. Installed Dec. 13. Died 1558, Sept. 29. In place of No. 305. (323)

1549, Dec. 1. THOMAS (WEST), 9th lord de la Warr. Installed Dec. 13. Died 1554, Sept. 25. In place of No. 320. (324)

1549, Dec. 1. Sir WILLIAM HERBERT, afterwards 20th earl of Pembroke. Installed Dec. 13. Died 1569-70, Mar. 17. In place of No. 288. (325)

1551, Apr. 24. HENRY II., king of France. Invested at Chateau Brienne, June 20. Installed by proxy Aug. 24. Died 1559, July 10. In place of No. 292. (326)

1551, Apr. 24. EDWARD (CLINTON), 9th lord Clinton, afterwards 13th earl of Lincoln. Installed June 30. Died 1584-5, Jan. 16. In place of No. 317. (327)

1551, Sept. 28. THOMAS (DARCY), 1st lord Darcy of Chiche. Installed Oct. 9. Died 1558, June 28 (or Nov. 28). In place of No. 313. (328)

1552, Sept. 28. HENRY (NEVILL), 5th earl of Westmorland. Installed Dec. 16. Died 1563, Aug., or 1563-4, Feb. 10. In place of No. 306. (329)

1552, Sept. 28. Sir ANDREW DUDLEY Installed Dec. 16. Degraded and attainted 1553, Nov. 27. In place of No. 321. (330)

MARY I., the twelfth Sovereign.

Succeeded 1553, July 6.

1554, Apr. 24. Philip, prince of Spain, afterwards Philip II. of Spain and King of England by courtesy. Invested with the Garter at Southampton July 21 and with the mantle and collar at Windsor and there installed as joint sovereign 1554, Aug. 3. Died 1598, Sept. 13. In place of No. 309.
(331)

1554, Apr. 24. Henry (Radclyffe), 9th earl of Sussex. Installed Aug. 4 Died 1556-7, Feb. 17. In place of No 310. (332)

1554, Aug. 6. Emanuel Philibert, duke of Savoy. Elected on the accession of king Philip to the joint sovereignty. Invested in camp at Auxy, Nov 6. Installed by proxy 1554-5, Jan. 31. Died 1580, Aug 30. (333)

1554, Oct. 9. William (Howard), 1st lord Howard of Effingham. Installed 1554-5, Jan. 31. Died 1572-3, Jan. 11 or 21. In place of No. 318. (334)

1555, Apr. 23. Sir Edward Hastings, afterwards lord Hastings of Loughborough Installed May 25. Died 1571-2, Mar. 5 (or Feb. 28). In place of No. 268. (335)

1555, Apr. 23. Anthony (Browne), 1st viscount Montagu. Installed Oct. 17. Died 1592, Oct. 19. In place of No. 324. (336)

1555, Apr. 23. Thomas (Radclyffe), 3rd earl of Sussex. Installed 1557-8, Jan. 9. Died 1583, June 9. In place of No. 301.
(337)

1557, Apr. 23. William (Grey), 13th lord Grey de Wilton. Installed by proxy 1558, Apr. 19, being then a prisoner in France. Died 1562, Dec. 14. In place of No 308. (338)

1557, Apr. 23. Sir Robert Rochester Died Nov. 28 following, without installation. In place of No. 332. (339)

ELIZABETH, the thirteenth Sovereign.
Succeeded 1558, Nov. 17.

1559, Apr. 24. THOMAS (HOWARD), 11th duke of Norfolk   Installed
June 3   Beheaded 1572, June 2. In place of No. 282. (340)

1559, Apr. 24. HENRY (MANNERS), 3rd earl of Rutland.   Installed
June 3. Died 1563, Sept. 17. In place of No 323.   (341)

1559, Apr. 24   Sir ROBERT DUDLEY, afterwards 11th earl of Leicester.
Installed June 3. Died 1588, Sept. 4. In place of No. 328.
(342)

1560, June 10. ADOLPHUS, duke of Holstein. Installed by proxy
Dec. 15. Died 1586, Oct. 1. In place of No. 302.   (343)

1561, Apr. 22. GEORGE (TALBOT), 9th earl of Shrewsbury. Installed
May 18. Died 1590, Nov. 18   In place of No. 315.   (344)

1561, Apr 22. HENRY (CAREY), 1st lord Hunsdon. Installed May 18.
Died 1596, July 23. In place of No. 316.   (345)

1563, Apr. 22   THOMAS (PERCY), 8th earl of Northumberland. In-
stalled May 23, attainted and degraded 1569, Nov. 27.
Beheaded 1572, Aug. 22. In place of No. 322.   (346)

1563, Apr. 22. AMBROSE (DUDLEY), 21st earl of Warwick. Invested
at Newhaven in France. Installed by proxy May 23. Died
1589-90, Feb 20 or 21. In place of No. 338.   (347)

1564, Apr. 23. CHARLES IX., king of France. Installed by proxy
1565-6, Jan. 22   Died 1574, May 30. In place of No. 326.
(348)

1564, Apr. 23   FRANCIS (RUSSELL), 4th earl of Bedford. Installed
May 14. Died 1585, July 28. In place of No. 321.   (349)

1564, Apr. 23. Sir HENRY SIDNEY. Installed May 14. Died 1586,
May 5. In place of No. 341.   (350)

1567, Apr. 23. MAXIMILIAN II., emperor of Germany. Invested at
Vienna 1567-8, Jan. 4. Achievements decreed to be placed
1571, Apr. 24. Died 1576, Oct. 12. In place of No. 279.
(351)

1570, Apr. 23   HENRY (HASTINGS), 20th earl of Huntingdon. In-
stalled June 19. Died 1595, Dec. 14. In place of No. 329.
(352)

1570, Apr. 23. WILLIAM (SOMERSET), 8th earl of Worcester. In-
stalled June 19. Died 1588-9, Feb. 21. In place of
No. 295.   (353)

1572, Apr. 23. FRANCIS, duc de Montmorency. Installed June 17. Died 1579, May 6. In place of No. 346 (354)

1572, Apr. 23. WALTER (DEVEREUX), 2nd viscount Hereford, afterwards 18th earl of Essex. Installed June 17. Died 1576, Sept. 22. In place of No. 325. (355)

1572, Apr. 23. WILLIAM (CECIL), 1st lord Burghley. Installed June 17. Died 1598, Aug. 4. In place of No. 312. (356)

1572, Apr. 23. ARTHUR (GREY), 14th lord Grey de Wilton. Installed June 17. Died 1593, Oct. 14. In place of No. 335 (357)

1572, Apr. 23. EDMUND (BRYDGES), 2nd lord Chandos of Sudeley. Installed June 17. Died 1573, Sept. 11. In place of No. 311. (358)

1574, Apr. 24. HENRY (STANLEY), 13th earl of Derby. Installed May 20. Died 1593, Sept. 25 In place of No. 319. (359)

1574, Apr. 24. HENRY (HERBERT), 21st earl of Pembroke. Installed May 20. Died 1600-1, Jan 19. In place of No. 334. (360)

1575, Apr. 23. HENRY III.,king of France and Poland. Invested at Paris 1585-6, Feb. 18. Died 1589, Aug 1. In place of No. 348. (361)

1575, Apr. 23. CHARLES (HOWARD), 2nd lord Howard of Effingham, afterwards 10th earl of Nottingham. Installed May 8. Died 1624, Dec 14. In place of No. 340. (362)

1578, Apr. 24. RODOLPHUS II , emperor of Germany. Election vacated by neglect of instalment. In place of No. 351. (363)

1578, Apr. 24 FREDERICK II., King of Denmark. Invested 1581, Aug. 14. Installed by proxy 1581-2, Jan. 8. Died 1588, Apr. 4. In place of No. 358. (364)

1578-9, Feb. 8. JOHN CASIMIR, count Palatine of the Rhine, duke of Bavaria. Invested same day. Installed by proxy 1581-2, Jan. 8. Died 1582-3, Jan. 6. In place of No. 355. (365)

1584, Apr. 23. EDWARD (MANNERS), 4th earl of Rutland. Installed 1585, Apr. 15. Died 1587, Apr. 14. In place of No. 354. (366)

1584, Apr. 23. WILLIAM (BROOKE), 10th lord Cobham. Installed 1585, Apr. 15. Died 1596-7, Mar. 6. In place of No. 314. (367)

1584, Apr. 23. HENRY (LE SCROPE), 9th lord Scrope of Bolton. Installed by proxy 1885, Apr. 15. Died 1591, May 10. In place of No. 333. (368)

1588, Apr. 23. ROBERT (DEVEREUX), 19th earl of Essex. Installed May 23. Executed 1600–1, Feb. 25. In place of No. 337. (369)

1588, Apr. 23. THOMAS (BUTLER), 11th earl of Ormonde. Installed May 23. Died 1614, Nov. 22. In place of No 327. (370)

1588, Apr 23. Sir CHRISTOPHER HATTON. Installed May 23. Died 1591, Nov. 20. In place of No. 349. (371)

1589, Apr. 22. HENRY (RADCLYFFE), 11th earl of Sussex. Installed Dec. 18. Died 1593, Dec. 14. In place of No. 350. (372)

1589, Apr. 22. THOMAS (SACKVILLE), 1st lord Buckhurst, afterwards 4th earl of Dorset. Installed Dec. 18. Died 1608, Apr. 19. In place of No 343. (373)

1590, Apr. 24. HENRY IV., king of France. Invested 1596, Oct. 10. installed by proxy 1600, Apr. 28. Died 1610, May 14. In place of No 361. (374)

1590, Apr. 24. JAMES VI., king of Scotland, afterwards James I. of England. Died 1625, Mar. 27. In place of No 366. (375)

1592, Apr. 23. GILBERT (TALBOT), 10th earl of Shrewsbury. Installed June 19. Died 1616, May 8. In place of No. 353. (376)

1592, Apr. 23. GEORGE (CLIFFORD), 3rd earl of Cumberland. Installed June 19. Died 1605, Oct. 30. In place of No. 364. (377)

1593, Apr. 23. HENRY (PERCY), 10th earl of Northumberland. Installed June 25. Died 1632, Nov. 5. In place of No. 342. (378)

1593, Apr. 23. EDWARD (SOMERSET), 9th earl of Worcester. Installed June 25. Died 1627–8, Mar. 3. In place of No. 347. (379)

1593, Apr. 23. THOMAS (BURGH), 5th lord Burgh. Installed June 25. Died 1597, Oct. 14. In place of No. 344. (380)

1593, Apr. 23. EDMUND (SHEFFIELD), 3rd lord Sheffield of Butterwicke, afterwards 1st earl of Mulgrave. Installed June 25. Died 1646, Oct. 6. In place of No. 368. (381)

1593, Apr. 23. Sir FRANCIS KNOLLYS. Installed June 25. Died 1595–6, Mar. 22. In place of No. 371. (382)

1597, Apr. 23. FREDERICK, duke of Wurtemberg. Invested at Stuttgart 1603, Nov. 6. Installed by proxy 1604, Apr. 20. Died 1607-8, Jan. 29. In place of No. 365. (383)

1597, Apr. 23. THOMAS (HOWARD), 1st lord Howard, afterwards 9th earl of Suffolk. Installed May 24. Died 1626, May 28. In place of No. 359. (384)

1597, Apr. 23. GEORGE (CAREY), 2nd lord Hunsdon. Installed May 24. Died 1603, Sept 9. In place of No. 372. (385)

1597, Apr. 23. CHARLES (BLOUNT), 8th lord Mountjoy, afterwards 1st earl of Devonshire. Installed May 24. Died 1606, Apr. 3. In place of No. 357. (386)

1597, Apr. 23. Sir HENRY LEA Installed May 24. Died 1610-1, Feb. 12. In place of No. 336. (387)

1599, Apr. 23. ROBERT (RATCLIFFE), 12th earl of Sussex. Installed June 6. Died 1629, Sept. 22. In place of No. 352 (388)

1599, Apr. 23. HENRY (BROOKE), 11th lord Cobham. Installed June 6. Degraded 1603-4, Feb. 12. Died 1618-9, Jan. 24. In place of No. 382. (389)

1599, Apr. 23. THOMAS (SCROPE), 10th lord Scrope de Bolton. Installed June 6. Died 1609, Sept. 3. In place of No. 345. (390)

1601, Apr. 23. WILLIAM (STANLEY), 15th earl of Derby. Installed May 26. Died 1642, Sept. 29. In place of No. 367. (391)

1601, Apr. 23. THOMAS (CECIL), 2nd lord Burghley, afterwards 1st earl of Exeter. Installed May 26. Died 1622-3, Feb. 8. In place of No. 380. (392)

JAMES I., the fourteenth Sovereign.

Succeeded 1602-3, Mar. 24.

1603, June 14. HENRY FREDERICK (STUART), 11th duke of Rothesay, afterwards prince of Wales. Elected upon the accession of the sovereign. Installed July 9. Died 1612, Nov. 6. (393)

1603, June 14. CHRISTIERN IV., king of Denmark. Installed by proxy, 1605, Sept. 8. Died 1648-9, Feb. 25. In place of No. 363. (394)

1603, June 25. LODOVICK (STUART), 2nd duke of Lennox, afterwards 2nd duke of Richmond Installed July 9. Died 1623–4, Feb 16. In place of No. 356.   (395)

1603, June 25. HENRY (WRIOTHESLEY), 4th earl of Southampton. July 9. Died 1624, Nov. 10. In place of No. 331. (396)

1603, June 25 JOHN (ERSKINE), 19th earl of Mar. Installed July 9. Died 1634, Dec. 14   In place of No. 360.   (397)

1603, June 25. WILLIAM (HERBERT), 22nd earl of Pembroke. Installed July 9. Died 1630, Apr. 10. In place of No. 369.
                                                         (398)

1605, Apr 24. ULRIC, duke of Holstein. Installed May 16. Died 1624, Mar. 27. In place of No. 385   (399)

1605, Apr. 24. HENRY (HOWARD), 7th earl of Northampton. Installed May 16. Died 1614, June 15. In place of No. 389.
                                                         (400)

1606, Apr. 24. ROBERT (CECIL), 14th earl of Salisbury. Installed May 20. Died 1612, May 24. In place of No 377. (401)

1606, Apr. 24. THOMAS (HOWARD), 3rd viscount Howard of Bindon. Installed May 20. Died 1610–11, Mar. 1. In place of No. 386.   (402)

1608, Apr. 23. GEORGE (HOME), 12th earl of Dunbar. Installed May 18. Died 1611–12, Jan. 29   In place of No. 383. (403)

1608, Apr. 23 PHILIP (HERBERT), earl of Montgomery, afterwards 23rd earl of Pembroke. Installed May 18. Died 1649–50, Jan. 23   In place of No. 373.   (404)

1611, Apr. 24. CHARLES (STUART), 7th duke of York, afterwards king Charles I. Installed May 13. Died 1648–9, Jan. 30. In place of No. 374.   (405)

1611, April 24. THOMAS (HOWARD), 26th earl of Arundel, 16th earl of Surrey, afterwards 15th earl of Norfolk. Installed May 13. Died 1646, Oct. 4. In place of No. 390.   (406)

1611, Apr. 24 ROBERT (CARR), 1st viscount Rochester, afterwards 6th earl of Somerset. Installed May 13   Died 1645, July. In place of No 402.   (407)

1612, Dec 19. FREDERICK CASIMIR, elector and count palatine of the Rhine, afterwards king of Bohemia. Installed 1612–13, Feb. 7. Died 1632, Nov. 19. In place of No. 387. (408)

1612, Dec. 19. MAURICE DE NASSAU, prince of Orange. Invested at the Hague, 1612-13, Feb. 4. Installed by proxy Feb. 7. Died 1625, Apr. 13. In place of No. 403. (409)

1615, Apr. 24. THOMAS (ERSKINE), 1st viscount Fentoun, afterwards 1st earl of Kellie. Installed May 22. Died 1639, June 12. In place of No. 401. (410)

1615, Apr. 24. WILLIAM (KNOLLYS), lord Knollys, afterwards 1st earl of Banbury. Installed May 22. Died 1632, May 25. In place of No. 393. (411)

1616, Apr. 24. FRANCIS (MANNERS), 7th earl of Rutland. Installed July 7. Died 1632, Dec. 17. In place of No. 400. (412)

1616, Apr. 24. Sir GEORGE VILLIERS, afterwards 4th duke of Buckingham. Installed July 7. Died 1628, Aug. 23. In place of No. 370. (413)

1616, May 26. ROBERT (SYDNEY), 8th viscount Lisle, afterwards 12th earl of Leicester. Installed July 7. Died 1626, July 13. In place of No. 376. (414)

1622-3, Feb. 2. JAMES (HAMILTON), 2nd Marquess of Hamilton, afterwards 7th earl of Cambridge. Installed 1623, Apr. 22. Died 1624-5, Mar. 2. In place of No. 392. (415)

1624, Apr. 22. ESME (STUART), 3rd duke of Lennox. Installed same day. Died 1624, July 30. In place of No. 395. (416)

1624, Dec. 31. CHRISTIAN, duke of Brunswick Wolfenbüttel. Installed by proxy, 1625, Dec. 13. Died 1626, June 6. In place of No. 399. (417)

1624, Dec. 31. WILLIAM (CECIL), 15th earl of Salisbury. Installed 1625, Dec. 13. Died 1668, Dec. 3. In place of No. 416. (418)

1624, Dec. 31. JAMES (HAY), 2nd earl of Carlisle. Installed 1625, Dec. 13. Died 1636, Apr. 25. In place of No. 396. (419)

CHARLES I., the fifteenth Sovereign.

Succeeded 1625, March 27.

1625, May 15. EDWARD (SACKVILLE), 7th earl of Dorset. Upon the succession of the Sovereign. Installed by proxy Dec. 13. Died 1652, July 17. (420)

1625, May 15. HENRY (RICH), 1st earl of Holland. Installed Dec. 13.
    Died 1648–9, Mar. 9. In place of No. 362.   (421)

1625, May 15. THOMAS (HOWARD), 1st viscount Andover, afterwards
    2nd earl of Berkshire. Installed Dec. 13. Died 1669, July
    16. In place of No 415   (422)

1625, July 4. CLAUDE DE LORRAINE, duc de Chevreuse. Installed by
    proxy, Dec. 13. Died 1656–7, Jan. 24. In place of No. 409.
                                                          (423)

1627, Apr. 24. GUSTAVUS ADOLPHUS, king of Sweden; commission to
    invest June 24; acceptance Oct. 6   Installed by proxy 1628,
    Sept 23. Died 1632, Nov 6. In place of No. 384.   (424)

1627, Apr. 24   HENRY FREDERICK DE NASSAU, prince of Orange.
    Invested at the Hague same month   Installed by proxy
    1628, Sept. 23. Died 1647, May 14. In place of No. 417.
                                                          (425)

1627, Apr. 24. THEOPHILUS (HOWARD), 10th earl of Suffolk. In-
    stalled 1628, Sept. 24. Died 1640, June 3. In place of
    No 414.   (426)

1628, Sept 25. WILLIAM (COMPTON), 8th earl of Northampton.
    Installed 1629, Apr. 21. Died 1630, June 24   In place of
    No 379.   (427)

1630, Apr 18. RICHARD (WESTON), 1st lord Weston, afterwards 1st
    earl of Portland. Installed 1630, Oct. 5. Died 1634–5,
    Mar. 13. In place of No. 413   (428)

1630, Apr. 18. ROBERT (BERTIE), 1st earl of Lindsey. Installed
    Oct. 5. Died 1642, Oct. 23. In place of No 388.   (429)

1630, Apr. 18. WILLIAM (CECIL), 2nd earl of Exeter   Installed
    Oct 5. Died 1640, July 6   In place of No. 398.   (430)

1630, Oct. 5. JAMES (HAMILTON), 3rd marquess, afterwards 1st duke
    of Hamilton. Beheaded 1648–9, Mar. 9. In place of
    No. 427.   (431)

1633, Apr. 18   CHARLES LEWIS, count palatine of the Rhine, duke of
    Bavaria, prince elector, nephew of king Charles I. Invested
    by special commission 1633, July 25, at Buckstal, near
    Balduck in Brabant, in the army of the States General.
    Installed by proxy Nov. 6   Died 1680, Aug. 28. In place
    of No. 411.   (432)

1633, Apr. 18. JAMES (STUART), 4th duke of Lennox, afterwards duke
    of Richmond   Installed Nov. 6. Died 1655, Mar. 30.
    In place of No. 378   (433)

1633, Nov. 7. HENRY (DANVERS), earl of Danby. Died 1643–4, Jan. 20. In place of No. 424. (434)

1633, Nov. 7. WILLIAM (DOUGLAS), 8th earl of Morton. Installed 1634, Apr. 21. Died 1648, Aug. 7. In place of No. 408. (435)

1635, Apr. 23. ALGERNON (PERCY), 11th earl of Northumberland. Installed May 13. Died 1668, Oct. 13. In place of No. 412. (436)

1638, May 21. CHARLES STUART, prince of Great Britain, afterwards Charles II. Died 1684–5, Feb. 6. In place of No. 428. (437)

1640, Oct. THOMAS (WENTWORTH), 1st earl of Strafford. Elected at York. Not installed. Executed 1641, May 12. In place of No. 419. (438)

1642, Apr. 20. JAMES (STUART), duke of York, afterwards James II. Elected and invested at York; installation dispensed with at Oxford 1644–5, Mar. 2. Died 1701, Sept. 6. In place of No. 426. (439)

1642, Apr. 20. RUPERT, count palatine of the Rhine, duke of Bavaria, afterwards duke of Cumberland. Elected at York. Invested at Nottingham Aug. following. Installation dispensed with *ut supra*. Personally installed 1663, Apr. 22. Died 1682, Nov. 29. In place of No. 430. (440)

1644–5, Mar. 2. WILLIAM DE NASSAU, prince of Orange, son-in-law to Charles I. Elected at Oxford; ensigns sent to him Mar. 4. Died 1650, Nov. 4. In place of No. 438. (441)

1644–5, Mar. 2. BERNARD DE NOGARET DE FOIX, duc d'Epernon, Captal de Buch. Elected at Oxford; ensigns sent to him Mar. 4. His banner, etc., placed over his stall by a warrant dated 1661, Apr. 15. Died 1660, July 25. In place of No. 391. (442)

CHARLES II., the sixteenth Sovereign

Succeeded 1648–9, Jan. 30.

1649, Sept. 18. MAURICE, count palatine of the Rhine, duke of Bavaria: the sovereign's cousin. Nominated at St. Germain-en-Laye; insignia sent to him then in Ireland with the duke of Ormonde and afterwards delivered to him at Lisbon. Not installed. Lost at sea about 1651. In place of the sovereign on his accession. (443)

1649, Sept. 18. JAMES (BUTLER), 1st marquess, afterwards 1st duke of Ormonde Nominated *ut supra*. Installed 1661, Apr. 15. Died 1688, July 21. In place of No. 429. (444)

1649, Sept. 19. EDWARD, count palatine of the Rhine, duke of Bavaria · the sovereign's cousin. Nominated and invested at St Germain-en-Laye, 1649, Sept. 19. Installed 1661, Apr. 15. Died 1662-3, Mar. 10 In place of No. 434. (445)

1649, Sept. 19 GEORGE (VILLIERS), 2nd duke of Buckingham. Nominated, invested and installed *ut supra*. Died 1687, Apr. 16. In place of No. 410. (446)

1649-50, Jan. 13. WILLIAM (SEYMOUR), 1st marquess of Hertford, afterwards 7th duke of Somerset. Nominated at Jersey, 1649-50, Jan. 13. Invested at Canterbury 1660, May 27; not installed. Died 1660, Oct. 24. In place of No. 407. (447)

1649-50, Jan 13 THOMAS (WRIOTHESLEY), 5th earl of Southampton; nominated and invested *ut supra*. Installed 1661, Apr. 15. Died 1667, May 16 In place of No. 406. (448)

1649-50, Jan. 12. WILLIAM (HAMILTON), 2nd duke of Hamilton. Elected at Jersey Riband and George sent to him in Holland; not installed. Died 1651, Sept. 12. In place of No. 381 (449)

1649-50, Jan. 12. WILLIAM (CAVENDISH), 1st marquess, afterwards 1st duke of Newcastle Elected *ut supra*. Riband and George sent to him in Flanders. Installed 1661, Apr. 15. Died 1676, Dec 25. In place of No. 425 (450)

1649-50, Jan. 12 JAMES (GRAHAM), 1st marquess of Montrose. Elected *ut supra*. Insigna sent to him in Norway; not installed. Executed 1650, May 21 In place of No. 435. (451)

1649-50, Jan. 12. JAMES (STANLEY), 16th earl of Derby. Elected *ut supra*. Riband and George sent to him in the Isle of Man; not installed. Beheaded 1651, Oct. 15. In place of No. 394. (452)

1652-3, Jan. GEORGE (DIGBY), 2nd earl of Bristol. Nominated and invested at Paris Installed 1661, Apr. 15. Died 1676-7, Mar 20. In place of No. 421. (453)

1653, Apr 4. HENRY (STUART), duke of Gloucester, brother of the sovereign Nominated by the sovereign's letter dated Palais Royal, Paris, 1653, Apr. 4. Invested at the Hague by Garter King of Arms Apr. 14; not installed. Died 1660, Sept. 13 In place of No. 431. (454)

1653, Apr. 4. HENRY CHARLES DE LA TREMOUILLE, prince of Tarent. Nominated and invested *ut supra*. Installed by dispensation 1661, Apr. 10. Died 1672, Sept. 14. In place of No. 404. (455)

1653, Apr. 25. WILLIAM HENRY DE NASSAU, prince of Orange, afterwards king William III. Nominated by the sovereign's letter dated Paris, 1653, Apr. 25 Invested at the Hague by Garter May 4. Installed by dispensation 1661, Apr. 10 Died 1702, Mar. 8. In place of No. 451. (456)

1653-4, Jan. 23. FREDERICK WILLIAM, margrave of Brandenburg, prince elector. Nominated by the sovereign's letter dated Paris, 1653-4, Jan. 23. Invested at Berlin by Garter Mar. 31. Installed by dispensation 1661, Apr. 10. Died 1688, Apr 29. In place of No. 441. (457)

1657-8, Feb. 26. JOHN GASPAR FERDINAND DE MARCHIN, comte de Graville. Elected and invested by the sovereign at Antwerp 1657-8, Feb 26. Installed by dispensation 1661, Apr. 10. Died 1672-3, Mar. 9 In place of No. 443. (458)

1660, May 26. Sir GEORGE MONCK, afterwards duke of Albemarle. Elected and invested at Canterbury. Installed 1661, Apr. 15. Died 1669-70, Jan. 3 In place of No. 449. (459)

1660, May 26. Sir EDWARD (MONTAGU), 1st earl of Sandwich. Invested May 27. Installed 1661, Apr. 15. Died 1672, May 28. In place of No. 452. (460)

1660, May 31. AUBREY (DE VERE), 20th earl of Oxford Installed 1661, Apr. 15. Died 1702-3, Mar. 12. In place of No. 420. (461)

1661, Apr. 1. CHARLES (STUART), 5th duke of Richmond, duke of Lennox. Installed Apr. 15. Died 1672, Dec. 12. In place of No. 397. (462)

1661, Apr. 1. MONTAGU (BERTIE), 2nd earl of Lindsey Installed Apr. 15. Died 1666, July 25. In place of No. 433. (463)

1661, Apr. 1. EDWARD (MONTAGU), 2nd earl of Manchester Installed Apr. 15. Died 1671, May 5. In place of No 423. (465)

1661, Apr. 1. WILLIAM (WENTWORTH), 2nd earl of Strafford. Installed Apr. 15. Died 1695, Oct. 16. In place of No 442. (465)

1662, Nov. 6. CHRISTIERN, prince royal of Denmark, afterwards Christiern V, king of Denmark. Installed by proxy 1663, Apr. 22. Died 1699, Aug 25   In place of No. 447.   (466)

1663, Mar. 28. JAMES (FITZROY afterwards SCOTT), duke of Monmouth, afterwards duke of Buccleuch. Installed Apr. 22. Degraded 1685, June 18.   Executed 1685, July 15.   In place of No. 445.   (467)

1666, Dec. 3. JAMES (STUART), duke of Cambridge, the sovereign's nephew. Not installed. Died 1667, June 20. In place of No. 463.   (468)

1668, June 19. CHARLES XI., king of Sweden. Invested at Stockholm July 29.   Installed by proxy 1671, May 28.   Died 1697, Apr. 15.   In place of No. 468.   (469)

1668, June 19. JOHN GEORGE II., duke of Saxony. Invested at Dresden 1669, Apr. 13.   Installed *ut supra*.   Died 1680, Aug. 22.   In place of No. 448.   (470)

1669–70, Feb. 4. CHRISTOPHER (MONCK), 4th duke of Albemarle. Installed 1671, May 28. Died 1688, Oct. 6. In place of No. 436.   (471)

1672, Apr 18   JOHN (MAITLAND), 2nd earl, afterwards duke of Lauderdale Installed by proxy June 3 Died 1682, Aug. 24. In place of No. 418   (472)

1672, May 29.   HENRY (SOMERSET), 3rd marquess of Worcester, afterwards 1st duke of Beaufort; installed June 3.   Died 1699–1700, Jan. 21.   In place of No. 459.   (473)

1672, May 29.   HENRY (JERMYN), 3rd earl of St. Albans.   Installed June 3   Died 1683–4, Jan. 2.   In place of No. 422.   (474)

1672, May 29.   WILLIAM (RUSSELL), 7th earl, afterwards 4th duke of Bedford.   Installed June 3.   Died 1700, Sept. 7.   In place of No. 464.   (475)

1672, June 15.   HENRY (BENNET), 1st earl of Arlington.   Installed by proxy, June 22.   Died 1685, July 28.   In place of No. 460.   (476)

1672, Sept. 30. Sir THOMAS BUTLER, commonly called earl of Ossory. Installed Oct 25.   Died 1680, July 30.   In place of No. 455.   (477)

1672–3, Jan. 25. Sir CHARLES FITZROY, commonly called earl of Southampton, afterwards 1st duke of Southampton and duke of Cleveland. Natural son of the sovereign. Installed 1673, Apr. 1. Died 1730, Sept. 9. In place of No. 462   (478)

1674, Apr. 23. JOHN (SHEFFIELD), 3rd earl of Mulgrave, afterwards duke of Buckingham and of Normandy. Installed May 28. Died 1720–1, Feb. 24. In place of No. 458.   (479)

1676–7, Feb. 17. HENRY (CAVENDISH), 2nd duke of Newcastle. Installed Apr. 19. Died 1691, July 26. In place of No. 450.   (480)

1676–7, Mar. 24. THOMAS (OSBORNE), 2nd earl of Danby, afterwards 1st duke of Leeds. Installed Apr. 19. Died 1712, July 26. In place of No. 453.   (481)

1680, Aug. 31. HENRY (FITZ-ROY), 1st duke of Grafton. Natural son of the sovereign. Installed by proxy Sept. 30. Died 1690, Oct. 9. In place of Charles XI. of Sweden, translated to the prince's stall.   (482)

1680, Aug. 31. JAMES (CECIL), 16th earl of Salisbury. Installed Sept. 30. Died 1683, June. In place of No. 477.   (483)

1680, Sept. 15. CHARLES II., count Palatine of the Rhine, duke of Bavaria, great grandson of James I. Installed by proxy 1680–1, Jan. 22. Died 1685, May 26. In place of No. 432.   (484)

1681, Apr. 7. CHARLES (LENNOX), 6th duke of Richmond, duke of Lennox. Natural son of the sovereign. Installed Apr. 20. Died 1723, May 27. In place of No. 470.   (485)

1682, Sept. 25. WILLIAM (DOUGLAS-HAMILTON), 3rd duke of Hamilton. Invested Nov. 4. Installed Nov. 21. Died 1694, Apr. 18. In place of No. 472.   (486)

1683–4, Jan. 1. GEORGE, prince of Denmark, afterwards duke of Cumberland, brother to Christiern V., king of Denmark and consort to the princess Anne, afterwards Queen of England. Installed 1684, Apr 8. Died 1708, Oct. 28. In place of No. 440.   (487)

1683–4, Jan. 10. CHARLES (SEYMOUR), 11th duke of Somerset. Installed 1684, Apr. 8. Died 1748, Dec. 2. In place of No. 483.   (488)

1683–4, Jan. 10. GEORGE (FITZ-ROY), 2nd duke of Northumberland, natural son of the sovereign. Installed 1684, Apr. 8. Died 1716, July 3 (? June 28). In place of No. 474.   (489)

JAMES II., the seventeenth Sovereign.

Succeeded 1684–5, Feb. 6.

1685, May 6. HENRY (HOWARD), 14th duke of Norfolk. Installed
        July 22. Died 1701, Apr. 2. In place of the Sovereign on
        the latter's accession.   (490)

1685, June 18. HENRY (MORDAUNT), 2nd earl of Peterborough.
        Installed July 22. Died 1697, June 19. In place of
        No. 484.   (491)

1685, June 29. LAWRENCE (HYDE), 4th earl of Rochester. Installed
        July 22. Died 1711, May 2. In place of No. 467.   (492)

1685, July 30. LEWIS (DE DURAS), 2nd earl of Feversham. Installed
        Aug. 25. Died 1709, Apr. 19. In place of No. 476.   (493)

1687, Apr. 26. ROBERT (SPENCER), 3rd earl of Sunderland. Installed
        May 23. Died 1702, Sept. 28. In place of No. 446.   (494)

1688, Sept. 28. JAMES (FITZ JAMES), duke of Berwick, natural son of
        the sovereign. Not installed. Slain 1734, June 12. In
        place of No. 457.   (495)

*1688, Sept. 28. JAMES (BUTLER), 2nd duke of Ormonde. Installed
        1689, Apr. 5. Degraded 1716, July 12. Died 1745, Nov.
        5–16. In place of No. 444.   (496)

WILLIAM and MARY, the eighteenth Sovereign.

Succeeded 1688–9, Feb. 13.

1689, Apr. 3. FREDERICK ARMAND DE SCHÖNBERG OR SCHOMBERG,
        1st duke of Schomberg. Installed May 14. Died 1690,
        July 1. In place of William, prince of Orange, on the
        latter's accession as sovereign.   (497)

* It may be of interest to append here a note of the Jacobite nominations of Knights of the Garter, as
made by the Stuarts when in exile. These nominations of course bear no authority. I am indebted to the
courtesy of the most Honourable the Marquis de Ruvigny for the permission to reprint these names from
"the Jacobite Peerage," p. 193. The titles of the persons named are Jacobite dignities, with the exception of
the Hamilton and Wharton titles, and are equally without authority.

1692, Apr. 19.   JAMES (STUART), prince of Wales, duke of Cornwall and Rothesay.
1692, Apr. 19.   WILLIAM (HERBERT), 1st duke of Powis.
1692, Apr. 19.   JOHN (DRUMMOND), 1st duke of Melfort.
1692, Apr. 19.   FRANCIS NOMPAR (DE CAUMONT), 1st duke of Lauzan.
1706, June 21.   JAMES (DRUMMOND), 1st duke of Perth.
[1714,   ?   PIERS (BUTLER), 1st earl of Newcastle.]
1716, Apr. 8.   JOHN ERSKINE, 1st duke of Mar.
1723, July 30.   JAMES (DOUGLAS-HAMILTON), 5th duke of Hamilton and 2nd duke of Brandon, K. T.
1726, Mar. 5.   PHILIP (WHARTON), 1st duke of Wharton and Northumberland.
1727, Apr. 3.   JAMES (FITZJAMES), duke of Liria [Spain], earl of Tynmouth.
1742,   ?   CHARLES, prince of Wales, duke of Cornwall and Rothesay.
1747.   DANIEL (O'BRIEN), 1st earl of Lismore.

1689, Apr. 3. WILLIAM (CAVENDISH), 5th earl afterwards 1st duke of Devonshire. Installed May 14. Died 1707, Aug. 18. In place of No. 471. (498)

1689–90, Jan. 1. FREDERICK III , Margrave of Brandenburg, afterwards Frederick I., king of Prussia. Invested at Berlin 1690, June 6. Installed by proxy 1694, June 5. Died 1713–4, Feb. 25. Elected to the stall of his late father, No. 457, in place of the duke of Berwick, No. 495, whose election was declared void 1689–90, Jan. 1. (499)

1690, Dec. 30. GEORGE WILLIAM, duke of Brunswick-Luneburg, afterwards duke of Zelle. Invested at the Hague, 1691, Apr. 8. Installed by proxy 1694, June 5. Died 1705, Aug. 28. In place of No. 497. (500)

1691–2, Feb. 2. JOHN GEORGE IV , duke of Saxony. Invested at Dresden 1692–3, Jan. 26; not installed. Died 1694 In place of No 482. (501)

1691–2, Feb. 2. CHARLES (SACKVILLE), 9th earl of Dorset, earl of Middlesex, etc. Installed Feb. 24. Died 1705–6, Jan. 29. In place of No. 480. (502)

1694, Apr. 25. CHARLES (TALBOT), 15th earl, afterwards 1st duke of Shrewsbury. Installed June 5. Died 1717–8, Feb. 1. In place of No. 486. (503)

1695–6, Jan. 6. WILLIAM, commonly called duke of Gloucester, son of the princess Anne by prince George of Denmark. Installed July 24. Died 1700, July 30 In place of No. 465 (504)

1696–7, Feb. 19. WILLIAM (BENTINCK), 5th earl of Portland. Installed Mar. 15. Died 1709, Nov. 23. In place of No 501. (505)

1698, May 30. JOHN (HOLLES), 3rd duke of Newcastle. Installed July 7. Died 1711, July 15. In place of No. 469. (506)

1700, May 14. THOMAS (HERBERT), 27th earl of Pembroke, earl of Montgomery Installed June 5. Died 1732–3, Jan. 22. In place of No. 491. (507)

1700, May 14. ARNOLD JOOST (VAN KEPPEL), 13th earl of Albemarle. Installed June 5. Died 1718, May 30. In place of No. 466. (508)

1701, June 18. GEORGE LEWIS, duke of Brunswick-Lüneburg, afterwards George I., of England. Invested at Hanover, 1701, Aug. 23 and 24. Installed by proxy, 1702–3, Mar. 13. In place of No. 473.   (509)

1701, June 18. JAMES (DOUGLAS), 2nd duke of Queensberry. Invested July 10. Died 1711, July 6. In place of No. 504.   (510)

ANNE, the nineteenth Sovereign.

Succeeded 1701–2, Mar. 8.

1701–2, Mar. 14. WRIOTHESLEY (RUSSELL), 5th duke of Bedford. Installed 1702–3, Mar. 13. Died 1711, May 26. In place of No. 475.   (511)

1701–2, Mar. 14. JOHN (CHURCHILL), 5th earl, afterwards 1st duke of Marlborough. Installed 1702–3, Mar. 13. Died 1722, June 16. In place of No. 490.   (512)

1703, Aug. 12. MEINHARDT (DE SCHÖNBERG OR SCHOMBERG), 3rd duke of Schomberg. Installed Sept. 2. Died 1719, July 5. In place of No. 494.   (513)

1704, July 6. SIDNEY (GODOLPHIN), 1st lord, afterwards 1st earl of Godolphin. Installed Dec. 13. Died 1712, Sept. 15. In place of No. 461.   (514)

1706, Apr. 4. GEORGE AUGUSTUS, electoral prince of Brunswick-Lüneburg, afterwards George II. of England. Invested at Hanover, June 13. Installed by proxy, 1710, Dec. 22. Died 1760, Oct. 25. In place of No. 500.   (515)

1709–10, Mar. 22. WILLIAM (CAVENDISH), 2nd duke of Devonshire. Installed Dec. 22. Died 1729, June 4. In place of No. 502.   (516)

1709–10, Mar. 22. JOHN (CAMPBELL), 2nd duke of Argyll. Installed Dec. 22. Died 1743, Oct. 4. In place of No. 498.   (517)

1712, Oct. 25. HENRY (SOMERSET), 2nd duke of Beaufort. Installed 1713, Aug. 4. Died 1714, May 24. In place of No. 487.   (518)

1712, Oct. 25. JAMES (HAMILTON), 4th duke of Hamilton. Not installed. Died 1712, Nov. 15. In place of No. 493.   (519)

1712, Oct. 25. HENRY (GREY), 1st duke of Kent. Installed 1713, Aug. 4. Died 1740, June 5. In place of No. 505.   (520)

1712, Oct. 25. JOHN (POULETT),1st earl Poulett. Installed 1713, Aug. 4. Died 1743, May 28. In place of No. 492. (521)

1712, Oct. 25. ROBERT (HARLEY), 21st earl of Oxford Installed 1713, Aug. 4. Died 1724, May 21. In place of No. 511. (522)

.1712, Oct. 25. THOMAS (WENTWORTH), 3rd earl of Strafford. Installed by proxy 1713, Aug. 4. Died 1739, Nov. 15. In place of No. 510. (523)

1713, Aug. 4. CHARLES (MORDAUNT), 3rd earl of Peterborough. Installed Aug. 4. Died 1735, Oct. 25. In place of No. 506. (524)

GEORGE I., the twentieth Sovereign.

Succeeded 1714, Aug 1.

1714, Oct. 16. CHARLES (POWLETT), 2nd duke of Bolton. Installed Dec. 9. Died 1721-2, Jan. 21. In place of No. 509 on the latter's accession as sovereign. (525)

1714, Oct. 16 JOHN (MANNERS), 2nd duke of Rutland. Installed Dec. 9. Died 1720-1, Feb. 22 In place of No. 481. (526)

1714, Oct. 16 LIONEL CRANFIELD (SACKVILLE),10th earl,afterwards 1st duke of Dorset. Installed Dec. 9. Died 1765, Oct. 10. In place of No. 514 (527)

1714, Oct. 16. CHARLES (MONTAGUE), 1st earl of Halifax. Installed Dec. 9. Died 1715, May 19 In place of No. 519. (528)

1717, July 3. FREDERICK LEWIS, prince of Brunswick-Luneburg, afterwards prince of Wales, grandson of the sovereign. Invested at Hanover Dec. 24 Installed by proxy 1718, Apr. 30. Died 1750-1, Mar. 20. In place of No. 499. (529)

1717, July 3. ERNEST AUGUSTUS, prince of Brunswick-Luneburg, afterwards duke of York and Albany, brother of the sovereign. Invested at Hanover Dec. 24. Installed by proxy 1718, Apr. 30. Died 1728, Aug. 14. In place of No. 518. (530)

1718, Mar. 31. CHARLES (BEAUCLERK), 1st duke of St. Albans, natural son of Charles II. Installed Apr. 30. Died 1726, May 10. In place of No. 528. (531)

1718, Mar. 31. JOHN (MONTAGU), 2nd duke of Montagu Installed Apr. 30. Died 1749, July 16. In place of No. 489. (532)

1718, Mar. 31. Thomas (Pelham-Holles), 4th duke of Newcastle.
Installed Apr. 30.   Died 1768, Nov. 17.   In place of
No. 496.   (533)

1718, Mar. 31. James (Berkeley), 3rd earl of Berkeley. Installed
Apr. 30.   Died 1736, Aug. (or Sept. 2).   In place of
No. 503.   (534)

1719, Apr. 29. Evelyn (Pierrepont), 1st duke of Kingston.   In-
stalled June 23.   Died 1725-6, Mar. 5.   In place of
No. 508.   (535)

1719, Nov. 21. Charles (Spencer), 4th earl of Sunderland.   In-
stalled 1720, May 24.   Died 1722, Apr. 19.   In place of
No. 513.   (536)

1721, Mar. 27. Charles (Fitz-Roy), 2nd duke of Grafton Installed
Apr. 25.   Died 1757, May 6.   In place of No. 479.   (537)

1721, Mar. 27. Henry (Clinton), 19th earl of Lincoln.   Installed
Apr. 25.   Died 1728, Sept. 7.   In place of No. 526.   (538)

1722, Oct. 10. Charles (Pawlet or Powlett), 3rd duke of Bolton.
Installed Nov. 13.   Died 1754, Aug. 26.   In place of
No. 525.   (539)

1722, Oct. 10. John (Manners), 3rd duke of Rutland.   Installed
Nov. 13.   Died 1779, May 29.   In place of No. 536.   (540)

1722, Oct. 10. John (Ker), 1st duke of Roxburghe.   Installed
Nov. 13.   Died 1740-1, Feb. 24.   In place of No. 512. (541)

1724, July 9. Richard (Lumley), 2nd earl of Scarborough.   In-
stalled July 28.   Died 1739-40, Jan. 29.   In place of
No. 485.   (542)

1724, July 9. Charles (Townshend), 2nd viscount Townshend of
Raynham.   Installed July 28   Died 1738, June 21.   In
place of No. 522   (543)

1726, May 26. Charles (Lennox), 7th duke of Richmond. Installed
June 16   Died 1750, Aug. 8.   In place of No. 535.   (544)

1726, May 26   Sir Robert Walpole, afterwards 1st earl of Orford.
Installed June 16.   Died 1744-5, Mar. 18.   In place of
No. 531.   (545)

GEORGE II., the twenty-first Sovereign.

Succeeded 1727, June 11

1730, May 18. WILLIAM AUGUSTUS, prince of Brunswick-Lüneburg, afterwards duke of Cumberland, second son of the sovereign. Installed June 18, in succession to the sovereign on the latter's accession. Died 1765, Oct. 31. (546)

1730, May 18. PHILIP DORMER (STANHOPE), 5th earl of Chesterfield, Installed June 18. Died 1773, Mar. 24. In place of No. 530. (547)

1730, May 18. RICHARD (BOYLE), 3rd earl of Burlington, earl of Cork. Installed June 18. Died 1753, Dec. 3. In place of No. 538. (548)

1733, June 12. WILLIAM CHARLES HENRY FRISO DE NASSAU, prince of Orange, son-in-law of the sovereign. Invested at the Hague, July 22 and 25 Installed by proxy Aug. 22. Died 1751, Oct. 11. In place of No. 516. (549)

1733, June 12. WILLIAM (CAVENDISH), 3rd duke of Devonshire. Installed Aug. 22. Died 1755, Dec. 5. In place of No. 478. (550)

1733, June 12 SPENCER (COMPTON), earl of Wilmington. Installed Aug. 22. Died 1743, July 2. In place of No. 507. (551)

1737-8, Feb. 20. WILLIAM (CAPELL), 23rd earl of Essex. Installed 1738, June 15. Died 1742-3, Jan. 8. In place of No. 524. (552)

1737-8, Feb. 20. JAMES (WALDEGRAVE), 1st earl Waldegrave. Installed by proxy, June 15. Died 1741, Apr. 11. In place of No 534 (553)

1740-1, Mar. 20. FREDERICK, prince, afterwards landgrave, of Hesse Cassel, son-in-law of the sovereign. Invested at Hanover 1741, June 29. Installed 1750, July 12. Died 1785, Oct. 31. In place of No. 543. (554)

1740-1, Mar. 20. CHARLES (BEAUCLERK), 2nd duke of St. Albans. Installed Apr. 21. Died 1751, July 27. In place of No. 523. (555)

1740-1, Mar. 20. CHARLES (SPENCER), 3rd duke of Marlborough. Installed Apr. 21. Died 1758, Oct. 20. In place of No. 542. (556)

1740–1, Mar. 20. EVELYN (PIERREPONT), 2nd duke of Kingston-upon-Hull. Installed Apr. 21. Died 1773, Sept. 23. In place of No. 520. (557)

1740–1, Mar. 20. WILLIAM (BENTINCK), 2nd duke of Portland. Installed Apr. 21. Died 1762, May 1. In place of No. 541. (558)

1741, May 2. FREDERICK III., duke of Saxe-Gotha. Invested at Gotha July 12 and 13 Installed by proxy 1750, July 12. Died 1772, Mar 10. In place of No. 553. (559)

1745, Apr. 24. JOHN ADOLPHUS, duke of Saxe-Weissenfels. Invested at Weissenfels 1745–6, Feb. 18; not installed. Died in 1746. In place of No. 552. (560)

1749, June 22. GEORGE WILLIAM FREDERICK, prince of Brunswick-Luneburg, eldest grandson of the sovereign, and afterwards George III. Installed by proxy 1750, July 12; died 1820, Jan. 29. In place of No. 521. (561)

1749, June 22. CHARLES WILLIAM FREDERICK, margrave of Brandenburg-Anspach. Invested at Anspach Aug. 26. Installed by proxy 1750, July 12. Died 1757, Aug. In place of No. 551. (562)

1749, June 22. THOMAS (OSBORNE), 4th duke of Leeds. Installed 1750, July 12. Died 1789, Mar. 23. In place of No. 517. (563)

1749, June 22. JOHN (RUSSELL), 7th duke of Bedford. Installed 1750, July 12. Died 1771, Jan. 14. In place of No. 545. (564)

1749, June 22 WILLIAM ANNE (VAN KEPPEL), 14th earl of Albemarle. Installed by proxy 1750, July 12. Died 1754, Dec 22. In place of No. 560. (565)

1749, June 22. JOHN (CARTERET), 2nd earl Granville. Installed 1750, July 12. Died 1763, Jan. 2. In place of No. 488. (566)

1752, Mar. 13. EDWARD AUGUSTUS, prince of Brunswick-Lüneburg, afterwards duke of York and Albany, second grandson of the sovereign Installed by proxy 1752, June 4. Died 1767, Sept. 17. In place of No. 532. (567)

1752, Mar. 13. WILLIAM V. DE NASSAU, prince of Orange, grandson of the sovereign. Invested at the Hague June 5. Installed by proxy June 4. Died 1806. In place of No. 544. (568)

1752, Mar. 13. HENRY (CLINTON, afterwards PELHAM-CLINTON), 21st earl of Lincoln, afterwards 2nd duke of Newcastle-under-Lyne. Installed June 4. Died 1794, Feb. 22. In place of No. 529. (569)

1752, Mar. 13. DANIEL (FINCH), 8th earl of Winchilsea, earl of Nottingham. Installed June 4. Died 1769, Aug. 2. In place of No. 555. (570)

1752, Mar. 13. GEORGE (MONTAGU), 4th earl of Cardigan, afterwards 3rd duke of Montagu. Installed June 4. Died 1790, May 23. In place of No. 549. (571)

1756, Nov. 18. WILLIAM (CAVENDISH), 4th duke of Devonshire. Installed 1757, Mar. 29. Died 1764, Oct. 2. In place of No. 548. (572)

1756, Nov. 18. HENRY (HOWARD), 7th earl of Carlisle. Installed 1757, Mar. 29. Died 1758, Sept. 3. In place of No 539. (573)

1756, Nov. 18. HUGH (PERCY), 15th earl, afterwards 3rd duke of Northumberland. Installed 1757, Mar. 29. Died 1786, June 6. In place of No 565. (574)

1756, Nov. 18. FRANCIS (SEYMOUR-CONWAY), 16th earl, afterwards 4th marquess of Hertford. Installed 1757, Mar. 29. Died 1794, June 14. In place of No. 550 (575)

1757, June 30. JAMES (WALDEGRAVE), 2nd earl Waldegrave. Installed Aug. 30. Died 1763, Apr. 28. In place of No. 537. (576)

1759, Aug. 16. FERDINAND, prince of Brunswick-Bevern. Invested at Kroffdorff near Giessen Oct. 16 and 17. Installed by proxy 1760, May 6. Died 1792, July 3. In place of No. 562. (577)

1760, Feb. 4. CHARLES (WATSON-WENTWORTH), 2nd marquess of Rockingham. Installed May 6. Died 1782, July 2. In place of No. 573. (578)

1760, Feb. 4. RICHARD (GRENVILLE-TEMPLE), earl Temple. Installed May 6. Died 1779, Sept. 11. In place of No. 556. (579)

GEORGE III., the twenty-second Sovereign.

Succeeded 1760, Oct. 25.

1762, May 27. WILLIAM HENRY, prince of Brunswick-Luneburg, afterwards duke of Gloucester and Edinburgh, brother of the sovereign. Installed Sept. 22. By virtue of a statute dated 1805, Jan. 10, he was as a descendant of George II. excepted from the original number of 25 knights. Died 1805, Aug. 25. In place of the sovereign on the latter's accession. (580)

1762, May 27. JOHN (STUART), 3rd earl of Bute. Installed Sept. 22. Died 1792, Mar. 10. In place of No. 558. (581)

1764, Apr. 23. ADOLPHUS FREDERICK, duke of Mecklenburg-Strelitz, brother of the queen consort. Invested at Strelitz May 29 and June 4. Installed by proxy 1771, July 25. Died 1794, June 2. In place of No. 566. (582)

1764, Apr. 23. GEORGE (MONTAGUE-DUNK), 5th earl of Halifax. Not installed. Died 1771, June 8. In place of No. 576. (583)

1765, Dec. 26. GEORGE AUGUSTUS FREDERICK, prince of Wales, afterwards king George IV Installed 1771, July 25. Died 1830, June 26. In place of No. 572. (584)

1765, Dec. 26. CHARLES WILLIAM FERDINAND, ·hereditary prince, afterwards duke, of Brunswick-Wolfenbuttel, brother-in-law of the sovereign. Installed by proxy 1771, July 25. Died 1806, Nov. 10. In place of No. 527. (585)

1765, Dec. 26 GEORGE (KEPPEL), 15th earl of Albemarle Installed 1771, July 25. Died 1772, Oct. 13. In place of No. 546. (586)

1767, Dec. 21. HENRY FREDERICK, prince of Brunswick-Luneburg, afterwards duke of Cumberland and Strathearn, brother of the sovereign. Installed 1771, July 25. Died 1790, Sept. 18. In place of No. 567. (587)

1768, Dec 12. GEORGE (SPENCER), 4th duke of Marlborough. Installed 1771, July 25. Died 1817, Jan. 29. In place of No 533 (588)

1769, Sept. 20. AUGUSTUS HENRY (FITZ-ROY), 3rd duke of Grafton. Installed 1771, July 25 Died 1811, Mar. 14. In place of No. 570. (589)

1771, Feb. 11. GRANVILLE (LEVESON-GOWER), 2nd earl Gower, afterwards 1st marquess of Stafford. Installed July 25. Died 1803, Oct. 26. In place of No. 564. (590)

1771, June 19. FREDERICK, prince of Brunswick-Lüneburg, bishop of Osnaburgh, afterwards duke of York and Albany, second son of the sovereign. Installed July 25. Died 1827, Jan. 5. In place of No. 583. (591)

1772, June 18. Sir FREDERICK NORTH, commonly called lord North, afterwards 4th earl of Guilford. Not installed. Died 1792, Aug. 5. In place of No. 559. (592)

1778, June 3. HENRY (HOWARD), 20th earl of Suffolk, earl of Berkshire. Not installed. Died 1779, Mar. 7. In place of No. 586. (593)

1778, June 3. WILLIAM HENRY (NASSAU DE ZULESTEIN), 4th earl of Rochford. Not installed. Died 1781, Sept. 28. In place of No. 547. (594)

1778, June 3. THOMAS (THYNNE), 3rd viscount Weymouth, afterwards 1st marquess of Bath. Not installed. Died 1796, Nov. 19. In place of No. 557. (595)

1782, Apr. 19. WILLIAM HENRY, prince of Brunswick Lüneburg, afterwards duke of Clarence and St. Andrews, and king William IV. of England, third son of the sovereign. Ensigns delivered to him at New York. Installed by dispensation, 1801, May 28. In place of No. 593. (596)

1782, Apr. 19. CHARLES (LENNOX), 8th duke of Richmond, duke of Lennox. Installed by dispensation 1801, May 29. Died 1806, Dec. 29. In place of No. 540. (597)

1782, Apr. 19. WILLIAM (CAVENDISH), 5th duke of Devonshire. Installed ut supra. Died 1811, July 29. In place of No. 579. (598)

1782, Apr. 19. WILLIAM (PETTY), 3rd earl of Shelbourne, afterwards 1st marquess of Lansdowne. Installed ut supra. Died 1805, May 7. In place of No. 594. (599)

1782, Oct. 3. CHARLES (MANNERS), 4th duke of Rutland. Not installed. Died 1787, Oct. 24. In place of No. 578. (600)

1786, June 2. EDWARD, prince of Brunswick-Lüneburg, afterwards duke of Kent and Strathearn, fourth son of the sovereign. Ensigns transmitted to him at Hanover. Installed by dispensation 1801, May 28. Died 1820, Jan. 23. Elected by virtue of a new statute dated 1786, May 31, admitting the sons of the sovereign for the time being into the Order in addition to the number of knights established by the ancient Statutes. (601)

1786, June 2. ERNEST AUGUSTUS, prince of Brunswick-Luneburg, afterwards duke of Cumberland and Tiviotdale and king of Hanover, fifth son of the sovereign. Elected and installed *ut supra.* Died 1851, Nov. 18.   (602)

1786, June 2. AUGUSTUS FREDERICK, prince of Brunswick-Luneburg, afterwards duke of Sussex, sixth son of the sovereign. Elected and installed *ut supra.* Died 1843, Apr. 21.   (603)

1786, June 2. ADOLPHUS FREDERICK, prince of Brunswick-Luneburg, afterwards duke of Cambridge, seventh son of the sovereign. Elected and installed *ut supra.* Died 1850, July 8.   (604)

1786, June 2. WILLIAM, landgrave of Hesse-Cassel, afterwards elector of the Holy Roman Empire. Invested at Cassel 1786, Aug. 7. Installed by dispensation 1801, May 29. Died 1821, Feb. 27. In place of No. 554.   (605)

1786, June 2. HENRY (SOMERSET), 5th duke of Beaufort. Installed *ut supra.* Died 1803, Oct. 11. In place of the prince of Wales, No 584, in consequence of the latter's exception from the original number by the statute of 1786, May 31.
          (606)

1786, June 2. GEORGE (NUGENT-TEMPLE-GRENVILLE), 1st marquess of Buckingham. Installed *ut supra.* Died 1813, Feb. 11. In place of No. 591 in consequence, etc., *ut supra.*   (607)

1786, June 2. CHARLES (CORNWALLIS), 2nd earl, afterwards 1st marquess Cornwallis. Ensigns delivered to him at Calcutta 1787, Mar. 4. Installed *ut supra* Died 1805, Oct. 5. In place of No. 596 in consequence, etc., *ut supra.*   (608)

1788, Apr. 9. JOHN FREDERICK (SACKVILLE), 3rd duke of Dorset. Installed *ut supra.* Died 1799, July 19. In place of No. 574.   (609)

1788, Apr. 9. HUGH (PERCY), 4th duke of Northumberland. Installed *ut supra.* Died 1817, July 10. In place of No. 600.
          (610)

1790, Dec. 15. ERNEST LEWIS, duke of Saxe-Gotha, cousin of the sovereign. Invested at Gotha 1791, Apr. 18. Installed *ut supra.* Died 1804, Apr. 20. In place of No. 563.   (611)

1790, Dec. 15. FRANCIS GODOLPHIN (OSBORNE), 5th duke of Leeds. Not installed. Died 1799, Jan. 31. In place of No. 571.
          (612)

1790, Dec. 15.   JOHN (PITT), 2nd earl of Chatham.   Installed by
    dispensation 1801, May 29.   Died 1835, Sept. 24.   In place
    of No. 587.   (613)

1793, June 12.   JAMES (CECIL), 1st marquess of Salisbury.   Installed
    ut supra.   Died 1823, June 13.   In place of No. 581.   (614)

1793, June 12.   JOHN (FANE), 16th earl of Westmorland.   Invested
    1795, Jan. 14.   Installed *ut supra.*   Died 1841, Dec. 15.
    In place of No. 577.   (615)

1793, June 12.   FREDERICK (HOWARD), 8th earl of Carlisle.   Installed
    ut supra.   Died 1825, Sept. 4.   In place of No. 592.   (616)

1794, May 28.   HENRY (SCOTT), 3rd duke of Buccleuch, afterwards
    also duke of Queensbury.   Installed *ut supra.*   Died 1812,
    Jan. 11.   In place of No. 569.   (617)

1794, July 16.   WILLIAM FREDERICK, prince of Brunswick-Luneburg,
    afterwards duke of Gloucester and Edinburgh; nephew of
    the sovereign.   Ensigns delivered to him by the duke of
    York, then in Flanders   Installed *ut supra.*   Excepted from
    the original number of knights by the statute of 1805, Jan.
    10.   Died 1857, Apr. 30.   In place of No. 582.   (618)

1794, July 16.   WILLIAM HENRY CAVENDISH (Bentinck, afterwards
    Cavendish-Bentinck), 3rd duke of Portland.   Installed *ut
    supra.*   Died 1809, Oct. 30.   In place of No. 575.   (619)

1797, June 2.   RICHARD (HOWE), 1st earl Howe; not installed.   Died
    1799, Aug. 5.   In place of No. 595.   (620)

1799, Mar. 1.   GEORGE JOHN (SPENCER), 2nd earl Spencer.   Installed
    by dispensation, 1801, May 29.   Died 1834, Nov. 10.   In
    place of No. 612.   (621)

1799, Aug. 14.   JOHN JEFFREYS (PRATT), 2nd earl, afterwards 1st
    marquess Camden.   Installed *ut supra.*   Died 1840, Oct. 8.
    In place of No. 609.   (622)

1801, June 3   JOHN (KER), 3rd duke of Roxburghe.   Nominated, in-
    vested and installed by dispensation.   Died 1804, March 19
    In place of No. 620.   (623)

1803, Nov. 25.   JOHN HENRY (MANNERS), 5th duke of Rutland.   In-
    stalled 1805, Apr. 23.   Died 1857, Jan. 20.   In place of
    No. 606.   (624)

4

1803, Nov. 25. PHILIP (YORKE), 3rd earl of Hardwicke. Received the ensigns at Dublin Castle 1805, Apr. 16. Installed by proxy Apr. 23. Died 1834, Nov. 18. In place of No. 590. (625)

1805, Jan. 17. HENRY CHARLES (SOMERSET), 6th duke of Beaufort. Installed Apr. 23. Died 1835, Nov. 23. In place of No. 623. (626)

1805, Jan. 17. JOHN JAMES (HAMILTON), 1st marquess of Abercorn. Installed Apr. 23 Died 1818, Jan. 27. In place of No. 611. (627)

1805, Jan. 17. GEORGE AUGUSTUS (HERBERT), 30th earl of Pembroke, earl of Montgomery. Installed Apr. 23. Died 1827, Oct 26. In place of No. 580 under the statute of 1805, Jan. 10. (628)

1805, Jan. 17 GEORGE (FINCH), 9th earl of Winchilsea, earl of Nottingham. Installed Apr. 23. Died 1826, Aug. 2. In place of No. 618 under the statute of 1805, Jan. 10 (629)

1805, Jan. 17. PHILIP (STANHOPE), 6th earl of Chesterfield. Installed Apr. 23. Died 1815, Aug. 29. In place of No. 568 under the statute of 1805, Jan. 10 (630)

1805, May 27. GEORGE (LEGGE), 3rd earl of Dartmouth. Not installed. Died 1810, Nov. 10. In place of No. 599. (631)

1806, Mar. 22. GEORGE GRANVILLE (LEVESON-GOWER), 2nd marquess of Stafford, afterwards duke of Sutherland. Installed by dispensation 1812, Mar. 31. Died 1833, July 5. In place of No. 608. (632)

1807, July 18. FRANCIS (INGRAM-SEYMOUR-CONWAY), 5th marquess of Hertford. Installed *ut supra*. Died 1822, June 17. In place of No. 585. (633)

1807, July 18. WILLIAM (LOWTHER), 2nd earl of Lonsdale. Installed *ut supra*. Died 1844, Mar. 19. In place of No. 597. (634)

1810, Mar. 3. RICHARD (WELLESLEY), marquess Wellesley. Installed *ut supra*. Died 1842, Sept. 26. In place of No. 619. (635)

1812, Mar. 26. CHARLES (LENNOX), 9th duke of Richmond. Installed *ut supra*. Received the ensigns at Dublin Castle Apr. 7. Died 1819, Aug. 28. In place of No. 631. (636)

1812, Mar. 26. JAMES (GRAHAM), 4th duke of Montrose. Installed *ut supra*. Died 1836, Dec. 30 In place of No. 589. (637)

1812, June 12. FRANCIS (RAWDON-HASTINGS), 2nd earl of Moira, afterwards 1st marquess of Hastings. Installed by dispensation June 13. Died 1826, Nov. 28. In place of No. 598. (638)

1812, June 19. HENRY PELHAM (PELHAM-CLINTON). 4th duke of Newcastle-under-Lyne. Installed by dispensation June 22. Died 1851, Jan. 12. In place of No. 617. (639)

1813, Mar. 4. ARTHUR (WELLESLEY), marquess, afterwards duke, of Wellington. Received the ensigns at Freneda in Portugal, May 6. Installed by dispensation 1814, April 19. Died 1852, Sept. 14. In place of No. 607. (640)

1813, July 27. ALEXANDER I., emperor of all the Russias. Elected a supernumerary knight by virtue of a special statute. Invested at Töplitz in Bohemia, Sept. 27. Installed *ut supra*. Died 1825, Sept. 4. (641)

1814, Apr. 21. LOUIS XVIII., king of France and Navarre. Elected a supernumerary knight by virtue of a special statute. Invested at Carlton House and installed by dispensation same day. Died 1824, Sept. 16. (642)

1814, June 9. FRANCIS I., emperor of Austria. Elected a supernumerary knight by virtue of a special statute. Invested at Vienna Sept. 21. Installed by dispensation Dec. 27. Died 1835, Mar. 2. (643)

1814, June 9. FREDERICK WILLIAM III., king of Prussia. Elected *ut supra*. Invested at Carlton House and installed same day by dispensation. Died 1840, June 7. (644)

1814, June 9. ROBERT BANKS (JENKINSON), 2nd earl of Liverpool. Elected *ut supra*. Knighted and invested on same day and installed by dispensation June 28. Died 1828, Dec. 4. Supernumerary till the death of No. 630. (645)

1814, June 9. Sir ROBERT STEWART, commonly called viscount Castlereagh, afterwards 2nd marquess of Londonderry. Elected and installed *ut supra*. Died 1822, Aug. 12. Supernumerary till the death of No. 588. (646)

1814, Aug. 10. FERDINAND VII., king of Spain. Elected a supernumerary knight by virtue of a special statute. Invested at Madrid, 1815, May 17. Installed by dispensation 1815, Aug. 26. Died 1833, Sept. 29. (647)

1814, Aug 10 WILLIAM FREDERICK DE NASSAU, prince of Orange, afterwards king of the Netherlands. Elected by virtue of the statute of 1805, Jan. 29, as a descendant of George II. Invested at Brussels Aug. 22. Installed by dispensation 1814, Dec. 27. Died 1843, Dec. 12. (648)

1816, May 23. LEOPOLD GEORGE FREDERICK, duke of Saxe-Coburg-Saalfeld, consort of the princess Charlotte Augusta, only child of the prince Regent, and afterwards king of the Belgians. Elected a supernumerary knight by special statute. Invested same day. Installed by dispensation May 25 Died 1865, Dec 10. (649)

1817, July 24. HENRY (BATHURST), 3rd earl Bathurst. Installed by dispensation July 26. Died 1834, July 27. In place of No. 610. (650)

1818, Feb. 19 HENRY WILLIAM (PAGET), 1st marquess of Anglesey. Installed by dispensation Mar. 2. Died 1854, Apr. 29. In place of No 627. (651)

1819, Nov. 25. HUGH (PERCY), 5th duke of Northumberland. Installed by dispensation Dec. 4. Died 1847, Feb. 11. In place of No. 636. (652)

GEORGE IV., the twenty-third Sovereign.

Succeeded 1820, January 29.

1820, June 7. RICHARD (TEMPLE-NUGENT-BRYDGES-CHANDOS-GRENVILLE), 2nd marquess, afterwards first duke of Buckingham. Installed by dispensation June 12. Died 1839, Jan. 17. In place of the sovereign on the latter's accession. (653)

1822, Feb. 13. FREDERICK VI , king of Denmark. Elected a supernumerary knight by virtue of a special statute. Invested at Copenhagen June 11. Installed by dispensation July 22. Died 1839, Dec. 3. (654)

1822, Feb. 13. JOHN VI., king of Portugal. Elected *ut supra*. Invested at the Palace of Ajuda near Lisbon 1823, Sept. 23. Installed by dispensation Nov. 23. Died 1826, Mar. 10. (655)

1822, July 22. GEORGE JAMES (CHOLMONDELEY), 1st marquess Cholmondeley. Elected, invested and installed by dispensation same day. Died 1827, Apr. 10. In place of No. 633. (656)

1822, Nov. 22. FRANCIS CHARLES (SEYMOUR-CONWAY), 6th marquess of Hertford. Elected, invested and installed by dispensation same day. Died 1842, Mar. 1. In place of No. 646.
(657)

1823, July 16. THOMAS (THYNNE), 2nd marquess of Bath. Installed by dispensation July 29. Died 1837, Mar. 27. In place of No. 614. (658)

1825, Mar. 9. CHARLES X., king of France and Navarre. Declared a supernumerary knight by special statute. Invested at Paris June 7. Installed by dispensation Dec. 20. Died 1836, Nov. 4. (659)

1826, Jan. 30. CHARLES (SACKVILLE-GERMAINE), 5th duke of Dorset. Elected, invested and installed by dispensation same day. Died 1843, July 29. In place of No. 616 (660)

1827, Mar. 16. NICHOLAS I., emperor of all the Russias. Declared a supernumerary knight by special statute. Invested at Czarskozelo July 8. Installed by dispensation Sept. 4 Died 1855, Mar. 2. (661)

1827, May 10. GEORGE WILLIAM FREDERICK (OSBORNE), 6th duke of Leeds. Elected, invested and installed by dispensation same day. Died 1838, July 10. In place of No. 629. (662)

1827, May 10. WILLIAM GEORGE SPENCER (CAVENDISH), 6th duke of Devonshire. Elected, etc., *ut supra*. Died 1858, Jan. 18. In place of No. 638 (663)

1827, May 10. BROWNLOW (CECIL), 2nd marquess of Exeter. Elected, etc., *ut supra*. Died 1867, Jan. 16. In place of No. 656.
(664)

1829, May 13. CHARLES (LENNOX afterwards GORDON-LENNOX), 10th duke of Richmond. Elected, etc., *ut supra*. Died 1860, Oct 21. In place of No. 628. (665)

1829, June 10. GEORGE (ASHBURNHAM), 3rd earl of Ashburnham. Installed by dispensation June 22. Died 1830, Oct. 27 (or 17). In place of No. 645. (666)

WILLIAM IV., the twenty-fourth Sovereign.

Succeeded 1830, June 26.

1830, July 17. BERNARD ERIC FREUND, reigning duke of Saxe-
Meiningen, brother of the queen consort. Declared a
supernumerary knight by special statute. Invested at
Windsor Castle July 26. Installed by dispensation 1831,
Aug. 20. Abdicated 1866, Sept 20. Died 1882, Dec. 3.
(667)

1830, July 26. WILLIAM I., king of Wurtemberg. Elected as a
lineal descendant of George II Invested at St. James's
Palace and installed by dispensation on same day. Died
1864, June 25.   (668)

1830, Nov. 25 JOHN (RUSSELL), 10th duke of Bedford. Elected,
invested and installed by dispensation same day. Died
1839, Oct. 20 In place of No. 666.   (669)

1831, May 27 CHARLES (GREY), 2nd earl Grey. Elected by a
special statute as an extra knight. Installed and invested
by dispensation same day. Died 1845, July 17. A super-
numerary knight till the death of No. 632.   (670)

1831, June 20. AUGUSTUS WILLIAM MAXIMILIAN FREDERICK LEWIS,
reigning duke of Brunswick-Wolffenbuttel Elected as a
lineal descendant of George II. Invested at St. James's
Palace and installed by dispensation same day. Died 1884,
Oct. 18   (671)

1834, Aug. 13. BERNARD EDWARD (HOWARD), 19th duke of Norfolk.
Elected, invested and installed by dispensation.* Died
1842, Mar. 16 In place of No. 650   (672)

1834, Dec 20. GEORGE HENRY (FITZ-ROY), 4th duke of Grafton.
Elected, invested and installed by dispensation Dec. 20.
Died 1844, Sept 28 In place of No. 621   (673)

1835, Feb. 23 WALTER FRANCIS (MONTAGU-DOUGLAS-SCOTT), 5th
duke of Buccleuch, duke of Queensberry. Elected, invested
and installed by dispensation Feb. 23 Died 1884, Apr. 16.
In place of No 625.   (674)

* From this point onward to the end of the Garter Knights the date in the margin, unless otherwise
stated, is that of installation or of the letters patent dispensing with all ceremonies of installation.

1835, Aug. 15. GEORGE FREDERICK ALEXANDER CHARLES ERNEST AUGUSTUS, prince of Brunswick-Luneburg, son and heir apparent of the duke of Cumberland and nephew of the sovereign. Elected, invested and installed Aug. 15 as a lineal descendant of king George I. Afterwards duke of Cumberland and Tiviotdale and king of Hanover. Died 1878, June 12, at his residence in the Rue de Presbourg, Paris. (675)

1835, Aug. 15. GEORGE WILLIAM FREDERICK CHARLES, prince of Brunswick-Luneburg, son and heir apparent of the duke of Cambridge and nephew of the sovereign. Elected, invested and installed Aug. 15 as a lineal descendant of George I. Afterwards 7th duke of Cambridge   Died 1904, Mar. 17. (676)

1836, Feb. 5. ALEXANDER (HAMILTON), 10th duke of Hamilton. Elected, invested and installed by dispensation Feb. 5. Died 1852, Aug. 12. In place of No. 613. (677)

1836, Feb. 5. HENRY (PETTY), 3rd marquess of Lansdowne. Elected, invested and installed by dispensation Feb. 5. Died 1863, Jan. 31. In place of No. 626. (678)

1837, Mar. 17. GEORGE (HOWARD), 9th earl of Carlisle. Elected invested and installed by dispensation Mar. 17. Died 1848, Oct. 7. In place of No. 637. (679)

1837, Apr. 19. EDWARD ADOLPHUS (SEYMOUR), 16th duke of Somerset. Elected, invested and installed by dispensation Apr. 19. Died 1855, Aug. 15. In place of No. 658. (680)

VICTORIA, the twenty-fifth Sovereign.

Succeeded 1837, June 20.

1837, July 14. CHARLES WILLIAM FREDERICK EMICON, prince of Leiningen, the sovereign's half brother. Declared a supernumerary knight by a special statute July 14. Invested and installed by dispensation same day. Died 1856, Nov. 13. (681)

1838, July 16 ERNEST ANTHONY CHARLES LEWIS, reigning duke of Saxe-Coburg and Gotha, the sovereign's uncle. Declared a supernumerary knight by special statute July 16. Invested and installed by dispensation same day. Died 1844, Jan. 29. (682)

1839, Apr. 2. EDWARD (SMITH-STANLEY), 22nd earl of Derby. Elected and installed by dispensation Apr. 2. Died 1851, June 30. In place of No. 662. (683)

1839, Apr. 17. WILLIAM HARRY (VANE), 4th duke of Cleveland. Elected, invested and installed by dispensation Apr. 17. Died 1842, Jan. 29. In place of No. 653. (684)

1839, Dec. 16. FRANCIS ALBERT AUGUSTUS CHARLES EMANUEL, duke of Saxe, prince of Saxe-Coburg and Gotha, the sovereign's cousin, afterwards prince Consort. Declared a supernumerary knight by special statute and installed by dispensation Dec. 16. Received the ensigns at Gotha 1840, Jan. 24. Died 1861, Dec. 14. (685)

1841, Mar. 11. GEORGE GRANVILLE (LEVESON-GOWER, afterwards SUTHERLAND-LEVESON-GOWER), 1st duke of Sutherland. knighted and invested at Buckingham Palace Mar. 11 and installed by dispensation same day. Died 1861, Feb. 28. In place of No. 669. (686)

1841, Mar. 11. ROBERT (GROSVENOR), 1st marquess of Westminster. Knighted and invested at Buckingham Palace and installed by dispensation same day. Died 1845, Feb. 17. In place of No. 622. (687)

1841, Dec. 8. For the prince of Wales see below under date 1858, Nov. 9.

1842, Jan. 25. FREDERICK WILLIAM IV., king of Prussia. Nominated as a lineal descendant of George I., Jan. 25. Invested at Windsor same day. Letters patent of dispensation of installation same day. Died 1861, Jan. 2. (688)

1842, Apr. 11. FREDERICK AUGUSTUS II., king of Saxony. Nominated as a descendant *ut supra* Apr. 11. Invested at Dresden by special commission Oct. 8. Letters patent of dispensation of installation Oct. 31. Died 1854, Aug. 9. (689)

1842,* Apr. 11. HENRY (SOMERSET), 7th duke of Beaufort. Nominated Apr. 11 in place of No. (?) 615. Knighted and invested Apr. 11. Letters patent of dispensation of installation Apr. 11. Died 1853, Nov. 17. (690)

1842, Apr. 11. RICHARD PLANTAGENET (TEMPLE-NUGENT-BRYDGES-CHANDOS-GRENVILLE), 2nd duke of Buckingham and Chandos. Nominated Apr. 11 in place of No. (?) 684. Invested Apr. 11. Letters patent of dispensation of installation Apr. 11. Died 1861, July 29. (691)

* From numbers 690 to 727 the succession of the Knights is not stated in the Register of the Order. It is here given from Young's MS. Register and from other MSS. at the College of Arms

1842, Apr. 11. JAMES BROWNLOW (GASCOYNE-CECIL, formerly CECIL), 2nd marquess of Salisbury. Nominated Apr. 11 in place of No. 635. Knighted and invested Apr. 11. Letters patent of dispensation of installation Apr. 11. Died 1868, Apr. 12. (692)

1842, Apr. 11. HENRY (VANE), 5th duke of Cleveland. Nominated Apr. 11 in place of No (?) 672. Invested Apr. 11. Letters patent of dispensation and installation Apr. 11. Died 1864, Jan. 18. (693)

1844, Oct. 11. LOUIS PHILIPPE, king of the French. Nominated by special statute Oct. 11. Invested Oct. 11. Letters patent of dispensation of installation Oct. 11. Died 1850, Aug 26. (694)

1844, Dec. 12. ERNEST II., duke of Saxe-Coburg and Gotha, brother-in-law to queen Victoria. Nominated by special statute Dec. 12. Invested Dec. 12. Letters patent of dispensation of installation Dec. 12 Died 1893, Aug. 22, at the Castle of Reinhardsbrunn, Gotha. (695)

1844, Dec. 12. THOMAS PHILIP (WEDDELL, afterwards DE GRAY), 2nd earl de Grey of Wrest. Nominated Dec. 12 in place of 635. Knighted and invested Dec. 12. Letters patent of dispensation and installation Dec. 12. Died 1859, Nov. 14. (696)

1844, Dec. 12. JAMES (HAMILTON), 2nd marquess, afterwards 1st duke of Abercorn. Nominated Dec. 12 in place of No. 660 Knighted and invested Dec. 12. Letters patent of dispensation of installation Dec. 12. Died 1885, Oct. 31. (697)

1844, Dec. 12. CHARLES CHETWYND (CHETWYND-TALBOT, formerly TALBOT), 3rd earl Talbot. Nominated Dec. 12 in place of No. 634. Invested Dec. 12. Letters patent of dispensation of installation Dec. 12. Died 1849, Jan 13. (698)

1844, Dec. 12. EDWARD HERBERT (HERBERT, formerly CLIVE), 7th earl of Powis. Nominated Dec. 12. Knighted and invested Dec. 12 in place of No. 673. Letters patent of dispensation of installation Dec. 12. Died 1848, Jan. 17. (699)

1846, Jan. 19. GEORGE CHARLES (PRATT), 2nd marquess of Camden. Nominated Jan. 19 in place of No. 687. Invested at Windsor Castle Jan. 19, he being there first knighted that day. Letters patent of dispensation of installation same day. Died 1866, Aug. 8. (700)

1846, Jan. 19. RICHARD (SEYMOUR-CONWAY), marquess of Hertford. Nominated Jan. 19 in place of No. 670. Invested at Windsor Castle Jan. 19, he being there first knighted that day. Letters patent of dispensation of installation same day. Died 1870, Aug. 24, at his residence in Paris. (701)

1847, Mar. 26. FRANCIS (RUSSELL), 7th duke of Bedford. Nominated Mar. 26 in place of No. 652. Knighted and invested at Buckingham Palace Mar. 26. Letters patent of dispensation of installation same day. Died 1861, May 14. (702)

1848, May 4. HENRY CHARLES (HOWARD), 20th duke of Norfolk. Nominated May 4 in place of No. 699. Knighted and invested at Buckingham Palace May 4. Letters patent of dispensation of installation same day. Died 1856, Feb. 18. (703)

1849, Mar. 23. GEORGE WILLIAM FREDERICK (VILLIERS), 8th earl of Clarendon. Nominated Mar. 23 in place of No. 679. Invested Mar. 23. Letters patent of dispensation of installation Mar. 23. Died 1870, June 27. (704)

1849, Mar. 23. FREDERICK (SPENCER), 4th earl Spencer. Nominated Mar. 23 in place of No. 698. Knighted and invested at Buckingham Palace Mar. 23. Letters patent of dispensation of installation same day. Died 1857, Dec. 27. (705)

1851, Feb. 19. CONSTANTINE HENRY (PHIPPS), 1st marquess of Normanby. Nominated Feb. 19 in place of No. 639. Invested Feb. 19. Letters patent of dispensation of installation Feb. 19. Died 1863, July (? Sept.) 28. (706)

1851, Nov. 4. CHARLES WILLIAM (WENTWORTH-FITZWILLIAM), 5th earl Fitzwilliam. Nominated Nov. 4 in place of No. 683. Knighted and invested at Windsor Castle Nov. 4. Letters patent of dispensation of installation Nov. 4. Died 1857, Oct. 4. (707)

1853, Jan. 19. ALGERNON (PERCY), 6th duke of Northumberland. Nominated Jan. 19 in place of No. 677. Knighted and invested Jan. 19 at Windsor Castle. Letters patent of installation same day. Died 1865, Feb. 12. (708)

1853, Jan. 19. CHARLES WILLIAM (VANE, formerly STEWART), 3rd marquess of Londonderry. Nominated Jan. 19 in place of No. 640. Invested at Windsor Castle Jan. 19. Letters patent of dispensation of installation Jan. 19. Died 1854, Mar. 6. (709)

1855, Feb. 7. GEORGE WILLIAM FREDERICK (HOWARD), 7th earl of Carlisle. Nominated Feb. 7 in place of No. 690 Knighted and invested at Windsor Castle Feb. 7. Letters patent of dispensation of installation same day. Died 1864, Dec. 5. (710)

1855, Feb. 7. FRANCIS (LEVESON-GOWER), 1st earl of Ellesmere. Nominated Feb 7 in place of No. 651. Knighted and invested at Windsor Castle Feb 7. Letters patent of dispensation of installation same day. Died 1857, Feb. 18. (711)

1855, Feb. 7. GEORGE (GORDON, *afterwards* HAMILTON-GORDON), 4th earl of Aberdeen Nominated Feb. 7 in place of No. 709. Invested Feb. 7. Letters patent of dispensation of installation Feb. 7. Died 1860, Dec. 14. (712)

1855, Apr 18. NAPOLEON III, emperor of the French. Nominated by special statute Apr. 18. Invested same day. Letters patent of dispensation of installation same day. Died 1873, Jan. 9. (713)

1855, Dec. 5. VICTOR EMMANUEL II, king of Sardinia, afterwards king of Italy. Nominated by special statute Dec 5. Invested same day. Letters patent of dispensation of installation same day. Died 1878, Jan. 9, at Rome. (714)

1856, July 12. HUGH (FORTESCUE), 2nd earl Fortescue. Nominated July 12 in place of No. 680. Knighted and invested July 12. Letters patent of dispensation of installation July 12. Died 1861, Sept. 14. ·(715)

1856, July 12. HENRY JOHN (TEMPLE), viscount Palmerston. Nominated July 12 in place of No. 703. Invested July 12. Letters patent of dispensation of installation July 12. Died 1865, Oct. 18 (716)

1856, Nov. 5. ABDUL MEDJID, sultan of Turkey Nominated by special statute Aug. 16. Invested by special commission at Constantinople Nov. 1 in the royal palace of Dolma Bajtche. Letters patent of dispensation of installation Dec. 12. Died 1861, June 25. (717)

1857, July 6. GRANVILLE GEORGE (LEVESON-GOWER), 5th earl Granville. Nominated July 6 in place of No. 624. Knighted and invested at Buckingham Palace July 6. Letters patent of dispensation of installation same day. Died 1891, Mar. 31. (718)

1857, July 6. RICHARD (GROSVENOR), 2nd marquess of Westminster. Nominated July 6 in place of No. 711. Knighted and invested at Buckingham Palace July 6. Letters patent of dispensation of installation same day. Died 1869, Oct. 31. (719)

1858, Jan. 28. H.R.H. FREDERICK WILLIAM NICHOLAS CHARLES, crown prince of Prussia, afterwards Frederick III., emperor of Germany. As a lineal descendant of George I. Invested Jan. 28 in the Chapter Room. Letters patent of dispensation of installation same day. Died 1888, June 15. (720)

1858, Mar. 25. ARTHUR RICHARD (WELLESLEY), 2nd duke of Wellington. Nominated Mar. 25 in place of No. 707. Knighted and invested at Buckingham Palace Mar. 25. Letters patent of dispensation of installation same day. Died 1884, Aug. 13. (721)

1858, Mar. 25. WILLIAM (CAVENDISH), 7th duke of Devonshire. Nominated Mar. 25 in place of No. 705. Knighted and invested at Buckingham Palace Mar. 25. Letters patent of dispensation of installation same day. Died 1891, Dec. 21. (722)

1858, June 24. PEDRO V., king of Portugal. Nominated by special statute Apr. 26. Invested at the palace of Belem, at Lisbon, May 28 by special commission. Letters patent of dispensation of installation June 24. Died 1861, Nov. 11. (723)

1858, Nov. 9. ALBERT EDWARD, prince of Wales. Invested by the Queen in the presence of prince Consort without any public ceremony, he having become a knight of the Garter in 1841, Dec. 8, by his creation as prince of Wales when less than a month old. Letters patent dispensing with installation dated 1858, Nov. 9. Afterwards King Edward VII. (724)

1859, June 28. DUDLEY (RYDER), 2nd earl of Harrowby. Nominated June 28 [in place of No. 663]. Knighted and invested at Buckingham Palace June 28. Letters patent of dispensation of installation same day. Died 1882, Nov. 19. (725)

1859, June 28. EDWARD GEOFFREY (SMITH-STANLEY), 28th earl of Derby. Created an extra knight by special statute June 28. Knighted and invested at Buckingham Palace June 28. Letters patent of dispensation of installation same day. Subsequently succeeded to No. 696. Died 1869, Oct. 28. (726)

1860, Dec. 17. HENRY PELHAM (PELHAM-CLINTON), 5th duke of Newcastle. Nominated Dec. 17 in place of No. (?) 665. Knighted and invested at Windsor Castle Dec. 17. Letters patent of dispensation of installation same day. Died 1864, Oct. 18.   (727)

1861, Apr. 12. WILLIAM I., king of Prussia, afterwards emperor of Germany. Nominated by special statute Feb. 6. Invested by special commission at Berlin Mar. 4. Letters patent of dispensation of installation Apr. 12. Died 1888, Mar. 9.
(728)

1862, May 21. CHARLES JOHN (CANNING), earl Canning. Nominated May 8 in place of No. 712. Letters patent of dispensation of installation May 21. Died 1862, June 17.   (729)

1862, May 21. EDWARD ADOLPHUS (SEYMOUR), 17th duke of Somerset. Knighted by letters patent May 6. Nominated May 8 in place of No. 702. Letters patent of dispensation of installation May 21. Died 1885, Nov. 28.   (730)

1862, May 21. JOHN (RUSSELL), 1st earl Russell. Knighted by letters patent May 6. Nominated May 8 in place of No. 686. Letters patent of dispensation of installation May 21. Died 1878, May 28.   (731)

1862, May 21. ANTHONY (ASHLEY-COOPER), 8th earl of Shaftesbury. Knighted by letters patent May 6. Nominated May 8 in place of No. 691. Letters patent of dispensation of installation May 21. Died 1885, Oct. 1.   (732)

1862, May 21. WILLIAM THOMAS SPENCER (WENTWORTH-FITZ-WILLIAM), 6th earl Fitzwilliam. Knighted by letters patent May 6. Nominated May 8 in place of No. 715. Letters patent of dispensation of installation May 21. Died 1902, Feb. 20.   (733)

1862, July 5. PRINCE FREDERICK WILLIAM LOUIS CHARLES of Hesse and the Rhine, afterwards grand duke Louis IV. of Hesse. Nominated June 27. Invested privately by the queen at Osborne July 5. Letters patent of dispensation of installation July 5. Died 1892, Mar. 13, at Darmstadt.   (734)

1862, Aug. 12. FREDERICK WILLIAM CHARLES GEORGE ERNEST ADOLPHUS GUSTAVUS, reigning grand duke of Mecklenburg-Strelitz. Nominated by special statute July 31. Received the ensigns from Garter by the queen's command Aug. 12 at Kew. Letters patent of dispensation of installation Aug. 12. Died 1904, May 30.   (735)

1863, June 10. PRINCE ALFRED ERNEST ALBERT; duke of Saxony and Prince of Saxe-Coburg-Gotha, afterwards duke of Edinburgh, duke of Saxe-Coburg and Gotha. Nominated May 24 (the queen's birthday) and invested privately by the queen [the same day] Letters patent of dispensation of installation June 10. Died 1900, July 30. (736)

1863, June 10. HENRY GEORGE (GREY), 3rd earl Grey. Knighted by letters patent May 30. Nominated May 30 in place of No. 729. Ensigns delivered to him by Garter June 1. Letters patent of dispensation of installation June 10. Died 1894, Oct. 9. (737)

1864, Apr. 30. GEORGE GRANVILLE WILLIAM (SUTHERLAND-LEVESON-GOWER), 3rd duke of Sutherland. Knighted by letters patent Apr. 22. Nominated Apr. 22 in place of No. 678. Ensigns delivered to him at Sutherland House by Garter. Letters patent of dispensation of installation Apr. 30. Died 1892, Sept. 22. (738)

1864, May 23. GEORGE WILLIAM FREDERICK (BRUDENELL-BRUCE), 2nd marquess of Ailesbury. Knighted by letters patent May 23. Nominated May 23 in place of No. 706. Ensigns subsequently delivered to him by Garter. Letters patent of dispensation of installation May 23. Died 1878, Jan. 6. (739)

1864, Oct. 10. HENRY (PETTY-FITZMAURICE), 4th marquess of Lansdowne. Knighted by letters patent Sept. 27. Nominated Sept. 30 in place of No. 693. Ensigns delivered to him by Garter Oct. 6 at Lansdowne House. Letters patent of dispensation of installation Oct. 10. Died 1866, July 5. (740)

1865, Jan. 14. JOHN POYNTZ (SPENCER), 5th earl Spencer. Knighted by letters patent 1864, Dec. 28. Nominated Dec. 30 in place of No. 727. Ensigns delivered to him by Garter 1865, Jan. 13. Letters patent of dispensation of installation Jan. 14. (741)

1865, Apr. 10. HARRY GEORGE (VANE afterwards POWLETT), 7th duke of Cleveland. Knighted by letters patent Apr. 6. Nominated Apr. 8 in place of No. 710. Letters patent of dispensation of installation Apr. 10. Died 1891, Aug. 21. (742)

1865, June 17. LOUIS I., king of Portugal and the Algarvas, duke of Saxony. Nominated by special statute Jan. 17. Invested at Ajuda near Lisbon by special commission June (? May) 4. Letters patent of dispensation of installation June (? May) 17. Died 1889, Oct. 19. (743)

1865, June 17. CHRISTIAN IX., king of Denmark. Nominated by special statute Jan. 17. Invested by special commission at Copenhagen Apr. 25. Letters patent of dispensation of installation June (? May) 17. (744)

1865, June 17. LOUIS III., grand duke of Hesse and the Rhine. Nominated by special statute Jan. 17. Invested by special commission at Darmstadt June 6. Letters patent of dispensation of installation June (? May) 17. Died 1877, June 19, at Darmstadt. (745)

1865, Aug. 5. FRANCIS THOMAS DE GRAY (COWPER), 7th earl Cowper. Nominated July 24 in place of No. 708. Ensigns delivered to him by Garter July 31. Letters patent of dispensation of installation Aug 5. (746)

1866, Feb. 3. HENRY RICHARD CHARLES (WELLESLEY), 1st earl Cowley. Nominated Jan. 23 in place of No. 716. Invested privately at Osborne Feb. 3. Letters patent of installation Feb. 3. Died 1884, July 15. (747)

1866, Feb. 23. LEOPOLD II., king of the Belgians. Nominated by special statute Jan. 6. Invested by special commission at Brussels Feb. 12. Letters patent of dispensation of installation Feb. 23. (748)

1866, July 9. PRINCE FREDERICK CHRISTIAN CHARLES AUGUSTUS of Schleswig-Holstein. Nominated by special statute July 3. Presented with the insignia by the queen in private at Windsor July 5 after his marriage with the princess Helena. Letters patent of dispensation of installation July 9. (749)

1867, Feb. 6. CHARLES HENRY (GORDON-LENNOX), 6th duke of Richmond and 1st duke of Gordon. Nominated Jan. 30 in place of No. 740. Knighted and invested Jan. 30 at Osborne. Letters patent of dispensation of installation Feb. 6. Died 1903, Sept. 27. (750)

1867, Feb. 6. CHARLES CECIL JOHN (MANNERS), 6th duke of Rutland. Nominated Jan. 30 in place of No. 700. Knighted and invested Jan. 30 at Osborne. Letters patent of dispensation of installation Feb. 6. Died 1888, Mar. 4. (751)

1867, Mar. 19. HENRY CHARLES FITZROY (SOMERSET), 8th duke of Beaufort. Nominated Mar. 18 in place of No. 664. Knighted and invested at Buckingham Palace Mar. 19. Letters patent of dispensation of installation Mar. 19. Died 1899, Apr. 30. (752)

1867, May 24. PRINCE ARTHUR WILLIAM PATRICK ALBERT, duke of
Saxony, prince of Coburg and Gotha, afterwards duke of
Connaught. Nominated May 24 (the queen's birthday).
Ensigns presented to him in private by the queen [same
day]. Letters patent of dispensation of installation May 24.
(753)

1867, Aug. 14. FRANCIS JOSEPH, emperor of Austria. Nominated
by special statute June 13. Invested at Vienna by special
commission July 25. Letters patent of dispensation of
installation Aug. 14. (754)

1867, Aug. 14. ALEXANDER II., emperor of Russia. Nominated by
special statute June 13. Invested at Tsarkoselo near St.
Petersburg by special commission July 28. Letters patent
of dispensation of installation Aug. 14. Died 1881, Mar. 13.
(755)

1867, Aug. 14. ABDUL AZIZ, sultan of Turkey. Nominated July
17 by special statute. Letters patent of dispensation of
installation Aug. 14. Died 1876, June 4. (756)

1868, May 23. JOHN WINSTON (SPENCER-CHURCHILL), 7th duke of
Marlborough. Nominated May 14 in place of No. 692 and
knighted at Windsor Castle the same day and immediately
afterwards invested. Letters patent of dispensation of in-
stallation May 23. Died 1883, July 5. (757)

1869, May 29. PRINCE LEOPOLD GEORGE DUNCAN ALBERT, after-
wards duke of Albany. Nominated May 24 (the queen's
birthday) and privately invested at Balmoral the same day.
Letters patent of dispensation of installation May 29. Died
1884, May 28, at Cannes. (758)

1869, Dec. 11. STRATFORD (CANNING), viscount Stratford de Red-
cliffe. Nominated Dec. 10 in place of No. 726. Invested
at Windsor Dec. 11. Letters patent of dispensation of
installation same day. Died 1880, Aug. 14. (759)

1869, Dec. 11. GEORGE FREDERICK SAMUEL (ROBINSON), earl de Grey
and Ripon, afterwards marquess of Ripon. Nominated
Dec. 4 in place of No. 705. Knighted and invested at
Windsor Dec. 11. Letters patent of dispensation of in-
stallation Dec. 11. (760)

1870, Dec. 6. HUGH LUPUS (GROSVENOR), 3rd marquess of West-
minster, afterwards 1st duke of Westminster. Nominated
Dec. 4 in place of No. 705. Knighted and invested at
Windsor Castle Dec. 6. Letters patent of dispensation of
installation Dec. 6. Died 1899, Dec. 22. (761)

1871, July 11. PEDRO II., emperor of Brazil. Nominated by statute July 5. Ensigns delivered to him personally by the queen at Claridge's Hotel July 5. Letters patent of dispensation of installation July 11. Died 1891, Dec. 5, at Paris. (762)

1872, Dec. 26. THOMAS (DUNDAS), 2nd earl of Zetland. Nominated Dec. 12 in place of No. 701. Ensigns delivered to him by Garter at Aske Hall near Richmond, Yorks, Dec. 23. Letters patent of dispensation of installation Dec. 26. Died 1873, May 6. (763)

1873, June 26. NASIR ED DIN, shah of Persia. Nominated by special statute June 20. Invested same day at Windsor Castle by the queen in the presence of prince Arthur, prince Leopold, and prince Christian of Schleswig-Holstein. Letters patent of dispensation of installation June 26. Died 1896, May 1. (764)

1873, June 30. THOMAS WILLIAM (COKE), 2nd earl of Leicester. Nominated June 28 in place of No. 763. Knighted and invested at Windsor Castle June 30. Letters patent of dispensation of installation June 30. (765)

1876, July 12. GEORGE I., king of the Hellenes. Nominated by special statute July 12. Invested at Frogmore House same day by the queen in the presence of the prince of Wales and prince Leopold. Letters patent of dispensation of installation same day. (766)

1877, Jan. 27. PRINCE FREDERICK WILLIAM VICTOR ALBERT of Prussia, son of the crown prince of Germany, afterwards emperor William II. of Germany. Nominated Jan. 27. Lord Odo Russell, the British Ambassador at Berlin, delivered the insignia the same day to the crown prince of Germany, who thereupon invested the prince. Letters patent of dispensation of installation Jan. 27. (767)

1878, Mar. 16. HUMBERT, king of Italy. Nominated by special statute Feb. 5. Invested at Rome by special commission Mar. 2. Letters patent of dispensation of installation Mar. 16. Died 1900, July 29, at Monza. (768)

1878, July 20. PRINCE ERNEST AUGUSTUS WILLIAM ADOLPHUS GEORGE FREDERICK of Hanover, duke of Cumberland and Teviotdale. Nominated June 22. Invested June 23 at Windsor in the presence of the prince of Wales and prince Leopold. Letters patent of dispensation of installation July 20. (769)

1878, July 22. BENJAMIN (D'ISRAELI), earl of Beaconsfield. Nominated July 22 in place of No. 739. Knighted and invested same day at Osborne. Letters patent of dispensation of installation July 22. Died 1881, Apr. 19. (770)

1878, July 30. ROBERT ARTHUR TALBOT (GASCOYNE-CECIL), 3rd marquess of Salisbury. Nominated July 30 in place of No. 731. Knighted and invested same day at Osborne. Letters patent of dispensation of installation same day. Died 1903, Aug. 22. (771)

1880, Dec. 1. FRANCIS CHARLES HASTINGS (RUSSELL), 9th duke of Bedford. Nominated Sept. 22 in place of No. 759. Knighted and invested Dec. 1 at Windsor in the presence of the duke of Connaught. Letters patent of dispensation of installation same day. Died 1891, Jan. 14. (772)

1881, Apr. 2. ALEXANDER III., emperor and autocrat of all the Russias. Nominated by special statute Mar. 21. Invested by the prince of Wales as a special commissioner in the Annutchkin Palace at St. Petersburg Mar. 28 in the presence of the crown prince of Germany, the duke of Edinburgh, and the grand duke of Hesse. Letters patent of dispensation of installation Apr. 2. Died 1894, Nov. 1, at the Summer Palace at Livadia. (773)

1881, May 17. OSCAR II., king of Sweden and Norway. Nominated by special statute May 17. Invested same day at Windsor Castle by the queen, assisted by prince Leopold. Letters patent of dispensation of installation same day. (774)

1881, Oct. 24. ALFONSO XII., king of Spain. Nominated by special statute Sept. 8. Invested Oct. 11 in the Royal Palace at Madrid by special commission. Letters patent of dispensation of installation Oct. 24. Died 1885, Nov. 25. (775)

1882, Feb. 20. ALBERT, king of Saxony. Nominated 1881, Dec. 12, by special statute. Invested in the Royal Palace at Dresden by special commission 1882, Feb. 7. Letters patent of dispensation of installation Feb. 20. Died 1902, June 19. (776)

1882, Apr. 24. WILLIAM III., king of the Netherlands. Nominated by special statute Apr. 24. Invested same day at Windsor Castle in the presence of the queen of the Netherlands and all the royal family. Letters patent of dispensation of installation same day. Died 1890, Nov. 23, at the Castle of Loo. (777)

1883, Feb. 3. AUGUSTUS CHARLES LENNOX (FITZ-ROY), 7th duke of Grafton. Nominated Jan. 9 in place of No. 770. Knighted and invested at Osborne Feb. 3. Letters patent of dispensation of installation same day. (778)

1883, Sept. 11. H.R.H. PRINCE ALBERT VICTOR CHRISTIAN EDWARD of Wales. Nominated Sept. 3. Invested same day at Balmoral. Letters patent of dispensation of installation same day. Afterwards duke of Clarence and of Avondale. Died 1892, Jan. 14, at Sandringham. (779)

1884, July 15. GEORGE DOUGLAS (CAMPBELL), 8th duke of Argyll. Nominated 1883, Oct. 22, in place of No. 725. Invested at Windsor 1884, July 15. Letters patent of dispensation of installation same day. Died 1900, Apr. 24. (780)

1884, July 15. EDWARD HENRY (STANLEY), 24th earl of Derby. Nominated June 21 in place of No. 757. Knighted and invested at Windsor July 15. Letters patent of dispensation of installation same day. Died 1893, Apr. 21. (781)

1884, Aug. 4. PRINCE GEORGE FREDERICK ERNEST ALBERT of Wales, afterwards duke of York and prince of Wales. Nominated Aug. 4. Invested same day at Osborne in the presence of the prince of Wales. Letters patent of dispensation of installation same day. (782)

1885, July 9. JOHN (WODEHOUSE), 1st earl of Kimberley. Nominated July 9 in place of No. 674. Knighted and invested same day at Windsor. Letters patent of dispensation of installation same day. Died 1902, Apr. 8. (783)

1885, July 9. WILLIAM (COMPTON), 4th marquess of Northampton. Nominated July 9 in place of No. 747. Knighted and invested same day at Windsor. Letters patent of dispensation of installation same day. Died 1897, Sept. 11. (784)

1885, July 9. WILLIAM PHILIP (MOLYNEUX), 4th earl of Sefton. Nominated July 9 in place of No. 721. Knighted and invested same day at Windsor. Letters patent of dispensation of installation same day. Died 1897, June 27. (785)

1885, July 23. PRINCE HENRY MAURICE of Battenberg. Nominated by special statute July 23. Married same day at Whippingham to princess Beatrice, and before that ceremony privately invested by the queen at Osborne. Letters patent of dispensation of installation same day. Died 1896, Jan. 20, on board H.M.S. " Blonde." (786)

1886, Feb. 22. ALGERNON GEORGE (PERCY), 8th duke of Northumberland. Nominated 1885, Nov. 24, in place of No. 732. Knighted and invested at Windsor 1886, Feb. 22. Letters patent of dispensation of installation same day. Died 1889, Jan. 2.   (787)

1886, Feb. 22. WILLIAM (NEVILL), 1st marquess of Abergavenny. Nominated 1885, Dec. 10, in place of No. 697. Knighted and invested at Windsor 1886, Feb. 22. Letters patent of dispensation of installation same day.   (788)

1886, Feb. 22. HENRY (FITZALAN-HOWARD), 22nd duke of Norfolk. Nominated 1885, Dec. 19, in place of No. 730. Knighted and invested at Windsor 1886, Feb. 22. Letters patent of dispensation of installation same day.   (789)

1887, June 20. RUDOLPH FRANCIS CHARLES JOSEPH, crown prince of Austria. Nominated by special statute June 20 on the occasion of the queen's Jubilee. Invested same day in the garden at Buckingham Palace. Letters patent of dispensation of installation same day. Died 1889, Jan. 29, at his villa of Meyerling near Baden.   (790)

1888, May 7. CHARLES STEWART (VANE-TEMPEST-STEWART), 6th marquess of Londonderry. Nominated May 7 in place of No. 751. Invested privately at Windsor Castle same day. Letters patent of dispensation of installation same day.
     (791)

1889, Aug. 8. PRINCE ALBERT WILLIAM HENRY of Prussia. Nominated by special statute Aug. 8 Invested at Osborne same day. Letters patent of dispensation of installation same day.
     (792)

1890, Apr. 23. CHARLES, king of Wurtemberg. Nominated by special statute Mar. 20. Invested by special commission in the Palace at Stuttgart Apr. 15. Letters patent of dispensation of installation Apr. 23. Died at Stuttgart 1891, Oct. 6.   (793)

1891, Aug. 3. VICTOR EMANUEL, prince of Naples. Nominated by special statute Aug. 3. Invested same day at Osborne. Letters patent of dispensation of installation same day. Afterwards Victor Emanuel III. of Italy.   (794)

1891, Aug. 5. JOHN JAMES ROBERT (MANNERS), 7th duke of Rutland. Nominated May 16 in place of No. 772. Invested at Osborne Aug. 5. Letters patent of dispensation of installation same day.   (795)

1891, Aug. 5. GEORGE HENRY (CADOGAN), 6th earl Cadogan. Nominated Aug. 1 in place of No. 718. Knighted and invested at Osborne Aug. 5. Letters patent of dispensation of installation same day. (796)

1892, May 16. H.R.H. ERNEST LOUIS CHARLES ALBERT WILLIAM, grand duke of Hesse and the Rhine. Nominated Apr. 27. Personally invested by the queen at Darmstadt same day. Letters patent of dispensation of installation May 16. (797)

1892, June 30. CHARLES, king of Roumania. Nominated by special statute June 30. Invested same day at Windsor Castle. Letters patent of dispensation of installation same day. (798)

1892, Aug. 10. SPENCER COMPTON (CAVENDISH), 8th duke of Devonshire. Nominated July 30 in place of No. 742. Knighted and invested at Osborne Aug. 10. Letters patent of dispensation of installation same day. (799)

1892, Aug. 10. JAMES (HAMILTON), 2nd duke of Abercorn. Nominated July 30 in place of No. 722. Knighted and invested at Osborne Aug. 10. Letters patent of dispensation of installation same day. (800)

1892, Nov. 23. ARCHIBALD PHILIP (PRIMROSE), 5th earl of Rosebery. Nominated Oct. 22 in place of No. 738. Knighted and invested at Windsor Nov. 21. Letters patent of dispensation of installation Nov. 23. (801)

1893, July 1. Grand duke CESAREVITCH NICHOLAS ALEXANDROVITCH of Russia, afterwards emperor Nicholas II. of Russia. Nominated 1893, July 1, by special statute. Invested at Windsor Castle by the queen same day. Letters patent of dispensation of installation same day. (802)

1894, Mar. 7. GAVIN (CAMPBELL), 1st marquess of Breadalbane. Nominated 1893, Dec. 4, in place of No. 781. Knighted and invested at Buckingham Palace 1894, Mar. 7. Letters patent of dispensation of installation same day. (803)

1894, Apr. 23. ALFRED ALEXANDER WILLIAM ERNEST ALBERT, hereditary prince of Saxe-Coburg and Gotha (prince Alfred of Edinburgh). Nominated by special statute Apr. 23. Personally invested by the queen at Coburg same day. Letters patent of dispensation of installation same day. Died 1899, Feb. 6, at Meran. (804)

1895, Mar. 6. HENRY CHARLES KEITH (PETTY-FITZMAURICE), 5th
marquess of Lansdowne.   Nominated 1894, Nov. 10, in
place of No. 737.   Knighted and invested 1895, Mar. 6, at
Buckingham Palace.   Letters patent of dispensation of
installation same day.   (805)

1895, Nov. 9. CHARLES I. (CARLO FERDINAND LOUIS MARIE VICTOR
MICHAEL RAPHAEL GABRIEL GONZAGUE XAVIER FRANÇOIS
D'ASSISE JOSEPH SIMON), king of Portugal and the Algarvas.
Nominated by special statute Nov. 9.   Personally invested
by the queen at Balmoral same day.   Letters patent of
dispensation of installation same day.   (806)

1896, July 21. H.R.H. prince FREDERICK (CHRISTIAN FREDERICK
WILLIAM CHARLES), crown prince of Denmark.   Nominated
by special statute July 21.   Invested same day at Marl-
borough House.   Letters patent of dispensation of installa-
tion same day.   (807)

1897, Aug. 19. FREDERICK ARTHUR (STANLEY), 25th earl of Derby.
Nominated Aug. 6 in place of No. 785.   Invested at Osborne
Aug. 19.   Letters patent of dispensation of installation
same day.   (808)

1897, Dec. 7. WILLIAM HENRY WALTER (MONTAGU-DOUGLAS-SCOTT),
6th duke of Buccleuch.   Nominated Dec. 2 in place of
No. 784.   Invested at Windsor Castle Dec. 7.   Letters patent
of dispensation of installation same day.   (809)

1899, Mar. 2. VICTOR ALEXANDER (BRUCE), 9th earl of Elgin, earl
of Kincardine.   Nominated Feb. 16 in place of No. 787.
Knighted and invested at Windsor Castle Mar. 2.   Letters
patent of dispensation of installation same day.   (810)

1899, July 11. HENRY GEORGE (PERCY), 9th duke of Northumber-
land.   Nominated May 22 in place of No. 752.   Knighted
and invested July 11 at Windsor Castle.   Letters patent of
dispensation of installation same day.   (811)

1900, Mar. 15. WILLIAM JOHN ARTHUR CHARLES JAMES (CAVENDISH-
BENTINCK), 6th duke of Portland.   Nominated Mar. 15 in
place of No. 761.   Knighted and invested same day at
Windsor Castle.   Letters patent of dispensation of in-
stallation same day.   (812)

1901, Jan. 24 Field-Marshal FREDERICK SLEIGH (ROBERTS), lord,
afterwards earl Roberts.   Nominated Jan. 2 in place of
No. 780.   Invested same day at Osborne by the queen.
Letters patent of dispensation of installation Jan. 24   (813)

EDWARD VII., the twenty-sixth Sovereign of the Garter.

Succeeded 1901, Jan. 22.

1901, Jan. 27. H.I. & R.H. FREDERICK WILLIAM VICTOR AUGUSTUS ERNEST, crown prince of Germany. Nominated by special Statute Jan. 28. Personally invested by the king at Osborne same day in the presence of the German emperor, duke of Connaught, duke of Cambridge, prince Christian of Schleswig-Holstein, duke of Norfolk and earl Roberts. Letters patent of dispensation of installation same day.
(814)

1901, Feb. 12. The Secretary of State for the Home Department signified to the Chancellor of the Garter the king's pleasure as Sovereign of the Order that a special statute under the seal of the Order shall be issued for conferring upon H.M. the queen Alexandra the title and dignity of a Lady of that most noble Order and fully authorising her Majesty to wear the insignia thereof.

1902, May 16. ALFONSO XIII., king of Spain. Nominated by special statute, Apr. 21. Invested by special commission at Madrid, May 16. Letters patent of dispensation of installation same day.
(815)

1902, May 30. HERBRAND ARTHUR (RUSSELL), 14th duke of Bedford. Nominated Mar. 26 in place of No. 733. Invested at Buckingham Palace, May 30. Letters patent of dispensation of installation same day.
(816)

1902, May 30. CHARLES RICHARD JOHN (SPENCER-CHURCHILL), 9th duke of Marlborough. Nominated May 28 in place of No. 783. Invested at Buckingham Palace, May 30. Letters patent of dispensation of installation same day.
(817)

1902, July 15. H.I.H. the hereditary grand duke MICHAEL ALEXANDROVITCH of Russia. Nominated by special statute in June. Invested at Buckingham Palace by the King ? June 29. Letters patent of dispensation of installation July 15.
(818)

1902, July 15. H.I. & R.H. the ARCHDUKE FRANCIS FERDINAND CHARLES LOUIS JOSEPH MARIE of Austria-Este. Nominated by special statute in June. Insignia delivered to him at the Castle of Konopischt in July by Sir Fr. Plunkett, H.M. ambassador at Vienna. Letters patent of dispensation of installation July 15.
(819)

1902, July 15. H.R H. EMMANUEL PHILIBERT VICTOR EUGÈNE
GENES JOSEPH MARIE, duke d'Aosta. Nominated by special
statute in June. Invested at Buckingham Palace by the
King ? June 29. Letters patent of dispensation of
installation July 15. (820)

1902, July 15. H.R H. LOUIS PHILIPPE MARIE CHARLES AMELIO
FERDINAND VICTOR MANUEL ANTOINE LAURENT MIGUEL
RAPHAËL GABRIEL GONZAGUE XAVIER FRANCIS D'ASSISE
BENOIT, crown prince of Portugal, duke of Braganza.
Nominated by special statute in June. Invested by the
duke of York at York House, June 27. Letters patent of
dispensation of installation July 15. (821)

1902, July 15. H.R.H. LEOPOLD CHARLES EDWARD GEORGE ALBERT,
duke of Albany, reigning duke of Saxe-Coburg and Gotha.
Nominated in June. Invested at Buckingham Palace
by the King ? July 7. Letters patent of dispensation of
installation July 15. (822)

1902, July 15. H.R.H. prince ARTHUR FREDERICK PATRICK ALBERT,
eldest son of the duke of Connaught. Nominated in June.
Invested at Buckingham Palace by the King ? July 7.
Letters patent of dispensation of installation July 15. (823)

1902, Aug. 8. ARTHUR CHARLES (WELLESLEY), 4th duke of
Wellington. An additional knight. Nominated June 26.
Invested Aug. 8 at Buckingham Palace. Letters patent of
dispensation of installation Aug. 8. (824)

1902, Aug. 8 CROMARTIE (SUTHERLAND-LEVESON-GOWER), 4th duke
of Sutherland. An additional knight. Nominated June 26.
Invested Aug. 8 at Buckingham Palace. Letters patent of
dispensation of installation Aug. 8. (825)

1903, Feb. 16. MUZAFFER-ED-DIN, shah of Persia. Nominated by
special statute 1902, Dec. 12. Invested at Teheran by
viscount Downe, the King's special envoy, 1903, Feb. 3.
Letters patent of dispensation of installation 1903, Feb. 16.
  (826)

1904, Feb. 23. WILLIAM II. (WILHELM CHARLES PAUL HENRY
FREDERICK), king of Wurtemberg. Nominated by special
statute Feb. 23. Invested at Stuttgart by the prince of
Wales, Apr. 25. Letters patent of dispensation of installa-
tion ? same day. (827)

The Most Ancient and Most Noble Order of the Thistle.

Knights of the Most Ancient and Most Noble Order of the Thistle.

JAMES II., first Sovereign.

1687, June 6. JAMES (DRUMMOND), 4th earl of Perth. Knighted and invested by the duke of Hamilton in the Council Chamber at Edinburgh shortly after June 6. Died 1716, May 11. (1)

1687, June 6. GEORGE (GORDON), 1st duke of Gordon. Invested at Edinburgh shortly after June 6. Died 1716, Dec. 7. (2)

1687, June 6. JOHN (MURRAY), 1st marquess of Atholl. Knighted and invested by the earl of Perth in the Council Chamber at Edinburgh shortly after June 6. Died 1703, May 6. (3)

1687, June 6. JAMES (HAMILTON), commonly called earl of Arran (afterwards 4th duke of Hamilton). Invested at Edinburgh shortly after June 6. Was allowed to retain the Order of the Thistle on his election as a K.G. Died 1712, Nov. 15. (4)

1687, June 6. KENNETH (MACKENZIE), 4th earl of Seaforth. Invested at Windsor Castle June 6. Died 1701, Jan. (5)

1687, June 6. JOHN (DRUMMOND), 1st earl of Melfort. Invested at Windsor Castle June 6. Died 1714–5, Jan. 25. (6)

1687, June 6. GEORGE (DOUGLAS), 1st earl of Dumbarton. Invested at Windsor Castle June 6. Died 1692. (7)

1687, June 6. ALEXANDER (STUART), 18th earl of Moray. Invested At Windsor Castle, June 6. Died 1701, Nov. 1. (8)

* It may be of interest to print here the Jacobite nominations to the order of the Thistle, as made by the Stuarts when in exile—premising only that (as in the case of the Jacobite nominations to the order of the Garter *supra* p. 38) they bear no authority. The titles of noblesse as stated in the following list are mostly Jacobite titles and equally devoid of authority. I am indebted to the courtesy of the Most Honourable the Marquis de Ruvigny for permission to reprint this list from his "*Jacobite Peerage*" p. 194.

1705, Mar.   JAMES (DRUMMOND), marquess of Drummond.
1705, Mar.   CHARLES (HAY), 13th earl of Errol.
1705 or 1708, Feb. ?   WILLIAM (KEITH), 9th earl Marischal.
1708, May 10.   JOHN BAPTISTE (GUALTERIO), 1st earl of Dundee.
1716, Apr. 3.   JAMES (BUTLER), 2nd duke of Ormonde.
1716, Apr. 3.   JAMES (MAULE), 4th earl of Panmure.
1722, May 26.   ARTHUR (DILLON), 1st earl (?) Dillon.
1723, July 30.   JAMES (DOUGLAS-HAMILTON), 5th duke of Hamilton. (See *infra*.)
1725, Dec. 29.   GEORGE (KEITH) 10th earl Marischal.
1725, Dec. 31.   JAMES (HAY), 1st earl of Inverness.
1725, Dec. 31.   WILLIAM (MAXWELL), 5th earl of Nithsdale.
1725, Dec. 31.   JAMES (MURRAY), 1st earl of Dunbar.
1739, May 15.   JAMES (DRUMMOND), 3rd duke of Perth.
1740, July 27.   JAMES (DOUGLAS-HAMILTON), 5th duke of Hamilton. (Fresh warrant.)
1742,   ?   CHARLES, prince of Wales, duke of Cornwall and Rothesay.
1768,   JOHN (CARYLL), 3rd baron Caryll of Dunford.
1784, Nov. 30.   CHARLOTTE (STUART), duchess of Albany.

QUEEN ANNE, second Sovereign.

Revived the Order 1703, December 31.

1703–4, Feb. 4. JOHN (CAMPBELL), 2nd duke of Argyll. Nominated and invested same day. Resigned the order on being elected K.G., 1709–10, Mar. 22.   (9)

1703–4, Feb. 7. JOHN (MURRAY), 1st duke of Atholl. Nominated and invested same day. Died 1724, Nov. 14.   (10)

1703–4, Feb. 7. WILLIAM (JOHNSTON), 1st marquess of Annandale. Nominated and invested same day. Died 1720–1, Jan. 14.   (11)

1703–4, Feb. 7. JAMES (SCOTT), commonly called earl of Dalkeith. Nominated and invested same day. Died 1704–5, Mar. 14.   (12)

1703–4, Feb. 7. GEORGE (HAMILTON), 6th earl of Orkney. Nominated and invested same day. Died 1736–7, Jan. 29.   (13)

1703–4, Feb. 7. JAMES (OGILVY), 1st earl of Seafield, afterwards earl of Findlater. Nominated and invested same day. Died 1730, Aug. 19.   (14)

1705, Oct. 30. WILLIAM (KERR), 2nd marquess of Lothian. Knighted and invested by the duke of Queensberry in the Council Chamber at Edinburgh Nov. 8. Died 1721–2, Feb. 28   (15)

1705, Oct. 30. CHARLES (BOYLE), 4th earl of Orrery. Nominated and invested by queen Anne at St. James's Palace same day. Died 1731, Aug. 28.   (16)

1706, Aug 10. · JOHN (ERSKINE), 23rd earl of Mar. Nominated and invested by queen Anne at Windsor Castle same day. Honours forfeited in 1715 by attainder.   (17)

1706, Aug. 10. HUGH (CAMPBELL), 3rd earl of Loudoun. Nominated and invested *ut supra*. Died 1731, Nov. 20.   (18)

1710, Mar. 25 JOHN (DALRYMPLE), 2nd earl of Stair. Invested by the duke of Marlborough at the Camp before Douay May 26. Died 1747, May 9.   (19)

1712–3, Jan. 17. DAVID (COLYEAR), 1st earl of Portmore. Nominated and invested by queen Anne at St. James's Palace same day. Died 1729–30, Jan. 2.   (20)

GEORGE I., third Sovereign.

1716, June 22. JOHN (GORDON), 16th earl of Sutherland. Nominated and invested by George I. at St. James's Palace same day. Died 1733, June 27. (21)

1716, June 22. WILLIAM (CADOGAN), 1st baron Cadogan. Nominated and invested at St. James's same day. Died 1726, July 17. (22)

1717, Mar. 1. THOMAS (HAMILTON), 6th earl of Haddington. Nominated and invested at St. James's same day. Died 1735, Oct. 26. (23)

1720-1, Feb. 28. CHARLES (BENNET), 2nd earl of Tankerville. Nominated in place of No. 11 and invested at St. James's same day. Died 1722, May 21. (24)

1724-5, Feb. 2. FRANCIS (SCOTT), earl of Dalkeith, afterwards 2nd duke of Buccleuch. Nominated and invested at St. James's same day. Died 1751, Apr. 22. (25)

1724-5, Feb. 2. WILLIAM (CAPELL), 23rd earl of Essex. Nominated and invested at St. James's same day. Resigned 1737-8, Feb. 20, on being elected K.G. (26)

1724-5, Feb. 2. ALEXANDER (HUME-CAMPBELL), 2nd earl of Marchmont. Invested at Cambray by lord Whitworth Mar. 10. Died 1739-40, Feb. 27. (27)

1726, Sept. 23. JAMES (HAMILTON), 5th duke of Hamilton and 2nd duke of Brandon. Invested by the earl of Findlater at Holyrood Oct. 31. Died 1742-3, Mar. 2. In place of No. 22. (28)

GEORGE II., fourth Sovereign.

1730, May 16. CHARLES (BENNET), 3rd earl of Tankerville. Nominated and invested at St. James's same day. Died 1753, Mar. 14. (29)

1731, Dec. 10. CHARLES (STUART), 19th earl of Moray. Invested by the earl of Haddington at Holyrood House 1731-2, Feb. 1. Died 1735, Oct. 7. In place of No. 14. (30)

1732, June 2. CHARLES (COLYEAR), 2nd earl of Portmore. Nominated and invested at St. James's same day. Died 1785, July 5. In place of No. 16. (31)

1734, Feb. 11. James (Murray), 2nd duke of Atholl. Nominated and invested at St. James's same day. Died 1764, Jan. 8. In place of No. 18.   (32)

1734, Feb. 11. William (Kerr), 3rd marquess of Lothian. Nominated and invested at St. James's same day. Died 1767, July 28. In place of No. 21.   (33)

1738, July 10. James (Douglas), 15th earl of Morton. Nominated and invested at Kensington same day. Died 1768, Oct. 12.   (34)

1738, July 10. John (Stuart), 3rd earl of Bute. Invested by the marquess of Lothian at Holyrood House Aug. 15. Resigned in 1762 on being elected K.G.   (35)

1738, July 10. Charles (Hope), 1st earl of Hopetoun. Invested *ut supra*. Died 1741-2, Feb. 26.   (36)

1739, June 7. Augustus (Berkeley), 4th earl of Berkeley. Nominated and invested at Kensington same day. Died 1755, Jan 9.   (37)

1741, Feb 23. James (Stuart), 21st earl of Moray. Nominated and invested at St. James's same day. Died 1767, July 5.   (38)

1742, June 22. John (Carmichael), 3rd earl of Hyndford. Invested at Charlottenburg by the king of Prussia Aug. 2 (new style). Died 1767, July 19. In place of No. 36.   (39).

1743, Mar. 29 Lionel (Tollemash), 4th earl of Dysart. Nominated and invested at St. James's same day. Died 1770, Mar. 10.   (40)

1747-8, Feb. 16. Cosmo George (Gordon), 3rd duke of Gordon. Nominated and invested at St. James's same day. Died 1752, Aug. 5.   (41)

1752, Mar. 11. William (Dalrymple-Crichton), 5th earl of Dumfries. Nominated and invested at St. James's same day. Died 1768, July 27.   (42)

1753, Mar. 29. Francis (Greville), 1st earl Brooke, afterwards earl of Warwick. Nominated and invested at St. James's same day. Died 1773, July 6.   (43)

1753, Mar. 29. John (Leslie), 10th earl of Rothes. Nominated and invested at St. James's same day. Died 1767, Dec. 10.   (44)

1755, Mar. 18. James (Hamilton), 6th duke of Hamilton and 3rd duke of Brandon. Invested by the duke of Hamilton at Holyrood House Apr. 3. Died 1758, Jan. 17.   (45)

GEORGE III., the fifth Sovereign.

1763, Apr. 13. CHARLES SCHAW (CATHCART), 9th lord Cathcart.
Nominated and invested at St. James's same day. Died 1776,
Aug. 14.   (46)

1763, Apr. 13. WILLIAM (DOUGLAS), 3rd earl of March and earl
of Ruglen, afterwards duke of Queensberry. Nominated
and invested at St. James's same day. Died 1810, Dec. 23.
                                                           (47)

1765, Aug. 7. JOHN (CAMPBELL), 4th duke of Argyll. Nominated
and invested at St. James's same day. Died 1770, Nov. 9.
                                                           (48)

1767, Dec. 23. HENRY (SCOTT), 3rd duke of Buccleuch. Nominated
and invested at St. James's same day. Resigned 1794, May,
on being elected K.G.   (49)

1767, Dec. 23. JOHN (MURRAY), 3rd duke of Athole. Nominated
and invested at St. James's same day. Died 1774, Nov 5.
                                                           (50)

1767, Dec. 23. FREDERICK (HOWARD), 8th earl of Carlisle. Invested
by the king of Sardinia at Turin 1768, Feb. 27. Resigned
on his election as K.G 1793, June 12.   (51)

1768, Oct. 26. WILLIAM HENRY (KERR), 4th marquess of Lothian.
Nominated and invested at St. James's same day. Died
1775, Apr. 12.   (52)

1768, Nov. 2. DAVID (MURRAY), 7th viscount Stormont, afterwards
earl of Mansfield. Knighted and invested by the Emperor
at Vienna Nov. 30. Died 1796, Sept. 1.   (53)

1768, Nov. 28. JOHN (KERR), 3rd duke of Roxburghe. Nominated
. and invested at St. James's same day. Retained the Order
of the Thistle on his election as K.G. 1801, June 3. Died
1804, Mar. 19.   (54)

1770, Apr. 5. WILLIAM HENRY, of Brunswick-Luneburg, third son
of the sovereign Nominated and invested same day. After-
wards duke of Clarence and St. Andrew and king William
IV. Elected K.G. in 1782, but retained the Order of the
Thistle. Died 1837, June 20.   (55)

1771, Mar. 4. NEIL (PRIMROSE), 3rd earl of Rosebery. Nominated
and invested same day. Died 1814, Mar. 25.   (56)

1773, Aug. 18. ROBERT (HENLEY), 2nd earl of Northington.
Nominated, knighted and invested at St. James's same day
Died 1786, July 5.   (57)

1775, Jan. 11. ALEXANDER (GORDON), 4th duke of Gordon. Nominated and invested at St. James's same day. Died 1827, June 17. (58)

1775, Nov. 1. JOHN (STEWART), 7th earl of Galloway. Nominated, knighted and invested at St. James's same day. Died 1806, Nov. 13. (59)

1776, Oct. 11. WILLIAM JOHN (KERR), 5th marquess of Lothian. Nominated, knighted and invested at St. James's same day. Died 1815, Jan. 4. (60)

1786, Mar. 3. DOUGLAS (HAMILTON), 8th duke of Hamilton and 5th duke of Brandon. Nominated and invested at St. James's same day. Died 1799, Aug. 2. (61)

1786, Nov. 29. THOMAS BRUCE (BRUDENELL-BRUCE), 4th earl of Ailesbury. Nominated and invested at St. James's same day. Died 1814, Apr. 19. (62)

1793, June 14. JAMES (GRAHAM), 4th duke of Montrose. Nominated, knighted and invested at St. James's same day. Resigned on being elected K.G., 1812, Mar. 26. (63)

1794, May 30. JOHN (POULETT), 4th earl Poulett. Nominated, knighted and invested at St. James's same day. Died 1819, Jan. 14. (64)

1797, July 26. GEORGE (DOUGLAS), 17th earl of Morton. Nominated, knighted and invested at St. James's same day. Died 1827, July 17. (65)

1800, Apr. 23 (? 4). JOHN (MURRAY), 4th duke of Atholl. Nominated, and invested at St. James's same day. Died 1830, Sept. 29. (66)

1805, Nov. 23. WILLIAM SCHAW (CATHCART), 10th baron, afterwards 1st earl Cathcart. Nominated and invested same day at Windsor. Died 1843, June 16. (67)

1808, Mar. 16. GEORGE (GORDON, afterwards Hamilton-Gordon), 4th earl of Aberdeen. Nominated, knighted and invested same day in the Queen's Palace in the presence of His Majesty. Was allowed to retain the Order of the Thistle on being elected K.G. in 1855, Feb. 7. Died 1860, Dec. 14. (68)

1812, May 22. CHARLES WILLIAM HENRY (MONTAGU-SCOTT), 4th duke of Buccleuch and duke of Queensbury. Nominated, knighted and invested same day by the Prince Regent at Carlton House. Died 1819, Apr. 20. (69)

1812, May 22. HUGH (MONTGOMERIE), 12th earl of Eglintoun. Nominated, knighted and invested *ut supra*. Died 1819, Dec. 14. (70)

1814, May 23. GEORGE (STEWART), 8th earl of Galloway. Knighted and invested May 30 in the Prince Regent's closet at Carlton House.* Died 1834, Mar. 27. (71)

1814, May 23. HENRY (NEVILL), 2nd earl of Abergavenny. Nominated, knighted and invested same day by the Prince Regent in his closet at Carlton House. Died 1843, Mar. 27. (72)

1815, Feb. 23. THOMAS (ERSKINE), 1st baron Erskine. Nominated and invested by the Prince Regent at Carlton House same day. Died 1823, Nov. 17. (73)

1819, May 20. CHARLES (BRUDENELL-BRUCE), 5th earl afterwards 1st marquess of Ailesbury. Nominated and invested same day by the Prince Regent at Carlton House. Died 1856, Jan. 4. (74)

GEORGE IV., the sixth Sovereign.

1820, Apr. 26. WILLIAM (KERR), 6th marquess of Lothian. Nominated and invested at Carlton House same day. Died 1824, Apr. 27. (75)

1820, May 22. GEORGE (HAY), 8th marquess of Tweeddale. Nominated and invested at Carlton House same day. Died 1876, Oct. 10. (76)

1821, July 17. ARCHIBALD (KENNEDY), 12th earl of Cassillis and 1st baron afterwards 1st marquess of Ailsa. An extra knight on the Coronation of George IV. Nominated and invested at Carlton House same day. Died 1846, Sept. 8. (77)

1821, July 17. JAMES (MAITLAND), 8th earl of Lauderdale. An extra knight nominated and invested *ut supra*. Died 1839, Sept. 15. (78)

1821, July 17. ROBERT (SAUNDERS-DUNDAS), 2nd viscount Melville. An extra knight, and nominated and invested *ut supra*. Died 1851, June 10. (79)

1821, July 17. CHARLES (DOUGLAS), 6th marquess of Queensberry. An extra knight nominated *ut supra*. Invested 1822, Apr. 19. Died 1837, Dec. 3. (80)

* The Register dates this investiture May 30. But it is possibly a clerical error for May 23. The Earl took the oath on May 23.

6

1827, May 10. GEORGE (GORDON), 5th earl of Aboyne, afterwards
      9th marquess of Huntley (extra knight). Nominated,
      knighted and invested in the King's closet at St. James's
      Palace same day. Died 1853, June 17.   (81)

1827, May 10. HENRY RICHARD (GREVILLE), 3rd earl Brooke of
      Warwick Castle. Nominated, knighted and invested *ut
      supra* (extra knight). Died 1853, Aug. 10.   (82)

1827, Sept. 3. JAMES (DUFF), 4th earl of Fife (extra knight).
      Knighted and invested at St James's Sept. 4. Died 1857,
      Mar. 9.   (83)

1827, Sept. 3. FRANCIS (STUART), 23rd earl of Moray (extra knight).
      Knighted and invested at St. James's 1830, Aug. 4. Died
      1848, Jan. 12.*   (84)

KING WILLIAM IV., the seventh Sovereign.

1830, July 19. AUGUSTUS FREDERICK of Brunswick-Luneburg, duke
      of Sussex, 6th son of George III. Nominated, knighted
      and invested at St. James's same day. Died 1843, Apr. 21.
      (85)

1830, Nov. 5. WALTER FRANCIS (MONTAGU-DOUGLAS-SCOTT), 5th
      duke of Buccleuch and duke of Queensberry (extra knight).
      Nominated, knighted and invested same day in the King's
      closet at St James's Warrant of dispensation of installa-
      tion same day. Resigned on being elected K G., 1835,
      Feb. 23.   (86)

1834, Apr. 16. WILLIAM GEORGE (HAY), 18th earl of Erroll. Elected
      in a Chapter at St James's Apr 16; invested same day;
      warrant of dispensation of installation same day. Died
      1846, Apr. 19.   (87)

1835, Mar. 4. DAVID WILLIAM (MURRAY), 3rd earl of Mansfield and
      8th viscount Stormont. Elected and invested same day at
      St. James's Palace. Died 1840, Feb 18.   (88)

* The warrant dispensing with a Chapter for the election of the Earl of Moray was dated 1827, Sept. 4 ;
and the warrant dispensing with his installation was dated Sept 3 (*sic*) For some reason the whole pro-
ceeding was incomplete After the accession of William IV fresh documents were issued, viz , warrant
dispensing with a Chapter 1830, Aug 4, warrant of nomination Aug 4, and warrant dispensing with
installation Aug 4 Accordingly in the Register the Earl of Moray is placed after the Duke of Sussex

QUEEN VICTORIA, the eighth Sovereign.

1838, Mar. 21. JOHN (CAMPBELL), 2nd marquess of Breadalbane.
Warrant of appointment Mar. 21. Invested same day,
warrant of dispensation of installation same day. Died
1862, Nov. 8   (89)

1840, Mar. 18. JAMES HENRY ROBERT (INNES-KER), 6th duke of
Roxburghe. Warrant of appointment Mar. 18; knighted
and invested same day, warrant of dispensation of installa-
tion same day. Died 1879, Apr. 23.   (90)

1840, Mar. 18. ARCHIBALD JOHN (PRIMROSE), 4th earl of Rosebery.
Appointed, knighted, invested and dispensed *ut supra.*
Died 1866, Mar. 14.   (91)

1842, Jan. 17. PRINCE ALBERT, consort of Her Majesty. Declared
a knight by special statute Jan. 17; warrant dispensing
with investiture and warrant dispensing with installation
both dated Jan. 17. Died 1861, Dec. 14.   (92)

1843, June 13. JOHN (CRICHTON-STUART), 2nd marquess of Bute.
Elected in a Chapter at Buckingham Palace June 13,
knighted and invested *ibid* same day; warrant of dispensa-
tion of installation same day. Died 1848, Mar. 18.   (93)

1843, June 13. WILLIAM DAVID (MURRAY), 4th earl of Mansfield.
Elected, knighted, invested and dispensed for installation
ut supra. Died 1898, Aug. 2.   (94)

1845, Mar. 12. JAMES (GRAHAM), 5th duke of Montrose Elected
in a Chapter held at St. James's Palace Mar. 12; knighted
and invested same day there; warrant of dispensation of
installation same day. Died 1874, Dec. 30.   (95)

1847, July 12. JOHN HAMILTON (DALRYMPLE), 8th earl of Stair.
Warrant of appointment July 12; knighted by Letters
patent dated Whitehall, 1847, June 16, warrant of
dispensation of investiture and warrant of dispensation of
installation both dated July 12. Died 1853, Jan. 10
Probably in place of No 87   (96)

1847, July 12 JAMES (BRUCE), 8th earl of Elgin, earl of Kincardine.
Warrant of appointment July 12; knighted by Letters
patent dated Whitehall, 1847, June 16; dispensed for
investiture and installation *ut supra.* Died 1863, Nov. 20.
Probably in place of No. 77.   (97)

1848, May 12. James Andrew (Ramsay), 10th earl, afterwards marquess, of Dalhousie. Elected in a Chapter at Buckingham Palace May 12; knighted by Letters patent dated Whitehall, May 12; investiture dispensed with (he being then in India as governor general) by warrant of May 12; warrant of dispensation of installation May 12. Died 1860, Dec. 19.
(98)

1848, May 12. Robert Dundas (Duncan), 1st earl of Camperdown. Elected in a Chapter at Buckingham Palace May 12; dispensed for installation May 12. Died 1859, Dec. 22.   (99)

1852, Mar. 25. Alexander George (Fraser), 16th lord Saltoun. Elected in a Chapter at Buckingham Palace Mar. 25; invested same day there; warrant of dispensation of installation same day. Died 1853, July 18.   (100)

1853, June 18. Archibald William (Montgomerie), 13th earl of Eglintoun, and afterwards earl of Winton. Elected in a Chapter at Buckingham Palace June 18; knighted and invested there same day; warrant of dispensation of installation same day. Died 1861, Oct. 4.   (101)

1853, Oct. 28. Thomas (Hamilton), 9th earl of Haddington. Elected in a Chapter at Windsor Castle Oct. 28; knighted and invested there same day; warrant of dispensation of installation same day. Died 1858, Dec. 1.   (102)

1853, Oct. 28. George Augustus Frederick John (Murray), 6th duke of Atholl. Elected, knighted, invested and dispensed for installation *ut supra*. Died 1864, Jan. 16.
(103)

1853, Oct. 28. Fox (Maule), 2nd lord Panmure of Brechin, afterwards 11th earl of Dalhousie. Elected, knighted, invested and dispensed for installation *ut supra*. Died 1874, July 6.
(104)

1856, May 2. George Douglas (Campbell), 8th duke of Argyll. Elected in a Chapter at Buckingham Palace May 2; knighted and invested there same day; warrant of dispensation of installation same day. Retained the Thistle on being made K.G. in 1883. Died 1900, Apr. 24.   (105)

1857, July 6. George William Fox (Kinnaird), 9th lord Kinnaird. Elected in a Chapter at Buckingham Palace July 6; knighted and invested there same day; warrant of dispensation of installation same day. Died 1878, Jan. 7.   (106)

1859, Mar. 7. Archibald (Kennedy), 2nd marquess of Ailsa. Elected in a Chapter at Buckingham Palace Mar. 7; knighted and invested there same day; warrant of dispensation of installation same day. Died 1870, Mar. 20.   (107)

1860, Mar. 2. JAMES (DUFF), 5th earl of Fife. Elected in a
Chapter at Buckingham Palace Mar. 2; knighted and
invested there same day; warrant of dispensation of
installation same day. Died 1879, Aug. 7. (108)

1861, July 1. THOMAS (DUNDAS), 2nd earl of Zetland. Elected in
a Chapter at Buckingham Palace on Monday, July 1;
knighted and invested there same day; warrant of dispensa-
tion of installation same day. Elected in place probably
of No. 98. Resigned the Thistle on being made K.G. 1872,
Dec. 26. (109)

1861, July 1. ROBERT MONTGOMERIE (HAMILTON), 8th lord Belhaven
and Stenton. Elected, knighted, invested and dispensed
for installation *ut supra*. Died 1868, Dec. 22. Probably in
place of No. 68. (110)

1862, Mar. 12. DAVID GRAHAM DRUMMOND (OGILVY), 7th earl of
Airlie. Warrant of appointment Mar. 12; warrant
dispensing with investiture and warrant dispensing with
installation both dated Mar. 12. Died 1881, Sept. 25. In
place of No. 101. (111)

1864, May 10. FRANCIS (NAPIER), 10th lord Napier and 1st lord
Ettrick. Warrant of appointment May 10; warrant
dispensing with investiture May 10; warrant dispensing
with installation May 10. Died 1898, Dec. 19. In place of
No. 89. (112)

1864, Oct. 15. Prince ALFRED ERNEST ALBERT, afterwards duke of
Edinburgh and duke of Saxe-Coburg and Gotha. An extra
knight; nominated by special statute and by warrant of
appointment both dated Oct. 15; invested at Balmoral same
day; warrant of dispensation of installation same day.
Died 1900, July 20. (113)

1865, July 28. THOMAS ALEXANDER (FRASER), 12th lord Lovat.
Warrant of appointment July 28; warrant of dispensation
of investiture and warrant of dispensation of installation
both dated July 28. Died 1875, June 28. In place of
No. 97. (114)

1865, Aug. 28. JOHN (HAMILTON-DALRYMPLE), 10th earl of Stair.
Warrant of appointment Aug. 28; warrant of dispensation
of installation same day. Dated 1903, Dec. 3. In place of
No. 103. (115)

1867, May 24. H.R H. ALBERT EDWARD, prince of Wales, afterwards Edward VII. An extra knight; nominated by special statute and by warrant of appointment both dated May 24; warrant of dispensation of installation same day. (116)

1868, May 14 JOHN JAMES HUGH HENRY (STEWART-MURRAY), 7th duke of Atholl. Warrant of appointment May 14; invested at Windsor Castle same day; warrant of dispensation of installation same day. In place of No. 91. (117)

1869, Mar. 1. JAMES (CARNEGIE), 6th earl of Southesk. Warrant of appointment Mar. 1; knighted and invested same day at Windsor Castle; warrant of dispensation of installation same day. In place of No 110 (118)

1869, May 24 H.R.H. prince ARTHUR WILLIAM PATRICK ALBERT, afterwards duke of Connaught. An extra knight. Nominated by special statute and by warrant of appointment both dated May 24; invested at Balmoral same day; warrant of dispensation of installation same day (119)

1870, May 13. WILLIAM HUGH (ELLIOT-MURRAY-KYNYNMOUND), 3rd earl of Minto. Warrant of appointment May 13; invested at Windsor Castle same day; warrant of dispensation of installation same day. Died 1891, Mar. 17. In place of No 107. (120)

1871, Mar 21. JOHN DOUGLAS SUTHERLAND (CAMPBELL), marquess of Lorne, afterwards 9th duke of Argyll. An extra knight. Nominated by special statute and by warrant of appointment both dated Mar. 21, knighted and invested same day by the Queen in the presence of prince Arthur and princess Louise in the Queen's private room at Windsor Castle, on the return from the marriage ceremony in the Chapel; warrant of dispensation of installation same day. (121)

1871, May 24 H R H. prince LEOPOLD GEORGE DUNCAN ALBERT, afterwards duke of Albany. An extra Knight. Special statute and warrant of appointment both dated May 24; invested in the Queen's private room at Balmoral same day in the presence of princess Beatrice; warrant of dispensation of installation same day Died 1884, Mar. 28. (122)

1874, Dec. 12 CHARLES JOHN (COLVILLE), 8th lord Colville of Culross, afterwards viscount Colville. Warrant of appointment 1874, July 30; invested at Windsor Castle Dec. 12; warrant of dispensation of installation Dec. 19. Died 1903, July 1. In place of No. 104 (123)

1875, May 13. JOHN PATRICK (CRICHTON-STUART), 3rd marquess of
Bute. Warrant of appointment Apr. 29; invested at
Windsor Castle May 13; warrant of dispensation of
installation May 18. Died 1900, Oct. 9. In place of No. 95.
(124)

1875, Aug. 5. WILLIAM HENRY WALTER (MONTAGU-DOUGLAS-SCOTT),
earl of Dalkeith, afterwards 6th duke of Buccleuch and
8th duke of Queensberry. Warrant of appointment Aug. 5;
invested at Osborne same day; warrant of dispensation of
installation same day. In place of No. 114. (125)

1876, Dec. 9. Sir WILLIAM STIRLING-MAXWELL, bart. Warrant of
appointment Dec. 9; invested at Windsor Castle same day;
warrant of dispensation of installation same day. Died
1878, Jan. 15. In place of No 76 (126)

1878, Feb. 22. WILLIAM ALEXANDER LOUIS STEPHEN (DOUGLAS-
HAMILTON), 12th duke of Hamilton and 9th duke of
Brandon. Warrant of appointment Feb. 20; invested at
Windsor Castle Feb. 22; warrant of dispensation of
installation Feb. 22. Died 1895, May 16. In place of
No. 106. (127)

1878, Feb. 22. SCHOMBERG HENRY (KERR), 9th marquess of Lothian.
Warrant of appointment Feb. 20; invested at Windsor
Castle Feb. 22; warrant of dispensation of installation
Feb. 22. Died 1900, Jan. 17. In place of No 126. (128)

1879, Nov. 29. JOHN CHARLES (OGILVIE-GRANT), 11th earl of
Seafield. Warrant of appointment June 30; invested at
Windsor Castle Nov. 29; warrant of dispensation of
installation Nov. 29. Died 1881, Feb. 18. In place of
No. 90. (129)

1879, Nov. 29. DOUGLAS BERESFORD MALISE RONALD (GRAHAM),
6th duke of Montrose. Warrant of appointment Nov. 22;
invested at Windsor Castle Nov. 29; warrant of dispensation
of installation Nov. 29. In place of No. 108. (130)

1881, Mar. 24. ALEXANDER WILLIAM GEORGE (DUFF), 6th earl,
afterwards duke of Fife Warrant of appointment Mar. 16;
invested at Windsor Castle Mar. 24; warrant of dispensation
of installation Mar. 26. In place of No. 129. (131)

1881, Dec. 7. JOHN WILLIAM (RAMSAY), 13th earl of Dalhousie.
Warrant of appointment Nov. 21; invested at Windsor
Castle Dec. 7; warrant of dispensation of installation Dec. 7.
Died 1887, Nov. 28. In place of No. 111. (132)

1881, Sept. 17. GEORGE WILLIAM FREDERICK CHARLES, duke of Cambridge. An extra knight; nominated by special statute and by warrant of appointment both dated Sept. 17; invested privately at Balmoral same day; warrant of dispensation of installation same day. Died 1904, Mar. 17.
(133)

1888, Feb. 21. ALAN PLANTAGENET (STEWART), 10th earl of Galloway. Warrant of appointment 1887, Dec. 28; invested at Windsor Castle 1888, Feb. 21; warrant of dispensation of installation Mar. 8. Died 1901, Feb 7. In place of No. 132
(134)

1891, Dec 10. JAMES LUDOVIC (LINDSAY), 26th earl of Crawford Warrant of appointment Dec. 7; invested at Windsor Castle Dec. 10; warrant of dispensation of installation Dec. 10. In place of No. 120.
(135)

1893, July 5. GEORGE FREDERICK ERNEST ALBERT, duke of York, afterwards prince of Wales. An extra knight; nominated by special statute and by warrant of appointment both dated July 5, and with precedence after the duke of Connaught and before the duke of Cambridge; warrant of dispensation of installation July 5.
(136)

1895, June 28. ARCHIBALD PHILIP (PRIMROSE), 5th earl of Rosebery. Warrant of appointment June 28; invested at Windsor Castle same day; warrant of dispensation of installation same day. In place of No. 127.
(137)

1898, Dec. 8. WILLIAM MONTAGU (HAY), 10th marquess of Tweeddale. Warrant of appointment Oct. 26; invested at Windsor Castle Dec 8; warrant of dispensation of installation Dec. 8 In place of No 94
(138)

1899, July 3. CHARLES ALEXANDER (DOUGLAS-HOME), 12th earl of Home. Warrant of appointment 1899, Feb. 25; invested at Windsor Castle July 3; warrant of dispensation of installation Aug. 17. In place of No. 112.
(139)

1900, July 14 LAWRENCE (DUNDAS), 1st marquess of Zetland. Warrant of appointment Mar. 29; invested in the Green Drawing Room at Windsor Castle July 14; warrant of dispensation of installation July 14. In place of No. 128.
(140)

1900, Sept 20. JOHN ADRIAN LOUIS (HOPE), 7th earl of Hopetoun, afterwards marquess of Linlithgow. Warrant of appointment July 12; invested at Balmoral Sept. 20; warrant of dispensation of installation Sept. 20. In place of No. 105.
(141)

KING EDWARD VII., the ninth Sovereign.

1901, Mar. 18. ALEXANDER HUGH (BRUCE), 6th lord Balfour of
Burghley. Appointed by queen Victoria by warrant dated
1901, Jan. 10; knighted and invested by Edward VII. at
Marlborough House 1901, Mar. 18; warrant of dispensation
of installation Mar. 26. In place of No. 124. (142)

1901, June 10. CHARLES GORE (HAY), 20th earl of Erroll. Warrant
of appointment June 1; knighted and invested in the
Throne Room at St. James's Palace June 10; warrant of
dispensation of installation June 21. In place of No. 134.
(143)

1902, Aug. 8. HENRY JOHN (INNES-KER), 8th duke of Roxburghe.
An extra knight appointed on the occasion of the Coronation
of Edward VII. Warrant of appointment Aug. 8; invested
at Buckingham Palace same day; warrant of dispensation
of installation same day. Succeeded as an ordinary knight
on the death of No. 123. (144)

1902, Aug. 8. GEORGE (BAILLIE-HAMILTON-ARDEN), 11th earl of
Haddington. An extra knight *ut supra*. Nominated,
invested, and dispensed for installation *ut supra*. Succeeded
as an ordinary knight on the death of No. 115. (145)

The Most Illustrious Order of St. Patrick.

THE SOVEREIGNS.

See the list of sovereigns given *seriatim supra* under the Order of the Garter.

GRAND MASTERS OF THE ORDER.
(The Lords Lieutenant of Ireland for the time being).
The dates being those of their investiture with the insignia of the Order.

GEORGE (NUGENT-TEMPLE-GRENVILLE), 3rd earl Temple. Invested 1783, Mar. 11.

ROBERT (HENLEY), 2nd earl of Northington, 1783, June 3.

CHARLES (MANNERS), 4th duke of Rutland, 1784, Feb. 24.

GEORGE (NUGENT-TEMPLE-GRENVILLE), marquess of Buckingham formerly earl Temple, 1787, Dec. 16, for the second time.

JOHN (FANE), 16th earl of Westmorland, 1790, Jan. 5.

WILLIAM (FITZWILLIAM), 2nd earl Fitzwilliam, 1795, Jan. 4.

JOHN JEFFREYS (PRATT), 2nd earl Camden, 1795, Mar. 31.

CHARLES (CORNWALLIS), 1st marquess Cornwallis, 1798, June 20.

PHILIP (YORKE), 3rd earl of Hardwicke, 1801, May 25.

JOHN (RUSSELL), 9th duke of Bedford, 1806, Mar. 28.

CHARLES (LENNOX), 9th duke of Richmond, 1807, Apr. 19.

CHARLES (WHITWORTH), 1st earl Whitworth, 1813, Aug. 26.

CHARLES CHETWYND (CHETWYND-TALBOT), 3rd earl Talbot, 1817, Oct. 9.

RICHARD (WELLESLEY), marquess Wellesley, 1821, Dec. 29.

HENRY WILLIAM (PAGET), 1st marquess of Anglesey, 1828, Mar. 1.

HUGH (PERCY), 5th duke of Northumberland, 1829, Mar. 6.

HENRY WILLIAM (PAGET), 1st marquess of Anglesey, 1830, Dec. 23, for a second time.

RICHARD (WELLESLEY), marquis Wellesley, 1833, Sept. 26, for a second time.

THOMAS (HAMILTON), 9th earl of Haddington, 1835, Jan. 6.

CONSTANTINE HENRY (PHIPPS), 2nd viscount, afterwards 3rd marquess of Normanby, 1835, May 11.

HUGH (FORTESCUE), viscount Ebrington, afterwards 2nd earl Fortescue, 1839, Apr. 3.

THOMAS PHILIP (DE GREY), 2nd earl de Grey, 1841, Sept. 15.

WILLIAM (A'COURT), 1st lord Heytesbury, 1844, July 26.

JOHN WILLIAM (PONSONBY), 4th earl of Bessborough, 1846, July 11.

GEORGE WILLIAM FREDERICK (VILLIERS), 8th earl of Clarendon, 1847, May 26.

ARCHIBALD WILLIAM (MONTGOMERIE), 13th earl of Eglintoun, 1852, Mar. 10.

EDWARD GRANVILLE (ELIOT), 3rd earl of St. Germans, 1853, Jan. 6.

GEORGE WILLIAM FREDERICK (HOWARD), 10th earl of Carlisle, 1855, Mar. 13.

ARCHIBALD WILLIAM (MONTGOMERIE), 13th earl of Eglinton, 1858, Mar. 12, for a second time.

GEORGE WILLIAM FREDERICK (HOWARD), 10th earl of Carlisle, 1859, June 18, for a second time.

JOHN (WODEHOUSE), 3rd lord Wodehouse, afterwards 1st earl of Kimberley, 1864, Nov. 8.

JAMES (HAMILTON), 2nd marquess, afterwards 1st duke of Abercorn, 1866, July 20.

JOHN POYNTZ (SPENCER), 5th earl Spencer, 1868, Dec. 23.

JAMES (HAMILTON), 1st duke of Abercorn, 1874, Mar. 2, for the second time.

JOHN WINSTON (SPENCER-CHURCHILL), 7th duke of Marlborough, 1876, Dec. 12.

FRANCIS THOMAS DE GREY (COWPER), 7th earl Cowper, 1880, May 5.

JOHN POYNTZ (SPENCER), 5th earl Spencer, 1882, May 6.

HENRY HOWARD MOLYNEUX (HERBERT), 9th earl of Carnarvon, 1885, June 30.

JOHN CAMPBELL (HAMILTON-GORDON), 7th earl of Aberdeen, 1886, Feb. 10.

CHARLES STEWART (VANE-TEMPEST-STEWART), 6th marquess of Londonderry, 1886, Aug 5.

LAWRENCE (DUNDAS), 3rd earl afterwards 1st marquess of Zetland, 1889, Oct. 5.

ROBERT OFFLEY ASHBURTON (MILNES), 2nd baron Houghton, 1892, Aug. 22.

GEORGE HENRY (CADOGAN), 6th earl Cadogan, 1895, July 8.

WILLIAM HUMBLE (WARD), 2nd earl of Dudley, 1902, Aug. 16.

Knights of the Most Illustrious Order of St. Patrick.

The fifteen original knights or "Knights Founders" as below were nominated on the 5th Feb., 1783, invested on the 11th March and installed on the 17th. The fifteenth knight, the earl of Ely, was, owing to ill health, absent from the investiture and installation. He is therefore not considered one of the knights founders, though named in the letters patents. At the investiture on the 11th Mar., 1783, knights Nos. 2—10 were knighted. No. 1, prince Edward, was represented by a proxy, lord Muskerry, who was knighted.

The marginal date is that of the investiture, except where otherwise stated.

1783, Mar. 11. H.R.H. prince EDWARD AUGUSTUS, afterwards duke of Kent and Strathearn. Died 1820, Jan. 23. (1)

1783, Mar. 11. WILLIAM ROBERT (FITZGERALD), 2nd duke of Leinster. Died 1804, Oct. 4 (2)

1783, Mar. 11. HENRY (DE BURGH), 12th earl of Clanrickarde. Died 1795, Dec. 18.* (3)

1783, Mar. 11. THOMAS (NUGENT), 6th earl of Westmeath. Died 1790, Sept. 7. (4)

1783, Mar. 11. MURROUGH (O'BRIEN), 5th earl of Inchiquin, afterwards marquess of Thomond. Died 1808, Feb. 10. (5)

1783, Mar. 11. CHARLES (MOORE), 6th earl of Drogheda. Died 1821, Dec. 22. (6)

1783, Mar. 11. GEORGE DE LA POER (BERESFORD), 2nd earl of Tyrone, afterwards marquess of Waterford. Died 1800, Dec. 3. (7)

1783, Mar. 11. RICHARD (BOYLE), 2nd earl of Shannon. Died 1807, May 20. (8)

1783, Mar. 11 JAMES (HAMILTON), 2nd earl of Clanbrassill. Died 1798, Feb. 6. (9)

---

* RANDALL, WILLIAM (MACDONNEL), 6th earl of Antrim, was nominated February after the earl of Clanrickarde, but relinquished his election as he did not wish to relinquish the order of the Bath.

1783, Mar. 11. RICHARD (WELLESLEY), 2nd earl of Mornington.
afterwards marquess Wellesley. Resigned 1810, Mar. 3, on
being elected K.G. (10)

1783, Mar. 11. ARTHUR SAUNDERS (GORE), 2nd earl of Arran. Died
1809, Oct. 8. Nominated as a knight founder on the refusal
of the earl of Antrim, who declined the honour. (11)

1783, Mar. 11. JAMES (STOPFORD), 2nd earl of Courtown. Died
1810, Mar. 30. (12)

1783, Mar. 11. JAMES (CAULFIELD), 1st earl of Charlemont. Died
1799, Aug. 4. (13)

1783, Mar. 11. THOMAS (TAYLOUR), 1st earl of Bective. Died 1795,
Feb. 14. (14)

1783, Mar. 11. HENRY (LOFTUS), earl of Ely. Died abroad 1783,
May 8, uninvested. (15)

1784, Feb. 5. JOHN JOSHUA (PROBY), 2nd baron Carysfoot. In
place of No. 15. Elected and invested 1784, Feb. 5.
Knighted Mar. 5. Installed by proxy 1800, Aug. 11. Died
1828, Apr. 7. (16)

1794, Dec. 12. CHARLES (LOFTUS *formerly* Tottenham), 1st earl of
Ely. In place of No 4 Elected, knighted and invested
1794, Dec. 12. Installed 1800, Aug. 11. Died 1806,
Mar. 22. (17)

1795, Mar. 30. WILLIAM HENRY (FORTESCUE), earl of Clermont. In
place of No. 14. Elected Mar. 30. Invested soon after by
the Sovereign in England. Installed by proxy 1800,
Aug. 11. Died 1806, Sept. 30. (18)

1798, Mar. 19. WALTER (BUTLER), earl of Ormonde and Ossory.
In place of No. 3. Knighted Mar. 9. Elected and invested
1798, Mar. 19. Installed 1800, Aug. 11. Died 1820,
Aug. 10. (19)

1798, Mar. 19. CHARLES (DILLON), 12th viscount Dillon. In place
of No. 9. Knighted Mar. 9. Elected and invested 1798,
Mar. 19. Installed by proxy 1800, Aug. 11. Died 1813,
Nov. 9. (20)

1800, Aug. 5. JOHN DENNIS (BROWNE), 3rd earl of Altamont. In
place of No. 13. Elected and invested Aug. 5. Installed
Aug. 11. Died 1809, Jan. 2. (21)

7

1801, Jan. 22. HENRY (CONYNGHAM), 2nd earl, afterwards 1st marquess, Conyngham   In place of No. 7.   Elected, knighted and invested 1801, Jan 22. Installed 1809, June 29. Died 1832, Dec. 28.   (22)

1806, Mar. 14. HENRY DE LA POER (BERESFORD), 2nd marquess of Waterford. In place of No. 2. Elected, knighted and invested 1806, Mar. 14. Installed 1809, June 29. Died 1826, July 16.   (23)

1806, May 15. THOMAS (TAYLOUR), 1st marquess of Headfort. In place of No 17. Elected May 15. Invested soon after by the sovereign in England. Installed by proxy 1809, June 29. Died 1829, Oct. 23.   (24)

1806, Nov. 13. ROBERT (JOCELYN), 2nd earl of Roden. In place of No 8. Elected, knighted and invested 1806, Nov. 13. Installed 1809, June 29. Died 1820, June 29.   (25)

1807, Nov. 3 JOHN (LOFTUS), 2nd marquess of Ely. In place of No. 8. Elected, knighted and invested 1807, Nov. 3. Installed 1809, June 29. Died 1845, Sept 23.   (26)

1808, Apr. 5. HENRY (BOYLE), 3rd earl of Shannon. In place of No. 5. Elected, knighted and invested 1808, Apr. 5. Installed 1809, June 29   Died 1842, Apr. 22.   (27)

1809, Feb. 13 CHARLES HENRY ST. JOHN (O'NEILL), 1st earl O'Neill. In place of No. 21. Elected, knighted and invested Feb. 13. Installed June 29. Died 1841, Mar. 25.   (28)

1809, Nov. 11 WILLIAM (O'BRYEN), 2nd marquess of Thomond. In place of No. 11. Elected, knighted and invested 1809, Nov. 11. Installed 1819, May 27. Died 1846, Aug. 21.   (29)

1810, Mar. 24. HOWE PETER (BROWNE), 2nd marquess of Sligo. In place of No 10, resigned. Invested at Malta by special dispensation 1811, June 11   Installed 1819, May 27. Died 1845, Jan 26.   (30)

1810, Apr. 27. JOHN WILLOUGHBY (COLE), 2nd earl of Enniskillen. In place of No. 12. Elected, knighted and invested 1810, Apr. 27. Installed 1819, May 27. Died 1840, Mar 31.   (31)

1813, Dec 17. THOMAS (PAKENHAM), 2nd earl of Longford. In place of No. 20. Elected, knighted and invested 1813, Dec. 17. Installed 1819, May 27. Died 1835, May 24.   (32)

1821, Aug. 20. H.R.H. ERNEST AUGUSTUS, duke of Cumberland and Teviotdale, afterwards king of Hanover. In place of No 1. Invested by proxy Aug. 20. Installed by proxy Aug. 28. Died 1851, Nov. 18.   (33)

1821, Aug. 20. GEORGE AUGUSTUS (CHICHESTER), 2nd marquess of Donegall. In place of No. 25. Knighted by George IV. and invested Aug. 20; installed Aug. 28. Died 1844, Oct. 5.   (34)

1821, Aug. 20. DU PRE (ALEXANDER), 2nd earl of Caledon. In place of No. 19. Installed Aug. 28. Died 1839, Apr. 8. (35)

Six knights extraordinary (No. 36—41) were nominated at the Coronation of George IV., 1821, July 19, to be gradually absorbed among the knights in ordinary.

1821, Aug. 20. CHARLES CHETWYND (CHETWYND-TALBOT), 3rd earl Talbot, viceroy of Ireland. Knighted by George IV. and invested Aug. 20. Installed Aug. 28. Became a knight in ordinary in place of No. 6. Resigned 1844, Oct. 11, on being made K.G.   (36)

1821, Aug. 20. JAMES (BUTLER), earl of Ormonde and Ossory. Knighted by George IV. and invested Aug. 20. Installed Aug. 28. Became a knight in ordinary in place of No. 23. Died 1838, May 18.   (37)

1821, Aug. 20. JOHN CHAMBRE (BRABAZON), 10th earl of Meath. Knighted by George IV. and invested Aug. 20. Installed Aug. 28. Became a knight in ordinary in place of No. 16. Died 1851, Mar. 15.   (38)

1821, Aug. 20. ARTHUR JAMES (PLUNKETT), 8th earl of Fingall. Knighted by George IV. and invested Aug. 20. Installed Aug. 28. Became a knight in ordinary in place of No. 24. Died 1836, July 30.   (39)

1821, Aug. 20. JAMES GEORGE (STOPFORD), 3rd earl of Courtown. Knighted by George IV. and invested Aug. 20. Installed Aug. 28. Became a knight in ordinary in place of No. 22. Died 1835, June 15.   (40)

1821, Aug. 20. ROBERT (JOCELYN), 3rd earl of Roden. Knighted by George IV. and invested Aug. 20. Installed Aug. 28. Became a knight in ordinary by the statute of 1833, Jan. 24. Died 1870, Mar. 20.   (41)

Four knights extraordinary (Nos. 42—5) were nominated at the Coronation of William IV, 1831, Sept. 8, to be gradually absorbed among the knights in ordinary.

1831, Nov. 24   ARTHUR BLUNDELL SANDYS TRUMBULL (HILL), 2nd
marquess of Downshire. Invested Nov. 24. Installed by
dispensation 1833, Jan. 30. Became a knight in ordinary
by the statute of 1833, Jan. 24. Died 1845, Apr. 12.   (42)

1831, Oct 19.   ULICK JOHN (DE BURGH), 1st marquess of Clanri-
carde. Invested by the sovereign 1831, Oct. 19. Installed
by dispensation 1833, Jan. 30. Became a knight in
ordinary *ut supra.* Died 1874, Apr 10.   (43)

1831, Oct. 19.   FRANCIS WILLIAM (CAULFIELD), 2nd earl of Charle-
mont. Invested and installed *ut supra* Became a knight
in ordinary *ut supra.* Died 1863, Dec. 26.   (44)

1831, Nov 24   FRANCIS JAMES (MATHEW), 2nd earl of Llandaff.
Knighted and invested 1831, Nov. 24. Installed by dis-
pensation 1833, Jan 30. Became a knight in ordinary *ut
supra* Died 1833, Mar. 12.   (45)

1833, Mar. 27. FRANCIS NATHANIEL (CONYNGHAM), 2nd marquess
Conyngham. By the increase of the order under the statute
of 1833, Jan. 24. Nominated and invested Mar. 27. In-
stalled by dispensation Apr. 3. Died 1876, July 17.   (46)

1834, Apr 8   NATHANIEL (CLEMENTS), 2nd earl of Leitrim. By the
increase *ut supra.* Elected and invested Apr. 8. Installed
by dispensation May 31. Died 1854, Dec. 31.   (47)

1834, Apr. 8   JOHN (HELY-HUTCHINSON), 3rd earl of Donoughmore.
In place of No 45. Elected, invested and installed *ut
supra* Died 1851, Sept. 14.   (48)

1835, July 22. EDMUND (BOYLE), 8th earl of Cork and earl of Orrery.
In place of No. 32. Nominated, knighted, invested and
installed by dispensation on same day. Died 1856, June 30.
(49)

1835, July 22. THOMAS (ST. LAWRENCE), 3rd earl of Howth. In
place of No. 40. Nominated, knighted, invested and
installed by dispensation on same day. Died 1874, Feb. 4.
(50)

1837, Sept 12   THOMAS ANTHONY (SOUTHWELL), 3rd viscount South-
well. In place of No 39. Knighted and invested Sept. 12.
Installed by dispensation Sept. 20 Died 1860, Feb. 29.   (51)

1839, Apr 15   THOMAS (TAYLOUR), 2nd marquess of Headfort. In
place of No 37. Elected, knighted and invested Apr. 15.
installed by dispensation Apr. 18. Died 1870, Dec. 6.   (52)

1839, Apr. 29. WILLIAM (HARE), 3rd earl of Listowel. In place of
No. 53. Elected, knighted and invested Apr. 29. Installed
by dispensation May 7. Died 1856, Feb. 3.   (53)

1841, Mar. 13. JOSEPH (LEESON), 4th earl of Milltown. In place of No. 31. Knighted and invested Mar. 13. Installed by dispensation Mar 21. Died 1866, Jan. 31. (54)

1841, May 6. PHILIP YORKE (GORE), 4th earl of Arran. In place of No. 28. Knighted and invested May 6 Installed by dispensation July 19. Died 1884, June 25. (55)

1842, Jan 20 H.R.H prince ALBERT (FRANCIS ALBERT AUGUSTUS CHARLES EMANUEL), duke of Saxony, prince of Saxe-Coburg and Gotha, K.G. Declared by sign manual an extra knight with precedence above all other knights and dispensation from investiture and installation Died 1861, Dec. 14. (56)

1842, June 5. WILLIAM (HOWARD), earl of Wicklow. In place of No. 27. Knighted and invested Nov 9. Dispensed from installation Nov. 5. Died 1869, Mar. 22. (57)

1845, Jan. 4. WILLIAM (PARSONS), 3rd earl of Rosse. In place of No. 34. Knighted Jan. 4. Dispensed from installation Jan. 9. Died 1867, Oct. 31. (58)

1845, Jan 4. HENRY DE LA POER (Beresford), 3rd marquess of Waterford In place of No 36. Knighted, invested and dispensed ut supra. Died 1859, Mar. 29 (59)

1845, Sept. 17. JOHN (FITZ GIBBON), 2nd earl of Clare. In place of No 30. Knighted Sept 17. Invested and dispensed from installation Sept. 20. Died 1851, Aug. 18 (60)

1845, Sept. 17. JOHN (BUTLER), 2nd marquess of Ormonde. In place of No 42 Knighted, invested and dispensed ut supra Died 1854, Sept. 25. (61)

1845, Nov. 12 HENRY (MAXWELL), 7th baron Farnham. In place of No. 26 Knighted Nov 12. Invested and dispensed from installation Nov 14. Died 1868, Aug. 20. (62)

1846, Oct. 9 ARTHUR JAMES (PLUNKETT), 9th earl of Fingall. In place of No. 29 Knighted Oct. 12 Invested and dispensed from installation Oct 21 Died 1869, Apr. 21. (63)

1851, July 3. JOHN SKEFFINGTON (FOSTER-SKEFFINGTON), viscount Massareene and viscount Ferrard In place of No 38. Knighted, invested and dispensed from installation July 3. Died 1863, Apr. 28. (64)

1851, Nov. 17. H R.H. GEORGE WILLIAM FREDERICK CHARLES, duke of Cambridge, etc., K.G., etc In place of No 60 Invested and dispensed from installation Nov. 17. Died 1904, Mar 17. (65)

1851, Nov. 18. Robert. Shapland (Carew), 1st baron Carew. Knighted Nov. 18. In place of No. 48. Died 1856, June 2. (66)

1855, Feb. 22. Richard (Dawson), 3rd baron Cremorne, afterwards earl of Dartrey. In place of No. 61. Dispensed from installation Apr. 21. Died 1897, May 11. (67)

1855, Feb. 22. Archibald (Acheson), 3rd earl of Gosford. In place of No. 47. Dispensed *ut supra*. Died 1864, June 22. (68)

1856, Aug. 28. Frederick William Robert (Stewart), 4th marquess of Londonderry. In place of No. 53. Dispensed from installation Dec. 23. Died 1872, Nov. 25. (69)

1857, Jan. 30. George Arthur Hastings (Forbes), 7th earl of Granard. In place of No. 66. Dispensed from installation Mar. 10. Died 1889, Aug. 25. (70)

1857, Jan. 30. Hugh (Gough), 1st viscount Gough of Goojerat and of Limerick. In place of No. 49. Dispensed *ut supra*. Died 1869, Mar. 2. (71)

1857, Feb. 3. *George Hamilton (Chichester), 3rd marquess of Donegall. Dispensed from installation Mar. 10. In place of No. 33. Died 1883, Oct. 20. (72)

1859, May 24. Arthur Wills Blundell Sandys Trumbull Windsor (Hill), 4th marquess of Downshire. In place of No. 59. Dispensed from installation July 2. Died 1868, Aug. 6. (73)

1860, June 13. Richard Edmund St. Lawrence (Boyle), 9th earl of Cork and earl of Orrery. Dispensed from installation June 20. In place of No. 51. Died 1904, June 22. (74)

1864, Jan. 28. Frederick Temple (Hamilton-Blackwood), baron Dufferin and Claneboye, afterwards marquess of Dufferin and Ava. Dispensed from installation Feb. 11. In place of No. 64. Died 1902, Feb. 12. (75)

1864, Mar. 31. Charles (Brownlow), 2nd baron Lurgan. Invested at Dublin Castle Mar. 31. Dispensed from investiture Apr. 12. In place of No. 44. Died 1882, Jan. 16. (76)

[1864, Sept. 14. George Ponsonby (O'Callaghan), 2nd viscount Lismore, was nominated in place of No. 68, but relinquished the honour.]

1865, Dec. 28. James Molyneux (Caulfield), 3rd earl of Charlemont. Dispensed from installation 1866, Feb. 26. In place of No. 68. Died 1892, Jan. 12. (77)

* The marquess of Donegall was nominated to fill the vacancy caused by the death of No. 33, the king of Hanover, but was not invested. He was permitted to wear the insignia by warrant of the grand master, 1857, Jan. 23, and these were delivered to him by Ulster King of Arms, Feb. 3.

1866, Mar. 13. EDWIN RICHARD WINDHAM (WYNDHAM-QUIN), 3rd earl of Dunraven and Mountearl. Dispensed from installation Mar. 31. In place of No. 54. Died 1871, Oct. 6. (78)

1868, Feb. 7. HENRY FRANCIS SEYMOUR (MOORE), 3rd marquess of Drogheda. Dispensed from installation Feb. 20. In place of No. 58. Died 1892, June 29. (79)

1868, Mar. 18. H.R.H. ALBERT EDWARD, prince of Wales, K.G., etc. Declared by sign manual an extra knight with precedence above all other knights. Installed at St. Patrick's cathedral 1868, Apr. 18. Succeeded as Edward VII., 1901, Jan. 22. (80)

1868, Nov. 17. JOHN HENRY DE LA POER (BERESFORD), 5th marquess of Waterford. Dispensed from installation 1869, Jan. 16. In place of No. 73. Died 1895, Oct. 23. (81)

1868, Nov. 17. JOHN (CRICHTON), 3rd earl Erne. Dispensed *ut supra*. In place of No. 62. Died 1885, Oct. 3. (82)

1869, Jan. 18. RICHARD SOUTHWELL (BOURKE), 6th earl of Mayo, governor-general of India. Created a knight extraordinary by sign manual 1868, Nov. 11, but became a knight in ordinary in place of No. 71. Ceremonies dispensed with 1868, Nov. 17. Invested at Calcutta 1869, Jan. 18. Installation dispensed with Apr. 12. Died 1872, Feb. 8. (83)

1869, Mar. 30. H.R.H. prince ARTHUR WILLIAM PATRICK ALBERT, K.G., afterwards duke of Connaught and Strathearn. Declared by sign manual an extra knight with precedence after the prince of Wales. Installation dispensed with May 1. (84)

1869, June 2. GRANVILLE LEVESON (PROBY), 4th earl of Carysfort. In place of No. 57. Died 1872, May 18. (85)

1869, June 2. ARCHIBALD BRABAZON SPARROW (ACHESON), 4th earl of Gosford. In place of No. 63. (86)

1871, Aug. 2. MERVYN (WINGFIELD), 7th viscount Powerscourt. In place of No. 41. Died 1904, June 5. (87)

1871, Aug. 2. THOMAS ARTHUR JOSEPH (SOUTHWELL), 4th viscount Southwell. In place of No. 52. Died 1878, Apr. 26. (88)

1872, Feb. 29. ROBERT SHAPLAND (CAREW), 2nd baron Carew. In place of No. 78. Died 1881, Sept. 8. (89)

1872, June 1. VALENTINE AUGUSTUS (BROWNE), 4th earl of Kenmare. Invested privately at the Vice-Regal Lodge June 3. In place of No. 83. (90)

1873, Feb. 20. WILLIAM (HARE), 3rd earl of Listowel. In place of No. 69. (91)

1874, Aug. 31. WILLIAM (PROBY), 5th earl of Carysfort. In place of No. 50 (92)

1874, Aug. 31. GEORGE HENRY ROBERT CHARLES WILLIAM (VANE-TEMPEST), 5th marquess of Londonderry. Nominated Apr. 23. In place of No. 50. Died 1884, Nov. 5. (93)

1876, May 13. WINDHAM THOMAS (WYNDHAM-QUIN), 4th earl of Dunraven and Mountearl Nominated 1872, Aug. 7, but not invested till 1876, May 13. In place of No. 85. (94)

1877, Mar. 3. WILLIAM DROGO (MONTAGU), 7th duke of Manchester. In place of No. 46. Died 1890, Mar. 21. (95)

1879, Feb 8 HENRY JOHN REUBEN (DAWSON-DAMER), 3rd earl of Portarlington. In place of No 88 Died 1889, Mar. 1. (96)

1880, May 14 (20). H.R H ALFRED ERNEST ALBERT, duke of Edinburgh, duke of Saxony, prince of Saxe-Coburg and Gotha, K.G., etc Declared by sign manual an extra knight with precedence next to the prince of Wales, as a mark of the sense entertained by Her Majesty of the services rendered by H R H in administering relief in Ireland. Died 1900, July 30. (97)

1882, Jan. 17. THOMAS (O'HAGAN),1st baron O'Hagan and formerly lord chancellor of Ireland. Invested in the Vice-regal Lodge Jan. 17. In place of No. 89. Died 1885, Feb 1. (98)

1882, Apr. 11. CHICHESTER SAMUEL (PARKINSON-FORTESCUE), baron Carlingford, afterwards baron Clermont. Nominated Feb. 9. In place of No. 76. Died 1898, Jan. 30. (99)

1884, May 8 WILLIAM ULICK TRISTRAM (ST LAWRENCE), 4th earl of Howth. In place of No. 72 (100)

1885, Feb. 9. LUKE (WHITE), 2nd baron Annaly. Nominated Jan. 1. Invested at Dublin Feb. 9. In place of No. 55. Died 1888, Mar. 17. (101)

1885, Feb. 9. THOMAS SPRING (RICE), 2nd baron Monteagle of Brandon. Nominated and invested *ut supra*. In place of No. 94. (102)

1885, Nov. 28. GARNET JOSEPH (WOLSELEY), viscount Wolseley. In
place of No. 98.   (103)

1885, Nov. 28. THOMAS (TAYLOUR),3rd marquess of Headfort
Invested at Dublin Nov. 28. In place of No. 82. Died 1894,
July 22   (104)

1887, June 28. H.R.H prince ALBERT VICTOR CHRISTIAN EDWARD,
of Wales, K.G., afterwards duke of Clarence. An extra
knight with precedence after the duke of Connaught. Died
1892, Jan. 14.   (105)

1888, Apr. 26. JAMES EDWARD WILLIAM THEOBALD (BUTLER), 3rd
marquess of Ormonde   In place of No. 101.   (106)

1889, Apr. 4. JOHN HENRY (CRICHTON), 4th earl Erne. In place of
No. 96   (107)

1890, Feb 7. EDWARD NUGENT (LEESON), 6th earl of Milltown.
Nominated 1889, Sept 26   Invested at Dublin Castle 1890,
Feb. 7 In place of No. 70. Died 1890, May 30.   (108)

1890, May 24   FRANCIS CHARLES (NEEDHAM), 3rd earl of Kilmorey.
- Nominated Apr. 22   Invested in St. Patrick's Hall, Dublin
Castle. In place of No. 95   (109)

1890, Aug 29. LAWRENCE (PARSONS), 4th earl of Rosse. Nominated
July 7. Invested Aug. 29 in St. Patrick's Hall, Dublin
Castle. In place of No. 108.   .(110)

1890, Dec. 18 Prince WILLIAM AUGUSTUS EDWARD, of Saxe
Weimar. Nominated Sept. 30. Invested at Windsor
Nov. 24. An extra knight with precedence after the duke
of Cambridge. Died 1902, Nov. 16   (111)

1892, Mar. 18. WILLIAM HALE JOHN CHARLES (PERY), 5th earl of
Limerick. Nominated Feb 8. In place of No. 77. Died
1896, Aug. 8.   (112)

1892, Aug. 5. EDWARD DONOUGH (O'BRIEN), 14th baron Inchiquin
In place of No. 79   Died 1900, Apr. 8.   (113)

1894, Nov. 3. FREDERICK EDWARD GOULD (LAMBART), 9th earl of
Cavan. Nominated Sept. 25. Invested privately at the
Vice-Regal Lodge. In place of No. 104. Died 1900,
July 14.   (114)

1896, Feb 25. EDWARD CECIL (GUINESS), 1st baron Iveagh.
Nominated 1895, Nov 27. Invested in St Patrick's Hall
1896, Feb. 25. In place of No. 81.   (115)

1897, Feb. 11. JAMES (ALEXANDER), 4th earl of Caledon. Nominated 1896, Nov 14. Invested at Dublin Castle 1897, Feb. 11. In place of No. 112. Died 1898, Apr. 27. (116)

1897, Aug. 20. H.R.H. GEORGE FREDERICK ERNEST ALBERT, duke of York, afterwards prince of Wales Nominated July 6 Invested in St Patrick's Hall Aug 20 An extra knight. (117)

1897, Aug 20. FREDERICK SLEIGH (ROBERTS), baron, afterwards earl Roberts Nominated June 4. Invested in St. Patrick's Hall Aug. 20. In place of No. 67. (118)

1898, Mar. 15. ARTHUS SAUNDERS WILLIAM CHARLES FOX (GORE), 7th earl of Arran. Nominated Mar. 9. Invested Mar. 15. In place of No 99. Died 1901, Mar 14. (119)

1899, Mar. 4. GEORGE (BINGHAM), 4th earl of Lucan. Nominated 1898, May 8. Invested in St. Patrick's Hall 1899, Mar. 2 In place of No. 116 (120)

1900, Aug. 29. JAMES FRANCIS (BERNARD), 4th earl of Bandon. Nominated Apr. 24. Invested privately at the Vice Regal Lodge, Aug. 29, the usual formalities being dispensed with in consequence of Court mourning. In place of No. 113. (121)

1900, Aug. 29. LUKE GERALD (DILLON), 4th baron Clonbrock. Nominated Aug. 2. Invested *ut supra*. In place of No 114. (122)

1901, June 10. THOMAS (PAKENHAM), 5th earl of Longford. Nominated May 15. Knighted and invested at St. James's Palace, June 11 In place of No. 119. (123)

1902, Mar. 15. HENRY DE LA POER (BERESFORD), 6th marquess of Waterford. In place of No 75. (124)

1902, Aug 11. LOWRY EGERTON (COLE), 4th earl of Enniskillen. An extra knight (on the King's Coronation), became an ordinary knight in place of No. 65 Privately invested in the Throne Room at Dublin Castle. (125)

1902, Aug. 11. DUDLEY CHARLES FITZGERALD-DE-ROS), 24th lord de Ros. An extra knight (on the King's Coronation), became an ordinary knight in place of No. 87. Invested *ut supra*. (126)

1904. DERMOT ROBERT WYNDHAM (BOURKE), 7th earl of Mayo. In place of No. 74. Invested Feb 3, 1905. (127)

Knights of the Bath.

Knights of the Bath.

SOVEREIGNS.

See list of sovereigns given seriatim under the Order of the Garter.

GRAND MASTERS and (subsequently) First and Principal Knights Grand Cross.

1725, May 27. JOHN (MONTAGU), 2nd duke of Montagu. Died 1749, July 16.

1767, Dec. 30. Prince FREDERICK, of Brunswick Luneburg, afterwards duke of York. Died 1827, Jan. 5.

1827. WILLIAM HENRY, duke of Clarence. Succeeded as Sovereign as William IV., in 1830, June 26.

1837, Dec. 16. AUGUSTUS FREDERICK, duke of Sussex. Died 1843, Apr. 21.

1843, May 31. FRANCIS ALBERT AUGUSTUS CHARLES EMANUEL, prince Consort. Died 1861, Dec. 14.

1897, June 22. ALBERT EDWARD, prince of Wales. Succeeded as Sovereign of the Order as Edward VII., in 1901, Jan. 22.

1901, Feb. 26. ARTHUR WILLIAM PATRICK ALBERT, duke of Connaught and Streathearn.

KNIGHTS OF THE BATH (K.B.).
From 1204 to 1815.

1127 at Pentecost. GEOFFREY, son of FULK, count of Anjou (by Henry I. at Rouen).

after 1204, July 18. THOMAS ESTURMY.

1205, Nov. 5. THEODORIC LE TYES.

1233, June 11. WILLIAM LONGSPÉE.

1233, June 11. ROGER (BIGOD), 5th earl of Norfolk.

1233, June 11. HUGH (DE VERE), 4th earl of Oxford.

1234, June 11. GILBERT (MARSHAL), 6th earl of Pembroke.

after 1249, July 26. STEPHEN DE SALINIS.

1249, Dec. 25. JOHN DE SIMNEVIL.

1252, Dec. 25. ALEXANDER III., king of Scotland, and 20 others.

1253, Oct. 6. REGINALD DE COKER' (to be made at the coming feast of St. Edward   Writ tested at the Camp before Benanges).

1253, Oct. 6. BERTRANDUS DE CRESSY, valettus to the king's half-brother Guy, of Lusignan (to be made, etc., *ut supra*).

1253, Oct. 6. INGERAM DE FENES (to be made, etc., *ut supra*).

1253, Oct. 7. WARIN DE FRUGES' (to be made at the coming feast of St. Edward and to have accoutrements sicut aliis novis militibus.   Writ tested at the Camp before Benanges).

1253, Oct. 15. WILLIAM DE COURTENAY and a companion (to be made at the coming feast of All Saints.   Writ tested *ut supra*).

1253, Oct. 15 GAUCHER DE GOMARCYN, a relative of Peter of Savoy; together with two companions (to be made, etc , *ut supra*).

1253, Oct. 15. ROBERT DE CRENEQUER (to be made, etc., *ut supra*, with accoutrements sicut novis militibus nostris).

1254–5. MATTHEW HANYBAL.

? 1256. DROGO DE BARENTINO, whom the king of England in Gascony decorated with the belt of a knight.

(EDWARD I.).

1302–3. PETER DE LA FOIX.

1302–3. JOHN DE HORNE, as a Banneret.

1302–3. ROBERT DE UFFORD, as a Banneret.

1302–3. JOHN DE FELTON, as a bachelor.

1302–3. RICHARD DE ————, as a simple knight.

1302–3. JOHN DE DAGWORTH, as a simple Banneret.

1302–3 (1303, May 23). RICHARD DE STRATTON, as a simple Banneret.

1302–3. JOHN DE CORMAILLES, as a simple Banneret.

1302–3. WILLIAM DE BOTECOURT, as a simple Banneret.

1302–3. JOHN DE BERKELEY, as a simple Banneret.

1302–3. JOHN GIFFARD, as a simple Banneret.

1302–3. PHILIP DE NEVILLE, as a Banneret.

1304–5 PAIN DE TIBETOT.

1304–5 GEORGE DE THORPE.

1304–5. JOHN DOUVEDALE.

1304–5. JOHN DE NEVILLE.

1304–5. THOMAS DE LATIMER.

1304–5. RICHARD GREY.

1304–5. PETER SKERK.

1304–5. WILLIAM CLERK.

1304–5. JOHN DE WATERVILLE.

1304–5. JOHN LE STRANGE.

1304–5. HUGH DE CROFTE.

1304–5. BARTHOLOMEW DYNEVILE.

The names of all the knights (267 in all) made at Whitsuntide, 34 Edward I., on the occasion of the knighting of Edward, prince of Wales, afterwards Edward II.*

1306, May 22. DOMINUS EDWARDUS, princeps Walliae.

1306, May 22. JOHANNES DE WARENNA [7th earl of Surrey], son [in-law] to the count of Bar.

1306, May 22. EDMUNDUS [John] DE ARUNDEL.

1306, May 22. THOMAS DE GREILLY.

1306, May 22. JOHANNES DE LA WARE [Mare] [lord de la Mare].

1306, May 22. THOMAS DE FERERS.

1306, May 22. BARTHOLOMEWS DE ENFEUD.

1306, May 22. JOHANNES [son of Roger] DE MOUBRAY [2nd lord Mowbray].

1306, May 22. ALANUS PLOKENET.

1306, May 22. AUNGERUS filius Henrici.

1306, May 22. GILBERTUS DE CLARE, filius domini Thomae de Clare.

---

* The above list of 267 knights made on the occasion of the knighting of Edward Prince of Wales, is printed by Ashmole, in the 1672 Edition of the 'Institutions, &c.'... of the Garter,' pp. 38-9. Ashmole there states as his authority the *Rotulus computi Johannis de Drokensford Custodis Magnae Guarderobae regis*, a MS. then in the possession of the King's Remembrancer. Drokensford's wardrobe account for the 34th year of Edward I. is still preserved at H.M. Record Office, among the Exchequer Q.R. But I have been quite unable to find in this account the lists of knights here printed. Running parallel or contemporaneous with the big yearly Wardrobe account for this year, 34 Edward I., there are several smaller files and accounts (in especial Miscellaneous Rolls Chancery, Wardrobe and Household Accounts, ⅓⅜, and Exchequer Accounts, Q. R. Bundle 369, Roll No. 4). These accounts give the names of a small proportion of the knights printed in the text here, frequently with variations in the form of the name or in the description. Where the difference is material, I have incorporated it in the text by printing the variant within square brackets. In addition, the smaller accounts give the names of two persons to be knighted, which do not appear in Ashmole; but are printed above. These two names are as follows :— Males [Malise] son of [and himself afterwards 8th] Earl of Stratherne, to be knighted at All Saints [Nov. 1] with 5 others unnamed. Walter Lislebone, banneret: to be knighted at Xmas.

1306, May 22.　EDMUNDUS DE CORNUBIA.

1306, May 22.　JOHANNES DE FRIVILL.

1306, May 22.　WILLELMUS DE FREIGNE.

1306, May 22.　AMARICUS DE FOSSAD [come from afar].

1306, May 22.　FULCIUS filius Warini.

1306, May 22.　WALTERUS DE HUGEFORD.

1306, May 22.　STEPHANUS DE BURGHASH.

1306, May 22.　JACOBUS DE NORTWOODE.

1306, May 22.　HUMPHRIDUS DE WALDENE.

1306, May 22.　ROGERUS DE CHAUNDOS.

1306, May 22.　JOHANNES DE DEEN.

1306, May 22.　WILHELMUS DE LA ZOUCHE.

1306, May 22.　RICHARDUS LOVEL.

1306, May 22.　ROGERUS DE MORTUOMARI.

1306, May 22.　WALTERUS HAKELUT.

1306, May 22.　ROGERUS DE BANFOU [Beaufoy].

1306, May 22.　GALFRIDUS DE SEYE.

1306, May 22.　RICHARDUS [DE] PORTESEIE [tanquam banerettus].

1306, May 22.　EGIDIUS DE BREHEUS.

1306, May 22.　WALTERUS DE MOLLESWORTH.

1306, May 22.　RETHERICUS DE ISPANIA.

1306, May 22.　PETRUS DE GAVASTON.

1306, May 22.　THOMAS DE VERDON.

1306, May 22.　HUMFRIDUS DE BASSINGBOURN.

1306, May 22. NICHOLAUS KRYELL.

1306, May 22. ROBERTUS, filius Roberti filii Pagani.

1306, May 22. JOHANNES DE HARECOURT.

1306, May 22. JOHANNES, filius domini Johannis de Sulleye.

1306, May 22. WILLIELMUS TRACY.

1306, May 22. HUGO, filius domini Hugonis le Despenser.

1306, May 22. WILLELMUS DE HUNTINGFEUD.

1306, May 22. THOMAS BARDOLF [tanquam banerettus].

1306, May 22. NICHOLAUS MALEMEYNS.

1306, May 22. ROBERTUS DE SCALES.

1306, May 22. WILLIELMUS TRUSSEL.

1306, May 22. JOHANNES DE HANTS.

1306, May 22. WILLELMUS DE MONTEACUTE.

1306, May 22. THOMAS DE MULTON.

1306, May 22. WALTERUS DE MONTGOMERIE.

1306, May 22. ROGERUS filius domini Rogeri de Mortuomari.

1306, May 22. EUSTACHIUS DE WHYTENEYE.

1306, May 22. JOHANNES MAUTRAVERS [tanquam banerettus].

1306, May 22. THOMAS DE VEER, filius comitis Oxonie.

1306, May 22. THOMAS DE LODELAWE.

1306, May 22. WILLELMUS DE BERNYNGHAM.

1306, May 22. GRIFFINUS filius Griffini de la Pole.

1306, May 22. WILLELMUS DE LODELAWE.

1306, May 22. PHILIPPUS DE COURTENAY.

8

1306, May 22.   URIANUS DE SANCTO PETRO.

1306, May 22.   WARINUS DE BASSINGBURN [nouveau chevalier].

1306, May 22.   JOHANNES LE BLOUNT, mayor of London.

1306, May 22.   JOHANNES DENRE.

1306, May 22.   JOHANNES DE INSULA.

1306, May 22.   THOMAS DE LUCY.

1306, May 22.   RADULPHUS DE BOTETOURTE.

1306, May 22.   HUGO [Hugelin] de Mailly.

1306, May 22.   RADULPHUS DE KAMOYS.

1306, May 22.   PETRUS filius domini Petri de Malolacu [Mauley]

1306, May 22.   EDMUNDUS DE WILLINGTON.

1306, May 22.   ROBERTUS DE KENDALE.

1306, May 22.   HENRICUS DE DEN.

1306, May 22.   JOHANNES DE NEVILL.

1306, May 22.   ROGERUS DE INGELFELD.

1306, May 22.   HUGO BRABOEF

1306, May 22.   JOHANNES DE WESTON.

1306, May 22   JOHANNES filius Warini.

1306, May 22   THOMAS DE PONYNGES.

1306, May 22   JOHANNES DE FOXLEY.

1306, May 22.   JOHANNES DE WALKINGHAM.

1306, May 22.   WILLELMUS DE HARDEN

1306, May 22.   RADULPHUS DE WEDEN.

1306, May 22.   JOHANES DE MERYETH.

1306, May 22.   RADULPHUS DE ROLLESTON.

1306, May 22. JOHANNES DE MAUDUIT.

1306, May 22. THOMAS DE BOIVILLE.

1306, May 22. WILLIELMUS CORBET.

1306, May 22. WILLIELMUS BRABAZON.

1306, May 22. GEORGIUS [Gregory] DE THORNETONE.

1306, May 22. JOHANNES DE LA PENNE [nouveau chevalier].

1306, May 22. JOHANNES DE BYKEBYRY.

1306, May 22. WILLIELMUS DE COSYNGTON.

1306, May 22. RADULPHUS BAGOT.

1306, May 22. WILLELMUS DE BASSINGES.

1306, May 22. ANDREAS DE SAKEVILLE.

1306, May 22. NICOLAUS PERSHOTS.

1306, May 22. MORGANUS AP MEREDUK.

1306, May 22. UMFRIDUS DE BOUNE.

1306, May 22. WALTERUS DE SKYDEMORE

1306, May 22. JOHANNES CHAUNDOS.

1306, May 22. WALTERUS DE DERLYNGHAM.

1306, May 22. WALTERUS DE STIRKELONDE.

1306, May 22. JOHANNES DE CLYNDON.

1306, May 22. INGELRAMUS BELET [simple knight].

1306, May 22. LAURENTIUS DE HOLLEBECHE.

1306, May 22. JOHANNES DE STAUNTONE.

1306, May 22. JOHANNES DE WACHESHAM.

1306, May 22. JOHANNES DE LA MARE.

1306, May 22.   HUGO HOWEL.

1306, May 22.   WILLELMUS DE MENYMRATE [Momyrate], socius Ameurey de Fossad.

1306, May 22.   WILLELMUS PYROT, socius Stephani de Burways

1306, May 22.,   JOHANNES SAUVAGE.

1306, May 22.   PHILIPPUS DE VYRELEY.

1306, May 22.   ROBERTUS LOVEL.

1306, May 22.   ADAM WALRAN.

1306, May 22.   JOHANNES DE PENBRUG.

1306, May 22   ROGERUS PYCHARD.

1306, May 22.   HENRICUS LE MOIGNE.

1306, May 22.   ROBERTUS DE LACY.

1306, May 22   JOHANNES DE BOILLAUNDE.

1306, May 22.   JOHANNES DE GUYSE.

1306, May 22.   WILLELMUS MOTOUN.

1306, May 22.   ROGERUS WALEYS.

1306, May 22.   PHILIPPUS LE LOU.

1306, May 22.   JOHANNES DE HINTON.

1306, May 22.   JOHANNES DE TWYFORD.

1306, May 22.   RICHARDUS DE BREHEUS.

1306, May 22.   STEPHANUS DE COBBEHAM.

1306, May 22.   JOHANNES DE HAULO.

1306, May 22   JOHANNES DE SANWICO.

1306, May 22.   JOHANNES DE MOUNTENEY.

1306, May 22.   ROBERTUS LE CONESTABLE.

1306, May 22.   JOHANNES MARTEYN.

1306, May 22. JOHANNES DE BELLO CAMPO.

1306, May 22. ROBERTUS DE ROS.

1306, May 22. RADULPHUS BASSET.

1306, May 22. PETRUS DE GRISLE.

1306, May 22. THOMAS MALORIE.

1306, May 22. RICHARDUS DE SCULTON.

1306, May 22 WILLELMUS DE HAUNDESACRE.

1306, May 22. JOHANNES DE THOUTHORP.

1306, May 22. WALTERUS DE ROMESEYE.

1306, May 22. JOHANNES DE RUDA [Routh].

1306, May 22. PETRUS DE BOSOUN.

1306, May 22. NICHOLAUS DE GENEVILLE.

1306, May 22. JOHANNES DE KNOVILLE [son of Gilbert de Knovill].

1306, May 22. JOHANNES DE LACY.

1306, May 22. WILLIELMUS BERNAK.

1306, May 22. RICHARDUS DANIEL.

1306, May 22. ROBERTUS DE WYGKHAM.

1306, May 22. ROBERTUS ACHARD.

1306, May 22. WILLELMUS DE HERPEDEN.

1306, May 22. JACOBUS DE LAMBOURNE.

1306, May 22. JOHANNES MAUNCEL.

1306, May 22. ROBERTUS DE WYVILL.

1306, May 22. PHILIPPUS LE ROUS.

1306, May 22. JOHANNES COMYN.

1306, May 22.   JOHANNES DE SOMERY.

1306, May 22.   JOHANNES DE LUNGEVILL.

1306, May 22.   JOHANNES DE HARPEFELD.

1306, May 22.   EGIDIUS DE ASTELE.

1306, May 22.   JOHANNES DE BOIVILL.

1306, May 22.   HENRICUS filius Conani.

1306, May 22.   ROGERUS DE BURTON.

1306, May 22.   JOHANNES DE MULTON.

1306, May 22.   GODEFRIDUS DE MEAUX.

1306, May 22.   JOHANNES DE PLESCIS.

1306, May 22.   EDMUNDUS DE PLESCIS.

1306, May 22.   WILLELMUS DE HOLLANDE.

1306, May 22.   HENRICUS DE RYPSFORD.

1306, May 22.   THOMAS DE ZEDESEN.

1306, May 22.   JOHANNES DE LYNGEYNE.

1306, May 22.   ROGERUS DE BAVENT.

1306, May 22.   GALFRIDUS DE COLEVILL.

1306, May 22.   JOHANNES, filius Johannis Mautravers.

1306, May 22.   JOHANNES CONQUEST.

1306, May 22.   WILLELMUS DE STOPHAM.

1306, May 22.   RADULPHUS DE DRYBY.

1306, May 22.   THOMAS DE GREY.

1306, May 22.   ROBERTUS DE LA MARE.

1306, May 22.   THOMAS CORBET.

1306, May 22. JOHANNES DE HERYE.

1306, May 22. ROBERTUS DE HOO.

1306, May 22. JOHANNES DE LACY.

1306, May 22. WILLELMUS DE MANNEBY.

1306, May 22. JOHANNES DE MORTONE.

1306, May 22. GERARDUS DE AILLESFORD.

1306, May 22. GILBERTUS DE ATON.

1306, May 22. RICARDUS DE BERLEY.

1306, May 22. JOHANNES DE NEUBOURGH.

1306, May 22. JOHANNES DE LA POILLE.

1306, May 22. ROBERTUS, filius GUIDONIS.

1306, May 22. HUGO HOSE.

1306, May 22. WILLELMUS DE GOLDINGTON.

1306, May 22. WALTERUS filius Domini J de Insula.

1306, May 22. THOMAS DE BROMPTON.

1306, May 22. WILLELMUS DE WROTESLE.

1306, May 22. RICHARDUS HUWYS.

1306, May 22. ROBERTUS DE HILDYARD.

1306, May 22. JOHANNES DE KYRKEBY.

1306, May 22. THOMAS DE LEUKENORE.

1306, May 22. PETRUS DE EVERCY.

1306, May 22. WARINUS DE SCARGIL.

1306, May 22. GERARDUS DE USFLET.

1306, May 22. PETRUS DE BURGATE.

1306, May 22. ROBERTUS DE FAUDON.

1306, May 22. WILLELMUS DE SAUSTONE.

1306, May 22. JOHANNES MAULEVERER.

1306, May 22. WILLELMUS DE LUCY.

1306, May 22. ROGERUS DE CHEDLE.

1306, May 22. HUGO DE DULTON.

1306, May 22. JOHANNES DE HAVERYNGTON.

1306, May 22. ROGERUS DE SOMERVILLE.

1306, May 22. ADAM DE WALTON.

1306, May 22. NICHOLAUS DE SHELDON.

1306, May 22. WILLELMUS DE WEILONDE.

1306, May 22. WALTERUS DE FAUCUMBERG.

1306, May 22. NICHOLAUS DE RYE.

1306, May 22. ROGERUS DE GRYMESTON.

1306, May 22. HENRICUS DE ERDYNGTON.

1306, May 22 WILLELMUS DAUTRIE.

1306, May 22. JOHANNES DE LAUNEY.

1306, May 22. JOHANNES DE RYSON.

1306, May 22. HENRICUS BEAUSUN [BEAUFOU].

1306, May 22. ROGERUS filius Domini Thomae Corbet.

1306, May 22. HUGO DE PYKEWORTH.

1306, May 22. BALDEWINUS DE COLNE.

1306, May 22. ROBERTUS DE SKALE.

1306, May 22. HENRICUS DE BIRY.

1306, May 22. HENRICUS DE BERMYNGHAM.

1306, May 22. WALTERUS LE POURE.

1306, May 22. THOMAS DE BECHUM.

1306, May 22. WALTERUS filius Humfridi.

1306, May 22. EDMUNDUS PECCHE.

1306, May 22. JOHANNES DE TREIAGU.

1306, May 22. RICHARDUS FOLIOT.

1306, May 22. RICHARDUS DE ECHEBASTON.

1306, May 22. ROBERTUS DE GODEMANSTON.

1306, May 22. ADAM DE EVERINGHAM.

1306, May 22. JOHANNES DE BASSINGBOURN.

1306, May 22. ADAM DE WANERVILLE

1306, May 22. WILLELMUS DE SOMERCOTES.

1306, May 22. THOMAS, filius Domini T. de Chaworth.

1306, May 22. RADULPHUS DE KELE.

1306, May 22. PETRUS DE LEKEBURNE.

1306, May 22. HUGO filius Henrici.

1306, May 22. JOHANNES DE SALSBIRI.

1306, May 22. RICHARDUS DE RYVERS.

1306, May 22. JOHANNES filius Johannis de Wegetone.

1306, May 22. JOHANNES LE ROUS.

1306, May 22. GEORGIUS DU CHASTEL.

1306, May 22. WILLELMUS DE LA MOTE.

1306, May 22. WILLELMUS DE BAYOUS.

1306, May 22. WILLELMUS MARMYON.

1306, May 22. WILLELMUS ROSEL.

1306, May 22. JOHANNES DE LANGETON.

1306, May 22. WILLELMUS LITTEBON [Villabon].

1306, May 22. JOHANNES DE PABENHAM [tanquam banerettus].

1306, May 22. THOMAS MORDAC [tanquam simplex miles].

1306, May 22. JACOBUS DE NORTON [tanquam simplex miles].

1306, May 22. JOHANNES DE BELHOUS [or his attorney].

1306, May 22. BRANKALEO DE BOLOIGNE [Drantaleon de Ordalo *or* Endalo de Bologne].

1306, May 22. JOHANNES PYKARD.

1306, May 22. WALTERUS DE KYNGESHEVEDE [Kingshemede; valettus of the Household].

1306, May 22. ROBERTUS DE WATERVILL.

1306, May 22 ROGERUS DE KERDESTON.

1306, May 22. JOHANNES DE DAVENTRE.

1316, July 3 RICHARD DE RODNEY (at Keynsham).

1322, Sept. 10. HENRY PERCY.

1323, June 1. JOHN DE LA HAYE.

1323. WILLIAM DE DOUNTON.

1323 WILLIAM WAYKAM.

1323. HENRY TILLY.

1323. HENRY LONGCHAMP.

1323. RAYMOND DURANT, as a Banneret with his companion as a simple knight.

1324, Aug. 10. HUGH DE POYNTZ, as a Banneret.

1324, Aug. 13. PETER DE BOXSTEDE, by the hand of his cousin, Sir Henry de Boxstede.

1324, Aug. 13. RICHARD PYKE, by the king's hand.

1324, Aug. 13. THOMAS DE MARLBERGH.

1324, Oct. 24. PETER DE LA HORSE.

1324, Oct. 31. HUGH DE PLESSIS, as a Banneret, by the king's hand.

1325, Apr. 2. HUGH DE NEVILL.

1326, Mar. 31. JAMES BOTILLER of Ireland, as a Banneret.

1326, Apr. 19. WILLIAM DE MONTACUTE, as a Banneret, by the hands of Thomas de Langford at London.

1326, Apr. 19. EBULO LE STRANGE, as a Banneret, by the hands of Thomas de Langford.

1326, Apr. 19. ROGER DE BOURNE, by same.

1326, Apr. 19. ROGER ONLY, by same.

1326, Apr. 19. MATTHEW FITZHERBERT, by same.

1326, Apr. 19. JOHN DE GRAS, by same.

1326, Apr. 19. THOMAS WEST, by same.

1326, Apr. 19. RYCE AP GRIFFITH, by same.

1326, Apr. 19. THOMAS DE WESTON, by same.

1326, Apr. 19. NICHOLAS DE CANTELOU, by same.

1326, Apr. 19. THOMAS DE GOUSHULL, by same.

1326, Apr. 19. HENRY DE HARNHALL, by same.

1326, Apr. 19. ADAM DE MOLESTON (MOLELESTON), by same.

1326, Apr. 19. WALTER DE FAUCONBERGE, by same.

1326, Apr. 19. WILLIAM DE ALBEMARLE, by same.

1326, Apr. 19. JOHN DE KIRKETON, by same.

1326, Apr. 19. HENRY LE VAVASOUR, by same.

1326, Apr. 19. ROGER DEYNCOURT, by the hands of Thomas de Langford.

1326, Apr. 19. WILLIAM PEVERELL, by same.

1327, Jan. 20. JOHN DE BOHUN, the king's cousin, as an earl.

1327, Jan. 20. EDMUND DE MORTIMER, as a Banneret.

1327, Jan. 20. ROGER DE MORTIMER, as a Banneret.

1327, Jan. 20. GEOFFRY DE MORTIMER, as a Banneret.

1327, Jan. 20. GERARD DE LA BRET, as a Banneret.

1327, Jan. 20. HUGH DE COURTENAY, as a Banneret.

1327, Jan. 20 RALPH DE WYLINTON, as a Banneret.

1327, Jan. 20. RALPH DAUBENEY, as a Banneret

1327, Jan. 20. JOHN DE WILLOUGHBY, as a Banneret.

1327, Jan. 20. EDWARD STRADLING, as a Banneret.

1327, Jan. 20 RALPH STAFFORD, afterwards lord and earl of Stafford, as a Banneret.

1327, Jan. 20. JOHN DE MOELES, as a Banneret.

1327, Jan. 20. WILLIAM DE PERCY, as a Banneret.

1327, Jan 20. GERARD DE LISLE, as a Banneret.

1327, Jan. 20. PETER BRETON, as a Banneret.

1327, Jan. 20. ROGER DE STRANGE, as a Banneret.

1327, Jan. 20. ERNOMVILLE DE POITIERS, as a Banneret.

1327, Jan. 20. JOHN DE NEVILLE, as a Banneret; and four others.

1327, Jan. 20. WILLIAM DE WILLOUGHBY, as a Banneret.

1327, Jan. 20. JOHN DE RALEE, as a Banneret.

1327, Jan. 20. RALPH DE BLOYON, as a Banneret.

1327, Jan. 20. OTO BOTETOURT, as a Banneret.

1327, Jan. 20. WILLIAM DAUBENEY, as a Banneret.

1327, Jan. 20. ROBERT BRENTE, as a Banneret.

1327, Jan. 20. JOHN DE CHERNSTONE, as a Banneret.

1327, Jan. 20. JOHN DE SUTTON, as a Banneret.

1327, Jan. 20. ALEXANDER DE COBLEDYL, as a Banneret.

1327, Jan. 20. SAYER DE ROCHEFORD, as a Banneret.

1327, Jan. 20. WILLIAM CHEYNEY, as a Banneret.

1327, Jan. 20. REGINALD DE LA MARE, as a Banneret.

1327, Jan. 20. ROBERT DE BREUS, as a Banneret.

1327, Jan. 20. SIMON FITZRALPH, as a Banneret.

1327, Jan. 20. HUGH ABETOT, as a Banneret.

1327, Jan. 20. JOHN DE ROUS, as a Banneret.

1327, Jan. 20. WILLIAM DE EVEREUX.

1327, Jan. 20. JOHN DE HOTHAM.

1327, Jan. 31. The king, EDWARD III.

1329, Oct. 22. JOHN DE CAMBRIDGE (Justice Itinerant), as a Banneret.

1329, Oct. 22. EDWARD LE BLOUNT, as a Banneret.

1329, Oct. 22. PETER DE THORNTONE, as a Banneret.

1329, Oct. 22. RICHARD DE BAJOCIS (BAICUS), as a Banneret.

1329, Oct. 22. BANCO DE LERE, a Lombard, as a Banneret.

1330. THOMAS DE BRADESTON, as a Banneret.

1330. EDMUND DE CORNWALL, as a Banneret (son of lord Edmund de Cornwall).

1330. WILLIAM DE POMEROY, as a Banneret, and three others.

1331. WALTER DE MANNY, as a Banneret.

1332. ROBERT DE SCORESBURGH (Justice Itinerant), as a Banneret.

1332. WILLIAM DE DENAM (Baron of the Exchequer), as a Banneret.

1332. RICHARD DE ALDEBURGH (a Justice of Common Pleas), as a Banneret.

1332. JOHN DE SHARDELOWE (a Justice of Common Pleas), as a Banneret.

1332. THOMAS BACON (a Justice of Common Pleas), as a Banneret.

1333. JOHN DE SHOREDITCH (Baron of the Exchequer), as a Banneret.

1333. WILLIAM DE SHARESHULL (a Justice of Common Pleas), as a Banneret.

1333. NATHANIEL DE BATH, as a Banneret.

1333. SIMON FITZRICHARD, as a Banneret.

1333. ROBERT DE SCARDEBURGH (a Justice of Common Pleas).

1333. JOHN PETIT.

1333. NICHOLAS GIFFARD.

1347, Dec. 25. MAURICE FITZTHOMAS, of Kildare, and his companion, by the king's hand.

1347, Dec. 25. PHILIP DE STAUNTON.

1347, Dec. 25. THOMAS DE FENCOTES (a Justice of Common Pleas), as a Banneret.

1360, Dec. 25. JOHN MOWBRAY (a Justice of Common Pleas), as a Banneret.

1360, Dec. 25. WILLIAM DE SKIPWITH (a Justice of Common Pleas), as a Banneret.

1377, Apr. 23.

Knights of the Bath made on the occasion of the making Richard prince of Wales, and Henry earl of Derby, knights of the Garter.

RICHARD prince of Wales, afterwards Richard III.

HENRY earl of Derby, afterwards Henry IV.

THOMAS OF WOODSTOCK, sixth son of Edward III., and afterwards duke of Gloucester.

ROBERT (DE VERE) 9th earl of Oxford.

JOHN (BEAUMONT) 4th lord Beaumont.

JOHN (DE MOWBRAY) 5th lord Mowbray, afterwards earl of Nottingham.

Two sons of the earl of Stafford.

Three sons of lord Percy, who was afterwards earl of Northumberland, one of the said sons being Henry Percy known as Hotspur.

JOHN DE SOTHEREYE.

A son of Sir JOHN ARUNDEL.

1377, July 15.

Knights made at the Coronation of Richard II. after dinner in the Palace of Westminster.

EDWARD (son of Edmund earl of Cambridge) afterwards 2nd duke of York.

JOHN (son of Thomas lord Ros of Hamlake) afterwards 6th lord Ros

ROBERT (GREY), 4th lord GREY DE ROTHERFIELD.

RICHARD (son of Gilbert lord Talbot) afterwards 4th lord Talbot

GERARD DE LISLE, son of Warine lord Lisle.

MICHAEL DE LA POLE (son of Michael lord De La Pole), afterwards 2nd lord De La Pole and 4th earl of Suffolk.

RICHARD (POYNINGS), 4th lord POYNINGS.

ROBERT (HARINGTON), 3rd lord HARINGTON.

THOMAS DE LA MARE (doubtless a misreading for Thomas La Warr, afterwards 5th lord La Warr).

1383, Dec. 25. JOHN HOLT (a Justice of Common Pleas), as a Banneret. At Eltham, by the King.

1383, Dec. 25. WILLIAM BURGH (a Justice of Common Pleas), as a Banneret. At Eltham, by the King.

1389, Feb. 28 GEOFFREY DE LA VALE, of Ireland, as a Banneret. At Windsor, by the King.

1389, Apr. 23. WALTER CLOPTON (Chief Justice King's Bench), as a Banneret. At Windsor.

1389, Apr. 23. ROBERT CHARLETON (Chief Justice of Common Pleas), as a Banneret. At Windsor.

1390, Apr. 23. ROGER (MORTIMER), 4th earl of March. By the King at Windsor.

1390, Apr. 23. THOMAS (STAFFORD), 3rd earl of Stafford.

1390, Apr. 23. ALPHONSO, son of the count of Denia in Arragon.

1394, Mar. 25. O'NEALE, king of Meath. By Richard II. in the Cathedral Church of Dublin.

1394, Mar. 25. BRIAN DE THOMOND, king of Thomond, *ibid*, by same.

1394, Mar. 25. ARTHUR MacMOROUGH, king of Leinster, *ibid.*, by same.

1394, Mar. 25. CONNOR, king of Chenow and de Erpe.

1394, Mar. 25. THOMAS OURGHAM

1394, Mar. 25. JOHNATHAS DE PADO.

1394, Mar. 25. JOHN DE PADO

On the eve of the Coronation of king Henry IV.

1399, Oct. 11. THOMAS (PLANTAGENET), afterwards duke of Clarence, son of king Henry IV.

1399, Oct. 11. JOHN (PLANTAGENET), afterwards duke of Bedford, son of the king.

1399, Oct. 11. HUMPHREY (PLANTAGENET), afterwards duke of Gloucester, son of the king.

1399, Oct. 11. THOMAS (FITZ-ALAN), 17th earl of Arundel.

1399, Oct. 11. RICHARD (BEAUCHAMP), afterwards 13th earl of Warwick.

1399, Oct. 11. EDMUND (STAFFORD), 5th earl of Stafford.

1399, Oct 11. HUGH (COURTENAY), son of and afterwards 13th earl of Devon.

1399, Oct. 11. ———— COURTENAY.

1399, Oct. 11. HENRY (BEAUMONT), 5th lord Beaumont, and thirty-three others [partly accounted for as follows]

1399, Oct. 11. ———— WILLOUGHBY, brother to William, 5th lord Willoughby.

1399, Oct. 11. HUGH STAFFORD, brother to the earl of Stafford.

1399, Oct. 11. RICHARD CAMOIS, son of Thomas, lord Camois.

1399, Oct. 11. The lord of Paule.

1399, Oct. 11. PETER (DE MAULEY), 4th lord Mauley.

1399, Oct. 11. JOHN NEVILL, 5th lord Latimer.

1399, Oct. 11. RALPH [erratum for John] DEINCOURT, 5th lord Deincourt.

1399, Oct. 11. ALMARIC DE ST. AMAND, 3rd lord Seyntismond or St. Amand.

1400, Mar. 17. THOMAS BEAUCHAMPE.

1400, Mar. 17. THOMAS PELHAM.

1400, Mar. 17. JOHN LUTTRELL.

1400, Mar. 17. JOHN LISLE (LISLEIE).

1400, Mar. 17. WILLIAM HANKFORD (a Justice of Common Pleas).

1400, Mar. 17. WILLIAM BRENCHESLEY (a Justice of Common Pleas).

1400, Mar. 17. BARTHOLOMEW ROCHFORD (RACHFORD).

1400, Mar. 17. GILES DAUBENEY.

1400, Mar. 17. WILLIAM BUTLER.

1400, Mar. 17. JOHN ASHTON.

1400, Mar. 17. RICHARD SNAPE or SANAPE.

1400, Mar. 17. JOHN TIPTOFT (TIPSTON).

1400, Mar. 17. RICHARD FRANCIS.

1400, Mar. 17. HENRY PERCY.

1400, Mar. 17. JOHN ARUNDELL.

1400, Mar. 17. WILLIAM STRALL or STRALLEY.

1400, Mar. 17. JOHN TURPINGTON.

1400, Mar. 17. AILMER SAINT.

1400, Mar. 17. EDWARD HASTINGS.

1400, Mar. 17. JOHN GREISLEY.

1400, Mar. 17. GERALD SOTILL (SATELL).

1400, Mar. 17. JOHN ARDEN.

1400, Mar. 17. ROBERT CHALONS.

1400, Mar. 17. THOMAS DYMOCK.

1400, Mar. 17. WALTER HUNGERFORD.

1400, Mar. 17. WILLIAM GIBETHORPE (GILETHORPE).

1400, Mar. 17. WILLIAM NEWPORT, and others to the number of 46 in all.

On the eve of the Coronation of Henry V., Apr., 1413.

1413, Apr. 8. EDMOND (MORTIMER), 5th earl of March.

1413, Apr. 8. ROGER MORTIMER, his brother.

1413, Apr. 8. JOHN (HOLAND), restored as 14th earl of Huntington, afterwards duke of Exeter.

1413, Apr. 8. [RICHARD] HOLAND, his brother.

1413, Apr. 8. RICHARD LE DESPENSER [wrongly styled] lord le Despencer.

1413, Apr. 8. JOHN PHELIP.

1413, Apr. 8. JOHN ROTHENHALE.

9

1413, Apr. 8.   THOMAS WEST.

1418, Apr. 23.   LEWIS ROBSART, on the celebration of the feast of St. George at Caen.

1418, Apr. 23.   ROGER SALVEINE *(ibid.)*.

1418, Apr. 23.   JOHN STEWART *(ibid.)*.

1418, Apr. 23.   JOHN SHOTESBROOKE *(ibid.)*.

1418, Apr. 23.   JOHN MONTGOMERY and 10 more *(ibid.)*.

1421, Apr. 23.   JAMES I., king of Scotland, on the feast of St. George at Windsor.

1421, Apr. 23.   HUMPHREY (STAFFORD), 6th earl of Stafford *(ibid.)*.

1426, May 19.   After the battle of Verneuil (Aug., 1424), the duke of Bedford came over into England and on Whitsuntide in 1426 at Leicester [at a Parliament there] he dubbed king Henry VI. knight and forthwith the said king dubbed the following 44 knights.   Prior to this ceremony writs had been issued dated from Leicester, 1426, May 4, to 24 out of the following 44 knights commanding them to present themselves at Leicester at the coming feast of Pentecost to receive the dignity of knighthood along with the king.*

1426, May 19.   RICHARD (PLANTAGENET), 3rd duke of York.

1426, May 19.   JOHN (DE MOWBRAY), son and heir to the duke of Norfolk, and afterwards 5th duke of Norfolk.

1426, May 19.   THOMAS (COURTENAY), 14th earl of Devon.

1426, May 19.   JOHN (DE VERE), 12th earl of Oxford.

1426, May 19.   RALPH (DE NEVILL), 2nd earl of Westmorland.

1426, May 19.   HENRY (PERCY), son and heir to and afterwards 3rd earl of Northumberland.

1426, May 19.   JAMES (BUTLER, *alias* Ormond), son and heir to and afterwards 5th earl of Ormond.

---

* The remaining knights elect who did not receive such summons are here printed in italics. As to the question whether the italicised knights in this list are to be considered knights bachelors, or knights of the Bath, see introduction, p. xv.

1426, May 19. THOMAS DE ROS, 9th lord Ros.

1426, May 19. JOHN (BEAUMONT), lord, afterwards viscount, Beaumont.

1426, May 19. *James Butler.*

1426, May 19. JOHN (FITZ-ALAN), lord Maltravers, afterwards 19th earl of Arundel.

1426, May 19. JOHN CORNWALL.

1426, May 19. HENRY (GREY), 2nd earl of Tankerville.

1426, May 19. WILLIAM (NEVILL), afterwards 6th lord Nevill de Fauconberge.

1426, May 19. GEORGE [erratum for John] (NEVILL), 6th lord Latimer.

1426, May 19. LIONEL (DE WELLES), 6th lord Welles.

1426, May 19. *James (de Berkeley), lord de Berkeley.*

1426, May 19. JOHN (TALBOT), son and heir to lord Talbot, and afterwards 5th earl of Shrewsbury.

1426, May 19. HUGH (DE CAMOYS), 2nd lord Camoys.

1426, May 19. HENRY BOURCHIER.

1426, May 19. *Rauf Grey, of Werke.*

1426, May 19. ROBERT VERE, brother of the earl of Oxford

1426, May 19. *Richard de Grey (Gray).*

1426, May 19. GILBERT DEBENHAM.

1426, May 19. *Edmond [? Robert] Hungerford, son and heir of Baron Hungerford.*

1426, May 19. *Robert Wingfield.*

1426, May 19. *John Butler* (Boteler).

1426, May 19. *Reginald Cobham.*

1426, May 19. *John Pasheley (Pasleu).*

1426, May 19. *Thomas Tunstall (Dunstall, Constable).*

1426, May 19. *John Chidioke.*

1426, May 19. *Rauf Longford (Alonghford).*

1426, May 19. WILLIAM (THOMAS) DRURY.

1426, May 19. *William ap Thomas.*

1426, May 19. RICHARD CARBONELL.

1426, May 19. *Richard Wydevill (Wodewyk).*

1426, May 19. *John (Ralph) Shirdelowe (Shadelowe, Shirley).*

1426, May 19. *Nicholas Blouket (Bloucat, Plouket).*

1426, May 19. *Rauf Radclif.*

1426, May 19. EDMOND TRAFFORD *(Canford).*

1426, May 19. WILLIAM CHEYNEY (SHEYNE, CHEYNE), Justice of the King's Bench.

1426, May 19. WILLIAM BABINGTON, Chief Justice of Common Pleas

1426, May 19 *John June (Juen), Justice of Common Pleas.*

1426, May 19. *Gilbert Beauchampe.*

Coronation of Henry VI., 1429, Nov. 6; 30 (32 or 36) knights made;
names not recorded. "And the morrow after was the
Prince's son of Portugal made knight in the Whitehall
at Westminster"

1449, Xmas (at Greenwich) EDMUND TUDOR, afterwards 15th earl of Richmond, half-brother to the king.

1449, Xmas JASPER TUDOR, afterwards 16th earl of Pembroke, half-brother to the king.

1449, Xmas. THOMAS NEVILL, son of Richard, 8th earl of Salisbury.

1449, Xmas. JOHN NEVILL, son of Richard, 8th earl of Salisbury.

1449, Xmas. WILLIAM HERBERT.

1449, Xmas. ROGER LEWKNOR.

1449, Xmas. WILLIAM CATESBY.

Knights of the Bath made at the Tower of London [on the eve before] the Coronation of Edward IV., 1461, June 27.

1461, June 27. GEORGE (PLANTAGENET), 3rd duke of Clarence, brother to the king.

1461, June 27. RICHARD (PLANTAGENET), brother to the king, 3rd duke of Gloucester, afterwards Richard III.

1461, June 27. JOHN DE MOWBRAY, son and heir to, and afterwards 6th duke of Norfolk.

1461, June 27. JOHN (STAFFORD), lord Stafford, afterwards 3rd earl of Wiltshire.

1461, June 27. THOMAS FITZALAN, commonly called lord FitzAlan, son of, and afterwards 22nd earl of Arundel.

1461, June 27. JOHN (LE STRANGE), 8th lord Strange of Knokyn.

1461, June 27. HUMPHRY BOURCHIER.

1461, June 27. JOHN MARKHAM.

1461, June 27. ROBERT DANBY.

1461, June 27. WILLIAM YELVERTON.

1461, June 27. JOHN WINGEFIELD.

1461, June 27. WALTER BLOUNT.

1461, June 27. ROBERT MARKHAM.

1461, June 27. ROBERT CLIFDEN or Clifton.

1461, June 27. WILLIAM STANLEY.

1461, June 27. NICHOLAS BYRON.

1461, June 27. WILLIAM CANTELEWE.

48 [? 40] of Knights of the Bath made on Ascension day in the Tower of London by Edward IV., on the Coronation of Elizabeth, Queen of Edward IV., 1465, May 26.

1465, May 26. HENRY (STAFFORD), 2nd duke of Buckingham.

1465, May 26. ———— STAFFORD, his brother.

1465, May 26. JOHN (DE VERE), 13th earl of Oxford.

1465, May 26. THOMAS (TALBOT), 2nd Viscount Lisle.

1465, May 26. JOHN FITZ-ALAN, styled lord Maltravers, son of John [sic for William], 21st earl of Arundel.

1465, May 26. GEORGE GREY, son of Edward [Edmund], who was afterwards 12th earl of Kent.

1465, May 26. RICHARD WYDVILE.

1465, May 26. JOHN WYDVILE, brother to the Queen.

1465, May 26. RALPH JOSSELYNE.

1465, May 26. RICHARD BINGHAM, a Justice of Common Pleas.

1465, May 26. ROBERT DANVERS, a Justice of the King's Bench.

1465, May 26. JOHN NEEDHAM, a Justice of Common Pleas.

1465, May 26. RICHARD CHOKE, a Justice of Common Pleas.

1465, May 26. WALTER MOYLE, a Justice of the King's Bench.

1465, May 26. Sir RICHARD ILLINGWORTH, Chief Baron of the Exchequer.

1465, May 26. ———— HYNGHAM.

1465, May 26. JOHN ARUNDELLE.

1465, May 26. WILLIAM CALTHORP.

1465, May 26. THOMAS BREWCE or BRUCE.

1465, May 26. GEORGE DARELLE.

1465, May 26. RICHARD HARECOURT.

1465, May 26. WALTER MAUNTELLE.

1465, May 26. EDMUND REDE.

1465, May 26. WILLIAM HAWTE.

1465, May 26. JOHN CLIFFORD.

1465, May 26. JOHN SAY.

1465, May 26. JOHN CHENEY, of Canterbury.

1465, May 26. ROBERT DARCY.

1465, May 26. THOMAS OVEDALE.

1465, May 26. JOHN DURWARD.

1465, May 26. JOHN HENYNGHAM.

1465, May 26. JOHN SAVAGE.

1465, May 26. ROGER CORBET, of Murtone.

1465, May 26. [NICHOLAS?] CULPEPER.

1465, May 26. HUGH WHYCHE.

1465, May 26. THOMAS COOKE, citizen of London.

1465, May 26. JOHN PLOMER.

1465, May 26. HENRY WAFYR (Waver), citizen of London.

1465, May 26. MATHEW PHILIP, citizen of London.

1465, May 26. Lord DURAS, a Gascon.

1465, May 26. BARTELOT DE ROBAIRE (RIBAIRE), of Bayonne, a Gascon.

At the creation of prince Edward, the king's eldest son, as prince of Wales, 1475, April 18, at Westminster, in Saint Edward's Chamber, on Whit Sunday, viz., on the right side of the Chamber, the following :—

1475, Apr. 18. EDWARD, prince of Wales, afterwards Edward V., the king's son.

1475, Apr. 18. RICHARD (PLANTAGENET), 5th duke of York, the king's son.

1475, Apr. 18. JOHN (DE LA POLE), earl of Lincoln, son and heir of John, duke of Suffolk.

1475, Apr. 18. GEORGE (TALBOT), 7th earl of Shrewsbury.

1475, Apr. 18. EDWARD (STAFFORD), 4th earl of Wiltshire.

1475, Apr. 18. RALPH (NEVILLE), 6th lord Neville, afterwards 3rd earl of Westmorland.

1475, Apr. 18 JAMES TUCHET, son of, and afterwards 7th lord Audley.

1475, Apr. 18. RICHARD BEAUCHAMP [afterwards 6th] lord St. Amand.

1475, Apr. 18. JOHN STOURTON, son of, and afterwards 3rd lord Stourton.

1475, Apr. 18. [WALTER?] HERBERT, brother to William, earl of Pembroke.

1475, Apr. 18. THOMAS BRYAN, Chief Justice of Common Pleas.

1475, Apr. 18. THOMAS LYTTELTON, Justice of Common Pleas.

1475, Apr. 18. HENRY BODRYNGAM.

1475, Apr. 18. RICHARD CHARLETON.

1475, Apr. 18. JOHN PILKYNTON.

On the left side of the chamber these following.

1475, Apr. 18. THOMAS (GREY), 16th earl of Huntingdon, the Queen's son, created marquess of Dorset the same day after dinner and so dined in his habit.

1475, Apr. 18. RICHARD GREY, his brother.

1475, Apr. 18. EDWARD WYDVILLE.

1475, Apr. 18. WILLIAM (BERKELEY), [lord, afterwards 1st marquess of Berkeley], son of James, lord Berkeley.

1475, Apr. 18. GEORGE STANLEY, son of Thomas, 2nd lord Stanley.

1475, Apr. 18. EDWARD HASTINGS, son of and afterwards 2nd lord Hastings.

1475, Apr. 18. JOHN (DEVEREUX), son of and afterwards 8th lord Ferrers of Chartley.

1475, Apr. 18. THOMAS VAUGHAN.

1475, Apr. 18. BRYAN STAPILTON.

In the chamber end these following.

1475, Apr. 18. WILLIAM KNYVETT.

1475, Apr. 18. RICHARD LUDLOW.

Knights of the Bath made on the marriage of Richard, duke of York, the King's 2nd son, to Ann, daughter of John, duke of Norfolk. The marriage was solemnised on the 15th Jan. These knights were elected on the 17th, and dubbed on the 18th Jan., 1477–8.

1477–8, Jan. 17. HENRY BOURCHIER, son of William, viscount Bourchier, and grandson of and afterwards 15th earl of Essex.

1477–8, Jan. 17. RICHARD (NEVILL), 2nd lord Latimer.

1477–8, Jan. 17. JOHN (BOURCHIER), 2nd lord Berners or Barnes.

1477–8, Jan. 17. JOHN (GREY), lord Powis.

1477–8, Jan. 17. HENRY (LOVEL), 8th lord Morley.

1477 8, Jan. 17. THOMAS (WEST), 8th lord de la Warr.

1477–8, Jan. 17. JOHN (BLOUNT), 3rd lord Mountjoy.

1477–8, Jan 17. JOHN BEAUCHAMP, son and heir of lord [Richard] Beauchamp.

1477–8, Jan. 17. THOMAS HOWARD (son and heir of John, 1st lord Howard), afterwards 9th duke of Norfolk.

1477–8, Jan. 17. THOMAS BOUCHIER.

1477–8, Jan. 17. THOMAS ST. LEGER.

1477–8, Jan. 17. JOHN ELRINGTON, treasurer of the Household.

1477–8, Jan. 17. GILES DAWBENEY.

1477–8, Jan. 17. WILLIAM STONER.

1477–8, Jan. 17. GUY FAIRFAX.

1477–8, Jan. 17. WILLIAM GASCOIGNE.

1477–8, Jan. 17. ROBERT BROUGHTON.

1477–8, Jan. 17. THOMAS FROWECK.

1477–8, Jan. 17. HENRY TALBOYS, or TAILBOYS.

1477–8, Jan. 17. WILLIAM REDMAN.

1477–8, Jan. 17. HENRY [RICHARD] WENTWORTH.

1477–8, Jan. 17. RICHARD DELADERE.

1477–8, Jan. 17. RICHARD LAKYN.

The following persons were summoned by writs dated 1483, June 5, to furnish themselves to receive knighthood at the intended Coronation of Edward V., on the 22nd June. The ceremony of the Coronation, however, did not take place.

OTES GILBERT, esquire.

JOHN SPEKE.

—— —— BEAUMONT.

EDWARD COURTENEY.

[1483, June.]   WILLIAM GARRAUNT.

THOMAS ARUNDELL.

WILLIAM BOLNEY.

ALEXANDER CRESSEMERE.

JOHN CLOPTON.

HENRY HAYDEN.

JOHN WYNKEFELD.

CHRISTOPHER WILLOUGHBY.

PHILIP CALTHORPE.

———— BEDYNGFELD.

THOMAS LEWKENORE.

WILLIAM BARKELEY.

JOHN STANLEY.

———— GRAVILE.

WILLIAM BIRMINGAM.

THOMAS BUTTELER, of Beawsey.

JOHN BERON.

WILLIAM TROWTBEK.

———— MILBOURN.

Lord DORMOND [? Sir John Drummond, afterwards
   1st lord Drummond].

EDWARD (SUTTON *alias* Dudley), 6th lord Dudley, or
   lord Sutton de Dudley.

[EDMUND] CORNEWALL, lord of Burford.

[GEORGE] NEVILL, son of, and afterwards 5th lord
   Abergavenny.

JOHN BROWN, of Stamford.

[1483, June.]   [GEORGE] (GREY), lord Grey, of Ruthen, afterwards 13th earl of Kent.

JOHN GIFFORD.

WILLIAM CHENAY, of Shepay.

ROBERT WHITE, of Southwarne Borrowe.

GERVASE CLYFTON, of Oddisake.

NICHOLAS LILE.

WILLIAM BERKELEY, of Beverston.

HENRY VERNON.

NICHOLAS MONTGOMERY.

———— GRENE.

WILLIAM OVEDALE.

WILLIAM SAY.

[? THOMAS BROOKE], son and heir of lord Cobham.

TH. HAMDEN, of Hamden.

THOMAS DARCY.

RAUF LANGFORD [SANFORD].

———— BABYNGTON.

HENRY COLET, alderman of London.

———— KYNGESTON.

JOHN PAWLET.

THOMAS WYNDESORE.

JOHN ROGER, of Frefolke.

At the Coronation of Richard III., 1483, July 6.

1483, July 6.   EDMUND DE LA POLE, afterwards 3rd duke of Suffolk.

1483, July 6.   JOHN [*sic* for George] GREY, son of and afterwards 13th earl of Kent.

1483, July 6.   WILLIAM ZOUCHE, brother of John, lord Zouche.

1483, July 6.   WILLIAM or HENRY [*sic* for George] NEVILL, son of and afterwards 5th lord Abergavenny.

1483, July 6.   CHRISTOPHER WILLOUGHBY.

1483, July 6.   WILLIAM BERKELEY of Beverston.

1483, July 6.   HENRY [? William] BANINGTON [Babington].

1483, July 6.   THOMAS ARUNDELL.

1483, July 6.   THOMAS BOLAYNE or Boleyn.

1483, July 6.   EDMUND BEDINGFIELD [Beningefeld].

1483, July 6.   GERVASE or BREWAS of Clifton.

1483, July 6.   WILLIAM SAY.

1483, July 6.   WILLIAM ENDERBY.

1483, July 6.   THOMAS [James] LEWKENOR.

1483, July 6.   THOMAS ORMOND.

1483, July 6.   JOHN BROWNE.

1483, July 6.   WILLIAM BARKELEY of Wyldy.

1483, July 6.   EDMUND CORNWALL, baron of Burford.

———

Twelve knights of the Bath made at [two or three days before] the Coronation of Henry VII., 1485, Oct. 28, in the Hall within the Tower of London.

1485, Oct. 28.   EDWARD STAFFORD, afterwards 3rd duke of Buckingham.

1485, Oct. 28. JOHN (RADCLIFF), 9th lord Fitz-Walter.

1485, Oct. 28. THOMAS COKESAY.

1485, Oct. 28. ROGER LEWKENOR.

1485, Oct. 28. HENRY HEYDON.

1485, Oct. 28. REGINALD BRAY.

1485, Oct. 28. JOHN VERNEY.

? 1485, Oct. 28. HUGH BRICE (Bryse), mayor of London.

---

*Eleven knights of the Bath created on the eve of the Coronation of
Elizabeth, queen of Henry VII., 1487, Nov. 24.*

1487, Nov. 24. WILLIAM COURTENAY, styled lord Courtenay, son of
and afterwards 19th earl of Devon.

1487, Nov. 24. EDWARD (SUTTON, *alias* Dudley), 6th lord Dudley.

1487, Nov. 24. JOHN or WILLIAM GASCOYNE.

1487, Nov. 24. THOMAS BUTLER of Warrington.

1487, Nov. 24. EDWARD BERKELEY.

1487, Nov. 24. WILLIAM LUCY.

1487, Nov. 24. THOMAS HUNGERFORD.

1487, Nov. 24. GUY of Wolston.

1487, Nov. 24. THOMAS or RICHARD PEMERY (Pomerey).

1487, Nov. 24. JOHN or RALPH SHELDON.

1487, Nov. 24. HUGH LUTTRELL.

1487, Nov. 24. THOMAS PULTENEY.

1487, Nov. 24. HUGH CONWAY.

1487, Nov. 24. NICHOLAS LISLEY (Lisle).

On the creation of prince Arthur as prince of Wales, 1489, Nov. 29,
on St. Andrew's eve.

1489, Nov. 29. ARTHUR, prince of Wales (the King's son).

1489, Nov. 29. HENRY ALGERNON (PERCY), 6th earl of Northumber-
land.

1489, Nov. 29. WILLIAM (FITZ-ALAN), lord Maltravers, afterwards
23rd earl of Arundel.

1489, Nov. 29. RICHARD GREY, commonly called lord Grey of
Ruthyn, son of and afterwards 14th earl of Kent.

1489, Nov. 29. WILLIAM (STOURTON), 5th lord Stourton.

1489, Nov. 29. THOMAS WEST, son of and afterwards 9th lord De
La Warr.

1489, Nov. 29. JOHN ST. JOHN.

1489, Nov. 29. HENRY VERNON.

1489, Nov. 29. JOHN HASTINGS.

1489, Nov. 29. WILLIAM GRIFFITH.

1489, Nov. 29. WILLIAM TYNDALL.

1489, Nov. 29. NICHOLAS MONTGOMERY.

1489, Nov. 29. WILLIAM UVEDALL.

1489, Nov. 29. MATTHEW BROWNE.

1489, Nov. 29. THOMAS DARCY.

1489, Nov. 29. THOMAS CHENEY.

1489, Nov. 29. EDMUND GORGES.

1489, Nov. 29. WALTER DENIS.

1489, Nov. 29. WILLIAM SCOTT.

1489, Nov.29. JOHN GUYSE.

On the creation of prince Henry as duke of York, 1494, Oct. 31.

1494, Oct. 31.   Prince HENRY, duke of York, afterwards Henry VIII.

1494, Oct. 31.   THOMAS GREY, styled lord Haryngton, son of and afterwards 5th marquess of Dorset.

1494, Oct. 31.   HENRY (CLIFFORD), 10th lord Clyfford.

1494, Oct. 31.   JOHN (BOURCHIER), 11th lord Fitz Warin.

1494, Oct. 31.   THOMAS (FIENNES), 8th lord Dacre of the South.

1494, Oct. 31.   THOMAS STANLEY, son of lord Strange and grandson of and afterwards 11th earl of Derby.

1494, Oct. 31   JOHN ARUNDELL of the West.

1494, Oct. 31.   WALTER GRYFFITH of Lancashire.

1494, Oct 31.   GERVASE CLIFTON of Yorkshire.

1494, Oct. 31.   EDWARD [EDMOND], TRAFORD.

1494, Oct. 31.   ROBERT HARCOURT or HARDECOURT of the West.

1494, Oct. 31.   HENRY MARNEY of Essex.

1494, Oct. 31.   ROGER NEWBURGH.

1494, Nov. 1.   RALPH RIDER of Yorkshire.

1494, Nov. 1.   THOMAS BAWDE of Harfordshire.

1494, Nov. 1.   JOHN SPEKE.

1494, Nov. 1.   HUMPHREY FULFORD.

1494, Nov. 1.   ROBERT LYTTON, or LITTEN.

1494, Nov. 1.   PIERS EDGECOMBE.

1494, Nov. 1.   ROBERT CLERE.

1494, Nov. 1.   THOMAS FAIRFAX.

1494, Nov. 1.   RICHARD KNIGHTLEY DE FALWESLEY.

1494, Nov. 1.   JOHN (WILLIAM) CHOOKE or CHEOKE.

On the marriage of Arthur, prince of Wales, 1501, Nov. 14.

1501, Nov. 14. RICHARD (HASTINGS), 8th lord Willoughby de Eresby.

1501, Nov. 14. JOHN (CLINTON), 7th lord Clinton.

1501, Nov. 14. GEORGE HASTINGS, son of Edward, 2nd lord Hastings, and afterwards 3rd lord Hastings and 18th earl of Huntingdon.

1501, Nov. 14. THOMAS FENYS or FINNIS.

1501, Nov. 14. GRYFFITHE AP RYS THOMAS.

1501, Nov. 14. ROBERT CORBET.

1501, Nov. 14. JOHN WOGAN.

1501, Nov. 14. THOMAS LAURENCE.

1501, Nov. 14. HENRY ROGERS.

1501, Nov. 14. WILLIAM WALGRAVE.

1501, Nov. 14 WILLIAM SEYMOUR.

1501, Nov. 14. ROBERT THROGMORTON.

1501, Nov. 14. JOHN BASSETT.

1501, Nov. 14. THOMAS GRENEFIELD or GRENVILLE.

1501, Nov. 14. JOHN ARUNDEL of Trerice.

1501, Nov. 14. ROGER STRANGE.

1501, Nov. 14. JOHN SCROPE of Castlecomb.

1501, Nov. 14. JOHN PAULET.

1501, Nov. 14. WALTER BASKERVYLE.

1501, Nov. 14. ROBERT WATERTON.

1501, Nov. 14. JOHN GYFFORD.

1501, Nov. 14. JOHN ASTON.

10

1501, Nov. 14. ——— ASTON.

1501, Nov. 14. WILLIAM FYLLOLL.

1501, Nov. 14. THOMAS INGILFIELD.

1501, Nov. 14. WILLIAM MARTYN.

1501, Nov. 14. WILLIAM CALLWEY.

1501, Nov. 14. GEORGE PUTNAM.

1501, Nov. 14. NICHOLAS BIRON (Byron)

1501, Nov. 14. THOMAS HAWTE.

1501, Nov 14. RICHARD DE LA WARR.

1501, Nov. 14. ALNATHE MALYVERER.

1501, Nov. 14. WILLIAM REDE.

1501, Nov 14. JOHN TREVELYAN.

1501, Nov. 14. JOHN (GEORGE) FOSTER.

1501, Nov 14. WALTER STRYKELAND.

1501, Nov. 14. THOMAS LONG

1501, Nov. 14. JOHN PHILPOT.

1501, Nov 14. JOHN LEE, of Wiltshire.

1501, Nov. 14. WILLIAM HARTWELL

1501, Nov. 14. NICHOLAS GRIFFIN.

1501, Nov. 14. LANCELOT THYRKYLL.

1501, Nov 14. JOHN NORTON.

1501, Nov. 14. ROGER ORMESTON.

1501, Nov. 14. GEORGE or GERARD [? EDWARD], Fyldenge.

1501, Nov. 14. THOMAS CURWYN.

1501, Nov. 14. HUGH LODER.

1501, Nov. 14. THOMAS SAMPSON.

1501, Nov. 14. RICHARD FOWLER.

1501, Nov. 14. THOMAS WOODHOUSE.

1501, Nov. 14. PHILIP BOTHE.

1501, Nov. 14. JOHN (GEORGE) IWARDBY (Inwardby).

1501, Nov. 14. HENRY FROWICK.

1501, Nov. 14 JOHN LEGHE, of Stokewell.

1501, Nov. 14. WILLIAM ASCUE.

1501, Nov. 14. THOMAS KEMP

1501, Nov. 14. MORGAN KYDWELL

1501, Nov. 14. JOHN GYLLOT.

On the creation of Henry, duke of York (afterwards Henry VIII.) as prince of Wales, 1503, Feb. 18 *

1503–4, Feb. 18. JOHN (GREY), 4th viscount Lisle.

1503–4, Feb. 18. THOMAS (DACRE), 3rd lord Dacre, of the North.

1503–4, Feb. 18. MYLES BUSSY.

1503–4, Feb. 18. EDWARD POMERY.

1503–4, Feb. 18. JOHN MORDAUNT.

1503–4, Feb. 18. BRIAN STAPILTON.

1503–4, Feb. 18. RAUFF GRAY.

1503–4, Feb. 18. JAMES HUBERT.

---

* See these eight names repeated as knights of the sword in the list of knights bachelors, *infra* Vol. ii p. 84

At the Coronation of Henry VIII., 1509, June 23.

1509, June 23.   ROBERT (RADCLIFFE), 10th lord FitzWalter.

1509, June 23.   HENRY (LE SCROPE), 7th lord Scrope of Bolton.

1509, June 23.   GEORGE (FITZ-HUGH), 7th lord Fitz-Hugh.

1509, June 23.   WILLIAM (BLOUNT), 4th lord Mountjoy.

1509, June 23   HENRY (DAUBENEY), 2nd lord Daubeney.

1509, June 23   ROBERT (WILLOUGHBY), 2nd lord Willoughby de
    Broke.

1509, June 23.   MORRIS BARKELEY.

1509, June 23.   HENRY CLYFFORD.

1509, June 23.   THOMAS KNEVET (Knyvet).

1509, June 23.   ANDREW WINDSOR.

1509, June 23.   THOMAS PARRE.

1509, June 23.   THOMAS BOLEYN.

1509, June 23.   RICHARD WENTWORTH.

1509, June 23.   HENRY OWTRED.

1509, June 23.   FRANCIS CHENEY.

1509, June 23.   HENRY WYOTTE or WYATT.

1509, June 23.   GEORGE HASTINGS.

1509, June 23   THOMAS METHAM.

1509, June 23.   GYLES ALLINGTON.

1509, June 23.   JOHN TREVANYON.

1509, June 23.   THOMAS BEDINGFIELD.

1509, June 23.   JOHN SKELTON.

1509, June 23.   WILLIAM CROWMER.

1509, June 23. JOHN HEYDON of Bakenthorpe.

1509, June 23. EDWARD or GODARD OXENBRIDGE.

1509, June 23. HENRY SACKVEYLE or SACHEVERELL.

1509, June 23. STEPHEN JENYNS, lord mayor of London 1508.

Knights of the Bath made on the Coronation of Anne Boleyn, queen of Henry VIII., 1533, May 30, on Whit-Sunday, the last day of May.

1533, May 30   HENRY (GREY), 6th marquess of Dorset.

1533, May 30. EDWARD (STANLEY), 12th earl of Derby.

1533, May 20. HENRY CLIFFORD, commonly called lord Clifford, son of and afterwards 2nd earl of Cumberland

1533, May 30. HENRY RATCLIFFE, commonly called lord Fitzwalter, son of and afterwards 9th earl of Sussex.

1533, May 30. FRANCIS HASTINGS, commonly called lord Hastings, son of and afterwards 19th earl of Huntingdon.

1533, May 30. WILLIAM STANLEY, son of and afterwards 3rd lord Monteagle

1533, May 30. THOMAS (VAUX), 2nd lord Vaux of Harrowden.

1533, May 30. HENRY PARKER, son of Henry, 10th lord Morley.

1533, May 30. WILLIAM WINDSOR, son of and afterwards 2nd lord Windsor.

1533, May 30. JOHN MORDAUNT, son of and afterwards 2nd lord Mordaunt.

1533, May 30. FRANCIS WESTON.

1533, May 30. THOMAS ARUNDELL.

1533, May 20. JOHN HUDLESTON.

1533, May 30. THOMAS POYNINGS.

1533, May 30   HENRY SAVELL.

1533, May 30.   GEORGE FITZ WILLIAMS, of Lincolnshire.

1533, May 30.   JOHN TYNDALL.

1533, May 30.   Sir HENRY (? John) JERMEY.

On the Coronation of Edward VI., 1547, Feb. 20.
Knights dubbed by the King on Sunday, the day of his Coronation,
the 20th of February, being crowned, to the number of 40,
in lieu of the Bath, which then could not be performed
according to all ceremonies thereto belonging, the time for
that purpose being too short. (See *infra* footnote, Vol. II.,
p. 59)

1546-7, Feb. 20   HENRY (BRANDON), 5th duke of Suffolk.

1546-7, Feb 20   EDWARD (SEYMOUR), 8th earl of Hertford, duke of
Somerset

1546-7, Feb 20.   JOHN (DE VERE), 16th earl of Oxford.

1546-7, Feb 20.   THOMAS (BUTLER), 11th earl of Ormond.

1546-7, Feb 20   HENRY (FITZ-ALAN), lord Maltravers [son of the
earl of Arundel].

1546-7, Feb 20.   GEORGE TALBOT, commonly called lord Talbot, son
of and afterwards 9th earl of Shrewsbury.

1546-7, Feb 20.   EDWARD [erratum for Henry] STANLEY, commonly
called lord Strange, son of and afterwards 13th earl of
Derby.

1546-7, Feb 20.   WILLIAM SOMERSET, commonly called lord Herbert,
son of and afterwards 8th earl of Worcester.

1546-7, Feb. 20.   JOHN (DUDLEY), viscount Lisle, son and heir of
John, 19th earl of Warwick.

1546-7, Feb 20.   GREGORY (CROMWELL), 1st lord Cromwell.

1546-7, Feb. 20.   HENRY HASTINGS, commonly called lord Hastings,
son of and afterwards 20th earl of Huntingdon..

1546-7, Feb. 20.   CHARLES BRANDON, brother of and afterwards 6th
duke of Suffolk.

1546–7, Feb. 20. HENRY SCROPE, son of and afterwards 9th lord Scrope, of Bolton.

1546–7, Feb. 20. THOMAS WINDSOR, son and heir to William, 2nd lord Windsor.

1546–7, Feb. 20. FRANCIS RUSSELL.

1546–7, Feb. 20. ANTHONY BROWNE, son to the Master of the Horse.

1546–7, Feb. 20. RICHARD DEVEREUX.

1546–7, Feb. 20. HENRY SEYMOUR.

1546–7, Feb. 20. JOHN GATES.

1546–7, Feb. 20. ANTHONY COOK, of Essex.

1546–7, Feb. 20. ALEXANDER UMPTON, of Oxfordshire.

1546–7, Feb. 20. GEORGE NORTON, of Somersetshire.

1546–7, Feb. 20. VALENTINE KNIGHTLEY.

1546–7, Feb. 20. ROBERT LYTTON.

1546–7, Feb. 20. GEORGE VERNON, of the Peak.

1546–7, Feb. 20. JOHN PORTE, of Derbyshire.

1546–7, Feb. 20. THOMAS JOSSELYN.

1546–7, Feb. 20. EDMUND MOLYNEUX, Sergeant-at-Law, afterwards Justice of Common Pleas.

1546–7, Feb. 20. CHRISTOPHER BARKER, Garter King of Arms.

1546–7, Feb. 20. JAMES HALES (Hailes or Halles).

1546–7, Feb. 20. WILLIAM BAPTHORPE (Babthorpe).

1546–7, Feb. 20. THOMAS BRYKENELL (Brudenall).

1546–7, Feb. 20. THOMAS NEVILLE, of the Holt.

1546–7, Feb. 20. ANGELL MAREYN (Marnia, Marian, Marina), an Italian from Cremona.

1546–7, Feb. 20. JOHN HOLCROFTE.

1546–7, Feb. 20. JOHN CUTTE (CUFF or CUYT), of Essex. (See *infra*, Vol. II., p 63).

1546–7, Feb. 20. HENRY TYRELL (TERRELL), of Heron.

1546–7, Feb. 20. WILLIAM SHERRINGTON (Scarrington).

1546–7, Feb. 20. WIMOND CAREWE.

1546–7, Feb. 20. WILLIAM SNEATH (Snathe, Smyth).

———————

Knights of the Bath made prior to the Coronation of queen Mary, 1553, Sept. 28.

1553, Sept 29. EDWARD (COURTENAY), 21st earl of Devon.

1553, Sept. 29. THOMAS HOWARD, son of and afterwards 15th earl of Surrey.

1553, Sept. 29. HENRY HERBERT, commonly called lord Cardiff, son of and afterwards 20th earl of Pembroke.

1553, Sept. 29. HENRY (NEVILL), 6th lord Abergavenny or Bergavenny.

1553, Sept. 29 HENRY (BERKELEY), 7th lord Berkeley.

1553, Sept. 29. JOHN (LUMLEY), 6th lord Lumley.

1553, Sept. 29. JAMES (BLOUNT), 6th lord Mountjoy.

1553, Sept. 29. HENRY CLINTON, son of and afterwards 10th lord Clinton.

1553, Sept. 29. WILLIAM PAULET, son of John, lord St. John, and grandson of and afterwards 3rd marquess of Winchester.

1553, Sept. 29. HUGH RICH, son of Richard, 1st lord Rich.

1553, Sept. 29. HENRY PAGET, son of and afterwards 2nd lord Paget.

1553, Sept. 29. HENRY PARKER.

1553, Sept. 29. ROBERT ROCHESTER, Comptroller of the Household.

1553, Sept. 29. HENRY JERNINGHAM.

1553, Sept. 29. WILLIAM DORMER.

Knights of the Bath made at the Coronation of Queen Elizabeth,
1558–9, Jan. 15.

1558–9, Jan. 15. JOHN DARCY, 2nd lord Darcy of the North [of Darcy and Mainhill].

1558–9, Jan. 15. JOHN SHEFFIELD, 2nd lord Sheffield of Butterwicke.

1558–9, Jan. 15. JOHN (DARCY), 2nd lord Darcy of Chiche.

1558–9, Jan. 15. ROBERT RICHE.

1558–9, Jan. 15. ROGER NORTH

1558–9, Jan 15. JOHN DE LA SOUWCHE or ZOUCHE.

1558–9, Jan. 15. NICHOLAS POYNES (POINTZ).

1558–9, Jan. 15. JOHN BERKELEY.

1558–9, Jan. 15. EDWARD UMPTON (UNTON).

1558–9, Jan. 15. HENRY WESTON.

1558–9, Jan. 15. GEORGE SPEKE.

Knights of the Bath made at the Coronation of king James I.,
1603, July 25.

1603, July 25. PHILIP HERBERT, afterwards 23rd earl of Montgomery.

1603, July 25. THOMAS BERKELEY, son and heir of Henry, 7th lord Berkeley.

1603, July 25. WILLIAM (EURE), son of and afterwards 4th lord Eure.

1603, July 25. GEORGE WHARTON.

1603, July 25. ROBERT RICH, afterwards 23rd earl of Warwick.

1603, July 25. ROBERT CARR, afterwards 6th earl of Somerset.

1603, July 25. JOHN EGERTON, afterwards earl of Bridgewater.

1603, July 25. HENRY COMPTON (brother of William, lord Compton, who was afterwards 8th earl of Northampton).

1603, July 25. JOHN ERSKINE (son of earl of Mar), afterwards 20th earl of Mar

1603, July 25. WILLIAM ANSTRUTHER, a Gentleman of the Bed-chamber.

1603, July 25. PATRICK MURRAY, afterwards 3rd earl of Tulli-bardine.

1603, July 25. JAMES (HAY), 7th lord Hay, of Yester.

1603, July 25. JOHN LINDESAY [of Lothian].

1603, July 25. RICHARD PRESTON, afterwards 17th earl of Desmond.

1603, July 25. OLIVER CROMWELL, of Huntingdonshire.

1603, July 25. EDWARD STANLEY, of Lancashire.

1603, July 25. WILLIAM HERBERT, afterwards 1st lord Powis.

1603, July 25. FULKE GREVILLE, afterwards 1st lord Brooke of Beauchamps Court.

1603, July 25. FRANCIS FANE, afterwards 7th earl of Westmorland.

1603, July 25. ROBERT CHICHESTER, of Devonshire.

1603, July 25. ROBERT KNOWLES, of Berkshire.

1603, July 25. GERVASE or WILLIAM CLIFTON, of Nottinghamshire.

1603, July 25. FRANCIS FORTESCUE, of Devonshire.

1603, July 25. EDWARD (? RICHARD) CORBET, of Shropshire.

1603, July 25. EDWARD HERBERT, afterwards 1st lord Herbert, of Chirbury.

1603, July 25. THOMAS LANGTON, of Lancashire.

1603, July 25. WILLIAM POPE, of Oxfordshire, afterwards 1st earl of Downe.

1603, July 25. ARTHUR HOPTON, of Somerset.

1603, July 25. CHARLES MORISON or MORYSON, of Hertfordshire.

1603, July 25 FRANCIS LEIGH, of Warwickshire, afterwards 1st earl of Chichester.

1603, July 25. EDWARD MONTAGU, afterwards 1st lord Montagu, of Boughton

1603, July 25. EDWARD STANHOPE, of Yorkshire.

1603, July 25. PETER MANWOOD, of Kent.

1603, July 25. ROBERT HARLEY, of Herefordshire.

1603, July 25. THOMAS STRICKLAND, of Yorkshire.

1603, July 25. CHRISTOPHER HATTON, of Northamptonshire.

1603, July 25 EDWARD GRIFFIN, of Northamptonshire.

1603, July 25. ROBERT BEVILL, of Huntingdonshire.

1603, July 25. WILLIAM WELBY, of Lincoln.

1603, July 25. EDWARD HARWELL, of Worcestershire.

1603, July 25 JOHN MALLET, of Somersetshire.

1603, July 25. WALTER ASTON, of Staffordshire, afterwards 1st lord Aston of Forfar.

1603, July 25. HENRY GAWDY, of Essex.

1603, July 25. RICHARD MUSGRAVE, of Westmorland.

1603, July 25. THOMAS LEEDS, of Suffolk.

1603, July 25. JOHN STOWELL, of Somersetshire.

1603, July 25. RICHARD AMCOTES, of Lincolnshire.

1603, July 25   THOMAS JERMYN, of Norfolk.

1603, July 25.   RALPH HARE, of Norfolk.

1603, July 25.   WILLIAM FORSTER, of Buckinghamshire.

1603, July 25.   GEORGE SPEKE, of Somersetshire.

1603, July 25.   GEORGE HYDE, of Berkshire.

1603, July 25.   ANTHONY FELTON, of Suffolk.

1603, July 25.   WILLIAM BROWNE, of Northamptonshire.

1603, July 25.   THOMAS WISE, of Essex.

1603, July 25.   ROBERT CHAMBERLAINE, of Oxfordshire

1603, July 25.   ANTHONY PALMER, of Suffolk.

1603, July 25.   EDWARD HERON, of Lincolnshire.

1603, July 25.   HENRY (? THOMAS) BURTON, of Surrey.

1603, July 25.   ROBERT BARKER, of Suffolk.

1603, July 25.   WILLIAM NORRIS, of Lancashire.

1603, July 25.   ROGER BODENHAM, of Herefordshire.

———

Knights of the Bath made on the creation of prince Charles (after-wards Charles I) as duke of York, 1604–5, Jan. 5–6.

1604–5, Jan. 6.   CHARLES, duke of York and Albany, afterwards Charles I.

1604–5, Jan. 6.   ROBERT BERTIE, 12th lord Willoughby de Eresby, afterwards 1st earl of Lindesey.

1604–5, Jan. 6.   WILLIAM COMPTON, commonly called lord Compton, afterwards 8th earl of Northampton.

1604–5, Jan 6.   GREY (BRYDGES), 5th lord Chandos.

1604–5, Jan. 6   FRANCIS (NORRIS), 2nd lord Norris, afterwards 1st earl of Berkshire.

1604–5, Jan. 6. WILLIAM CECIL, afterwards 15th earl of Salisbury.

1604–5, Jan. 6. ALLAN PERCY, brother of Henry, earl of Northumberland.

1604–5, Jan. 6. FRANCIS MANNERS, afterwards 7th earl of Rutland.

1604–5, Jan. 6. FRANCIS CLIFFORD, brother of and afterwards 4th earl of Cumberland.

1604–5, Jan. 6. THOMAS SOMERSET, afterwards viscount Somerset, of Cashel, in Ireland.

1604–5, Jan. 6. THOMAS HOWARD, afterwards 2nd earl of Berkshire.

1604–5, Jan. 6. JOHN HARRINGTON, son of and afterwards 2nd lord Harrington of Exton.

Knights of the Bath made on the creation of prince Henry as prince of Wales, at Durham House, 1610, June 2 (? 4).

1610, June 2 (? 4). HENRY (DE VERE), 18th earl of Oxford.

1610, June 2. GEORGE GORDON, commonly called lord Gordon, afterwards 2nd marquess of Huntley.

1610, June 2. HENRY CLIFFORD, styled lord Clifford, afterwards 5th earl of Cumberland.

1610, June 2. HENRY RATCLIFFE, commonly called lord Fitzwalter [son and heir to the earl of Sussex].

1610, June 2. EDWARD (BOURCHIER), lord FitzWarine, afterwards 5th earl of Bath.

1610, June 2. FRANCIS [*sic*: erratum for JAMES] HAY, commonly called lord Hay, afterwards 2nd earl of Carlisle.

1610, June 2. JAMES ERSKINE, commonly called lord Erskine (son of earl of Mar), and afterwards 18th earl of Buchan.

1610, June 2. THOMAS (WINDSOR), 6th lord Windsor.

1610, June 2. THOMAS (WENTWORTH), 4th lord Wentworth, afterwards 1st earl of Cleveland.

1610, June 2. CHARLES SOMERSET, 3rd son of Edward, earl of Worcester.

1610, June 2. EDWARD SOMERSET, 4th son of Edward, earl of Worcester.

1610, June 2 THOMAS RATCLIFFE, 2nd son of earl of Sussex.

1610, June 2. FRANCIS STUART, son of earl of Moray.

1610, June 2. WILLIAM STEWART, son of and afterwards 2nd lord Blantyre

1610, June 2. FERDINANDO SUTTON, son of Edward, lord Dudley.

1610, June 2. HENRY CAREY, afterwards 4th Lord Hunsdon and 1st earl of Dover.

1610, June 2 OLIVER ST. JOHN, commonly called lord St. John, afterwards 1st earl of Bolingbroke.

1610, June 2. GILBERT GERARD, son of and afterwards 2nd lord Gerard.

1610, June 2 CHARLES STANHOPE, son of and afterwards 2nd lord Stanhope of Harrington

1610, June 2 EDWARD BRUCE, son of and afterwards 2nd lord Kinlosse

1610, June 2 ROBERT SYDNEY, commonly called lord Sydney, afterwards 12th earl of Leicester.

1610, June 2. FERDINANDO TOUCHET, second son of George, lord Audley.

1610, June 2. PEREGRINE BERTIE, brother of Robert, 12th lord Willoughby de Eresby.

1610, June 2. HENRY RICH, afterwards 1st earl of Holland.

1610, June 2. EDWARD SHEFFIELD (son of lord Sheffield).

1610, June 2. WILLIAM CAVENDISH, afterwards 1st duke of Newcastle.

Knights of the Bath made on the creation of Charles, duke of York (afterwards Charles I.) as prince of Wales, at Whitehall, 1616, Nov. 3 (? 4).

1616, Nov. 3 (? 4). JAMES HOWARD, commonly called lord Maltravers, son of Thomas, earl of Arundel.

1616, Nov. 3. ALGERNON PERCY, commonly called lord Percy, afterwards 11th earl of Northumberland.

1616, Nov. 3. JAMES WRIOTHESLEY, commonly called lord Wriothesley, son of Henry, earl of Southampton.

1616, Nov. 3 THEOPHILUS CLINTON, commonly called lord Clinton, afterwards 16th earl of Lincoln.

1616, Nov. 3. EDWARD SEYMOUR, lord Beauchamp, grandson of Edward, 9th earl of Hertford.

1616, Nov. 3. GEORGE BERKELEY, 8th lord Berkeley.

1616, Nov. 3. JOHN (MORDAUNT), 5th lord Mordaunt, afterwards 1st earl of Peterborough.

1616, Nov. 3. ALEXANDER (ERSKINE), master of Fentoun or viscount of Fentoun, son of Thomas, who was afterwards 1st earl of Kellie.

1616, Nov. 3. HENRY FREDERICK HOWARD, afterwards 27th earl of Arundel.

1616, Nov. 3 ROBERT HOWARD, 3rd or 5th son of Thomas, earl of Suffolk.

1616, Nov. 3. EDWARD SACKVILLE, afterwards 7th earl of Dorset.

1616, Nov. 3. WILLIAM HOWARD, 4th or 6th son of Thomas, earl of Suffolk.

1616, Nov. 3. EDWARD HOWARD, 5th or 7th son of Thomas, earl of Suffolk.

1616, Nov. 3. WILLIAM SEYMOUR, afterwards 1st marquess of Hertford.

1616, Nov. 3.   MONTAGU BERTIE, afterwards 2nd earl of Lindsey.

1616, Nov. 3.   WILLIAM STOURTON, afterwards 11th lord Stourton.

1616, Nov. 3.   HENRY PARKER, afterwards 6th lord Monteagle.

1616, Nov. 3.   DUDLEY NORTH, afterwards 4th lord North.

1616, Nov. 3.   WILLIAM SPENCER, afterwards 2nd lord Spencer.

1616, Nov. 3.   SPENCER COMPTON, afterwards 9th earl of Northampton

1616, Nov. 3.   ROWLAND ST. JOHN, brother to Oliver, lord St. John.

1616, Nov. 3.   JOHN CAVENDISH, 2nd son of William, earl of
Devonshire.

1616, Nov. 3.   THOMAS NEVILL, son of Edward, lord Abergavenny.

1616, Nov. 3.   JOHN ROPER, afterwards 3rd lord Teynham.

1616, Nov. 3.   JOHN NORTH, brother of Dudley, lord North.

1616, Nov. 3.   HENRY CAREY, afterwards 1st viscount of Falkland.

---

*Knights of the Bath made at the Coronation of Charles I., 1625-6,
Feb. 1.*

1625-6, Feb. 1.   GEORGE FEILDING, viscount Callan, afterwards
18th earl of Desmond.

1625-6, Feb. 1.   JAMES STANLEY, commonly called lord Strange,
afterwards 16th earl of Derby.

1625-6, Feb. 1.   CHARLES CECIL, commonly called viscount Cran-
borne, son of William, earl of Salisbury.

1625-6, Feb. 1.   CHARLES HERBERT, commonly called lord Herbert
of Shurland, son of Philip, earl of Montgomery.

1625-6, Feb. 1.   ROBERT RICH, commonly called lord Rich, after-
wards 24th earl of Warwick.

1625-6, Feb. 1.   JAMES HAY, commonly called lord Hay, afterwards
3rd earl of Carlisle.

1625–6, Feb. 1. BASIL FIELDING, commonly called viscount Fielding, afterwards 2nd earl of Denbigh.

1625–6, Feb. 1. OLIVER ST. JOHN, commonly called lord St. John, son of Oliver, earl of Bolingbroke.

1625–6, Feb. 1. MILDMAY FANE, commonly called lord Burghersh, afterwards 8th earl of Westmorland

1625–6, Feb. 1. HENRY PAULET, commonly called lord Henry Paulet, son of William, marquess of Winchester.

1625–6, Feb. 1. EDWARD MONTAGU, afterwards 2nd earl of Manchester.

1625–6, Feb. 1. JOHN CAREY, afterwards 2nd earl of Dover.

1625–6, Feb. 1. CHARLES HOWARD, afterwards 3rd earl of Berkshire.

1625–6, Feb. 1. WILLIAM HOWARD, son of Thomas, earl of Arundel.

1625–6, Feb. 1. ROBERT STANLEY, 2nd son of William, 15th earl of Derby.

1625–6, Feb. 1. PAWLET ST. JOHN, 2nd son of Oliver, earl of Bolingbroke.

1625–6, Feb. 1. FRANCIS FANE, 2nd son of Francis, earl of Westmoreland.

1625–6, Feb. 1. JAMES HOWARD, afterwards 11th earl of Suffolk.

1625–6, Feb. 1. WILLIAM CAVENDISH, afterwards 4th earl of Devonshire.

1625–6, Feb. 1. THOMAS WENTWORTH, afterwards 5th lord Wentworth.

1625–6, Feb. 1. WILLIAM PAGET, afterwards 6th lord Paget.

1625–6, Feb. 1. WILLIAM RUSSELL, afterwards 4th duke of Bedford.

1625–6. Feb. 1. HENRY STANHOPE, son of Philip, lord Stanhope of Shelford.

1625–6, Feb. 1. RICHARD VAUGHAN, afterwards 2nd earl of Carbery.

11

1625–6, Feb. 1. CHRISTOPHER NEVILLE, 2nd son of Edward, lord Abergavenny.

1625–6, Feb. 1. ROGER BERTIE, 2nd son of Robert, lord Willoughby de Eresby.

1625–6, Feb. 1. THOMAS WHARTON, 2nd son of Thomas, lord Wharton.

1625–6, Feb. 1. ST. JOHN BLUNT or BLOUNT, brother of Mountjoy, lord Mountjoy.

1625–6, Feb. 1. RALPH (ST.) CLARE, of Worcestershire, the king's servant of the Privy Chamber.

1625–6, Feb. 1. JOHN MAYNARD (brother to lord Maynard), the king's servant of the Privy Chamber.

1625–6, Feb 1. FRANCIS CAREW, of Devonshire, the king's servant of the Privy Chamber.

1625–6, Feb 1. JOHN BYRON, of Nottinghamshire, the king's servant of the Privy Chamber.

1625–6, Feb 1. ROGER PALMER, Master of the Household.

1625–6, Feb. 1. HENRY EDMONDS, son of the Treasurer of the Household.

1625–6, Feb. 1. RALPH HOPTON, of Somersetshire.

1625–6, Feb. 1. WILLIAM BROOKE, of Kent.

1625–6, Feb. 1. ALEXANDER RATCLIFFE, of Lancashire.

1625–6, Feb. 1. EDWARD SCOTT, of Kent.

1625–6, Feb. 1. CHRISTOPHER HATTON, of Northampton.

1625–6, Feb. 1. THOMAS SACKVILLE, of Sussex.

1625–6, Feb. 1. JOHN MUNSON, or MONSON, of Lancashire, son of Sir Thomas Munson.

1625–6, Feb. 1. PETER WENTWORTH, of Oxfordshire.

1625–6, Feb. 1. JOHN BUTLER, of Hertfordshire.

1625–6, Feb 1. EDWARD HUNGERFORD, of Wiltshire.

1625–6, Feb. 1. RICHARD LEWSON, of Kent.

1625–6, Feb. 1. NATHANIEL BACON, of Culford, in Suffolk.

1625–6, Feb. 1. ROBERT POYNTZ, of Gloucestershire.

1625–6, Feb. 1. ROBERT BEVILL, of Huntingdonshire.

1625–6, Feb. 1. GEORGE SANDES, of Kent.

1625–6, Feb. 1. THOMAS SMITH, or SMYTHE, afterwards 1st viscount Strangford.

1625–6, Feb. 1. THOMAS FANSHAWE, of Warparke, in Hertfordshire.

1625–6, Feb. 1. MILES HOBART, of Plumstead, in Norfolk.

1625–6, Feb. 1. HENRY HART, of Kent, son of Sir Percival Hart.

1625–6, Feb. 1. FRANCIS CAREW, alias THROGMORTON, of Bedington, Surrey.

1625–6, Feb. 1. JOHN BACCUS, or BACKHOUSE, of Berkshire.

1625–6, Feb. 1. MATTHEW MONINS, of Kent.

1625–6, Feb. 1. JOHN STOWELL, or STAWELL, of Somersetshire.

1625–6, Feb. 1. JOHN JENNINGS, of Hertfordshire.

1625–6, Feb. 1. STEPHEN HARVEY, of Northampton, son of Justice Harvey.

Knights of the Bath made with prince Charles as preparatory to his receiving the Order of the Garter, 1638, May 21 (? 22).

1638, May 21. Prince CHARLES, afterwards Charles II.

1638, May 21. ROBERT (DEVEREUX), 20th earl of Essex.

1638, May 21. ULICK (BOURKE), 2nd earl of St. Albans.

1638, May 21. ROBERT (BRUCE), 1st earl of Elgin.

1638, May 21. WILLIAM (VILLIERS), 2nd viscount Grandison.

Knights of the Bath made at the Coronation of Charles II., 1661, Apr. 23.

1661, Apr. 23. EDWARD CLINTON, commonly called Lord Clinton, afterwards 17th earl of Lincoln.

1661, Apr. 23. JOHN EGERTON, commonly called lord Brackley, afterwards 4th earl of Bridgewater.

1661, Apr. 23. PHILIP HERBERT, 2nd son of Philip, earl of Pembroke and Montgomery.

1661, Apr. 23 WILLIAM EGERTON, 2nd son of John, earl of Bridgewater.

1661, Apr. 23. VERE FANE, afterwards 10th earl of Westmorland.

1661, April 23. CHARLES BERKELEY, afterwards 2nd earl of Berkeley.

1661, Apr. 23. HENRY BELASYSE, son and heir apparent of John, who was afterwards 1st lord Belasyse.

1661, April 23. HENRY HYDE, afterwards 2nd earl of Clarendon.

1661, Apr. 23. ROWLAND BELLASYSE, brother to Thomas, viscount Fauconberg.

1661, Apr. 23. HENRY CAPELL, 2nd son of Arthur, earl of Essex.

1661, Apr. 23. JOHN VAUGHAN, 2nd son of earl of Carbery.

1661, Apr. 23. CHARLES STANLEY, grandson of Charles, 17th earl of Derby.

1661, Apr 23 FRANCIS FANE, grandson of the late earl of Westmorland.

1661, Apr. 23. HENRY FANE, grandson of the late earl of Westmorland.

1661, Apr. 23. Sir WILLIAM PORTMAN, bart.

1661, Apr. 23. Sir RICHARD TEMPLE, bart

1661, Apr. 23 Sir WILLIAM DUCIE, bart, afterwards 1st viscount Downe.

1661, Apr. 23. Sir THOMAS TREVOR, bart.

1661, Apr. 23. Sir JOHN SCUDAMORE, bart.

1661, Apr. 23. Sir WILLIAM GARDINER, bart.

1661, Apr. 23. CHARLES CORNWALLIS, afterwards 2nd lord Cornwallis.

1661, Apr. 23. JOHN NICHOLAS, son of Sir Edward Nicholas, Secretary of State.

1661, Apr. 23. JOHN MONSON.

1661, Apr. 23. BOURCHIER WREY (Wray).

1661, Apr. 23. JOHN COVENTRY.

1661, Apr. 23. EDWARD HUNGERFORD.

1661, Apr. 23. JOHN KNYVET (KNEVET).

1661, Apr. 23. PHILIP BUTLER.

1661, Apr. 23. ADRIAN SCROOPE.

1661, Apr. 23. RICHARD KNIGHTLEY.

1661, Apr. 23. HENRY HERON.

1661, Apr. 23. JOHN LEWKENOR.

1661, Apr. 23. GEORGE BROWNE.

1661, Apr. 23. WILLIAM TERRINGHAM, or TIRINGHAM

1661, Apr. 23. FRANCIS GODOLPHIN.

1661, Apr. 23. EDWARD BAYNTON.

1661, Apr. 23. GREVILL VERNEY.

1661, Apr. 23. EDWARD HARLEY.

1661, Apr. 23. EDWARD WALPOLE.

1661, Apr. 23. FRANCIS POPHAM.

1661, Apr. 23. EDWARD WISE.

1661, Apr. 23. CHRISTOPHER CALTHORPE.

1661, Apr. 23. RICHARD EDGCUMBE.

1661, Apr. 23. WILLIAM BROMLEY.

1661, Apr. 23. THOMAS BRIDGES.

1661, Apr. 23. THOMAS FANSHAWE.

1661, Apr. 23. JOHN DENHAM.

1661, Apr. 23. NICHOLAS BACON.

1661, Apr. 23. JAMES ALTHAM.

1661, Apr. 23. THOMAS WINDY, or WENDY.

1661, Apr. 23. JOHN BRAMPSTON.

1661, Apr. 23. GEORGE FREEMAN.

1661, Apr. 23. NICHOLAS SLANING.

1661, Apr. 23. RICHARD INGOLDSBY.

1661, Apr. 23. JOHN ROLLES.

1661, Apr. 23. EDWARD HEATH.

1661, Apr. 23. WILLIAM MORLEY.

1661, Apr. 23. JOHN BENNET.

1661, Apr. 23. HUGH SMITH.

1661, Apr. 23. SIMON LEECH.

1661, Apr. 23. HENRY CHESTER.

1661, Apr. 23. ROBERT ATKINS.

1661, Apr. 23. ROBERT GAYER or GAYRE

1661, Apr. 23. RICHARD POWLE.

1661, Apr. 23. HUGH DARCY or DUCIE.

1661, Apr. 23. STEPHEN HALES.

1661, Apr. 23. RALPH BASH.

1661, Apr 23. THOMAS WHITMORE.

The Most Honourable Order
of the Bath.

The Most Honourable Order of the Bath.

SOVEREIGNS

See list of sovereigns given seriatim under the Order of the Garter.

GRAND MASTERS and (subsequently) First and Principal Knights Grand Cross.

1725, May 27. JOHN (MONTAGU), 2nd duke of Montagu. Died 1749, July 16.

1767, Dec. 30 Prince FREDERICK, of Brunswick Luneburg, afterwards duke of York. Died 1827, Jan. 5.

1827. WILLIAM HENRY, duke of Clarence. Succeeded as Sovereign as William IV., in 1830, June 26.

1837, Dec 16. AUGUSTUS FREDERICK, duke of Sussex. Died 1843, Apr. 21.

1843, May 31. FRANCIS ALBERT AUGUSTUS CHARLES EMANUEL, prince Consort. Died 1861, Dec. 14.

1897, June 22. ALBERT EDWARD, prince of Wales. Succeeded as Sovereign of the Order as Edward VII., in 1901, Jan. 22.

1901, Feb. 26 ARTHUR WILLIAM PATRICK ALBERT, duke of Connaught and Streathearn.

Original Knights Companions (K.B.) invested May 27, and installed June 17.

1725, May 27. Prince WILLIAM AUGUSTUS, 2nd son of George, prince of Wales, and grandson of George I., afterwards duke of Cumberland. Installed by proxy

1725, May 27. JOHN (MONTAGU), 2nd duke of Montagu (Great Master).

1725, May 27. CHARLES (LENNOX), 7th duke of Richmond (not invested). Knighted by the Grand Master. Installed by proxy.

1725, May 27. WILLIAM (MONTAGU), 2nd duke of Manchester.

1725, May 27 CHARLES BEAUCLERK, commonly called earl of Burford, afterwards 2nd duke of Saint Albans.

1725, May 27. JOHN (SYDNEY), 17th earl of Leicester.

1725, May 27. WILLIAM ANNE (Van Keppel), 14th earl of Albemarle.

1725, May 27. HENRY (SCOTT), 1st earl of Deloraine.

1725, May 27. GEORGE (MONTAGUE), 2nd earl of Halifax.

1725, May 27. TALBOT (YELVERTON), 17th earl of Sussex.

1725, May 27. THOMAS (FERMOR), 1st earl of Pomfret.

1725, May 27. NASSAU PAULET, commonly called Lord Nassau Paulet, son of Charles, 3rd duke of Bolton.

1725, May 27. Adm. GEORGE (BYNG), 1st viscount Torrington.

1725, May 27. GEORGE CHOLMONDELEY, commonly called viscount Malpas, afterwards 3rd earl of Cholmondeley.

1725, May 27. JOHN CAMPBELL, commonly called viscount Glenorchy, afterwards 3rd earl of Breadalbane. Knighted in Denmark. Installed by proxy.

1725, May 27. JOHN (WEST), lord De la Warr, afterwards 1st earl De la Warr.

1725, May 27. HUGH (FORTESCUE), 13th lord Clinton, afterwards 1st earl Clinton.

1725, May 27. ROBERT (WALPOLE), lord Walpole, afterwards 2nd earl of Orford.

1725, May 27. The Honourable SPENCER COMPTON, afterwards earl of Wilmington (quitted for the Garter 1733, Aug.).

1725, May 27. WILLIAM STANHOPE, 2nd son of Philip, earl of Chesterfield.

1725, May 27. CONIERS D'ARCY, uncle of Robert, earl of Holder-nesse.

1725, May 27. THOMAS LUMLEY-SAUNDERSON, afterwards 3rd earl of Scarbrough

1725, May 27. PAUL METHUEN.

1725, May 27. ROBERT WALPOLE, afterwards 1st earl of Orford (quitted for the Garter 1726).

1725, May 27. ROBERT SUTTON.

1725, May 27. Lieut. Gen. CHARLES WILLS (Willis).

1725, May 27. Sir JOHN HOBART, bart., afterwards earl of Bucking-hamshire.

1725, May 27. Sir WILLIAM GAGE, bart.

1725, May 27. ROBERT CLIFTON, son of Sir Gervase Clifton, bart.

1725, May 27. MICHAEL NEWTON (afterwards bart.).

1725, May 27. WILLIAM YONGE, afterwards bart.

1725, May 27. THOMAS WATSON-WENTWORTH, afterwards 1st marquess of Rockingham.

1725, May 27. JOHN MONSON, afterwards 1st lord Monson.

1725, May 27. WILLIAM MORGAN, of Tredegar.

1725, May 27. THOMAS COKE, afterwards 19th earl of Leicester.

1725, May 27. WILLIAM (O'BRIEN), 4th earl of Inchiquin. Invested 1725, May 28. Installed June 15.

1725, May 27. JOHN (BROWNLOW), 1st viscount Tyrconnell. Invested 1725, May 28. Installed June 15.

(Dates of Investiture.)

1732, Jan. 12. HENRY BRYDGES, commonly called marquess of Carnarvon, afterwards 2nd duke of Chandos. Installed June 30.

1732, Jan. 12 WILLIAM (BATEMAN), 1st viscount Bateman. Installed June 30.

1732, Jan 12 Sir GEORGE DOWNING, bart. Installed June 30.

1732, Jan. 17. CHARLES GUNTER NICOLL. Installed June 30.

1742, June 26. Sir THOMAS ROBINSON, bart., afterwards 1st lord Grantham. Invested at Vienna Dec. 8. Installed 1744, Oct. 20.

1743, July 12. Lieut. Gen. PHILIP HONYWOOD. Installed 1744, Oct. 20.

1743, July 12. The Hon. JAMES CAMPBELL, Lieut. Gen., second son of the earl of Loudoun. Installed 1744, Oct. 20.

1743, July 12. Lieut. Gen. JOHN COPE. Installed 1744, Oct. 20.

1743, July 12. Sir JOHN LOUIS LIGONIER, afterwards earl Ligonier. Installed 1744, Oct. 20.

1744, May 28. RICHARD (FITZWILLIAM), 6th viscount Fitzwilliam of Meryon.* Installed Oct. 20.

1744, May 28. THOMAS WHITMORE. Installed Oct. 20.

1744, May 28. HENRY CALTHORPE. Installed Oct. 20.

1744, May 28. Sir WILLIAM MORDEN HARBORD, bart. Installed Oct. 20.

1744, May 28. CHARLES HANBURY WILLIAMS. Installed Oct. 20.

1747, May 29. R. Adm. PETER WARREN. Installed 1749, June 26.

1747, Nov. 14. V. Adm. EDWARD HAWKE, afterwards 1st Lord Hawke. Installed by proxy 1749, June 26.

1749, May 2. The Hon. CHARLES HOWARD, Lieut. Gen., brother of Henry, earl of Carlisle. Installed 1749, June 26.

1749, May 2. Maj. Gen. CHARLES ARMAND POWLETT. Installed 1749, June 26.

1749, May 2. Maj. Gen. JOHN MORDAUNT. Installed 1749, June 26.

1749, May 2. JOHN SAVILE, afterwards 1st earl of Mexborough. Installed 1749, June 26.

1752, Mar. 12. RICHARD (ONSLOW), 3rd lord Onslow. Installed 1753, Dec. 27.

1753, Aug. 27. The Hon. EDWARD WALPOLE, 2nd son of Robert, 1st earl of Orford. Installed Dec. 27.

1753, Aug. 27. Lieut. Gen. CHARLES POWLETT, afterwards 5th duke of Bolton. Installed Dec. 27.

1753, Aug. 27. Lieut. Gen. the Hon RICHARD LYTTELTON, brother of George, lord Lyttelton. Installed Dec. 27.

1753, Aug. 27. EDWARD HUSSEY-MONTAGU, afterwards earl of Beaulieu Installed Dec 27.

1753, Dec. 12. Adm. WILLIAM ROWLEY. Installed Dec. 27.

1754, Sept. 23. BENJAMIN KEENE Nominated Aug. 17. Invested Sept. 23 at Madrid by the king of Spain. Not installed.

1756, Nov. 27. Lieut Gen. WILLIAM BLAKENEY, afterwards lord Blakeney. Installed by proxy 1761, May 26.

1761, Mar. 23. JOHN (PROBY), 1st lord Carysfort. Installed May 26.

1761, Mar. 23. Lieut. Gen. the Hon. JOSEPH YORKE, afterwards lord Dover. Installed May 26.

1761, Mar. 23 Sir JAMES GRAY, bart. Appointed Mar 23; installed by proxy May 26; invested at Naples by king Ferdinand June 6

1761, Mar. 23. Sir WILLIAM BEAUCHAMP PROCTOR, bart. Installed by proxy May 26.

1761, Mar. 23. Sir JOHN GIBBONS, bart. Installed May 26.

Date of nomination
1761, Mar. 23 Adm. GEORGE POCOCK. Invested May 6. Installed May 26.

1761, Mar. 23. Maj Gen. Sir JEFFERY AMHERST, afterwards 1st lord Amherst. Invested at Staten Island, in North America, by Maj. Gen. Monckton, Oct. 25 Installed by proxy May 26.

Date of investiture
1761, Mar. 23. Maj. Gen. JOHN GRIFFIN GRIFFIN, afterwards 4th lord Howard de Walden. Installed by proxy May 26.

1761, Mar. 23. FRANCIS BLAKE DELAVAL. Installed May 26.

1761, Mar. 23. CHARLES FREDERICK. Installed May 26.

1761, Mar. 26. GEORGE WARREN. Installed May 26.

Date of nomination
1761, May 16. V. Adm. CHARLES SAUNDERS. Invested at Gibraltar by Maj. Gen. Parslow, July 6. Installed by proxy May 26.

Date of investiture

1764, Jan. 16. CHARLES COOTE, afterwards 5th earl of Bellomont. Invested by the Lord Lieutenant at Dublin Castle. Installed 1772, June 15.

1764, Apr. 24. Maj. Gen. ROBERT (CLIVE), 1st lord Clive. Installed 1772, June 15.

1765, Dec. 13. ANDREW MITCHELL. Not installed.

1765, Dec. 27. Maj. Gen. WILLIAM DRAPER. Installed 1772, June 15.

1767, Dec. 30. Prince FREDERICK, of Brunswick-Luneburg, Bishop of Osnaburgh, afterwards duke of York. Nominated First and Principal Companion. Installed by proxy 1772, June 15.

1768, Oct. 25. Sir HORATIO MANN, bart Invested at Florence by the grand duke of Tuscany. Installed by proxy, 1772, June 15. *

1770, May 18 ROBERT (KNIGHT), 1st earl of Catherlough. Not installed.

1770, May 18. V. Adm Sir JOHN MOORE, bart. Installed by proxy 1772, June 15.

Date of nomination

1770, June 28. R. Adm. Sir JOHN LINDSAY, bart. Invested by the Nabob of the Carnatic, near Madras, 1771, Mar. 11. Installed 1772, June 15

1770, June 28. Maj. Gen. EYRE COOTE. Invested 1771, Aug. 30. Installed 1772, June 15.

Date of investiture

1771, Feb. 18. Lieut. Gen. CHARLES MONTAGU. Installed 1772, June 15.

1771, Feb. 18 RALPH PAYNE, afterwards lord Lavington. Installed by proxy 1772, June 15.

Date of nomination

1771, Feb. 18. WILLIAM LYNCH. Invested at Turin Mar. 11. Installed 1772, June 15.

Date of investiture

1772, Jan. 15. Sir CHARLES HOTHAM (afterwards Hotham-Thompson), bart. Installed June 15.

1772, Jan 15. WILLIAM HAMILTON. Installed June 15.

1772, Feb. 29. Lieut. Col. ROBERT MURRAY KEITH. Nominated a
supernumerary knight. Succeeded as an ordinary knight
on the death of the earl of Caterlough. Installed by proxy
June 15.

1772, May 29. Rt. Hon. Sir GEORGE MACARTNEY, afterwards earl
Macartney. Invested at Dublin, June 25. Installed by
proxy June 15.

Date of investiture
1773, Feb. 22. Lieut. Gen. JAMES ADOLPHUS OUGHTON. Installed
by proxy 1779, May 19.

Date of nomination
1773, June 2. ROBERT GUNNING, afterwards bart. Invested at St.
Petersburg by the empress of Russia, July 9. Installed
by proxy 1779, May 19.

Date of investiture
1774, Aug. 3. Lieut. Gen. Sir GEORGE HOWARD, bart. Installed
1779, May 19

1774, Aug 3. Lieut. Col. Rt. Hon. JOHN BLAQUIERE, afterwards 1st
lord de Blaquiere. Installed 1779, May 19.

1775, Feb. 3. WILLIAM GORDON. Installed 1779, May 19

1775, Dec 15. Lieut. Gen. Rt. Hon. JOHN IRWINE. Installed 1779,
May 22.

Date of nomination
1776, July 6. Gen. GUY CARLETON, afterwards 1st lord Dorchester.
Installed 1779, May 19.

1776, Oct. 13. Maj. Gen. the Hon. WILLIAM HOWE, afterwards 5th
viscount Howe. Invested at New York by viscount Howe,
1777, Jan. 18. Installed 1779, May 19.

1776, Nov. 9. Lieut. Gen. JOHN CLAVERING. Invested by himself
at Calcutta, 1777, June 30. Not installed.

Date of investiture.
1777, Apr. 11. Maj Gen. HENRY CLINTON. A supernumerary
knight till the death of the earl of Inchiquin in July
following. Installed by proxy 1779, May 19.

1778, Dec 9. R. Adm. EDWARD HUGHES. Installed by proxy 1779,
May 19

Date of nomination
1779, Feb. 24 JAMES HARRIS, afterwards 1st earl of Malmesbury.
Invested by the Empress of Russia at St. Petersburg,
Mar. 21. Installed by proxy May 19.

1779, Mar. 23. Maj. Gen. Hector Monro. Invested by the nabob of Arcot, near Madras, Oct. 13. Installed by proxy May 19.

Date of Investiture
1779, May 5. Randall William (MacDonnell), 6th earl, afterwards 1st marquess of Antrim. Installed 1779, May 19.

Date of nomination
1780, Nov. 13. Thomas Wroughton. Invested at Stockholm by the king of Sweden, Dec. 5. Not installed.

1780, Nov. 13. Lieut. Gen. Richard Pierson. Invested Nov. 13. Not installed.

1780, Nov. 14. Adm Sir George Brydges Rodney, bart., afterwards 1st Lord Rodney. A supernumerary knight till the death of Sir Richard Pierson in 1781, Feb Installed 1788, May. 19.

Date of investiture
1781, Dec. 17. Lieut. Gen. Edward (Ligonier), 1st earl Ligonier Died before installation.

1782, May 29. Capt. John Jervis, afterwards earl of St. Vincent. Installed 1788, May 19

Date of nomination
1783, Jan. 8 The Hon. George Ausgustus Elliott, afterwards 1st lord Heathfield. Invested at Gibraltar by Lieut. Gen. Boyd, 1783, Apr. 23. Installed 1788, May 19.

Date of investiture
1783, Jan. 8. Lieut. Gen. Charles Grey, afterwards 1st earl Grey, of Howick. A supernumerary knight till the death of Sir Eyre Coote, 1783, Apr. 26. Installed 1788, May 19.

1785, Jan. 28. Lieut. Gen. Robert Boyd. Installed 1788, May 19.

1785, Sept. 30. Lieut. Gen. Frederick Haldimand. Installed 1788, May 19.

1785, Sept. 30. Maj. Gen. Archibald Campbell. A supernumerary knight till the death of Sir Charles Frederick, 1785, Dec. Installed by proxy 1788, May 19

1786, Dec. 20. Lieut. Gen. William Fawcett. Installed 1788, May 19.

1786, Dec. 20. Robert (Monckton-Arundell), 8th viscount Galway. A supernumerary knight till the death of Sir William Draper, 1787, Jan. Installed 1788, May 19.

1788, May 7. Rt Hon. Sir George Yonge, bart. Installed May 19.

1788, May 7. V. Adm. Alexander Hood, afterwards 1st viscount Bridport. Installed May 19.

1788, June 6. Gen. Robert Sloper. Not installed.

Date of nomination
1791, Dec. 16. Morton Eden, afterwards 1st lord Henley. Invested at Berlin by the king of Prussia, 1792, Jan. 1. Installed 1803, May 19.

Date of investiture
1792, Aug. 15 Lieut. Gen the Rt. Hon. William Augustus Pitt. Installed 1803, May 19.

1792, Aug. 15 Lieut. Gen. the Hon. John Vaughan. Not installed.

Date of nomination
1792, Aug. 15. Maj Gen. William Medows. Invested Dec. 14. Installed by proxy 1803, May 19

1792, Aug. 15. Maj. Gen. Robert Abercromby. Invested at Bombay by Sir C. W Malet, 1793, June 4. Installed by proxy 1803, May 19.

1793, Sept 27. Charles Whitworth, afterwards lord Whitworth. Invested at St. Petersburg by the Empress of Russia, 1793, Nov. 17. Installed by proxy 1803, May 19.

Date of investiture
1794, May 30. R. Adm. the Hon. George Keith Elphinstone, afterwards 1st viscount Keith. Installed by proxy 1803, May 19.

1794, May 30 Capt the Rt. Hon. Sir John Borlase Warren, bart. Installed by proxy 1803, May 19.

Date of nomination
1794, Nov. 18. Maj. Gen. Adam Williamson. Invested at Kingston, Jamaica, by the earl of Balcarres, 1795, Apr. 21. Not installed.

Date of investiture
1795, July 1. Sir Joseph Banks, bart. Installed 1803, May 19.

1795, July 22. Maj. Gen. Ralph Abercromby. Not installed.

1796, Feb. 17. R. Adm. Hugh Cloberry Christian. Not installed.

Date of nomination

1797, Jan. 14. Maj. Gen. ALURED CLARKE. Installed 1803, May 19.

1797, Jan. 14. Maj. Gen. JAMES HENRY CRAIG. Installed 1803, May 19.

1797, May 27. R. Adm. HORATIO NELSON, afterwards viscount Nelson. Invested Sept. 27. Installed by proxy 1803, May 19.

Date of investiture

1798, Feb. 14. V. Adm. JOHN COLPOYS. Installed 1803, May 19.

Date of nomination

1799, Jan. 8. Lieut. Gen. the Hon. CHARLES STUART. Invested 1800, Jan. 8. Not installed.

Date of investiture

1800, Jan. 8. V. Adm. HENRY HARVEY. Installed 1803, May 19.

1800, Jan. 8. V. Adm. ANDREW MITCHELL. Installed by proxy 1803, May 19.

Date of nomination

1801, May 14. R. Adm. THOMAS GRAVES. Invested by lord Nelson in Kiego Bay, 1801, June 14. Installed by proxy 1803, May 19.

1801, May 28. Maj. Gen. the Hon. JOHN HELY-HUTCHINSON, afterwards 2nd earl of Donoughmore. Installed 1803, May 19.

1801, June 6. Lieut. Gen. THOMAS TRIGGE. Installed by proxy 1803, May 19.

1801, June 6. R. Adm. JOHN THOMAS DUCKWORTH. Invested at Antigua by lord Lavington, 1801, Nov. 30. Installed by proxy 1803, May 19.

1801, Sept. 5. R. Adm. Sir JAMES SAUMAREZ, bart. Invested at Gibraltar by Gen. O'Hara, 1801, Nov. 17. Installed by proxy 1803, May 19.

Date of investiture

1802, May 19. Maj. Gen. EYRE COOTE. A supernumerary knight till the death of Sir Robert Sloper, 1802, Aug. Installed 1803, May 19.

1803, Feb. 16. Maj. Gen. JOHN FRANCIS CRADDOCK. Installed May 19.

12

1803, Apr. 28. Lieut. Gen. DAVID DUNDAS. Installed May 19.

Date of nomination

1804, May 21. Rt. Hon. ARTHUR PAGET. Installed 1812, June 1.

1804, Aug. 28. Maj. Gen. the Hon. ARTHUR WELLESLEY, afterwards duke of Wellington. A supernumerary knight till the death of viscount Nelson in Oct., 1805. Invested in India about March, 1805. Installed by proxy 1812, June 1.

1804, Sept. 26. Maj. Gen. the Hon. GEORGE JAMES LUDLOW, afterwards 3rd earl Ludlow. A supernumerary knight till the death of Sir Hector Munro in Jan., 1806. Invested 1804, Nov. 14. Installed 1812, June 1.

1804, Sept. 26. Maj. Gen. JOHN MOORE. A supernumerary knight till the death of Sir Andrew Mitchell in Feb., 1806. Invested 1804, Nov. 14. Not installed.

1804, Sept. 26. Commodore SAMUEL HOOD. A supernumerary knight till the death of earl Macartney in March, 1806. Invested at Antigua by lord Lavington in May, 1805. Installed by proxy 1812, June 1.

1806, Jan. 29. R. Adm. WILLIAM (CARNEGIE), 7th earl of Northesk. A supernumerary knight till the death of lord Lavington in Aug., 1807. Invested 1806, June 5. Installed 1812, June 1.

1806, Jan. 29. R. Adm. Sir RICHARD JOHN STRACHAN, bart. A supernumerary knight till the death of earl Grey in Nov., 1807. Invested 1807, Mar. 4. Installed 1812, June 1.

1806, Mar. 29. R. Adm. the Hon. ALEXANDER FORRESTER INGLIS COCHRANE. A supernumerary knight till the death of lord Dorchester in Nov., 1808. Installed by proxy 1812, June 1.

1806, Sept. 13. Maj. Gen. JOHN STUART. A supernumerary knight till the death of Sir John Moore in Jan., 1809. Invested 1807, Mar. 4. Installed 1812, June 1.

1806, Oct. 29. PHILIP FRANCIS. A supernumerary knight till the death of Sir William Pitt in Dec., 1809. Invested 1806, Oct. 29. Installed 1812, June 1.

1806, Oct. 29. Sir GEORGE HILARO BARLOW, bart. A supernumerary knight till the death of viscount Galway in July, 1810. Invested at Calcutta by lord Minto, 1807, Aug. 12. Installed by proxy 1812, June 1.

1808, Mar. PERCY CLINTON SYDNEY (SMYTHE), 6th viscount Strangford. A supernumerary knight till the death of Sir Henry Harvey in Dec., 1810. Invested 1808, Mar. 16. Installed by proxy 1812, June 1.

1808, Oct. 15. R. Adm. RICHARD GOODWIN KEATS. A supernumerary knight till the death of Sir James Craig in Jan., 1812. Invested 1809, July 12.

1809, Apr. 21. Lieut. Gen. Sir DAVID BAIRD, bart. A supernumerary knight till the death of lord Blaquiere in Aug., 1812. Invested 1809, Apr. 26. Installed 1812, June 1.

1809, Apr. 21. Lieut. Gen. the Hon. JOHN HOPE, afterwards 4th earl of Hopetoun. A supernumerary knight till the death of Sir George Yonge in Sept., 1812. Invested 1809, Apr. 26. Installed by proxy 1812, June 1.

1809, Apr. 21. Maj. Gen. BRENT SPENCER. A supernumerary knight till the resignation of the marquess of Wellington in May, 1813. Invested 1809, Apr. 26. Installed 1812, June 1.

1809, Apr. 24. Lieut. Gen. the Rt. Hon. GEORGE BECKWITH. A supernumerary knight till the death of Sir William Medows in Nov., 1813. Invested at Martinique by Sir Alexander Cochrane, 1809, Aug. 20. Installed by proxy 1812, June 1.

1809, Apr. 24. Capt. the Hon. THOMAS COCHRANE, commonly called lord Cochrane,, afterwards 10th earl of Dundonald. A supernumerary knight till the death of Sir Thomas Trigge in Jan., 1814. Invested 1809, Apr. 26. Installed 1812, June 1. Expelled the Order 1814, July 15, but re-admitted as G.C.B. 1847, May 22.

1809, Sept. 16. Maj. Gen. JOHN COPE SHERBROOKE. A supernumerary knight till the death of lord Bridport in May, 1814. Invested at Badajoz by viscount Wellington, 1809, Oct. 7. Installed by proxy 1812, June 1.

1810, Oct. 16. Lieut. Gen. WILLIAM CARR BERESFORD, afterwards viscount Beresford. A supernumerary knight till the death of Sir Thomas Graves in June, 1814. Invested by viscount Wellington at Mafra, 1810, Nov. 7. Installed by proxy 1812, June 1.

1812, Feb. 22. Lieut. Gen. THOMAS GRAHAM, afterwards lord Lynedoch. A supernumerary knight till the death of viscount Howe in July, 1814. Invested by the earl of Wellington, 1812, Mar. 10. Installed by proxy June 1.

1812, Feb 22. Lieut. Gen ROWLAND HILL, afterwards 1st viscount Hill. A supernumerary knight till the expulsion of lord Cochrane in July, 1814. Invested by the earl of Wellington, 1812, Mar. 10, at Elvas. Installed by proxy June 1.

1812, Feb 22. Maj. Gen. SAMUEL AUCHMUTY A supernumerary knight till the death of Sir Samuel Hood in Dec., 1814. Installed by proxy, June 1.

1812, Mar. 10. The Rt Hon. HENRY WELLESLEY, afterwards 1st lord Cowley. A supernumerary knight. Invested at Cadiz by the President of the Regency. Installed by proxy June 1.

Date of investiture

1812, June 12. Lieut. Gen. the Hon. EDWARD PAGET. A supernumerary knight.

Date of nomination

1812, Aug. 21. Lieut Gen Sir STAPLETON COTTON, bart., afterwards 1st viscount Combermere. A supernumerary knight. Invested by the marquess of Wellington in Sept. or Oct., 1812.

1812, Sept. 26. CHARLES STUART, afterwards 1st lord Stuart de Rothesay. A supernumerary knight. Invested at Lisbon, 1813, Jan. 17, by the marquess of Wellington.

1812, Oct. 10. Maj. Gen ISAAC BROCK. An extra knight. Slain in North America on the 13th of the same month.

1813, Feb. 1. Adm. the Hon. GEORGE CRANFIELD BERKELEY. A supernumerary knight. Invested 1813, Mar. 4.

1813, Feb. 1. Lieut. Gen the Rt. Hon. Sir GEORGE NUGENT, bart. A supernumerary knight. Invested by the earl of Moira, gov. gen. of India.

1813, Feb 1. Lieut. Gen. WILLIAM KEPPEL. A supernumerary knight.

1813, Feb 1. Lieut. Gen. Sir JOHN DOYLE, bart. A supernumerary knight. Knighted and invested same day at Carlton House.

1813, Feb. 1. Lieut. Gen. WILLIAM CAVENDISH BENTINCK, commonly called lord William Cavendish Bentinck. A supernumerary knight.

1813, Feb 1. Maj. Gen. JAMES LEITH. A supernumerary knight. Invested 1813, Mar. 4

1813, Feb. 1. Maj. Gen. THOMAS PICTON. A supernumerary knight. Invested 1813, Feb. 1.

1813, Feb. 1. Maj. Gen. GALBRAITH LOWRY COLE. A supernumerary knight. Invested by the marquess of Wellington at Ciudad Rodrigo in April, 1813.

1813, Feb. 1. Maj. Gen. the Hon CHARLES WILLIAM STEWART, afterwards 3rd marquess of Londonderry. A supernumerary knight.

1813, June 29. Lieut. Gen. the Hon. ALEXANDER HOPE. A supernumerary knight.

1813, June 29. Maj. Gen. HENRY CLINTON. A supernumerary knight. Invested 1814, July 28.

1813, Sept. 11. GEORGE (RAMSEY), 9th earl of Dalhousie, lieut. gen. A supernumerary knight. Invested by the marquess of Wellington, 1813, Sept. 27, at Lesaca.

1813, Sept. 11. Lieut. Gen. the Hon. WILLIAM STUART or STEWART. A supernumerary knight. Invested *ut supra.*

1813, Sept. 11. Maj. Gen. GEORGE MURRAY. A supernumerary knight. Invested *ut supra.*

1813, Sept. 11. Maj. Gen. the Hon. EDWARD MICHAEL PAKENHAM. a supernumerary knight. Invested *ut supra.*

1814, July 12. Adm. WILLIAM YOUNG. A supernumerary knight. Invested 1814, July 12.

1814, Aug. 16. WILLIAM FREDERICK HENRY, of Nassau, hereditary prince of Orange, afterwards William I, king of the Netherlands. A supernumerary knight. Invested at Brussels by viscount Castlereagh, 1814, Aug. 16.

ORDER REMODELLED, JAN. 2, 1815.

KNIGHTS GRAND CROSS—MILITARY DIVISION.

(G.C.B).

Existing Knights of the Bath declared to be Knights Grand Cross
under the new organisation of the Order.

1815, Jan. 2.   FREDERICK, duke of York.

1815, Jan. 2   Adm JOHN (JERVIS), 1st earl of St Vincent.

1815, Jan. 2.   Gen. Sir ROBERT ABERCROMBY.

1815, Jan. 2   Adm. GEORGE KEITH (ELPHINSTONE), 1st viscount Keith.

1815, Jan. 2.   Adm Sir JOHN BORLASE WARREN, bart.

1815, Jan. 2.   Gen Sir ALURED CLARKE.

1815, Jan. 2.   Adm. Sir JOHN COLPOYS

1815, Jan 2.   Gen JOHN (HELY-HUTCHINSON), lord Hutchinson, afterwards 2nd earl of Donoughmore.

1815, Jan. 2.   Adm. Sir JOHN THOMAS DUCKWORTH.

1815, Jan. 2.   Adm Sir JAMES SAUMAREZ.

1815, Jan. 2.   Gen. Sir EYRE COOTE.

1815, Jan. 2.   Gen Sir JOHN FRANCIS CRADOCK.

1815, Jan. 2.   Gen. Sir DAVID DUNDAS.

1815, Jan. 2.   F. Marsh. ARTHUR (WELLESLEY), duke of Wellington.

1815, Jan 2.   Gen. GEORGE JAMES (LUDLOW), 3rd earl Ludlow.

1815, Jan. 2.   Adm. WILLIAM (CARNEGIE), 7th earl of Northesk.

1815, Jan. 2.   V. Adm. Sir RICHARD JOHN STRACHAN.

1815, Jan. 2.   V. Adm. Sir ALEXANDER FORRESTER INGLIS COCHRANE.

1815, Jan. 2. Lieut. Gen. Sir JOHN STUART.

1815, Jan. 2. V. Adm. Sir RICHARD GOODWIN KEATS.

1815, Jan. 2. Gen. Sir DAVID BAIRD

1815, Jan. 2. Gen Sir GEORGE BECKWITH.

1815, Jan. 2. Lieut. Gen. JOHN (HOPE), lord Niddry, afterwards 4th earl of Hopetown.

1815, Jan. 2. Lieut. Gen. Sir BRENT SPENCER.

1815, Jan. 2. Lieut. Gen. Sir JOHN COPE SHERBROKE.

1815, Jan. 2. Lieut. Gen. WILLIAM CARR (BERESFORD), lord afterwards viscount Beresford.

1815, Jan. 2. Lieut. Gen. THOMAS (GRAHAM), 1st lord Lynedoch.

1815, Jan. 2. Lieut. Gen. ROWLAND (HILL), lord afterwards viscount Hill.

1815, Jan. 2. Lieut. Gen. Sir SAMUEL AUCHMUTY.

1815, Jan 2. Lieut. Gen. Sir EDWARD PAGET.

1815, Jan. 2. Lieut. Gen. STAPLETON (COTTON), lord afterwards Viscount Combermere.

1815, Jan. 2. Adm Sir GEORGE CRANFIELD BERKELEY.

1815, Jan. 2. Gen Sir GEORGE NUGENT, bart.

1815, Jan. 2. Gen. Sir WILLIAM KEPPELL

1815, Jan. 2. Lieut Gen. Sir JOHN DOYLE, bart.

1815, Jan. 2. Lieut. Gen. Sir WILLIAM CAVENDISH BENTINCK, commonly called lord William Cavendish Bentinck.

1815, Jan. 2. Lieut. Gen. Sir JAMES LEITH.

1815, Jan. 2. Lieut. Gen. Sir THOMAS PICTON.

1815, Jan 2. Lieut. Gen. Sir GALBRAITH LOWRY COLE

1815, Jan. 2. Lieut. Gen CHARLES WILLIAM (VANE), lord Stewart, afterwards 3rd marquess of Londonderry.

1815, Jan. 2.   Lieut. Gen. Sir ALEXANDER HOPE.

1815, Jan. 2.   Lieut. Gen. Sir HENRY CLINTON.

1815, Jan. 2.   Lieut. Gen. GEORGE (RAMSAY), 9th earl of Dalhousie.

1815, Jan. 2.   Lieut. Gen. Sir WILLIAM STEWART.

1815, Jan. 2.   Maj. Gen. Sir GEORGE MURRAY.

1815, Jan. 2.   Maj. Gen. Sir EDWARD MICHAEL PAKENHAM.

1815, Jan. 2   (Honorary) WILLIAM FREDERICK HENRY of NASSAU, hereditary prince of Orange, afterwards William I., king of the Netherlands

Subsequent appointments.

Date of nomination

1815, Jan 2   WILLIAM HENRY, duke of Clarence, afterwards William IV., acting Great Master, 1827.

1815, Jan. 2.   F. Marsh. EDWARD, duke of Kent.

1815, Jan. 2.   F. Marsh. ERNEST AUGUSTUS, duke of Cumberland, afterwards king of Hanover

1815, Jan. 2.   F. Marsh. ADOLPHUS FREDERICK, duke of Cambridge.

1815, Jan. 2.   F. Marsh WILLIAM FREDERICK, duke of Gloucester.

1815, Jan. 2.   Adm. SAMUEL (HOOD), 1st viscount Hood.

1815, Jan 2   Adm. Sir RICHARD ONSLOW, bart.

1815, Jan. 2.   Adm the Hon WILLIAM CORNWALLIS.

1815, Jan. 2.   Adm. WILLIAM (WALDEGRAVE), 1st lord Radstock.

1815, Jan. 2.   Adm. Sir ROGER CURTIS, bart.

1815, Jan 2.   Adm. GEORGE MONTAGU.

1815, Jan. 2.   Lieut. Gen. HENRY WILLIAM (PAGET), earl of Uxbridge, afterwards 1st marquess of Anglesey.

1815, Jan 2.   Gen. Sir ROBERT BROWNRIGG, bart

1815, Jan. 2.   Lieut. Gen. Sir HENRY CALVERT, bart.

1815, Jan. 2.   Lieut. Gen. the Rt. Hon. THOMAS MAITLAND.

1815, Jan. 2.   Gen. WILLIAM HENRY CLINTON.

1815, Apr. 1.   RICHARD (LE POER TRENCH), 6th earl of afterwards
1st viscount Clancarty.

1815, Apr. 7.   Lieut. Gen. the Hon. Sir JOHN ABERCROMBY.

1815, Apr. 7.   Maj. Gen. the Hon. CHARLES COLVILLE.

1815, June 7.   Adm. JAMES (GAMBIER), lord Gambier.   Invested
1816, July 5.

1815, Aug. 18.   F. Marsh. KARL PHILIP, prince Schwartzenburg.
Invested on that day as an honorary G.C.B. by the duke of
Wellington at Paris.

1815, Aug. 18.   F. Marsh. ALBERT LOUIS LEOPOLD, prince Blucher.
Invested *ut supra.*

1815, Aug. 18.   F. Marsh. Count BARCLAY DE TOLLY.   Invested
ut supra.

1815, Aug. 18.   F. Marsh. CHARLES PHILIP, prince von Wrede.
invested *ut supra.*

1815, Aug. 18.   WILLIAM FREDERICK CHARLES, prince and after-
wards king William I. of Wurtemburg.   Invested *ut supra.*

1815, June 22.   Maj. Gen. the Rt. Hon. Sir JAMES KEMPT.

1816, Mar. 16.   Adm. EDWARD (PELLEW), 1st lord Exmouth.

1816, May 23.   Gen. LEOPOLD GEORGE FREDERICK, duke of Saxe, etc.,
afterwards Leopold I., king of the Belgians.

1816, Dec. 10.   Maj. Gen. Sir DAVID OCHTERLONY, bart.

1817, Jan. 7.   Lieut. Gen. Sir GORDON DRUMMOND.

1817, Mar. 11.   Maj. Gen. Sir GEORGE TOWNSHEND WALKER, bart.

1818, Feb. 20.   Adm. Sir CHARLES MORICE POLE, bart.

1818, Feb. 20.   R. Adm. Sir THOMAS FRANCIS FREMANTLE.

1818, Feb. 20.   R. Adm. Sir GEORGE COCKBURN, afterwards bart.

1818, Oct. 14.   Gen. FRANCIS (RAWDON-HASTINGS), 1st marquess of Hastings.

1818, Oct. 14.   Lieut. Gen. Sir THOMAS HISLOP, bart.   Invested at Calcutta by the marquess of Hastings, 1819, May 11.

1819, Apr 17.   Prince VOLKOUSKY, gen. of the Russian Service (Honorary).

1819, Apr. 17.   Count WORONZOW, gen. of the Russian Service (Honorary)

1819, Apr. 17.   ERNST KARL COUNT VON ZIETEN, gen. of the Prussian Service (Honorary).

1819, Apr. 17.   JOHANN MARIA FRIMONT, afterwards count von Palota, etc. of the Austrian Service (Honorary).

1819, Nov. 20.   Maj. Gen. Sir JOHN MALCOLM.   Invested at Bombay by lieut, gen. Sir Charles Colville.

1820, Mar. 17.   Lieut Gen. KENNETH ALEXANDER (HOWARD), 12th lord Howard, of Effingham, afterwards 5th earl of Effingham.

1820, May 16.   Adm. Sir WILLIAM DOMETT

1820, May 16.   V. Adm. Sir THOMAS FOLEY.

1820, May 16.   Gen WILLIAM (HARCOURT), 3rd earl Harcourt, an extra G.C.B. in contemplation of the coronation of George IV.

1820, May 16.   Adm. BENJAMIN CALDWELL.   Extra *ut supra*

1820, May 16.   Adm. Sir RICHARD RODNEY BLIGH.   Extra *ut supra.*

1820, May 16   Gen. Sir HENRY JOHNSON, bart..   Extra *ut supra.*

1820, May 16.   Gen. HENRY (PHIPPS), 1st earl of Mulgrave.   Extra *ut supra.*

1820, May 16.   Adm Sir CHARLES HENRY KNOWLES, bart.   Extra *ut supra.*

1820, May 16.   Adm. the Hon Sir THOMAS PAKENHAM.   Extra *ut supra.*

1820, May 16. Gen. GEORGE (HARRIS), 1st lord Harris. Extra *ut supra.*

1820, May 16. Gen. Sir BANASTRE TARLETON, bart. Extra *ut supra.*

1820, May 16. Gen the Rt. Hon. Sir GEORGE HEWETT, bart. Extra *ut supra.*

1820, May 20. Gen. Sir GEORGE DON. Extra *ut supra.*

1820, May 20. Gen. JAMES (ST. CLAIR-ERSKINE), 2nd earl of Rosslyn, 9th Dragoons. Extra *ut supra.*

1820, May 20. Gen. GEORGE (GORDON), commonly called marquess of Huntley, afterwards 5th duke of Gordon. Extra *ut supra.*

1820, May 20. Lieut. Gen. CHARLES CREGAN CRAUFURD. Extra *ut supra.*

1820, May 20. Lieut. Gen Sir HILDEBRAND OAKES, bart. Extra *ut supra.*

1820, June 8. Adm. Sir GEORGE CAMPBELL.

1820, Aug. 12. Gen. CHARLES COUNT ALTEN, of the Hanoverian Service. An Honorary G.C.B.

1821, Feb. 23. V. Adm. Sir GEORGE MARTIN.

1822, Sept. 14. V. Adm Sir THOMAS BOULDEN THOMPSON, bart.

1822, Sept. 14. V. Adm. Sir HARRY NEALE, bart.

1824, Feb. 25. Lieut. Gen. Sir JOHN OSWALD, 35th Foot.

1825, Jan. 11. Adm. Sir EDWARD THORNBROUGH.

1825, Jan. 11. Adm Sir ELIAB HARVEY.

1825, Oct. 4. V. Adm. Sir WILLIAM JOHNSTONE HOPE.

1826, Jan. 24. Lieut. Gen. Sir HENRY FANE (Vane).

1826, Dec. 26. Maj. Gen. Sir ARCHIBALD CAMPBELL, bart.

1827, Nov. 13. V. Adm. Sir EDWARD CODRINGTON.

1830, Mar. 3. V. Adm. Sir THOMAS BYAM MARTIN.

1830, July 22. BERNARD, duke of Saxe-Weimar (Honorary).

1830, Nov. 17. Adm. Sir JAMES HAWKINS WHITSHED, bart.

1830, Nov. 17. Sir PHILIP CHARLES HENDERSON-DURHAM, afterwards Calderwood-Henderson-Durham.

1831, Feb. 16. ERNEST FREDERICK HERBERT, count Munster, minister of State and Cabinet of Hanover (Honorary).

1831, Feb. 24. Lieut. Gen. Sir WILLIAM HOUSTON, bart.

1831, Feb. 24. Lieut. Gen. Sir EDWARD BARNES.

1831, May 19. Adm. Sir HENRY TROLLOPE.

1831, June 6. Adm the Hon Sir ROBERT STOPFORD.

1831, June 6. Adm. Sir BENJAMIN HALLOWELL CAREW (extra).

1831, June 6. Lieut. Gen. Sir JOHN BYNG, afterwards 6th earl of Strafford.

1831, Sept. 13. Gen. the Hon. Sir HENRY GEORGE GREY. (Extra, on the Coronation of William IV.).

1831, Sept. 13. Gen. Sir RONALD CRAUFURD FERGUSON. Extra ut supra.

1831, Sept. 13. Gen. Sir HENRY WARDE. Extra ut supra.

1831, Sept. 13. Adm. Sir THOMAS WILLIAMS. Extra ut supra.

1831, Sept. 13. Adm. Sir WILLIAM HARGOOD. Extra ut supra.

1831, Sept. 13. Lieut Gen. the Hon. Sir WILLIAM LUMLEY. Extra ut supra.

1831, Sept 13. Lieut. Gen. Sir JAMES WILLOUGHBY GORDON, bart. Extra ut supra.

1831, Sept. 13. R. Adm. Sir THOMAS MASTERMAN HARDY, bart. Extra ut supra.

1833, Jan. 24. Adm. Sir DAVIDGE GOULD.

1833, Jan. 29. Adm. Sir CHARLES TYLER.

1833, Apr. 24. V. Adm. Sir PULTENEY MALCOLM.

1833, July 29. Lieut. Gen. Sir GEORGE ANSON.

1833, July 29. Lieut. Gen. Sir JOHN ORMSBY VANDELEUR.

1833, Aug. 1. Lieut. Gen. Sir THOMAS DALLAS, of the East India Company's Service.

1834, Apr. 16. Lieut. Gen. Sir HERBERT TAYLOR.

1834, May 23. F. Marsh. CHARLES, archduke of Austria (Honorary).

1834, Aug. 19. Lieut. Gen. LUDWIG GEORG THEDEL, count of Walmoden-Gimborn (Honorary).

1834, Oct. 6. Adm Sir JOHN WELLS.

1834, Oct. 17. Lieut. Gen. Sir ROBERT EDWARD HENRY SOMERSET, commonly called lord Robert Edward Henry Somerset.

1834, Dec. 19. Lieut. Gen. Sir WILLIAM HENRY PRINGLE.

1835, Mar. 28. Lieut. Gen. the Hon. Sir EDWARD STOPFORD.

1835, Aug. 3. Adm. Sir AMELIUS BEAUCLERK, commonly called lord Amelius Beauclerk.

1835, Aug. 29. Lieut. Gen ERNEST FREDERICK FERDINAND CHARLES WILLIAM PHILIP LOUIS, prince of Hesse Philippsthal Barchfeld (Honorary).

1836, Mar. 11. V. Adm Sir GRAHAM MOORE.

1836, June 11. Gen. LOUIS WILLIAM FREDERICK, landgrave of Hesse-Homburg (Honorary).

1836, Sept. 10. Lieut. Gen. MATTHEW (WHITWORTH-AYLMER), 5th lord Aylmer.

1837, Feb. 6. Lieut. Gen. Sir THOMAS MAKDOUGALL-BRISBANE, bart.

1837, Feb. 24. Adm. Sir LAWRENCE WILLIAM HALSTED.

1837, Mar. 10. Lieut. Gen Sir JOHN DOVETON, of the East India Company's Army. Invested at Madras by lord Elpinstone, 1839, Jan. 11.

1837, Mar. 10. Maj. Gen. Sir JOHN WHITTINGTON ADAMS. Nominated but died 1837, Mar 9, in India.

1837, May 30. Lieut. Gen. Sir RICHARD HUSSEY VIVIAN, bart.

1838, Jan. 29. Lieut. Gen. Sir JOHN COLBORNE, afterwards 1st lord Seaton Invested in Canada by Maj. Gen. Sir James Macdonnel, 1839, Oct. 22 (additional).

1838, Feb. 15. Lieut Gen Sir THOMAS BRADFORD.

1838, Feb 16. Maj Gen. Sir HENRY WORSLEY, of the East India Company's Army

1838, Apr. 20 Lieut. Gen. Sir FREDERICK PHILIPSE ROBINSON.

1838, July 19. Adm. Sir WILLIAM SIDNEY SMITH (extra on the Queen's coronation).

1838, July 19. Lieut. Gen. Sir JOHN LAMBERT (extra).

1838, July 19. Lieut Gen. the Hon. Sir ROBERT WILLIAM O'CALLAGHAN (extra).

1838, July 20. Maj. Gen. Sir ALEXANDER CALDWELL, of the East India Company's Army (extra).

1838, July 20. Maj Gen. Sir JAMES LAW LUSHINGTON, of the East India Company's Army (extra).

1838, July 23 Maj. Gen Sir ALEXANDER DICKSON (extra).

1839, June 12. FERDINAND GEORGE AUGUSTUS, prince of Saxe Coburg Saalfeld (Honorary)

1839, Aug. 12. Lieut. Gen. Sir JOHN KEANE, afterwards 1st lord Keane (additional).

1839, Oct. 25. Adm. Sir HENRY WILLIAM BAYNTUN.

1840, Jan. 21. Maj Gen Sir WILLOUGHBY COTTON. Invested at Jellalabad by Sir W. H. Macnaughten (additional).

1840, Mar 6. F. Marsh. H.R.H. FRANCIS ALBERT AUGUSTUS CHARLES EMANUEL, duke of Saxony, prince of Saxe Coburg and Gotha, consort of Queen Victoria. Invested at St. James's Palace, Mar 6. Nominated 1843, May 31, as First and Principal G.C B and acting Great Master in the room of H R H. the duke of Sussex deceased.

1840, June 20. Lieut. Gen. the Rt. Hon. Sir FREDERICK ADAM.

1840, June 20 Lieut. Gen Sir BENJAMIN D'URBAN.

1840, June 20. Lieut. Gen. Sir ANDREW FRANCIS BARNARD.

1840, July 4. Adm. Sir WILLIAM HOTHAM.

1840, July 4. Adm. Sir JOSIAS ROWLEY, bart.

1840, July 4. V. Adm. Sir CHARLES ROWLEY, bart.

1840, July 4. V. Adm. Sir DAVID MILNE.

1840, July 20. Gen. BALDOMERO ESPARTERO, count of Luchana, and duke de la Victoria y de Morella. In the service of the Queen of Spain (Honorary). Appointed on or before July 18; dispensed for investiture and installation July 20.

1841, Feb. 12. Maj. Gen. Sir JOSEPH O'HALLORAN, of the Bengal Army.

1841, Oct. 14. Maj. Gen. HUGH GOUGH, afterwards 1st viscount Gough, commanding the forces in China.

1842, Feb. 23. Adm. the Hon. Sir JOHN TALBOT.

1842, Feb. 23. Adm. Sir ROBERT BARLOW.

1842, Feb. 23. Adm. Sir HENRY DIGBY.

1842, May 30. Lieut. Gen. EMANUEL, count MENSDORFF-POUILLY.

1842, June 16. Col. Sir ROBERT HENRY SALE, serving with the rank of Maj. Gen. in Afghanistan.

1842, Nov. 5. Archduke FREDERICK CHARLES, of Austria (Honorary). Dispensed of all ceremonies Nov. 10; appointed a G.C.B. 1841, Jan. 12, but on the representation of the Austrian Court invested only as a C.B. by Adm. Stopford by warrant of 1841, Jan. 16.

1842, Dec. 2. V. Adm. Sir WILLIAM PARKER.

1842, Dec. 2. Maj. Gen. GEORGE POLLOCK.

1842, Dec. 2. Maj. Gen. WILLIAM NOTT, of the East India Company's Service.

1843, July 4. Maj. Gen. Sir CHARLES JAMES NAPIER.

1843, Aug. 18. Prince FREDERICK WILLIAM CHARLES, of Prussia (Honorary).

1845, May 8. Adm. Sir ROBERT WALLER OTWAY, bart.

1845, May 8.   V. Adm. Sir EDWARD WILLIAM CAMPBELL RICH OWEN.

1846, Apr 7.   Col. Sir HENRY GEORGE WAKELYN SMITH, serving with the rank of Maj Gen in India.

1846, Nov. 10.   Prince WALDEMER of Prussia (Honorary). Warrant on that day to the earl of Westmorland, British ambassador at Berlin, to invest him.

1847, May 22. V Adm THOMAS (COCHRANE), 10th earl of Dundonald (see "Cochrane" under K.B., 1809, Apr. 21, p. 177, *supra*).

1847, Sept. 17.   FITZROY JAMES HENRY SOMERSET, called lord Fitzroy Somerset, afterwards 1st lord Raglan.

1847, Sept. 17.   Lieut. Gen. Sir John MACDONALD, adj. gen. of the Forces.

1847, Dec. 30.   Gen. Sir COLIN HALKETT.

1848, Jan. 31.   Maj. Gen. Sir JOHN HUNTER LITTLER, of the Bengal Infantry.

1848, Aug. 25.   Sir JAMES LILLYMAN CALDWELL.

1849, May 7.   Lieut. Gen. Sir EDWARD BLAKENEY.

1849, June 5.   Maj. Gen. Sir JOSEPH THACKWELL.

1849, June 5.   Maj. Gen. Sir WALTER RALEIGH GILBERT, in the service of the East India Company.

1852, Apr 6.   Adm. Sir CHARLES EKINS.

1852, Apr. 6.   Gen. Sir PEREGRINE MAITLAND.

1852, Apr. 6.   Adm. the Hon. Sir THOMAS BLADEN CAPEL.

1852, Apr. 6.   Lieut. Gen Sir ALEXANDER WOODFORD.

1852, Apr. 6   Lieut. Gen. Sir HENRY FREDERICK BOUVERIE.

1852, Apr. 6.   V. Adm. Sir CHARLES BULLEN.

1852, Apr. 6.   Lieut. Gen. Sir JOHN FOX BURGOYNE, inspector general of fortifications.

1854, Aug. 12. F. Marsh. H.H. OMAR LUTFI PACHA, generalissimo of the Turkish Forces (Honorary).

1855, July 5. Lieut. Gen. Sir GEORGE BROWN.

1855, July 5. V. Adm. JAMES WHITLEY DEANS DUNDAS.

1855, July 5. Lieut. Gen. H.R.H. GEORGE WILLIAM FREDERICK CHARLES, duke of Cambridge.

1855, July 5. Lieut. Gen. Sir DE LACY EVANS.

1855, July 5. Lieut. Gen. Sir RICHARD ENGLAND, Maj. Gen. with the rank of Lieut. Gen. in Turkey.

1855, July 5. Lieut. Gen. Sir COLIN CAMPBELL, afterwards lord Clyde, Maj. Gen. with the rank of Lieut. Gen. in Turkey.

1855, July 5. R. Adm. Sir EDMUND LYONS, bart.

1855, July 5. Lieut. Gen. Sir GEORGE CATHCART, would have been recommended for the G.C.B. had he survived.

1855, July 5. Adm. Sir GRAHAM EDEN HAMOND, bart.

1855, July 5. Adm. Sir JAMES ALEXANDER GORDON.

1855, July 5. Gen. Sir JAMES MCDONELL.

1855, July 5. Gen. Sir HEW DALRYMPLE ROSS.

1855, Sept. 5. Gen. FRANCOIS CERTAIN CANROBERT (Honorary).

1855, Sept. 5. H.I.H. Prince NAPOLEON (Honorary).

1855, Oct. 16. His Excellency JEAN BAPTISTE PHILIBERT COMTE VAILLANT, senator and marshall of France, grand marshall of the Palace of Napoleon, and secretary of state for war (Honorary).

1855, Oct. 16. Gen. JAMES SIMPSON.

1855, Oct. 25. Gen. ALFONSO FERRERO DELLA MARMORA, commanding-in-chief his Sardinian Majesty's forces in the Crimea (Honorary).

1855, Nov. 12. His Excellency marshall AIMABLE JEAN JACQUES PÉLISSIER, afterwards duc de Malakoff, commanding-in-chief the French army in the Crimea (Honorary).

13

1856, Jan. 3. Gen. PIERRE FRANCOIS JOSEPH BOSQUET, gen. of division, an officer of his Imperial Majesty the emperor of the French, afterwards marsh. of France (Honorary).

1856, Jan 3. Gen. CHARLES MARIE JOSEPH MARIUS COMTE DE SALLES, general of division, an officer of his Imperial Majesty the Emperor of the French (Honorary).

1856, Jan. 3. Gen. MARIE EDME PATRICK MAURICE DE MACMAHON, general of division, an officer of his Imperial Majesty the Emperor of the French, afterwards duc de Magenta and marsh. of France (Honorary).

1856, Jan. 3. Gen. AUGUSTE MICHEL ETIENNE count REGNAULT DE SAINT JEAN D'ANGELY, general of division, an officer of his Imperial Majesty the Emperor of the French, afterwards marsh. of France (Honorary).

1856, Jan. 3. LOUIS MICHEL MORRIS, gen of division, an officer of his Imperial Majesty the Emperor of the French (Honorary).

1857, Jan. 1 H R H. prince FREDERICK WILLIAM LEWIS, of Prussia, afterwards king William I., of Prussia, and emperor William I., of Germany, col. gen. in the Service of His Majesty the king of Prussia (Honorary). Warrant of appointment dated 1856, Dec. 10.

1857, May 7. Adm. FERDINAND ALPHONSE HAMELIN, senateur, ministre secretaire d'Etat au département de la Marine et des colonies, officer of the marine of the Emperor of the French (Honorary)

1857, July 30. Lieut. Gen. Sir JAMES OUTRAM, of the Bombay Army.

1858, July 6. Maj. Gen. Sir HUGH HENRY ROSE, afterwards lord Strathnairn.

1858, July 6. H.H. the MAHARAJAH JUNG BAHADOOR KOONWAR RANAJEE, commander-in-chief of the Goorkha troops lately acting with the British Army in India.

1859, May 20. R Adm Sir MICHAEL SEYMOUR, late commander-in-chief of Her Majesty's Naval Forces in the East Indies and China.

1859, June 21. Gen. Sir THOMAS McMAHON, bart.

1859, June 21 Gen. CHARLES MURRAY (CATHCART), 2nd earl Cathcart.

1859, June 21. Gen Sir WILLIAM MAYNARD GOMM.

1859, June 21. Gen. Sir ROBERT WILLIAM GARDINER.

1860, May 18. Adm. Sir JOHN WEST.

1860, May 18. Adm Sir WILLIAM HALL GAGE, knight.

1860, May 18. Adm. Sir FRANCIS WILLIAM AUSTEN.

1860, May 18. Adm. Sir THOMAS JOHN COCHRANE.

1860, May 18. Adm. Sir GEORGE FRANCIS SEYMOUR.

1860, May 18. Gen. Sir JAMES DAWES DOUGLAS.

1860, May 18. Gen. Sir GEORGE SCOVELL.

1860, May 18. ULYSSES (BURGH), 2nd lord Downes, gen.

1860, May 18. Gen. Sir FREDERICK STOVIN.

1860, May 18. Gen. Sir JAMES FERGUSSON.

1860, May 18 Gen. Sir JOHN BELL.

1860, June 29. Lieut. Gen. Sir CHARLES YORKE, military secretary to H R.H the [duke of Cambridge] general commanding-in-chief

1860, Nov 9. Lieut. Gen. Sir JAMES HOPE GRANT, commanding Her Majesty's Military Forces in China.

1861, Mar. 1. Maj. Gen. Sir PATRICK GRANT, of the Bengal Infantry, serving with the local rank of Lieut. Gen. in the East Indies, late commander-in-chief at Madras.

1861, June 28. Gen. Sir ARTHUR BENJAMIN CLIFTON.

1861, June 28. Adm. Sir PHIPPS HORNBY.

1861, June 28. Gen. Sir JAMES ARCHIBALD HOPE.

1861, June 28. Gen. Sir THOMAS WILLIAM BROTHERTON.

1861, June 28. Gen. Sir SAMUEL BENJAMIN AUCHMUTY.

1861, June 28. Adm. Sir BARRINGTON REYNOLDS.

1861, June 28.   Gen. Sir THOMAS WILLSHIRE, bart.

1861, June 28.   V. Adm. the Rt. Hon. Sir MAURICE FREDERICK FITZHARDINGE BERKELEY, afterwards 1st lord Fitzhardinge.

1861, June 28.   Lieut. Gen. Sir HARRY DAVID JONES.

1862, Nov. 10.   Gen. Sir JOHN WRIGHT GUISE, bart. (on the occasion of the coming of age of H.R.H. the prince of Wales).

1862, Nov. 10.   Gen. Sir JOHN FORSTER FITZGERALD (same occasion).

1862, Nov. 10.   Adm. ANTHONY (MAITLAND), 10th earl of Lauderdale (same occasion).

1862, Nov. 10.   Adm. Sir EDWARD TUCKER, reserved half pay of the Navy (same occasion).

1865, Feb. 10.   Gen. H.R.H. ALBERT EDWARD, prince of Wales.

1865, Mar. 28.   Adm. Sir EDWARD HARVEY.

1865, Mar. 28.   Adm Sir FAIRFAX MORESBY.

1865, Mar. 28.   Gen. Sir WILLIAM ROWAN.

1865, Mar. 28.   Adm. Sir HOUSTON STEWART.

1865, Mar. 28.   Gen. Sir WILLIAM JOHN CODRINGTON.

1865, Mar. 28.   Gen. Sir GEORGE AUGUSTUS WETHERALL.

1865, Mar. 28.   Adm. Sir HENRY DUCIE CHADS.

1865, Mar. 28.   Gen. Sir JAMES FREDERICK LOVE.

1865, Mar. 28   Gen. Sir JAMES JACKSON.

1865, Mar. 28.   Lieut. Gen. Sir JOHN CHEAPE, Royal (late Bengal) Engineers.

1865, Mar. 28.   Lieut. Gen. HENRY (DUNDAS), 3rd viscount Melville.

1865, Mar. 28.   V. Adm. the Hon. Sir FREDERICK WILLIAM GREY.

1865, Mar. 28.   V. Adm. Sir JAMES HOPE.

1865, June 7.   Adm. Sir GEORGE ROBERT LAMBERT.

1867, Mar. 13. Adm. Sir STEPHEN LUSHINGTON.

1867, Mar. 13. Lieut. Gen. Sir JOHN LYSAGHT PENNEFATHER.

1867, Mar. 13. Lieut. Gen. Sir RICHARD AIREY.

1867, Mar. 13. Adm. Sir CHARLES HOWE FREMANTLE.

1867, Mar. 13. Maj Gen. Sir ARCHDALE WILSON, bart.

1867, Mar. 13. Lieut. Gen. Sir EDWARD LUGARD.

1867, Mar. 13. Gen. Sir JOHN AITCHISON.·

1867, Mar. 13. Gen. the Hon. Sir CHARLES STEPHEN GORE.

1867, Mar. 13. GEORGE (HAY), 8th marquess of Tweeddale, gen.

1868, Apr. 27. Lieut. Gen. Sir ROBERT CORNELIS NAPIER, after-
wards lord Napier of Magdala. Lieut. Gen. commanding
Her Majesty's forces in Abyssinia.

1869, June 2. Adm. Sir HENRY PRESCOTT.

1869, June 2. GEORGE CHARLES (BINGHAM), 3rd earl of Lucan, gen

1869, June 2. Gen. Sir RICHARD JAMES DACRES.

1869, June 2. Lieut. Gen. the Hon. Sir JAMES YORKE SCARLETT.

1869, June 2. Lieut. Gen. Sir GEORGE BULLER.

1869, June 2. V. Adm. Sir AUGUSTUS LEOPOLD KUPER.

1870, May 14. Lieut. Gen. Sir WILLIAM ROSE MANSFIELD, after-
wards 1st lord Sandhurst (late commander-in-chief in
India).

1871, May 20. Adm. the Hon. Sir HENRY KEPPEL.

1871, May 20. Gen. Sir WILLIAM FENWICK WILLIAMS, bart.

1871, May 20. Adm. Sir ALEXANDER MILNE.

1871, May 20. Gen. Sir ROBERT JOHN HUSSEY VIVIAN.

1871, May 20. Lieut. Gen. Sir JOHN MICHEL.

1871, May 20. Lieut. Gen. Sir WILLIAM PAULET, commonly called lord William Paulet.

1871, May 20. Adm. Sir SYDNEY COLPOYS DACRES.

1873, May 24. Gen. Sir HENRY GEORGE ANDREW TAYLOR, Madras Army.

1873, May 24. Gen. Sir GEORGE BOWLES.

1873, May 24. Adm. Sir PROVO WILLIAM PARRY WALLIS.

1873, May 24. Adm Sir WILLIAM FANSHAWE MARTIN, bart.

1873, May 24. Gen. Sir ABRAHAM ROBERTS.

1873, May 24. Gen. Sir JAMES CHARLES CHATTERTON, bart.

1873, May 24. THOMAS (MAITLAND), 11th earl of Lauderdale, adm.

1873, May 24. Adm. Sir LEWIS TOBIAS JONES.

1873, May 24. Gen. Sir WILLIAM HENRY ELLIOTT.

1873, May 24. Lieut. Gen. Sir SYDNEY JOHN COTTON.

1873, May 24. Lieut. Gen. Sir JOHN BLOOMFIELD.

1873, May 24. Lieut. Gen. Sir DUNCAN ALEXANDER CAMERON.

1875, May 29. Gen. Sir THOMAS REED.

1875, May 29. HENRY (MONTAGU), 6th lord Rokeby, gen.

1875, May 29. Gen. Sir JOHN BLOOMFIELD GOUGH.

1875, May 29. Gen. Sir CHARLES THOMAS VAN STRAUBENZEE.

1875, May 29. Lieut. Gen. the Hon. Sir AUGUSTUS ALMERIC SPENCER.

1875, May 29. V. Adm. Sir HASTINGS REGINALD YELVERTON.

1875, May 29. Lieut. Gen. Sir CHARLES SHEPHERD STUART, Bombay Army.

1875, May 29. Lieut. Gen. Sir JOHN GARVOCK.

1875, May 29. Lieut. Gen. Sir NEVILLE BOWLES CHAMBERLAIN, Bengal Army.

1875, May 29. Maj. Gen. Sir ALFRED HASTINGS HORSFORD.

1877, Jan. 1. (Honorary) Gen. H.H. JIOJI RAO SINDIA, Maharaja of Gwalior.

1877, June 2. Adm. Sir GEORGE RODNEY MUNDY.

1877, June 2. Gen. Sir WILLIAM WYLLIE.

1877, June 2. Lieut. Gen. Sir FREDERICK EDWARD CHAPMAN.

1877, June 2. Lieut. Gen. Sir FREDERICK PAUL HAINES.

1877, June 2. Lieut. Gen. Sir DAVID EDWARD WOOD

1877, June 2. Maj. Gen. Sir JOHN DOUGLAS.

1878, June 13. Gen Sir ARTHUR AUGUSTUS THURLOW CUNYNGHAME.

1878, July 3. (Honorary) Gen H R H. prince FREDERICK CHARLES NICHOLAS, of Prussia.

1878, July 29. Gen. Sir JOHN LINTON ARABIN SIMMONS.

1879, Aug. 19. Maj. Gen FREDERICK AUGUSTUS (THESIGER), 2nd lord Chelmsford, with rank of lieut. gen. while in command of the forces at the Cape of Good Hope.

1880, Apr. 23. SIR GEORGE ROSE SARTORIUS, adm. of the Fleet.

1880, Apr. 23. Sir THOMAS MATTHEW CHARLES SYMONDS, adm. of the Fleet.

1880, Apr. 23. Adm. the Hon. Sir JAMES ROBERT DRUMMOND.

1880, June 19. Lieut. Gen. Sir GARNET JOSEPH WOLSELEY, afterwards viscount Wolseley, late governor and high commissioner of the Colonies of Natal and Transvaal and commanding the forces in South Africa.

1880, Sept. 21. Lieut. Gen. Sir DONALD MARTIN STEWART.

1880, Sept. 21. Maj. Gen. Sir FREDERICK SLEIGH ROBERTS.

1881, May 24. Gen. WILLIAM LYGON (PAKENHAM), 6th earl of Longford.

1881, May 24. V. Adm Sir FREDERICK BEAUCHAMP PAGET SEYMOUR, afterwards lord Alcester.

1882, Apr. 15. Gen. Sir CHARLES HENRY ELLICE.

1882, Nov. 17. Lieut. Gen. Sir JOHN MILLER ADYE.

1882, Nov. 24 Adm. Sir ASTLEY COOPER KEY.

1882, Nov. 24. Adm. Sir WILLIAM ROBERT MENDS, director of transports (extra).

1883, Jan. 25. F. Marsh. FREDERICK WILLIAM NICHOLAS CHARLES, crown prince of Prussia, afterwards emperor Frederick III. of Germany.

1884, May 24. Gen. Sir CHARLES WILLIAM DUNBAR STAVELEY.

1884, May 24. Gen. Sir COLLINGWOOD DICKSON, V.C.

1884, May 24. Gen. Sir ARTHUR BORTON.

1884, May 24. Gen Sir HENRY CHARLES BARNSTON DAUBENEY.

1884, May 24 Gen. Sir JAMES BRIND.

1885, July 3. Maj. Gen. Sir PETER STARK LUMSDEN.

1885, July 22. (Honorary) Gen. his highness prince ALEXANDRE LOUIS GEORGE FRÉDÉRIC EMILE, of Hesse.

1885, Dec. 19. Adm. Sir GEOFFREY THOMAS PHIPPS HORNBY.

1886, Jan. 30. Lieut. Gen. Sir FREDERICK CHARLES ARTHUR STEPHENSON.

1886, May 29. Adm. lord CLARENCE EDWARD PAGET, P.C.

1886, May 29. Gen. GEORGE FREDERICK (UPTON), 3rd viscount Templetown.

1886, May 29. Gen Sir WILLIAM JONES.

1886, May 29. Gen. Sir CHARLES REID, Bengal Staff Corps.

1886, May 29. Gen. Sir GEORGE MALCOLM, Bombay Staff Corps.

1886, May 29. Gen. Sir DANIEL LYSONS.

1886, May 29. Lieut. Gen. and Honorary Gen. Sir FREDERICK FRANCIS MAUDE, V.C.

1886, July 30. Adm. Sir JOHN HAY, commonly called lord John Hay.

1886, Dec. 10. (Honorary) His Highness Prince ALEXANDER JOSEPH, of Bulgaria, in lieu of the Civil distinction of the G.C.B. to which he was gazetted 1879, June 6.

1887, June 21. Adm. Sir GEORGE GREVILLE WELLESLEY.

1887, June 21. Adm. Sir EDWARD GENNYS FANSHAWE.

1887, June 21. Gen. Sir EDWARD COOPER HODGE.

1887, June 21. Gen. the Rt. Hon. Sir THOMAS MONTAGUE STEELE.

1887, June 21. Gen. Sir EDWIN BEAUMONT JOHNSON, Royal Artillery.

1887, June 21. Gen. Sir HENRY WYLIE NORMAN, Bengal Staff Corps.

1887, June 21. (Additional) prince WILLIAM AUGUSTUS EDWARD, of Saxe-Weimar, gen. (gazetted on the 21st to civil division but on the 28th June to the military division, G.C.B.).

1887, June 21. (Additional) Adm. Sir WILLIAM HOUSTON STEWART.

1887, June 21. (Additional) Adm. Sir JOHN EDMUND COMMERELL, V.C.

1887, June 21. (Additional) Lieut. Gen. and Honorary Gen. Sir CHARLES LAWRENCE D'AGUILAR, Royal Artillery.

1887, June 21. (Additional Lieut. Gen. Sir ARCHIBALD ALISON, bart., commanding the Division, Aldershot.

1887, June 21. (Additional) Lieut. Gen. Sir CHARLES HENRY BROWNLOW, Bengal Staff Corps.

1887, July 1, and Sept. 27. (Additional) Adm. H.S.H. ERNEST LEOPOLD VICTOR CHARLES AUGUSTE JOSEPH EMICH, of Leiningen, Royal Navy [promoted from G.C.B. civil division], gazetted as Honorary G.C.B. on July 1 and as additional G.C.B. on Sept. 27, with precedence as from 1866, June 29.

1889, May 25. Adm. H.R.H. ALFRED ERNEST ALBERT, duke of Edinburgh, personal aide-de-camp to the Queen, late commander-in-chief on the Mediterranean station.

1889, May 25. Gen. Sir FREDERICK HORN.

1889, May 25. Gen. Sir JOHN ST. GEORGE, Royal Artillery.

1889, May 25.   Gen. Sir ARCHIBALD LITTLE.

1889, May 25.   Gen. Sir HENRY DALY, Bombay Staff Corps.

1889, May 25.   Lieut. Gen. and Honorary Gen. Sir ALEXANDER
TAYLOR, Royal Engineers.

1889, Sept. 3.   Adm. Sir ARTHUR WILLIAM ACLAND HOOD.

1890, July 1.   (Honorary) His Imperial Highness Prince AKIHITO
of Komatsu, general-in-chief of the Japanese Imperial
Household Troops.

1891, May 30.   Gen. Sir SAMUEL JAMES BROWNE, V.C., Indian Staff
Corps.

1891, May 30.   Gen. Sir CHARLES PATTON KEYES, Indian Staff
Corps.

1891, May 30.   Gen. Sir JOHN ROSS, commanding the troops in the
Dominion of Canada.

1891, May 30.   Lieut. Gen. Sir JOHN CHETHAM McLEOD.

1891, May 30.   Lieut. Gen. Sir HENRY EVELYN WOOD, V.C., com-
manding the troops, Aldershot.

1892, May 16.   (Honorary) His Grand Ducal Highness gen. prince
HENRY LOUIS WILLIAM ADALBERT WALDEMAR ALEXANDER,
of Hesse.

1892, May 25.   Adm. Sir GEORGE OMMANNEY WILLES.

1893, June 3.   Lieut. Gen. Sir JAMES HILLS-JOHNES, V.C., Royal
(late Bengal) Artillery.

1893, June 3.   Gen. Sir WILLIAM MONTAGU SCOTT McMURDO.

1893, June 3.   Gen. lord MARK KERR.

1893, Nov. 17.   Adm. Sir ANTHONY HILEY HOSKINS.

1894, May 26.   Gen. Sir ROBERT ONESIPHORUS BRIGHT.

1894, May 26.   Gen. Sir ROBERT PHAYRE, Indian Staff Corps.

1894, May 26.   Honorary Maj. Gen. Sir CHARLES HENRY PALLISER,
retired full pay, late Indian Staff Corps.

1894, May 26. Gen. Sir CHARLES GEORGE ARBUTHNOT, Royal Artillery.

1894, May 26. Lieut. Gen. (temporary Gen.) the Rt. Hon. Sir REDVERS HENRY BULLER, V.C., adjut. gen. to the Forces.

1895, May 25. Gen. Sir MICHAEL ANTHONY SHRAPNEL BIDDULPH, col. commandant Royal Artillery.

1895, May 25. Gen. Sir GEORGE HARRY SMITH WILLIS, col. the Devonshire Regiment.

1895, May 25. Gen. Sir CHARLES JOHN STANLEY GOUGH, V.C., Indian Army.

1895, May 25. Lieut. Gen. Sir DRURY CURZON DRURY-LOWE, col. 17th Lancers.

1895, May 25. Adm. Sir WILLIAM MONTAGU DOWELL.

1895, May 25. RICHARD JAMES (MEADE), 4th earl of Clanwilliam, Admiral of the Fleet.

1895, May 25. Adm. Sir RICHARD VESEY HAMILTON.

1895, June 28. Adm. Sir FREDERICK WILLIAM RICHARDS.

1896, Jan. 21. Maj. Gen. Sir ROBERT CUNLIFFE LOW, Indian Army, commanding a first-class district in India, in recognition of services during the operation of the Chitral Relief Force.

1896, May 20. Gen. Sir HUGH HENRY GOUGH, V.C., Indian Staff Corps.

1896, May 20. Lieut. Gen. Sir GERALD GRAHAM, V.C., Royal Engineers.

1896, May 20. Gen. Sir GEORGE RICHARDS GREAVES.

1897, June 22. (Additional) Gen. Sir ANTHONY BLAXLAND STRANSHAM, Royal Marines.

1897, June 22. (Additional) Lieut. Gen. (Local Gen.) Sir GEORGE STEWART WHITE, V.C., commander-in-chief, East Indies.

1897, June 22. (Additional) Maj. Gen. and Hon. Lieut. Gen. Sir HENRY MARSHMAN HAVELOCK-ALLAN, bart., V.C., col. the Royal Irish Regiment.

1897, June 22. (Additional) Adm. Sir NOWELL SALMON, V.C., commander-in-chief, Portsmouth.

1897, June 22. (Additional) Adm. Sir ALGERNON McLENNAN LYONS, principal naval A.D C

1897, June 22. (Additional) Adm. Sir MICHAEL CULME-SEYMOUR, bart.

1898, May 20. Gen. Sir WILLIAM STEPHEN ALEXANDER LOCKHART, Indian Army, in recognition of services during the recent operations on the North-West Frontier of India.

1898, May 21. Gen. H R.H. ARTHUR WILLIAM PATRICK ALBERT, duke of Connaught and Strathearn, A.D.C., commanding the Troops, Aldershot.

1898, Nov. 15. Lieut. Gen. Sir FRANCIS WALLACE GRENFELL, commanding the Force in Egypt, in recognition of services in Egypt and the Sudan, including the battles of Atbara and Khartum. Afterwards lord Grenfell.

1898, Nov. 15. Maj. Gen. HORATIO HERBERT, LORD KITCHENER, Royal Engineers, Sirdar of the Egyptian Army (same occasions)

1899, June 3. Gen. Sir JOHN FORBES, Bombay Cavalry.

1899, June 3. Adm Sir WALTER JAMES HUNT-GRUBBE.

1899, June 3. Adm. the Hon. Sir EDMUND ROBERT FREMANTLE.

1899, June 3. Adm. Sir JOHN OMMANNEY HOPKINS.

1899, June 3. Gen. Sir ROBERT BIDDULPH, Royal Artillery, governor and commander-in-chief Gibraltar.

1900, May 23 Gen. Sir CHARLES COOPER JOHNSON, Indian Staff Corps.

1900, May 23 Lieut. Gen. Sir BAKER CREED RUSSELL, col. 13th Hussars, commanding the Troops Southern District.

1900, May 23. Gen. Sir WILLIAM OLPHERTS, V.C., col. commandant Royal (late Bengal) Artillery.

1900, Nov. 9. V. Adm. Sir EDWARD HOBART SEYMOUR.

1900, Nov. 29. Lieut. Gen. (temporary gen.) Sir HENRY BRACKEN-BURY, col. commandant, Royal Artillery, in recognition of services in connection with the campaign in South Africa, 1899–1900. (*See* footnote on p. 347.)

1900, Nov. 29. Lieut. Gen. Sir CHARLES MANSFIELD CLARKE, bart., (same occasion).

1901, Mar. 19. (Honorary) prince LUITPOLD CHARLES JOSEPH GUILLAUME LOUIS, regent of Bavaria.

1901, Aug. 16. (Honorary) field-marshal count VON WALDERSEE.

1902, June 26. Adm. the lord WALTER TALBOT KERR, 4th son of 7th marquess of Lothian.

1902, June 26. Adm. Sir JOHN ARBUTHNOT FISHER.

1902, June 26. V. Adm. Sir FREDERICK GEORGE DENHAM BEDFORD.

1902, June 26. (Additional) Adm. the Rt. Hon. Sir JOHN CHARLES DALRYMPLE HAY, bart. (retired).

1902, June 26. (Additional) Sir WILLIAM GRAHAM (retired).

1902, June 26. (Additional) Adm. Sir ALGERNON CHARLES FIESCHI HENEAGE (retired).

1902, June 26. (Additional) Adm. Sir ALEXANDER BULLER (retired).

1902, June 26. Gen. Sir RICHARD CHAMBRE HAYES TAYLOR.

1902, June 26. Gen. Sir HARRY NORTH DALRYMPLE PRENDERGAST. V.C., unemployed supernumerary list, Royal (late Madras) Engineers.

1902, June 26. Gen. Sir JOHN WATSON, V.C., unemployed supernumerary list, Indian Staff Corps.

1902, June 26. Lieut. Gen. Sir ROBERT HUME.

1902, June 26. Gen. Sir MARTIN DILLON.

1902, June 26. Gen. Sir REGINALD GIPPS.

1902, June 26. Lieut. Gen. Sir ROBERT GRANT.

1902, Sept. 19. His Majesty MENELEK II., emperor of Ethiopia.

1902, Oct. 31. (Additional) Lieut. Gen. PAUL SANFORD (METHUEN), 3rd lord Methuen (for services in South Africa).

1902, Nov. 9. (Additional) Adm. Sir ROBERT HENRY MORE MOLYNEUX

1902, Nov. 9. (Additional) Adm Sir CHARLES FREDERICK HOTHAM.

1902, Nov. 9. (Additional) Adm. the lord CHARLES THOMAS MONTAGU-DOUGLAS-SCOTT, 4th son of 5th duke of Buccleuch.

1903, June 26. Gen. Sir ARTHUR POWER PALMER, Indian Army.

1903, June 26. Gen. Sir GEORGE WENTWORTH ALEXANDER HIGGINSON.

1903, June 26. Gen. Sir RICHARD HARRISON, Royal Engineers.

1903, Nov 9. Adm. Sir CYPRIAN ARTHUR GEORGE BRIDGE.

1904, April 26. (Honorary) FRIEDRICK ADOLPHE HERMANN, reigning prince of Waldeck and Pyrmont.

1904, June 10 (Honorary) H.I. and R.H. Archduke FREDERICK MARIE ALBERT WILLIAM CHARLES, duke of Teschen of Austria.

1904, June 24 Gen. Sir EDWARD ALAN HOLDICH.

1904, June 24. Gen Sir JOHN ALEXANDER EWART, since deceased.

1904, June 24. Gen. Sir WILLIAM GORDON CAMERON.

1904, June 24. Lieut. Gen Sir THOMAS KELLY-KENNY.

1904, June 24 Lieut. Gen Sir CHARLES COMYN EGERTON, Indian Army, in recognition of his services in command of the Somaliland Field Force.

1904, Nov. 9. Adm. Sir COMPTON EDWARD DOMVILE.

KNIGHTS GRAND CROSS—CIVIL DIVISION (G.C.B.).

Existing knights of the Bath declared Civil G.C.B. at the extension of the Order.

1815, Jan. 2. Sir ROBERT GUNNING.

1815, Jan. 2. JAMES (HARRIS), 1st earl of Malmesbury.

1815, Jan. 2. MORTON (EDEN), 1st lord Henley.

1815, Jan 2. CHARLES (WHITWORTH), lord afterwards earl Whitworth.

1815, Jan. 2. Sir JOSEPH BANKS, bart.

1815, Jan. 2. Rt. Hon. Sir ARTHUR PAGET.

1815, Jan. 2. Sir PHILIP FRANCIS.

1815, Jan. 2. Sir GEORGE HILARO BARLOW.

1815, Jan. 2. PERCY CLINTON SYDNEY (SMYTHE), 6th viscount Strangford in Ireland, afterwards lord Penshurst in Great Britain.

1815, Jan. 2. The Hon Sir HENRY WELLESLEY, afterwards 1st lord Cowley.

1815, Jan. 2. The Hon. Sir CHARLES STUART (Stewart).

Subsequent Appointments.

1816, Oct. 21. Sir ROBERT LISTON.

1819, Oct. 20. Sir WILLIAM A'COURT, bart., afterwards 1st lord Heytesbury. Invested by the king of Naples.

1820, May 20. Sir CHARLES LONG, afterwards lord Farnborough An extra G.C.B. in contemplation of the coronation of George IV. Invested May 22.

1820, May 20. Sir CHARLES BAGOT. Extra *ut supra.*

1822, Mar. 8. The Rt. Hon. EDWARD THORNTON.

1822, Apr. 1. Maj. Gen. the Rt. Hon. Sir BENJAMIN BLOOMFIELD, afterwards 1st lord Bloomfield.

1825, May. GRANVILLE (LEVESON-GOWER), 1st viscount, afterwards 4th earl Granville. Invested by the king of France 1825, June 9.

1827, Dec. 13 Rt. Hon. FREDERICK JAMES LAMB, afterwards lord Beauvale and 3rd viscount Melbourne.

1829, Dec. 7. Rt. Hon. Sir STRATFORD CANNING, afterwards viscount Stratford de Redcliffe.

1829, Dec. 7. Rt. Hon. Sir ROBERT GORDON.

1831, Aug. 3. Rt. Hon. Sir ROBERT ADAIR.

1832, June 6. HENRY JOHN (TEMPLE), 3rd viscount Palmerston.

1833, Aug. 31. CHARLES MANNERS SUTTON, afterwards 1st viscount Canterbury.

1834, Mar. 3. JOHN (PONSONBY), 2nd lord and afterwards 1st viscount Ponsonby.

1834, Sept 16. GILBERT (ELLIOT-MURRAY-KYNYNMOUND), 2nd earl of Minto.

1835, Aug. 29 GEORGE (EDEN), 2nd lord, afterwards 1st earl of Auckland.

1835, Sept. 12. Rt. Hon. Sir CHARLES THEOPHILUS METCALFE, bart. Invested by lord Auckland, gov. gen. of India, 1836, Mar. 14.

1837, June 27. JOHN GEORGE (LAMBTON), 1st earl of Durham.

1837, July 12. PAUL ANTHONY, prince Esterhazy (Honorary).

1837, Oct. 19. GEORGE WILLIAM FREDERICK VILLIERS, afterwards 8th earl of Clarendon.

1837, Dec. 15 AUGUSTUS FREDERICK, duke of Sussex. Appointed first and principal G.C.B. Dec. 15, and acting Great Master of the Order Dec. 16. Invested 1838, Feb 21.

1838, July 19. ARCHIBALD (ACHESON), 2nd earl of Gosford. An extra civil G.C.B.

1838, July 19. Col. George William Russell, commonly called called lord George William Russell, envoy extraordinary and minister plenipotentiary to the king of Prussia. An extra civil G.C.B.

1838, July 19. Charles Augustus (Ellis), 6th lord Howard de Walden, envoy extraordinary and minister plenipotentiary to Portugal. An extra civil G.C.B.

1838, July 20. Richard Jenkins, formerly of the East India Company's Civil Service. An extra civil G.C.B.

1839, Apr. 15. John McNeill.

1841, Aug. 19. Rt. Hon. Charles Edward (Poulett Thomson), 1st lord Sydenham, gov. gen. of British North America.

1841, Aug. 27. Lieut. Gen. Sir Howard Douglas, bart.

1841, Aug. 27. Lieut. Gen. Sir Lionel Smith, bart., gov. of Mauritius.

1842, Dec. 2. Maj. Gen. Sir Henry Pottinger.

1843, Nov. 10. Arthur Aston, late H.M. envoy extraordinary and minister plenipotentiary to the queen of Spain.

1844, July 1. Lieut. Gen. Sir Henry Hardinge, afterwards 1st viscount Hardinge.

1844, July 10. Sir Edmund Lyons, bart., capt. R.N., H.M. minister plenipotentiary to the king of Greece.

1844, Oct. 30. Rt. Hon. Edward (Law), 1st earl of Ellenborough.

1845, Dec. 11. Rt. Hon. Charles Cecil Cope (Jenkinson), 3rd earl of Liverpool.

1846, June 24. Lieut. Gen. John (Fane), 17th earl of Westmorland, envoy extraordinary and minister plenipotentiary at Berlin.

1847, Jan. 28. Sir George Hamilton Seymour, envoy extraordinary and minister plenipotentiary to the queen of Portugal.

1847, Dec. 10. Constantine Henry (Phipps), 3rd marquess of Normanby, ambassador extraordinary and plenipotentiary to the king of the French.

14

1848, Jan. 22.   ERNEST CHRISTIAN CHARLES, prince of Hohenlohe-Langenburg.

1848, Jan. 22.   FREDERICK WILLIAM CHARLES GEORGE ERNEST ADOLPHUS GUSTAVUS, hereditary (subsequently reigning) grand duke of Mecklenburg-Strelitz.

1849, Mar. 31.   Sir GEORGE GREY, bart., one of her majesty's principal secretaries of state.

1851, Mar. 1.   Sir WILLIAM HENRY LYTTON EARLE BULWER, afterwards lord Dalling and Bulwer, envoy extraordinary and plenipotentiary to the United States of America.

1852, Feb. 23.   Rt. Hon. JOHN CAM (HOBHOUSE), lord Broughton.

1853, Feb. 21.   HENRY RICHARD CHARLES (WELLESLEY), 2nd lord and 1st earl Cowley, ambassador extraordinary and plenipotentiary to his majesty the emperor of the French.

1854, Apr. 15.   Rt. Hon. Sir JAMES ROBERT GEORGE GRAHAM, bart., a lord of the admiralty.

1855, Oct. 29.   Fox (MAULE), 2nd lord Panmure, afterwards 11th earl of Dalhousie, secretary of state for war.

1856, June 19.   Rt. Hon. Sir CHARLES WOOD, bart., afterwards 1st viscount Halifax, of Monk Bretton, a lord of the admiralty.

1857, Jan. 24.   EDWARD GRANVILLE (ELIOT), 3rd earl of St. Germans.

1857. Nov. 11.   Sir JOHN LAIRD MAIR LAWRENCE, afterwards lord Lawrence, chief commissioner and agent to the gov. gen. of India for the affairs of the Punjab.

1858, Mar 5.   JOHN HOBART (CARADOC), 2nd lord Howden, maj. gen., envoy extraordinary and minister plenipotentiary to the queen of Spain.

1858, Sept. 3.   JOHN ARTHUR DOUGLAS (BLOOMFIELD), 2nd lord Bloomfield, envoy extraordinary and minister plenipotentiary to the king of Prussia.

1858, Sept. 28.   (Extra) JAMES (BRUCE), 8th earl of Elgin, and 12th earl of Kincardine, high commissioner and plenipotentiary on a special mission to the emperor of China.

1859, Mar 31.   (Extra) Rt. Hon CHARLES JOHN (CANNING), 2nd viscount Canning, gov. gen. of India.

1859, Mar. 31.   (Extra) Rt. Hon. JOHN (ELPHINSTONE), 13th lord Elphinstone, gov. of the Presidency of Bombay.

1859, June 15. (Extra) Rt. Hon. JAMES HOWARD (HARRIS), 3rd earl of Malmesbury, secretary of state for foreign affairs.

1859, June 15. (Extra) Rt. Hon. Sir JOHN SOMERSET PAKINGTON, bart, afterwards 1st lord Hampton, one of the commissioners of the admiralty.

1862, Jan. 24. RICHARD BICKERTON PEMELL (LYONS), 2nd lord, and afterwards 1st viscount Lyons, envoy extraordinary and minister plenipotentiary to the United States of America.

1863, Mar. 10. Rt. Hon. JOHN ROBERT (TOWNSHEND), 3rd viscount and afterwards 1st earl Sydney, lord chamberlain of her majesty's household.

1863, Mar. 20. CHRISTIAN IX., king of Denmark. Nominated by queen Victoria 1863, Mar. 20, he being then prince Christian of Denmark; warrant of appointment dated 1865, Mar. 11, but his precedence to be as of date 1863, Mar. 20

1863, Aug. 11. Sir JAMES HUDSON, envoy extraordinary and minister plenipotentiary to the king of Italy.

1864, July 1. Maj. Gen. Sir HENRY KNIGHT STORKS, late high commissioner of the Ionian Islands.

1865, Mar. 17. The Hon Sir FREDERICK WILLIAM ADOLPHUS BRUCE, envoy extraordinary and minister plenipotentiary to the emperor of China, and now envoy extraordinary and minister to the United States of America.

1865, June 1. (Honorary) His Highness the MUSHIR MOHAMMED EL SADECK BASHA BEY, Bey of Tunis.

1866, Jan. 5. The Rt. Hon. Sir ROBERT PEEL, bart.

1866, Jan. 29. H.S.H. ERNEST LEOPOLD VICTOR CHARLES AUGUSTE JOSEPH EMICH, prince of Leiningen, capt. R.N. (nephew to the sovereign).

1866, June 12. H.S.H. FRANCIS PAUL CHARLES LOUIS ALEXANDER, prince of Teck. (Honorary.)

1866, July 6. (Extra) Sir ANDREW BUCHANAN, ambassador extraordinary and plenipotentiary to the emperor of Russia.

1866, July 6. (Extra) The Hon. Sir AUGUSTUS WILLIAM FREDERICK SPENCER LOFTUS, commonly called lord Augustus Loftus, ambassador extraordinary and plenipotentiary to the king of Prussia.

1866, July 6. (Extra) Sir Arthur Charles Magenis, late envoy extraordinary and minister plenipotentiary to the king of Portugal.

1866, Dec. 18 (Honorary) H H. Ismail Pacha, viceroy of Egypt.

1867, May 8. (Honorary) H.S.H. Herman Ernest Francis Bernhard, prince of Hohenlohe-Langenburg, the queen's nephew.

1868, Nov. 13. (Extra) The Rt. Hon. Sir John Young, bart., late capt. gen. and governor-in-chief in and over the colony of New South Wales, afterwards lord Lisgar.

1869, Nov. 22. (Extra) The Rt. Hon. Henry George Elliot, ambassador extraordinary and plenipotentiary to the Ottoman Porte.

1872, July 13. The Rt. Hon. Robert Vernon (Smith), 1st lord Lyveden.

1872, July 13. Sir Henry Francis Howard, late envoy extraordinary and minister plenipotentiary to the king of Bavaria.

1873, Feb. 12. (Extra) Sir Alexander James Edmund Cockburn, bart., lord chief justice, king's bench.

1874, Feb. 21. The Hon. Odo William Leopold Russell, commonly called lord Odo Russell, afterwards 1st lord Ampthill, ambassador extraordinary and plenipotentiary to the emperor of Germany.

1876, May 17. The Rt Hon. Sir Henry Bartle Edward Frere, afterwards bart.

1877, Apr. 17. (Honorary) H.R.H. George Adolphus Frederick Augustus Victor Ernest Adalbert Gustavus William Wellington, hereditary grand duke of Mecklenburg-Strelitz.

1878, Jan 1. The Rt. Hon. Edward Robert (Lytton), 2nd lord afterwards 1st earl of Lytton, viceroy and governor-general of India.

1878, June 11. Rt. Hon. Henry Austen Layard, ambassador extraordinary and plenipotentiary to the sultan of Turkey.

1879, Jan. 24. Francis Hugh George (Seymour), 8th marquess of Hertford, gen., lord chamberlain of her majesty's household.

1879, June 6. (Honorary) Prince ALEXANDER JOSEPH of Battenberg, prince elect of Bulgaria.

1880, Mar. 20. Rt. Hon. STEPHEN CAVE, paymaster-general of the Forces.

1880, Apr. 20. Rt. Hon. RICHARD ASSHETON CROSS, afterwards viscount Cross.

1880, Apr. 20. Rt. Hon. Sir STAFFORD HENRY NORTHCOTE, bart, afterwards earl of Iddlesleigh.

1880, Apr. 20. Rt. Hon. lord JOHN JAMES ROBERT (MANNERS), afterwards 7th duke of Rutland.

1881, Aug. 13. Prince HENRY (ALBERT WILLIAM HENRY), of Prussia.

1881, Sept. 20. HENRY BOUVERIE WILLIAM BRAND, M.P., speaker of the House of Commons, afterwards viscount Hampden.

1882. GEORGE VICTOR, prince of Waldeck (Honorary).

1883, June 15. The Rt. Hon. FREDERICK TEMPLE (BLACKWOOD), earl afterwards marquess of Dufferin.

1883, Aug. 21. Rt. Hon. Sir EDWARD THORNTON, ambassador extraordinary and minister plenipotentiary at St. Petersburg.

1883, Aug. 21. Rt. Hon. Sir AUGUSTUS BERKELEY PAGET, ambassador extraordinary and minister plenipotentiary at Rome.

1884, Nov. 21. Rt. Hon. Sir JOHN ALEXANDER MACDONALD, prime minister of the Dominion of Canada.

1885, Jan. 7. Rt. Hon. HENRY AUSTIN (BRUCE), 1st lord Aberdare, P.C.

1885, Jan. 9. The most hon. GEORGE AUGUSTUS CONSTANTINE (PHIPPS), 4th marquess of Normanby, P.C.

1885, June 15. His Excellency Sir JOHN SAVILE LUMLEY, ambassador extraordinary and minister plenipotentiary at Rome.

1885, June 30. Rt. Hon. CHARLES (SHAW-LEFEVRE), viscount Eversley, P.C.

1885, June 30. Rt. Hon. ROBERT (LOWE), viscount Sherbrooke, P.C.

1885, Aug 3. (Honorary) His Highness prince PHILIPPE, of Saxe-Coburg and Gotha [Ferdinand Philippe Marie Auguste Raphael, 2nd son of August, 3rd son of duke Ernest I. of Saxe-Coburg-Gotha.].

1886, Feb 2. Rt. Hon FREDERICK ARTHUR STANLEY, M.P., one of Her Majesty's aides-de-camp, afterwards 25th earl of Derby.

1886, Feb 2. Rt. Hon Sir EDWARD BALDWIN MALET, ambassador extraordinary and minister plenipotentiary at Berlin.

1887, June 21. (Honorary) His Imperial Highness the grand duke SERGE ALEXANDROVITCH, of Russia.

1887, June 21. H.R.H. ERNEST LOUIS CHARLES ALBERT WILLIAM, hereditary grand duke of Hesse. (Honorary)

1887, June 21. His Highness BERNARD FREDERICK WILLIAM ALBERT GEORGE, hereditary prince of Saxe-Meiningen. (Honorary.)

1887, June 21. His Highness MEHEMED TEWFIK, the khedive of Egypt. (Honorary.)

1887, June 21. Hon. Gen. the Rt. Hon Sir HENRY FREDERICK PONSONBY, private secretary and Extra Equerry to the Queen

1887, June 21. (Additional) V. Adm. H.S.H. prince VICTOR FERDINAND FRANZ EUGEN GUSTAF ADOLPH CONSTANTIN FRIEDRICH, of Hohenlohe Langenburg.

1887, June 21. (Additional) H.S.H. prince LOUIS ALEXANDER of Battenberg, commander Royal Navy.

1887, Sept. 30. The Rt. Hon. Sir ROBERT BURNETT DAVID MORIER, ambassador extraordinary and minister plenipotentiary at St. Petersburg.

1888, Mar. 10. Prince CHRISTIAN FREDERICK WILLIAM CHARLES, crown prince of Denmark.

1888, June 2 The Rt Hon. Sir WILLIAM ARTHUR WHITE, ambassador extraordinary and minister plenipotentiary at Constantinople.

1889, Jan. 2. The Rt. Hon. Sir HENRY DRUMMOND WOLFF, envoy extraordinary and minister plenipotentiary to Persia.

1889, Apr. 29. The Rt. Hon. Sir FRANCIS CLARE FORD, ambassador extraordinary and minister plenipotentiary to Madrid (in connexion with her majesty's recent meeting with the queen regent of Spain at San Sebastian).

1889, May 25. Sir WILLIAM JENNER, bart., M.D., one of the physicians in ordinary to her majesty.

1889, July 23. Maj. Gen. Sir HENRY CRESWICKE RAWLINSON, member of the council of the secretary of state for India.

1889, Aug. 2. MIRZA ALI ASGHER KHAN, Amin-es-Sultan, grand vizier to the shah of Persia.

1890, July 18. (Honorary) baron FRANCOIS AUGUSTE LAMBERMONT, minister of state to the king of the Belgians.

1890, July 19. (Extra) his highness prince CHRISTIAN VICTOR ALBERT LUDWIG ERNEST ANTON, of Schleswig-Holstein.

1891, July 14. (Honorary) his highness prince ARIBERT JOSEPH ALEXANDER, of Anhalt.

1891, Oct. 23. Gen. the Rt. Hon. ALEXANDER NELSON (HOOD), 3rd lord, afterwards viscount Bridport, retired pay, one of Her Majesty's lords-in-waiting in ordinary and one of Her Majesty's extra equerries.

1892, May 16. (Honorary) his serene highness prince ADOLPHE GEORGE, of Schaumbourg-Lippe.

1892, May 25. Sir JULIAN PAUNCEFOTE, envoy extraordinary and minister plenipotentiary to the United States.

1892, June 10. H.H. prince ABBAS PASHA, khedive of Egypt.

1892, Aug. 1. The Rt. Hon. EDWARD (BOOTLE-WILBRAHAM), 1st earl of Lathom, P.C., lord chamberlain of her majesty's household.

1892, Aug. 1. Sir ROBERT GEORGE WYNDHAM HERBERT, late under-secretary of state, colonial office.

1892, Aug. 1. Sir PHILIP WODEHOUSE CURRIE, under-secretary of state for foreign affairs, afterwards lord Currie.

1892, Aug. 20. Sir HENRY BROUGHAM LOCH, gov. and commander-in-chief of the Cape of Good Hope and its dependencies, and high commissioner of South Africa, afterwards 1st lord Loch.

1892, Aug. 20. Sir REGINALD EARLE WELBY, permanent secretary of the treasury, afterwards lord Welby.

1892, Dec. 21. H R.H. prince FERDINAND VICTOR ALBERT MAINRAD, crown prince of Roumania (honorary).

1893, May 19. (Extra) Rt. Hon. FARRER (HERSCHELL), 1st lord Herschell, lord high chancellor of England.

1893, Dec. 29. (Honorary) his highness ABDUL RAHMAN KHAN, amir of Afghanistan.

1895, Jan 8. EVELYN (BARING), lord, afterwards earl of Cromer, minister plenipotentiary in Egypt.

1895, May 25. The Rt. Hon LYON (PLAYFAIR), lord Playfair.

1895, May 25. The Rt. Hon. JAMES STANSFELD.

1895, June 29. Rt. Hon HENRY CAMPBELL-BANNERMAN.

1895, July 4 H.R.H. CONSTANTINE, crown prince of Greece.

1896, May 20 The Rt. Hon Sir EDMUND JOHN MONSON, ambassador extraordinary and minister plenipotentiary at Vienna.

1896, July 21. (Honorary) H.R.H. Prince CHRISTIAN FREDERICK CHARLES GEORGE WALDEMAR AXEL, of Denmark, wrongly gazetted as military G.C.B.

1897, Jan. 1. The Rt. Hon. Sir FRANK CAVENDISH LASCELLES, ambassador extraordinary and minister plenipotentiary at Berlin.

1897, Mar. 23. The Hon. Sir ROBERT HENRY MEADE, late under secretary of state for the Colonial Department.

1897, June 22 (Honorary) His highness prince FREDERIC CHARLES LOUIS CONSTANTIN, of Hesse.

1897, June 22. (Additional) The Hon. Sir SPENCER CECIL BRABAZON PONSONBY-FANE, comptroller of accounts, lord chamberlain's department.

1897, June 22. (Additional) Sir ARTHUR LAWRENCE HALIBURTON, afterwards lord Haliburton, permanent under secretary of state, War Office.

1897, June 22. (Additional) Col. Sir EDWARD RIDLEY COLBORNE BRADFORD, aide-de-camp to the queen, commissioner of the Metropolitan Police.

1897, June 22. (Additional) The Rt. Hon. Sir NICHOLAS RODERICK O'CONOR, ambassador extraordinary and minister plenipotentiary at St. Petersburg.

1897, June 22. (Additional) The Rt. Hon Sir HORACE RUMBOLD, bart., ambassador extraordinary and minister plenipotentiary at Vienna.

1897, Oct. 22. H.S.H. ERNEST WILLIAM FREDERICK CHARLES MAXIMILIAN, hereditary prince of Hohenlohe-Langenburg.

1899, Jan. 2. Sir HUGH OWEN, late permanent secretary to the Local Government Board.

1899, Jan. 2. Sir CHARLES LENNOX PEEL, late clerk of the Council.

1899, June 9. Rt. Hon. Sir CHARLES STEWART SCOTT, ambassador extraordinary and minister plenipotentiary at St. Petersburg.

1899, June 9. HENRY MORTON STANLEY, M.P.

1900, May 23. The Rt. Hon. VICTOR ALBERT GEORGE (CHILD-VILLIERS), 7th earl of Jersey.

1900, June 29. (Honorary) H.R.H. prince GEORGE of Greece

1900, Nov. 16. Sir THOMAS HENRY SANDERSON, permanent under secretary of state for Foreign Affairs.

1900, Nov. 27. (Extra) His Highness prince ALBERT JOHN CHARLES FREDERICK ALFRED GEORGE, of Schleswig-Holstein.

1901, Jan. 1. Sir ALFRED MILNER, high commissioner for South Africa, afterwards viscount Milner.

1901, Jan. 1. Sir FRANCIS MOWATT, secretary to the Treasury.

1901, Feb. 13. The Rt. Hon. lord justice Sir ROBERT ROMER.

1901, Feb. 15. (Honorary) His Imperial Highness the grand duke MICHAEL ALEXANDROWICH, of Russia.

1901, Feb. 19. (Honorary) His Imperial Highness the archduke FRANZ FERDINAND, of Austria.

1901, Feb. 19. (Honorary) H.R.H. OSCAR GUSTAVE ADOLPHE, crown prince of Sweden and Norway.

1901, July 2. (Honorary) MOULAI ABDUL-EL-AZIZ, sultan of Morocco.

1901, Sept. 17. (Honorary) H.R.H. prince WALDEMAR, of Denmark.

1901, Nov. 9. The Rt. Hon. Sir FRANCIS RICHARD PLUNKETT, ambassador extraordinary and plenipotentiary at Vienna.

1902, Jan. 14. (Honorary) The marquess ITO.

1902, June 26 (Additional) EDWARD HYDE (VILLIERS), 9th earl of Clarendon, P C., lord chamberlain.

1902, June 26. (Additional) The Rt. Hon. Sir FRANCIS HENRY JEUNE, P.C., judge advocate general.

1902, June 26 (Additional) The Rt. Hon. Sir ALGERNON EDWARD WEST, P.C.

1902, June 26. (Additional) Gen The Rt. Hon. Sir DIGHTON MACNAGHTEN PROBYN, V.C , P.C , keeper of the privy purse.

1902, Nov 28 (Honorary) His Imperial Highness prince ARISUGAWA, of Japan, on the occasion of His Majesty's birthday.

1903, Jan. 1. (Honorary) His Highness ASAF YAH MUZAFFAR-UL-MAMALIK, NIZAM-UL-MULK NIZAM-UD-DAULA NAWAB MIR SIR MAHBUB ALI KHAN BAHADUR FATEH YANG, of Hyderabad.

1903, Jan 27. (Honorary) prince CHARLES of Bourbon, prince of the Asturias.

KNIGHT COMMANDERS—MILITARY DIVISION
K.C.B. (MILITARY).

1815, Jan. 2. Adm. JAMES (GAMBIER), lord Gambier. Invested
Apr. 12.

1815, Jan. 2. Adm. Sir CHARLES MORICE POLE, bart. Invested
Apr. 12.

1815, Jan. 2. Adm. JAMES HAWKINS WHITSHED. Invested Apr. 12.

1815, Jan. 2. Adm. Sir ROBERT CALDER, bart. Invested Apr. 12.

1815, Jan. 2. Adm. Sir RICHARD BICKERTON, bart. Invested
June 29.

1815, Jan. 2. Adm. JOHN KNIGHT. Invested Apr. 12

1815, Jan. 2. Adm. EDWARD THORNBROUGH. Invested Apr. 12.

1815, Jan. 2. Adm. GEORGE CAMPBELL. Invested Apr. 12.

1815, Jan. 2. Adm. Sir ALBEMARLE BERTIE, bart. Invested 1817,
Apr. 21.

1815, Jan. 2. Adm. EDWARD (PELLEW), 1st lord, afterwards 1st earl
Exmouth.

1815, Jan. 2. V. Adm. WILLIAM DOMETT. Invested 1818, Feb. 12.

1815, Jan. 2. V. Adm. GEORGE MURRAY. Invested Apr. 12.

1815, Jan. 2. V. Adm. JOHN SUTTON. Invested Apr. 12.

1815, Jan. 2. V. Adm. WILLIAM ESSINGTON. Invested Apr. 12.

1815, Jan. 2. V. Adm. ELIAB HARVEY. Invested Apr. 20.

1815, Jan. 2. V. Adm. Sir EDMUND NAGLE. Invested Apr. 12.

1815, Jan. 2. V. Adm. RICHARD GRINDALL   Invested by dispensa-
tion 1816, May 30.

1815, Jan. 2. V. Adm. Sir GEORGE MARTIN. Invested Apr. 12.

1815, Jan. 2. ·V. Adm. Sir WILLIAM SYDNEY SMITH. Invested at
Paris by the duke of Wellington 1815, Dec. 29.

1815, Jan. 2 Lieut. Gen. GORDON DRUMMOND. Invested 1816, July 1.

1815, Jan 2. V. Adm. HERBERT SAWYER. Invested Dec 4.

1815, Jan. 2. Lieut. Gen. the Hon. JOHN ABERCROMBY.

1815, Jan. 2. V. Adm. the Hon. ROBERT STOPFORD. Invested Apr. 12.

1815, Jan 2. V. Adm. THOMAS FOLEY. Invested Apr. 12

1815, Jan. 2. Lieut. Gen RONALD CRAUFORD FERGUSON. Invested Apr. 12.

1815, Jan. 2. Lieut. Gen. HENRY WARDE. Invested Apr. 12.

1815, Jan. 2. V. Adm. CHARLES TYLER. Invested 1816, Apr. 20.

1815, Jan. 2. V. Adm. ALAN HYDE (GARDNER), 2nd lord Gardner.

1815, Jan. 2. V. Adm. WILLIAM MITCHELL.

1815, Jan. 2. V. Adm. Sir THOMAS WILLIAMS. Invested Apr. 12.

1815, Jan. 2. V. Adm Sir THOMAS BOULDEN THOMPSON, bart. Invested Apr. 12.

1815, Jan. 2. Lieut. Gen. WILLIAM HOUSTON. Invested Apr. 12.

1815, Jan. 2. Lieut. Gen. the Hon. WILLIAM LUMLEY. Invested Apr. 12.

1815, Jan 2. Lieut. Gen. WROTH PALMER ACLAND. Invested Apr. 12.

1815, Jan 2. Lieut Gen. MILES NIGHTINGALE. Invested 1819, July 23.

1815, Jan 2. Lieut. Gen. HENRY FREDERICK CAMPBELL. Invested Apr. 12.

1815, Jan. 2. V. Adm. WILLIAM HARGOOD Invested Apr. 12.

1815, Jan. 2. V. Adm. ROBERT MOORSOM. Invested Apr. 12.

1815, Jan. 2. V. Adm. LAWRENCE WILLIAM HALSTED. Invested Apr. 12.

1815, Jan. 2. V. Adm. Sir HARRY NEALE, bart. Invested Aug. 12.

1815, Jan. 2. V. Adm. Sir JOSEPH SIDNEY YORKE. Invested Apr. 12.

1815, Jan. 2. V. Adm. the Hon. ARTHUR KAYE LEGGE. Invested Apr. 12.

1815, Jan. 2. Maj. Gen. ALAN CAMERON. Invested Apr. 12.

1815, Jan. 2. Maj. Gen. the Hon. CHARLES COLVILLE.

1815, Jan. 2. Maj. Gen. HENRY FANE. Invested Apr. 12.

1815, Jan. 2. Maj. Gen. GEORGE ANSON. Invested Apr. 12.

1815, Jan. 2. Maj. Gen. KENNETH ALEXANDER HOWARD, afterwards 12th lord Howard of Effingham, and 5th earl of Effingham. Invested Apr. 12.

1815, Jan. 2. R. *Adm. THOMAS FRANCIS FREMANTLE. Invested Apr. 12.

1815, Jan. 2. R. Adm. Sir FRANCIS LAFOREY, bart. Invested Apr. 12.

1815, Jan. 2. R. Adm. PHILIP CHARLES HENDERSON DURHAM. Invested by dispensation 1815, July 10. Knighted and invested 1816, May 14.

1815, Jan. 2. R. Adm. ISRAEL PELLEW. Invested by dispensation 1815, July 10. Knighted and invested 1816, July 1.

1815, Jan. 2. Maj. Gen. HENRY BELL. Invested Apr. 12.

1815, Jan. 2. Maj. Gen. JOHN OSWALD. Invested 1818, Feb. 12.

1815, Jan. 2. Maj. Gen. Sir WILLIAM ANSON, bart. Invested Apr. 12.

1815, Jan. 2. Maj. Gen. EDWARD HOWORTH. Invested Apr. 12.

1815, Jan. 2. Maj. Gen. CHARLES WALE. Invested Apr. 20.

1815, Jan. 12. Maj. Gen. JOHN ORMSBY VANDELEUR. Invested at Brussels by the duke of Wellington.

1815, Jan. 2. Maj. Gen. the Hon. EDWARD STOPFORD. Invested Apr. 12.

1815, Jan. 12. Maj. Gen. GEORGE TOWNSHEND WALKER. Invested Apr. 12.

1815, Jan. 2. R. Adm. BENJAMIN HALLOWELL (afterwards Carew). Invested Apr. 12.

1815, Jan. 2. R. Adm. GEORGE HOPE. Invested Apr. 12.

1815, Jan. 2. R Adm. AMELIUS BEAUCLERK, commonly called lord Amelius Beauclerk Invested Apr. 12.

1815, Jan. 2. R. Adm. JAMES NICOLL MORRIS. Invested Apr. 12.

1815, Jan. 2. R. Adm. THOS. BYAM MARTIN. Invested Nov. 27.

1815, Jan. 2 Maj. Gen. JAMES KEMPT. Invested Apr. 12.

1815, Jan. 2 Maj Gen ROBERT ROLLO GILLESPIE Nominated but died in India 1814, Oct. 31.

1815, Jan. 2. Maj. Gen. WILLIAM HENRY PRINGLE. Invested Apr. 12.

1815, Jan. 2. R. Adm WILLIAM JOHNSTONE HOPE. Invested Sept. 29.

1815, Jan 2. R. Adm HENRY PAULET, commonly called lord Henry Paulet. Invested Apr 12.

1815, Jan 2. R. Adm GEORGE COCKBURN. Invested June 29.

1815, Jan. 2. R. Adm. GRAHAM MOORE Invested Apr. 12.

1815, Jan. 2. R. Adm. HENRY WILLIAM BAYNTUN. Invested Apr. 12.

1815, Jan. 2. R. Adm. Sir RICHARD KING, bart. Invested Apr. 12.

1815, Jan. 2. R. Adm. RICHARD LEE. Invested Apr. 12.

1815, Jan. 2 Maj. Gen. FREDERICK PHILIPSE ROBINSON. Invested by dispensation in 1828.

1815, Jan. 2. Maj. Gen. EDWARD BARNES. Never invested.

1815, Jan. 2. Maj Gen. the hon. WILLIAM PONSONBY. Invested Apr. 12.

1815, Jan. 2. Maj. Gen. JOHN BYNG. Invested Apr. 12.

1815, Jan 2. Maj. Gen. THOMAS BRISBANE (afterwards Makdougall-Brisbane).

1815, Jan. 2. Maj. Gen. DENIS PACK. Invested Apr. 12.

1815, Jan. 2. Maj. Gen. ROBERT EDWARD HENRY SOMERSET, commonly called lord Robert Edward Henry Somerset. Invested Apr. 12.

1815, Jan. 2. Maj. Gen. THOMAS BRADFORD. Invested June 8.

1815, Jan. 2. Maj. Gen. JOHN LAMBERT.

1815, Jan. 2. Maj. Gen. JAMES WILLOUGHBY GORDON. Invested Apr. 12.

1815, Jan. 2. Maj. Gen. MANLEY POWER Invested June 8.

1815, Jan. 2. Maj. Gen. SAMUEL GIBBS. Never invested

1815, Jan. 2. MATTHEW (AYLMER, afterwards Whitworth-Aylmer), 5th lord Aylmer, maj. gen. Knighted and invested by the lord lieutenant at Dublin, 1815, June 5.

1815, Jan. 2 R Adm. WILLIAM HOTHAM. Invested Apr. 12.

1815, Jan. 2. R. Adm. PULTENEY MALCOLM. Invested June 8.

1815, Jan. 2. R. Adm. JOHN GORE Invested Apr. 12.

1815, Jan. 2. R. Adm. HENRY HOTHAM. Invested Apr. 12.

1815, Jan. 2. R. Adm. GEORGE BURLTON. Invested by dispensation July 10.

1815, Jan. 2. R. Adm. HOME RIGGS POPHAM. Invested Apr. 12.

1815, Jan. 2. R. Adm. Sir JOSIAS ROWLEY, bart. Invested by dispensation July 10. Knighted and invested Nov. 27.

1815, Jan. 2. R. Adm. EDWARD CODRINGTON. Invested Apr. 20.

1815, Jan. 2. R. Adm. Sir CHARLES ROWLEY, bart. Knighted and invested May 25.

1815, Jan. 2. Maj Gen COLQUHOUN GRANT. Invested Apr. 20.

1815, Jan. 2. Maj. Gen. Sir THOMAS SIDNEY BECKWITH. Invested 1816, July 5.

1815, Jan. 2. Maj. Gen. the Hon. ROBERT WILLIAM O'CALLAGHAN. Invested Apr 12.

1815, Jan. 2.   Maj. Gen. JOHN KEANE.   Invested June 8.

1815, Jan 2.   Maj. Gen. COLIN HALKETT.

1815, Jan. 2.   Maj. Gen Sir HENRY EDWARD BUNBURY, bart.
Invested Apr. 12.

1815, Jan. 2.   Maj. Gen. RICHARD HUSSEY VIVIAN. Invested Apr. 12.

1815, Jan. 2.   Maj. Gen. HENRY TORRENS   Invested Apr. 13.

1815, Jan. 2.   Capt Sir GEORGE EYRE.   Invested 1819, Nov. 26.

1815, Jan. 2.   Capt. Sir CHARLES BRISBANE.

1815, Jan. 2.   Capt. the Hon. JOHN TALBOT.   Knighted 1815,
Apr. 12.   Invested 1820, May 22.

1815, Jan. 2   Capt. Sir EDWARD BERRY, bart. Invested 1822, Feb. 8.

1815, Jan. 2.   Capt. Sir EDWARD HAMILTON, bart.   Invested by
dispensation in 1829.

1815, Jan 2.   Capt. Sir EDWARD WILLIAM CAMPBELL RICH OWEN.
Knighted 1816, May 14.

1815, Jan. 2.   Capt. Sir THOMAS MASTERMAN HARDY, bart. Knighted
1815, June 29   Invested 1825, June 29.

1815, Jan. 2.   Capt. Sir YAHLEEL BRENTON, bart   Invested 1830,
July 28.

1815, Jan. 2.   Capt. Sir MICHAEL SEYMOUR, bart.   Knighted 1816,
Apr 20   Invested 1832, July 25

1815, Jan. 2.   Capt. Sir THOMAS LAVIE.

1815, Jan. 2.   Capt. Sir PHILIP BOWES VERE BROKE, bart.   Knighted
1815, June 29   Invested 1830, July 28

1815, Jan. 2.   Sir WILLIAM HOSTE, bart.   Knighted 1815, June 8.

1815, Jan. 2.   Capt. Sir CHRISTOPHER COLE.

1815, Jan. 2.   Capt. Sir GEORGE RALPH COLLIER, bart.

1815, Jan 2.   Capt. Sir JAMES LIND.

1815, Jan 2.   Capt. JAMES ALEXANDER GORDON.   Knighted 1815,
June 29.   Invested 1837, Mar. 17.

1815, Jan. 2.   Capt. Sir THOMAS STAINES.

1815, Jan. 2.   Capt. Sir EDWARD TUCKER. Invested 1837, Apr. 19.

1815, Jan. 2.   Capt. Sir JAMES LUCAS YEO.

1815, Jan. 2.   Col. JOHN ELLEY. Knighted Apr. 12.

1815, Jan. 2.   Col. CHARLES PHILIP BELSON, 28th regiment. Knighted 1815, Apr. 12. Invested 1821, July 25.

1815, Jan. 2.   WILLIAM HOWE DE LANCEY, deputy quarter master general.

1815, Jan. 2.   Col. BENJAMIN D'URBAN, 2nd West India Regiment. Knighted 1817, Apr. 21. Invested 1819, Nov. 26.

1815, Jan. 2.   Col. GEORGE RIDOUT BINGHAM, 53rd Foot. Knighted 1815, Apr. 12. Invested 1819, Nov. 26.

1815, Jan. 2.   Col. the Hon. CHARLES JAMES GREVILLE, 38th Foot. Knighted 1815, Apr. 20. Invested 1819, Nov. 26.

1815, Jan. 2.   Col. HAYLETT FRAMINGHAM, Royal Artillery. Knighted Apr. 12.

1815, Jan. 2.   Col. ANDREW FRANCIS BARNARD, 95th Foot. Knighted 1815, Apr. 12. Invested 1819, Nov. 26.

1815, Jan. 2.   Col. WILLIAM ROBE, Royal Artillery. Knighted Apr. 12.

1815, Jan. 2.   Col. HENRY WALTON ELLIS, 23rd Foot.

1815, Jan. 2.   Col. JOHN CAMERON, 9th Foot. Knighted and invested 1822, Apr. 19.

1815, Jan. 2.   Col. the Hon. ROBERT LE POER TRENCH. Knighted by the lord lieut. of Ireland, Dec. 22.

1815, Jan. 2.   Col. CHARLES PRATT, 5th Foot. Knighted 1815, June 29. Invested 1830, Aug. 4.

1815, Jan. 2.   Col. EDWARD BLAKENEY, 7th Foot. Knighted and invested 1825, June 29.

1815, Jan. 2.   Col. JOHN M'LEAN, 27th Foot. Knighted 1815, Apr. 12. Invested 1825, June 29.

15

1815, Jan. 2. Col RICHARD DOWNES JACKSON, Coldstream Guards. Knighted 1815, Apr. 12. Invested 1825, June 29.

1815, Jan. 2. Col. WILLIAM DOUGLAS, 91st Foot.

1815, Jan 2. Col. COLIN CAMPBELL, Coldstream Guards   Knighted Apr. 12.

1815, Jan 2. Col. JOHN COLBORNE, 52nd Foot.

1815, Jan 2. Col. ARCHIBALD CAMPBELL, Portuguese Service.

1815, Jan 2   Col. THOMAS ARBUTHNOT, 57th Foot.   Knighted 1816, July 1.

1815, Jan. 2. Col. HENRY FREDERICK BOUVERIE, Coldstream Guards. Knighted 1815, Apr 12. Invested 1825, June 29

1815, Jan 2   Lieut Col. WILLIAM WILLIAMS, 13th Foot.   Knighted 1815, Dec 4   Invested 1830, Aug. 4.

1815, Jan. 2. Lieut. Col. HENRY HOLLIS BRADFORD, 1st Guards.

1815, Jan. 2. Lieut. Col. ALEXANDER LEITH, 31st Foot.   Knighted 1820, June 8.

1815, Jan. 2. Lieut Col. the Hon. ROBERT LAWRENCE DUNDAS, Royal Staff Corps   Knighted 1816, July 1.

1815, Jan 2. Lieut. Col. ROBERT ARBUTHNOT, Coldstream Guards. Knighted Dec 4.

1815, Jan. 2. Lieut. Col. CHARLES SUTTON, 23rd Foot.

1815, Jan. 2. Lieut. Col. JAMES DAWES DOUGLAS, Portuguese service. Knighted 1815, Apr. 12   Invested 1831, Sept. 28.

1815, Jan. 2. Lieut. Col the Rt. Hon. HENRY HARDINGE, afterwards 1st viscount Hardinge, 1st Guards.   Invested 1830, July 28.

1815, Jan 2. Lieut Col. GEORGE HENRY FREDERICK BERKELEY, 35th Foot

1815, Jan. 2. Lieut Col JEREMIAH DICKSON, assistant quartermaster general. Knighted Apr. 12.

1815, Jan 2. Lieut Col Sir JOHN MILLEY DOYLE. Authorised to wear the Star by royal warrant, dated 1838, Oct. 31.

1815, Jan. 2   Lieut. Col. Sir THOMAS NOEL HILL, 1st Guards.

1815, Jan. 2   Lieut. Col. ROBERT MACARA, 42nd Foot.

1815, Jan. 2.   Lieut. Col. the Hon. ALEXANDER GORDON, 3rd Foot Guards.

1815, Jan. 2.   Lieut Col. HENRY WILLIAM CARR, 83rd Foot. Knighted Apr. 12.

1815, Jan 2.   Lieut. Col. CHARLES BROKE, assistant quartermaster-general. Knighted Apr. 12.

1815, Jan. 2.   Lieut. Col CHARLES BROKE VERE.

1815, Jan 2.   Lieut. Col. FITZROY JAMES HENRY SOMERSET, commonly called lord Fitzroy Somerset, afterwards 1st lord Raglan: 1st Guards   Knighted and invested 1825, June 29.

1815, Jan. 2.   Lieut. Col JAMES WILSON, 48th Foot. Knighted 1820, May 22

1815, Jan. 2.   Lieut. Col ALEXANDER J. DICKSON, Royal Artillery. Knighted 1815, June 8.   Invested 1837, Mar. 17.

1815, Jan. 2.   Lieut. Col. JOHN MAY, Royal Artillery. Knighted 1815, Apr. 12.   Invested 1837, Apr. 19.

1815, Jan. 2.   Lieut Col. GEORGE SCOVELL, late Staff Corps Cavalry. Knighted and invested 1837, Mar. 17.

1815, Jan. 2.   Lieut. Col. WILLIAM MAYNARD GOMM (Gomme), Coldstream Guards. Knighted 1815, Apr. 12.   Invested 1837, Mar. 17.

1815, Jan. 2.   Lieut Col. ULYSSES BURGH, afterwards 2nd lord Downes: 1st Guards.   Knighted and invested 1837, May 17.

1815, Jan. 2.   Lieut. Col. FRANCIS D'OYLEY, 1st Guards.

1815, Jan. 2.   Lieut Col. RICHARD WILLIAMS, of the Royal Marines. Knighted 1815, May 25.   Invested 1838, Aug 15.

1815, Jan. 2.   Lieut. Col. JAMES MALCOLM, of the Royal Marines. Knighted May 25.

1815, Jan. 2.   Lieut. Col. JAMES ARCHIBALD HOPE, 3rd Guards. Knighted 1815, May 25.   Invested 1837, Apr. 19.

1815, Jan. 2. Lieut Col AUGUSTUS SIMON FRAZER, Royal Artillery. Knighted Apr 12.

1815, Jan. 2. Lieut. Col HEW DALRYMPLE Ross, Royal Artillery. Knighted 1815, May 25 Invested 1837, Apr. 19.

1815, Jan. 2. Lieut Col. EDMUND KEYNTON WILLIAMS, 81st Foot. Knighted and invested 1837, Apr. 19.

1815, Jan. 2. Lieut. Col. MAXWELL GRANT, 42nd Foot. Knighted Apr. 12.

1815, Jan 2. Lieut. Col. FREDERICK STOVIN, 28th Foot. Knighted June 8.

1815, Jan. 2. Lieut. Col JOSEPH HUGH CARNCROSS, Royal Artillery. Knighted by the lord lieutenant of Ireland Dec. 22.

1815, Jan. 2 Lieut Col ROBERT WILLIAM GARDINER, Royal Artillery. Knighted 1815, Apr. 12. Invested 1837, May 17.

1815, Jan. 2. Lieut. Col. JOHN DYER, Royal Artillery. Knighted Apr. 12.

1815, Jan. 2. Lieut. Col. CHARLES, baron, afterwards count, LIN-SINGEN Invested Apr 12 (honorary).

1815, Jan. 2. Lieut. Gen. LUDWIG GEORG THEDEL, count of Walmoden Gimborn (honorary).

1815, Jan 2. Lieut. Col. count NUGENT (honorary).

1815, Jan. 2. Maj. Gen. SIGISMUND, baron LOW (honorary).

1815, Jan. 2. Maj. Gen CHARLES, baron ALTEN (honorary).

1815, Jan. 2. Maj. Gen. HENRY DE HINUBER (honorary).

1815, Jan. 2. Maj. Gen WILHELM DE DORNBERG (honorary).

1815, Jan. 2. Col. FREDERICK, baron DE ARENTSCHILDT (honorary).

1815, Jan. 2. Lieut. Col. FREDERICK AUGUSTUS DE HERTZBERG (honorary).

1815, Jan 2. Lieut. Col. JULIUS HARTMANN (honorary).

1815, Apr. 7. Lieut. Gen. MOORE DISNEY. Invested Apr. 12.

1815, Apr. 7. Maj. Gen. WILLIAM INGLIS. Invested Apr. 12.

1815, Apr. 7. Maj. Gen. JAMES LYON.

1815, Apr. 7. Lieut. Gen. JOHN MACDONALD, of the East India Company's service.

1815, Apr. 7. Maj. Gen. ROBERT BLAIR, of the East India Company's service.

1815, Apr. 7. Maj. Gen. GEORGE WOOD, of the East India Company's service.

1815, Apr. 7. Maj. Gen. HECTOR McLEAN, of the East India Company's service. Invested Apr. 12.

1815, Apr. 7. Maj. Gen. THOMAS DALLAS, of the East India Company's service. Invested Apr. 12.

1815, Apr. 7. Maj. Gen. JOHN MARY CHALMERS, of the East India Company's service.

1815, Apr. 7. Maj. Gen. JOHN HORSFORD, of the East India Company's service.

1815, Apr. 7. Maj. Gen. HENRY WHITE, of the East India Company's service.

1815, Apr. 7. Maj. Gen. GABRIEL MARTINDELL, of the East India Company's Service.

1815, Apr. 7. Maj. Gen. GEORGE SACKVILLE BROWNE, of the East India Company's Service. Invested Apr. 12.

1815, Apr. 7. Maj. Gen. GEORGE HOLMES, of the East India Company's Service.

1815, Apr. 7. Maj. Gen. DAVID OCHTERLONY, of the East India Company's Service.

1815, Apr. 7. Col. JOHN MALCOLM, of the East India Company's Service.

1815, Apr. 7. Col. AUGUSTUS FLOYER, of the East India Company's Service.

1815, Apr. 7. Col. ROBERT BARCLAY, of the East India Company's Service. Knighted 1816, Apr. 20.

1815, June 7. V. Adm. Sir DAVIDGE GOULD. Invested June 29.

1815, June 20. Maj. Gen GEORGE COOKE. Invested Oct. 19.

1815, June 22. Maj Gen. PEREGRINE MAITLAND.

1815, June 22. Maj. Gen. FREDERICK ADAM.

1815, Oct. 10. Lieut. Gen. MIGUEL D'ALAVA, of the Spanish Service. (Honorary).

1815, Oct. 20 [FREDERICK FERDINAND KARL] BARON DE MUFFLING (Honorary).

1816, Jan 3. R Adm CHARLES VINICOMBE PENROSE. Invested by dispensation May 30.

1816, Jan 23. Maj. Gen. Sir HUDSON LOWE. Invested 1822, Apr. 19.

1816, Sept. 19. R. Adm. Sir DAVID MILNE. Invested Oct. 2.

1816, Oct. 4 V Adm. [THEODORUS FREDERIK] VAN CAPELLEN, of. the king of Netherland's Navy (Honorary).

1817, Jan 7. Lieut. Gen. Sir ALEXANDER CAMPBELL, bart. Invested Feb 6.

1817, Feb. 3. Lieut. Gen. RICHARD JONES, of the East India Company's Service. Invested Mar. 6.

1817, Mar. 11 Lieut. Gen. ROBERT MACFARLANE. Invested Apr. 21.

1818, Sept. 5. Lieut Gen Sir THOMAS HISLOP, bart.

1818, Oct. 14. Maj Gen. DYSON MARSHALL, of the East India Company's Service.

1818, Oct. 14 Lieut Gen. RUFANE SHAW DONKIN. Invested 1822, Apr 19.

1819, Apr. 17. Gen. NICHOLAS CHARLES BARON VINCENT, of the Austrian Service (Honorary)

1819, Apr 17. Count CARLO ANDREA POZZO DI BORGO, of the Russian Service (Honorary).

1819, Apr. 17. Gen. DE REEDE, of the Netherlands Service [Honorary].

1819, Apr. 17. Lieut. Gen. LAMOTTE [Honorary].

1819, Aug. 12. V. Adm. MANLEY DIXON Invested Nov. 26.

1819, Aug. 12. R. Adm. the Hon. Sir HENRY BLACKWOOD, bart. Invested Sept. 16.

1819, Aug. 12. R. Adm. Sir JOHN POO BERESFORD, bart. Invested Sept. 16.

1819, Nov. 26. Maj. Gen. Sir THOMAS MUNRO, bart, of the East India Company's service.

1819, Nov. 26. Maj. Gen. WILLIAM TOONE, of the East India Company's service

1819, Nov. 26. Maj. Gen. JOHN DOVETON, of the East India Company's service.

1820, Mar. 17. Lieut. Gen. HENRY TUCKER MONTRESOR. Invested May 6

1820, May 20. Adm. HENRY TROLLOPE Invested July 19.

1820, May 20. Adm. HENRY D'ESTERRE DARBY. Invested July 19.

1820, May 20. V. Adm. JOHN WELLS. Invested May 29.

1820, May 20. V. Adm. HENRY NICHOLLS.

1820, May 20 Capt. Sir ROBERT BARLOW Invested May 29.

1820, May 20. Capt the Hon Sir GEORGE GREY, bart. Invested May 29.

1822, Dec 3 Maj. Gen Sir WILLIAM KEIR GRANT. Invested 1823, Apr. 21.

1822, Dec. 3. Maj. Gen. JAMES CAMPBELL. Invested 1825, June 29.

1822, Dec. 3. Maj. Gen LIONEL SMITH, afterwards bart.

1822, Dec. 3. Maj. Gen. THEOPHILUS PRITZLER. Invested 1823, Jan. 4.

1823, July 23. Maj. Gen. THOMAS BROWN, of the East India Company's service. Invested by dispensation 1828.

1825, Jan 13. R. Adm. WILLIAM CHARLES FAHIE. Invested 1825, Apr. 27.

1826, June 8. R. Adm ROBERT WALLER OTWAY, afterwards bart. Invested Aug 4 by dispensation.

1826, Dec 26. Maj Gen THOMAS REYNELL, afterwards bart. Invested by dispensation in 1827.

1826, Dec. 26. Maj. Gen. JASPER NICHOLLS Invested *ut supra.*

1826, Dec. 26. Maj. Gen SAMUEL FORD WHITTINGHAM. Invested *ut supra.*

1827, Jan. 18. Maj. Gen. Sir THOMAS McMAHON, bart. Invested by dispensation July 18.

1827, Jan. 18. Lieut. Gen. THOMAS BOWSER, of the East India Company's service. Invested *ut supra.*

1827, Jan. 18. Maj. Gen JOHN ARNOLD, of the East India Company's service. Invested by dispensation in 1827.

1827, Oct. 2. Lieut. Gen. Baron von HUGEL, of the Wurtemberg service (honorary).

1828, Mar. 14. Adm. LOUIS count von HEYDEN, of the Russian service (honorary).

1828, Mar. 14. R. Adm. HENRI GAUTHIER LE CHEVALIER DE RIGNY, afterwards comte de Rigny in the service of the French King.

1830, Nov. 17. V. Adm. Sir WILLOUGHBY THOMAS LAKE Invested Dec. 1.

1830, Nov. 17. R Adm Sir FREDERICK LEWIS MAITLAND. Invested 1831, Feb. 23.

1831, Mar. 14 V. Adm HENRY DIGBY. Invested Mar. 16.

1831, May 19. V. Adm. EDWARD GRIFFITH COLPOYS.

1831, May 19. V. Adm. EDWARD JAMES FOOTE. Invested May 25.

1831, June 8. V. Adm. CHARLES EKINS. Invested June 15.

1831, June 8. R. Adm. THOMAS BAKER. Invested 1833, Mar. 13.

1831, Sept. 13. Lieut. Gen. SAMUEL VENABLES HINDE. Invested Sept. 28.

1831, Sept. 13. Maj. Gen. JOHN WRIGHT GUISE, afterwards bart. Invested Sept. 28.

1831, Sept. 13. Maj. Gen. JAMES BATHURST. Invested Sept. 28.

1831, Sept. 13. Maj Gen. JAMES STEVENSON BARNS. Invested 1835, June 3.

1831, Sept. 13. R. Adm. Sir ROBERT LAURIE, bart. Invested 1836, Apr. 28.

1831, Sept. 13. Maj. Gen. JOHN MACDONALD. Invested Sept. 28

1831, Sept 13. Maj. Gen. ALEXANDER WOODFORD. Invested 1831, Sept. 28.

1831, Sept. 13. Maj. Gen. the hon. FREDERICK CAVENDISH PONSONBY. Invested Sept. 28

1831, Sept. 13. R. Adm. GEORGE SCOTT. Invested Sept. 13.

1831, Sept. 13. R. Adm. THOMAS DUNDAS. Invested Sept. 13.

1831, Sept. 13. R. Adm. Sir GRAHAM EDEN HAMOND, bart. Invested Sept. 28.

1831, Sept. 13. Maj. Gen. JOHN BUCHAN. Invested Sept. 28.

1831, Sept. 13. Maj. Gen HUGH GOUGH, afterwards 1st viscount Gough. Invested Sept. 28.

1831, Sept. 13. Maj. Gen. CHARLES ASHWORTH.

1831, Sept. 13. Maj. Gen. CHARLES BRUCE. Invested Sept. 28.

1831, Sept. 13. Maj. Gen. JOHN FOSTER FITZGERALD. Invested Sept. 28.

1831, Sept. 13. Maj. Gen. JOHN ROSS. Invested Sept. 28.

1831, Sept. 13. Maj. Gen. DUGALD LITTLE GILMOUR Invested Sept. 28.

1831, Sept. 13. Maj. Gen. WILLIAM MACBEAN. Invested Sept. 28.

1831, Sept. 13. Maj. Gen. GEORGE ELDER. Invested Sept. 28.

1831, Sept. 26. Maj. Gen. ALEXANDER KNOX, of the East India Company's service: at the Coronation of William IV.

1831, Sept. 26 Maj. Gen. Sir JOHN WHITTINGTON ADAMS, of the East India Company's service.

1831, Sept. 26. Maj. Gen. HENRY WORSLEY, of the East India Company's service. Invested Sept. 28.

1831, Sept. 26. HOPTON STRATFORD SCOTT Invested Sept. 28.

1831, Sept 26 Maj. Gen. ROBERT SCOT, of the East India Company's service. Invested Sept. 28.

1831, Sept. 26. Maj. Gen. ANDREW MACDOWALL, of the East India Company's service.

1832, Feb. 20. R. Adm. JOHN TREMAYNE RODD. Invested Feb. 22.

1832, Feb 20 R. Adm the hon. THOMAS BLADEN CAPEL. Invested Feb. 22.

1832, Mar 1. Maj. Gen. JOHN WATERS. Invested Mar. 28.

1832, Apr. 7. Maj. Gen. HUGH FRASER, of the East India Company's service. Invested 1834, Feb. 21.

1833, Jan 29 Adm. Sir CHARLES HAMILTON, bart. Invested Feb. 7

1833, Apr. 24. R Adm THOMAS HARVEY. Invested May 1.

1833, Apr. 24. R. Adm. RICHARD HUSSEY HUSSEY. Invested May 16

1833, June 1. V. Adm. JOHN HARVEY. Invested June 12.

1833, June 1. V. Adm GEORGE PARKER. Invested June 12.

1833, Sept 16. Maj. Gen. ARTHUR BROOKE. Invested 1834, Mar. 19.

1833, Sept. 16. Maj Gen. Sir JOHN ALEXANDER WALLACE, bart. Invested 1834, Apr. 23.

1834, July 14. R. Adm. Sir WILLIAM PARKER. Invested July 16.

1834, Oct. 6. R. Adm. EDWARD BRACE. Invested Oct. 29.

1834, Oct. 17. Maj. Gen. JOHN TAYLOR. Invested Oct 29.

1835, Jan. 26. Maj. Gen. RICHARD BOURKE. Invested by dispensa-
tion 1835, Feb. 23.

1835, Mar. 28. Maj. Gen. the hon. HENRY KING. Invested May 13.

1835, Aug. 10. R. Adm. CHARLES ADAM. Invested Aug. 12.

1836, Apr. 11. R. Adm. PATRICK CAMPBELL. Invested by dis-
pensation Nov. 29.

1836, Sept. 16. Maj. Gen. WILLIAM THORNTON. Invested 1837,
Mar. 17.

1836, Dec. 21. Maj. Gen. HENRY SHEEHY KEATING. Invested 1838,
Feb. 21.

1837, Feb. 6. Maj. Gen. Sir JOHN WILSON.

1837, Feb 28. V. Adm. ROSS DONNELLY. Invested Mar. 17.

1837, Feb. 28. R. Adm. FRANCIS WILLIAM AUSTEN. Invested
Mar. 17.

1837, Feb. 28. R. Adm. GEORGE MUNDY. Invested Mar. 17.

1837, Mar. 10. Maj. Gen. JAMES LILLYMAN CALDWELL, of the East
India Company's service. Invested May 10.

1837, Mar. 10. Maj Gen. ALEXANDER CALDWELL, of the East India
Company's service Invested Mar. 17.

1837, Mar. 10. Maj. Gen. DAVID LEIGHTON, of the East India
Company's service. Invested Apr. 26.

1837, Mar. 10. Maj. Gen. CHARLES DEACON, of the East India
Company's service. Invested Mar. 17.

1837, Mar. 10. Maj. Gen. JAMES RUSSELL, of the East India
Company's service. Invested Apr. 19.

1837, Mar. 10. Maj. Gen. Sir JOSEPH O'HALLORAN, of the East
India Company's service. Invested Mar. 17.

1837, Mar. 10. Maj. Gen. Sir ROBERT HOUSTOUN, bart , of the East
India Company's service. Invested Apr. 26.

1837, Mar 10. Maj. Gen. ROBERT STEVENSON, of the East India Company's service

1837, Mar. 10. Maj. Gen. WILLIAM CASEMENT, of the East India Company's service.

1837, Mar. 10 Maj. Gen. JAMES LAW LUSHINGTON, of the East India Company's service. Invested Mar. 17

1837, June 2. Maj. Gen WILLIAM JOHNSTON. Invested 1838, Feb. 21.

1838, Feb 13. Col. DE LACY EVANS, a lieut gen. in the service of the queen of Spain Invested 1838, Feb. 21.

1838, Feb 15. Maj Gen. JOHN FANE, commonly called lord Burghersh, afterwards 17th earl of Westmorland. Invested 1838, Mar. 21.

1838, Feb 16. Maj Gen. DONALD MACLEOD, of the East India Company's service. Invested 1838, Mar. 21.

1838, Apr. 20. Maj. Gen. CHARLES HENRY SOMERSET MANNERS, commonly called lord Charles Manners. Invested 1839, June 5

1838, Apr. 20. Maj Gen. Sir JAMES MACDONELL. Invested by Sir John Colborne in Canada, 1839, Aug. 23.

Queen Victoria's Coronation

1838, July 19 Adm. JOHN LAWFORD Invested Aug 15.

1838, July 19 Maj. Gen. ANDREW PILKINGTON. Invested Aug. 15.

1838, July 19. Maj. Gen. JOHN GARDINER. Invested Aug. 15.

1838, July 19. Maj. Gen. Sir ARTHUR BENJAMIN CLIFTON. Invested Aug. 15.

1838, July 19. Maj Gen. CHARLES MURRAY CATHCART, commonly called lord Greenock, afterwards 2nd earl Cathcart Invested by dispensation 1839, Sept. 5.

1838, July 19. Maj. Gen. WILLOUGHBY COTTON. Invested by dispensation 1839, Jan 14.

1838, July 19. Maj. Gen. Sir JOHN GEORGE WOODFORD.

1838, July 19. Maj. Gen PATRICK LINDESAY.

1838, July 19. Maj. Gen. CHARLES JAMES NAPIER. Invested 1839, June 5.

1838, July 19. Maj. Gen. Sir EVAN JOHN MURRAY MACGREGOR, bart. Invested by dispensation Nov. 16.

1838, July 19. Maj. Gen. EDWARD GIBBS. Invested Aug. 15

1838, July 19. Maj. Gen. GEORGE THOMAS NAPIER. Invested by dispensation Nov. 16.

1838, July 19. Maj. Gen. the Hon. HERCULES ROBINSON PAKENHAM. Invested 1839, June 5.

1838, July 19. Maj Gen Sir JOHN THOMAS JONES, bart. Invested 1839, June 5

1838, July 19. Maj. Gen. JOHN HARVEY. Invested by dispensation 1839, Jan. 3

1838, July 19 Maj. Gen LEONARD GREENWELL. Invested 1839, June 5.

1838, July 19. Maj. Gen. ROBERT HENRY DICK. Invested by dispensation Sept. 22.

1838, July 19. Maj. Gen. NEIL DOUGLAS. Invested 1840, July 17.

1838, July 19. R. Adm. JOHN ACKWORTH OMMANEY. Invested by dispensation Oct. 31.

1838, July 19. Maj. Gen. ALEXANDER CAMERON.

1838, July 19. Maj. Gen. JOHN FOX BURGOYNE Invested 1839, June 5.

1838, July 20. Maj. Gen. JOHN ROSE, of the Bengal Infantry, East India Company's service. Invested 1840, Apr. 6.

1838, July 20. Maj. Gen. THOMAS CORSELLIS, of the Bombay Infantry, East India Company's service. Invested by dispensation 1839, Jan. 3.

1838, July 20. Maj. Gen. WILLIAM RICHARDS, of the Bengal Infantry, East India Company's service.

1838, July 20. Maj. Gen. THOMAS WHITEHEAD, of the Bengal Infantry, East India Company's service.

1838, July 20. Maj Gen. JOHN DOVETON, of the Madras Cavalry, East India Company's service.

1838, July 20. Maj Gen. DAVID FOULIS, of the Madras Cavalry, East India Company's service

1838, July 20. Maj. Gen. Sir THOMAS ANBUREY, of the Bengal Engineers, East India Company's service. Invested by dispensation 1839, Apr. 6.

1839, Apr. 18 R. Adm. Sir CHARLES BULLEN. Invested 1839, June 5.

1839, Apr. 18. R. Adm. Sir SAMUEL WARREN. Invested 1839, June 5

1839, July 5. Lieut. Gen. JAMES WATSON. Invested 1840, Apr. 6.

1839, Oct 25. R. Adm. SAMUEL PYM. Invested 1840, Apr. 6.

1839, Oct 25 Maj. Gen. Sir JOHN BOSCAWEN SAVAGE, of the Royal Marines. Invested 1840, Apr. 6.

1839, Dec. 20. Col. THOMAS WILLSHIRE, commanding Bombay troops, with rank of maj gen. in India. Invested by dispensation 1840, June 24.

1839, Dec 20. Col. JOSEPH THACKWELL, commanding the Cavalry, with rank of maj gen. in India. Invested *ut supra*.

1839, Dec. 20. Col ROBERT HENRY SALE, commanding 13th Light Infantry, with rank of maj. gen in Afghanistan. Invested *ut supra*.

1840, July 4. V. Adm. JOHN WEST. Invested July 17.

1840, July 4 R. Adm. Sir CHARLES DASHWOOD. Invested July 17.

1840, July 4. R. Adm. Sir JOHN WENTWORTH LORING. Invested July 17.

1840, July 4 R. Adm. Sir ROBERT BARRIE. Invested July 17.

1840, July 4. R. Adm. Sir JOHN HILLYAR. Invested July 17.

1840, July 4. R. Adm. WILLIAM FITZROY, commonly called lord William Fitzroy. Invested 1841, Mar. 26

1840, July 18. Lieut. Gen. Sir EDWARD KERRISON, bart. Invested 1841, Mar. 26.

1840, July 18. Lieut. Gen. Sir HOWARD DOUGLAS, bart., lord high commissioner to the Ionian Isles. Invested by dispensation 1841, Jan. 30.

1840, Dec 4. Capt. and Commodore CHARLES NAPIER, commander-in-chief in the Mediterranean. For services on the coast of Syria. Invested by Sir Robert Stopford.

1841, Jan. 12. R. Adm. FRANCIS DE BANDIERA, of the Austrian Service; an honorary K.C.B. For services *ut supra*. Invested by dispensation Feb. 11.

1841, Jan. 12. R. Adm BALDWIN WAKE WALKER, of the Turkish Service; a Captain in the Royal Navy (Honorary) For services *ut supra*. Invested *ut supra*.

1841, June 29. Adm. JOHN CHAMBERS WHITE.

1841, June 29. R. Adm. CHARLES RICHARDSON.

1841, June 29. R. Adm. Sir ARTHUR FARQUHAR.

1841, June 29. Commodore Sir JAMES JOHN GORDON BREMER.

1841, Aug. 24. R. Adm. FRANCIS MASON

1841, Oct 14. THOMAS HERBERT, Capt R.N.

1842, Dec 24. Maj. Gen. ALEXANDER GEORGE (FRASER), 16th lord Saltoun.

1842, Dec. 24. Col. ROBERT BARTLEY, of the 49th Foot, with the local rank of maj. gen. in India.

1842, Dec. 24. Col. JAMES HOLMES SCHOEDDE, of the 55th Foot, with the local rank of maj. gen. in India.

1842, Dec. 24 Capt. THOMAS BOURCHIER, R.N.

1842, Dec. 24. Col. JOHN McCASKILL, of the 9th Foot, with the local rank of maj. gen. in India.

1843, July 12. Lieut. Gen WILLIAM WASHINGTON, in the service of the king of Bavaria [Honorary].

1843, July 12. Lieut. Gen. MAXIMILIAN VON SCHREIBERSHOFER, in the service of the king of Saxony [Honorary].

1843, Sept. 23 (27). Maj. Gen. Sir CHARLES FELIX SMITH.

1843, Sept. 23 (27). Col. RICHARD ENGLAND, with the local rank of maj. gen. in India.

1844, May 2. Maj. Gen JOHN GREY.

1844, May 2. Maj. Gen. HENRY GEORGE WAKELYN SMITH.

1844, May 2. Maj. Gen. JAMES RUTHERFORD LUMLEY, Bengal Infantry, adjutant general of the army; in the East India Company's service.

1844, May 2. Maj. Gen. JOHN HUNTER LITTLER, Bengal Infantry; in the East India Company's service.

1844, Oct. 30 Col JAMES DENNIS, of the 3rd Foot, with the local rank of maj. gen. in India.

1844, Oct. 30. Col. THOMAS VALIANT, of the 40th Foot, with the local rank of maj. gen. in India.

1845, May 8. R. Adm Sir EDWARD CHETHAM, afterwards Chetham-Strode.

1846, Mar. 9. Capt. CHARLES HOTHAM, R.N.

1846, Apr. 3. Maj Gen. WALTER RALEIGH GILBERT.

1846, Dec. 21. Maj. Gen. CHARLES WILLIAM PASLEY.

1847, July 8. R. Adm. Sir HUGH PIGOT.

1847, Oct. 28. R. Adm. Sir THOMAS JOHN COCHRANE.

1848, Mar. 2. Maj Gen. Sir DUDLEY ST. LEGER HILL.

1848, Mar 2. Maj Gen. JOHN ROLT.

1848, Apr. 27. Maj. Gen WILLIAM FRANCIS PATRICK NAPIER.

1848, Aug. 25. Maj Gen ARCHIBALD GALLOWAY.

1849, June 5. Col. the Hon. HENRY DUNDAS, of the 60th Rifles, afterwards 3rd viscount Melville.

1849, June 5 Col. COLIN CAMPBELL, of the 98th Foot, afterwards lord Clyde.

1849, June 5. Maj. Gen. WILLIAM SAMSON WHISH, in the service of the East India Company.

1849, June 5. Col. JOHN CHEAPE, of the Bengal Engineers.

1850, Aug. 16. Sir JOHN BISSET, commissary general.

1850, Aug. 16. Sir JAMES McGRIGOR, bart., M.D., director general of the medical department of the Army.

1850, Aug. 16. Sir WILLIAM BURNETT, M.D., director general of the medical department of the Navy.

1850, Aug. 16. JAMES THOMSON, inspector general of hospitals on the Bengal establishment of the East India Company's service.

1850, Aug. 16. Col. HUGH MASSEY WHEELER, of the Bengal Infantry.

1851, July 22. Maj. Gen. GEORGE BOWLES, late master of the Household, and now lieutenant of the Tower.

1852, Feb. 23. Maj. Gen. JOHN OWEN, late deputy adjutant general of the Royal Marines.

1852, Apr. 6. Lieut. Gen. Sir THOMAS DOWNMAN.

1852, Apr. 6. V. Adm. Sir GEORGE FRANCIS SEYMOUR.

1852, Apr. 6. V. Adm. the Hon. Sir ANTHONY MAITLAND.

1852, Apr. 6. Lieut. Gen. Sir ARCHIBALD MACLAINE, knt.

1852, Apr. 6. Lieut. Gen. GEORGE CHARLES D'AGUILAR.

1852, Apr. 6. Lieut. Gen. Sir RICHARD ARMSTRONG, knt.

1852, Apr. 6. Lieut. Gen. HENRY GOLDFINCH.

1852, Apr. 6. Lieut. Gen. JOHN BELL.

1852, Apr. 6. Lieut. Gen. GEORGE BROWN, adjutant general of Her Majesty's Forces.

1852, Apr. 6. R. Adm. PHIPPS HORNBY, commissioner of the Admiralty.

1852, Apr. 6. R. Adm. WILLIAM FAIRBROTHER CARROLL.

1852, Apr. 6. Col. JAMES TENNANT, of the Bengal Artillery.

1852, June 29. Lt. Gen. CHARLES McLEOD, of the East India Company's Service.

16

1853, May 30. Lieut. Gen. the Hon. GEORGE CATHCART, governor of the Cape of Good Hope.

1853, May 30. Maj Gen. HENRY SOMERSET.

1853, Dec. 9. Maj. Gen. HENRY GODWIN.

1853, Dec. 9. Brig. Gen. SCUDAMORE WINDE STEEL, of the Madras Army.

1853, Dec. 9. Commodore GEORGE ROBERT LAMBERT, of the Royal Navy.

1855, July 5. Lieut. Gen. GEORGE CHARLES (BINGHAM), 3rd earl of Lucan.

1855, July 5. Lieut. Gen. HENRY JOHN WILLIAM BENTINCK, major gen. with rank of lieut. gen. in Turkey.

1855, July 5. Lieut. Gen. JOHN LYSAGHT PENNEFATHER, same.

1855, July 5. R. Adm. HOUSTON STUART, same.

1855, July 5. R. Adm. JAMES HANWAY PLUMRIDGE.

1855, July 5. Maj. Gen. JAMES THOMAS (BRUDENELL), 17th earl of Cardigan.

1855, July 5 Maj. Gen. WILLIAM JOHN CODRINGTON.

1855, July 5. Maj. Gen. RICHARD AIREY.

1855, July 5. Maj. Gen. the Hon. JAMES YORKE SCARLETT.

1855, July 5. Maj. Gen. HARRY DAVID JONES, Royal Engineers.

1855, July 5. Maj. Gen. ARTHUR WELLESLEY TORRENS.

1855, July 5. Maj. Gen. GEORGE BULLER.

1855, July 5. Maj. Gen. WILLIAM EYRE.

1855, July 5. Maj. Gen. RICHARD JAMES DACRES, Royal Artillery.

1855, July 5. R. Adm. the Hon MONTAGUE STOPFORD.

1855, July 5. R. Adm. HENRY DUCIE CHADS.

1855, July 5. R. Adm. MICHAEL SEYMOUR.

1855, July 5. R. Adm. HENRY BYAM MARTIN.

1855, July 5. Capt. STEPHEN LUSHINGTON, R.N.

1855, July 5. Adm. FREDERICK WHITWORTH WILLIAM (AYLMER), 6th lord Aylmer.

1855, July 5. Gen. EDWARD NICOLLS, Royal Marines.

1855, July 5. Lieut. Gen. JAMES FERGUSON.

1855, July 5. Lieut. Gen. THOMAS WILLIAM BROTHERTON.

1855, July 5. V. Adm. HENRY HOPE.

1855, July 5. V. Adm. JOHN HENRY COODE.

1855, July 5. R. Adm. MAURICE FREDERICK FITZHARDINGE BERKELEY, a lord of the Admiralty.

1855, July 5. * R. Adm. FAIRFAX MORESBY.

1855, Oct. 16. Maj. Gen. HUGH HENRY ROSE, afterwards lord Strathnairn, Military Commissioner at the Headquarters of the French Army in the East.

1856, Jan. 3. Gen. EDMOND CHARLES DE MARTIMPREY, Gen. of Division; an officer in the service of the emperor of the French. [Honorary.]

1856, Jan. 3. FRANCOIS AUGUSTE THIRY, Gen. of Division, Artillery; an officer in the service of the emperor of the French. [Honorary.]

1856, Jan. 3. Gen. ADOLPHE NIEL, Gen. of Division, Engineers; an officer in the service of the emperor of the French. [Honorary.]

1856, Jan. 3. Gen. JACQUES CAMOU, Gen. of Division, Infantry; an officer in the service of the emperor of the French. [Honorary.]

* [List of officers of the Army and Navy who would have been recommended for the honours of the 2nd class of the Order of the Bath, had they survived.].
July 5, 1855 ?   Rear-Admiral Armar Lowry Corry.
  ,,   ,,   Rear-Admiral Edward Boxer, C.B.
  ,,   ,,   Maj.-Gen. James Bucknall Bucknall-Estcourt.
  ,,   ,,   Maj,-Gen. Sir John Campbell, Bart.
  ,   ,,   Brig.-Gen. William Burton Tylden, Royal Engineers.
  ,,   ,,   Brig.-Gen, Henry William Adams, 49th Foot.
  ,,   ,,   Brig.-Gen. Andrew Goldie, 57th Foot.
  ,,   ,,   Brig.-Gen. Thomas Fox-Strangways, Commanding Royal Artillery.
In the *Gazette* of 1856, Sept. 8, the Queen ordained that the widows of the above should have the precedence and title to which they would have been entitled had their husbands survived as above.

1856, Jan. 3.   Gen. CHARLES PATÉ, Gen. of Division, Infantry; an officer in the service of the emperor of the French. [Honorary.]

1856, Jan. 3.   Gen. CHARLES D'AUTEMARRE D'ERVILLÉ, Gen. of Division, Infantry; an officer in the service of the emperor of the French. [Honorary.]

1856, Jan. 3.   Gen. ARMAND OCTAVE MARIE D'ALLONVILLE, Gen. of Division, Cavalry; an officer in the service of the emperor of the French. [Honorary.]

1856, Jan. 3.   Gen. CHARLES LEVAILLANT, Gen. of Division, Infantry; an officer in the service of the emperor of the French. [Honorary.]

1856, Jan. 3.   Gen. JOSEPH DULAC, Gen. of Division, Infantry; an officer in the service of the emperor of the French. [Honorary.]

1856, Jan 3.   Gen. JEAN BAPTISTE CASIMIR DALESME, Gen. of Division, Engineers; an officer in the service of the emperor of the French. [Honorary.]

1856, Jan. 3.   Gen. EMILE HERBILLON, Gen. of Division, Infantry; an officer in the service of the emperor of the French. [Honorary.]

1856, Jan. 3   Gen. MARIE JOSEPH GUILLAUME BOUAT, Gen. of Division, Infantry; an officer in the service of the emperor of the French. [Honorary.]

1856, Jan. 3.   CHARLES RIGAULT DE GENOUILLY, contre amiral; an officer in the service of the emperor of the French. [Honorary.]

1856, Jan. 3.   Gen. CLAUDE MICHEL LOUIS D'AURELLES DE PALADINES, Gen. of Division, Infantry; an officer in the service of the emperor of the French. [Honorary.]

1856, Jan. 3.   Gen. EMILE MELLINET, Gen. of Division, Infantry; an officer in the service of the emperor of the French. [Honorary]

1856, Jan. 3.   Adm. CHARLES PENAUD, contre-amiral, an officer in the service of the emperor of the French. [Honorary.] Warrant of appointment dated Jan 22.

1856, Feb. 5.   Gen. JAMES WALLACE SLEIGH.

1856, Feb. 5.   Lieut. Gen. RICHARD GODDARD HARE CLARGES.

1856, Feb. 5.   V. Adm. HENRY PRESCOTT.

1856, Feb. 5.   Lieut. Gen. JOHN McDONALD.

1856, Feb. 5. Lieut. Gen. WILLIAM ROWAN.

1856, Feb. 5. V. Adm. BARRINGTON REYNOLDS.

1856, Feb. 5. Lieut. Gen. WILLIAM GEORGE MOORE.

1856, Feb. 5. Maj. Gen. JAMES FREDERIC LOVE.

1856, Feb. 5. Maj. Gen. JAMES JACKSON.

1856, Feb. 5. Maj. Gen. CHARLES YORKE, military secretary to the commander-in-chief.

1856, Feb. 5. R. Adm. the Hon. RICHARD SAUNDERS DUNDAS.

1856, Feb. 5. Maj. Gen. LOVELL BENJAMIN LOVELL.

1856. Feb. 5. Sir GEORGE MACLEAN, knt., commissary general.

1856, Feb. 5. JOHN HALL, inspector general of hospitals.

1856, Feb. 5. Maj. Gen. GEORGE AUGUSTUS WETHERALL, adjutant general.

1856, Feb. 5. Maj. Gen. WILLIAM FENWICK WILLIAMS, afterwards bart.

1856, May 3. Maj. Gen HENRY WILLIAM BARNARD.

1856, May 3. Maj. Gen. HENRY (MONTAGU), 6th lord Rokeby.

1857, Jan. 2. Lieut. Gen. SAMUEL BENJAMIN AUCHMUTY.

1857, Jan. 2. Lieut. Gen. NATHANIEL THORN.

1857, Jan. 2. R. Adm. CHARLES HOWE FREMANTLE.

1857, Jan. 2. R. Adm. the Hon. FREDERICK WILLIAM GREY.

1857, Jan. 2. Col. ROBERT GARRETT.

1857, Jan. 2. Col HENRY KNIGHT STORKS. Unattached.

1857, Jan. 2. Lieut. Gen. GEORGE PETRE WYMER, of the Bengal Army.

1857, Jan. 2. Lieut. Gen. PATRICK GRANT, of the Bengal Army.

1857, Jan. 2. (Honorary) V. Adm. LÉONARD VICTOR JOSEPH CHARNER.

1857, Jan. 2. (Honorary) MARIE JOSEPH ALPHONSE ODET-PELLION, contre amiral.

1857, Jan. 2. (Honorary) JEAN LUGEOL, contre amiral.

1857, Jan. 2. (Honorary) LOUIS EDOUARD COMTE BOUËT-WILLAUMEZ, contre amiral.

1857, Jan. 2. (Honorary) OCTAVE PIERRE ANTOINE DE CHABANNES-CURTON, contre amiral.

1857, Jan. 2. (Honorary) PIERRE EDMOND JURIEU JEAN DE LA GRAVIÈRE, contre amiral.

1857, Jan. 2. (Honorary) Lieut. Gen. chevalier GIOVANNI DURANDO, commanding the First Division of the Sardinian Army in the East.

1857, Jan. 2. (Honorary) Lieut. Gen. chevalier ARDINGO TROTTI, commanding the Second Division of the Sardinian Army in the East.

1857, Jan. 22. Maj. Gen. ROBERT JOHN HUSSEY VIVIAN, of the Madras Army, late serving with the local rank of lieut. gen. while in the command of the Turkish contingent.

1857, July 4. (Extra) Maj. Gen. JOHN BENNETT HEARSEY, col. of the 6th Regiment of Bengal Light Cavalry, in the East India Company's service.

1857, Sept. 12. R. Adm. the Hon. HENRY KEPPEL.

1857, Nov. 11. Maj. Gen. HENRY HAVELOCK.

*1857, Nov. 14. Col. ARCHDALE WILSON, of the Bengal Artillery.

1858, Jan. 21. Maj. Gen. JOHN EARDLEY WILMOT INGLIS.

1858, Jan. 21. Capt. WILLIAM PEEL, R.N.

1858, Jan. 21. Col. EDWARD LUGARD.

1858, Jan. 21. Col. JAMES HOPE GRANT.

1858, Mar. 24. Col. SIDNEY JOHN COTTON, serving with the local rank of Maj. Gen. in the East Indies.

※ The following would have been recommended for the dignity had they survived.
Nov. 17, 1857. Col. JAMES GEORGE NEILL, of the Madras Fusiliers.
    ,,   ,,   Lt.-Col. JOHN NICHOLSON, of the 27th Regiment of Bengal Native Infantry.
    In the *Gazette* of 1857, Nov. 26, the Queen ordained that ISABELLA NEILL, the widow of the late Col. JAMES GEORGE NEILL, of the Madras Fusiliers, should have and hold, etc., the same precedence as if he had survived, etc., etc.

1858, Mar. 24. Col. WILLIAM ROSE MANSFIELD, afterwards lord Sandhurst, serving with the local rank of maj. gen. in the East Indies.

1858, Mar. 24. (Extra) Col. THOMAS SEATON, Bengal Army.

1858, June 18. Maj. Gen. CHARLES THOMAS VAN STRAUBENZEE, commanding Land Forces in China.

1858, July 27. Maj. Gen. THOMAS HARTE FRANKS.

1858, July 27. (Extra) Col. ROBERT CORNELIS NAPIER, afterwards lord Napier of Magdala, of the Bengal Engineers.

1858, Aug. 18. Capt. ADOLPHUS SLADE, R.N., V. Adm. in the Ottoman Navy.

1858, Oct. 1. R. Adm. Sir HENRY JOHN LEEKE, sometime commander-in-chief and superintendent of the Indian Navy.

1858, Nov. 16. Col. JOHN JONES, of the 60th Regiment.

1859, Mar. 22. Maj. Gen. JOHN MICHEL.

1859, Mar. 22. (Extra) Col. CHARLES SHEPHERD STUART, of the Bombay Infantry.

1859, May 16. (Extra) Col. ROBERT WALPOLE, Rifle Brigade.

1859, May 16. (Extra) Col. GEORGE ROBERT BARKER, Royal Artillery.

1859, May 16. (Extra) Col. JOHN DOUGLAS, 79th Regiment.

1859, May 16. (Extra) Maj. Gen. HENRY GEE ROBERTS, Bombay Army.

1859, May 16. (Extra) Maj. Gen. GEORGE CORNISH WHITLOCK, Madras Army.

1859, June 10. JOHN MACANDREW, M.D., insp. gen. of Hospitals : on half pay.

1859, June 21. Gen. HENRY WYNDHAM.

1859, June 21. Lieut. Gen. JOHN AITCHISON.

1859, Aug. 17. (Extra) Col. DAVID EDWARD WOOD, of the Royal Artillery.

1860, May 9. Col. ALFRED HASTINGS HORSFORD.

1860, May 18. Lieut. Gen. SAMUEL BURDON ELLIS, of the Royal Marines.

1860, May 18. V. Adm. ARTHUR FANSHAWE.

1860, May 18. V. Adm. PROVO WILLIAM PARRY WALLIS.

1860, May 18. R. Adm. ROBERT LAMBERT BAYNES.

1860, May 18. Gen. the Hon. HENRY MURRAY.

1860, May 18. Lieut. Gen. PHILIP BAINBRIGGE.

1860, May 18. Lieut. Gen. THOMAS ERSKINE NAPIER.

1860, May 18. Lieut. Gen. the Hon. CHARLES STEPHEN GORE.

1860, May 18. Lieut. Gen. EDWARD CHARLES WHINYATES.

1860, May 18 Lieut. Gen. GEORGE JUDD HARDING.

1860, July 21. Col. ANTHONY CONINGHAM STERLING, sometime Military Secretary to the Commander-in-Chief in the East Indies.

1860, July 30. Col. RICHARD DENIS KELLY, of the 34th Regiment.

1860, Nov. 9. V. Adm. JAMES HOPE, Commander-in-chief of the Naval Forces in the East Indies and China.

1861, Mar. 1. (Honorary) CHARLES GUILLAUME MARIE APPOLINAIRE ANTOINE COUSIN-MONTAUBAN [Comte de Palikao] Gen. of Division, Commander-in-chief of the French Land Forces in China; officer of the French Army.

1861, June 28. Adm. EDWARD HARVEY.

1861, June 28. Lieut. Gen. WILLIAM HENRY SEWELL.

1861, June 28. Lieut. Gen. GEORGE WILLIAM PATY.

1861, June 28. Lieut. Gen. JAMES SHAW KENNEDY.

1861, June 28. Lieut. Gen. GEORGE LEIGH GOLDIE.

1861, June 28. Lieut. Gen. JOHN MITCHELL.

1861, June 28. V. Adm. HENRY WILLIAM BRUCE.

1861, June 28. V. Adm. WILLIAM FANSHAWE MARTIN.

1861, June 28. Maj. Gen. WILLIAM BRERETON.

1861, June 28. R. Adm. LEWIS TOBIAS JONES.

1861, June 28. Col. WILLIAM LYGON (PAKENHAM), 6th earl of Longford.

1861, July 16. Maj. Gen. THOMAS SIMSON PRATT.

1862, Jan. 28. Maj. Gen. STUART CORBETT, Bengal Infantry.

1862, Nov. 10. Gen. the Hon. HUGH ARBUTHNOTT (on the occasion of the coming of age of H.R.H. the prince of Wales).

1862, Nov. 10. Gen. Sir JOHN HANBURY, knt. (same occasion).

1862, Nov. 10. Gen. GEORGE (HAY), 8th marquess of Tweeddale (same occasion).

1862, Nov. 10. Gen. WILLIAM GREENSHIELDS POWER (same occasion).

1862, Nov. 10. Gen. HENRY GEORGE ANDREW TAYLOR, Madras Army (same occasion).

1862, Nov. 10. Gen. ALEXANDER LINDSAY, Bengal Army (same occasion).

1862, Nov. 10. Gen. Sir JAMES HENRY REYNETT, knt. (same occasion).

1862, Nov. 10. Gen. RICHARD LLUELLYN (same occasion).

1862, Nov. 10. Gen. CHARLES GRENE ELLICOMBE (same occasion).

1862, Nov. 10. Lieut. Gen. GEORGE TURNER (same occasion).

1862, Nov. 10. Lieut. Gen. JAMES FREETH (same occasion).

1862, Nov. 10. Lieut. Gen. JOHN LOW, Madras Army (same occasion).

1862, Nov. 10. Lieut. Gen. Sir JAMES CHARLES CHATTERTON, bart. (same occasion).

1862, Nov. 10. Lieut. Gen. ALEXANDER KENNEDY CLARK KENNEDY (same occasion).

1862, Nov. 10. Lieut. Gen. MICHAEL WHITE (same occasion).

1862, Nov. 10. Lieut. Gen. DAVID CAPON, Bombay Army (same occasion).

1862, Nov. 10. Maj. Gen. Sir ABRAHAM JOSIAS CLOETE (same occasion).

1862, Nov. 10. Maj. Gen. WILLIAM HENRY ELLIOTT (same occasion).

1862, Nov 10. Adm. the Hon. GEORGE ELLIOTT (same occasion).

1862, Nov. 10. Adm. Sir LUCIUS CURTIS, bart. (same occasion).

1862, Nov. 10. Adm. WILLIAM BOWLES (same occasion).

1862, Nov. 10. V. Adm. WILLIAM JAMES HOPE JOHNSTONE (same occasion).

1862, Nov. 10 V. Adm. JAMES SCOTT (same occasion).

1862, Nov. 10. R. Adm CHARLES TALBOT (same occasion).

1862, Nov 10 R. Adm. JOHN McDOUGALL (same occasion).

1862, Nov. 10. R. Adm. GEORGE RODNEY MUNDY (same occasion).

1862, Nov. 10 Lieut. Gen. SAMUEL ROBERT WESLEY, Royal Marines (same occasion).

1863, Apr. 11. Col. NEVILLE BOWLES CHAMBERLAIN, of the Bengal Army.

1863, Dec. 31. JOHN WILLIAM SMITH, commissary gen. in chief.

1864, Feb 9. Sir JOHN LIDDELL, knt., M D , late director-gen. of the Medical Department of the Navy.

1864, Feb. 20 Maj. Gen. DUNCAN ALEXANDER CAMERON (having the local rank of lieut. gen. while in command of the Troops in New Zealand).

1864, Feb. 25. R. Adm. Sir ALEXANDER MILNE, promoted from K.C B. (Civil) with temporary rank as V. Adm. while commander-in-chief on the North American and West Indian Station.

1864, Feb. 25. R. Adm. AUGUSTUS LEOPOLD KUPER, with temporary rank as V. `Adm. while commander-in-chief on the East Indian and China Station.

1864, Aug. 25. Maj. Gen. JOHN GARVOCK.

1865, Feb. 23. (Honorary) V. Adm. JEAN LOUIS CHARLES JAURES, officer of the French Marine.

1865, Mar. 28. Gen. WILLIAM WOOD.

1865, Mar. 28. Gen. THOMAS KENAH.

1865, Mar. 28. Adm. Sir GEORGE ROSE SARTORIUS, knt.

1865, Mar. 28. Gen. ABRAHAM ROBERTS.

1865, Mar. 28. Lieut. Gen. THOMAS MONTEATH-DOUGLAS, Bengal Army.

1865, Mar. 28. Lieut. Gen. WILLIAM CATOR.

1865, Mar. 28. Lieut. Gen. PATRICK MONTGOMERIE, Royal (late Madras) Artillery.

1865, Mar. 28. Lieut. Gen. THOMAS REED.

1865, Mar. 28. Lieut. Gen. JOHN SCOTT.

1865, Mar. 28. Lieut. Gen. WILLIAM WYLLIE.

1865, Mar. 28. Lieut. Gen. CHARLES ASH WINDHAM.

1865, Mar. 28. V. Adm. THOMAS (MAITLAND), 11th earl of Lauderdale.

1865, Mar. 28. V. Adm. ROBERT SMART.

1865, Mar. 28. V. Adm. JOHN KINGCOME.

1865, Mar. 28. V. Adm. HORATIO THOMAS AUSTIN.

1865, Mar. 28. Lieut. Gen. JOHN EDWARD DUPUIS.

1865, Mar. 28. Lieut. Gen. FORTESCUE GRAHAM, Royal Marines

1865, Mar. 28. R. Adm. Sydney Colpoys Dacres.

1865, Mar. 28. Maj. Gen. lord William Paulet.

1865, Mar. 28. Maj. Gen. the Hon. Augustus Almeric Spencer.

1865, Mar. 28. Maj. Gen. Robert William Honner, Bombay Army.

1865, Mar. 28. Col. John William Gordon.

1865, Mar. 28. Col. Edward Harris Greathed.

1865, Mar. 28. Col. Charles William Dunbar Staveley.

1865, Mar. 28. James Brown Gibson, M.D., Director-General of the Army Medical Department.

1865, Mar. 28. William Linton, M D., Inspector-General of Hospitals on half-pay.

1865, Mar. 28. William James Tyrone Power, Commissary-General-in-Chief.

1865, Apr. 19. Gen. Charles Menzies, of the Royal Marine Artillery.

1865, Apr. 19. Maj. Gen. Charles Warren.

1865, June 7. Adm. Edward Collier.

1865, June 7. V. Adm. Peter Richards.

1867, Mar. 13. V. Adm. Henry John Codrington.

1867, Mar. 13. V. Adm. Joseph Nias.

1867, Mar. 13. V. Adm. Sir Edward Belcher, knt.

1867, Mar. 13. Lieut. Gen Edmund Finucane Morris.

1867, Mar. 13. Lieut. Gen. Peter Edmondstone Craigie

1867, Mar. 13. Lieut. Gen. John Bloomfield Gough.

1867, Mar. 13. Lieut. Gen. George Henry Lockwood.

1867, Mar. 13. Maj. Gen. MAURICE STACK, Bombay Army.

1867, Mar. 13. Maj. Gen. EDWARD GREEN, Bombay Army.

1867, Mar. 13. Lieut. Gen. GEORGE BROOKE, Bengal Army.

1867, Mar. 13. Maj. Gen. JOHN ROWLAND SMYTH.

1867, Mar. 13. Adm. FREDERICK THOMAS MITCHELL.

1867, Mar. 13. V. Adm. THOMAS MATTHEW CHARLES SYMONDS.

1867, Mar. 13. R. Adm. WILLIAM HUTCHEON HALL.

1867, Mar. 13. Maj. Gen. GEORGE BELL.

1867, Mar. 13. Col. FREDERICK EDWARD CHAPMAN.

1867, Mar. 13. DAVID DEAS, M.D., inspector general of hospitals and fleets.

1867, Mar. 13. Lieut. Gen. THOMAS HOLLOWAY, Royal Marine Artillery,

1867, Mar. 13. Capt. Sir WILLIAM SALTONSTALL WISEMAN, bart., R.N.

1867, Mar. 13. Lieut. Gen. WILLIAM BELL.

1867, Mar. 13. Lieut. Gen. JOHN BLOOMFIELD.

1867, Mar. 13. Lieut. Gen. ANTHONY BLAXLAND STRANSHAM, Royal Marine Light Infatry.

1867, Mar. 13. Maj. Gen. WILLIAM BATES INGILBY.

1867, Mar. 13. Maj. Gen. TREVOR CHUTE.

1868, Mar. 14. Maj. Gen. HENRY TOMBS, V.C., of the Royal (late Bengal) Artillery.

1868, Aug. 14. Maj. Gen. GEORGE MALCOLM, Bombay Army.

1868, Aug. 14. Capt. LEOPOLD GEORGE HEATH, R.N.

1869, June 2. V. Adm. WILLIAM RAMSAY.

1869, June 2. Lieut. Gen. GEORGE FREDERICK (UPTON), 3rd viscount Templetown.

1869, June 2.   V. Adm. the Rt. Hon. CLARENCE EDWARD PAGET, commonly called lord Clarence Paget.

1869, June 2.   Lieut. Gen. EDWARD HUTHWAITE.

1869, June 2.   V. Adm. HENRY KELLETT.

1869, June 2.   Maj. Gen. FREDERICK HORN.

1869, June 2.   Maj. Gen. ARTHUR AUGUSTUS THURLOW CUNYNGHAME.

1869, June 2.   Lord GEORGE AUGUSTUS FREDERICK PAGET, maj. gen.

1869, June 2.   Maj. Gen. ARTHUR JOHNSTONE LAWRENCE.

1869, June 2.   Maj. Gen. HORATIO SHIRLEY.

1869, June 2.   R. Adm. HASTINGS REGINALD YELVERTON.

1869, June 2.   Maj. Gen. WILLIAM JONES.

1869, June 2.   R. Adm. BARTHOLOMEW JAMES SULIVAN.

1869, June 2.   Maj Gen. JOHN ST. GEORGE.

1869, June 2.   Maj. Gen. EDWARD CHARLES WARDE.

1869, June 2.   Maj. Gen. JAMES BRIND.

1869, June 2.   Maj. Gen. the Rt Hon. PERCY EGERTON HERBERT.

1869, June 2.   Maj. Gen. JOHN LINTORN ARABIN SIMMONS.

1869, June 2.   Maj. Gen. ARCHIBALD LITTLE.

1869, June 2.   Col. ALFRED THOMAS WILDE, Madras Army.

1869, June 2   THOMAS GALBRAITH LOGAN, M.D., director-gen. of the Medical Department of the Army.

1871, May 20.   Lieut. Gen. JAMES ALEXANDER.

1871, May 20.   Lieut Gen EDWARD WALTER FORESTIER WALKER.

1871, May 20.   Lieut. Gen. JOHN FOWLER BRADFORD.

1871, May 20.   Maj. Gen. DAVID RUSSELL.

1871, May 20. Maj. Gen. HENRY WILLIAM STISTED.

1871, May 20. Maj. Gen. CHARLES RICHARD (SACKVILLE-WEST), 6th earl De La Warr.

1871, May 20. Maj. Gen. FREDERICK PAUL HAINES.

1871, May 20. Maj. Gen. THOMAS MONTAGU STEELE.

1871, May 20. Maj. Gen. COLLINGWOOD DICKSON, V.C.

1871, May 20. Maj. Gen. CHARLES REID.

1871, May 20. Maj. Gen. JAMES WILLIAM FITZMAYER.

1871, May 20. Maj. Gen. HENRY CHARLES BARNSTON DAUBENEY.

1871, May 20. R. Adm. WILLIAM ROBERT MENDS.

1871, May 20. R. Adm. WILLIAM KING HALL.

1871, May 20. DAVID DUMBRECK, M.D., insp.-gen. of Hospitals on half pay.

1871, May 20. WILLIAM HENRY DRAKE: controller, War Office.

1871, June 17. ALEXANDER ARMSTRONG, M.D , director-gen. of the Medical Department of the Navy.

1872, Sept. 10. (Honorary) Maj. Gen. GEORGE BOURCHIER, Royal (late Bengal) Artillery.

1872, Sept. 10. Col. CHARLES HENRY BROWNLOW, Bengal Staff Corps.

1873, May 24. Adm. HENRY SMITH.

1873, May 24. Adm. Sir THOMAS SABINE PASLEY, bart.

1873, May 24. Adm. CHARLES EDEN.

1873, May 24. Lieut Gen. FRANCIS WARDE.

1873, May 24. V. Adm. GEORGE ST. VINCENT KING.

1873, May 24. Lieut. Gen. FREDERICK WILLIAM HAMILTON.

1873, May 24. V. Adm. the Hon. JAMES ROBERT DRUMMOND

1873, May 24. Lieut. Gen. ARTHUR MITFORD BECHER.

1873, May 24. Lieut. Gen. CHARLES TROLLOPE.

1873, May 24. Lieut. Gen EDWARD COOPER HODGE.

1873, May 24. Lieut. Gen. the Hon. ALEXANDER HAMILTON-GORDON.

1873, May 24. Lieut. Gen. JOHN FORDYCE.

1873, May 24. Lieut. Gen. PHILIP MELMOTH NELSON GUY

1873, May 24   V. Adm. ASTLEY COOPER KEY.

1873, May 24. Maj. Gen HENRY HUGH MANVERS PERCY, commonly called lord Henry Percy, V.C.

1873, May 24. Maj. Gen. CHARLES HENRY ELLICE.

1873, May 24. Maj. Gen RICHARD WILBRAHAM.

1873, May 24. Maj. Gen. JAMES DUNCAN MACPHERSON.

1873, May 24. Maj. Gen. EDMUND HAYTHORNE.

1873, May 24   Maj. Gen. HENRY DRURY HARNESS.

1873, May 24. R. Adm. JOHN WALTER TARLETON.

1873, May 24. R. Adm. CHARLES FREDERICK ALEXANDER SHADWELL.

1873, May 24. Maj. Gen. HENRY WYLIE NORMAN.

1873, May 24. Col. JOHN MILLER ADYE.

1873, May 24. Surg Gen. WILLIAM MURE MUIR, M.D.

1874, Mar. 31. Maj. Gen SIR GARNET JOSEPH WOLSELEY, afterwards viscount Wolseley.

1874, Mar. 31. Capt. JOHN EDMUND COMMFRELL, R.N., V.C.

1874, Mar. 31. Capt. WILLIAM NATHAN WRIGHTE HEWETT, R.N., V.C.

1874, Mar. 31. Col. Sir ARCHIBALD ALISON, bart.

1874, Mar. 31. Col. JOHN CHETHAM McLEOD, 42nd Regt.

1874, Mar. 31. Deputy-Surgeon Gen. ANTHONY DICKSON HOME, V.C.

1875, May 29. Lieut. Gen. BURKE CUPPAGE.

1875, May 29. V. Adm. RICHARD COLLINSON.

1875, May 29. V. Adm. CLAUDE HENRY MASON BUCKLE.

1875, May 29. V. Adm. GEORGE GIFFARD

1875, May 29. Lieut. Gen. the Hon. GEORGE CADOGAN.

1875, May 29. V. Adm. WILLIAM LORING.

1875, May 29. Lieut. Gen. Sir FRANCIS SEYMOUR, bart.

1875, May 29. Lieut. Gen. WILLIAM O'GRADY HALY.

1875, May 29. V. Adm. EDWARD SOUTHWELL SOTHEBY.

1875, May 29. Lieut. Gen. EDWARD ALAN HOLDICH.

1875, May 29. Maj. Gen. EDWIN BEAUMONT JOHNSON.

1875, May 29. Maj. Gen. HENRY DERMOT DALY

1875, May 29. Surgeon Gen. JOHN CAMPBELL BROWN, Bengal Army.

1876, Mar. 23. Maj. Gen the Hon. FRANCIS COLBORNE, commanding Her Majesty's Troops in China and the Straits Settlements

1877, June 2. Adm. GEORGE ELLIOT.

1877, June 2. Lieut. Gen. ARTHUR BORTON.

1877, June 2. Lieut. Gen. RICHARD WADDY.

1877, June 2. V. Adm. FREDERICK BEAUCHAMP PAGET SEYMOUR.

1877, June 2. Lieut. Gen. HENRY DALRYMPLE WHITE.

1877, June 2. Maj. Gen. WILLIAM SHERBROOKE RAMSAY NORCOTT.

1877, June 2. Maj. Gen. DANIEL LYSONS.

17

1877, June 2. Maj. Gen. CHARLES LAWRENCE D'AGUILAR.

1877, June 2. Maj. Gen. JAMES TALBOT AIREY.

1877, June 2 Maj. Gen. ALEXANDER TAYLOR.

1877, June 2. Maj. Gen MICHAEL GALWEY, Madras Army.

1877, June 2. Maj. Gen GEORGE WADE GUY GREEN, Bengal Army.

1877, June 2. R. Adm. WILLIAM HOUSTON STEWART.

1877, June 2. Maj. Gen. THOMAS HURDLE, late Royal Marines.

1877, June 2. WILLIAM RICHARD EDWIN SMART, M.D., inspector
general of hospitals and fleets.

1878, July 29. Lieut. Gen Sir ARNOLD BURROWES KEMBALL.

1878, Aug. 12. V. Adm. GEOFFREY THOMAS PHIPPS HORNBY,
commander-in-chief of Her Majesty's Naval Forces in the
Mediterranean.

1878, Nov. 11. FREDERICK AUGUSTUS (THESIGER), 2nd lord
Chelmsford, maj. gen., having the local rank of lieut. gen.
while serving in command of the Forces at the Cape of Good
Hope.

1879, June 23. Col HENRY EVELYN WOOD, V.C.

1879, June 23. Commissary General EDWARD STRICKLAND.

1879, June 28 Gen. HENRY BATES.

1879, July 25. Lieut. Gen. DONALD MARTIN STEWART.

1879, July 25. Lieut. Gen. Sir SAMUEL JAMES BROWNE, V.C.

1879, July 25. Lieut. Gen FREDERICK FRANCIS MAUDE, V.C.

1879, June 25. Maj.Gen. MICHAEL ANTHONY SHRAPNEL BIDDULPH,
R.A.

1879, July 25. Maj. Gen. FREDERICK SLEIGH ROBERTS, R.A., V.C.

1879, July 25. Col. and Local Maj Gen. PETER STARK LUMSDEN.

1879, Nov. 27. R. Adm. FRANCIS WILLIAM SULLIVAN.

1880, Mar. 6   Col. CHARLES PATTON KEYES, Madras Staff Corps.

1880, Mar. 6   Col. CAMPBELL CLAYE GRANT ROSS, Bengal Staff Corps.

1880, Apr. 23.   Maj. Gen. FREDERICK ALEXANDER CAMPBELL, director of Artillery and Stores.

1880, Apr. 23.   Adm. GEORGE GREVILLE WELLESLEY.

1881, Feb. 22.   Lieut. Gen. ROBERT ONESIPHORUS BRIGHT.

1881, Feb. 22.   Maj. Gen. JOHN ROSS.

1881, Feb. 22.   Maj. Gen. JAMES HILLS, V.C.

1881, Feb. 22.   Maj. Gen. ROBERT PHAYRE, Bombay Staff Corps.

1881, Feb 22.   Col. HERBERT TAYLOR MACPHERSON (having local rank of maj. gen.), V.C., Bengal Staff Corps.

1881, Feb. 22.   Col. CHARLES HENRY PALLISER, Bengal Staff Corps.

1881, Feb. 22.   Col. CHARLES JOHN STANLEY GOUGH, V.C., Bengal Cavalry.

1881, Feb. 22.   Col. THOMAS DURAND BAKER, 18th Regiment.

1881, Feb. 22.   Col CHARLES METCALFE MACGREGOR, Bengal Staff Corps.

1881, Feb. 22   Col. HUGH HENRY GOUGH, V.C., Bengal Staff Corps.

1881, May 24.   Adm. the Hon. CHARLES GILBERT JOHN BRYDONE ELLIOT.

1881, May 24.   Adm. EDWARD GENNYS FANSHAWE.

1881, May 24.   Gen. GEORGE COLT LANGLEY.

1881, May 24.   Gen. WILLIAM MONTAGU SCOTT MCMURDO.

1881, May 24.   Gen. lord MARK KERR.

1881, May 24.   Gen. H.S.H. prince EDWARD (WILLIAM AUGUSTUS EDWARD) of Saxe-Weimar.

1881, May 24.   Gen. JOHN THORNTON GRANT.

1881, May 24.   Lieut. Gen. GEORGE VAUGHAN MAXWELL.

1881, May 24.   Lieut. Gen. ALEXANDER MACDONELL.

1881, May 24.   Lieut. Gen. CHARLES PYNDAR BEAUCHAMP WALKER.

1881, May 24.   Lieut Gen. JOHN FORBES

1881, May 24.   V Adm. the Rt. Hon. lord JOHN HAY.

1881, May 24.   Hon. Maj. Gen. JOHN COKE.

1881, May 24.   Capt. FREDERICK WILLIAM RICHARDS, R.N.

1881, May 24.   Col. CHARLES GEORGE ARBUTHNOT.

1881, May 24   Col. CHARLES COOPER JOHNSON, Bengal Staff Corps.

1882, Aug. 14.   Capt. WALTER JAMES HUNT-GRUBBE.

1882, Nov. 18   V Adm WILLIAM MONTAGU DOWELL.

1882, Nov. 18.   Lieut. Gen GEORGE HARRY SMITH WILLIS.

1882, Nov. 18.   Lieut. Gen Sir EDWARD BRUCE HAMLEY.

1882, Nov. 18.   R. Adm. ANTHONY HILEY HOSKINS.

1882, Nov. 18.   Commissary Gen EDWARD MORRIS, Commissariat
and Transport Staff.

1882, Nov. 18   Maj. Gen. GERALD GRAHAM.

1882, Nov 18.   Maj Gen. DRURY CURZON DRURY-LOWE.

1882, Nov 18.   Col CHARLES BUTLER PETER HODGES NUGENT.

1882, Nov 18.   Col ORIEL VIVEASH TANNER.

1882, Nov 18.   Col. Sir BAKER CREED RUSSELL.

1882, Nov. 18.   Deputy Surg. Gen. JAMES ARTHUR HANBURY.

1882, Nov. 18.   Col. CROMER ASHBURNHAM.

1882, Nov. 24.   Lieut Gen RICHARD CHAMBRE HAYES TAYLOR.

1882, Nov. 24.   Lieut. Gen. ARTHUR JAMES HERBERT.

1882, Nov. 24.   Lieut. Gen. EDMUND AUGUSTUS WHITMORE.

1882, Nov. 24. Maj. Gen. CHARLES WILLIAM ADAIR.

1882, Nov. 24. JOHN WATT REID, M.D., director general of the Medical Department of the Navy.

1882, Nov. 24. Maj. Gen. JOHN CARSTAIRS McNEILL, V.C.

1884, May 21. (Extra) Lieut. Gen. FREDERICK CHARLES ARTHUR STEPHENSON.

1884, May 21. (Extra) Col. HERBERT STEWART, aide-de-camp to the queen.

1884, May 24. (Extra)Adm. ALFRED PHILLIPPS RYDER.

1884, May 24. (Extra) V. Adm. GEORGE OMMANEY WILLES.

1885, Aug. 11. Adm. Rt. Hon. Sir JOHN CHARLES DALRYMPLE HAY, bart., F.R.S.

1885, Aug. 25. (Extra) Maj. Gen. Sir GEORGE RICHARDS GREAVES.

1885, Aug. 25. (Extra) Maj. Gen. Sir REDVERS HENRY BULLER, V.C.

1885, Aug. 25. (Extra) THOMAS CRAWFORD, M.D., director general of the Army Medical Department.

1885, Aug. 25. (Extra) Col. JOHN HUDSON, Bengal Staff Corps.

1885, Aug. 25. (Extra) Col. HENRY PETER EWART, half-pay.

1885, Aug. 25. (Extra) Col. Sir CHARLES WILLIAM WILSON, Royal Engineers.

1885, Nov. 7. (Extra) Capt. ROBERT HENRY MORE MOLYNEUX, Royal Navy.

1885, Dec. 8. (Extra) Maj. Gen. HARRY NORTH DALRYMPLE PRENDERGAST, V.C.

1885, Dec. 19. (Extra) V. Adm. ARTHUR WILLIAM ACLAND HOOD.

1886, Jan. 9. (Extra) Gen. the Hon. ARTHUR EDWARD HARDINGE, an extra equerry to the Queen.

1886, Jan. 16. (Extra) Lieut. Gen. the Hon. Sir LEICESTER SMYTH.

1886, Feb. 18. V. Adm. H.R.H. ALFRED ERNEST ALBERT, duke of Edinburgh.

1886, Apr. 1. (Extra) Maj. Gen. EDWARD GASCOIGNE BULWER.

1886, May 29. Gen. FRANK TURNER, Royal Artillery.

1886, May 29. Adm. ARTHUR FARQUHAR, Royal Navy.

1886, May 29. Gen. HENRY JAMES WARRE.

1886, May 29 Lieut. Gen. and Hon. Gen. the Hon. ST GEORGE
GERALD FOLEY.

1886, May 29. Lieut. Gen. and Hon Gen. HENRY ERRINGTON
LONGDEN.

1886, May 29. Gen. WILLIAM OLPHERTS, V.C , Royal (Bengal)
Artillery.

1886, May 29. Adm JOHN CORBETT, Royal Navy.

1886, May 29. V. Adm Sir GEORGE HENRY RICHARDS, knt., Royal
Navy.

1886, May 29. Lieut. Gen. JULIUS RICHARD GLYN.

1886, May 29. Lieut. Gen. WILLIAM POLLEXFEN RADCLIFFE.

1886, May 29. Lieut. Gen. WILLIAM PAYN.

1886, May 29. Maj Gen JOHN WATSON, V C., Bombay Staff Corps.

1886, Nov 25. Lieut Col. and Col. FRANCIS BOOTH NORMAN, Bengal
Staff Corps

'1886, Nov. 25. Lieut. Col. and Col. FRANCIS WALLACE GRENFELL,
aide-de-camp to the queen; on half-pay list.

1886, Nov. 25. Lieut. Col. and Col. WILLIAM FRANCIS BUTLER,
aide-de-camp to the queen; on half-pay list.

1886, Nov. 25 Lieut. Col. and Col. GEORGE STEWART WHITE, V.C.,
having local rank of maj. gen. while commanding in Upper
Burmah; on half-pay list.

1887, June 21. Adm. HENRY CHADS.

1887, June 21. Gen. JAMES MACLEOD BANNATYNE FRASER-TYTLER,
Bengal Staff Corps.

1887, June 21. Adm. CHARLES FARRELL HILLYAR.

1887, June 21. Gen. PENROSE CHARLES PENROSE, Royal Marine Light Infantry.

1887, June 21. Adm. Sir EDWARD AUGUSTUS INGLEFIELD, knt.

1887, June 21. Adm. ARTHUR CUMMING.

1887, June 21. Adm. Sir REGINALD JOHN MACDONALD.

1887, June 21. Gen. JOHN ALEXANDER EWART.

1887, June 21. Adm. EDWARD BRIDGES RICE.

1887, June 21. Adm. AUGUSTUS PHILLIMORE.

1887, June 21. Adm. the Rt. Hon. RICHARD JAMES (MEADE), 4th earl of Clanwilliam.

1887, June 21. Gen. CHARLES LOUDON BARNARD, Royal Marine Artillery.

1887, June 21. Lieut. Gen. and Hon. Gen. WILLIAM PARKE.

1887, June 21. Lieut. Gen. JOHN LUTHER VAUGHAN, Bengal Staff Corps.

1887, June 21. Lieut. Gen. LOTHIAN NICHOLSON, Inspector Gen. of Fortifications.

1887, June 21. Lieut. Gen. ROBERT HUME.

1887, June 21. Lieut. Gen. HENRY D'OYLEY TORRENS, commanding the Troops in South Africa.

1887, June 21. V. Adm. RICHARD VESEY HAMILTON.

1887, June 21. V. Adm. THOMAS BRANDRETH.

1887, June 21. Surgeon Gen. JOHN HARRIE KER INNES, honorary surgeon to the Queen.

1887, June 21. Maj. Gen. Sir HENRY MARSHAM HAVELOCK-ALLAN, bart., V.C.

1887, June 21. (Additional) V. Adm. WILLIAM GRAHAM.

1887, June 21.　(Additional) V. Adm. NOWELL SALMON, V.C.

1887, June 21.　(Additional) Maj. Gen. (Honorary) GEORGE HUTT, V.C.

1887, June 21.　(Additional) WILLIAM MACKENZIE, inspector gen. of hospitals, Indian Medical Service; honorary physician to the queen.

1887, June 21.　(Additional) JAMES JENKINS, inspector gen. of Hospitals and Fleets, Royal Navy.

1887, June 21.　(Additional) Maj. Gen. MARTIN DILLON, commanding a division, Bengal.

1887, June 21.　(Additional) Maj. Gen. GEORGE BYNG HARMAN, military secretary, head quarters of the Army.

1887, June 21.　(Additional) R. Adm. GEORGE TRYON.

1887, July 1 (Nov. 25).　Lieut. Col. and Col. (having the local and temporary rank of brig. gen) ROBERT CUNLIFFE LOW, Bengal Cavalry, commanding a Brigade, Bengal.

1887, July 1 (Nov. 25).　Lieut. Col. and Col. (having the local and temporary rank of brig. gen.) WILLIAM STEPHEN ALEXANDER LOCKHART, Bengal Infantry, commanding a Brigade, Bengal.

1888, Jan. 16.　Maj. Gen. REGINALD GIPPS, commanding the Home District.

1889, Apr. 10.　Lieut. Col. and Col. (having local and temporary rank of Maj. Gen.) JOHN WITHERS McQUEEN, A.D.C., Bengal Staff Corps, commanding Hazara Field Force.

1889, May 25.　Adm. the Hon. ARTHUR AUCKLAND LEOPOLD PEDRO COCHRANE, retired list Royal Navy.

1889, May 25.　Gen. JOHN WILLIAM SCHNEIDER, Bombay Infantry.

1889, May 25.　Adm ALGERNON McLENNAN LYONS, Royal Navy.

1889, May 25.　Lieut. Gen. and Hon. Gen. CHARLES CAMERON SHUTE.

1889, May 25.　Lieut Gen GEORGE WENTWORTH ALEXANDER HIGGINSON, lieut. of the Tower of London.

1889, May 25. Lieut. Gen. and Hon. Gen. the Hon. DAVID MACDOWALL FRASER, Royal Artillery.

1889, May 25. Lieut. Gen. ALLEN BAYARD JOHNSON, Bengal Staff Corps.

1889, May 25. Maj. Gen. and Hon. Lieut. Gen. WILLIAM AUGUSTUS FYERS.

1889, May 25. Maj. Gen. the Hon. JAMES CHARLEMAGNE DORMER, commanding the Force in Egypt.

1889, May 25. R. Adm. the Hon EDMUND ROBERT FREMANTLE, Royal Navy.

1889, May 25 Maj. Gen. RICHARD HARRISON, Royal Engineers.

1890, Jan. 1. Lieut. Gen. GEORGE TOMKYNS CHESNEY (Royal Engineers), member of the Council of the Viceroy and Gov. Gen. of India.

1890, Feb. 18. (Honorary) His Excellency V. Adm. CARL AUGUST DEINHARD, commander-in-chief of the German Cruising Squadron.

1890, May 16. V. Adm. JOHN KENNEDY ERSKINE BAIRD, Royal Navy.

1890, July 8. Lieut. Gen. H.R.H. ARTHUR WILLIAM PATRICK ALBERT, duke of Connaught and Strathearn (wrongly gazetted on July 1 to G.C.B. military; gazetted on July 8 to K.C.B. military).

1891, May 30. Adm. Sir FRANCIS LEOPOLD McCLINTOCK, knt., Royal Navy.

1891, May 30. Gen. WILLIAM TEMPLER HUGHES, Indian Staff Corps.

1891, May 30. Gen. CHARLES CURETON, Indian Staff Corps.

1891, May 30. Gen. JOHN FIELD, Bombay Infantry.

1891, May 30. V. Adm. GEORGE WILLES WATSON, Royal Navy, commander-in-chief North America and West Indies.

1891, May 30. Lieut. Gen. CHARLES CRAUFURD FRASER.

1891, May 30. Lieut. Gen. WILBRAHAM OATES LENNOX, V.C., Royal Engineers.

1891, May 30. Lieut. Gen. WILLIAM JOHN WILLIAMS, Royal Artillery.

1891, May 30. Maj. Gen. and Hon. Lieut Gen. HENRY EDWIN WEARE.

1891, May 30. Maj. Gen. and Hon. Lieut. Gen. ALEXANDER ABERCROMBY NELSON.

1891, May 30. WILLIAM ALEXANDER MACKINNON, direc. gen. of the Army Medical Department.

1891, May 30. Lieut. Col. and Col. HENRY JAMES ALDERSON (temporary maj. gen.), half-pay Royal Artillery, director of artillery.

1891, Nov. 19. Maj. Gen. WILLIAM KIDSTON ELLES, commanding a first-class district, Bengal.

1891, Nov. 19. Col. (having local and temporary rank of brig. gen.) GEORGE BENJAMIN WOLSELEY, aide-de-camp to the Queen, commanding a second-class district, Madras.

1891, Nov. 19. Lieut. Col. and Col. (having local and temporary rank of brig. gen.) HENRY COLLETT, Indian Staff Corps, commanding a second-class district, Bengal.

1892, May 25. V. Adm. JOHN OMMANEY HOPKINS.

1892, May 25 V. Adm. ALGERNON CHARLES FIESCHI HENEAGE.

1892, May 25. Gen. JOHN WILLIAM COLLMAN WILLIAMS, Royal Marine Artillery.

1893, June 3. Gen. RICHARD THOMAS FARREN.

1893, June 3. Maj. Gen. and Hon. Lieut. Gen. WILLIAM DRYSDALE.

1893, June 3. Lieut. Gen. and Hon. Gen JULIUS AUGUSTUS ROBERT RAINES.

1893, June 3. Gen. WILLIAM GORDON CAMERON, commanding the Troops in South Africa.

1893, June 3. Gen. the Hon. PERCY ROBERT BASIL FIELDING.

1893, June 3. Gen. ALFRED WILLIAM LUCAS, Indian Staff Corps.

1893, June 3. Maj. Gen. and Hon. Lieut. Gen. JOHN BLICK SPURGIN.

1893, June 3. Gen. THOMAS WRIGHT, Indian Staff Corps.

1893, June 3. Lieut. Gen. JOHN DORAN, Indian Staff Corps.

1893, June 3. Gen. ROBERT WHITE.

1893, June 3. Gen. MARK WALKER, V.C.

1893, June 3. Lieut. Gen. and Hon. Gen. CHARLES JOHN FOSTER.

1893, June 3. Lieut. Gen. WILLIAM STIRLING, Royal Artillery, governor and commandant Royal Military Academy.

1893, Nov. 17. Adm. Sir MICHAEL CULME-SEYMOUR, bart.

1894, May 8. Maj. Gen. ARTHUR POWER PALMER, Indian Staff Corps, commanding a second-class district in India (in recognition of services during the operations in the Chin Hills in 1892–3).

1894, May 8. Maj. Gen. RICHARD CAMPBELL STEWART, Madras Cavalry, commanding a first-class district in India (same occasion).

1894, May 26. Gen. JAMES FRANKFORT MANNERS BROWNE, Royal Engineers.

1894, May 26. Surg. Gen. JAMES MOUAT, V.C., half pay, late Army Medical Department, hon. surg. to the queen.

1894, May 26. Honorary Maj. Gen. JAMES MANSFIELD NUTTALL, retired half pay, late Indian Staff Corps.

1894, May 26. Gen. JAMES ABBOTT, Royal (late Bengal) Artillery.

1894, May 26. Gen. ROBERT CADELL, Royal (late Madras) Artillery.

1894, May 26. Gen. HENRY HASTINGS AFFLECK WOOD, Indian Staff Corps.

1894, May 26. Maj. Gen. FREDERICK WILLIAM EDWARD FORESTIER-WALKER, commanding the Force in Egypt.

1894, May 26. Lieut. Gen. EDWARD NEWDIGATE NEWDIGATE.

1894, May 26. Lieut. Gen. HENRY BRACKENBURY, Royal Artillery, ordinary member of the Council of the gov. gen. of India.

1894, May 26. Honorary Maj. Gen. ROBERT JOHN HUGHES, retired pay.

1894, May 26. Col. WILLIAM GREEN, retired pay.

1894, May 26. Lieut. Gen. ROBERT JOHN HAY, Royal Artillery, director of Artillery.

1894, May 26. R. Adm. JOHN ARBUTHNOT FISHER, Controller of the Navy.

1894, July 17. Lieut. Gen. (with the local and temporary rank of Col) ALFRED BURDON ELLIS, the West India Regiment, commanding the Troops on the West Coast of Africa; would have been recommended for the dignity of knt. commander of the Order of the Bath (Military Division) had he survived.

1894, Dec. 21. R Adm. FREDERICK GEORGE DENHAM BEDFORD.

1895, May 25. V. Adm. CHARLES FREDERICK HOTHAM.

1895, May 25. V. Adm. ROBERT O'BRIEN FITZROY.

1895, May 25   Lieut Gen. HENRY BRASNELL TUSON, Royal Marine Artillery.

1895, May 25. JAMES NICHOLAS DICK, inspec. gen. of Hospitals and Fleets and direc gen. of the Medical Department of the Navy.

1895, June 11. Honorary Lieut. Col. RAJA RAM SINGH, commander-in-chief Kashmir State Troops   (Honorary).

1896, Jan. 21. Col. BINDON BLOOD, in recognition of services during the operations of the Chitral Relief Force.

1896, Mar. 31. Honorary Maj. Gen. Sir FRANCIS CUNNINGHAM SCOTT, in recognition of services in the recent expedition to Ashanti.

1896, May 20   Maj. Gen. and Hon Lieut. Gen. JOHN WILLIAM COX, col. the Bedfordshire Regiment.

1896, May 20. Gen. GEORGE AUGUSTUS SCHOMBERG, Royal Marine Artillery.

1896, May 20. Gen. DAVID SCOTT DODGSON, Bengal Infantry.

1896, May 20. Gen. ARTHUR HOWLETT, Indian Staff Corps.

1896, May 20. V. Adm. ALEXANDER BULLER.

1896, May 20. Gen. Sir ROBERT BIDDULPH, col. commandant Royal Artillery, governor and commander-in-chief, Gibraltar.

1896, May 20. Lieut. Gen. CHARLES MANSFIELD CLARKE, commanding the Forces, Madras.

1896, May 20. V. Adm. HENRY FAIRFAX.

1896, May 20. Maj. Gen. (temporary lieut. gen) ROBERT GRANT, Royal Engineers, insp. gen. of Fortifications.

1896, May 20. Adm. RICHARD WELLS.

1896, May 20. V. Adm. lord WALTER TALBOT KERR.

1896, Nov. 17. Maj. Gen Sir HORATIO HERBERT KITCHENER, Royal Engineers (Sirdar of the Egyptian Army) in recognition of services during the recent operations in the Soudan

1897, May 7. Maj. Gen Sir FREDERICK CARRINGTON, commanding Infantry Brigade, Gibraltar, in recognition of services during the operations in South Africa, 1896.

1897, May 25. R Adm. HARRY HOLDSWORTH RAWSON, in recognition of services during the recent expedition to Benin.

1897, June 22. (Additional) Lieut. Gen. and Hon. Gen. Sir WILLIAM HOPE, bart.

1897, June 22. (Additional) Surg. Gen. CHARLES ALEXANDER GORDON, hon. physician to the Queen.

1897, June 22. (Additional) Adm. WILLIAM GARNHAM LUARD.

1897, June 22. (Additional) Adm. GEORGE GRANVILLE RANDOLPH.

1897, June 22. (Additional) Maj. Gen. and Hon. Lieut. Gen. JAMES CLERK-RATTRAY.

1897, June 22. (Additional) Gen. JOHN IRVINE MURRAY, Indian Staff Corps.

1897, June 22. (Additional) Gen. FREDERICK RICHARD MAUNSELL, col. commandant Royal (late Bengal) Engineers).

1897, June 22. (Additional) Maj. Gen. and Hon Lieut. Gen. HENRY LE GEYT BRUCE, Royal (late Bengal) Artillery.

1897, June 22. (Additional) Maj. Gen. ALEXANDER JAMES HARDY ELLIOTT, col. 6th Dragoon Guards.

1897, June 22. (Additional) gen. ÆNEAS PERKINS, col. commandant Royal (late Bengal) Engineers.

1897, June 22. Col. FRANCIS HOWELL JENKINS, Indian Staff Corps.

1897, June 22 (Additional) Lieut. Gen. HENRY RICHARD LEGGE NEWDIGATE.

1897, June 22 (Additional) Lieut. Gen. HENRY MOORE, Indian Staff Corps.

1897, June 22. (Additional) Maj. Gen. GEORGE LUCK, inspec. gen. of Cavalry in Great Britain and Ireland.

1897, June 22. (Additional) HENRY FREDERICK NORBURY, inspec. gen. of Hospitals and Fleets.

1897, June 22. (Additional) Gen. WILLIAM ANTHONY GIB, Indian Staff Corps.

1897, June 22. (Additional) Hon. Maj. Gen. JOSEPH PHILIPS, Royal Marines.

1897, June 22. (Additional) V. Adm. HENRY FREDERICK NICHOLSON, commander-in-chief, Sheerness.

1897, June 22. (Additional) Gen. HOWARD SUTTON JONES, Royal Marines.

1897, June 22. (Additional) Lieut. Gen. HENRY CLEMENT WILKINSON, col. 4th Dragoon Guards

1897, June 22. (Additional) Lieut. Gen. WILLIAM HOWLEY GOODENOUGH, Royal Artillery, commanding the Troops, South Africa.

1897, June 22. (Additional) Maj. Gen. JAMES MAKGILL HERIOT MAITLAND, Royal Engineers.

1897, June 22. (Additional) Lieut. Gen. CHARLES EDWARD NAIRNE, Royal Artillery, commanding the Forces, Bombay.

1897, June 22. (Additional) V. Adm. EDWARD HOBART SEYMOUR.

1897, June 22. (Additional) Lieut. Gen. CECIL JAMES EAST, gov. and commandant, Royal Military College.

1897, June 22. (Additional) Maj. Gen. WILLIAM GALBRAITH, commanding a first-class district in India.

1897, June 22. (Additional) V. Adm. HENRY FREDERICK STEPHENSON.

1897, June 22. (Additional) Maj. Gen. JAMES ALLEYNE, commanding Royal Artillery, Aldershot.

1897, June 22. (Additional) JAMES JOHN LOUIS DONNET, inspec. gen. of Hospitals and Fleets.

1897, June 22. (Additional) V. Adm. JAMES ELPHINSTONE ERSKINE, commander-in-chief, North America and West Indies.

1897, June 22. (Additional) V. Adm. NATHANIEL BOWDEN-SMITH.

1897, June 22. (Additional) Lieut. Gen. EDWIN MARKHAM, Royal Artillery, insp. gen. of Ordnance, Head Quarters.

1897, June 22. (Additional) V. Adm. WILLIAM ROBERT KENNEDY.

1898, May 20. Col. (brig. gen) WILLIAM PENN SYMONS, commanding a second-class district in India, in recognition of services during the recent operations on the North-west Frontier of India.

1898, May 20. Col. (brig. gen.) RICHARD WESTMACOTT, commanding a second-class district in India (same occasion).

1898, May 20 Col. (brig. gen.) WILLIAM GUSTAVUS NICHOLSON, deputy adj. gen , Punjab command (same occasion).

1898, May 20. Col. (brig. gen) ALFRED GASELEE, A.D.C., Indian Staff Corps (same occasion).

1898, May 20. Col. (brig. gen.) EDMOND ROCHE ELLES, commanding a second-class district in India (same occasion).

1898, May 20. Col. WILLIAM HOPE MEIKLEJOHN, Indian Army (same occasion).

1898, May 20. Surg. Col. GEORGE THOMSON, Indian Medical Service (same occasion).

1898, May 21. Gen HUGH ROWLANDS, V.C.

1898, May 21 Gen. JOHN JAMES HOOD GORDON, Indian Staff Corps, member of the Council of India.

1898, May 21. Gen. STANLEY DE BURGH EDWARDES, Indian Army.

1898, May 21. V. Adm. lord CHARLES THOMAS MONTAGU-DOUGLAS-SCOTT.

1898, May 21. Gen JOHN DAVIS, commanding the Troops, Southern District.

1898, May 21. Maj. Gen COLERIDGE GROVE, military secretary at Headquarters

1898, May 21. V. Adm. RICHARD EDWARD TRACEY, president of the Royal Naval College.

1898, May 21. V Adm. COMPTON EDWARD DOMVILE, adm. superintendent of Naval Reserves.

1898, May 21. Maj. Gen. RAYMOND HERVEY, viscount Frankfort de Montmorency.

1898, Nov. 15. Maj Gen. WILLIAM FORBES GATACRE.

1898, Nov 15 Maj Gen. ARCHIBALD HUNTER, governor of Dongola Province and commandant Frontier Field Force, Egypt.

1898, Nov 15. Maj. Gen HENRY MACLEOD LESLIE RUNDLE, Royal Artillery, employed with Egyptian Army.

1899, May 16 Col (brig. gen) REGINALD CLARE HART, V.C., commanding a second-class district in India in recognition of services rendered during recent operations on the North-West Frontier of India.

1899, June 3. Lieut. Gen FREDERICK ARTHUR WILLIS (since deceased)

1899, June 3. Maj. Gen. and Hon. Lieut. Gen. HENRY RADFORD NORMAN.

1899, June 3. Maj. Gen. and Hon. Lieut. Gen. ALEXANDER HUGH COBBE.

1899, June 3. Lieut. Gen. ROBERT GORDON ROGERS, Indian Staff Corps.

1899, June 3. Lieut. Gen. BENJAMIN LUMSDEN GORDON, Royal (late Madras) Artillery.

1899, June 3. Maj. Gen. CORNELIUS FRANCIS CLERY, deputy adj. gen. to the Forces.

1899, June 3. V. Adm. CYPRIAN ARTHUR GEORGE BRIDGE.

1900, Mar. 13. Col. (local maj. gen.) Sir FRANCIS REGINALD WINGATE, A.D.C., in recognition of his services during the pursuit and defeat of the Khalifa in November last.

1900, May 23. Gen. ALEXANDER GEORGE MONTGOMERY MOORE, col. 18th Hussars, commanding Aldershot district (temporarily).

1900, May 23. Gen. JOHN LOUIS NATION, Indian Staff Corps.

1900, May 23. Gen. Sir THOMAS EDWARD GORDON, Indian Staff Corps.

1900, May 23. Lieut. Col. and Col. (Hon. Maj. Gen.) JOHN HILLS, Royal (late Bombay) Engineers.

1900, May 23. Maj. Gen. HUGH McCALMONT, commanding Cork district.

1900, May 23. Lieut. Gen. EDWARD HOPTON, col. Connaught Rangers, lieut. gov. and gen. officer commanding the Troops, Jersey.

1900, May 23. Lieut. Gen. GEORGE DIGBY BARKER, governor and commander-in-chief, Bermuda.

1900, May 28. Lieut. Gen. HENRY LE GUAY GEARY, Royal Artillery, president Ordnance Committee.

1900, May 23. Maj. Gen. THOMAS FRASER, Royal Engineers, commanding Thames district.

1900, May 23. Maj. Gen. JOHN FREDERICK MAURICE, Royal Artillery, commanding Woolwich district.

1900, May 23. Col. FREDERICK JOHN KEEN, Indian Staff Corps.

1900, Nov. 6. R. Adm. Sir ROBERT HASTINGS HARRIS, in recognition of services during the war in South Africa.

18

1900, Nov. 29.   R. Adm. BOUVERIE FRANCIS CLARK, R.N. (in recognition of services during the operations in South Africa. Gazetted 1901, Apr. 19, but with precedence as of date 1900, Nov. 29. *See* footnote on p. 341).

1900, Nov 29   Maj. Gen (local lieut. gen.) CHARLES TUCKER (same occasion).

1900, Nov. 29   Lieut. Gen. Sir PAUL SANFORD (METHUEN), 3rd lord Methuen (same occasion).

1900, Nov 29.   Col. (local maj. gen.) ELLIOTT WOOD, R.E. (same occasion).

1900, Nov. 29.   Maj Gen. (local lieut. gen.) REGINALD POLE-CAREW (same occasion).

1900, Nov. 29.   Col. (local maj. gen.) WILLIAM GEORGE KNOX (same occasion).

1900, Nov. 29.   Maj. Gen. (local lieut. gen.) HENRY JOHN THOROTON HILDYARD (same occasion).

1900, Nov. 29.   Col. WODEHOUSE DILLON RICHARDSON (same occasion).

1900, Nov. 29.   Maj. Gen. WILLIAM FREEMAN KELLY (same occasion).

1900, Nov 29.   Col. (local lieut. gen., now promoted maj. gen.) IAN STANDISH MONTEITH HAMILTON (same occasion).

1900, Nov. 29.   Col. EDWARD WILLIS DUNCAN WARD (same occasion).

1900, Nov. 29   Col. FRANCIS HOWARD, A D.C. to the king (same occasion).

1900, Nov. 29.   Col. (local maj gen.) HECTOR ARCHIBALD MACDONALD, A D.C. (same occasion).

1900, Nov. 29   Col. (temporary brig. gen.) HENRY HAMILTON SETTLE (same occasion).

1900, Nov. 29.   Maj. Gen. (local lieut. gen.) JOHN DENTON PINKSTONE FRENCH (same occasion).

1900, Nov 29.   Col. (local maj. gen , now promoted maj. gen.) CHARLES EDMOND KNOX (same occasion).

1900, Nov. 29.   Col. (local maj. gen) GEORGE HENRY MARSHALL (same occasion).

1900, Nov. 29. Maj. and Brev. Col. (local maj. gen.) JOHN GRENFELL MAXWELL (same occasion).

1900, Nov. 29. Col. (local maj. gen.) JAMES WOLFE MURRAY (same occasion).

1900, Nov. 29. Hon. Col. (local maj. gen.) CHARLES COMPTON WILLIAM (CAVENDISH), 3rd lord Chesham, Imperial Yeomanry (same occasion).

1900, Nov. 29. Brig. Gen. EDWARD YEWD BRABANT, Colonial Defence Force (same occasion).

1900, Nov. 29. Col. (local brig. gen.) JOHN GEORGE DARTNELL, Natal Volunteer Force (same occasion).

1901, July 24. Col. Sir CLAUDE MAXWELL MACDONALD, promoted from K.C.B. (civil): Reserve of Officers.

1901, July 24. Col. ALEXANDER JOHN FORSYTH REID, Indian Staff Corps.

1901, July 24. Col. EDMUND GEORGE BARROW, Indian Staff Corps.

1901, July 24. Col. ARTHUR ROBERT FORD DORWARD, in recognition of services during the recent operations in China.

1901, July 24. Hon. Col. His Highness the Maharaja SINDHIA of Gwalior. (Honorary.)

1901, July 24. (Honorary) Col. His Highness the Maharaja Dhiraj Sir PERTAB SINGH.

1901, Nov. 9. Adm. GEORGE DIGBY MORANT.

1901, Nov. 9. V. Adm. CHARLES GEORGE FANE.

1901, Nov. 9. Col. THALES PEASE.

1902, June 26. Adm. Sir ERASMUS OMMANNEY (retired).

1902, June 26. Adm. ST. GEORGE CAULFIELD D'ARCY IRVINE (retired).

1902, June 26. V. Adm. HILARY GUSTAVUS ANDOE.

1902, June 26. V. Adm. ARTHUR KNYVET WILSON, V.C.

1902, June 26. V. Adm. ARCHIBALD LUCIUS DOUGLAS.

1902, June 26. V. Adm. Sir GERARD HENRY UCTRED NOEL.

1902, June 26   R. Adm. ARTHUR WILLIAM MOORE

1902, June 26. (Additional) JOHN DENIS MACDONALD, M.D., R.N., insp. gen. of Hospitals and Fleets (retired).

1902, June 26. WILLIAM EAMES, R.N., chief inspector of machinery (retired).

1902, June 26. (Additional) HENRY BENBOW, R N., chief inspector of machinery (retired).

1902, June 26 (Additional) JAMES WILLIAM MURRAY ASHBY, paymaster-in-chief (retired).

1902, June 26. (Additional) Fleet paymaster FREDERICK CLEEVE (retired).

1902, June 26. Surg. Gen. JOHN ANDREW WOOLFRYES, M.D., hon. physician to the King.

1902, June 26. Lieut Gen. ALEXANDER ROBERT BADCOCK, Indian Staff Corps

1902, June 26. Surg. Gen. ANNESLEY CHARLES CASTRIOTT DE RENZY, Indian Medical Service (retired).

1902, June 26. Gen. ROWLEY SALE SALE-HILL, unemployed, supernumerary list, Indian Staff Corps.

1902, June 26 (Additional) Maj Gen. JOHN FREDERICK CREASE (retired)

1902, June 26. (Additional) Gen SAMUEL JAMES GRAHAM (retired).

1902, June 26. Lieut. Gen. Sir MONTAGUE GILBERT GERARD, Indian Staff Corps.

1902, June 26. Maj. Gen. (honorary) ALEXANDER BRUCE TULLOCH.

1902, June 26. Maj. Gen. REGINALD THOMAS THYNNE.

1902, June 26. Maj. Gen. the Hon. REGINALD ARTHUR JAMES TALBOT.

1902, June 26. Maj. Gen Sir EDWARD STEDMAN, Indian Staff Corps.

1902, June 26. Lieut. Gen. THOMAS KELLY-KENNY.

1902, June 26 (Additional) Col. HENRY GREY DIXON.

1902, June 26. (Additional) Col: EDWARD LOCKE ELLIOT, Indian Staff Corps.

1902, June 26. (Additional) Lieut. Gen. the Hon. NEVILLE GERALD LYTTELTON.

1902, June 26. Maj. Gen. ALFRED EDWARD TURNER.

1902, June 26. Col. (ranking as maj. gen.) JOHN STEEVENS

1902, June 26. Surg. Gen. (ranking as lieut. gen) WILLIAM TAYLOR, M.D., hon. physician to the King.

1902, June 26. (Additional) Hon. Col. AUBREY WOOLS-SAMPSON, lieut. col. Imperial Light Horse.

1902, June 26. (Additional) Maj. Gen. BRUCE MEADE HAMILTON.

1902, Oct. 17. (Honorary) Maj. Gen. FUKUSHIMA, Imperial Japanese Army.

1902, Oct. 17. Adm. IGUIN, Imperial Japanese Navy. [Honorary.]

1902, Aug. 22 (Oct. 31). (Additional) Maj. Gen. MILDMAY WILLSON WILLSON, staff services in South Africa. (Warrant of appointment Nov. 20.)

1902, Aug. 22 (Oct. 31). (Additional) Maj. Gen ROBERT MACGREGOR STEWART. (Warrant of appointment Nov. 20.)

1902, Aug. 22 (Oct. 31). (Additional) Maj. Gen. WILLIAM SALMOND (Warrant of appointment Nov. 20.)

1902, Nov. 9. (Honorary) His Excellency Gen. R. GORJAO, of the Portuguese Army, governor general of the province of Mozambique (on the occasion of His Majesty's birthday).

1903, Jan. 1. Col. (local maj. gen) CHARLES COMYN EGERTON, A.D.C.

1903, Jan. 1. Col. ARTHUR GEORGE HAMMOND, V.C.

1903, June 26. Lieut. Gen. and Hon. Gen. FOWLER BURTON.

1903, June 26. Gen. lord ALEXANDER GEORGE RUSSELL.

1903, June 26. Lieut. Gen. JOHN FRYER.

1903, June 26. Maj. Gen. CHARLES BENJAMIN KNOWLES.

1903, June 26. Surg. Gen. COLVIN COLVIN - SMITH, late Indian Medical Service.

1903, June 26 Maj. Gen GEORGE ROBERTSON HENNESSY, Indian Army.

1903, June 26. Surg. Maj. Gen. JOHN BY COLE READE, late Army Medical Staff.

1903, June 26. Col. (local maj gen.) O'MOORE CREAGH, V.C., Indian Army, commanding the Forces in China (in recognition of services during the occupation of China by International Troops).

1903, Nov. 9. Adm. ALGERNON FREDERICK ROUS DE HORSEY.

1903, Nov. 9. Adm. ALBERT HASTINGS MARKHAM.

1903, Nov. 9. V. Adm. JOHN FELLOWES.

1903, Nov. 9. V. Adm. lord CHARLES WILLIAM DE LA POER BERESFORD.

1904, June 24 Lieut Gen. and Hon. Gen. WILLIAM HENRY SEYMOUR.

1904, June 24. Maj Gen. and Hon. Lieut. Gen. JOHN WELLESLEY THOMAS.

1904, June 24. Gen. ALEXANDER LOW.

1904, June 24. Maj. Gen and Hon. Lieut. Gen. FREDERICK WILLIAM TRAILL-BURROUGHS.

1904, June 24. Deputy Surg. Gen. JAMES HOWARD THORNTON, late Indian Medical Service.

1904, June 24. Lieut. Gen. ADAM GEORGE FORBES HOGG, Indian Army.

1904, June 24. Surg Gen. EDMOND TOWNSEND, Army Medical Staff.

1904, June 24. V. Adm. HUGO LEWIS PEARSON.

1904, Nov. 9. V. Adm. ARTHUR DALRYMPLE FANSHAWE.

1904, Nov. 9. V. Adm. Sir LEWIS ANTHONY BEAUMONT.

1904, Nov. 9. Lieut. Gen. WILLIAM PURVIS WRIGHT

KNIGHTS COMMANDERS—CIVIL DIVISION (K.C.B.).

Under Statutes of 1847, May 15, Victoria.

1847, Aug. 10.   Count ALEXANDER MENSDORF-POUILLY.

1848, Apr. 27.   Rt. Hon. HENRY LYTTON EARLE BULWER, afterwards lord Dalling and Bulwer, envoy extraordinary and minister plenipotentiary to the queen of Spain.

1848, Apr. 27.   Rt. Hon. HENRY ELLIS, sometime employed on an extraordinary and special mission to the emperor of Brazil.

1848, Apr. 27.   Rt. Hon. RICHARD PAKENHAM, envoy extraordinary and minister plenipotentiary to the United States of America.

1848, Apr. 27.   JAMES BROOKE, governor and commander-in-chief of the Island of Labuan.

1848, Apr. 27.   GEORGE RUSSELL CLERKE, governor of Bombay.

1848, Apr. 27.   HENRY LIGHT, governor and commander-in-chief of British Guiana.

1848, Apr. 27.   GEORGE GREY, governor of New Zealand.

1848, Apr. 27.   CHARLES EDWARD TREVELYAN, assistant secretary to the Treasury.

1848, Apr. 27.   Sir RANDOLPH ISHAM ROUTH, commissary gen. employed on a particular service in Ireland.

1848, Apr. 27.   R. Adm. FRANCIS BEAUFORT, hydrographer to the Admiralty.

1848, Apr. 27.   Rt. Hon. JAMES STEPHEN, one of the under secretaries of State for the War and Colonial Department.

1848, Apr. 27.   Maj. Gen. WILLIAM MORISON, of the Madras Artillery.

1848, Apr. 27.   Lieut. Col. HENRY MONTGOMERY LAWRENCE, of the ·Bengal Artillery.

1848, Dec. 26.   DUNCAN McGREGOR, inspec. gen. of the Constabulary Force of Ireland.

1848, Dec. 26. Lieut. Col. CHARLES ROWAN, one of the Commissioners of the Police of the Metropolis.

1849, June 5. HENRY MIERS ELLIOT, secretary to the gov. gen. of India in Council, in the Foreign Department.

1849, Aug. 28. THOMAS NICHOLAS REDINGTON, under secretary to the lord lieut. of Ireland.

1850, Nov. 22 SAMUEL GEORGE BONHAM, chief superintendent of the trade of H.M. subjects trading with China and governor of Hong Kong.

1850, Nov. 22 Sir GEORGE WILLIAM ANDERSON, sometime governor of Mauritius and now governor of Ceylon.

1851, Mar. 1. JOHN ARTHUR DOUGLAS (BLOOMFIELD), 2nd lord Bloomfield, envoy extraordinary and minister plenipotentiary to Russia.

1851, Mar. 1 HENRY RICHARD CHARLES (WELLESLEY), 2nd lord, afterward 1st earl Cowley, minister plenipotentiary on a special mission at Frankfort.

1851, Mar. 1. GEORGE NICHOLLS, late secretary to the Poor Law · Board.

1851, Mar. 1. Sir HENRY WATKIN WILLIAMS-WYNN, bart., envoy extraordinary and minister plenipotentiary to Denmark.

1851, Mar. 1 The Hon. WILLIAM TEMPLE, envoy extraordinary and minister plenipotentiary to the king of the Two Sicilies.

1851, Mar. 1. The Hon. RALPH ABERCROMBY, afterwards 2nd lord Dunfermline, envoy extraordinary and minister plenipotentiary to the king of Sardinia.

1851, Oct. 25. Lieut. Col WILLIAM REID, Royal Engineers, formerly governor of Bermudas, sometime chairman of the executive committee of the Exhibition of Industry.

1851, Oct. 25 RICHARD MAYNE, commissioner of Police, London.

1852, Feb. 23. JOHN HOBART (CARADOC), 2nd lord Howden, envoy extraordinary and minister plenipotentiary to the queen of Spain.

1852, June 29. WILLIAM GORE OUSELEY, sometime minister plenipotentiary to the Argentine Confederation.

1852, Dec. 23. BELFORD HINTON WILSON, sometime chargé d'affaires and consul gen. to the Republic of Venezuela.

1853, July 18. HENRY BARKLY, sometime governor of the colony of British Guiana.

1853, Sept. 5. JAMES COSMO MELVILL, secretary to the Court of Directors of the East India Company.

1854, June 12. Sir CHARLES AUGUSTUS FITZ-ROY, knt., capt. gen and governor-in-chief in and over the colony of New South Wales.

1854. June 12. Sir JOHN FRANCIS DAVIS, bart., sometime governor and commissioner-in-chief in and over the colony of Hong Kong and plenipotentiary and chief superintendent of British trade in China.

1854, July 29. PROBY THOMAS CANTLEY, late lieut. col. in the Bengal Artillery and director of the Ganges Canal.

1855, Jan. 30. Lieut. Col. JUSTIN SHEIL, sometime envoy extra-ordinary and minister plenipotentiary to the shah of Persia.

1855, May 2. JAMES HUDSON, envoy extraordinary and minister plenipotentiary to the king of Sardinia.

1856, Feb. 5. Maj. HENRY CRESWICKE RAWLINSON, of the Bombay Army

1856, Feb. 5. JOHN LAIRD MAIR LAWRENCE, afterwards lord Lawrence, chief commissioner and agent to the gov. gen. of India, for the Punjab.

1856, Feb. 5. Maj. Gen. WILLIAM HENRY SLEEMAN, of the Bengal Army.

1856, Feb. 5. Maj. Gen. JAMES OUTRAM, of the Bombay Army, acting as political agent at Lucknow.

1856, Feb. 5. BENJAMIN HAWES.

1856, May 26. Lieut. Gen. MARK CUBBON, of the East India Company's Service, commissioner for the Government of Mysore.

1856, July 19. Lieut. Col. Sir WILLIAM THOMAS DENISON, knt., R.E., capt. gen. and governor-in-chief in and over the colony of New South Wales.

1856, July 19. R. Adm. CHARLES ELLIOT, governor and commander-in-chief in and over the Island of Trinidad.

1856, Sept 30. The Hon. JOHN DUNCAN BLIGH, sometime envoy extraordinary and minister plenipotentiary to the king of Hanover.

1856, Sept 30. ARTHUR CHARLES MAGENIS, envoy extraordinary and minister plenipotentiary to the king of Sweden and Norway.

1856, Sept. 30 JOHN FIENNES TWISLETON CRAMPTON, sometime envoy extraordinary and minister plenipotentiary to the United States of America

1857, Jan. 2. JAMES MACAULAY HIGGINSON, governor and commander-in-chief of Mauritius and its dependencies.

1857, Jan. 22. JOHN GEORGE SHAW-LEFEVRE, clerk of the parliaments.

1857, Mar. 27. Rt. Hon. THOMAS WYSE, minister plenipotentiary to the king of Greece.

1857, Apr. 17. Col. ALEXANDER MURRAY TULLOCH, military super-intendent of the pensioners of the Army.

1858, Jan. 21. Col the Hon. CHARLES BEAUMONT PHIPPS, keeper of the Privy Purse

1858, July 9 ANDREW SMITH, M.D., late direc. gen of the Army Medical Department.

1858, Sept 6 RICHARD MADOX BROMLEY, accountant gen. of the Navy.

1858, Sept. 6 THOMAS TASSELL GRANT, late comptroller of the Victualling and Transport Service of the Navy.

1858, Dec. 20 R. Adm. ALEXANDER MILNE, a commissioner of the Admiralty.

1859, Feb. 4 Rt Hon. Sir JOHN YOUNG, bart , sometime lord high commissioner in and for the United States of the Ionian Islands.

1859, Mar 9. R. Adm. Sir THOMAS HASTINGS, knt., sometime principal storekeeper of the Ordnance.

1859, Mar. 25. Col. Joshua Jebb, surveyor gen. of prisons, inspec. gen. of military prisons, and chairman of the directors of convict prisons.

1859, May 20. Henry Bartle Edward Frere, the resident in the Province of Scinde.

1859, May 20. Robert Montgomery, lately the chief commissioner in Oude.

1860, Feb. 10. Rowland Hill, secretary to the Post Office.

1860, Feb. 25. Andrew Buchanan, envoy extraordinary and minister plenipotentiary to H.M. the queen of Spain.

1860, May 18. Frederick James Halliday, late lieut. gov. of Bengal.

1860, May 18. Sir Robert North Collie Hamilton, bart., late political agent in Central India.

1860, May 18. Maj. Gen. Richard James Hollwell Birch, secretary to the government of India in the Military Department.

1860, May 18. Col. Peter Melvill Melvill, secretary to the government of Bombay in the Military and Naval Departments.

1860, May 18. Lieut. Col. Herbert Benjamin Edwardes, commissioner of Peshawur.

1860, May 22. Charles Lennox Wyke, envoy extraordinary and minister plenipotentiary to the Mexican Republic.

1860, June 19. Maj. Gen. Thomas Aiskew Larcom, under secretary to the lord lieut. of Ireland.

1860, Aug. 6. George Lloyd Hodges, late chargé d'affaires to the Free Hanseatic Cities of Hamburg, Bremen and Lubeck.

1860, Dec. 11. (Extra) Richard Bickerton Pemell (Lyons), 2nd lord afterwards viscount Lyons, envoy extraordinary and minister plenipotentiary to the United States of America.

1860, Dec. 11. (Extra) the Rt. Hon. Sir EDMUND WALKER HEAD, bart., capt. gen and governor-in-chief in and over the Provinces of Canada, Nova Scotia, New Brunswick and the Island of Prince Edward.

1861, June 18. FREDERICK TEMPLE (BLACKWOOD), lord Dufferin and Clandeboye, afterwards marquess of Dufferin and Ava, the British member of the late European Commission in Syria.

1861, June 25. Maj. Gen. GEORGE HALL MACGREGOR, sometime employed as military commissioner attached to the camp of Jung Bahadoor during the late mutiny in India.

1862, Feb. 14. JOHN PETER GRANT, lieut. gov. of Bengal.

1862, May 20. JOHN HAY DRUMMOND-HAY, minister resident at the Court of Morocco.

1862, May 20. HARRY SMITH PARKES, consul at Shanghai.

1862, June 20. RUTHERFORD ALCOCK, envoy extraordinary and minister plenipotentiary in Japan.

1862, July 23. WILLIAM STEVENSON, governor and commander-in-chief in and over the Island of Mauritius and its dependencies.

1862, July 23. PHILIP EDMOND WODEHOUSE, governor and commander-in-chief in and over the colony of the Cape of Good Hope and its dependencies, and high commissioner for the settling and adjustment of the affairs of the territories adjacent or contiguous to the eastern frontier of that colony

1862, July 23. CHARLES HENRY DARLING, capt. gen and governor-in-chief in and over the Island of Jamaica and its dependencies.

1862, July 23. Maj Gen. EDWARD MACARTHUR, sometime administering the government of the colony of Victoria.

1862, Dec. 12. AUGUSTUS WILLIAM FREDERICK SPENCER LOFTUS, commonly called lord Augustus Loftus, envoy extraordinary and Minister plenipotentiary at the Court of Bavaria.

1862, Dec. 12. The Hon. FREDERICK WILLIAM ADOLPHUS BRUCE, envoy extraordinary and minister plenipotentiary to the emperor of China.

1863, Feb. 3. Sir RODERICK IMPEY MURCHISON, knt., director gen. of the Geological Survey of the United Kingdom and director of the Royal School of Mines and Museum of Practical Geology.

1863, Mar. 3. HENRY FRANCIS HOWARD, envoy extraordinary and minister plenipotentiary at the Court of Hanover.

1863, Mar. 10. Col. THOMAS MYDDELTON BIDDULPH, master of Her Majesty's Household.

1863, Mar. 17. AUGUSTUS BERKELEY PAGET, envoy extraordinary and minister plenipotentiary at the Court of Denmark.

1863, Aug. 7. Capt. H.S.H. ERNEST LEOPOLD VICTOR CHARLES AUGUSTE JOSEPH EMICH, prince of Leiningen, R.N.

1863, Aug. 11. JAMES DOUGLAS, governor and commander-in-chief in and over Vancouver's Island and the colony of British Columbia. •

1863, Dec. 11. GEORGE FREDERICK EDMONSTONE, late lieut. gov. of the North-Western Provinces of Bengal.

1864, June 7. Maj. Gen. WILLIAM MARCUS COGHLAN, of the Royal Artillery, sometime political resident and commandant at Aden.

1865, May 30. ROBERT GILMOUR COLQUHOUN, agent and consul gen. in Egypt.

1865, June 7. ALEXANDER BRYSON, M D., director general of the Medical Department of the Navy.

1865, Aug. 23. Maj. JOHN CLAYTON COWELL, of the Royal Engineers, in recognition of his services as governor for nine years to H.R.H. prince Alfred Ernest Albert, who has attained his majority on the 6th inst.

1865, Oct. 9. Lieut. Gen. Sir JOHN GASPARD LE MARCHANT, late governor and commander-in-chief in and over the island of Malta and its dependencies.

1865, Nov. 27. (Extra) Rt. Hon. WILLIAM HUTT, vice president of the Board of Trade.

1866, Jan. 29. (Honorary) H.S H. HERMAN ERNEST FRANCIS BERNHARD, prince of Hohenlohe-Langenburg (nephew of the Queen).

1866, June 23   Sir ALEXANDER MALET, bart , envoy extraordinary and minister plenipotentiary to the Germanic Confederation.

1866, June 23.   The Hon. CHARLES AUGUSTUS MURRAY, late envoy extraordinary and plenipotentiary to the king of Saxony and now envoy extraordinary and minister plenipotentiary to the king of Denmark.

1866, June 23.   The Hon. JOHN HENRY THOMAS MANNERS-SUTTON, governor and commander-in-chief of the colony of Victoria.

1866, July 6   Sir JAMES CLARK, bart., M.D., one of the physicians in ordinary to Her Majesty.

1866, July 6   THOMAS ERSKINE MAY, afterwards lord Farnborough, clerk assistant of the House of Commons.

1866, July 6   CHARLES PRESSLY, late chairman of the Board of Inland Revenue.

1867, Apr. 23.   (Extra) Gen. WILLIAM THOMAS KNOLLYS, comptroller and treasurer of the Household of H.R.H. the prince of Wales.

1867, June 29.   (Extra) JOHN ALEXANDER MACDONALD, chairman of the recent conference of delegates from British North America on the measure of confederation.

1867, Oct. 14.   (Extra) WILLIAM ROSE, deputy clerk of the Parliaments.

1868, Dec. 7.   R. Adm. JAMES CRAWFORD CAFFIN, director of Stores, War Department.

1868, Dec. 7.   V. Adm. ROBERT SPENCER ROBINSON, controller of the Navy.

1869, July 27.   ANTONY PANIZZI, late principal librarian and secretary to the British Museum.

1869, July 27.   Lieut. Gen. EDWARD SABINE.

1870, Feb. 1.   Maj Gen WILLIAM ERSKINE BAKER of the Royal (Bengal) Engineers, a member of the Council of India.

1870, June 24.   Maj. Gen. GEORGE BALFOUR, of the Royal (Madras) Artillery, assistant to the controller-in-chief, War Department.

1870, Aug. 9. EDWARD THORNTON, envoy extraordinary and minister plenipotentiary to the United States of America

1870, Dec. 6. WILLIAM GEORGE ANDERSON, assistant comptroller and auditor gen. of the Exchequer and Audit Department.

1870, Dec. 19. Col. JOHN STEWART WOOD, inspec. gen. of the Royal Irish Constabulary.

1871, June 13. Maj. Gen. THOMAS TOWNSEND PEARS, military secretary to the secretary of state for India in Council.

1871, July 3. Lieut. Col HOWARD CRAUFURD ELPHINSTONE, V.C., of the Royal Engineers, late governor to H.R.H. the prince Arthur.

1871, Nov. 7. WILLIAM HENRY STEPHENSON, chairman of the Board of Inland Revenue.

1872, Jan. 20. Sir WILLIAM JENNER, bart., M.D., one of the physicians-in-ordinary to Her Majesty.

1872, June 17. GEORGE BIDDELL AIRY, the astronomer royal.

1872, July 13. V. Adm. the Hon. EDWARD ALFRED JOHN HARRIS, envoy extraordinary and minister plenipotentiary to the king of the Netherlands.

1872, July 18. ARTHUR HELPS, clerk of the Council.

1873, Mar. 27. HENRY THRING, afterwards lord Thring, the parliamentary counsel.

1873, Mar. 27. ALFRED POWER, vice-president of the Local Government Board for Ireland.

1874, May 16. Lieut. Col. JAMES MACNAGHTEN HOGG, afterwards McGarel-Hogg and lord Magheramorne, chairman of the Metropolitan Board of Works.

1875, Mar. 25. HENRY COLE, late secretary of the Science and Art Department of the Committee of Council on Education and general superintendent and director of the South Kensington Museum.

1875, Mar. 25. Col. HENRY ATWELL LAKE, chief commissioner of Dublin Metropolitan Police.

1875, Nov. 25. THOMAS FRANCIS WADE, envoy extraordinary and minister plenipotentiary and chief superintendent of Trade in China.

1876, May 17 CHARLES (HARBORD), 5th lord Suffield, a lord of the Bedchamber to H R.H. the prince of Wales.

1876, Nov. 29. (Extra) Capt. GEORGE STRONG NARES, of the Royal Navy.

1877, July 23. Col. JOHN STOKES, of the Royal Engineers.

1877, Aug. 6. Lieut. Col. EDMUND FREDERICK DU CANE, of the Royal Engineers, surveyor gen. of prisons, chairman of directors of convict prisons, and commissioner under the provisions of the Prisons Act, 1877.

1877, Aug. 6. Col. Sir LEWIS PELLY, of the Bombay Staff Corps, agent of the gov. gen. of India in Rajpootana.

1877, Aug. 6 HENRY WILLIAM GORDON, commissary general in the Ordnance Store Department

1878, Mar. 15. EDMUND YEAMANS WALCOT HENDERSON, late lieut. col. in the Corps of Royal Engineers, the commissioner of police of the Metropolis

1878, July 29. CHARLES STUART AUBREY (ABBOTT), 3rd lord Tenterden, under secretary of state for Foreign Affairs.

1878, Oct. 10. JOHN SAVILE LUMLEY, envoy extraordinary and minister plenipotentiary to the king of the Belgians.

1878, Nov. 14 Sir RICHARD WALLACE, bart , one of Her Majesty's commissioners for the Paris Universal Exhibition of 1878.

1879, Mar. 12 Lieut Gen. HENRY FREDERICK PONSONBY, keeper of Her Majesty's Privy Purse and private secretary to Her Majesty.

1879, Mar 31. Sir FRANCIS RICHARD JOHN SANDFORD, knt., secretary to the Committee of Council on Education, afterwards lord Sandford.

1879, Mar. 31. RALPH ROBERT WHEELER LINGEN, afterwards lord Lingen, permanent secretary of the Treasury.

1879, Mar. 31. JOHN LAMBERT, secretary to the Commissioners of the Local Government Board.

1879, July 19. Maj. PIERRE LOUIS NAPOLEON CAVAGNARI, Bengal
Staff Corps, deputy commissioner second class for the
Punjab.

1879, Sept. 24. Sir HENRY DRUMMOND WOLFF, late Her Majesty's
commissioner in Eastern Roumelia

1880, Mar. 20. Sir THEODORE MARTIN.

1880, Apr. 20. The Hon. ADOLPHUS FREDERIC OCTAVIUS LIDDELL,
Q.C., permanent under secretary of State for the Home
Department.

1880, Apr. 20 JOHN TILLEY, late secretary to the Post Office.

1880, May 24. Hon. Col. LUITBERT ALEXANDER GEORGE LIONEL
ALPHONSE, FREIHERR VON PAWEL-RAMMINGEN

1880, Aug. 14. EDWARD JAMES REED, late chief instructor of the
Navy.

1880, Sept. 18. HENRY BROUGHAM LOCH, afterwards lord Loch,
lieutenant governor of the Isle of Man.

1880, Oct. 27. CHARLES JOHN HERRIES, chairman of the Board of
Inland Revenue.

1881, May 24. Lieut. Col. and Hon. Col WILLIAM FITZWILLIAM
LENNOX CONYNGHAM, Londonderry Militia.

1881, May 24. Lieut. Col. and Hon. Col. HAMBLETON FRANCIS
CUSTANCE, West Norfolk Militia.

1881, May 24. Lieut. Col. THOMAS HERON (JONES), 7th viscount
Ranelagh, 2nd (South) Middlesex Rifle Volunteer Corps.

1881, May 24. Lieut. Col. ROBERT JAMES LOYD-LINDSAY, V.C., 1st
Berkshire Rifle Volunteer Corps, afterwards lord Wantage.

1881, May 24. THOMAS BRASSEY, hon. commander of the Liverpool
Brigade of Royal Naval Artillery Volunteers, afterwards
lord Brassey.

19

1881, May 24. Rt Hon. ALFRED COMYNS LYALL, secretary of the Foreign Department of the Government of India

1881, May 24. Capt FREDERICK JOHN OWEN EVANS, R.N , hydrographer of the Navy.

1881, Oct. 8. EDWARD BALDWIN MALET, Consul General in Egypt.

1882, June 2 JAMES CAIRD, senior copyhold, inclosure and tithe commissioner for England and Wales.

1882, June 2 RALPH WOOD THOMPSON, under-secretary of state for the War Department.

1882, June 24. GEORGE KETTILBY RICKARDS, late counsel to the Speaker of the House of Commons.

1882, Oct 16. ROBERT BURNETT DAVID MORIER, minister at the Court of Spain

1882, Dec. 26. ROBERT GEORGE WYNDHAM HERBERT, permanent under secretary of State, Colonial Office.

1882, Dec. 26 REGINALD EARLE WELBY, afterwards lord Welby, auditor of the Civil List and financial secretary to the Treasury.

1883, Apr. 9. Rt Hon LYON PLAYFAIR, afterwards 1st lord Playfair.

1883, Sept. 15. Col. JOHN GRAHAM McKERLIE, Royal Engineers (retired list), chairman of the Board of Public Works in Ireland.

1884, Jan. 5 Professor RICHARD OWEN, F.R.S., late superintendent department of Natural History, British Museum.

1884, Jan. 12. ROBERT GEORGE CROOKSHANK HAMILTON, under secretary to the lord lieut of Ireland.

1884, Apr 15. ROBERT HAWTHORN COLLINS, comptroller of the Household of His late Royal Highness the duke of Albany.

1884, Apr. 29. H S.H prince LOUIS ALEXANDER, of Battenberg, lieut. in the Royal Navy

1884, May 24 Hon SPENCER CECIL BRABAZON PONSONBY-FANE, comptroller of accounts, Lord Chamberlain's Department.

1884, May 24. HENRY WENTWORTH DYKE ACLAND, M.D., regius professor of medicine in the University of Oxford, afterwards bart.

1885, June 15 NATHANIEL BARNABY, director of naval construction at the Admiralty.

1885, June 30. AUGUSTUS FREDERICK WILLIAM KEPPEL STEPHENSON, solicitor to the Treasury.

1885, July 22. Gen. ALEXANDER NELSON (HOOD), 1st viscount Bridport, one of Her Majesty's equerries.

1885, Aug. 11. RALPH ALLEN GOSSET, late sergeant-at-arms, House of Commons.

1885, Aug. 25. ARTHUR LAWRENCE HALIBURTON, director of supplies and transport, War Office.

1885, Dec. 1. PHILIP HENRY WODEHOUSE CURRIE, assistant under secretary of State for Foreign Affairs, afterwards lord Currie.

1885, Dec. 26. GEORGE EDWARD PAGET, M.D., F.R.S., regius professor of physic in the University of Cambridge.

1886, Feb. 2. Col. JAMES FRASER, commissioner of police for the City of London.

1886, Feb. 2. WILLIAM STUART WALKER, chairman of the Board of Supervision for the Relief of the Poor, and of Public Health, Scotland.

1886, Feb. 2. FRANCIS BROCKMAN MORLEY, chairman of the Middlesex Quarter Sessions, exon of Her Majesty's Royal Bodyguard of Yeomen of the Guard.

1886, Feb. 5. Hon. Col. and Lieut. Col. Commandant FREDERICK WINN KNIGHT, commanding 1st Volunteer Battalion Worcestershire Regiment.

1886, May 29. HENRY ROBINSON, vice-president of the Local Government Board, Ireland.

1886, June 28. (Additional) Sir FRANCIS PHILIP CUNLIFFE-OWEN, secretary to the Royal Commission and executive commissioner for the Indian Empire and for several colonies for services in connection with Colonial and Indian Exhibition of 1886.

1886, July 30. ALGERNON EDWARD WEST, chairman of the Board of Inland Revenue.

1887, June 21. (Additional) Lieut. Col. and Hon. Col. DONALD MATHESON, 1st Lanarkshire Engineer Volunteer Corps, in connection with Her Majesty's Auxiliary Forces.

1887, June 21 Lieut. Gen. Sir DIGHTON MACNAGHTEN PROBYN, V C, controller and treasurer of the Household of H.R H. the prince of Wales.

1887, June 21. Maj Sir EVELYN BARING, afterwards viscount Cromer, agent and consul gen. in Egypt.

1887, June 21. STEVENSON ARTHUR BLACKWOOD, secretary to the General Post Office.

1887, June 21. CHARLES THOMAS NEWTON, late of the British Museum.

1887, June 21. JOHN SIMON, M.D., late medical officer, Privy Council Office

1887, June 21. HUGH OWEN, permanent secretary, Local Government Board.

1887, June 21. WILLIAM FRASER, LL.D., deputy keeper of Records of Scotland.

1887, June 21. CHARLES LISTER RYAN, assistant comptroller and auditor, Exchequer and Audit Department

1887, June 21. Sir EDWARD WALTER, knt., founder and commanding officer, Corps of Commissionaires.

1887, June 21. Capt. DOUGLAS GALTON, late Royal Engineers.

1887, June 21. Maj. FLEETWOOD ISHAM EDWARDS, Royal Engineers, assistant keeper of the Privy Purse and assistant private secretary to the queen.

1887, June 21 (Additional) ARTHUR MITCHELL, M.D., LL.D., commissioner in lunacy in Scotland.

1887, June 21. (Additional) Col. GEORGE ASHLEY MAUDE, crown equerry.

1887, June 21. (Additional) Hon. Col. WALTER RICE OLIVEY, chief paymaster, Army Pay Department.

1888, Jan. 7. Sir ROBERT RAWLINSON, knt., chief engineering inspector, Local Government Board.

1888, Jan. 7. Sir CHARLES WARREN, chief commissioner of Metropolitan Police, col. in the Corps of Royal Engineers.

1888, June 2. Sir JULIAN PAUNCEFOTE, permanent under-secretary of state, Foreign Office.

1888, June 2. EDWARD GEORGE JENKINSON, late assistant under secretary, police and crime, for Ireland.

1888, June 15. EDWARD CHARLES BLOUNT.

1889, Mar. 4. EDWIN CHADWICK.

1889, May 25 HENRY LONGLEY, chief charity commissioner for England and Wales.

1889, July 3. Hon Col. ROBERT NIGEL FITZHARDINGE KINGSCOTE, honorary col , 4th Battalion Gloucester Regiment, and late lieut. col , Scots Fusilier Guards, one of Her Majesty's commissioners of Woods and Forests.

1889, Aug. 16 JOHN THOMAS BANKS, M D , one of the physicians in ordinary to the queen in Ireland

1890, Jan. 7. The Hon. CHARLES WILLIAM FREMANTLE, deputy-master and comptroller of the Mint.

1890, Jan 7. CHARLES LENNOX PEEL, clerk of the Council

1890, May 21. Col. Sir EDWARD RIDLEY COLBORNE BRADFORD, A.D.C. to the Queen, Madras Staff Corps.

1890, May 21. HENRY GEORGE CALCRAFT, permanent secretary to the Board of Trade.

1890, July 18. Sir JOHN KIRK, M D , late plenipotentiary to the Slave Trade Conference at the Court of Brussels.

1890, Aug. 26. Sir HENRY PERCY ANDERSON, of the Foreign Office.

1890, Nov. 21. Col. CHARLES BEAN EUAN-SMITH (Madras Infantry, on the retired list), Her Majesty's agent and consul gen. for the dominions of the sultan of Zanzibar.

1890, Dec. 19. Lieut Col and Hon Col. ALEXANDER MONCRIEFF (retired list), formerly commanding the duke of Edinburgh's Own Edinburgh Artillery (Southern Division, Royal Artillery).

1891, Jan 13. Col the Rt Hon Sir JOSEPH WEST RIDGEWAY (Bengal Infantry retired list), under secretary to the lord lieut. and gen. gov. of Ireland.

1891, Feb 3 Sir FREDERICK AUGUSTUS ABEL, knt , president of Committee on Explosives, War Department.

1891, Nov 5. EYRE MASSEY SHAW, late chief officer of the Metropolitan Fire Brigade

1892, May 10. Col GEORGE GUSTAVUS WALKER, 3rd Battalion the King's Own Scottish Borderers.

1892, May 10. Lieut Col Commandant and Hon. Col. EDWARD STOCK HILL, 1st and 2nd Glamorganshire Artillery Volunteers

1892, May 10 Col. Sir WILLIAM HENRY HUMPHERY, bart., 1st Volunteer Battalion the Hampshire Regiment, and commanding the Portsmouth Infantry Volunteer Brigade.

1892, May 25. GODFREY LUSHINGTON, under secretary of State, Home Office

1892, May 25 Lieut Gen. RICHARD HIERAM SANKEY, chairman Board of Public Works, Ireland.

1892, May 25 HENRY JENKYNS, parliamentary counsel to the Treasury.

1892, May 25 COURTENAY BOYLE, assistant secretary, Board of Trade (Railway Department)

1892, May 25 Lieut Col GEORGE ARCHIBALD LEACH, late Royal Engineers, late secretary to the Board of Agriculture.

1892, May 25 Adm. WILLIAM WINDHAM HORNBY, commissioner Prison Department, Home Office

1892, May 25. JOHN EVANS, D C.L., LL D , late president of the Society of Antiquaries.

1892, Aug. 20 Sir EDWARD HERTSLET, knt , librarian and keeper of the papers of the Foreign Office.

1892, Aug. 20. HORACE GEORGE WALPOLE, assistant under secretary of State, India Office.

1892, Aug 20. EVAN MacGREGOR, permanent secretary to the Admiralty.

1892, Aug. 20. Professor WILLIAM HENRY FLOWER, director of the Natural History Department, British Muesum.

1892, Aug. 20. REGINALD FRANCIS DOUCE PALGRAVE, clerk of the House of Commons.

1893, Jan. 24 Rt. Hon. JOHN TOMLINSON HIBBERT, financial secretary to the Treasury.

1893, Jan 24. ARTHUR GODLEY, under secretary of State for India.

1893, June 3. ANDREW NOBLE, late capt., Royal Artillery.

1893, June 3. FRANCIS MOWATT, assistant secretary to the Treasury.

1893, June 3. JOHN FRETCHEVILLE DYKES DONNELLY, hon. maj. gen., Royal Engineers (retired list), secretary to the Science and Art Department

1893, Dec. 29 Sir THOMAS HENRY SANDERSON, assistant under-secretary of state, Foreign Office.

1894, Jan. 9. ROBERT HENRY MEADE, commonly called the Hon. Robert Henry Meade, under-secretary of state for the Colonial Department.

1894, Mar. 13. Hon. Col. DAVID CARRICK ROBERT CARRICK-BUCHANAN, 3rd and 4th Battalions, the Cameronians (Scottish Rifles).

1894, May 26. EDWARD WALTER HAMILTON, assistant secretary to the Treasury.

1894, May 26. AUGUSTUS WOLLASTON FRANKS, keeper, Department of British and Mediæval Antiquities and Ethnography, British Museum.

1895, Jan. 8. HERBERT HARLEY MURRAY, late chairman of the Board of Customs.

1895, Jan. 8. GEORGE WILLIAM KEKEWICH, secretary to the Committee of Council on Education.

1895, Jan 8. WILLIAM HENRY WHITE, assistant controller and director of Naval Construction.

1895, Feb. 12. GEORGE SCHARF, director, keeper and secretary of the National Portrait Gallery.

1895, May 25. RALPH HENRY KNOX, accountant gen. of the Army.

1895, May 25. STAIR ANDREW AGNEW, registrar gen. and deputy keeper of Records, Scotland.

1895, May 25 Lieut. Col. ARTHUR JOHN BIGGE, private secretary to the queen.

1895, May 25. NICHOLAS RODERICK O'CONOR, envoy extraordinary and minister plenipotentiary at Pekin

1895, May 25. Sir DAVID HARREL, knt., under secretary for Ireland

1895, May 25. EDWARD MAUNDE THOMPSON, principal librarian and secretary, British Museum.

1895, June 28. JAMES REID, one of the physicians in ordinary to Her Majesty.

1895, July 2. Col. VIVIAN DERING MAJENDIE, inspector of explosives, Home Office.

1895, July 2. ROBERT GIFFEN, comptroller gen. of the Commercial, Labour, and Statistical Department, Board of Trade.

1895, July 2. ALFRED MILNER, chairman of the Board of Inland Revenue.

1896, Jan. 10. HENRY HAMILTON JOHNSTON, imperial commissioner and consul gen. for British Central Africa.

1896, Feb 6. (Honorary) H S.H. prince FRANCIS JOSEPH of Battenberg.

1896, Feb. 10. Col. lord EDWARD WILLIAM PELHAM-CLINTON, master of the Household

1896, Feb. 28. Maj. Gen. CHARLES TAYLOR DU PLAT (retired pay), late Royal Artillery, extra equerry to the Queen

1896, May 20. CLEMENTS ROBERT MARKHAM, president of the Royal Geographical Society.

1897, Jan. 1. Sir ELWIN MITFORD PALMER, financial adviser to His Highness the khedive of Egypt.

1897, Jan. 1. WILLIAM ANDERSON, director gen. of Ordnance Factories.

1897, Jan. 1. Hon. Col. the Hon. WELLINGTON PATRICK MANVERS CHETWYND-TALBOT, sergeant-at-arms, House of Lords.

1897, June 1. Hon. Col. DAVID DAVIDSON, the Queen's Rifle Volunteer Brigade, the Royal Scots (Lothian Regiment).

1897, June 22. (Additional) Sir FRANCIS KNOLLYS, private secretary to H.R.H. the prince of Wales, afterwards lord Knollys.

1897, June 22. (Additional) GEORGE LAWSON, assistant under secretary of state, War Office.

1897, June 22. (Additional) Sir JOHN GARDNER DILLMAN ENGLE-HEART, knt., clerk of the Council of the Duchy of Lancaster.

1897, June 22. (Additional) EDWIN HENRY EGERTON, envoy extraordinary and minister plenipotentiary at Athens.

1897, Jun 22. (Additional) Col. EDWARD TALBOT THACKERAY, V.C.

1897, June 22. (Additional) HENRY CRAIK, secretary, Scotch Education Department.

1897, June 22. (Additional) JOHN SKELTON, vice-president, Local Government Board for Scotland.

1897, June 22. (Additional) Sir ALBERT WILLIAM WOODS, garter principal king-of-arms.

1897, June 22. (Additional) HENRY CHURCHILL MAXWELL-LYTE, deputy keeper Public Record Office.

1897, June 22. (Additional) FREDERIC LACEY ROBINSON, deputy chairman Board of Inland Revenue.

1897, June 22. (Additional) Sir ANDREW REED, knt., insp. gen. Royal Irish Constabulary.

1897, June 22. (Additional) RICHARD THORNE THORNE, medical officer to the Local Government Board.

1897, June 22. (Additional) JOSEPH NORMAN LOCKYER, professor of astronomy, Royal College of Science.

1897, June 22. (Additional) JOHN WOLFE BARRY.

1897, June 22. (Additional) JOHN TAYLOR, surveyor, Office of Works.

1897, June 22. (Additional) Hon. Lieut Col. (retired) HENRY SMITH, commissioner of the City of London Police.

1897, June 22. (Additional) The Rt. Hon. Sir FRANCIS HENRY JEUNE, knt., president of the Probate, Divorce, and Admiralty Division of the High Court of Justice, judge advocate gen.

1897, June 22 (Additional) Sir JOHN HASSARD, knt., apparitor gen. Consistory Court of the bishop of London

1897, June 22 (Additional) HENRY CHARLES BURDETT.

1897, June 22 (Additional) EDWARD FRANKLAND, water analyst to the Local Government Board

1897, June 22 (Additional) WILLIAM HUGGINS.

1897, June 22. (Additional) WILLIAM BLAKE RICHMOND.

1897, June 22. (Additional) R. Adm. WILLIAM JAMES LLOYD WHARTON, hydrographer of the Admiralty.

1897, June 22. (Additional) ALBERT JOHN DURSTON, chief inspector of machinery, engineer-in-chief of the Navy.

1897, June 22. (Additional) Hon. Col SAMUEL BRISE RUGGLES BRISE, 4th Battalion the Essex Regiment

1897, June 22. (Additional) Lieut Col. and Hon. Col. Sir CHARLES WATKIN SHAKERLEY, bart., late 5th Volunteer Battalion, the Cheshire Regiment.

1897, June 22. (Additional) Hon. Col. Sir HENRY WILMOT, bart., V C., 1st Volunteer Battalion the Sherwood Foresters (Derbyshire Regiment).

1897, June 22. (Additional) Lieut. Col. and Hon. Col. ROBERT THOMAS WHITE-THOMSON, late 4th Battalion the Devonshire Regiment.

1898, Jan. 1. EDWARD AUGUSTUS BOND, late principal librarian of the British Museum.

1898, Jan. 1 WILLIAM TENNANT GAIRDNER, physician in ordinary to Her Majesty in Scotland, dean of the Faculty of Medicine, Glasgow University.

1898, Jan. 1. GEORGE MORRIS, vice-president, Local Government Board for Ireland.

1898, Jan. 1. SPENCER WALPOLE, secretary to the General Post Office.

1898, Feb. 8. Lieut Col. and Hon. Col. JOHN WILLIAMS WALLINGTON, late 4th Battalion the Gloucestershire Regiment.

1898, Mar. 25. Maj. Sir CLAUDE MAXWELL MACDONALD, envoy extraordinary, minister plenipotentiary, and chief superintendent of Trade at Pekin.

1898, May 21. Col. Sir RICHARD EDWARD ROWLEY MARTIN.

1898, May 21. KENNETH AUGUSTUS MUIR MACKENZIE, Q.C., permanent secretary of the lord Chancellor's office and clerk of the Crown.

1898, May 21. HAMILTON JOHN AGMONDESHAM CUFFE (commonly called the Hon. Hamilton John Agmondesham Cuffe), solicitor to the Treasury, director of Public Prosecutions, afterwards 5th viscount Desart.

1898, May 21. EDWARD LEIGH PEMBERTON, late assistant under secretary of state, Home Office.

1898, May 21. Sir KENELM EDWARD DIGBY, under secretary of state, Home Office.

1898, May 21. JOHN MURRAY, F.R.S., LL.D.

1899, Jan. 2. CAREY JOHN KNYVETT, late principal clerk, Home Office.

1899, Jan. 2. EDWARD WINGFIELD, under secretary of State for the Colonies.

1899, Jan. 2. WILLIAM CHANDLER ROBERTS-AUSTEN, F.R.S., chemist and assayer to the Royal Mint.

1899, Jan. 2. HENRY WILLIAM PRIMROSE, chairman of the Board of Customs.

1899, June 9. Col. JOHN FARQUHARSON, Royal Engineers, late director gen. of the Ordnance Survey.

1899, June 9. GEORGE HERBERT MURRAY, secretary to the General Post Office.

1899, June 9. WILLIAM HENRY PREECE, consulting engineer to the General Post Office.

1899, June 9. MICHAEL FOSTER, secretary to the Royal Society.

1899, Nov 21 EDWARD PAYSON WILLS.

1900, Jan. 16. Capt. WILLIAM DE WIVELESLIE ABNEY, F.R.S., director of the Science and Art Department.

1900, May 23 JOHN SAMUEL PURCELL, late comptroller of Stamps and Stores and registrar of Joint Stock Companies, Inland Revenue Department.

1900, May 23 DAVID GILL, Her Majesty's astronomer, Cape of Good Hope.

1900, May 23. WILLIAM CONYNGHAM GREENE, of Her Majesty's diplomatic service, late British agent at Pretoria

1900, May 23. HENRY AUGUSTUS ROBINSON, vice president Local Government Board, Ireland

1900, Oct 16 Col the Rt. Hon JOHN HAY ATHOL MACDONALD, commanding the Forth Volunteer Infantry Brigade, and formerly commanding the Queen's Rifle Volunteer Brigade, the Royal Scots (Lothian Regiment).

1900, Nov. 29. Sir WILLIAM MACCORMAC, bart. (*See* footnote on p 347)

1901, Jan. 1. The Hon. EDWARD CHANDOS LEIGH, Q C., counsel to the Speaker, House of Commons.

1901, Jan. 1. RICHARD MILLS, late comptroller and auditor gen.

1901, Jan. 1. Sir WILLIAM TURNER, D.C.L.

1901, July 2 Sir ARTHUR NICHOLSON, bart.

1901, Nov. 9 Sir MONTAGUE FREDERICK OMMANNEY, under secretary of State, Colonial Office.

1901, Nov. 9. ROBERT ANDERSON, *LL.D*, assistant commissioner of Metropolitan Police

1901, Nov. 9. FRANCIS JOHN STEPHENS HOPWOOD, permanent secretary to the Board of Trade.

1901, Nov. 9. SAMUEL BUTLER PROVIS, permanent secretary to the Local Government Board

1901, Nov. 9. GEORGE LISLE RYDER, chairman of the Board of Customs

1901, Nov. 26. The Rt. Hon. BEILBY (LAWLEY), 5th lord Wenlock, P C., lord of the Bedchamber to H.R.H. the prince of Wales.

1902, Jan. 21. ARCHIBALD JOHN SCOTT MILMAN.

1902, June 26. (Additional) Maj. HENRY PILKINGTON, Royal Engineers.

1902, June 26. Hon. Col. ALFRED PLANTAGENET FREDERICK CHARLES SOMERSET, 7th Battalion the Rifle Brigade (the prince Consort's Own).

1902, June 26. Lieut. Col. and Hon. Col ROBERT BRIDGFORD, late 2nd Volunteer Battalion the Manchester Regiment.

1902, June 26. Hon. Col. CHARLES GERVAISE BOXALL, 1st Sussex Royal Garrison Artillery (Volunteers).

1902, June 26. Col. ARTHUR PENDARVES VIVIAN, South Wales Border Volunteer Infantry Brigade.

1902, July 11. (Additional) RICHARD DAVIS AWDRY, accountant gen. of the Royal Navy.

1902, July 11. (Additional) The Hon. BERNARD ERIC BARRINGTON.

1902, July 11. (Additional) The Hon. FRANCIS LEVESON BERTIE, assistant under secretary of state for Foreign Affairs.

1902, July 11. (Additional) Sir WILLIAM SELBY CHURCH, bart., M.D., president of the Royal College of Physicians.

1902, July 11. (Additional) CLINTON EDWARD DAWKINS.

1902, July 11. (Additional) THOMAS HENRY ELLIOTT, secretary to the Board of Agriculture

1902, July 11. (Additional) REGINALD BALIOL (BRETT), 2nd viscount Esher, secretary to H.M.'s Office of Works

1902, July 11. (Additional) JOHN LOWNDES ELDON GORST, financial adviser to the Egyptian Government.

1902, July 11. (Additional) HENRY JOHN LOWNDES GRAHAM, clerk of the Parliaments.

1902, July 11 (Additional) The Hon. SCHOMBERG KERR MACDONNELL.

1902, July 11. (Additional) HENRY JAMES VANSITTART NEALE, assistant secretary of the Admiralty.

1902, July 11 (Additional) ALFRED DE BOCK PORTER, secretary to the Ecclesiastical Commission.

1902, July 11. (Additional) Professor WILLIAM RAMSAY, F.R.S.

1902, July 11. (Additional) EVELYN JOHN RUGGLES BRISE, chairman of the Prisons Commission.

1902, July 11. (Additional) LESLIE STEPHEN.

1902, July 11. (Additional) GEORGE WHITEHOUSE, engineer-in-chief of the Uganda Railway.

1902, July 11. (Additional) HENRY FRANCIS REDHEAD YORKE, director of victualling of the Royal Navy.

1902, July 17 HORACE ALFRED DAMER SEYMOUR, deputy master of the Mint, would have been made K.C B. had he survived.

1902, Nov 9. Sir ANDREW CHARLES HOWARD, late assistant commissioner of the Metropolitan Police.

1902, Nov 9. GEORGE CHRISTOPHER TROUT BARTLEY, M.P.

1902, Nov. 9. ROBERT WILLIAM ARBUTHNOT HOLMES, treasury remembrancer in Ireland.

1902, Dec. 30. Sir BENJAMIN BAKER, LL.D , F.R.S.

1903, June 26 WILLIAM DAVIDSON NIVEN, F.R.S., director of studies, Royal Naval College.

1903, June 26. Lieut. Col and Hon. Col. HENRY MONTAGUE HOZIER, 3rd Kent Royal Garrison Artillery (Volunteers).

1903, June 30. Col EDMOND BAINBRIDGE, chief superintendent of Ordnance Factories.

1903, July 10. Sir JOHN HENRY GIBBS BERGNE, late of the Foreign Office.

1903, July 10. Sir PATRICK COLL, chief Crown solicitor, Ireland.

1903, July 10. CHARLES HENRY ALDERSON, late chief charity commissioner.

1903, Aug. 11 Col. NEVILLE FRANCIS FITZGERALD CHAMBERLAIN, inspec. gen., Royal Irish Constabulary.

1903, Aug. 11. Lieut. Col. JOHN FOSTER GEORGE ROSS-OF-BLADENS-BURG, chief commissioner of the Dublin Metropolitan Police.

1904, June 24. CHARLES JOHN REED, hon. col. of the Northumberland Royal Garrison Artillery (Volunteers)

1904, June 24. Sir DAVID GAMBLE, bart , hon col , 2nd Volunteer Battalion, prince of Wales's Volunteers (South Lancashire Regiment).

1904, June 24. WALTER SPENCER STANHOPE, hon. col , 2nd Volunteer Battalion the York and Lancaster Regiment.

1904, June 24 Hon. Col. ANGUS WILLIAM HALL, late 3rd Battalion Dorsetshire Regiment.

1904, June 24. Hon Col. Sir FITZROY DONALD MACLEAN, bart., late West Kent Imperial Yeomanry.

1904, Nov 9. Sir ARTHUR HENRY HARDINGE.

1904, Nov. 9. WILLIAM HENRY MAHONEY CHRISTIE.

The Most Exalted Order of the Star of India.

The Most Exalted Order of the Star of India.

CHARLES JOHN (CANNING), 1st earl Canning. Appointed gov. gen July, 1855. Proclaimed 1st viceroy, 1858, Nov. 1.

JAMES (BRUCE), 8th earl of Elgin. Appointed 1862, Jan. 21. Assumed government 1862, Mar. 12. Died 1863, Nov. 20.

Sir JOHN LAIRD MAIR LAWRENCE (afterwards 1st lord Lawrence). Appointed 1863, Dec. 5. Assumed government 1864, Jan. 12.

RICHARD SOUTHWELL (BOURKE), 6th earl of Mayo. Appointed 1868, Oct. 27. Assumed government 1869, Jan. 12. Assassinated 1872, Feb. 8.

THOMAS GEORGE (BARING), 2nd lord afterward 1st earl of Northbrook. Appointed 1872, Mar. 14. Assumed government 1872, May 3.

EDWARD ROBERT LYTTON (BULWER-LYTTON), 2nd lord afterwards 1st earl of Lytton. Appointed 1876, Feb. 12. Took the oath at Calcutta, 1876, Apr. 12.

GEORGE FREDERICK SAMUEL (ROBINSON), 1st marquess of Ripon. Appointed 1880, May 6. Assumed government 1880, June 8.

FREDERICK TEMPLE (HAMILTON-BLACKWOOD, afterwards HAMILTON-TEMPLE-BLACKWOOD), 1st earl of Dufferin, afterwards marquess of Dufferin and Ava. Appointed 1884, Oct. 21. Assumed government 1884, Dec. 13.

HENRY CHARLES KEITH (PETTY-FITZMAURICE), 5th marquess of Lansdowne. Installed 1888, Dec. 10.

VICTOR ALEXANDER (BRUCE), 9th earl of Elgin. Appointed about 1893, Oct. 10. Assumed government 1894, Jan 27.

GEORGE NATHANIEL (CURZON), 1st lord Curzon of Kedleston. Appointed 1898, Dec. 3. Assumed government 1899, Jan. 6. Re-appointed for a second term, 1904, Sept. 3.

KNIGHTS OF THE ORDER OF THE STAR OF INDIA.

Original Knights before the enlargement of the Order.

1861, June 25. CHARLES JOHN (CANNING), 1st earl Canning, ex. officio as Grand Master. Died 1862, June 17.

1861, June 25. FRANCIS ALBERT AUGUSTUS CHARLES EMANUEL, prince consort of queen Victoria. (Extra.)

1861, June 25 ALBERT EDWARD, prince of Wales. (Extra.)

1861, June 25. H.H. NIZAM-OOL-MOOLK NUWAB TUYINAT ALI KHAN, Nizam of Hydrabad.

1861, June 25. Gen. HUGH (GOUGH), 1st viscount Gough, sometime commander-in-chief of H.M. Forces in the East Indies.

1861, June 25. H.H. JYAJEE RAO SINDHIA, Maharaja of Gwalior.

1861, June 25. GEORGE FRANCIS ROBERT (HARRIS), 3rd lord Harris, sometime governor of the Presidency of Madras.

1861, June 25. H.H. Maharaja DULEEP SINGH.

1861, June 25. Gen. COLIN (CAMPBELL), lord Clyde, late commander-in-chief of H M. Forces in the East Indies.

1861, June 25. H.H. RUNBEER SING, Maharaja of Cashmere.

1861, June 25. Sir GEORGE RUSSELL CLERK, governor of the Presidency of Bombay.

1861, June 25. H.H. TOOKOOJEE RAO HOLKAR, Maharaja of Indore.

1861, June 25 H.H. Maharaja KHUNDE RAO, Guicowar of Baroda.

1861 June 25. Sir JOHN LAIRD MAIR LAWRENCE, bart., lately lieut. governor of the Punjab (afterwards lord Lawrence). From 1864, Jan. 12, Grand Master and first and principal G.C.S.I.

1861, June 25. H.H. NURENDUR SINGH, Maharaja of Putiala.

1861, June 25. Lieut. Gen. Sir JAMES OUTRAM, bart., lately member of the Council of the gov. gen. of India.

1861, June 25. NUWAB SEKUNDER, Begum of Bhopal.

1861, June 25. Gen. Sir HUGH HENRY ROSE, commander-in-chief of H.M. Forces in the East Indies. Afterwards lord Strathnairn

1861, June 25. H.H.YOOSUF ALI KHAN, Nuwab of Rampore.

Subsequent Appointments.

1861, Aug. 19. F. Marsh STAPLETON (COTTON), 1st viscount Combermere, sometime commander-in-chief of the Forces in the East Indies.

1861, Aug. 19. Gen. Sir GEORGE POLLOCK, afterwards bart, who commanded the British Forces which advanced to Kabul in 1842; sometime member of the Council of the gov. gen. of India.

1862, Mar. 12. JAMES (BRUCE), 8th earl of Elgin, *ex-officio* as grand master. Died 1863, Nov. 20.

1863, Nov. 11. H.H. SERAMUDI RAJAHYE HINDOSTAN RAJ-RAJENDER SREE MAHARAJA DHEERAJ SEWEE RAM SING, Bahadoor or Maharaja of Jyepore.

1863, Nov. 11. H.H. FURZUND DILBUND RASEKOOL ITHAGAD DOWLUT-I-ENGLISHIA RAJA SUROOP SING, Bahadoor or Maharaja of Jheend.

1864, Dec. 10. H.H. FURZUND DILBUND RASEKHUL ITGAD DOWLUT-I-ENGLISHIA RAJAH RAJEGAN RAJAH RUNDHEER SING, Bahadoor of Kuppoorthulla.

1864, Dec. 10. H.H. Maharaja RUGHOO RAJ SING, Bahadoor of Rewah.

Enlargement of the Order in 1866.

STAR OF INDIA.

KNIGHTS GRAND COMMANDERS OF THE ORDER OF
THE STAR OF INDIA, (G.C.S I.).

*Promotion of Knights Commanders on the Enlargement of the
Order in 1866.*

1866, May 24. *ALBERT EDWARD, prince of Wales.

1866, May 24. *NIZAM-OOL-MOOLK NUWAB TUYINAT ALI KHAN,
Nizam of Hyderabad.

1866, May 24. *Gen. HUGH viscount GOUGH.

1866, May 24. *TYAJEE RAO SINDHIA, Maharaja of Gwalior.

1866, May 24. *GEORGE FRANCIS ROBERT (HARRIS), 3rd lord Harris.

1866, May 24. *Maharaja DHULEEP SING.

1866, May 24. *RUNBEER SINGH, Maharaja of Cashmere.

1866, May 24. *Sir GEORGE RUSSELL CLERK.

1866, May 24. *TOOKOOJEE RAO HOLKAR, Maharaja of Indore.

1866, May 24. *Maharaja KHUNDE RAO, Guicowar of Baroda.

1866, May 24. *Sir JOHN LAIRD MAIR LAWRENCE, bart., afterwards
lord Lawrence, Grand Master and first and principal
G.C.S I.

1866, May 24   *NUWAB SEKUNDER, Begum of Bhopal.

1866, May 24. *Gen. Sir HUGH HENRY ROSE, afterwards lord
Strathnairn.

1866, May 24. *YOOSUF ALI KHAN, Nuwab of Rampore.

1866, May 24. *Gen. Sir GEO. POLLOCK, bart.

*The names marked with an asterisk were the K.S I. existing at the date
of the enlargement of the order in 1866, and were made G.C.S.I. by that
enlargement.

1866, May 24. *H.H. SERAMUDI RAJAHYE HINDOSTAN RAJ-RAJENDER SREE MAHARAJA DHEERAJ SEWEE RAM SING, Bahadoor of Jyepore.

1866, May 24. *H.H. FURZUND DILBUND RASEKHUL ITGAD DOWLUT-I-ENGLISHIA, etc , Bahadoor of Kuppoorthulla.

1866, May 24. *H.H. Maharaja RUGHOO RAJ SING, Bahadoor of Rewah.

1866, May 24. *Sir HENRY BARTLE EDWARD FRERE.

1866, May 24. *H.H. the Maharaja of Joudpore.

1866, May 24. *Sir ROBERT MONTGOMERY.

1866, May 24. *H.H. the Maharaja of Travancore.

1866, May 24. *Gen. Sir WILLIAM ROSE MANSFIELD, afterwards 1st lord Sandhurst.

1866, May 24. *H.H. the Maharaja of Kerowlee.

Subsequent Appointments.

1867, May 24.   H.H. KRISHNAH RAJ WADYAR, Maharaja of Mysore.

1867, Sept. 16. Lieut. Gen. Sir ROBERT NAPIER, commander-in-chief of the Bombay Army, afterwards lord Napier of Magdala.

1868, Aug. 27. ISMAIL PASHA, viceroy of Egypt. (Honorary.)

1868, Dec. 8. Sir WILLIAM ROBERT SEYMOUR VESEY FITZGERALD, governor of the Presidency of Bombay. (Extra.)

1869, Jan. 12. RICHARD SOUTHWELL (BURKE), 6th earl of Mayo, *ex-officio* as Grand Master.

1869, June 2. The Rana of Dholepore.

1870, Feb. 7. H.R.H. ALFRED ERNEST ALBERT, duke of Edinburgh. (Extra.)

1870, May 28. H.H MOHENDER SING, Maharaja of Puttiala.

1870, May 28   The Nawab SALAR JUNG, Bahadoor, minister of the Hyderabad State.

1870, Aug. 19.   FERDINAND DE LESSEPS   (Honorary.)

1871, May 20.   H.H. DHERAJ SUMBHO SING, Maharana of Oodeypore.

1871, May 20.   H.H. the RAO PRAGMULJEE of Cutch.

1872, May 3.   THOMAS GEORGE (BARING), 2nd lord afterwards 1st earl of Northbrook, *ex officio* as Grand Master.

1872, May 31.   H.H. the NAWAB SHAH JEHAN, Begum of Bhopal.

1873, May 24.   H.E. Maharajah JUNG BAHADOOR KUNWAR RANAJEE, prime minister of Nepal.

1873, May 24   Gen. Sir JOHN LOW, Madras Infantry, formerly political resident at Lucknow and Hyderabad, and member of the Council of the gov. gen of India

1873, May 24   Lieut Gen. Sir NEVILLE BOWLES CHAMBERLAIN, Bengal Infantry, late commanding Punjab Irregular Force.

1873, July 1.   H.H. HAJEE MEERZA HUSSEIN KHAN, grand vizier and minister of war to the shah of Persia.   (Honorary.)

1875, May 3   H.H prince TEWFIK PASHA, heir apparent to the viceroy of Egypt, afterwards khedive of Egypt.   (Honorary.)

1875, Dec 31.   H.H. RAJ RAJESSUR MAHARAJAH DHIRAJ JESWNT SING, Bahadur of Jodhpore.

1875, Dec. 31.   H.H. FURZUND DILPIZIR NAWAB MAHUMMAD KULB ALI KHAN, Bahadur of Rampore.

1875, Dec. 31   H H. FURZUND DILBUND RASEKHUL ITGAD DOWLUT-I-ENGLISHIA RAJAH RUGBIR SING, Bahadur of Jheend.

1876, Apr. 12   EDWARD ROBERT LYTTON (BULWER-LYTTON), 2nd lord afterwards 1st earl of Lytton, *ex officio* as Grand Master.

1876, June 28.   RICHARD PLANTAGENET CAMPBELL (TEMPLE-NUGENT-BRYDGES-CHANDOS-GRENVILLE), 3rd duke of Buckingham and Chandos, governor of the Presidency of Madras.   (Extra.)

1876, June 28.   Sir PHILIP EDMOND WODEHOUSE, governor of the Presidency of Bombay.   (Extra.)

1877, Jan. 1. ARTHUR WILLIAM PATRICK ALBERT, duke of Connaught. (Extra.) (On the occasion of the proclamation of queen Victoria as empress of India at Delhi).

1877, Jan. 1. H.H. RAM SINGH MAHARAS, Raja of Bundi (on same occasion).

1877, Jan. 1. H.H. JASWANT SING, Maharaja of Bhurtpore (on same occasion).

1877, Jan. 1. H.H. SHRI PRASAD NARAIN SINGH, Maharaja of Benares (on same occasion).

1877, Jan. 1. H.H. AZIM JAH ZAHIR-UD-DOWLA, Bahadur, prince of Arcot (on same occasion).

1877, Jan. 25. Prince LEOPOLD GEORGE DUNCAN ALBERT, duke of Saxony, prince of Saxe-Coburg and Gotha, afterwards duke of Albany. (Extra.)

1877, June 2. GEORGE WILLIAM FREDERICK CHARLES, duke of Cambridge. (Extra.)

1878, Jan. 1. H.E. CHERIF PASHA, minister for Foreign Affairs to H.H. the khedive of Egypt. (Honorary).

1878, Jan. 1. Sir RICHARD TEMPLE, bart., governor of the Presidency of Bombay. (Extra.)

1878, May 3. Sir JOHN STRACHEY. (Extra.) Member of the Council of the gov. gen. of India.

1878, Aug. 27. H.H. SAFVET PASHA, grand vizier and minister of foreign affairs to the sultan of Turkey. (Honorary).

1879, July 29. H.H. MIR KHODADAD, khan of Khelat. (Honorary.)

1879, July 29. Hon. Col. H H. Raja Sir HIRA SINGH MALVINDAR, Bahadur of Nabha.

1879, July 29. Gen Sir FREDERICK PAUL HAINES, commander-in-chief of H.M. Forces in the East Indies. (Extra.)

1880, Apr. 23. (Extra) Rt. Hon. GATHORNE (GAYTHORNE-HARDY), 1st viscount Cranbrook, principal secretary of State for India. Invested at Windsor Castle, April 21.

1880, June 8. GEORGE FREDERICK SAMUEL (ROBINSON), 1st marquess of Ripon, ex officio as Grand Master.

1880, Nov. 9. His Highness the Nawab of Bahawulpur.

1881, May 24 His Highness Sujjun Singh, Maharana of Udaipur.

1882, May 23. His Highness the Maharajah of Travancore.

1882, May 23. His Highness Nawab Ikbal-ud-dowlah, of Oudh (Baghdad).

1884, May 23 His Highness Chama Rajendra Wadeir, Maharajah of Mysore.

1884, Nov. 17. His Highness Asaf Jah Nawab Mahub Ali Khan, Bahadur Fath Jang, Nizam of Hyderabad.

1884, Dec. 13. Frederick Temple (Hamilton-Blackwood, afterwards Hamilton-Temple-Blackwood), 1st earl of Dufferin, afterwards marquess of Dufferin and Ava, *ex officio* as Grand Master.

1885, Feb 25 (Extra) Rt. Hon. Sir James Fergusson, bart., governor of the Presidency of Bombay.

1885, Apr. 11. Abdul Rahman Khan, amir of Afghanistan. (Honorary)

1885, Dec. 7. (Extra) Gen. Sir Donald Martin Stewart, bart., late commander-in-chief in the East Indies.

1886, Jan. 1. His Highness Syud Toorkee, sultan of Muscat.

1886, Jan. 1. His Highness Maharao Raja Mangal, Sinh of Ulwar.

1886, Jan. 1. His Highness Takht Sinhji Thakur Sahib, of Bhaunagar.

1886, July 28. Sir Mountstuart Elphinstone Grant-Duff. (Extra.)

1887, Feb 15 His Highness Maharaja Sayaji Rao, Bahadur Gaekwar of Baroda.

1887, Feb. 15. His Highness Maharana Fateh Singh Bahadur, of Meywar (Oodeypore)

1887, Feb 15. His Highness Raja Sir Shamsher Prakash, Bahadur of Sirmur (Nahun)

1887, June 30. H.H. Maharaja Shivaji Rao Holker, Bahadur, Maharaja of Indore.

1887, Nov. 1. H.R.H. Sultan Massoud Mirza Yemin-ed-Dowlah Zil-es-Sultan, of Persia, gov. gen. of Ispahar, Fars, Arabistan, Kurdestan, Yezd. etc. (Honorary.)

1888, Jan. 2. H.H. the Maharajah Sawai Madhu Singh, of Jeypore (H.H. Saramad-i-Rajaha-i-Hindustan Raj Rajindra Sri Maharaja Maharaja-dhiraj Sawai Madhu Singh Bahadur, Maharaja of Jaipur).

1888, May 24. His Highness the Maharajah Bala Rama Varma, of Travancore.

1888, Dec. 10. Henry Charles Keith (Petty-Fitzmaurice), 5th marquess of Lansdowne, *ex officio* as Grand Master.

1890, Mar. 18. (Extra) Donald James (Mackay), 11th lord Reay, governor of the Presidency of Bombay.

1890, Nov. 8. (Honorary) His Highness Seyyid Ali bin Said bin Sultan, sultan of Zanzibar.

1892, May 25. Col. His Highness Maharaja Partab Singh Indar Mahinder, Bahadur, Sipar-i-Saltanat of Jummu and Kashmir.

1892, Aug. 1. (Extra) Rt. Hon. Richard Assheton (Cross), viscount Cross, His Majesty's principal secretary of State for India.

1893, June 3. (Extra) Gen. Frederick Sleigh, baron Roberts, of Kandahar, V.C., afterwards earl Roberts.

1894, Jan. 27. Victor Alexander (Bruce), 9th earl of Elgin, *ex officio* as Grand Master.

1894, Feb. 23. (Honorary) His Highness Saiyad Hamad-bin-Thowani, sultan of Zanzibar. Died May, 1896.

1895, Jan. 1. His Highness Shahu Chatrapati Maharaj, Raja of Kolhapur.

1895, May 25. His Highness the Maharaja Sindhia, of Gwalior (H.H. Maharaj Adhiraj Sir Madho Rao Sindhia, Bahadur of Gwalior).

1895, May 25. The Rt. Hon. George Robert Canning (Harris), 4th baron Harris. (Extra.)

1895, June 29. (Extra) Rt. Hon. Henry Hartley Fowler.

1896, Jan. 1. (Extra) the Rt. Hon. BEILBY (LAWLEY), lord Wenlock, governor of the Presidency of Madras.

1896, Feb. 29. His Excellency NUBAR PASHA. (Honorary).

1897, June 22. His Highness Maharaja VYANKATESH RAMANI PRASAD SINGH BAHADUR of Rewa.

1897, June 22. Sir JOSEPH DALTON HOOKER, M D.

1897, June 22. His Excellency Maharaja Sir BIR SHAMSHER JANG RANA BAHADUR, prime minister of Nepal.

1897, June 22. Sir ANTHONY PATRICK MACDONNELL, lieut. gov. of the North-Western Provinces.

1897, June 22. Lieut. Col. Maharaj Dhiraj Sir PARTAB SINGH BAHADUR, of Jodhpur [Sir PRATAB SINGHJI, of Idar].

1897, June 22. Lieut. Gen. RICHARD STRACHEY, Royal Engineers

1898, Jan. 11. Gen. Sir GEORGE STEWART WHITE, V.C., commander-in-chief in India.

1898, Apr. 20. H.H. SAID HAMUD BIN MAHOMED, the sultan of Zanzibar. (Honorary).

1898, May 21. His Highness the Maharaja of Patiala.

1899, Jan. 6. GEORGE NATHANIEL (CURZON), 1st lord Curzon of Kedleston, *ex-officio* as Grand Master.

1900, Mar. 9. (Extra) WILLIAM (MANSFIELD), 2nd lord Sandhurst, late governor of the Presidency of Bombay.

1901, Apr. 29. (Extra) Sir ARTHUR ELIBANK HAVELOCK, late governor of the Presidency of Madras.

1903, Jan 1. Rt. Hon. GEORGE FRANCIS HAMILTON, commonly called lord George Francis Hamilton (on the occasion of the Durbar).

1903, Jan. 1. His Highness Raja Sir RAMA VARMA, of Cochin (on the same occasion).

1904, Sept. 2. Rt. Hon. ARTHUR OLIVER VILLIERS (RUSSELL), 2nd lord Ampthill, acting gov. gen of India [during the absence of lord Curzon].

KNIGHTS COMMANDERS OF THE STAR OF INDIA (K.C.S.I.).

Order Enlarged.

1866, Feb. 12. Sir HENRY BARTLE EDWARD FRERE, governor of the Presidency of Bombay.

1866, Feb. 12. H.H. the Maharaja of Joudphore.

1866, Feb. 12. Sir ROBERT MONTGOMERY, late lieut. gov. of the Punjab.

1866, Feb. 12. H.H. the Maharaja of Travancore

1866, Feb. 12. Gen. Sir WILLIAM ROSE MANSFIELD, commander-in-chief of H.M. Forces in the East Indies, afterwards 1st lord Sandhurst.

1866, Feb. 12. H.H. the Maharaja of Kerowlee.

1866, May 24 The rajah SHREEMUN MAHARAJA CHUTTROPUTTEE SHAHABE DAM ALTAPHOO, of Kolhapoor.

1866, May 24. CECIL BEADON, Bengal Civil Service, lieut. gov. of Bengal.

1866, May 24. The nawab SALAR JUNG BAHADOOR, of Hyderabad, in the Deccan.

1866, May 24. DONALD FRIELL McLEOD, Bengal Civil Service, lieut. gov. of the Punjab.

1866, May 24. The Maharaja JEYPERCASH SING BAHADOOR, of Deo, in Behar.

1866, May 24. HENRY RICKETTS, Bengal Civil Service (retired), late member of the Council of the gov. gen. of India.

1866, May 24. The Maharaja MIRZA GAJAPATI RAZ MAUNE, Sultan Bahadoor Zemindar of Vizianagram, member of the Council of the gov. gen of India for making laws and regulations.

1866, May 24. HENRY BYNG HARRINGTON, Bengal Civil Service (retired), late member of the Council of the gov. gen. of India.

1866, May 24. The Maharaja Dig Bijye Singh, of Bulrampoor (Oudh).

1866, May 24. Walter Elliot, Madras Civil Service (retired), late member of the Council of the governor of Madras.

1866, May 24. Sharf-ul-Omrah, Bahadoor of Hyderabad, member of the Council of the gov. gen. of India for making laws and regulations.

1866, May 24 Thomas Pycroft, Madras Civil Service, member of the Council of the governor of Madras .

1866, May 24. Rajah Jymungul Singh, of Gidhore in Monghyr.

1866, May 24 John Macpherson McLeod, Madras Civil Service (retired) and member of the Indian Law Commission.

1866, May 24. The Rajah Dinkur Rao, late member of the Council of the gov. gen of India for making laws and regulations.

1866, May 24. Maj. Gen. Isaac Campbell Coffin, Madras Army, late commanding the Hyderabad Subsidiary Force.

1866, May 24 The Rajah Redhakanth Deb.

1866, May 24. Maj. Gen. George St. Patrick Lawrence, Bengal Staff Corps, late agent to the gov. gen. of India at Rajpootana.

1866, May 24. The Rajah of Drangadra.

1866, May 24 Maj. Gen. George Moyle Sherer, late Bengal Army, sometime commanding the 73rd Regiment of Bengal Native Infantry.

1866, May 24. Rajah Deo Narain Singh, of Benares.

1866, May 24. Maj Gen. Sir Arthur Thomas Cotton, knt., Royal (late Madras) Engineers.

1866, May 24. Meer Shere Mahomed, of Meerpur.

1866, May 24. Maj Gen. Sir Neville Bowles Chamberlain, Bengal Army, late commanding the Punjab Irregular Force

.1866, May 24 The Rajah Sahib Dyal Missar, member of the Council of the gov. gen of India for making laws and regulations

1866, May 24. GEORGE UDNEY YULE, Bengal Civil Service, resident at Hyderabad.

1866, May 24. TANJORE MADAVA RAO, Dewan of Travancore.

1866, May 24. CHARLES JOHN WINGFIELD, Bengal Civil Service, late chief commissioner of Oude.

1866, May 24. The Thakoor RAWUL JESWUNT SINGJEE, of Bhownuggur.

1866, May 24. Col. Sir HERBERT BENJAMIN EDWARDES, Bengal Army, commissioner and agent to the gov. gen. of India in the Cis-Sutlej States.

1866, May 24 HAKEEM SAADUT ALI KHAN.

1866, May 24. Col. ARNOLD BURROWES KEMBALL, Royal (late Bombay) Artillery, political agent in Turkish Arabia.

1866, May 24. Sirdar NIHAL SING CHACHI.

1866, May 24. Lieut. Col. THOMAS WILKINSON, late Bengal Army, sometime resident in Nagpoor.

1866, May 24. Lieut. Col. ROBERT WALLACE, Bombay Staff Corps, late resident at Baroda.

1866, May 24. Lieut. Col. WILLIAM HENRY RODES GREEN, Bombay Staff Corps, political superintendent in Upper Scinde.

1866, May 24. Maj. GEORGE WINGATE, late Bombay Engineers, sometime member of the Survey Commission at Bombay.

1866, Sept. 17. H.H. DATU TUMMONGONG ABUBAKR SRI, Maharajah of Johore.

1867, Feb. 8. Col. HENRY MARION DURAND, Royal (late Bengal) Engineers, fifth ordinary member of the Council of the viceroy and gov. gen. of India.

1867, Feb. 8. WILLIAM MUIR, Bengal Civil Service, secretary to the Government of India in the Foreign Department.

1867, May 24. H.H. the Maharajah SREE JOWAN SINGJEE, chief of Edur.

1867, May 24. DANIEL ELLIOTT, Madras Civil Service (retired), late member of the Law Commission of the Legislative Council of India and of the Council of the governor of Madras.

1867, May 24. GEORGE FREDERICK HARVEY, Bengal Civil Service (retired), late commissioner of Agra.

1867, May 24. Maj. Gen. WILLIAM HILL, late Madras Army, commanding the Nizam's contingent during the mutinies of 1857-8.

1867, May 24. Maj. Gen. VINCENT EYRE, Royal (late Bengal) Artillery.

1867, May 24. The Rajah JODHBIR CHUND, of Nadown.

1867, May 24. HENRY LACON ANDERSON, Bombay Civil Service (retired), late chief secretary to the Government of Bombay and member of the Council of the gov. gen. of India for making laws and regulations.

1867, May 24. RICHARD TEMPLE, Bengal Civil Service, resident at Hyderabad, afterwards bart.

1867, May 24. Col. ARTHUR PURVES PHAYRE, Bengal Staff Corps, chief commissioner in British Burmah.

1867, Sept. 16 The Maharajah MAUN SING, of Oude.

1867, Sept. 16. Col EDWARD ROBERT WETHERALL, late chief of the staff of the Central India Field Force.

1867, Sept. 16 Col. WILLIAM WEST TURNER, late 97th Regiment, sometime brig. commanding the second column of the Bundlecund Field Force.

1867, Oct. 22. The Rt Hon. WILLIAM ROBERT SEYMOUR VESEY FITZGERALD, governor of the Presidency of Bombay.

1868, Aug. 24. Maj. Gen. EDWARD LECHMERE RUSSELL, Bombay Army, political resident at Aden.

1868, Aug. 24. Col. WILLIAM LOCKYER MEREWETHER, Bombay Staff Corps, chief commissioner in Sindh, and lately political resident at Aden. (Extra.)

1869, June 2. H.H. the Rajah of Cochin.

1869, June 2. Lieut. Gen. JOHN CAMPBELL, Madras Army.

1869, June 2. Maj. Gen. GEORGE LE GRAND JACOB, late Bombay Army.

1870, May 28. H.H. prince GHOLAM MAHOMED.

1870, May 28. WILLIAM GREY, Bengal Civil Service, lieut. gov. of Bengal.

1871, May 20. The Nawab MOHSIN-OOD-DOWLAH, bahadoor of Oude.

1871, May 20. H.H. MOHUBUT KHAN, Nawab of Joonaghur

1871, May 20. Maj. Gen. GEORGE INGLIS JAMESON, Bombay Army, late president of the Military Finance Commission for India, now auditor of the accounts of the Department of the secretary of State for India in Council.

1871, May 20. JOHN WILLIAM KAYE, formerly of the Bengal Artillery, now secretary in the political and secret department of the secretary of State for India in Council.

1871, May 20. HENRY SUMNER MAINE, late member of the Council of the gov. gen. of India.

1871, Nov. 3. Col. FREDERICK JOHN GOLDSMID, Madras Staff Corps, employed on a special mission to Persia with the local rank of maj. gen., and late superintendent of the Indo-European Telegraph.

1872, May 31. JOHN STRACHEY, Bengal Civil Service, member of the Council of the gov. gen. of India.

1872, May 31. JOHN CRACROFT WILSON, Bengal Civil Service (retired), late civil and sessions judge at Moradabad and special commissioner for the trial of rebels and mutineers in 1857–8.

1873, Feb. 6. Lieut. Col. FREDERICK RICHARD POLLOCK, Bengal Staff Corps, lately employed (with local rank of maj. gen.) on a special mission in Sistan, commissioner and superintendent Peshawar Division.

1873, May 23. NAWAB KHAN BAHADOOR KHWAJAH MUHAMMED KHAN KUTTUK, of Kohat.

1873, May 23. GEORGE CAMPBELL, Bengal Civil Service, lieut. gov. of Bengal.

1873, May 23. ALEXANDER JOHN ARBUTHNOT, Madras Civil Service, late member of the Council of the governor of Madras.

1873, May 23. Maj. Gen. HARRY BURNETT LUMSDEN, Bengal Staff Corps, late envoy to Candahar.

21

1874, May 30.   ROBERT HENRY DAVIES, Bengal Civil Service, lieut.
gov. of the Punjab.

1874, May 30.   Col. RICHARD JOHN MEADE, Bengal Staff Corps,
chief commissioner of Mysore and Coorg.

1874, May 30.   Col. LEWIS PELLY, Bombay Staff Corps, agent to the
gov. gen. for the States of Rajpootana and late political
resident in the Persian Gulf.

1874, July 27.   (Extra) THOMAS DOUGLAS FORSYTH, Bengal Civil
Service, commissioner of the Fyzabad Division, Oude, and
lately employed on a special mission to Kashgar.

1875, Oct. 5.   BARROW HELBERT ELLIS, Bombay Civil Service
(retired), member of the council of the secretary of state for
India, and lately one of the members of the council of the
viceroy and gov. gen. of India.

1875, Dec. 31.   WILLIAM ROSE ROBINSON, Madras Civil Service,
member of the council of the governor of Madras.

1875, Dec. 31.   RUDUR PERTAB SING MAHUNDUR BAHADOOR, Maha-
rajah of Punnah.

1875, Dec. 31.   SHAMSHIR PRAKASH BAHADOOR, Rajah of Nahun.

1875, Dec. 31.   RAS KASEE RAO HOLKAR, Dada Saheb, of Indore.

1875, Dec. 31.   Gen. RUNNODEEP SING, Rana Bahadoor of Nepal,
commander-in-chief of the Nepalese Army.

1875, Dec. 31.   RAO RAJAH GUNPUT RAO KIRKEE SHAMSHIR
BAHADOOR, Dewan of Gwalior.

1875, Dec. 31.   MUMTAZ-UD-DOWLAH NAWAB MAHUMMAD FAIZ ALI
KHAN BAHADOOR, prime minister of Kotah.

1875, Dec. 31.   Col. the Hon. HENRY RAMSAY, Bengal Staff Corps,
commissioner, Kumaon.

1876, Mar. 7.   Maj. Gen. SAMUEL JAMES BROWNE, V.C., Bengal Staff
Corps, president of the Stud Commission and on special
duty with the prince of Wales.   (Extra.)

1876, Mar. 7.   Maj. Gen. DIGHTON MACNAGHTEN PROBYN, V.C.,
Bengal Cavalry, equerry to H.R.H. the prince of Wales.
(Extra.)

1876, Mar. 7. Surg. Gen. JOSEPH FAYRER, M.D., hon. physician to the queen and physician to H.R.H. the prince of Wales. (Extra.)

1877, Jan. 1. H.H. SHIVAJI CHATRAPATI, Raja of Kolhapore, on the occasion of the proclamation at Delhi of queen Victoria as empress of India.

1877, Jan. 1. JAMES FITZJAMES STEPHEN, Q.C., late member of the Council of the gov. gen. of India (same occasion).

1877, Jan. 1. H.H. raja ANAND RAO PUAR, of Dhar (same occasion).

1877, Jan. 1. ARTHUR HOBHOUSE, Q.C., second ordinary member of the Council of the gov. gen. of India. Afterwards lord Hobhouse (same occasion).

1877, Jan. 1. H.H. MAN SINGJEE RAJ SAHIB of Drangdra (same occasion).

1877, Jan. 1. EDWARD CLIVE BAYLEY, Bengal Civil Service, third ordinary member of the Council of the gov. gen. of India (same occasion).

1877, Jan. 1. H.H. the JAM SHRI VIBHAJEE, of Naunagar (same occasion).

1877, Jan. 1. Sir GEORGE EBENEZER WILSON COUPER, bart., Bengal Civil Service, lieut. gov. of the North-Western Provinces (same occasion).

1877, Jan. 1. R. Adm. REGINALD JOHN MACDONALD, commander-in-chief of H.M. Naval Forces in the East Indies (same occasion).

1877, June 2. JOSEPH DALTON HOOKER, M.D., director of the Royal Botanical Gardens at Kew.

1877, June 2. THOMAS LAWRENCE SECCOMBE, financial secretary to the Secretary of State for India in Council.

1878, Jan. 1. Maj. Gen. MICHAEL KAVANAGH KENNEDY, Royal (late Bombay) Engineers, additional member of the Council of the governor of Bombay for making laws and regulations, secretary to the Government of Bombay in the Public Works and Railway Departments, and lately employed on a special mission as a personal assistant to the governor of Madras.

1878, May 25. Hon. ASHLEY EDEN, lieut. gov. of Bengal.

1878, May 25. STEUART COLVIN BAYLEY, Bengal Civil Service, secretary to the Government of Bengal in the Judicial and Political Departments.

1879, July 29. ROBERT EYLES EGERTON, Bengal Civil Service, lieut. gov. of the Punjab.

1879, July 29. Lieut. Col. OWEN TUDOR BURNE, secretary in the Political and Secret Department of the India Office.

1879, July 29. Col. GEORGE POMEROY COLLEY, 2nd Regiment, private secretary to the viceroy and gov. gen. of India.

1879, July 29. Maj. ROBERT GROVES SANDEMAN, Bengal Staff Corps, agent to the viceroy and gov. gen. of India in Beluchistan.

1879, July 29. The nawab GHOLAM HUSSAN KHAN ALAZAI KHAN BAHADOOR.

1880, Feb. 18. (Extra) The Maharaja KIRTEE SING, of Muneepore.

1880, Dec. 9. Sirdar DEWA SINGH, prime minister of His Highness the Maharaja of Patiala.

1881, May 24. Gen. ORFEUR CAVENAGH, Bengal Staff Corps.

1881, May 24. CHARLES UMPHERSTON AITCHISON, Bengal Civil Service, chief commissioner British Burmah.

1881, May 24. His Highness TUKHT. SINGH, Thakur Saheb of Bhaunagur.

1881, May 24. JAMES DAVIDSON GORDON, Bengal Civil Service, Resident at Mysore.

1881, May 24. JOHN FORSYTH, insp. gen. of hospitals (retired), Bengal Medical Service.

1881, May 24. LEPEL HENRY GRIFFIN, Bengal Civil Service, agent to the gov. gen. in Central India.

1881, Oct. 29. MONESHUR BUX SINGH Maharajah of Domraon.

1882, May 23. The Maharajah JOTENDRO MOHUN TAGORE.

1882, May 23. Lieut. Col. OLIVER BEAUCHAMP COVENTRY ST. JOHN, royal (late Bengal) engineers, late Resident at Kandahar.

1882, Nov. 17. R. Adm. Sir WILLIAM NATHAN WRIGHTE HEWETT.

1882, Nov. 17. (Extra) Maj. Gen. Sir HERBERT TAYLOR MACPHERSON.

1883, May 24. JOHN HENRY MORRIS, Bengal Civil Service, late chief commissioner Central Provinces.

1883, Aug. 4. (Extra) Maj. EVELYN BARING, member of the Council of the gov. gen. of India, afterwards 1st earl of Cromer.

1885, Jan. 1. AUGUSTUS RIVERS THOMPSON, Bengal Civil Service, lieut. gov. of Bengal.

1885, Jan. 1. CHARLES GRANT, Bengal Civil Service, Secretary to the Government of India in the Foreign Department.

1885, June 6. Col. EDWARD RIDLEY COLBORNE BRADFORD, Madras Staff Corps, agent to the gov. gen., Rajpootana, and chief commissioner, Ajmere. Afterwards baronet.

1885, July 20. JOSEPH WEST RIDGEWAY, Bengal Infantry, under-secretary to the Government of India in the Foreign Department, and now in charge of the Afghan Boundary Commission.

1886, Jan. 1. Maharaj PERTAB SINGH.

1886, Feb. 8. JULAND DANVERS, secretary to the Public Works Department of the India Office.

1886, May 29. THEODORE CRACRAFT HOPE, Bombay Civil Service, member of the Council of the gov. gen. of India.

1886, May 29. CHARLES EDWARD BERNARD, Bengal Civil Service, chief commissioner of Burmah.

1886, May 29. Nawab KHWAJA ABDUL GHANI MEEAH, of Dacca.

1886, May 29. WILLIAM CHICHELE PLOWDEN, Bengal Civil Service (retired), late census commissioner for India.

1887, Feb. 15. CHARLES ALFRED ELLIOTT, Bengal Civil Service, chief commissioner of Assam.

1887, Feb. 15. WILLIAM WILSON HUNTER, Bengal Civil Service, direc. gen. of Statistics.

1887, Feb. 15. His Highness Maharaja SRI KESHRI SINGHJI of Idar.

1887, Feb. 15   Col. WILLIAM GEORGE DAVIES, Bengal Staff Corps, financial commissioner, Punjab.

1887, Feb. 15.   Col. JAMES JOHNSTONE, Bengal Infantry, late political agent at Manipur.

1888, Jan. 2.   JAMES BRAITHWAITE PEILE, Bombay Civil Service, member of the Council of India.

1888, Jan. 2.   MOULVIE SAIYID AHMAD KHAN BAHADUR, member of the Legislative Council of the lieut. gov. of the North-Western Provinces.

1888, Jan. 2.   Col. JAMES BROWNE, R.E., Public Works Department of the Government of India.

1888, May 24.   JAMES BROADWOOD LYALL, Bengal Civil Service, lieut. gov. of the Punjab.

1888, May 24.   CHARLES HAUKES TOD CROSTHWAITE, Bengal Civil Service, chief commissioner Burma.

1889, Jan. 1.   DAVID MILLER BARBOUR, Bengal Civil Service, ordinary member of the Council of the gov. gen. of India.

1889, Jan. 1.   NAWAB MUHAMAD AKRAM KHAN, chief of Amb.

1889, May 25.   Col. HENRY YULE, royal (late Bengal) engineers, member of the Council of the Secretary of State for India.

1890, May 21.   ANDREW RICHARD SCOBLE, ordinary member of the Council of the gov. gen. of India.

1890, May 21.   DENNIS FITZPATRICK, Bengal Civil Service, resident at Hyderabad.

1891, Jan. 1.   ALEXANDER MACKENZIE, Bengal Civil Service, chief commissioner of Burma.

1891, May 30.   PHILIP PERCEVAL HUTCHINS, Madras Civil Service, member of the Council of the gov. gen. of India.

1891, Oct. 31.   RAJA AMAR SINGH, president of the Council, Kashmir

1892, May 25.   Sir AUCKLAND COLVIN, Bengal Civil Service, lieut. gov. of the North-Western Provinces and chief commissioner of Oudh.

1892, May 25. HENRY EDWARD STOKES, Madras Civil Service, member of the Council of the governor of Madras.

1892, May 25. His Excellency Maharaja BIR SHAMSHER JUNG RANA Bahadur, prime minister of Nepal.

1892, May 25. Maharaja MANA VIKRAMA Bahadur Zamorin of Calicut.

1893, Jan. 2. ANTHONY PATRICK MACDONNELL, Indian Civil Service, chief commissioner of the Central Provinces.

1893, Jan. 2. KUMARAPURAM SHESHADRI AIYAR, Dewan of Mysore.

1893, July 3. HENRY WATERFIELD, financial secretary to the secretary of State for India in Council.

1894, Jan. 1. Sir HENRY MORTIMER DURAND, secretary to the Government of India in the Foreign Department.

1894, May 26. Maj. Gen. OLIVER RICHARDSON NEWMARCH, military secretary at the India Office.

1895, Jan. 1. JAMES WESTLAND, member of the Council of the gov. gen. of India.

1895, Jan. 1. FREDERICK WILLIAM RICHARDS FRYER, officiating financial commissioner, Punjab.

1895, Jan. 1. His Highness MAHARAO KAISHRI SINGH, of Sirohi.

1895, Jan. 1. COURTENAY PEREGRINE ILBERT.

1895, May 25. Lieut. Gen. Sir WILLIAM STEPHEN ALEXANDER LOCKHART.

1895, July 15. Surg. Maj. GEORGE SCOTT ROBERTSON, Indian Medical Service, British agent, Gilgit.

1896, Jan. 1. Lieut. Gen. Sir HENRY BRACKENBURY, R.A., member of the Council of the gov. gen. of India.

1896, Jan. 1. MANSINGHJI SARSINGHJI THAKORE Saheb of Palitana.

1896, May 20. WILLIAM ERSKINE WARD, chief commissioner of Assam.

1896, May 20. Brigade Surgeon Lieut. Col. ALFRED SWAINE LETH-BRIDGE, M.D.

1897, Jan. 1. JOHN WOODBURN, member of the Council of the gov. gen. of India.

1897, Jan. 1. His Highness MAHARAO RAO RANGHUBIR SINGH BAHADUR, Raja of Bundi.

1897, Jan. 1. Sir EDWARD CHARLES BUCK, secretary to the Government of India in the Department of Revenue and Agriculture.

1897, June 22. WILLIAM MACKWORTH YOUNG, lieut. gov. of the Punjab.

1897, June 22. His Highness SRI RAJA RAMA VARMA of Cochin.

1897, June 22. CHARLES JAMES LYALL, chief commissioner of the Central Provinces.

1897, June 22. ROBERT JOSEPH CROSTHWAITE, agent to the gov. gen. in Rajputana.

1897, June 22. WILLIAM JOHN CUNINGHAM, secretary to the Government of India in the Foreign Department.

1897, June 22. Maj. Gen. MONTAGU GILBERT GERARD, Indian Staff Corps.

1897, June 22. His Highness RAJA JAGATJIT SINGH Bahadur, of Kapurthala.

1897, June 22. RICHARD UDNY, Indian Civil Service.

1897, June 22. Col. HOWARD MELLISS, insp. gen. of Imperial Service Troops.

1898, Jan. 1. His Highness Maharaja LOKINDRA BHAWANI SINGH, Bahadur of Datia.

1898, Jan. 1. ARTHUR CHARLES TREVOR, Indian Civil Service.

1898, Jan. 1. JOHN FREDERICK PRICE, Indian Civil Service.

1898, May 21. WILLIAM LEE-WARNER, political secretary, India Office.

1898, May 21. TREVOR JOHN CHICHELE CHICELE-PLOWDEN, Indian Civil Service.

1898, Dec. 31. His Highness RASUL KHANJI MAHABBAT KHANJI, Nawab of Junagarh.

1898, Dec. 31. CHARLES CECIL STEVENS, Indian Civil Service.

1900, May 23. His Highness MAHARAO UMAID SINGH Bahadur, of Kotah.

1901, Jan. 1. CHARLES MONTGOMERY RIVAZ, ordinary member of the Council of the gov. gen. of India.

1901, Nov. 9. JAMES JOHN DIGGES LA TOUCHE, Indian Civil Service.

1901, Nov. 9. His Highness RAJA SURINDAR BIKRAM PRAKASH BAHADUR, of Sirmur.

1901, Nov. 9. Sultan AHMAD BIN FADTHL, of Lahej.

1902, June 26. Lieut. Col. DAVID WILLIAM KEITH BARR, Indian Staff Corps.

1902, June 26. HENRY JOHN STEDMAN COTTON, Indian Civil Service.

1902, June 26. AMARAVATI SESHAYYA SASTRI.

1903, Jan. 1. DENZIL CHARLES JELF IBBETSON, Indian Civil Service, member of the Council of the gov. gen. of India (on the occasion of the Durbar).

1903, Jan. 1. R. Adm. CHARLES CARTER DRURY, commander-in-chief of His Majesty's Naval Forces in the East Indies (same occasion).

1903, Jan. 1. HENRY MARTIN WINTERBOTHAM, Indian Civil Service, member of the Council of the governor of Fort St. George (same occasion).

1903, Jan. 1. JAMES MONTEATH, Indian Civil Service, member of the Council of the governor of Bombay (same occasion).

1903, Jan. 1. Lieut. Col. DONALD ROBERTSON, Indian Staff Corps, resident in Mysore and chief commissioner of Coorg (same occasion).

1903, Jan. 1. ANDREW HENDERSON LEITH FRASER, Indian Civil Service, chief commissioner of the Central Provinces (same occasion).

1903, Jan. 1. HUGH SHAKESPEAR BARNES, Indian Civil Service, secretary to the Government of India, in the Foreign Department (same occasion).

1903, Jan. 1. Surg. Gen. WILLIAM ROE HOOPER, Indian Medical Service (retired), president of the Medical Board at the India office (same occasion).

1903, Jan. 1. Col. Sir COLIN CAMPBELL SCOTT MONCRIEFF, Royal Engineers (retired) president of the Indian Irrigation Commission (same occasion).

1903, Jan. 1. His Highness RAJA KIRTI SAH, of Tehri, Garhwal, (same occasion).

1903, Jan. 1. KUNWAR RANBIR SINGH, of Patiala (same occasion).

1904, Jan. 1. ARUNDEL TAGG ARUNDEL, Esq., Indian Civil Service, an ordinary member of the Council of the gov. gen.

1904, Jan. 1. JAMES AUSTIN BOURDILLON, Esq., Indian Civil Service, resident in Mysore and chief commissioner of Coorg, lately acting lieut. gov. of Bengal.

1904, Mar. 18. THOMAS RALEIGH, a member of the Council of the go. gen. of India.

1904, June 24. Maj. His Highness Maharaja RAJ RAJESHWAR SHIROMANI SRI SIR GANGA SINGH BAHADUR, of Bikaner.

1904, June 24. H.H. THAKUR SAHIB BHAVSINGHJI TAKHTSINGHJI, of Bhaunagar.

1904, June 24. ARTHUR HENRY TEMPLE MARTINDALE, Indian Civil Service, agent to the gov. gen., Rajputana.

1904, Sept. 2. JAMES THOMSON, a member of the Council of the gov. of Madras and acting gov. of Madras.

The Most Distinguished Order of
St. Michael and St. George.

The Most Distinguished
Order of St. Michael and St. George.

Grands Masters and Principal Knights Grand Cross.

*1818. Lieut. Gen. the Rt. Hon. Sir THOMAS MAITLAND, Grand Master, Apr. 27, governor of Malta and high commissioner in the Ionian Islands. Died 1824, Jan. 17.

1825. F. Marsh. H.R.H. ADOLPHUS FREDERICK, duke of Cambridge, Grand Master 1825, June 20. Declared 1st and principal G.C.M.G. 1832, Aug. 16. Died 1850, July 8.

1851, [Dec. 31]. GEORGE WILLIAM FREDERICK CHARLES, duke of Cambridge, appointed 1st or principal G.C.M.G., re-appointed Grand Master and 1st or principal G.C.M.G. 1869, May 23, and 1877, May 30. Died 1904.

Knights Grand Cross (G.C.M.G.).

*1818, Apr. 27. Lieut. Gen. Sir THOMAS MAITLAND, Apr. 27, Grand Master. Invested at Corfu Nov. 17.

1818, Nov. 18. EMANUEL, baron THEOTOKY, president of the Ionian Senate. Invested at Corfu.

1818, Nov. 18. STAMO CALICHIOPULO, of Corfu, a senator of the Ionian Islands. Invested ut supra.

1818, Nov. 18. ANTONIO, count COMUTO, of Zante.

1818, Dec. 16. V. Adm. Sir CHARLES VINICOMBE PENROSE, naval commander-in-chief in the Mediterranean. Invested at Malta.

1818, Dec. 16. GIUSEPPE BORG OLIVIER, sometime president of the Court of Appeal at Malta. Invested ut supra.

* Throughout the following lists of the order of St. Michael and St. George the dates in the margin are (unless otherwise specifically stated) the dates of the warrant of appointment. Very frequently these dates will be found to differ greatly from the date of gazetting.

1818, Dec. 16. Doctor RAFFAELE CRISPINO XERRI. Invested *ut supra*, member of the Supreme Council of Justice for the Island of Malta and its Dependencies.

1819, Oct. 26. V. Adm. Sir THOMAS FRANCIS FREMANTLE, sometime naval commander-in-chief in the Mediterranean.

1819, Oct. 26. FREDERICK (NORTH), 7th earl of Guilford, sometime chancellor of the University of the Ionian Islands.

1820, Sept. 28. Adm. Sir GRAHAM MOORE, commander-in-chief in the Mediterranean. Resigned 1823, re-invested 1832, Aug. 24.

1821, Dec. 27. Sir FREDERICK ADAM, serving on the staff of the troops in the Ionian Islands. Invested 1822, Jan. 15.

1823, Mar. 1. Count NICOLO ANINO, sometime a senator in the Ionian Islands.

1824, Jan. 16. Adm. Sir HARRY BURRARD NEALE, bart., naval commander-in-chief in the Mediterranean, resigned 1826, re-invested 1832, Aug. 24.

1825, June 20. F. Marsh. prince ADOLPHUS FREDERICK, duke of Cambridge Grand Master, etc.).

1825, July 30. MARINO VEJA, of Cephalonia, sometime president of the Ionian Senate. Invested at Corfu Oct. 15.

1827, Apr. 23. Adm. Sir EDWARD CODRINGTON, sometime naval commander-in-chief in the Mediterranean. Resigned the order in 1828, re-invested 1832, Aug. 24.

1828, Nov. 5. Maj Gen. the Hon. Sir FREDERICK CAVENDISH PONSONBY, lieut gov. of Malta. Invested at Malta.

1829, Jan. 21 Adm. Sir PULTENEY MALCOLM, naval commander-in-chief in the Mediterranean. Invested at Malta. Resigned the Order in 1831. Re-appointed 1832, Aug. 16, and invested Oct. 12.

1831, July 4. V. Adm. the Hon. Sir HENRY HOTHAM, naval commander-in-chief in the Mediterranean. Invested at Malta.

1832, May 28. GUISEPPE CALCÉDONIO DEDONO, member of the Supreme Council of Justice at Malta. Invested at Malta.

1832, June 6. GIOVANNI CAPPADOCA, sometime a member of the supreme Council of Justice of the Ionian Islands.

1832, June 6. ANGIOLO CONDARI, of Santa Maura, a senator of the Ionian Islands. Invested at Corfu.

1832, June 22. Sir JAMES MACDONALD, bart., high commissioner for the Ionian Islands. Died before investiture.

1832, June 30. Lieut. Gen. Sir ALEXANDER WOODFORD, commander of the Forces in the Ionian Islands. Invested at Corfu.

1832, Aug. 12. GEORGE (NUGENT-TEMPLE-GRENVILLE), lord Nugent son of George, 3rd earl Temple and 1st marquess of Buckingham), high commissioner in the Ionian Islands. Invested Aug. 24.

1833, May 4. Col.* FREDERICK HANKEY, chief secretary to the governor of Malta. Invested at Malta, May 28

1833, June 26. R Adm. THOMAS BRIGGS, superintendent of the dockyard at Malta. Invested at Malta, July 24.

1833, July 17. SPIRIDION VITTOR, count Bulgari, president of the Ionian Senate. Invested at Corfu, Nov. 30.

1834, Feb. 22. Adm. Sir JOSIAS ROWLEY, bart., commander-in-chief in the Mediterranean. Invested at Malta, Apr. 4.

1835, Mar. 18. Lieut. Gen. Sir HOWARD DOUGLAS, bart., high commissioner in the Ionian Islands.

1836, Apr. 2. PAOLO, count Parisio, one of the lords lieut. of Malta. Invested at Malta, July 13

1836, Sept. 28. Lieut. Gen. Sir HENRY FREDERICK BOUVERIE, governor of Malta.

1837, May 10. Gen. HENRY PIGOT.

1837, May 10. Gen. THOMAS (GRAHAM), lord Lynedoch.

1837, May 10. Adm. the Hon. ROBERT STOPFORD, commander-in-chief in the Mediterranean.

1837, May 10. Gen. Sir MARTIN HUNTER. Investiture dispensed
with by warrant, 1838, May 1.

1837, May 10. Gen. Sir WILLIAM WILKINSON. Investiture *ut supra*.

1837, May 10. Lieut. Gen. Sir CHARLES BULKELEY EGERTON.

1837, May 10. Gen. Sir JOHN OSWALD.

1837, May 10. Lieut Gen. Sir HUDSON LOWE.

1837, May 10. V. Adm. Sir RICHARD HUSSEY HUSSEY. Invested
May 17.

1837, May 17. Adm. Sir GEORGE MARTIN.

1837, May 17. Maj. Gen. Sir PATRICK ROSS.

1838, Apr. 26. PIETRO PETRIZZOPULO, of Santa Maura, president
of the Ionian Senate. Invested at Corfu July 5.

1838, May 2. V. Adm. Sir GEORGE EYRE.

1839, Aug. 30. Sir VITTOR CARIDI, of Cephalonia. Invested at
Corfu Nov. 18.

1840, July 7. Sir FRANCISCO MUZZAN, of Zante. Invested Sept. 29.

1840, July 7. Sir PIETRO COIDAN, of Cephalonia. Invested at
Cephalonia Sept. 24.

1840, Oct. 6. Sir NICHOLAS HARRIS NICOLAS, chancellor and
Senior Knight Commander of the Order.

1842, Jan. 15. Prince FRANCIS ALBERT AUGUSTUS CHARLES
EMANUEL, prince of Saxe-Coburg and Gotha, consort of
queen Victoria.

1842, Jan. 21. Demetrio count DELLA DECIMA, of Cephalonia.

1842, Mar. 18. Sir AGOSTINO RANDON.

1843, July 3. Lieut. Gen. JOHN (COLBORNE), 1st lord Seaton, com-
manding the forces in the United States of the Ionian
Islands, and Her Majesty's lord high commissioner in and
for said States.

1843, July 3. Lieut. Gen. the Hon. PATRICK STUART, governor of
Malta.

1844, Dec. 16. Antonio count THEOTOKY.

1845, June 26. Prince GEORGE FREDERICK WILLIAM CHARLES,
duke of Cambridge.

1847, Mar. 31. His Highness Dr. SPIRIDIONE FOCCA STEFANO, president of the Senate of the Ionian Islands.

1849, June 25. HENRY GEORGE WARD, high commissioner for the Ionian Islands.

1850, Sept. 7. Demetrio count SALOMON, president of the Senate of the Ionian Islands.

1852, Nov. 23. Candiano count ROMA, president of the Senate of the Ionian Islands.

1852, Nov. 23. Demetrio count CARUSO, regent of Cephalonia.

1853, June 27. VINCENZO CASOLANI, collector of the land revenue of Malta.

1855, Mar. 31. ALESSANDRO DAMASCHINO.

1855, May 16. Sir JOHN YOUNG, bart., afterwards 1st lord Lisgar, on appointment as lord high commissioner of the Ionian Islands.

1856, Jan. 11. Col. Sir WILLIAM REID, governor of Malta.

1856, Jan. 28. Sir IGNATIUS GAVIN BONAVITA.

1856, Jan. 28. GUISEPPE MARIA, barone de Piro.

1857, July 9. Sir DEMETRIO, count Valsamachi.

1857, July 9. Dionisio count FLAMBURIARI, for long official services to the Ionian Government.

1858, May 15. EDMUND (LYONS), 1st lord Lyons, commander-in-chief in the Mediterranean.

1859, Feb. 15. Col. Sir HENRY KNIGHT STORKS, on appointment as lord high commissioner of the Ionian Islands.

1860, Apr. 16. Maj. Gen. Sir JOHN GASPARD LE MARCHANT, on appointment as governor of Malta.

1860, Apr. 16. GEORGE FERGUSON BOWEN, on appointment as first governor of Queensland.

1860, Apr. 16. Sir PAOLO DINGLI, late president of the Court of Appeal in Malta.

1864, May 21. Sir PIETRO ARMENI BRAILA, secretary of the Senate on the transfer of the Ionian Islands to the Kingdom of Greece.

1867, Mar. 2. Sir GEORGIO MARCORAN, LL.D., for services as judge
of the Supreme Court of the Ionian Islands, up to the
cession of those Islands to the Kingdom of Greece in 1864.

1868, Apr. 24. Sir ADRIANO DINGLI, for long services as Crown Law
Officer in Malta, Crown advocate of Malta from July, 1854.

1868, Apr. 24. Sir EDWARD VICTOR LOUIS HOULTON, for services
as chief secretary to the Government of Malta, chief secre-
tary to the Government of Malta.

1868, Apr. 23. Lieut. Gen. Sir PATRICK GRANT, on appointment as
governor of Malta.

1869, Feb. 13. The Rt. Hon. CHARLES STANLEY (MONCK), 4th
viscount Monck. late gov. gen. of the Dominion of Canada
and capt. gen. and governor-in-chief of the Island of Prince
Edward.

1869, Mar. 25. The Rt. Hon. EDWARD GEOFFREY (SMITH-STANLEY),
23rd earl of Derby, sometime secretary of State having the
Department of War and Colonies.

1869, Mar. 25. The Rt. Hon. HENRY GEORGE (GREY), 3rd earl
Grey, sometime secretary of State, having the Department
of War and Colonies.

1869, Mar. 25. The Rt. Hon. JOHN RUSSELL, 1st earl Russel, some-
time secretary of State, having the Department of War and
Colonies.

1869, June 29. H.R.H. ALFRED ERNEST ALBERT, duke of Edinburgh,
captain in the Fleet.

1869, Nov. 24. The Rt. Hon. EDWARD GEORGE EARLE LYTTON
(BULWER-LYTTON), 1st lord Lytton, formerly secretary of
State for the Colonies.

1870, Apr. 16. H.R.H. prince ARTHUR WILLIAM PATRICK ALBERT,
afterwards duke of Connaught and Strathearn.

1873, June 23. The Rt. Hon. JOHN HENRY THOMAS (MANNERS
SUTTON), 3rd viscount Canterbury, late governor and
commander-in-chief of the Colony of Victoria, on his
retirement from that Government.

1874, Feb. 20. Sir HENRY BARKLY, governor and commander-in-chief of the Colony of the Cape of Good Hope, governor and commander-in-chief of the Province of Griqua Land West, and Her Majesty's high commissioner for the settling and adjustment of the affairs of the territories adjacent to or contiguous to the Eastern Frontier of the Cape of Good Hope.

1874, Feb. 20. Sir JOHN PETER GRANT, late capt. gen. and governor-in-chief of the Island of Jamaica with the territories depending thereon.

1874, Mar. 31. Maj. Gen. Sir GARNET JOSEPH WOLSELEY, afterwards viscount Wolseley, for distinguished services in command of the expedition against the Ashantees.

1874, Apr. 23. JOHN HAWLEY GLOVER, sometime commander in H.M. Navy, and lately H.M. special commissioner to the friendly native chiefs in the eastern district of the protected territories near to H.M. settlements on the Gold Coast.

1875, Jan. 21. Sir HERCULES GEORGE ROBERT ROBINSON, now governor and commander-in-chief of the Colony of New South Wales and its dependencies. For special services in connection with the cession of the Fiji Islands.

1876, Mar. 20. (Honorary) H.H. Sir DATU TUMMONGONG ABUBAKR SRI, Maharajah of Johore, K.C.S.I., for various services to the Government of the Straits Settlements, especially during the disturbances in the Malay Peninsula, in 1875–76.

1876, May 11. The Rt. Hon. FREDERICK TEMPLE, earl of Dufferin, etc., afterwards marquess of Dufferin and Ava, gov. gen. of the Dominion of Canada.

1877, May 30. F. Marsh. H.R.H. GEORGE WILLIAM FREDERICK CHARLES, duke of Cambridge, to be Grand Master and first or principal knight Grand Cross.

1877, May 31. (Extra) F. Marsh. H.R.H. ALBERT EDWARD, prince of Wales.

1877, May 31. The Most Hon. GEORGE AUGUSTUS CONSTANTINE (PHIPPS), 4th marquess of Normanby, governor of the Colony of New Zealand.

1877, Dec. 12. Lieut. Gen. Sir ARTHUR PURVES PHAYRE, governor and commander-in-chief of the Island of Mauritius and its dependencies.

1878, Feb 6. Hon. Sir ARTHUR HAMILTON-GORDON, governor of Fiji and high commissioner for the Western Pacific, 1877 to 1883.

1878, May 25. Maj. Gen. Sir WILLIAM FRANCIS DRUMMOND JERVOIS, R.E., governor of the Colony of South Australia.

1878, May 25. Sir ALEXANDER TILLOCH GALT, member of the Halifax Fisheries Commission.

1878, Aug. 7. Sir HENRY DRUMMOND WOLFF, Her Majesty's commissioner on the European Commission for the organisation of Eastern Roumelia under the 18th article of the Treaty of Berlin.

1878, Aug. 3. SOMDITCH PRA PARAMINDR MAHA CHULULONKORN, king of Siam (Honorary), for services to the Government of the Straits Settlements, more particularly during the late disturbances in the Malay States in 1875–76. Invested at Bangkok, 1878, Nov. 22, by Sir William Cleaver Francis Robinson, governor of the Straits Settlements.

1878, Sept. 14. The Rt Hon. Sir JOHN DOUGLAS SUTHERLAND CAMPBELL, marquess of Lorne, afterwards 9th duke of Argyll, gov. gen. of Canada.

1878, Oct 30. Sir JOHN ROSE, bart , executive commissioner for the Dominion of Canada, and member of the Finance Committee, for services rendered to the Colonies as colonial commissioner and otherwise, in connection with the representation of British Colonial products at the Paris Universal Exhibition of 1878.

1879, May 24. RICHARD BICKERTON PEMELL (LYONS), 2nd lord afterwards 1st viscount Lyons, ambassador extraordinary and plenipotentiary to the French Republic.

1879, May 24. The Rt. Hon. Sir ODO WILLIAM LEOPOLD RUSSELL, C C., styled lord Odo Russell, afterwards lord Ampthill, ambassador extraordinary and plenipotentiary to the German Emperor.

1879, May 24 Sir ANTONIO MICALLEF, president of the Court of Appeal in the Island of Malta

1879, Sept. 10 Sir CHARLES LENNOX WYKE, envoy extraordinary and minister plenipotentiary to the king of Denmark.

1879, Sept. 10. Sir RICHARD WOOD, for services in connexion with the Maltese imigrants, introduced into Tunis, and to colonists in his capacity as Her Majesty's agent and consul gen. in the Regency of Tunis since 1855

1879, Oct. 9. (Honorary) His Excellency NUBAR PASHA, late president of the Council of Ministers, and minister for Foreign Affairs in Egypt.

1880, May 12. (Extra member) H.R.H. prince LEOPOLD GEORGE DUNCAN ALBERT, duke of Saxony, prince of Saxe-Coburg and Gotha, afterwards duke of Albany.

1880, May 29. Gen Sir ARTHUR BORTON, governor of the Island of Malta.

1881, May 24. Sir ARTHUR EDWARD KENNEDY, governor and commander-in-chief of the Colony of Queensland.

1881, May 24. Maj. Gen. Sir HARRY ST. GEORGE ORD, R.E, formerly governor of Western Australia.

1881, July 28 (Honorary) His Majesty king KALAKANA, of the Hawaiian Islands.

1881, Nov. 30 Sir HARRY SMITH PARKES, envoy extraordinary and minister plenipotentiary in Japan.

1882, Feb. 20. Maj. Gen. Sir HENRY EVELYN WOOD, V.C , lately in command of the Forces in Natal and Transvaal and one of the commissioners for the Settlement of the Transvaal Territory.

1882, Mar. 30 (Honorary) His Honour JOHN HENRY BRAND, president of the Orange Free State

1883, May 24. Rt. Hon. FREDERICK (ROGERS), loid Blachford, P.C , formerly under secretary of state for the Colonies.

1883, May 24. Sir HENRY ERNEST GASCOIGNE BULWER, governor of the Colony of Natal, and special commissioner for Zulu Affairs, 1882.

1883, May 24. Sir JAMES ROBERT LONGDEN, governor of Ceylon.

1883, July 4. (Honorary) His Highness SEYYID BARGHASH-BIN-SAID, sultan of Zanzibar. Invested at Zanzibar Sept 14, by Sir John Kirk.

1884, Jan. 28. The Most Hon. HENRY CHARLES KEITH (PETTY-FITZMAURICE), 5th gov. gen. of the Dominion of Canada.

1884, May 24. Sir ROBERT RICHARD TORRENS.

1884, May 24. Sir ALFRED STEPHEN, formerly chief justice of New South Wales, now lieut gov. of that Colony.

1884, Dec. 3 Sir JOHN HAY DRUMMOND-HAY, envoy extraordinary and minister plenipotentiary to the emperor of Morocco.

1885, June 6 Rt. Hon. CHARLES ROBERT (CARRINGTON),3rd lord Carrington), on appointment to be governor of the Colony of New South Wales.

1885, June 6. Sir ANDREW CLARKE, maj. gen. R.E., inspec. gen. of Fortifications and director of Works.

1885, June 6. Sir ANTHONY MUSGRAVE, governor of the Colony of Queensland.

1885, June 6. Sir FREDERICK ALOYSIUS WELD, governor of the Straits Settlements.

1885, June 26. Sir EDWARD BALDWIN MALET, ambassador extraordinary and plenipotentiary at Berlin.

1885, Aug. 25. Lieut. gen. Sir GERALD GRAHAM, R.E., V.C.

1885, Oct. 14 Maj. Gen. Sir CHARLES WARREN, R.E , special commissioner for Bechuanaland.

1885, Dec 1. Sir JULIAN PAUNCEFOTE, under secretary for Foreign Affairs.

1886, Feb. 18 Sir WILLIAM ARTHUR WHITE, envoy extraordinary and minister plenipotentiary to the sultan of Turkey.

1886, Feb 18 Rt. Hon. Sir HENRY THURSTAN HOLLAND, bart., M.P., afterwards lord Knutsford (a commissioner for the Colonial and Indian Exhibition of 1886, and member of the Finance Committee).

1886, Feb. 18. Sir CHARLES TUPPER, high commissioner in London for the Dominion of Canada.

1886, Feb. 18. Sir JOHN KIRK, agent and consul gen. at Zanzibar.

1886, Feb 20. Rt. Hon. Sir ROBERT BURNETT DAVID MORIER, ambassador extraordinary and plenipotentiary to the emperor of Russia.

1886, May 29. Maj. Gen. Sir ROBERT BIDDULPH, R A , late Her Majesty's high commissioner and commander-in-chief of the Island of Cyprus.

1886, May 29. Sir FRANCIS CLARE FORD, envoy extraordinary and minister plenipotentiary at Madrid.

1887, Jan 29. Sir GEORGE CUMINE STRAHAN, governor of the Colony of Tasmania.

1887, May 24. Gen. Sir JOHN LINTORN ARABIN SIMMONS, governor of the Island of Malta.

1887, May 24. Gen. Sir HENRY WYLIE NORMAN, capt. gen. and governor-in-chief of the Island of Jamaica.

1887, May 24. Sir HENRY BROUGHAM LOCH, governor of the Colony of Victoria, afterwards lord Loch.

1887, May 24. Sir WILLIAM CLEAVER FRANCIS ROBINSON, governor of the Colony of South Australia.

1887, June 21. Sir EDWARD WILLIAM STAFFORD, formerly for many years prime minister of New Zealand.

1887, June 21. Sir THOMAS ELDER, knt , for many years a member of the Legislative Council of South Australia.

1888, Jan. 10. Sir RONALD FERGUSON THOMSON, late envoy extraordinary and minister plenipotentiary at Teheran.

1888, Jan. 28. Sir HENRY PARKES, premier and colonial secretary of the Colony of New South Wales.

1888, Jan. 28. Sir HENRY TURNER IRVING, on retirement from the Government of British Guiana.

1888, May 24. Sir DANIEL COOPER, bart.

1888, June 2. Sir EVELYN BARING, C I.E., Her Majesty's agent and consul gen. at Cairo, afterwards viscount Cromer.

1888, June 2. CHARLES JOHNSON BROOKE, rajah of Sarawak.

1888, Sept. 10. The Hon. Sir LIONEL SACKVILLE SACKVILLE-WEST, envoy extraordinary and minister plenipotentiary at Washington (in recognition of services rendered at the recent Conference at Washington on the subject of the North American Fisheries), afterwards 2nd lord Sackville, of Knole.

1889, Jan. 2. Sir HUGH Low, late British resident at Perak, Malay Peninsula.

1889, Feb. 4 The Rt. Hon. WILLIAM HILLIER (ONSLOW), 4th earl of Onslow, on appointment to be governor and commander-in-chief of the Colony of New Zealand.

1889, Feb. 4. The Rt. Hon. ALGERNON HAWKINS THOMOND (KEITH-FALCONER), 9th earl of Kintore, on appointment to be governor and commander-in-chief of the Colony of South Australia.

1889, May 24 (Honorary) RIAZ PASHA, prime minister of Egypt.

1889, May 24. Sir THOMAS FRANCIS WADE, late envoy extraordinary and minister plenipotentiary at Pekin.

1889, May 24 Sir ROBERT HART, insp. gen. of Chinese Imperial Maritime Customs

1889, Sept. 11. The Rt. Hon. JOHN ADRIAN LOUIS (HOPE), 7th earl of Hopetoun, on appointment to be governor and commander-in-chief of the Colony of Victoria

1889, Nov. 1. (Honorary) His Highness KHALIFA BIN SAEED BIN SULTAN BIN IMAM, sultan of Zanzibar. Originally appointed by warrant dated 1888, June 13, but this warrant was subsequently cancelled and fresh warrants issued dated 1889, Nov. 1. The insignia were presented to him at Zanzibar 1889, Dec. 16, by Col Charles Bean Euan-Smith, agent and consul general at Zanzibar.

1890, Jan. 1. The Rt Hon. SOMERSET RICHARD (LOWRY-CORRY), 4th earl of Belmore, formerly governor and commander-in-chief of the Colony of New South Wales.

1890, May 21. The Rt. Hon. HENRY CRESPIGNY (VIVIAN), 3rd baron Vivian, envoy extraordinary and minister plenipotentiary to the king of the Belgians.

1890, Aug. 14 The Rt. Hon VICTOR ALBERT GEORGE (CHILD-VILLIERS), 7th earl of Jersey, P.C., on appointment to be governor and commander-in-chief of the Colony of New South Wales.

1891, Apr 2. (Honorary) V. Adm. baron VON DER GOLTZ, of the Imperial German Navy

1891, July 23 (Honorary) His Highness prince ABBAS BEY, of Egypt.

1892, Jan. 1. Sir CECIL CLEMENTI SMITH, governor and commander-in-chief of the Straits Settlements, and consul gen. and high commissioner for North Borneo and Sarawak.

1892, Feb. 22. The Rt. Hon. DAVID (BOYLE), 7th earl of Glasgow, on appointment to be governor and commander-in-chief of the Colony of New Zealand.

1892, May 25. Sir HORACE RUMBOLD, bart., envoy extraordinary and minister plenipotentiary at the Hague.

1892, May 25. Maj. Gen. Sir FRANCIS WALLACE GRENFELL, for services rendered in Egypt.

1892, Aug. 6. The Hon. Sir EDMUND JOHN MONSON, envoy extraordinary and minister plenipotentiary to the king of the Belgians.

1892, Aug. 6. Sir FRANK CAVENDISH LASCELLES, envoy extraordinary and minister plenipotentiary to the shah of Persia.

1892, Aug. 16. Sir JOHN PENDER, M.P., in recognition of his services in connection with the telegraphic communication of the Empire.

1893, Mar. 24. Rt. Hon. ROBERT WILLIAM DUFF, on appointment to be governor and commander-in-chief of the Colony of New South Wales and its dependencies.

1893, June 3. Sir GEORGE WILLIAM DES VOEUX, late governor of Hongkong.

1893, July 4. Sir FRANCIS WALTER DE WINTON, comptroller and treasurer of the Household of H.R.H. the duke of York [notwithstanding that the number of Knights Grand Cross in the said class is complete].

1893, Dec. 7. Sir CHARLES RUSSELL, Q.C., M.P., attorney-general, in recognition of services rendered in connection with the recent Behring Sea Arbitration.

1893, Dec. 7. Sir RICHARD EVERARD WEBSTER, knt., Q.C., M.P. (in recognition of services rendered in connexion with the Behring Sea Arbitration at Paris, 1893).

1894, Mar. 3. Sir SPENSER BUCKINGHAM ST. JOHN, envoy extraordinary and minister plenipotentiary to the king of Sweden and Norway.

1894, Mar. 15.   The Hon. Sir FRANCIS RICHARD PLUNKETT, envoy
extraordinary and minister plenipotentiary to the king of
the Belgians

1894, May 26.   The Hon. Sir HENRY AYERS, five times premier of
South Australia and subsequently for many years president
of the Legislative Council of that Colony.

1895, Jan 1.   Sir ARTHUR ELIBANK HAVELOCK, governor and com-
mander-in-chief of the Island of Ceylon.

1895, Jan. 1.   The Hon. Sir SAMUEL WALKER GRIFFITH, chief justice
and formerly premier of the Colony of Queensland.

1895, Mar. 14.   Sir CHARLES RIVERS WILSON.

1895, May 25.   The Rt. Hon. JOHN CAMPBELL (HAMILTON-GORDON),
7th earl of Aberdeen; gov. gen. of the Dominion of Canada.

1895, May 25.   Lieut. Col. Sir CHARLES BULLEN HUGH MITCHELL,
governor and commander-in-chief of the Straits Settlements
and their Dependencies.

1896, Feb. 27.   Sir NICHOLAS RODERICK O'CONNOR, ambassador
extraordinary and plenipotentiary to the emperor of Russia.

1896, Apr. 23.   (Honorary) Shahzada HABIBULLA KHAN, of Afghan-
istan.

1896, Apr. 23.   (Honorary) Shahzada NASRULLA KHAN, of Afghan-
istan.

1896, May 20.   Sir DONALD ALEXANDER SMITH, high commissioner
in London for the Dominion of Canada, afterwards lord
Strathcona.

1897, Jan 11.   (Honorary) His Excellency Monsieur LUIZ DE
SOVERAL, minister for Foreign Affairs of His Majesty the
king of Portugal and the Algarves.

1897, June 4.   (Honorary) Signor PAUL HONORÉ VIGLIANI, formerly
president of the Court of Cassation of Florence, minister of
State and senator of the Kingdom of Italy (in recognition of
services rendered as arbitrator between Great Britain and
Portugal on the Manica Boundary question).

1897, June 22.   The Rt. Hon. JENICO WILLIAM JOSEPH (PRESTON),
14th viscount Gormanston, governor and commander-in-
chief of the Colony of Tasmania.

1897, June 22. The Hon. Sir WALTER FRANCIS HELY-HUTCHINSON, commander-in-chief of the Colony of Natal.

1897, June 22. Sir ALFRED MILNER, governor and commander-in-chief of the Colony of the Cape of Good Hope and high commissioner for South Africa, afterwards viscount Milner.

1897, June 22. The Hon. WILFRID LAURIER, president of the Privy Council and premier of the Dominion of Canada.

1897, June 22. The Hon. Sir RICHARD JOHN CARTWRIGHT, minister of Trade and Commerce for the Dominion of Canada.

1897, June 22. Sir WILLIAM ROBINSON, governor and commander-in-chief of the Colony of Hong Kong.

1897, June 22. Sir HENRY ARTHUR BLAKE, capt. gen. and governor-in-chief of the Island of Jamaica.

1897, June 22. The Hon. Sir OLIVER MOWAT, minister of justice for the Dominion of Canada.

1897, June 22. Sir DONALD CURRIE, M.P., for services to British African Trade.

1897, June 22. Sir THOMAS SUTHERLAND, M.P., director of the Suez Canal Company.

1897, June 22. His Excellency ABOUL KASSEM KHAN, styled Nasr-ul-Mulk, envoy from the Shah of Persia to announce his said Majesty's accession. (Honorary.)

1897, July 6. (Honorary) H I.H. prince AMIR KHAN, Sirdar, special envoy from the Shah of Persia (on the occasion of the celebration of the sixtieth anniversary of the queen's accession to the Throne).

1897, Aug. 12. (Honorary) His Excellency CHANG YEN HOON, late special ambassador from the emperor of China (on same occasion).

1897, Oct. 25. (Honorary) H.M. MENELEK II , emperor of Ethiopia.

1898, May 21. Gen. Sir ARTHUR JAMES LYON FREMANTLE, governor and commander-in-chief of the Island of Malta and its Dependencies.

1898, May 21. (Honorary) His Excellency MOUSTAPHA FEHMY, Pasha, president of the Egyptian Council of Ministers.

1898, Oct. 31.   The Rt. Hon. GILBERT JOHN (ELLIOT-MURRAY-KYNYNMOUND), 4th earl of Minto, on appointment to be gov. gen. of the Dominion of Canada.

1899, Jan. 2.   The Rt. Hon. HENRY ROBERT (BRAND), 2nd viscount Hampden, governor and commander-in-chief of the Colony of New South Wales

1899, Jan. 2.   Sir THOMAS FOWELL BUXTON, bart, governor and commander-in-chief of the Colony of South Australia.

1899, Jan. 2.   His Excellency the Rt. Hon. Sir CHARLES STEWART SCOTT, ambassador extraordinary and plenipotentiary to the emperor of Russia.

1899, Jan 2.   Maj. Gen. Sir HERBERT CHARLES CHERMSIDE, R.E., for distinguished services in Crete

1899, June 3   Sir WALTER JOSEPH SENDALL, governor and commander-in-chief of the Colony of British Guiana.

1899, June 3   Sir HUGH GUION MACDONELL, envoy extraordinary and minister plenipotentiary to the king of Portugal.

1899, June 3.   Sir GODFREY LUSHINGTON, lately British delegate at the Anarchist Conference at Rome.

1899, Dec. 2.   Sir ROBERT THRESHIE REID, Q C., M.P., for his services in connection with the Venezuela Boundary Arbitration Commission.

1900, Jan. 1.   The Rt. Hon. Sir JOSEPH WEST RIDGEWAY, governor and commander-in-chief of the Island of Ceylon and its Dependencies.

1900, Jan. 1.   Sir JOHN BRAMSTON, D.C.L., late assistant under secretary of State for the Colonies.

1900, May 23.   The Right. Hon. CHARLES WALLACE ALEXANDER NAPIER ROSS (COCHRANE-BAILLIE), 2nd lord Lamington, governor and commander-in-chief of the Colony of Queensland and its Dependencies.

1900, May 23.   Sir AUGUSTUS WILLIAM LAWSON HEMMING, capt. gen and governor-in-chief of the Island of Jamaica and its Dependencies.

1900, May 23. Maj. Sir CLAUDE MAXWELL MACDONALD, envoy extraordinary and minister plenipotentiary to His Majesty the emperor of China (for his services in China).

1900, May 23. Sir HENRY MORTIMER DURAND, envoy extraordinary and minister plenipotentiary to the Shah of Persia (for his services in Persia).

1900, June 28. H.H. prince MOHAMED ALI, of Egypt (Honorary).

1901, Jan. 1. The Rt. Hon. Sir JOHN FORREST, LL.D., premier and colonial treasurer of Western Australia (in recognition of services rendered in connection with the Federation of the Australian Colonies and the establishment of the Commonwealth of Australia).

1901, Mar. 9. (Extra) H.R.H. the duke of Cornwall and York.

1901, Mar. 20. (Honorary) His Highness IDRIS BIN ALMARHOM BANDHARA ISKANDER SAH, sultan of Perak in the Federated Malay States (on the occasion of the visit of the duke and duchess of York to Ceylon and the Straits Settlements).

1901, Apr. 19.* Gen. the Rt. Hon. Sir REDVERS HENRY BULLER, V.C. In recognition of services rendered in connection with the war in South Africa.

1901, Apr. 19. Lieut. Gen. (local general) HORATIO HERBERT (KITCHENER), lord Kitchener of Khartoum, Royal Engineers, commander-in-chief of the Forces in South Africa (same occasion).

1901, Apr. 19. Lieut. Gen. Sir FREDERICK WILLIAM EDWARD FORESTIER FORESTIER-WALKER (same occasion).

1901, Apr. 19. Gen. Sir GEORGE STEWART WHITE, V.C. (same occasion).

1901, May 6. Sir FREDERICK MATTHEW DARLEY, lieut. gov. of the State of New South Wales and chief justice of the Supreme Court of that State (on the occasion of the visit of the duke and duchess of York to Australia).

---

* The "Gazette" notice of the promotions for the South African War stated that such promotions were to rank as from date 1900, Nov. 29. In all the promotions within the Order of the Bath this has been accordingly followed. (See supra pp. 198, 267, 298.) But such stipulation, which originated merely at the War Office, and was intended only to have bearing on the course of army promotions, did not and could not apply to the Order of St. Michael and St. George. Accordingly in this present list these promotions are arranged according to their strict and proper dates—viz. : the dates of the warrants of appointment.

1901, May 23 The Rt. Hon. UCHTER JOHN MARK (KNOX), 5th earl of Ranfurley, governor and commander-in-chief of the Colony of New Zealand (on the occasion of the visit of the duke and duchess of York to New Zealand).

1901, June 27. (Honorary) His Excellency MEHEDI BEN EL ARBI EL MENEBHI, special ambassador of His Imperial Majesty the Sultan of Morocco.

1901, June 28. Sir CHARLES BRUCE, governor and commander-in-chief of the Colony of Mauritius and its Dependencies.

1901, Nov. 9. Sir GUISEPPE CARBONE, LL.D., chief justice, president of the Court of Appeal, and vice-president of the Council of Government of the Island of Malta.

1901, Nov. 9. Sir HENRY HAMILTON JOHNSTON, lately His Majesty's special commissioner, commander-in-chief and consul gen. for the Uganda Protectorate and the adjoining Territories.

1902, June 2. (Honorary) V. Adm FELIX ROBERT EDUARD EMIL BENDEMANN, officer of the Imperial German Navy.

1902, June 26. The Rt Hon Sir JOHN GORDON SPRIGG, prime minister of the Colony of the Cape of Good Hope.

1902, June 26. The Rt. Hon. EDMUND BARTON, K.C., prime minister of the Commonwealth of Australia.

1902, June 26. Sir EDWIN HENRY EGERTON, His Majesty's minister at Athens.

1902, June 26. Sir ERNEST MASON SATOW, His Majesty's minister at Pekin.

1902, Nov. 9. [King's birthday] Sir JAMES LYLE MACKAY, late His Majesty's special commissioner and plenipotentiary for commercial negotiations with China.

1902, Nov 9. (Honorary) His Excellency count MATSUKATA, formerly prime minister of Japan.

1902, Dec. 6. Sir WILLIAM EDMUND GARSTIN, under secretary of State for Public Works in Egypt.

1902, Dec. 6. The Rt. Hon. EDWARD (MACNAGHTEN), lord Macnaghten, P.C.

1903, Feb. 9. (Honorary) H.R.H. the MOAYYED-ED-DOWLEH, of Persia.

1903, Feb. 9. His Excellency MIRZA MOHAMED KHAN, Vazir-i-Darbar to His Majesty the Shah of Persia.

1903, Mar. 5. His Excellency the Rt. Hon. Sir MICHAEL HENRY HERBERT, ambassador extraordinary and plenipotentiary to the United States of America.

1903, June 26. His Excellency the Rt. Hon. HALLAM (TENNYSON), 2nd lord Tennyson, gov. gen. and commander-in-chief of the Commonwealth of Australia.

1904, May 3. (Ordinary) His Excellency HENRY STAFFORD (NORTH-COTE) 1st lord Northcote, gov. gen. and commander-in-chief of the Commonwealth of Australia.

1904, June 24. Col. Sir HENRY EDWARD MCCALLUM, R.E., A D.C, governor and commander-in-chief of the Colony of Natal.

1904, June 24. Sir ROBERT BANNATYNE FINLAY, K.C, M P, His Majesty's attorney general, for services before the tribunal at the Hague on the question of priority in the payment of sums due by Venezuela to foreign countries.

1904, Oct. 7. ALBERT HENRY GEORGE (GREY), 4th earl Grey; on his appointment as gov. gen. of the Dominion of Canada.

1904, Nov 9. Sir MONTAGU FREDERICK OMMANEY, permanent under-secretary of State for the Colonies and secretary to the Order of St Michael and St. George.

1904, Nov. 9. His Excellency the Rt. Hon. Sir FRANCIS LEVESON BERTIE, ambassador extraordinary and plenipotentiary to Italy.

*KNIGHT COMMANDERS of the Order of St. Michael and
St. George (K.C.M.G)

1818, Nov. 18. VITTOR CARIDI, of Cephalonia. Invested at Corfu.

1818, Nov. 18. ANTONIO, count Theotoky, of Corfu. Invested at
Corfu.

1818, Nov. 18. DIONIZIO BULZO, of Zante. Invested at Corfu.

1818, Nov. 18. Col. FREDERICK HANKEY, secretary to the High
Commissioner of the Ionian Islands, etc. Invested at Corfu.

1818, Dec. 16. GUISEPPE NICOLO ZAMMIT, one of the judges and
sometime vice-president of the Court of Appeal at Malta.

1818, Dec 16. RICHARD PLASKET, chief secretary to the Government
of Malta. Invested at Malta

1819, Nov. 9   Lieut. Col. Sir PATRICK ROSS, resident for the High
Commissioner at Zante. Invested at Corfu.

1820, Feb. 26   Capt. the Hon. ANTHONY MAITLAND, afterwards 10th
earl of Lauderdale, sometime commodore in command in
the Mediterranean. Investiture dispensed with by warrant
of that date.

1820, Feb. 26   Count NICOLO ANINO [ANASTASIO, of Cephalonia],
sometime a senator of the Ionian Islands. Invested at
Corfu.

1820, Feb 26. GIOVANNI CAPPADOCA, of Corfu, a member of the
Supreme Council of Justice of the Ionian Islands. Invested
at Corfu.

1820, Feb. 26. MARINO VEJA, of Cephalonia, president of the
Legislative Assembly of the Ionian Islands. Invested at
Corfu.

1820, Feb. 26. Col. Sir FREDERICK STOVIN, military commander
and resident for the High Commissioner at Santa Maura.
Invested at Corfu.

---

* For a list of the Cavalieri of the 3rd class who between the years 1818 and 1832 were entitled to be
styled Sir, see introduction, p xxviii.

1820, Feb. 26. ALEXANDER WOOD, resident agent for the Ionian Islands in London and sometime chief secretary at Malta. Investiture dispensed with by warrant of that date. Knighted by the Sovereign 1821, Feb. 23.

1820, July 19. BASILIO ZAVO, a senator of the Ionian Islands.

1821, Mar. 14. DEMETRIO, count Foscardi, of Zante, sometime president of the Ionian Senate. Invested at Corfu.

1821, Mar. 14. GIACOMO CALICHIOPULO MANZARO, of Corfu, president of the Primary Council and advocate general of the Ionian Islands. Invested at Corfu.

1822, Jan. 31. Count PAOLO PARISIO, one of the lords lieutenant of Malta. Investiture dispensed with by warrant of that date.

1823, Feb. 20. Lieut. Col. ROBERT TRAVERS, inspecting field officer of militia in the Ionian Islands and resident for the lord High Commissioner at Cephalonia Investiture dispensed with by warrant of that date.

1823, Mar. 1. FRANCESCO MUZZAN, of Zante. Investiture dispensed with by warrant of that date.

1825, June 30. PIETRO COIDAN, of Cephalonia, member of the Supreme Council of Justice of the Ionian Islands. Invested at Corfu Oct. 11.

1825, June 30. ANGIOLO CONDARI, a senator of the Ionian Islands. Invested *ut supra*.

1832, June 22. JOSEPH RUDSDELL, sometime secretary to the High Commissioner in the Ionian Islands and secretary of the Primary Council there. Investiture dispensed with by warrant of date Aug. 16.

1832, Aug. 16. Sir NICHOLAS HARRIS NICOLAS, appointed chancellor and a knight commander with the rank of senior knight commander by the statutes of 1832, Aug. 16. Investiture dispensed with by warrant of same date.

1833, Feb. 9. VINCENZO CASOLANI, of Malta. Invested at Malta May. 28.

1833, Feb. 9. Guiseppe marquis TESTAFERRATA, one of the lords lieutenants of Malta. Invested *ut supra*.

23

1833, Feb. 9. SPIRIDION VITTOR, count Bulgari, sometime regent of Corfu. Invested at Corfu Apr. 23.

1833, Feb. 9. PIETRO PETRIZZOPULO, regent of Santa Maura. Invested *ut supra*.

1833, June 26. EDWARD STUART BAYNES, secretary to the Ionian Senate. Invested at Corfu Nov. 30.

1833, July 17. Count VINCENZO MANDUCA, of Malta. Invested at Malta Aug. 21.

1835, June 11. CLAUDIO VINCENZO BONNICI, a member of the Supreme Council of Justice at Malta.

1836, Apr. 2. IGNATIUS GAVIN BONAVITA, president of the Court of Appeal at Malta. Invested Apr. 28.

1839, Jan. 26. HECTOR GREIG, chief secretary at Malta. Invested at Malta Dec. 27.

1839, Aug. 30. STAMO GANGADI, sometime senator for Corfu and now Archon of the Ionian University. Invested at Corfu Nov. 18.

1839, Aug 30. AGOSTINO RANDON, one of the judges at Malta. Invested at Malta Dec. 27.

1839, Nov. 11. Maj. Gen. FRANCIS, count Rivarola, col. of the Royal Malta Fencible Regiment. Investiture dispensed with by warrant dated Nov. 30.

1840, July 7. Demetrio count DELLA DECIMA, member of the Supreme Council of Justices of the Ionian Islands. Invested at Corfu Sept. 9.

1840, Sept. 14. ALTAVILLA VILLETTA CALICHIOPULO, president of the Legislative Assembly of the Ionian Islands. Investiture dispensed with by warrant of Sept. 24.

1842, Jan. 21. ANGIOLO CALICHIOPULO, of Corfu, a senator of the Ionian Islands

1842, Mar. 18. Guiseppe Maria baron DE PIRO

1844, May 27. Demetrio VALSAMACHI.

1844, May 27. PLATO PETRIDES.

1844, May 27. Count DIONISIO FLAMBURIARI.

1844, Dec. 16. GEORGIO CAZZAITI.

1849, Sept. 26. Count ANTONIO LEFCOCHILO DUSMANI, for services to the Ionian Government from 1829, chiefly as secretary to the Senate from 1843, Nov. 3.

1849, Sept. 26. ANASTASIO TIPALDO XIDIAN.

1849, Sept. 26. ALESANDRO DAMASCHINO.

1850, Jan. 3. AGOSTINO PORTELLI

1853, June 27. Dr. GEORGIO MARCORAN, for services as judge of the Supreme Court of the Ionian Islands up to the cession of those Islands to the Kingdom of Greece in 1864.

1853, June 27. JOHN FRASER, secretary to the High Commissioner for the Ionian Islands.

1855, Mar. 31. SPIRIDIONE VALSAMACHI.

1855, May 16. PIETRO ARMENI BRAILA, LL D , president of the Legislative Assembly, Ionian Islands.

1856, Jan 28. WILLIAM HENRY THORNTON, auditor gen. at Malta and officer of arms of the Order of St. Michael and St. George there

1856, Jan. 28. Dr. PAOLO DINGLI, president of the Court of Appeal at Malta.

1856, Apr. 9. GEORGE FERGUSON BOWEN, chief secretary to the Ionian Government.

1857, July 9. Dr. DEMETRIO CURCUMELLI, LL.D , for services as procurator general to the Ionian Government from 1833.

1857, July 9. ANDREA MUSTOXIDI.

1859, Mar. 30. JAMES PHILIP LACAITA, appointed whilst acting as secretary to Mr. Gladstone's Mission of Enquiry into the affairs of the Ionian Government.

1859, Apr. 4. Sir CHARLES EURWICKE DOUGLAS, knight.

1860, Apr. 16. ANTONIO MICALLEF, LL D., for services as judge from Jan., 1854, and president of the Court of Appeal at Malta July, 1895.

1860, Apr. 16.   ADRIANO DINGLI, LL.D., Crown advocate for Malta,
for long services as Crown law officer in Malta.

1860, Apr. 16.   EDWARD VICTOR LOUIS HOULTON, for services as
chief secretary to the Government of Malta.

1860, Apr. 16.   PETER SMITH [late chief clerk at the Colonial Office
and secretary to the Order of St. Michael and St. George].

1862, July 14.   SPIRIDIONE VALAORITI, for services as senator of the
Ionian Islands.

1862, Oct. 8   HENRY DRUMMOND WOLFF, on his appointment as
commissioner from the Ionian Islands to the Industrial
Exhibition, 1832, and for services as public secretary to the
lord High Commissioner from 1859.

1864, May 21.   CHARLES SEBRIGHT, Esq. (baron d'Everton) for
services as resident of the Island of Santa Maura until the
cession of the Ionian Islands to the Kingdom of Greece in
1864.

1864, Oct. 13.   Maj. WILFRED BRETT, for services at Malta as officer
of arms and on resignation, of that office.

1868, Apr 24.   Baron PASQUALE SCEBERRAS TRIGONA.

1868, Apr. 24.   Count NICOLA SCEBARRAS BOLOGNA.

1868, Apr 24.   Maj. Gen. WILLIAM JOHN RIDLEY, senior member of
the Council of Government of Malta.

1869, Feb 13.   Maj. Gen. CHARLES HASTINGS DOYLE, lieut. gov. of
the Province of Nova Scotia, in the Dominion of Canada.

1869, Feb 13.   FRANCIS HINCKS, late governor and commander-in-
chief of the Colony of British Guiana, on his retirement
from that Government.

1869, Feb. 13.   JAMES WALKER, governor and commander-in-chief
of the Bahama Islands.   For services as governor for several
years, and on appointment to the Government of Bahamas.

1869, Feb. 13.   Col. THOMAS GORE BROWNE, late capt. gen. and
governor-in-chief of the Island of Tasmania on his retire-
ment from that office.

1869, June 23.   PAUL EDMUND DE STRZELECKI

1869, June 23   The Rt. Hon. GEORGE WILLIAM (LYTTLETON), 6th
baron Lyttleton, sometime under secretary of State for War
and Colonies.

1869, June 23. The Rt. Hon. FREDERICK PEEL, sometime under secretary of State for War and Colonies.

1869, June 23. The Rt. Hon. CHARLES BOWYER ADDERLEY, afterwards 1st lord Norton, late under secretary of State for the Colonies.

1869, June 23. Sir FREDERIC ROGERS, afterwards 1st lord Blachford, for services as permanent under secretary of State for the Colonies, 1860 to 1871.

1869, June 23. Sir HERCULES GEORGE ROBERT ROBINSON, knt., governor and commander-in-chief of the Island of Ceylon.

1869, June 23. ALEXANDER TILLOCK GALT, late minister for finance in the Dominion of Canada.

1869, June 23. HENRY TAYLOR. For long official services in connection with the Colonies, senior clerk in the Colonial Office 1825 to 1872.

1869, June 23. THOMAS FREDERICK ELLIOT, late assistant under secretary of State for the Colonies.

1870,* Jan. 13. JOHN ROSE, late finance minister for the Dominion of Canada.

1870, Jan. 13. THOMAS WILLIAM CLINTON MURDOCH, one of Her Majesty's commissioners for Colonial Land and Emigration.

1870, Aug. 16. Rt. Hon. WILLIAM COUTTS (KEPPEL), styled viscount Bury, afterwards 19th earl of Albemarle, formerly civil secretary and superintendent of Indian Affairs in the Province of Canada.

1870, Dec. 16. Lieut. Gen. the Hon. JAMES LINDSAY, for special military services, as commander of the Troops in Canada.

1870, Dec. 16. Col. GARNET JOSEPH WOLSELEY, afterwards viscount Wolseley, for special military services in Canada.

1871, Feb. 18. The Hon. ARTHUR HAMILTON GORDON, governor of the Island of Mauritius.

Mem. : In the *Gazette* of 1870, Aug. 5, Charlotte Christiana, the widow of Captain Charles Sturt, late of the 39th Regiment, and formerly Colonial Secretary of South Australia, was allowed the same rank and precedence as if her husband had lived to enjoy the distinction of a Knight Commander of the order, to which he was nominated a short time previous to his death in 1869. Captain Sturt was an eminent explorer of the Australian Continent, and had been Colonial Secretary for the Colony of South Australia.

1871, Feb. 18. Sir RICHARD GRAVES MacDONNELL, knt , governor
of the Colony of Hong Kong.

1871, Sept. 18. Sir ARTHUR EDWARD KENNEDY, knt., governor of
Her Majesty's West African Settlements.

1871, Sept. 18. Sir BENJAMIN CHILLEY CAMPBELL PINE, knt.,
governor of the Leeward Islands.

1872, Feb. 20. CHARLES COWPER, late first minister of the Govern-
ment of New South Wales and now agent general in
England for that Colony.

1872, Feb. 20   GEORGE FREDERIC VERDON, late treasurer of the
Colony of Victoria and now agent general in England for
that Colony.

1872, Mar. 22. SOMERSET RICHARD (LOWRY-CORRY), 4th earl of
Belmore, late governor and commander-in-chief of the
Colony of New South Wales, on his retirement from that
Government.

1872, Aug. 1. ROBERT RICHARD TORRENS, M.P., formerly a
member of the Assembly and chief secretary and treasurer
for the Colony of South Australia, for his long official
service in South Australia, especially in connection with
the passage of the measure for the Transfer of Land under
Registration.

1872, Nov. 22. HENRY AYERS, first minister of the Government of
the Colony of South Australia, on completion of telegraphic
communication with England, of which he was an active
supporter.

1873, Mar. 21. Col ANDREW CLARKE, R.E., formerly surveyor
general and a member of the Executive Government and
Executive Council of the Colony of Victoria.

1874, Feb 20. The most Hon. GEORGE AUGUSTUS CONSTANTINE
(PHIPPS), marquis of Normanby, governor and commander-
in-chief of the Colony of Queensland.

1874, Feb. 20   Sir ALFRED STEPHEN, knt , late chief justice of the
Colony of New South Wales

1874, Feb. 20. Sir JAMES McCULLOCH, knt., formerly first minister
of the Colony of Victoria.

1874, Feb. 20. JOHN O'SHANASSY, formerly first minister of the Colony of Victoria.

1874, Feb. 20. JOHN SCOTT, late governor and commander-in-chief of the Colony of British Guiana.

1874, Apr. 23. Col. FRANCIS WORGAN FESTING, R.M.A., lately in command of H.M. Troops within H.M. Settlements on the Gold Coast, during the recent Ashantee War, 1873–4.

1874, May 28. Col. STEPHEN JOHN HILL, governor of the Colony of Newfoundland.

1874, May 28. Col. WM. FRANCIS DRUMMOND JERVOIS, R.E. deputy director of Works for Fortifications, War Department, for his work in making Colonial surveys, and his advice on questions of Colonial fortification, also for his scheme of military defence for the Dominion of Canada.

1874, May 28. PENROSE GOODCHILD JULYAN, Crown agent for the Colonies, for special services chiefly in connection with Canada.

1874, July 15. HENRY ERNEST GASCOIGNE BULWER, governor and commander-in-chief of the Island of Labuan and its Dependencies.

1874, July 15. DONALD MACLEAN, minister for Native Affairs in the Colony of New Zealand.

1874, Sept. 24. The Rt. Hon. Sir JAMES FERGUSON, bart., lately governor of the Colony of New Zealand and its Dependencies.

1874, Sept. 24. EDWARD DEAS THOMSON, member of the Legislative Council of the Colony of New South Wales, and formerly, for many years, colonial secretary for that Colony.

1874, Sept. 24. JOHN SEALY, member of the Legislative Council of the Island of Barbadoes, and lately attorney general for that Island.

1875, Feb. 27. CHARLES DU CANE, late governor of the Colony of Tasmania.

1875, Feb. 27. GEORGE MACLEAY, formerly a member of the Legislative of the Colony of New South Wales.

1875, May 29. FRANCIS FORTESCUE TURVILLE.

1875, May 29. The Hon. GEORGE WILLIAM HAMILTON (FITZ-MAURICE), styled viscount Kirkwall, afterwards earl of Orkney.

1875, May 29. CHARLES SLADEN [formerly chief secretary to the Government of Victoria].

1875, May 29. JULIUS VOGEL, colonial treasurer and first minister of New Zealand 1873 to 1876.

1875, Aug. 17. Rt. Hon. WILLIAM HENRY GREGORY, governor and commander-in-chief of the Island of Ceylon and its Dependencies.

1875, Aug. 18. ANTHONY MUSGRAVE, governor of the colony of South Australia.

1875, Aug. 18. RAWSON WILLIAM RAWSON, lately governor of the Windward Islands.

1876, Mar. 7. JAMES ROBERT LONGDEN, governor of the colony of British Guiana.

1876, Mar 7. PETER LAYARD, Government agent for the Western Province of the Island of Ceylon.

1876, Aug. 11. THEOPHILUS SHEPSTONE, member of the executive and legislative councils and secretary for Native Affairs for the Colony of Natal, special commissioner to the Transvaal 1876.

1877, Apr. 14 Sir HENRY THURSTAN HOLLAND, bart., afterwards viscount Knutsford, late assistant under secretary of State for the Colonies.

1877, Apr. 14. WILLIAM WELLINGTON CAIRNS, governor of the Colony of South Australia.

1877, Apr. 14. Lieut Col. HENRY FITZHARDING BERKELEY MAXSE, governor of the Island of Heligoland.

1877, Apr. 14. WILLIAM FITZHERBERT, formerly colonial treasurer and member of the Executive Government and Executive Council of New Zealand and special agent for that Colony.

1877, May 31. Maj. Gen. Sir HARRY SAINT GEORGE ORD, R.E, knt., lately governor of the Straits Settlements.

1877, May 31. Sir REDMOND BARRY, knt., senior puisne judge of the Supreme Court of the Colony of Victoria.

1877, May 31. Sir HENRY WATSON PARKER, knt., formerly first minister of the Colony of New South Wales.

1877, May 31. JOHN BAYLEY DARVALL, formerly attorney general of the Colony of New South Wales.

1877, May 31. STEPHEN WALCOTT, Her Majesty's commissioner for emigration.

1877, May 31. WILLIAM CLEAVER FRANCIS ROBINSON, governor of the Colony of Western Australia.

1877, May 31. Maj. ROBERT MILLER MUNDY, lately lieut. gov. of the Colony of British Honduras.

1877, May 31. Maj. Gen. PATRICK LEONARD M'DOUGALL, deputy quartermaster gen., formerly adjutant gen. of the Militia of the Dominion of Canada.

1877, May 31. Maj. Gen. JOHN HENRY LEFROY, R.A., lately governor of the Bermuda Islands.

1877, May 31. Maj. Gen. EDWARD SELBY SMYTH, commanding the Militia of the Dominion of Canada.

1877, May 31. Brig. Gen. ROBERT MICHAEL LAFFAN, R.E., governor of the Bermuda Islands.

1877, May 31. JOHN ROBERTSON, lately first minister of the Colony of New South Wales.

1877, May 31. HENRY PARKES, first minister of the Colony of New South Wales.

1877, May 31. ARTHUR BLYTH, lately first minister of the Colony of South Australia.

1877, Dec. 1. Sir CHARLES GAVAN DUFFY, knt., speaker of the Legislative Assembly of the Colony of Victoria.

1877, Dec. 1. Gen. JOHN JARVIS BISSET, administered the government of Natal from 1865 to 1867.

1877, Dec. 1. RICHARD WOOD, for services in connection with the Maltese immigrants introduced into Tunis, and to Colonists, in his capacity as Her Majesty's agent and consul general in the Regency of Tunis since 1855.

1878, May 25. Sir JAMES MILNE WATSON, knt., lately premier of the Colony of Tasmania, and now president of the Legislative Council of that Colony.

1878, May 25 HENRY TURNER IRVING, governor of the Island of Trinidad.

1878, May 25. SANFORD FREELING, governor of the Gold Coast Colony.

1878, May 25. ALBERT SMITH, minister of the marine for the Dominion of Canada and lately employed in connection with the Halifax Fisheries Commission.

1878, May 25. JOHN HAY, president of the Legislative Council of the Colony of New South Wales.

1878, May 25. ARCHIBALD MICHIE, Q.C., formerly attorney general and minister of justice in the Colony of Victoria, and now agent general in England for that Colony.

1878, May 25. FREDERICK BOWKER TERRINGTON CARTER, Q.C., late premier and attorney general of the Island of Newfoundland.

1878, Oct. 20. FRANCIS PHILIP CUNLIFFE OWEN, secretary to the British Commissioners at the Paris Exhibition of 1878, for services rendered to the Colonies in connection with the representation of British Colonial Products.

1879, Jan. 20. (Honorary) H.H. the Somdetch CHAO PHYA SURAWONGSE, formerly regent of the kingdom of Siam, for services to the Government of the Straits Settlements, especially during the late disturbances in the Malay Peninsula in 1875–76.

1879, Apr. 5. (Honorary) H.H. the Raja AHMED TAJ UDIN BIN SULTAN ZAIN ALRASHID KEDAH [the Raja of Kedah], for similar services to the Government of the Straits Settle-

1879, May 24. (Honorary) His Excellency RÉCHAD PACHA, late governor of Gallipoli, for services to the Foreign Office as late governor of the town of Gallipoli.

1879, May 24. Sir NARCISSE FORTUNAT BELLEAU, knt., formerly lieut. gov. of Quebec.

1879, May 24. WILLIAM TAYLOR THOMSON, late envoy extraordinary and minister plenipotentiary to the Shah of Persia.

1879, May 24. WILLIAM PEARCE HOWLAND, formerly lieut. gov. of the Province of Ontario.

1879, May 24. CHARLES TUPPER, minister of Public Works for the Dominion of Canada.

1879, May 24. SAMUEL LEONARD TILLEY, minister of Finance for the Dominion of Canada.

1879, May 24. GEORGE BUCKLEY MATTHEW, late envoy extraordinary and minister plenipotentiary to the emperor of Brazil.

1879, May 24. GEORGE WELSH KELLNER, late financial commissioner in Cyprus.

1879, May 24. Maj. Gen. EDWARD WOLSTENHOLME WARD, late deputy master of the Branch Mint at Sydney.

1879, May 24. Dr. FERDINAND VON MUELLER, Ph.D., M.D., Government botanist for the Colony of Victoria

1879, May 24. GEORGE BROWN, member of the Senate of the Dominion of Canada.

1879, May 24. ALEXANDER CAMPBELL, receiver general of the Dominion of Canada.

1879, May 24. RICHARD JOHN CARTWRIGHT, lately finance minister for the Dominion of Canada.

1879, May 24. EDWARD WILLIAM STAFFORD, formerly prime minister of New Zealand.

1879, May 24. WILLIAM FOX, formerly prime minister of Queensland.

1879, July 30. (Honorary) His Excellency RIAZ PASHA, for services to the Foreign Office as late Egyptian minister of the Interior.

1879, Sept. 10. Sir DANIEL BROOKE ROBERTSON, knt., late consul general at Shanghai.

1879, Oct. 9. JOHN LUKE GEORGE (HELY-HUTCHINSON), 5th earl of Donoughmore, Her Majesty's assistant commissioner for the organisation of Eastern Roumelia under the 18th Article of the Treaty of Berlin.

1879, Dec. 9.   Maj. Gen. the Hon. HENRY HUGH CLIFFORD, V.C., for special services in the Zulu War, 1879.

1879, Dec. 9.   Col. CHARLES KNIGHT PEARSON, for distinguished service in the Zulu War, 1879.

1879, Dec. 22.   Sir JULIAN PAUNCEFOTE, knt., assistant under secretary of State for Foreign Affairs.

1879, Dec. 22.   Maj. Gen. EDWARD BRUCE HAMLEY, R.A., late Her Majesty's commissioner for the delimitation of Bulgaria, under the Treaty of Berlin.

1879, Dec. 22.   CHARLES RIVERS WILSON, secretary and comptroller general of the National Debt Office, for special services in Egypt.

1880, Apr. 17.   Col. WILLIAM OWEN LANYON, administrator of the Government of the Transvaal (for services rendered in South Africa.

1880, Apr. 17.   Col. BAKER CREED RUSSELL, 13th Hussars, lately in command of the Troops employed against Sikukuni in South Africa (for services in South Africa).

1880, Apr. 22.   JOHN POPE HENNESSY, governor of Hong Kong.

1880, Apr. 22.   Surgeon maj. SAMUEL ROWE, governor of West Africa Settlements.

1880, Apr. 27.   THOMAS GEORGE KNOX, late Her Majesty's agent and consul general in Siam.

1880, Apr. 27.   Maj. Gen. ROBERT BIDDULPH, R.A., Her Majesty's high commissioner and commander-in-chief in and over the Island of Cyprus.

1880, May 29.   Maj. GEORGE CUMINE STRAHAN, governor of the Colony of Tasmania.

1880, May 29.   FREDERICK ALOYSIUS WELD, governor of the Straits Settlements.

1880, May 29.   WILLIAM VALLANCE WHITEWAY, attorney general and premier of the Island of Newfoundland.

1880, July 2.   (Honorary) His Excellency CHAO PHYA BHANU-WONGSE MAHA KOSA TIPODI TI PHRAKLANG, ambassador extraordinary and plenipotentiary of the king of Siam.

1880, Aug. 12. Col. JOHN CARSTAIRS MCNEILL, V.C., for special services in Canada.

1880, Oct. 22. Sir DANIEL COOPER, bart., for services rendered to the Colony of New South Wales more particularly in connexion with the International Exhibition held at Sydney in 1879–80.

1880, Oct. 22. PATRICK JENNINGS, executive commissioner at the International Exhibition held at Sydney in 1879–80.

1880, Oct. 22. VIRGILE NAZ, member of the Council of the Government of Mauritius, for services in connection with that Colony.

1881, Mar 16. SPENSER BUCKINGHAM ST. JOHN, Her Majesty's minister resident to the Republic of Peru.

1881, May 24. Maj. Gen. GEORGE RICHARDS GREAVES adjutant gen. in India, late chief secretary and chief of the staff in Cyprus.

1881, May 24. GEORGE BERKELEY, governor and commander-in-chief of the Leeward Islands.

1881, May 24. HECTOR LOUIS LANGEVIN, Q.C., minister of Public Works in the Dominion of Canada.

1881, May 24. ARTHUR HUNTER PALMER, colonial secretary and late premier of Queensland.

1881, May 24. Sir FRANCIS DILLON BELL, knt, agent general in England for New Zealand and late speaker of the House of Representatives in that Colony.

1881, May 24. JOHN SUMMERFIELD HAWKINS lieut. gen., R E., formerly employed on the North American Boundary Commission.

1881, May 24. CHARLES WILLIAM WILSON, lieut. col., R E., Her Majesty's consul general in Anatolia.

1881, Aug. 5. DONALD CURRIE, for special services in connexion with the Cape, Natal and South Africa.

1881, Aug. 5. PATRICK JOSEPH KEENAN, resident commissioner of national education in Ireland, for services in connexion with education in Trinidad and Malta.

1881, Nov. 30.   JOHN KIRK, M.D., agent and consul general at Zanzibar.

1881, Nov. 30.   AUCKLAND COLVIN, controller general in Egypt.

1881, Nov. 30.   JOSHUA PETER BELL, president of the Legislative Council of Queensland.

1882, Feb. 13.   Gen. EDWARD STANTON, chargé d'affaires at Munich.

1882, Feb. 20.   Sir JOHN HENRY DE VILLIERS, knt., chief justice of the Colony of the Cape of Good Hope and lately one of the commissioners for the Settlement of the Transvaal Territory.

1882, Mar. 3.   V. Adm. RICHARD JAMES (MEADE), 4th earl of Clanwilliam (in command of the Detached Squadron, 1880—82).

1882, May 6.   FRANCIS SAVAGE REILLY, Q.C., in recognition of legal services rendered to the Foreign and Colonial Departments.

1882, May 6   ROBERT HART, inspec. gen. of Chinese Imperial Maritime Customs.

1882, May 24.   CORNELIUS HENDERICKSEN KORTRIGHT, late governor of British Guiana.

1882, May 24.   WILLIAM BRAMPTON GURDON, for services on special missions in 1879 and 1881 to South Africa for the settlement of financial questions.

1882, May 24.   Col. WILLIAM BELLAIRS, for services in South Africa.

1882, May 24.   Col GEORGE STODDART WHITMORE, formerly commandant of local forces in New Zealand and member of the Legislative Council of that Colony.

1882, May 24   SAUL SAMUEL, agent general in London for New South Wales and previously member of several administrations in that Colony.

1882, May 24   GEORGIO SERAFINO, count CIANTAR-PALEOLOGO, barone di San Giovanni, president of the Assembly of the Maltese nobility.

1882, May 24.   JOHN HALL, lately first minister in New Zealand.

1882, Aug. 26. EDWARD MORTIMER ARCHIBALD, H.M. consul gen. at New York.

1882, Aug. 26. JOHN CHARLES MOLTENO, first chief minister of the Cape of Good Hope under responsible government and lately colonial secretary of that Colony.

1882, Aug. 26. WILLIAM CHARLES SARGEAUNT, one of the Crown agents for the Colonies.

1882, Aug. 26. Maj. Gen. ARCHIBALD EDWARD HARBORD ANSON, R.A., late administrator of the government of the Straits Settlements and lieut. gov. of Prince of Wales Island.

1882, Nov. 1. (Honorary) MOHAMED SULTAN PASHA, president of the Chamber of Notables of Egypt.

1882, Nov. 17. WILLIAM MCARTHUR, alderman and M.P., late lord mayor of London.

1882, Nov. 17. THOMAS MCILWRAITH, Esq., first minister of the Colony of Queensland.

1882, Nov. 24. Col. REDVERS HENRY BULLER, V.C., for services rendered as head of the intelligence department in Egypt.

1883, May 24. WILLIAM ROBINSON, governor of the Windward Islands.

1883, May 24. GEORGE WILLIAM DES VOEUX, governor of the Colony of Fiji.

1883, May 24. Col. ROBERT WILLIAM HARLEY, lieut. gov. of the Colony of British Honduras.

1883, May 24. CHARLES CAMERON LEES, governor of the Bahamas.

1883, May 24. FREDERICK PALGRAVE BARLEE, lately lieut. gov. of the Colony of British Honduras.

1883, May 24. JOHN DOUGLAS, lieut. gov. and colonial secretary of Ceylon.

1883, May 24. CHARLES HUTTON GREGORY, C.E., past president of the Institute of Civil Engineers, consulting engineer to several Colonial Governments.

1883, May 24.   Lieut. Col. CHARLES BULLEN HUGH MITCHELL, R.M., colonial secretary and lately administrator of the government of Natal.

1883, May 24.   HUGH LOW, British resident at Perak in the Malay Peninsula.

1883, May 24.   WILLIAM MORGAN, for some time first minister of the Colony of South Australia.

1883, May 24.   AMBROSE SHEA, for many years member and sometime speaker of the Legislative Assembly, Newfoundland.

1883, May 24.   Col CHARLES WARREN, R E., in recognition of his services in connection with the bringing to justice the murderers of the late Professor Palmer and his party.

1883, July 9.   (Honorary) CONSTANTINE GEORGE ZEROUDACCHI, in recognition of the services rendered by him to Her Majesty's Forces in Egypt.

1884, Feb 1.   Lieut. Gen. the Hon. LEICESTER SMYTH, commander of Her Majesty's Troops in South Africa, and at present administering the Government of the Cape of Good Hope during the absence of the governor.

1884, Feb. 1.   Sir GEORGE WIGRAM ALLEN, knt., speaker of the Legislative Assembly of New South Wales.

1884, Feb. 1.   FREDERICK WHITAKER, late premier of New Zealand.

1884, Feb. 1.   FRANCIS WALTER DE WINTON, lieut. col., R.A., military secretary to the late gov. gen. of the Dominion of Canada

1884, Feb. 19.   Sir CHARLES AUGUSTUS HARTLEY, knt., in recognition of his services as engineer-in-chief to the European Commission for the Navigation of the Danube.

1884, Feb. 19.   Surg. Gen. WILLIAM GUYER HUNTER, M D., in recognition of services during the recent outbreak of cholera in Egypt.

1884, May 24.   THOMAS CHARLES SCANLEN, late first minister of the Cape of Good Hope.

1884, May 24.   Col. WILLIAM CROSSMAN, R.E., one of Her Majesty's commissioners appointed in 1882 to inquire into the revenue and expenditure, etc., of certain of the West Indian Colonies.

1884, May 24. FREDERICK NAPIER BROOME, governor of Western Australia.

1884, May 24. ARTHUR ELIBANK HAVELOCK, governor of the West Africa Settlements.

1884, Aug. 1. DAVID LEWIS MACPHERSON, minister of the Interior in the Dominion of Canada.

1884, Aug. 14. RONALD FERGUSON THOMPSON, envoy extraordinary and minister plenipotentiary at Teheran.

1884, Sept. 25. (Honorary) MOUSTAPHA BEY YAWER, Mudir of Dongola, in recognition of the services rendered by him to the British Troops and Government in the Soudan. On the same day (Sept. 25) were issued the warrant of appointment, the warrant granting the dignity, the warrant dispensing with investiture and the royal licence to wear the insignia and to assume the appellation of a Knight Bachelor.

1885, Mar. 23. WILLIAM ARTHUR WHITE, envoy extraordinary and minister plenipotentiary at Bucharest.

1885, Mar. 23. HENRY PERCY ANDERSON, of the Foreign Office.

1885, May 15. GERALD FITZGERALD, late direc. gen. of Public Accounts in Egypt.

1885, June 6. ADAMS GEORGE ARCHIBALD, late lieut. gov. of the Province of Nova Scotia, in the Dominion of Canada.

1885, June 6. CHARLES MILLS, agent gen. in London for the Cape of Good Hope.

1885, June 6. Maj. Gen. PETER HENRY SCRATCHLEY, R.E., Her Majesty's special commissioner for the protected Territory in New Guinea.

1885, June 6. ALEXANDER STUART, premier and colonial secretary of New South Wales.

1885, June 26. LIONEL SACKVILLE SACKVILLE-WEST, commonly called the Hon. Lionel Sackville Sackville-West, her Majesty's envoy extraordinary and minister plenipotentiary at Washington.

24

1885, June 26. FRANCIS CLARE FORD, Her Majesty's envoy extraordinary and minister plenipotentiary at Madrid.

1885, June 26. THOMAS VILLIERS LISTER, assistant under secretary of State for Foreign Affairs.

1885, Aug. 13. HALLIDAY MACARTNEY, M.D., English secretary to the Chinese Legation in London.

1885, Aug. 25. JOSEPH PHILIPPE RENÉ ADOLPHE CARON, minister of Militia and Defence for the Dominion of Canada.

1885, Aug. 25. Maj. Gen. FREDERICK DOBSON MIDDLETON, in command of the militia in the Dominion of Canada, for services while in command of the Force in the North-West Territory.

1885, Aug. 25. (Honorary) Maj. Gen. EDWARD ZOHRAB PASHA, unattached, in the army of the Khedive of Egypt, for services rendered in connection with the recent operations in the Soudan.

1885, Sept. 1. JOHN FOWLER, C.E., for services rendered in connection with recent operations in Egypt and the Soudan.

1886, Feb. 18. Col. JOHN UNDERWOOD BATEMAN-CHAMPAIN, R.E., for services of many years standing in connection with the Indo-European telegraph.

1886, Feb. 18. FRANK CAVENDISH LASCELLES, agent and consul gen. in Bulgaria.

1886, Feb. 20. Hon. FRANCIS RICHARD PLUNKETT, envoy extraordinary and minister plenipotentiary to the emperor of Japan.

1886, Feb. 20. Capt. RICHARD FRANCIS BURTON, consul at Trieste.

1886, May 29. Sir JOHN COODE, C.E., knt., in recognition of services rendered in connection with Colonial Harbours and Marine Works.

1886, May 29. Lieut. Col. MARSHALL JAMES CLARKE (late R.A.), resident magistrate in Basutoland.

1886, May 29. CECIL CLEMENTI SMITH, lieut. gov. and colonial secretary of Ceylon.

1886, May 29. DONALD ALEXANDER SMITH, of Montreal, in the Dominion of Canada.

1886, May 29. ROBERT STOUT, premier of New Zealand.

1886, May 29. (Honorary) His Highness ABDUL SAMAT, Sultan of Selangore.

1886, May 29. Hon. WILLIAM STUART, envoy extraordinary and minister plenipotentiary at the Hague.

1886, May 29. The Rt. Hon. HUSSEY CRESPIGNY (VIVIAN), 3rd lord Vivian, envoy extraordinary and minister plenipotentiary at Brussels.

1886, May 29 The Hon. EDMUND JOHN MONSON, envoy extraordinary and minister plenipotentiary at Copenhagen.

1886, May 29. Lieut. Col. ROBERT LAMBERT PLAYFAIR, consul gen. for Algeria and Tunis.

1886, June 28. (Additional) Sir SAMUEL DAVENPORT, knt., assistant executive commissioner for South Australia

1886, June 28. (Additional) FRANCIS KNOLLYS, for special services in connection with the colonial and Indian Exhibition.

1886, June 28 (Additional) ARTHUR NONUS BIRCH, formerly lieut. gov. and colonial secretary of Ceylon, executive commissioner for that Colony.

1886, June 28. (Additional) ARTHUR HODGSON, a royal commissioner and general secretary to the Reception Committee.

1886, June 28. (Additional) JOHN FRANCIS JULIUS VON HAAST, Ph.D , commissioner in charge of New Zealand exhibits.

1886, June 28 (Additional) AUGUSTUS JOHN ADDERLEY, late member of the Legislative Council of the Bahama Islands, a royal commissioner, also executive commissioner for the West Indian Islands.

1886, June 28. (Additional) JAMES FRANCIS GARRICK, a member of the Executive Council of Queensland, agent gen. for the Colony in London and a royal commissioner, also executive commissioner for the Colony.

1886, June 28. (Additional) GRAHAM BERRY, formerly premier of Victoria, agent gen. in London and executive commissioner for the Colony

1886, July 23 SAMUEL WALKER GRIFFITH, vice-president of the Executive Council, colonial secretary and premier of the Colony of Queensland.

1886, Aug 6. Sir HORACE RUMBOLD, bart , envoy extraordinary and minister plenipotentiary at Athens.

1886, Aug. 6. FRANCIS OTTIWELL ADAMS, envoy extraordinary and minister plenipotentiary at Berne.

1886, Aug. 6 FRANCIS BEILBY ALSTON, chief clerk of the Foreign Office.

1886, Oct. 25. Sir WILLIAM FOSTER STAWELL, knt., late chief justice of the Supreme Court of the Colony of Victoria.

1886, Oct. 25. JOHN GORDON SPRIGG, premier of the Cape of Good Hope.

1886, Nov. 8. (Additional) Rt. Hon. JOHN STAPLES, lord mayor of London, a royal commissioner for the Colonial and Indian Exhibition of 1886

1886, Nov 8 (Additional) WALTER LAWRY BULLER, a member of the New Zealand commission in London for the said exhibition.

1887, Apr. 18. CHARLES COX, chancellor of the most distinguished order of Saint Michael and Saint George (with rank as senior knight commander in accordance with the Tenth Article of the Statutes of 1832, Aug. 16, making provision for the office of chancellor).

1887, Apr. 18 ROBERT THORBURN, premier of Newfoundland, and one of the representatives of that Colony at the Colonial Conference.

1887, Apr. 18 JOHN WILLIAM DOWNER, premier of South Australia and one of the representatives of that Colony at the Colonial Conference

1887, Apr. 19. THOMAS UPINGTON, late premier and now attorney general of the Cape of Good Hope and one of the representatives of that Colony at the Colonial Conference.

1887, Apr. 19. JAMES LORIMER, member of the Legislative Council and minister of Defence of Victoria and one of the representatives of that Colony at the Colonial Conference.

1887, Apr. 19. ROBERT WISDOM, member of the Legislative Council and late attorney general of New South Wales and one of the representatives of that Colony at the Colonial Conference.

1887, May 24. The Rt. Hon. WILLIAM HILLIER (ONSLOW), 4th earl of Onslow, parliamentary under secretary of State for the Colonies.

1887, May 24. The Rt. Hon. JENICO WILLIAM JOSEPH (PRESTON), 14th viscount Gormanston, governor of the Leeward Islands.

1887, May 24 JAMES HECTOR, M.D., director of geological surveys and curator of the Colonial Museum for the Colony of New Zealand.

1887, May 24. WILLIAM BRANDFORD GRIFFITH, governor of the Gold Coast Colony.

1887, May 24. Lieut. Col. JOHN TERENCE NICOLLS O'BRIEN, governor of the Island of Heligoland.

1887, May 24. Col. FREDERICK CARRINGTON, commandant of the Police Force of British Bechuanaland.

1887, May 24. JOHN BATES THURSTON, lieut. gov. and colonial secretary of the Colony of Fiji.

1887, June 21. EDWARD NEWTON, late lieut. gov. and colonial secretary of Jamaica.

1887, June 21. MALCOLM FRASER, colonial secretary of Western Australia.

1887, June 21. WILLIAM HENRY MARSH, late colonial secretary and auditor general of Hong Kong.

1887, June 21. SIDNEY GODOLPHIN ALEXANDER SHIPPARD, M A., D.C.L., administrator and chief magistrate of British Bechuanaland.

1887, June 21. JOHN WILLIAM AKERMAN, speaker of the Legislative Council of Natal.

1887, June 21. JAMES ALEXANDER GRANT, M.D., of Ottawa, in the Dominion of Canada.

1887, June 21. Maj. Gen. CHRISTOPHER CHARLES TEESDALE, R.A., V.C.

1887, June 21. Col. COLIN CAMPBELL SCOTT-MONCRIEFF, late R.E., for services rendered in Egypt.

1887, June 21. WILLIAM KIRBY GREEN, Her Majesty's envoy extraordinary and minister plenipotentiary to the emperor of Morocco.

1887, June 21. Col. CHARLES EDWARD MANSFIELD, minister resident and consul general in the Republic of Peru.

1887, June 21. CLEMENT LLOYD HILL, of the Foreign Office.

1887, June 21. JOHN HENRY FAWCETT, consul general and judge of the Supreme Consular Court at Constantinople.

1887, June 21. GEORGE DASHWOOD TAUBMAN-GOLDIE, founder of the Royal Niger Company.

1887, June 21. (Honorary) MUSTAPHA FEHMY PASHA.

1887, July 30. (Honorary) Monsieur JOHN ANTONIADAS, for services rendered in Egypt.

1887, Aug. 1. EDGAR VINCENT, Esq., financial adviser to the Egyptian Government.

1887, Aug. 18. THOMAS HENRY SANDERSON, of the Foreign Office.

1888, Jan. 10 (Jan. 2). JOHN PENDER.

1888, Jan. 10 (Jan. 2). Col. ROBERT MURDOCH SMITH, R.E.

1888, Jan. 28. GEORGE SMYTH BADEN-POWELL, M.P., for various services rendered in connection with the Colonies.

1888, Jan. 28. HARRY ALBERT ATKINSON, premier of the Colony of New Zealand.

1888, Jan. 28. EDWIN THOMAS SMITH, mayor of Adelaide and member of the House of Assembly of the Colony of South Australia.

1888, Jan. 28. FREDERICK YOUNG, for some years honorary secretary and now one of the vice-presidents of the Royal Colonial Institute.

1888, May 24. MICHAEL HENRY GALLWEY, attorney general of the Colony of Natal.

1888, May 24. The Hon. WALTER FRANCIS HELY-HUTCHINSON, lieut. gov. of the Island of Malta.

1888, May 24. JOHN FREDERICK DICKSON, colonial secretary of the Straits Settlements

1888, May 24. EDWARD NOEL WALKER, colonial secretary of the Island of Ceylon.

1888, May 24. Capt JOHN CHARLES READY COLOMB, R.M.A , M.P.

1888, June 2. CHARLES ALFRED COOKSON, Her Majesty's consul and judge at Alexandria.

1888, June 2. JAMES WILLIAM REDHOUSE, Oriental translator to the Foreign Office.

1888, June 2. ALFRED DENT, founder of the British North Borneo Company.

1888, June 2. FREDERICK WILLIAM SMYTHE, general manager of the Imperial Ottoman Bank, Constantinople

1888, June 2. (Honorary) ZULFIKAR PASHA, chamberlain to His Highness the Khedive of Egypt.

1888, June 2. (Honorary) OSMAN PASHA ORPHI, governor of Alexandria.

1888, Sept. 10. JOHN SPARROW DAVID THOMPSON, Q C., minister of justice for the Dominion of Canada (in recognition of services rendered at the recent Conference at Washington on the subject of the North American Fisheries).

1888, Sept. 10. JAMES SPEARMAN WINTER, Q C., attorney general of the Island of Newfoundland (same occasion).

1888, Sept. 10. JOHN HENRY GIBBS BERGNE, superintendent of the Treaty Department of the Foreign Office (same occasion).

1888, Nov. 7. HENRY ARTHUR BLAKE, governor of Newfoundland.

1889, Jan. 2. Col. Sir HERBERT BRUCE SANDFORD, R.A , late secretary in Australia of the Royal Commission for the Adelaide Jubilee International Exhibition, 1887

1889, Jan. 2. ROGER TUCKFIELD GOLDSWORTHY, governor of the Colony of British Honduras.

1889, Jan. 2. JOSEPH WILLIAM TRUTCH, late resident agent for the Dominion of Canada in British Columbia.

1889, Jan. 2. Lieut. Gen. THOMAS LIONEL JOHN GALLWEY, R.E., late governor of the Bermuda Islands.

1889, May 24. Lieut. Gen. Sir HENRY D'OYLEY TORRENS, governor and commander-in-chief of the Island of Malta.

1889, May 24. Sir JAMES MACBAIN, knt., president of the Legislative Council of the Colony of Victoria.

1889, May 24. CHARLES BRUCE, lieut. gov. and government secretary of the Colony of British Guiana.

1889, May 24. WILLIAM MACGREGOR, M.D., administrator of the Possession of British New Guinea.

1889, May 24. WALTER JOSEPH SENDALL, governor and commander-in-chief of the Windward Islands.

1889, May 24. JAMES SHAW HAY, governor and commander-in-chief of the Colony of Sierra Leone.

1889, May 24. JOHN ROBINSON, member of the Legislative Council of Natal.

1889, May 24. LANGHAM DALE, M.A., LL.D., superintendent general of Education of the Cape of Good Hope, and vice-chancellor of the University of that Colony.

1889, May 24. Capt. JOHN SYDNEY WEBB, deputy master of the Corporation of the Trinity House for services in connection with lighthouses in the colonies and abroad.

1889, Oct. 11. *MEDHI KULI KHAN, styled Majd-ud-Dowleh, high steward to the shah of Persia. (Honorary.)

1889, Oct. 11. MUHAMMED HASAN KHAN, styled Etimad-us-Sultaneh. (Honorary.)

1889, Oct. 11. ABULKASSIM KHAN, styled Nasr-ul-Mulk. (Honorary.)

1889, Oct. 11. Dr. JOSEPH DÉSIRÉE THOLOZAN. (Honorary.)

* The four persons appointed on October 11th had had the honour conferred on them on the previous 29th of July by the Queen at Osborne House. They were not knighted on that occasion. Furthermore, they were never gazetted. The warrant of appointment, the warrant granting the dignity, the warrant dispensing with investiture, and the royal licence to wear the insignia of their rank and to assume the appellation of a knight bachelor are all dated October 11th.

1890, Jan. 1. CÉLICOURT AUGUSTE ANTELME, member of the Executive Council and senior elected member of the Council of Government of the Colony of Mauritius.

1890, Jan. 1. MONTAGU FREDERICK OMMANNEY, one of the crown agents for the Colonies.

1890, Jan. 1. CORNELIUS ALFRED MOLONEY, governor and commander-in-chief of the Colony of Lagos.

1890, Jan. 1. JOHN COX BRAY, speaker of the House of Assembly of the Colony of South Australia.

1890, Jan. 1. JACOBUS ALBERTUS DE WET, secretary for native affairs of the Colony of the Cape of Good Hope.

1890, Feb. 17. Lieut. Gen. HENRY AUGUSTUS SMYTH, R.A., on appointment to the governor and commander-in-chief of the the Island of Malta and its dependencies.

1890, Mar. 4. BENJAMIN BAKER, C.E., joint engineer of the Forth Bridge, who has rendered eminent professional services to the Dominion of Canada and the Colony of the Cape of Good Hope.

1890, May 21. Sir ALBERT WILLIAM WOODS, knt., Garter Principal King of Arms, and King of Arms of the said most distinguished Order.

1890, May 21. AUGUSTUS WILLIAM LAWSON HEMMING, of the Colonial Office.

1890, May 21. Lieut. Col FREDERICK THOMAS SARGOOD, formerly minister of Defence of the Colony of Victoria.

1890, May 21. WILLIAM FREDERICK HAYNES SMITH, governor and commander-in-chief of the Leeward Islands.

1890, May 21. Col. CASIMIR STANISLAUS GZOWSKI, honorary aide-de-camp to the queen, for valuable services rendered to the Dominion of Canada.

1890, May 21. GEORGE GLYNN PETRE, Her Majesty's envoy extraordinary and minister plenipotentiary to His Majesty the king of Portugal.

1890, May 21. JOSEPH ARCHER CROWE, Her Majesty's commercial attaché for Europe.

1890, May 21. CHARLES HALL, Q C , M.P., first British delegate to the Maritime Conference at Washington.

1890, Aug. 28. (Honorary) BLUM PASHA, late under secretary of finance in Egypt.

1890, Nov. 27. (Honorary) Count JACQUES HENRI EDWARD DE LALAING, of Belgium, for services in connexion with the Waterloo Memorial at Brussels.

1891, Jan. 1. Maj. Gen. JAMES BEVAN EDWARDS, R E , for services rendered in connection with the Australasian Military Forces.

1891, Jan. 1 JAMES ARNDELL YOUL, of the Colony of Tasmania.

1891, Jan. 1. FREDERICK McCOY, professor of natural science in the University of Melbourne in the Colony of Victoria.

1891, Jan. 1 GUISEPPE CARBONE, LL.D., Crown advocate of the Island of Malta.

1891, Jan. 1. EDWARD NICHOLAS COVENTRY BRADDON, agent general in London for the Colony of Tasmania

1891, Jan. 7. THOMAS SUTHERLAND, M P., chairman of the Peninsular and Oriental Steam Navigation Company and director of the Suez Canal Company.

1891, May 30 RICHARD SOUTHEY, formerly colonial secretary of the Colony of the Cape of Good Hope and lieut. gov of the Province of Griqualand West.

1891, May 30. JOHN FORREST, premier and treasurer of the Colony of Western Australia.

1891, May 30. GEORGE WILLIAM ROBERT CAMPBELL, on retirement from the office of inspec. gen of police and prisons of the Island of Ceylon.

1892, Jan. 1. (Honorary) His Highness IDRIS BIN ALMARHOM BANDHARA ISKANDER SAH, sultan of Perak.

1892, Jan. 1. Commander GRAHAM JOHN BOWER, late R.N., Imperial secretary and accountant to the High Commissioner for South Africa.

1892, Jan. 1. FRANCIS FLEMING, colonial secretary of Hong Kong.

1892, Jan. 1. JOHN COLTON, formerly premier of the Colony of South Australia.

1892, Jan. 1. HENRY JOHN WRIXON, member of the Executive Council and of the Legislative Assembly of the Colony of Victoria.

1892, May 25. Sir WILLIAM MONTAGU MANNING, knt., LL.D., member of the Legislative Council of the Colony of New South Wales.

1892, May 25. Sir DAVID TENNANT, knt., speaker of the House of Assembly of the Colony of the Cape of Good Hope.

1892, May 25. JOHN JOSEPH CALDWELL ABBOTT, D.C.L., Q C., prime minister of the Dominion of Canada and president of the Queen's Privy Council for the Dominion.

1892, May 25. OLIVER MOWAT, LL.D., Q.C., attorney general and premier of the Province of Ontario in the Dominion of Canada.

1892, May 25. PATRICK ALPHONSUS BUCKLEY, attorney general and colonial secretary of the Colony of New Zealand.

1892, May 25. FERDINANDO VINCENZO INGLOTT, late postmaster general of the Island of Malta.

1892, May 25. ELWIN MITFORD PALMER, for services rendered in Egypt.

1892, May 25. CHALONER ALABASTER, consul general for Canton.

1892, May 25. HUGH GUION MACDONNELL, envoy extraordinary and minister plenipotentiary to the king of Denmark.

1892, July 22. GEORGE RICHARD DIBBS, premier of the Colony of New South Wales.

1892, July 30. The Rt. Hon. DAVID EVANS, the lord mayor of London.

1892, Aug. 6. GERALD HERBERT PORTAL, Her Majesty's agent and consul general for the Dominions of His Highness the sultan of Zanzibar.

1892, Aug. 4. Maj. CLAUDE MAXWELL MACDONALD, Her Majesty's commissioner and consul general in the Oil Rivers Protectorate.

1892, Aug. 16   Col FRANCIS CUNNINGHAM SCOTT, inspec. gen. of the Gold Coast Constabulary for services rendered while in command of the Expeditionary Force against the Jebus.

1892, Aug. 16. Col. CHARLES HOLLED SMITH, King's Royal Rifle Corps, in recognition of his services as governor of Suakin.

1892, Aug. 16. JAMES SIVEWRIGHT, commissioner of Crown Lands and Public Works for the Colony of the Cape of Good Hope.

1893, Jan 2. HUBERT EDWARD HENRY JERNINGHAM, lieut. gov. and colonial secretary of the Colony of Mauritius.

1893, Jan. 2 ANTHONY COLLING BROWNLESS, LL D., M.D., chancellor of the University of Melbourne.

1893, Jan. 2. Maj. GEORGE SYDENHAM CLARKE, R.E., late secretary to the Colonial Defence Committee.

1893, June 3. JOHN CARLING, senator and member of the Government of the Dominion of Canada.

1893, June 3. CHARLES TODD, postmaster general and superintendent of telegraphs of the Colony of South Australia.

1893, June 3. MELMOTH OSBORN, late commissioner and chief magistrate, Zululand.

1893, June 3   GILBERT THOMAS CARTER, governor of the Colony of Lagos.

1893, June 3. GEORGE BERKLEY, C.E, past president of the Institution of Civil Engineers, for services rendered as consulting engineer to the Government of Natal and in connection with other Colonies.

1893, June 3. FRANCIS HENRY EVANS, M.P., for services in connection with the Colonies as deputy chairman of the Union Steamship Company and otherwise.

1893, July 24. (Honorary) V. Adm. JOSE DE CORRANZA Y DE ÉCHEVARRIA, capt. gen. of Ferrol, in recognition of services rendered in connection with the salving of H.M. ship "Howe"

1893, Sept. 14. The Hon. CHARLES HIBBERT TUPPER, LL.B., Q.C., minister of Marine and Fisheries of the Dominion of Canada, in recognition of his services as British agent at the recent Behrings Sea Arbitration in Paris.

1893, Dec. 15. CHARLES MALCOLM KENNEDY, of the Foreign Office.

1894, Jan. 1. NEALE PORTER, colonial secretary of the Island of Jamaica.

1894, Jan. 1. The Hon. JENKIN COLES, speaker of the House of Assembly of the Colony of South Australia.

1894, Jan. 1. WESTBY BROOK PERCEVAL, agent general in London for the Colony of New Zealand.

1894, Jan. 1. Brig. Gen. HORATIO HERBERT KITCHENER, R.E., A.D.C., sirdar of the Egyptian Army.

1894, Feb. 12. JOHN SCOTT, judicial adviser to His Highness the khedive of Egypt.

1894, Mar. 3. LLOYD WILLIAM MATHEWS, president of the Ministry and gen. in the Army of His Highness the sultan of Zanzibar.

1894, Mar. 15. GEORGE HUGH WYNDHAM, envoy extraordinary and minister plenipotentiary at Rio de Janeiro.

1894, Mar. 15. JOHN ROBERT SEELEY, M.A., regius professor of Modern History at the University of Cambridge.

1894, Apr. 25. ALEXANDER CONDIE STEPHEN, Her Majesty's chargé d'affaires at Coburg.

1894, May 26. Lieut. Gen. ARTHUR JAMES LYON FREMANTLE, governor and commander-in-chief of the Island of Malta.

1894, May 26. The Hon. JAMES BROWN PATTERSON, premier and chief secretary of the Colony of Victoria.

1894, May 26. The Hon. JOHN LACKEY, president of the Legislative Council of the Colony of New South Wales.

1894, May 26. GEORGE THOMAS MICHAEL O'BRIEN, colonial secretary of the Colony of Hong Kong.

1894, May 26. EDWYN SANDYS DAWES, for services in connection with the Colony of Queensland, and in developing steam communication between England and certain of Her Majesty's Colonial Possessions.

1894, May 26. (Honorary) WILLIAM CORNELIUS VAN HORNE, president of the Canadian Pacific Railway Company.

1895, Jan 1. The Hon MACKENZIE BOWELL, prime minister of the Dominion of Canada, president of the recent Colonial Conference at Ottawa.

1895, Jan. 1. The Hon. JAMES WILSON AGNEW, M.D., member of the Executive Council and formerly premier of the Colony of Tasmania.

1895, Feb. 18. Sir JOHN WALSHAM, bart., lately Her Majesty's envoy extraordinary and minister plenipotentiary at Bucharest.

1895, May 25. Sir THOMAS FOWELL BUXTON, bart., on appointment as governor and commander-in-chief of the Colony of South Australia.

1895, May 25 The Hon. Sir JOSEPH PALMER ABBOTT, knt., speaker of the Legislative Assembly of the Colony of New South Wales.

1895, May 25. The Hon. RICHARD CHAFFEY BAKER, president of the Legislative Council of the Colony of South Australia.

1895, May 25. Col. RICHARD EDWARD ROWLEY MARTIN, British representative on the late Provisional Government Committee in Swaziland

1895, May 25 JOHN CHRISTIAN SCHULTZ, M.D., LL.D , late lieut. gov of the Province of Manitoba in the Dominion of Canada.

1895, May 25. HENRI GUSTAVE JOLY DE LOTBINIÈRE, formerly premier of the Province of Quebec in the Dominion of Canada.

1895, May 25. The Hon WILLIAM AUSTIN ZEAL, president of the Legislative Council of the Colony of Victoria.

1895, May 25. ERNEST MASON SATOW, envoy extraordinary and minister plenipotentiary at Tangier.

1895, July 5.   Col. HENRY EDWARD COLVILLE, maj. and lieut. col Grenadier Guards, lately acting British commissioner in Uganda.

1895, Nov. 15.   LOUIS ANTOINE AIMÉ DE VERTEUIL, for many years member of the Legislative Council of the Colony of Trinidad and Tobago.

1895, Nov. 22.   Rt. Hon. CHARLES WALLACE ALEXANDER NAPIER Ross (COCHRAINE-BAILLIE), 2nd lord Lamington, on appointment as governor and commander-in-chief of Queensland.

1895, Nov. 22.   Lieut. Col. GERARD SMITH, on appointment as governor and commander-in-chief of Western Australia.

1896, Jan. 1.   The Hon. PHILIP OAKLEY FYSH, treasurer and formerly premier of the Colony of Tasmania.

1896, Jan 1.   WILLIAM CROFTON TWYNAM, on retirement, after fifty years' service, from the office of Government agent for the Northern Province of the Island of Ceylon.

1896, Apr. 10.   WILLIAM EDWARD MAXWELL, governor and commander-in-chief of the Gold Coast Colony, in recognition of services rendered in the recent expedition to Ashanti, etc.

1896, Apr. 17.   The Hon. MAURICE RAYMOND GIFFORD; in recognition of services rendered in Matabeleland.

1896, May 20.   The Hon. HUGH MUIR NELSON, premier, chief secretary and colonial treasurer of the Colony of Queensland.

1896, May 20   The Hon. JOSEPH ADOLPHE CHAPLEAU, LL.D., lieut. gov. of the Province of Quebec, in the Dominion of Canada.

1896, May 20.   CHARLES STEWART SCOTT, envoy extraordinary and minister plenipotentiary at Copenhagen.

1896, Sept. 21.   ALFRED BILIOTTI, Her Majesty's consul for the Island of Crete.

1896, Nov. 5.   The Rt. Hon. Sir WALTER HENRY WILKIN, knt., lord mayor of London.

1897, Jan. 1.   The Hon. GEORGE TURNER, premier and treasurer of the Colony of Victoria.

1897, May 4.   JOHN BRAMSTON, D.C.L., assistant-under-secretary of State for the Colonies.

1897, June 10.   The Rt Hon. UCHTER JOHN MARK (KNOX), 5th earl of Ranfurly, on his appointment as governor and commander-in-chief of the Colony of New Zealand and its Dependencies.

1897, June 22   The Hon. Sir WILLIAM LAMBERT DOBSON, knt., chief justice of the Colony of Tasmania, who has on several occasions administered the government of the Colony in the absence of the governor.

1897, June 22.   Sir FREDERICK MATTHEW DARLEY, knt., lieut. gov. of the Colony of New South Wales, and chief justice of the Supreme Court of that Colony.

1897, June 22.   Col. FREDERIC CARDEW, governor and commander-in-chief of the Colony of Sierra Leone.

1897, June 22.   His Honour the Hon. GEORGE AIREY KIRKPATRICK, lieut gov. of the Province of Ontario, in the Dominion of Canada.

1897, June 22.   WILLIAM ALEXANDER BAILLIE-HAMILTON, chief clerk of the Colonial Department.

1897, June 22   SANDFORD FLEMING, for services connected with the Dominion of Canada.

1897, June 22.   FREDERICK RICHARD SAUNDERS, treasurer of the Island of Ceylon.

1897, June 22.   FRANK ATHELSTANE SWETTENHAM, resident general for the Federation of the Protected States of the Malay Peninsula

1897, June 22.   CLEMENT COURTENAY KNOLLYS, colonial secretary of the Colony of Trinidad and Tobago.

1897, June 22.   GERALD STRICKLAND, count della Catena, chief secretary to the Government of the Island of Malta.

1897, June 22.   CAVENDISH BOYLE, government secretary of the Colony of British Guiana

1897, June 22.   CHARLES GAGE BROWN, M.D., medical adviser to the Colonial Office.

1897, June 22.   WALTER PEACE, agent general in London for the Colony of Natal.

1897, June 22. GODFREY YEATMAN LAGDEN, government secretary and accountant of Basutoland.

1897, June 22. The Hon. HORACE TOZER, colonial secretary of the Colony of Queensland.

1897, June 22. The Hon. LEWIS HENRY DAVIES, minister of Marine and Fisheries for the Dominion of Canada.

1897, June 22. The Hon. HENRY CUTHBERT, solicitor general of the Colony of Victoria.

1897, June 22. EDWARD MONTAGUE NELSON, for services in connection with the Australian Colonies.

1897, June 22. Hon. His Highness IBRAHIM, sultan of the State and Territory of Johore.

1897, June 22. Col. HERBERT CHARLES CHERMSIDE (late Royal Engineers).

1897, June 22. ARTHUR HARDINGE, Her Majesty's agent and consul general at Zanzibar.

1897, June 22. Lieut. Gen. FREDERICK MARSHALL, col. 1st Royal Dragoons.

1897, June 22. JAMES MACKIE, M.B., late British delegate on the Egyptian Board of Health.

1897, June 22. ROBERT HAMILTON LANG, late English controller of the Egyptian Daira Sanieh.

1897, June 22. Maj. FRANCIS ARTHUR MARINDIN, late Royal Engineers (inspector of railways, Board of Trade).

1897, June 22. WILLIAM EDMUND GARSTIN, under secretary of State, Egyptian Public Works Department.

1897, June 22. RALPH DENHAM RAYMENT MOOR, Her Majesty's commissioner and consul general in the Niger Coast Protectorate.

1897, June 22. WALTER CAINE HILLIER, late Her Majesty's consul general in Corea.

25

1897, Aug. 12. (Honorary) CHENTUNG LIANG-CHENG, late secretary to the special embassy from the emperor of China on the occasion of the 60th anniversary of queen Victoria's accession.

1898, Jan. 1. ROBERT BAXTER LLEWELYN, administrator of the Colony of the Gambia.

1898, Jan. 1. The Hon. PIETER HENDRIK FAURE, secretary for agriculture of the Colony of the Cape of Good Hope.

1898, Jan. 1. The Hon. JAMES PENN BOUCAUT, judge of the Supreme Court of the Colony of South Australia.

1898, Jan. 1. The Hon. FRANCIS JOHN PAKENHAM, envoy extraordinary and minister plenipotentiary to His Majesty the king of Sweden and Norway.

1898, Jan. 1. ALONZO MONEY, British commissioner on the Egyptian "Caisse de la Dette."

1898, Jan. 1. FERIK GEORGE MORICE, PASHA, comptroller general of Egyptian Ports and Lighthouses.

1898, Jan. 1. WALTER FREDERICK MIÉVILLE, late president of the Egyptian Maritime and Quarantine Board of Health

1898, Feb. 4. R Adm. ROBERT HASTINGS HARRIS, commanding the Second Division of the Mediterranean Fleet.

1898, Apr. 16. (Honorary) His Excellency Maj. JOAQUIM AUGUSTO MOUSINHO DE ALBUQUERQUE, royal commissioner and gov. gen of the Province of Mozambique, in recognition of services rendered to Her Majesty's Government during military operations in Mashonaland and Matabeleland by assisting the passage of British Troops through Portuguese Territory.

1898, May 21. The Hon. CHARLES ALPHONSE PANTALÉON PELLETIER, speaker of the Senate of the Dominion of Canada.

1898, May 21. The Hon. JAMES DAVID EDGAR, Q.C., speaker of the House of Commons of the Dominion of Canada.

1898, May 21. JOHN GEORGE BOURINOT, LL.D., D.C.L., clerk of the House of Commons of the Dominion of Canada.

1898, May 21. JAMES ALEXANDER SWETTENHAM, colonial secretary of the Straits Settlements.

1898, May 21. Surg. Lieut. Col. JOHN GODFREY ROGERS, pasha, head of the Egyptian Sanitary Department.

1898, May 21. Maj. EDWARD FITZGERALD LAW, Her Majesty's commissioner on the International Financial Committee at Athens.

1898, May 21. ALEXANDER GOLLAN, Her Majesty's consul general at Havana.

1898, May 21. THOMAS BERRY CUSACK-SMITH, Her Majesty's consul general at Valparaiso.

1898, June 27. MARTIN LE MARCHANT HADSLEY GOSSELIN, Her Majesty's minister plenipotentiary at Paris, for services in connection with recent negotiations in Paris relative to the Niger delimitation.

1898, June 27. Col. WILLIAM EVERETT (for services on same occasion).

1898, July 4. Lieut. Col. HENRY EDWARD McCALLUM, R.E , governor and commander-in-chief of the Colony of Lagos, in recognition of services in the Protectorate adjoining that Colony.

1898, Aug. 17. The Hon. HENRY BINNS, prime minister and colonial secretary of the Colony of Natal, in recognition of services rendered in connection with the establishment of a Customs Union between Natal, the Cape of Good Hope and the Orange Free State.

1898, Nov. 5. Lieut. Col. the Rt. Hon. HORATIO DAVID DAVIES, M.P., lord mayor of London.

1898, Nov. 11. Brevet Col. FRANCIS REGINALD WINGATE, R.A., A.D.C , in recognition of services in the Soudan.

1898. Col. RUDOLF CHARLES RITTER VON SLATIN PASHA, of the Egyptian Army (for services same occasion)   (Honorary).

1898, Nov. 25. R. Adm. GERARD HENRY UCTRED NOEL, in recognition of his services in Crete.

1899, Jan. 2. Sir JOHN MADDEN, knt., chief justice of the Supreme Court of the Colony of Victoria, who has on several occasions administered the Government of the Colony.

1899, Jan. 2. WILLIAM TURNER THISTLETON DYER, director of the Royal Botanic Gardens, Kew, in recognition of services rendered to Colonial Governments.

1899, Jan. 2. NEVILE LUBBOCK, chairman of the West India Committee, for services rendered in connection with the West Indian Colonies.

1899, Jan. 2. HENRY HOWARD, envoy extraordinary and minister plenipotentiary to Her Majesty the queen of the Netherlands.

1899, Jan. 2. EDMUND DOUGLAS VEITCH FANE, envoy extraordinary and minister plenipotentiary to His Majesty the king of Denmark.

1899, Jan. 2. Col. JAMES HAYES SADLER, late Her Majesty's consul general at Valparaiso.

1899, Jan. 2. (Honorary) His Excellency BOUTROS GHALY, Pasha, minister for Foreign Affairs to His Highness the khedive of Egypt.

1899, Feb. 16. The Rt. Hon. WILLIAM (LYGON) 7th earl BEAUCHAMP, on appointment as governor and commander-in-chief of the Colony of New South Wales and its Dependencies.

1899, Feb. 16. The Rt. Hon. HALLAM (TENNYSON), 2nd lord Tennyson, on appointment as governor and commander-in-chief of the Colony of South Australia and its Dependencies.

1899, June 3. FREDERICK MITCHELL HODGSON, governor and commander-in-chief of the Gold Coast Colony.

1899, June 3. DAVID WILSON, governor and commander-in-chief of the Colony of British Honduras.

1899, June 3. Maj. HENRY GEORGE ELLIOT, chief magistrate of Tembuland, Transkei and Pondoland, in the Colony of the Cape of Good Hope.

1899, June 3. HENRY MOORE JACKSON, colonial secretary of Gibraltar.

1899, June 3. Col. Sir CHARLES EDWARD HOWARD VINCENT, knt., M.P., lately British delegate at the Anarchist Conference at Rome.

1899, June 3. JAMES RENNELL RODD, secretary of Legation in Her Majesty's service attached to Her Majesty's agency at Cairo.

1899. June 3. PERCY SANDERSON, Her Majesty's consul general at New York.

1899, June 3. ERNEST JOSEPH CASSEL, for services in connexion with EGYPT.

1899, July 17. Sir DAVID MILLER BARBOUR, in recognition of his services as one of the royal commissioners appointed in 1896 to enquire into the condition and prospects of the West India sugar growing Colonies, and subsequently as commissioner appointed to enquire into the Finance of the Island of Jamaica.

1899, July 28. Col. CHARLES SIM BREMRIDGE PARSONS, late Royal Artillery, in recognition of his recent services in Egypt.

1900, Jan. 1. MALACHY BOWES DALY, Q.C., lieut. gov. of the Province of Nova Scotia, in the Dominion of Canada.

1900, Jan. 1. The Hon. Sir JAMES GEORGE LEE STEERE, knt., speaker of the Legislative Assembly of Western Assembly.

1900, Jan. 1. The Hon. JOHN ALEXANDER COCKBURN, M.D., formerly premier of South Australia, now agent general in London for that Colony.

1900, Jan. 1. HENRY JOHN JOURDAIN, formerly member of the Legislative Council of the Colony of Mauritius.

1900, Jan. 1. GEORGE CHARDIN DENTON, colonial secretary of the Colony of Lagos.

1900, Jan. 1. CHARLES NORTON EDGCUMBE ELIOT, late British commissioner in Samoa.

1900, Jan. 8. Maj. Gen. EDWARD ROBERT PREVOST WOODGATE.

1900, May 23. Lieut. Col. the Hon. ALBERT HENRY HIME, prime minister and minister of Lands and Works of the Colony of Natal.

1900, May 23. The Hon. WILLIAM JOHN LYNE, premier and colonial treasurer of the Colony of New South Wales.

1900, May 23. GEORGE MELVILLE, colonial secretary of the Leeward Islands and Island Secretary of Antigua.

1900, May 23. CHARLES ANTHONY KING-HARMAN, administrator of the Island of St. Lucia and its Dependencies.

1900, May 23. HARRY LANGHORNE THOMPSON, administrator of the Island of St. Vincent and its Dependencies.

1900, May 23. The Hon. EDWARD HORNE WITTENOOM, agent general in London for the Colony of Western Australia.

1900, May 23. ALFRED EDMUND BATEMAN, comptroller general of the Commercial, Labour, and Statistical Department of the Board of Trade, for services in connection with commercial negotiations with foreign countries.

1900, May 23. EWEN CAMERON, managing director of the Hong Kong and Shanghai Banking Corporation, for services to Her Majesty's Government with regard to affairs in China.

1900, June 28. (Honorary) DE MARTINO PASHA, controller of the Civil List of the khedive of Egypt.

1900, June 28. HASSAM PASHA ASSEM, Grand Master of the Ceremonies to the khedive of Egypt. (Honorary).

1900, July 28. Brevet Col. (local Col.) JAMES WILCOCKS, commandant of the West African Frontier Force, in recognition of his services while in command of the expedition to Ashanti.

1900, Nov. 8. R. Adm. JAMES ANDREW THOMAS BRUCE, second in command, China station.

1901, Jan. 1. The Hon. JAMES ROBERT DICKSON, D.C.L., chief secretary of Queensland (in recognition of services rendered in connection with the Federation of the Australian Colonies and the establishment of the Commonwealth of Australia).

1901, Jan. 1. WILLIAM MCMILLAN, formerly colonial treasurer of New South Wales, chairman of the Finance Committee of the Australian Federal Convention (same occasion).

1901, Jan. 1. JOSIAH HENRY SYMON, Q.C., formerly attorney general of South Australia, chairman of the Judiciary Committee of the Australian Federal Convention (same occasion).

1901, Jan. 28. Brig. Gen. FREDERICK JOHN DEALTRY LUGARD, high commissioner for the Protectorate of Northern Nigeria.

1901, Jan. 29. Sir HENRY NEVILL DERING, bart., envoy extraordinary and minister plenipotentiary to the United States of Brazil.

1901, Jan. 29. The Hon. WILLIAM AUGUSTUS CURZON BARRINGTON, envoy and minister plenipotentiary to the Argentine Republic.

1901, Jan. 29. JOHN GORDON KENNEDY, envoy extraordinary and minister plenipotentiary at the Court of the king of Roumania.

1901, Jan. 29. Col. HERBERT JEKYLL, Royal Engineers, secretary to the Royal Commission for the Paris Universal International Exhibition of 1900.

1901, Feb. 11. Capt. the Hon. ARTHUR LAWLEY, on his appointment as governor of the State of Western Australia.

1901, Feb. 22. JOHN ANDERSON, of the Colonial Department, who has been selected as one of the staff of the duke of Cornwall and York, on the occasion of the approaching visit of his Royal Highness to the Colonies.

1901, Apr. 19. Maj. Gen. (local Lieut. Gen.) Sir CORNELIUS FRANCIS CLERY, for services in connection with the War in South Africa. (See footnote supra p. 347),

1901, Apr. 19. Maj. Gen. (local Lieut. Gen.) Sir HENRY MACLEOD LESLIE RUNDLE (for same).

1901, Apr. 19. Maj. Gen. GEORGE TINDAL PRETYMAN, Royal Artillery (for same).

1901, Apr. 19. Surg. Gen. WILLIAM DEANE WILSON, M.B., Army Medical Staff (for same).

1901, Apr. 19. Col. (temporary Maj. Gen.) EDWARD THOMAS HENRY HUTTON (for same).

1901, Apr. 19. Col. the Hon. FREDERICK WILLIAM STOPFORD (for same).

1901, Apr. 19. Col. THOMAS JOSEPH GALLWEY, M.D., Royal Army Medical Corps (for same).

1901, Apr. 19. Capt. and Brevet Maj. (local Lieut. Col.) EDWARD PERCY CRANWILL GIROUARD, Royal Engineers (for same).

1901, May 6. The Hon. Sir JOHN STOKELL DODDS, knt., chief justice of the Supreme Court of the State of Tasmania and at present administering the government of that State (on the occasion of T.R.H. the duke and duchess of Cornwall and York's visit to Australia).

1901, May 23. The Hon. JOSEPH GEORGE WARD, postmaster general of the Colony of New Zealand (on the occasion of the visit of T.R H. the duke and duchess of Cornwall and York to New Zealand).

1901, May 23. The Hon. JOHN McKENZIE, late minister of Lands in the colony of New Zealand (same occasion).

1901, June 27. KAID HARRY MACLEAN, attached to the special embassy from His Imperial Majesty the Sultan of Morocco (for services in Morocco).

1901, July 23. R. Adm. LEWIS ANTHONY BEAUMONT, commander-in-chief on the Australian Station (on the occasion of the visit of T.R H. the duke and duchess of Cornwall and York to Australia and New Zealand).

1901, July 24. Maj. Gen. WILLIAM JULIUS GASCOIGNE, in recognition of his services during the recent operations in China.

1901, July 25. The Hon. HENRY BALE, K.C., attorney general and minister of education of the Colony of Natal (on the occasion of the visit of T R II. the duke and duchess of Cornwall and York to Natal).

1901, July 25. DAVID HUNTER, general manager of the Natal Government Railways (same occasion)

1901, Aug. 13. The Hon. JAMES ROSE INNES, K.C., attorney general of the Colony of the Cape of Good Hope (on the occasion of the visit of T.R.H. the duke and duchess of Cornwall and York to the Cape of Good Hope).

1901, Aug. 13. The Hon. RICHARD SOLOMON, K.C., member of the Legislative Assembly of the Cape of Good Hope (same occasion)

1901, Aug. 13 CHARLES BLETTERMAN ELLIOTT, LL.B., late general manager of railways of the Cape of Good Hope (same occasion).

1901, Aug. 13. SOMERSET RICHARD FRENCH, postmaster general (same occasion).

1901, Sept. 13. WILLIAM EDWARD GOSCHEN, envoy extraordinary and minister plenipotentiary at the Court of His Majesty the king of Denmark.

1901, Sept. 27. The Hon. THOMAS KEIR MURRAY, for services in connection with the South African War. (*See* note *supra*, p. 347.)

1901, Sept. 27. JOHN DENISON PENDER, vice-chairman and managing director, Eastern Telegraph Company (for civil services during same).

1901, Sept. 17. Sir JOHN ALEXANDER BOYD, chancellor of the High Court of Justice of the Province of Ontario (on the occasion of the visit of T.R.H. the duke and duchess of Cornwall and York to the Dominion of Canada)

1901, Sept. 17. LOUIS AMABLE JETTÉ, lieut. gov. of the Province of Quebec (same occasion).

1901, Sept. 17. The Hon. ROBERT BOND, premier and colonial secretary of the Island of Newfoundland (on the occasion of the visit of T.R.H. the duke and duchess of Cornwall and York to Newfoundland).

1901, Nov. 9. ERNEST EDWARD BLAKE, one of the Crown agents for the Colonies.

1901, Nov. 9. ALFRED LEWIS JONES, president of the Liverpool Chamber of Commerce, in recognition of services to the West African Colonies and to Jamaica.

1901, Nov. 9. FREDERICK ROBERT ST. JOHN, on retirement from the post of envoy extraordinary and minister plenipotentiary at Berne.

1901, Nov. 9. AUDLEY CHARLES GOSLING, on retirement from the post of envoy extraordinary and minister plenipotentiary at Santiago.

1901, Nov. 26. Lieut. Col. Sir ARTHUR JOHN BIGGE, private secretary to H.R.H. the prince of Wales.

1902, June 2. (Honorary) Capt. ERNEST ADOLPH JULIUS GUIDO VON USEDOM, an officer of the Imperial German Navy.

1902, June 26. Maj. MATTHEW NATHAN, Royal Engineers, governor and commander-in-chief of the Gold Coast Colony.

1902, June 26. Maj. HAMILTON JOHN GOOLD-ADAMS, lieut. gov. of the Orange River Colony.

1902, June 26. His Honour DANIEL HUNTER MCMILLAN, lieut. gov. of the Province of Manitoba, in the Dominion of Canada.

1902, June 26   The Hon NEIL ELLIOTT LEWIS, M.A., B.C.L., prime minister of the State of Tasmania.

1902, June 26.   The Hon. FREDERICK WILLIAM HOLDER, speaker of the House of Representatives of the Commonwealth of Australia.

1902, June 26.   The Hon JOHN SEE, prime minister of the State of New South Wales.

1902, June 26.   The Hon. ALEXANDER JAMES PEACOCK, late prime minister of the State of Victoria.

1902, June 26.   The Hon. FREDERICK WILLIAM BORDEN, M.D., minister of Militia and Defence of the Dominion of Canada.

1902, June 26   The Hon. WILLIAM MULOCK, K.C., LLD., M.A., postmaster general of the Dominion of Canada.

1902, June 26.   EDMUND CONSTANTINE HENRY PHIPPS, His Majesty's minister at Brussels, for services in connection with the Sugar Conference.

1902, June 26.   The Hon. MICHAEL HENRY HERBERT, His Majesty's ambassador at Washington.

1902, June 26.   Capt. FRANCIS POWELL, R.N., for services in China.

1902, June 26.   PELHAM LAIRD WARREN, His Majesty's consul general at Shanghai, for services in China.

1902, June 26.   Maj. HORACE HENDERSON PINCHING, head of Sanitary Department in Cairo.

1902, June 26.   GEORGE SUTHERLAND MACKENZIE, for services in connection with Persia.

1902, June 26.   FRANCIS LANGFORD O'CALLAGHAN, managing director of the Uganda Railway.

1902, Aug. 12.   (Honorary) HIS Highness RAS MAKUNAN, special envoy of HIS Majesty the emperor Menelik II., of Ethiopia, on the occasion of the Coronation.   Invested by the king at Buckingham Palace Aug. 8, but the warrant of appointment dated Aug. 12.

1902, Aug. 15.   Capt. GEORGE RAWLINSON VYVYAN, deputy master of the Corporation of the Trinity House.

1902, Oct. 31. (Additional) Lieut. Gen. Sir JOHN DENTON PINK-STONE FRENCH, for services in South Africa.

1902, Nov. 9. (King's birthday) HENRY AUSTIN LEE, secretary of the Embassy and commercial attaché in Paris and to His Majesty's Legations at Brussels and Berne.

1902, Nov. 9. (Honorary) Col. JOAQUIM JOS MACHADO, of the Portuguese Army, late gov. gen. of Mozambique.

1902, Nov. 9. Capt. CORNELIUS ALVARO DA COSTA FERREIRA, of the Portuguese Navy, late gov. gen. of Mozambique.

1902, Nov. 9. Viscount MEIRELLES DO CANTO E CASTRO, governor of the Mozambique Company.

1902, Nov. 9. Maj. Gen. GEORGE ARTHUR FRENCH, late com-mandant of the Military Forces of the State of New South Wales.

1902, Nov. 9. DONALD WILLIAM STEWART, chief commissioner, Ashanti.

1902, Nov. 9. (Honorary) His Highness AHMAD MAÄTHAM SHAH, Sultan of Pahang.

1902, Dec. 6. Maj. ROBERT HANBURY BROWN, R.E., inspec. gen. of Irrigation, Lower Egypt.

1902, Dec. 6. WILLIAM WILLCOCKS, of the Egyptian Irrigation Department.

1902, Dec. 6. (Honorary) HUSSEIN FAKHRY PASHA, Egyptian Ministry of Public Works.

1902, Dec. 6. Maj. Gen. Sir JOHN CHARLES ARDAGH.

1902, Dec. 6. Col. Sir THOMAS HUNGERFORD HOLDICH.

1903, Feb. 9. (Honorary) His Excellency MIRZA NEZAM GAFFARY, Mohandes-el-Mamalek, minister of Public Works to His Majesty the Shah of Persia.

1903, Mar. 17. (Honorary) His Excellency FATHULLAH KHAN HALAR AFKHAM, governor of Enzeli, in recognition of services rendered to the special mission to His Majesty the Shah of Persia.

1903, June 26   GEORGE RUTHVEN LE HUNTE, M.A., governor of the State of South Australia.

1903, June 26.   WILLIAM HENRY MILTON, senior administrator of the Protectorate of Southern Rhodesia.

1903, June 26.   DANIEL MORRIS, D.Sc., M.A., Imperial commissioner of Agriculture for the West Indies.

1903, June 26.   The Hon. ALFRED JEROME CADMAN, member of the Legislative Council of the Colony of New Zealand and late minister for railways in that Colony.

1903, June 26.   PATRICK MANSON, LL.D., M.D., F.R.S, medical adviser to the Colonial Office, for special services in connection with Tropical Diseases.

1903, June 26   VICTOR ARTHUR WELLINGTON DRUMMOND, His Majesty's minister resident at the Courts of Munich and Stuttgart, on retirement from the Diplomatic Service.

1903, June 26   ALFRED SHARPE, His Majesty's commissioner, commander-in-chief and consul general for the British Central Africa Protectorate.

1903, Nov. 9   The Hon. AUGUSTUS CHARLES GREGORY, formerly surveyor general of Queensland, member of the Legislative Council of that State.

1904, Mar. 26.   Rt. Hon. CHARLES HARDINGE, ambassador designate to the emperor of Russia.

1904, June 24.   Hon. GEORGE MORRIS SUTTON, prime minister and treasurer of Natal

1904, June 24.   WILLIAM SHELFORD, Esq , member of the Institute of Civil Engineers, consulting engineer for West African Railways.

1904, June 24.   The Hon. JOHN FROST, member of the House of Assembly of the Cape of Good Hope.

1904, June 24   WILLIAM HOOD TREACHER, resident general for the Federated States of the Malay Peninsula.

1904, June 24.   The Hon. GEORGE ALEXANDER DRUMMOND, president of the Bank of Montreal, Canada.

1904, June 24. JOHN NEWELL JORDAN, minister resident in Korea.

1904, June 24. ROBERT EDWARD BREDON, Esq., deputy inspec. gen. of the Chinese Imperial Maritime Customs.

1904, June 24. R. Adm. RICHARD MASSIE BLOMFIELD, controller general of the Egyptian ports and lighthouses.

1904, June 24. FRANCIS EDMUND HUGH ELLIOT, envoy extra-ordinary and minister plenipotentiary at Athens.

1904, Sept. 6. Brevet Lieut. Col. (local Brig. Gen.) WILLIAM HENRY MANNING, inspec. gen. of the King's African Rifles (for services during the operations in Somaliland).

1904, Nov. 9. JOHN PICKERSGILL RODGER, governor and commander-in-chief of the Gold Coast Colony.

1904, Nov. 9. WILLIAM GREY-WILSON, governor and commander-in-chief of the Bahama Islands.

1904, Nov. 9. ERNEST BICKHAM SWEET-ESCOTT, governor and com-mander-in-chief of British Honduras.

1904, Nov. 9. THOMAS EKINS FULLER, agent-general in London for the Colony of the Cape of Good Hope.

1904, Nov. 9. V. Adm. REGINALD NEVILLE CUSTANCE.

The Most Eminent Order of the Indian Empire.

The Most Eminent Order of the Indian Empire.

. GRAND MASTERS

And (by virtue thereof) First and Principal Knights Grand Commanders.

See the list of Viceroys of India, supra p. 305, from 1887 onwards.

KNIGHT COMMANDERS INDIAN EMPIRE (K.C.I.E.).

Original Knights on the first enlargement of the Order, 1887, Feb. 15th.

1887, Feb. 15. Gen. Sir FREDERICK SLEIGH ROBERTS, bart., V.C., commander-in-chief in India.

1887, Feb. 15. Hon. EDMUND DRUMMOND, late member of the Council of the secretary of state for India.

1887, Feb. 15. Sir ALFRED COMYNS LYALL, Bengal Civil Service, lieut. gov. of the North-West Provinces and chief commander of Oudh.

1887, Feb. 15. ROBERT ANSTRUTHER DALYELL, member of the Council of the secretary of state for India.

1887, Feb. 15. MAXWELL MELVILL, Bombay Civil Service, member of the Council of the governor of Bombay.

1887, Feb. 15. Maj. Gen. ALEXANDER CUNNINGHAM, R E.

1887, Feb. 15. THAKUR SAHEB BHAGWUT SINGH, of Gondal.

1887, Feb. 15. RANA SHANKAR BAKSH SINGH, Bahadur, additional member of the Council of the viceroy and gov. gen. of India for making Laws and Regulations.

1887, Feb. 15. DIETRICH BRANDIS, late inspec. gen. of forests in India.

1887, Feb. 15. Sir MONIER WILLIAMS BODEN, professor of Sanskrit in the University of Oxford.

1887, Feb. 15 Maharaja PASUPATI ANANDA GAJAPATI RAZ of Vizianagram.

1887, Feb. 15. ALEXANDER MEADOWS RENDEL, consulting engineer to the India Office.

1887, Feb. 15. DONALD CAMPBELL MACNABB, late Bengal Civil Service and Commissioner at Peshawur

1887, Feb 15 Nawab MUNIR-UD-DAULA SALAR JUNG, Bahadur, prime minister of Hyderabad.

1887, Feb. 15. Sir GEORGE CHRISTOPHER MOLESWORTH BIRDWOOD, M.D., special assistant in the Statistics and Commerce Department of the India Office.

1887, Feb. 15. His Highness RAJA RANJIT SINGH, of Rutlam.

1887, Feb 15. Surg. Gen. BENJAMIN SIMPSON, M.D., sanitary commissioner and surg. gen. with the Government of India.

1887, Feb 15. ALBERT JAMES LEPPOC CAPPEL, direc. gen. of the Telegraph Department of the Government of India.

1887, Feb 15 Nawab ALI KADIR SAYID HUSON ALI, Bahadur of Moorshidabad.

1887, Feb. 15. Maharaja LACHMESSUR SINGH, Bahadur, of Darbhanga.

1887, Feb. 15. BAPU SAHIB AVAR, commander-in-chief, Gwalior.

1887, Feb 15 DONALD MACKENZIE WALLACE, private secretary to the viceroy and gov. gen. of India.

1887, Feb. 15 ALFRED WOODLEY CROFT, director of Public Instruction, Bengal.

1887, Feb. 15. BRADFORD LESLIE, agent to the East Indian Railway Company.

KNIGHT GRAND COMMANDERS INDIAN EMPIRE
(G.C.I.E.).

On the second enlargement of the Order, 1887, June 21.

1887, June 21. FREDERICK (TEMPLE-BLACKWOOD, afterwards Hamilton-Temple-Blackwood), earl of Dufferin, afterwards marquess of Dufferin and Ava, *ex officio* as Grand Master of the Order.

1887, June 21. (Extra) F. Marsh. H.R.H ALBERT EDWARD, the prince of Wales.

1887, June 21. (Extra) V. Adm. H.R.H ALFRED ERNEST ALBERT, duke of Edinburgh

1887, June 21. (Extra) Maj. Gen. H R.H. ARTHUR WILLIAM PATRICK ALBERT, duke of Connaught and Strathearn.

1887, June 21. (Extra) F Marsh. H.R.H. GEORGE WILLIAM FREDERICK CHARLES, duke of Cambridge.

1887, June 21. The Rt. Hon. DONALD JAMES (MACKAY), lord Reay, governor of the Presidency of Bombay. In celebration of the 50th year of the queen's reign.

1887, June 21. The Rt Hon ROBERT (BOURKE), 1st lord Connemara, governor of the Presidency of Madras (same occasion).

1887, June 21. Gen. Sir FREDERICK SLEIGH ROBERTS, bart , V C., commander-in-chief in India (same occasion).

1887, June 30. His Highness MAHARAO KHENGARJI, Bahadur Rao of Kutch.

1888, Feb. 23. Maharaja NRIPENDRA NARAYAN BHUP, Bahadur of Cooch Behar

1888, Dec. 10. HENRY CHARLES KEITH (PETTY-FITZMAURICE), 5th marquess of Lansdowne, ex officio as Grand Master.

1890, May 21. The Rt Hon. GEORGE ROBERT CANNING (HARRIS), 4th lord Harris, governor of the Presidency of Bombay.

1890, May 21. His Highness the Nawab of Junagarh.

1890, May 21. His Highness the Nawab of Tonk.

1890, May 21. The Nawab SAIYID SIR HASSAN ALI, Khan, Bahadur of Murshidabad (Nawab Ali Kadir Sayid Husan Ali, Bahadur, of Murshidabad).

1891, Jan. 24. Rt. Hon. BEILBY (LAWLEY), 5th lord Wenlock, gov. of the Presidency of Madras.

1891, May 30. His Highness MIR ALI MURAD KHAN, Talpur of Khairpur.

1892, Jan. 1. His Highness Maharaja ADHIRAJ SARDUL SINGH Bahadur, Maharaja of Kishengarh.

1892, May 25. Sir JAMES BROADWOOD LYALL, Bengal Civil Service, late lieut. gov. of the Punjab.

1892, May 25. Maharaja Mirza Sir PUSAPATI ANANDA GUJAPATI RAZ MANI, Sultan Bahadur Goru, Zamindar of Vizianagram.

1892, Aug. 2. Sir THOMAS LAWRENCE SECCOMBE.

1893, Mar. 6. Maj. Gen. Sir GEORGE STEWART WHITE, V.C.

1894, Jan. 27. VICTOR ALEXANDER (BRUCE), 9th earl of Elgin, ex officio as Grand Master.

1894, Aug. 10. H.H. BEGLAR BEGI MIR MAHMUD, Khan of Khelat.

1895, Feb. 25. WILLIAM (MANSFIELD), 2nd lord Sandhurst, governor of the Presidency of Bombay.

1896, Jan. 1. Rt. Hon. Sir ALFRED COMYNS LYALL, member of the Council of India.

1896, Mar. 16. Sir ARTHUR ELIBANK HAVELOCK, governor of the Presidency of Madras.

1897, Jan. 1. Maj. Gen. Sir OWEN TUDOR BURNE.

1897, June 22. His Highness Sir BHANWAR PAL DEO Bahadur Yadukul Chandra Bhal, Maharaja of Karauli.

1897, June 22. His Highness FAIZ MUHAMMAD Khan, Talpur, Mir of Khairpur in Sind.

1897, June 22. Sir LACHHMESHWAR SINGH, Bahadur, Maharaja of Darbhanga.

1897, June 22. His Highness Sir BHAGWUT SINGH Thakur Saheb Sagrami of Gondal. Invested Oct. 8.

1897, June 22. Gen. CRAWFORD TROTTER CHAMBERLAIN.

1897, July 31. H.H. WAGHJI, Thakur Sahib of Morvi.

1897, Oct. 15. Rt. Hon. Sir GEORGE FAUDEL-PHILLIPS, bart.

1898, Jan. 1. His Highness Maharaja Sir PRABHU NARAYAN SINGH Bahadur of Benares.

1898, Jan. 1. His Highness Sir SHER MUHAMMAD KHAN, Diwan of Palanpur.

1899, Jan. 6. GEORGE NATHANIEL (CURZON), 1st lord Curzon of Kedleston, ex officio as Grand Master.

1900, Feb. 17. HENRY STAFFORD (NORTHCOTE), 1st lord Northcote, governor of the Presidency of Bombay (additional).

1900, May 23. H.H. Saramad-i-Rajaha-i-Hindustan, Raj Rajindra Sri Maharaja-dhiraj Sawai Sir MADHA SINGH, Bahadur of Jaipur.

1900, May 23. H.H. Saramad-i-Rajaha-i-Bundelkund, the Maharaja Mahindra Sawai Sir PRATAB SINGH, Bahadur of Orchha.

1900, Dec. 17. (Honorary) His Majesty the Emperor of Korea.

1900, Dec. 28 [? Dec. 4]. ARTHUR OLIVER VILLIERS (RUSSELL), 2nd lord Ampthill, governor of the Presidency of Madras (additional).

1901, Jan. 1. Maj. Gen. Sir EDWIN HENRY HAYTER COLLEN, military member of the Council of the gov. gen. of India.

1901, Jan. 1. His Highness Maharao Raja Sir RAGHUBIR SINGH Bahadur, of Bundi.

1901, July 24. Maj. Gen. Sir ALFRED GASELEE.

1901, Nov. 9. Gen. Sir ARTHUR POWER PALMER, commander-in-chief in India.

1901, Nov. 9. His Highness Maharao Sir KAISHRI SINGH Bahadur, of Sirohi, in Rajputana.

1902, June 26. His Highness Agha Sultan Sir Muhammad Shah AGHA KHAN, of Bombay.

1902, June 26. Sir HENRY WATERFIELD, secretary in the Financial Department of the India Office.

1903, Jan. 1. His Highness Sri Padmanabha Dasa Vanji Sir Bala Rama Varma Kulashekhara Kiritapati Mani Sultan Maharaja Raja Rama Raja, Bahadur Shamsher Jang, of Travancore (on the occasion of the Durbar).

1903, Jan. 1. His Highness Farzand-i-Arjumand Akidat-Paiwand Daulat-i-Inglishia Barar Bans Sarmur Raja-i-Rajagan Raja Sir Hira Singh Malwandar Bahadur, of Nabha (on same occasion).

1903, Jan. 1. Sir JOHN WOODBURN, would have been appointed G C S.I. on the same occasion in recognition of his long and distinguished services in India, but he died at Calcutta 1902, Nov. 21, being then lieut. gov. of Bengal.

1903, Nov. 15. H.H. SAIYID FAISAL BIN TURKI, Sultan of Muskat.

1903, Dec. 12. CHARLES WALLACE ALEXANDER NAPIER (COCHRANE-BAILLIE), 2nd lord Lamington [governor of Bombay].

1904, June 24. H H. Nawab Sultan JAHAN, Begum of Bhopal.

KNIGHTS COMMANDERS OF THE INDIAN EMPIRE.

(From the date of the second enlargement of the Order.)

1887, June 30.   His Highness the Thakore Sahib of Morvi.

1887, June 30.   Sir JASWANT SINGHJI, Thakur Sahib of Limri.

1887, Aug. 17.   WILLIAM GERALD SEYMOUR VESEY FITZGERALD, political aide-de-camp to the Secretary of State for India.

1888, Jan. 1.   Sir CHARLES ARTHUR TURNER, late chief justice of the Madras High Court.

1888, Jan. 1.   Nawab Bushir-ud-Dowlah Amir-i-Akbar ASMAN JAH Bahadur.

1888, Jan. 1.   Nawab Shams-ul-Amara Amir-i-Kabir KHUSHED JAH Bahadur, member of the Hyderabad Council of State.

1888, Jan. 1.   EDWIN ARNOLD.

1888, Jan. 1.   Maharajah RADHA PROSAD SING of Dumraon.

1888, Jan. 1.   VINAKERALA VARMA, Elaya Raja of Cochin.

1888, Mar. 20.   ARTHUR NICOLSON, Her Majesty's chargé d'affaires at Teheran.

1888, May 24.   RAYMOND WEST, Bombay Civil Service, member of the Council of the governor of Bombay.

1888, May 24.   Nawab NAWAZISH ALI Khan.

1888, May 24.   GUILFORD LINDSAY MOLESWORTH, consulting engineer to the Government of India for State Railways.

1888, May 24.   FREDERICK RUSSELL HOGG, Bengal Civil Service, direc. gen. of the Post Office of India.

1888, May 24. Sirdar NAOROZ Khan of Kharan.

1888, May 24. Surg. Gen. WILLIAM JAMES MOORE, surg. gen. with the Government of Bombay and honorary surgeon to the viceroy of India.

1888, May 24. Nawab IMAM BAKSH Khan.

1888, May 24. Sirdar ATAR SING of Bhadour.

1888, May 24. Raja VELUGOTI-SRI-KRISHNA YACHENDRA, of Venkatagiri (Raja Velugoti Sri Raja Gopala Yachendralavaru, of Venkatagiri).

1888, June 28. Maharaja HARENDRA KISHOR SINGH, Bahadoor of Bettia.

1888, June 28. Sir GREGORY CHARLES PAUL.

1888, June 28. Maharaja NARENDRA KRISNA DEB Bahadoor.

1889, Jan. 1. Rt. Hon HENRY MORTIMER DURAND, Bengal Civil Service, secretary to the Government of India in the Foreign Department.

1889, Jan. 1. Maharaja KRISHNA PARTAB SAHI, Bahadur, of Hatwa.

1889, Jan. 1. Sir ARTHUR GEORGE MACPHERSON, secretary in the Judicial and Public Department of the India Office.

1889, Jan. 1. WILLIAM MARKBY, D.C.L., University reader of Indian law at Oxford, late judge of the High Court at Calcutta.

1889, Jan. 1. HENRY STUART CUNNINGHAM, late judge of the High Court at Calcutta.

1889, May 25   Maharana SRI WAKHTSINGHJI, Raja of Lunawara.

1889, May 25. JOHN WARE EDGAR, Bengal Civil Service, chief secretary to the Government of Bengal.

1890, Jan. 1. Sir ROPER LETHBRIDGE, late press commissioner in India.

1890, Jan. 1. Sir GEORGE STEWART WHITE, V.C.

1890, May 21. JAMES BELLETT RICHEY, Bombay Civil Service.

1891, Jan. 1. His Highness PARBHU NARAYAN SINGH, Maharaja Bahadur of Benares.

1891, May 30. CHARLES BRADLEY PRITCHARD, Bombay Civil Service, member of the Council of the governor of Bombay.

1892, Jan. 1. His Excellency ALI KULI, Khan Mukhbar-ud-Dowla, of Persia. (Honorary.)

1892, May 25. TIRAVARUR MUTHUSWAMI AIYAR, one of the Puisne Judges, High Court of Judicature, Madras.

1892, May 25. GRIFFITH HUMPHREY PUGH EVANS, barrister-at-law, additional member of the Council of the Viceroy of India for making Laws and Regulations.

1892, May 25. Hon. EDWARD CHARLES KAYLL OLLIVANT, Bombay Civil Service, Political Agent and Collector of Stamp Revenue, Kathiawar.

1892, May 25. Sir CHARLES PONTIFEX, late legal adviser and solicitor to the secretary of state for India.

1892, May 25. Sir HENRY HOYLE HOWORTH, M.P.

1892, Aug. 15. Sir HENRY SEYMOUR KING.

1893, Jan. 2. His Highness SHER MAHOMED KHANJI JORAWAR KHANJI LOHANI, Dewan of Pahlanpur.

1893, Jan. 2. Mir Jam ALI KHAN, Jam of Las Bela.

1893, Jan. 2. Maj. Gen. EDWIN HENRY HAYTER COLLEN, Indian Staff Corps, Secretary to the Government of India in the Military department.

1893, Jan. 2. Raja AMIR HASSAN, Muhammad Bahadur, of Mahmoodabad.

1893, Jan. 2. Lieut. Col. WILLIAM BRERETON HUDSON, commandant of the Behar Light Horse.

1893, June 3. Lieut. Gen. THOMAS EDWARD GORDON, Indian Staff Corps.

1893, June 3. Lieut. Gen. EDWARD CHARLES SPARSHOTT WILLIAMS, R.E.

1893, June 3.   Sardar ASAD KHAN, of Sarawan.

1893, June 3.   JOHN LAMBERT, commissioner of police, Calcutta.

1893, Aug. 31.   (Honorary) Monsieur LEON EMILE CLÉMENT THOMAS, gouverneur des establishments français dans L'Inde.

1894, Jan. 1.   HIS Highness the Maharao Raja of Bundi.

1894, Jan. 1.   His Highness the Maharaja of Karauli.

1894, Jan. 1.   His Highness the Maharaja of Orchha.

1894, Jan. 1.   Prince JEHAN KADER MIRZA BAHADUR, of Oudh.

1894, Jan. 1.   Col. JOHN CHARLES ARDAGH, private secretary to His Excellency the viceroy.

1894, Jan. 1.   Col. lord WILLIAM LESLIE DE LA POER BERESFORD, V.C., military secretary to His Excellency the viceroy.

1894, Jan. 1.   JAMES LYLE MACKAY.

1895, Jan. 1.   Raja SUDHAL Deo of Bamra.

1895, Jan. 1.   Col. HENRY RAVENSHAW THUILLIER, R.E., surveyor general of India.

1895, Jan. 1.   Nawab Sidi Ahmad Khan Sidi Ibrahim Khan of Janjira.

1895, Jan. 1.   Raja Sri Rao Vencatesveta Chalapati [Ventaka Svetachalapati] Ranga Rao Bahadur of Bobbili.

1895, May 25.   WILLIAM ROBERT BROOKE, late direc. gen. of telegraphs in India

1895, May 25.   H.H. Maharaja PARTAB NARAYAN SINGH of Ajudhya.

1895, May 25.   Maharaja RAVENESHWAR PRASAD SINGH BAHADUR, of Gidhaur.

1895, May 25.   Sirdar Krishna Rao BAPU SAHEB JADU.

1895, Aug. 12.   Lieut. Col. ADELBERT CECIL TALBOT, Indian Staff Corps.

1896, Jan. 1. Nawab Secundar Jung Ikbal-ud-Dowlah, Iktadar-ul-Mulk, Vikar-ul-Umara, Bahadur, prime minister to His Highness the Nizam of Hyderabad.

1896, Jan. 1. (Extra) Maj. Gen. THOMAS DENNEHY, Bengal Army (retired).

1897, Jan. 1. His Highness Maharaja SAWAI RANJOR SINGH, Bahadur of Ajaigarh.

1897, June 22. HENRY WILLIAM BLISS.

1897, June 22. Nawab AMIR-UD-DIN AHMAD KHAN, Bahadur, chief of Loharu.

1897, June 22. Col. WILLIAM SINCLAIR SMITH BISSET, Royal Engineers, secretary to the Government of India in the Public Works Department.

1897, June 22. Maj, Gen. EDWARD STEDMAN, Indian Staff Corps

1897, June 22. JOHN JARDINE, Indian Civil Service (retired).

1897, June 22. R. Adm. JOHN HEXT, Royal Navy (retired), director of the Royal Indian Marine.

1897, June 22. MANCHERJEE MERWANJEE BHOWNAGGREE.

1897, June 22. Col. THOMAS HUNGERFORD HOLDICH, Royal Engineers.

1897, June 22. JAMES MACNABB CAMPBELL, Indian Civil Service.

1897, June 22. Munawwar ALI MUHAMMAD, Khan Bahadur, prince of Arcot.

1897, June 22. GEORGE WILLIAM ALLEN.

1897, June 22. Nawab Bahadur KHWAJA AHSAN-ULLA, of Dacca.

1898, Jan. 1. Hon. Baba, KHEM SINGH BEDI, of Kallar.

1898, Jan. 1. Brig. Surg. Lieut. Col. GEORGE KING.

1898, Jan. 1. ARTHUR WILSON, legal adviser and solicitor, Indian Office.

1898, Jan. 11. Hon. Sir FRANCIS WILLIAM MACLEAN, knt., Q.C., chief justice of the High Court of Justice, Calcutta.

1898, May 21.   His Highness Aga Sultan Muhammad SHAH AGA Khan.

1898, May 21.   Col. ROBERT WARBURTON, Indian Staff Corps.

1898, Dec. 31.   ANDREW WINGATE, Indian Civil Service.

1898, Dec. 31.   H.H. KUNWAR HARNAM SINGH, Ahluwalia of Kapurthala.

1898, Dec. 31.   Maj. Gen. GERALD DE COURCY MORTON.

1898, Dec. 31.   Maj. Gen. GEORGE CORRIE BIRD, Indian Staff Corps.

1900, Jan. 1   EDWARD SPENCE SYMES, Indian Civil Service, chief secretary to the Government of Burma.

1900, Jan. 1.   S. SUBRAMANIYA AIYAR, Dewan Bahadur, puisne judge of the High Court of Judicature at Fort St. George

1900, May 23   Sahib-Zada Muhammad OBEIDULLAH Khan, minister of Tonk, in Rajputana.

1901, Jan. 1   ALEXANDER FREDERICK DOUGLAS CUNNINGHAM, Indian Civil Service.

1901, Jan. 1.   HENRY EVAN MURCHISON JAMES, Indian Civil Service.

1901, Jan. 1.   (Honorary) His Excellency Col. EDUARDO AUGUSTO RODRIGUES GALHARDO, gov. gen. of Portuguese India.

1901, July 24.   Maj. His Highness Maharaja Raj Rajeshwar Siromani, Sri Gunga Singh, Bahadur of Bikanir.

1901, Nov. 9.   Nawab SHAHBAZ KHAN, Bugti of Baluchistan.

1901, Nov. 9   JAMES GEORGE SCOTT, deputy commissioner in Burma.

1901, Nov. 9.   Raja JANG Bahadur Khan of Nanpara, in the Bahraich District of Oudh.

1902, June 26.   (Honorary) His Excellency Mukhtsar-ed-Dowleh Husein Kuli Khan Mukhber-ul-Mulk, Persian minister of telegraphs.

1902, June 26. His Highness Maharaja-Dhiraj Sipahdar-ul-Mulk Mulkhan Singh Bahadur, of Charkhari, in Bundelkhand.

1902, June 26. Maharaja RAMESHWAR SINGH BAHADUR, of Darbhanga.

1902, June 26. THOMAS HIGHAM, secretary to the Government of India in the Public Works Department, Irrigation, etc., branch.

1902, June 26. Col SAMUEL SWINTON JACOB, Indian Staff Corps.

1902, Sept. 23. WILLIAM HUTT CURZON WYLIE.

1903, Jan. 1. Sir LAWRENCE HUGH JENKINS, chief justice of the High Court of Judicature at Bombay (on the occasion of the Durbar).

1903, Jan. 1 HERBERT THIRKELL WHITE, Indian Civil Service, chief judge of the Chief Court of Lower Burma (same occasion).

1903, Jan. 1. CHARLES LEWIS TUPPER, Indian Civil Service, financial commissioner of the Punjab and a member of the Council of the lieut. gov. of the Punjab for making Laws and Regulations (same occasion).

1903, Jan. 1. Surg. Gen. BENJAMIN FRANKLIN, Indian Medical Service, hon. physician to the King, direc. gen. Indian Medical Service, and sanitary commissioner with the Government of India (same occasion).

1903, Jan. 1. FREDERICK AUGUSTUS NICHOLSON, Indian Civil Service, first member of the Board of Revenue, Madras, and an additional member of the Council of the governor of Fort St. George for making Laws and Regulations (same occasion).

1903, Jan. 1. ARTHUR UPTON FANSHAWE, Indian Civil Service, direc. gen. of the Post Office of India (same occasion).

1903, Jan. 1. WALTER ROPER LAWRENCE, Indian Civil Service (retired), private secretary to His Excellency the Viceroy of India (same occasion).

1903, Jan. 1. JOHN ELIOT, meteorological reporter to the Government of India and direc. gen. of Indian Observatories (same occasion)

1903, Jan. 1. Raja Dhiraj NAHAR SINGH, of Shahpura, in Rajputana (same occasion).

1903, Jan. 1. GANGADHAR RAO GANESH, *alias* BALA SAHIB PATWAR-DHAN, chief of Miraj (senior branch) in the Southern Mahratta Country (same occasion)

1903, Jan. 1. Sardar GHAUS BAKHSH, RAISANI, the premier chief of the Sarawans, Baluchistan (same occasion).

1903, Jan 1. Maharaja HARBALLABH NARAYAN SINGH Bahadur of Sonbursa, Bengal (same occasion)

1903, Jan. 1. Maharaja PESHKAR KISHN PARSHAD, minister to His Highness the Nizam of Hyderabad (same occasion).

1903, Jan 1. PURNA NARASINGHARAO KRISHNA MURTI, Dewan of Mysore (same occasion).

1903, Jan. 1. Maharaja GODE NARAYANA GAJAPATI RAO, of Vizagapatam (same occasion).

1903, Nov. 15 (Honorary) H.H. SAIYID FAISAL BIN TURKI, sultan of Muskat.

1904, Jan. 1. Maj. Gen. Sir EDMOND ROCHE ELLES, Royal Artillery, an ordinary member of the Council of the gov. gen. of India.

1904, Jan. 1 SARDAR SULTAN JAN SADDOZAI, lately extra assistant commissioner, headquarters, Kohat.

1904, Mar. 25. Sir HENRY THOBY PRINSEP, knt., judge of the High Court, Calcutta.

1904, June 24. PHIROZSHAH MERWANJI MEHTA, additional member of the Council of the governor of Bombay for making Laws and Regulations.

1904, June 24. Col. BUCHANAN SCOTT, R E , mint master, Calcutta.

1904, June 24 Col. JOHN WALKER OTTLEY, R E., president of the Royal Indian Engineering College, Cooper's Hill.

1904, June 24. Raja JASWANT SINGH, Bahadur of Sailana, Central India.

The Royal Victorian Order.

Royal Victorian Chain.

A Personal Decoration created by King Edward VII., and given by His Majesty to Sovereigns, Princes, and other Royal Personages, as also to a few eminent British Subjects.

It does *not* form part of the Royal Victorian Order.

Alphabetical List of those to whom His Majesty has given the Royal Victorian Chain.

1902, Aug. 10. ARGYLL, duke of, K.T., G.C.M.G., G.C.V.O.

1904, Aug. 16. AUSTRIA, His Imperial Majesty the emperor of, king of Hungary, K.G.

1902, Aug. 9. CONNAUGHT, Field Marsh. His Royal Highness the duke of, K.G., K.T., K.P., G.C.B., G.C.S I., G.C.M.G., G.C.I.E , G.C.V.O.

1903, Jan. 1. CURZON OF KEDLESTON, His Excellency lord (Viceroy of India), G.M.S.I., G.M.I.E.

1904, Apr. 8. DENMARK, His Majesty the king of, K.G., G.C.B.

1902, Aug. 9. DENMARK, His Royal Highness the crown prince of, K.G., G.C.B., G C.V.O.

1902, Aug. 9. DENMARK, His Royal Highness prince Christian Frederick Charles George Waldemar Axel of, G.C.B., G.C.V.O.

1902, Aug. 11. FIFE, duke of, K T., G C.V.O.

1902, Nov. 9. GERMAN EMPEROR AND KING OF PRUSSIA, His Imperial Majesty the, K.G., G.C.V.O.

1902, Aug. 10. HESSE, His Royal Highness the grand duke of, K.G., G.C.B.

27

1903, Nov. 18   ITALY, His Majesty the king of, K.G.

1902, Nov. 19.   PORTUGAL, His Majesty the king of, K.G.

1904, June.   PRUSSIA, His Imperial and Royal Highness the crown
      prince of.

1902, Aug. 9   PRUSSIA, His Royal Highness prince Henry of, K.G.,
      G.C.B.

1904, Aug. 25.   RUSSIA, His Imperial Majesty the emperor of, K G.

1902, Aug. 10.   SCHLESWIG-HOLSTEIN, General His Royal Highness
      prince Christian of, K G , G.C.V.O.

1902, Aug. 9.   SPARTA, His Royal Highness the duke of, G.C.B.

1902, Aug. 9.   WALES, V. Adm. His Royal Highness the prince of,
      K.G , K T., K.P., G.C.M.G., G.C.V.O.

The Royal Victorian Order.

Sovereigns:

QUEEN VICTORIA.

KING EDWARD VII.

Knights Grand Cross

1896, May 6.   F. Marsh. H R H ALBERT EDWARD, prince of Wales

1896, May 6.   Gen. H.R.H. ARTHUR WILLIAM PATRICK ALBERT, duke of Connaught and of Strathearn.

1896, May 25   WILLIAM JOHN ARTHUR CHARLES JAMES (CAVENDISH-BENTINCK), 6th duke of Portland, master of the Horse.

1896, May 25.   SIDNEY (HERBERT), 31st earl of Pembroke and Montgomery, lord steward of the Household.

1896, May 25.   Rt. Hon. CHARLES JOHN (COLVILLE), lord, afterwards 1st viscount Colville, of Culross, chamberlain to H.R.H. the princess of Wales.   Died 1903, July 1.

1896, May 25.   Gen Sir DIGHTON MACNAGHTEN PROBYN, comptroller and treasurer of the Household to H R.H. the prince of Wales

1896, July 7.   WILLIAM (THOMPSON), lord Kelvin

1897, Jun 30.   Capt. H.R.H. GEORGE FREDERICK ERNEST ALBERT, duke of York, Royal Navy, afterwards prince of Wales

1897, June 30.   F. Marsh H.R.H. GEORGE WILLIAM FREDERICK CHARLES, duke of Cambridge.   Died 1904, Mar 17.

1897, June 30.   H.H. prince ALBERT JOHN CHARLES FREDERICK ALFRED GEORGE, of Schleswig-Holstein.

1897, June 30.   H.H. FRANCIS, 1st duke of Teck.   Died 1900, Jan. 20.

1897, June 30.   Gen. RICHARD WILLIAM PENN (CURZON-HOWE), 4th earl Howe.   Died 1900, Sept. 25

1897, June 30. WILLIAM HENRY (EDGCUMBE), 4th earl of Mount Edgcumbe, formerly lord chamberlain and lord steward to queen Victoria.

1898, Sept. 8. H.S.H. EMICH EDWARD CHARLES, hereditary prince of Leiningen.

1898, Dec. 8. Maj. H.H. prince CHRISTIAN VICTOR ALBERT LOUIS ERNEST ANTHONY, of Schleswig-Holstein, King's Royal Rifle Corps. Died 1900, Oct. 29.

1899, May 24. H.R.H. ALFRED ERNEST ALBERT, reigning duke of Saxe-Coburg and Gotha (duke of Edinburgh). Died 1900, July 30.

1899, May 24. H.R.H. prince ARTHUR FREDERICK PATRICK ALBERT, of Connaught and Strathearn.

1900, May 7. Lieut. Gen. Sir GEORGE STEWART WHITE, on his return from active service in South Africa.

1900, Sept. 19. JOHN ADRIAN LOUIS (HOPE), 7th earl of Hopetoun, Afterwards marquess of Linlithgow, governor general of Australia, late lord chamberlain to queen Victoria.

1901, Jan. 22. Gen. H.R.H. prince FREDERICK CHRISTIAN CHARLES AUGUSTUS, of Schleswig-Holstein-Sonderburg-Augustenburg, one of the personal aides-de-camp to queen Victoria.

1901, Jan. 27. H.S.H. ADOLPHUS CHARLES ALEXANDER ALBERT EDWARD GEORGE PHILIP LOUIS LADISLAUS, 2nd duke of Teck, capt. 1st Life Guards.

1901, Feb. 1. V. Adm. Sir JOHN REGINALD THOMAS FULLERTON, groom in waiting to king Edward VII.

1901, Feb. 2. Capt. H.S.H. prince LOUIS (LUDWIG ALEXANDER) of Battenberg.

1901, Feb. 2. JOHN DOUGLAS SUTHERLAND (CAMPBELL), 9th duke of Argyll, governor and constable of Windsor Castle.

1901, Feb. 2. ALEXANDER WILLIAM GEORGE (DUFF), duke of Fife.

1901, Feb. 2. Col. lord EDWARD WILLIAM PELHAM-CLINTON, late master of queen Victoria's Household, groom in waiting to king Edward VII.

1901, Feb. 2. Maj. Gen. Sir JOHN CARSTAIRS MCNEILL, V.C., senior equerry to queen Victoria, extra equerry to king Edward VII. Died 1904, May 25.

1901, Feb. 2. Sir FRANCIS KNOLLYS, afterwards lord Knollys, private secretary to the King.

1901, Feb. 2. Lieut. Col. the Rt. Hon. Sir FLEETWOOD ISHAM EDWARDS, extra equerry to the King, keeper of the Privy Purse to queen Victoria.

1901, Feb. 2. Lieut. Col. Sir ARTHUR JOHN BIGGE, on his retirement as private secretary to queen Victoria.

1901, Feb. 2. Sir JAMES REID, bart., M.D., on his retirement as resident physician to queen Victoria.

1901, Mar. 8. F. Marsh. H.H. prince EDWARD (WILLIAM AUGUSTUS EDWARD), of Saxe-Weimar. Died 1902, Nov. 16.

1901, Mar. 8. Rt. Hon. CHARLES (HARBORD), 5th lord Suffield, lord in waiting to the King.

1901, Mar. 8. Adm. Sir MICHAEL CULME-SEYMOUR, bart., first and principal aide-de-camp to queen Victoria.

1901, Mar. 8. Sir FREDERICK AUGUSTUS ABEL, bart., secretary of the Imperial Institute. Died 1902, Sept. 6.

1901, Mar. 8. Adm. Sir CHARLES FREDERICK HOTHAM, commander-in-chief at Portsmouth

1902, May 2. ARTHUR CHARLES (WELLESLEY), 4th duke of Wellington, Col. late Grenadier Guards.

1902, July 22. ROBERT ARTHUR TALBOT (CECIL), 8th marquess of Salisbury, in recognition of his long, faithful and valuable services to the Crown and the Empire. Died

1902, Aug. 22. HENRY (FITZALAN-HOWARD), 15th duke of Norfolk, earl marshal of England.

1902, Aug. 22. NATHAN MEYER (ROTHSCHILD), lord Rothschild.

1902, Aug. 22. HENRY (JAMES), lord James of Hereford, on the occasion of the Coronation and of his retirement from the office of chancellor of the Duchy of Lancaster.

1902, Aug. 22. Sir FRANCIS HENRY LAKING, bart., M.D., physician in ordinary to the King.

1902, Aug. 22. Maj Gen. Sir HENRY PETER EWART, crown equerry.

1902, Aug. 22. Sir ARTHUR EDWARD AUGUSTUS ELLIS, extra
        equerry to the King, and comptroller in the Lord
        Chamberlain's Department.

1902, Aug. 22. Maj. Gen. Sir STANLEY DE ASTEL CALVERT CLARKE,
        equerry to the King.

1902, Nov. 9. VICTOR ALBERT FRANCIS CHARLES (SPENCER), 1st
        viscount Churchill, lord in waiting to the King.

1902, Nov. 9. Gen. FREDERICK AUGUSTUS (THESIGER), 2nd lord
        Chelmsford, gold stick in waiting at the Coronation of
        Edward VII., Col. 2nd Life Guards.

1902, Nov. 9 HORACE BRAND TOWNSEND (FARQUHAR), 1st lord
        Farquhar, master of the Household.

1902, Nov. 9. Col Sir EDWARD RIDLEY COLBORNE BRADFORD, bart.,
        commissioner of the Metropolitan Police.

1902, Nov. 9. Col. Sir ROBERT NIGEL FITZ-HARDINGE KINGSCOTE,
        extra equerry to the King, paymaster of the Household.

1902, Nov. 9. Adm. Sir HENRY FREDERICK STEPHENSON, extra
        equerry to the King.

1902, Nov. 9. Maj. Gen Sir HENRY TROTTER, commanding Home
        District

1903, Mar. 31. H.H. the Maharaja of Gwalior, on the occasion of
        the Coronation of Edward VII. Invested by the duke of
        Connaught in India, Jan., 1903.

1903, Mar. 31. H.H. the Maharaja of Jaipur (same occasion).
        Invested *ut supra.*

1903, Mar 31. H H. the Maharaja of Kolhapur (same occasion).
        Invested *ut supra.*

1903, Apr. 21 Gen. Sir CHARLES MANSFIELD CLARKE, bart., governor
        and commander-in-chief of Malta (during His Majesty's
        visit to Malta).

1903, Apr. 21. Adm Sir COMPTON EDWARD DOMVILE, commanding-
        in-chief in the Mediterranean (same occasion).

1903, Apr. 27. The Rt. Hon. Sir FRANCIS LEVESON BERTIE, ambassador extraordinary and minister plenipotentiary at Rome (during His Majesty's visit to Italy).

1903, May 4. The Rt. Hon. Sir EDMUND JOHN MONSON, ambassador extraordinary and minister plenipotentiary in Paris (during King Edward VII.'s visit to Paris).

1903, June 30. Sir ALBERT WILLIAM WOODS, garter principal king of Arms. For services in connexion with the preparation of warrants, etc., of the Royal Victorian Order. Died 1904, Jan. 7.

1903, Aug. 11. CHARLES STEWART (VANE-TEMPEST-STEWART), 6th marquess of Londonderry, president of the Board of Education (on the occasion of king Edward VII.'s visit to Ireland).

1903, Aug. 11. WILLIAM HUMBLE (WARD), 3rd earl of Dudley, lord lieutenant of Ireland (same occasion).

1903, Oct. 9. Rt. Hon. Sir FRANCIS RICHARD PLUNKETT, ambassador and minister plenipotentiary at Vienna (on the occasion of king Edward VII.'s visit to Austria)

1903, Nov. 9. RICHARD GEORGE PENN (CURZON-HOWE), 5th earl Howe, lord chamberlain to Her Majesty Queen Alexandra.

1904, Jan. 23. The most Reverend and Rt. Hon. RANDALL THOMAS DAVIDSON, D.D., archbishop of Canterbury.

1904, Feb. 10. H.R.H. prince ALEXANDER AUGUSTUS FREDERICK WILLIAM ALFRED GEORGE, of Teck (on his marriage with princess Alice of Albany).

1904, July 1. Rt. Hon Sir FRANK CAVENDISH LASCELLES, His Majesty's ambassador, Berlin (on the occasion of Edward VII.'s visit to Kiel).

1904, Nov. 9. CHARLES HENRY (GORDON-LENNOX), 12th duke of Richmond and Gordon, A.D C., col 3rd Battalion Royal Sussex Regiment.

1904, Nov. 21. Sir MARTIN LE MARCHANT HADSLEY GOSSELIN, envoy extraordinary and minister plenipotentiary to Portugal (on the occasion of the visit of the king and queen of Portugal to England)

KNIGHTS GRAND CROSS (HONORARY).

1896, May 8. Monsieur ARSÈNE HENRY, préfet des Alpes Maritimes (on the occasion of the Queen's visit to Cimiez, Nice).

1896, June 30. Count HILARION VORONTSOV DASHKOV, minister of the Imperial [Russian] Court, adj. gen. and gen. of Cavalry. On the occasion of the emperor of Russia's Coronation.

1896, June 30. Gen. OTTO DE RICHTER, commandant of the Imperial [Russian] Headquarters, gen. adj. and gen. of Infantry (same occasion).

1896, June 30. Count CONSTANTINE PAHLEN, secretary of state and actual privy counsellor and arch grand marshal [of Russia] (same occasion).

1896, June 30. Prince ALEXIS DOLGOROUKY, grand master of the ceremonies [Russia] (same occasion).

1896, June 30. Maj. Gen. Prince DMITRI GALITZIN (Caucasian Cossacks of the line), on the staff of H.I.M. the emperor of Russia (same occasion).

1896, July 21. Count JOACHIM MOLTKE, comptroller and treasurer of the household of their Royal Highnesses the crown prince and crown princess of Denmark, and chamberlain to the king of Denmark. On the occasion of the wedding of H.R.H. prince Charles, son of the crown prince of Denmark with princess Maud.

1896, Aug. 5. His Excellency LI HUNG CHANG, special envoy from China (on the occasion of the emperor of China's mission).

1896, Oct. 31. Maj. Gen. Count PAUL BENCKENDORF, master of the household of H.I.H. the emperor of Russia (on the occasion of the emperor of Russia's visit to queen Victoria).

1897, Mar. 6. His Excellency Count GÖTZ BURKHARD SECKENDORFF, comptroller of the household of the empress Frederick.

1897, Mar. 26. H.H. NICHOLAS I., prince and Hospodar of Montenegro.

1897, Mar. 28. Lieut. Gen. EDWARD VON MÜLLER, inspec. gen. of Rifles, Berlin, in attendance on the duke of Connaught (on His Royal Highness's visit to Berlin).

1897, Apr. 26. H.S.H. prince FRANCIS JOSEPH of Battenberg.

1897, June 30. Count ARTHUR AUGUST VON MENSDORFF-POUILLY. Died 1904, Apr. 23.

1897, July 28. H.M. ALFONSO XIII., king of Spain.

1898, Aug. 26. Gen. FRANCOIS DE NEGRIER, membre du Conseil Superieur de la Guerre; inspecteur d'Armée (on the occasion of the attendance of the duke of Connaught at the French Manœuvres).

1899, Sept. 29. H.R.H. prince FREDERICK LEOPOLD of Prussia.

1899, Nov. 21. H.I.M. FREDERICK WILLIAM VICTOR ALBERT, the emperor William II. of Germany, king of Prussia.

1899, Nov. 23. Count BERNARD VON BULOW, foreign secretary of the German Empire, in attendance on the German emperor (on the occasion of the German emperor's visit to queen Victoria).

1899, Nov. 23. Count AUGUST ZU EULENBERG, grand marshal of the Court of the German emperor, in attendance on the German emperor (same occasion).

1899, Nov. 23. Gen. HANS VON PLESSEN, gen. of Infantry; aide-de-camp gen. of the emperor of Germany and commandant of the Headquarters Staff, in attendance on the German emperor (same occasion).

1899, Nov. 23. Adm. Baron GUSTAV VON SENDEN-BIBRAN, adm. à la suite of the German emperor and chief of the Marine Cabinet, in attendance on the German emperor (same occasion).

1900, Mar. 31. GUSTAVUS ERNEST, count of Erbach-Schönberg, col. à la suite of the Grand Ducal Hessian Army.

1900, Mar. 31. FREIHERR AUGUST VON WOELLWARTH-LAUTERBURG, chamberlain and grand marshal of the Court of the king of Wurtemberg, col. à la suite of the Army.

1900, June 28. H.H prince ABBAS PACHA, khedive of Egypt (on
the occasion of His Highness's visit to the queen, at
Windsor).

1900, July 16. H.S.H. prince HENRY XXX., of Reuss.

1900, Dec. 20. His Excellency Gen. GUSTAV CARL HEINRICH
FERDINAND EMIL VON ARNIM, à la suite of the Guard, Jäger
Battalion.

1901, Jan. 18. His Excellency Lieut. Gen. GUSTAV VON KESSEL,
aide-de-camp gen. of the German emperor (on the occasion
of the duke of Connaught's visit to Berlin for the
bicentenary of the foundation of the kingdom of Prussia).

1901, Jan. 27. H R.H. LEOPOLD CHARLES EDWARD GEORGE ALBERT,
duke of Saxe-Coburg and Gotha and duke of Albany.

1901, Feb 1. Count PAUL WOLFF METTERNICH, the German
emperor's ambassador to the Court of St. James's.

1901, Feb. 2. H.R.H. prince CHARLES (CHRISTIAN FREDERICK
CHARLES GEORGE VALDEMAR AXEL), of Denmark.

1901, Mar. 8   H M GEORGE I (CHRISTIAN WILLIAM FERDINAND
ADOLPHE GEORGEI, king of the Hellenes.

1901, Mar 8. H.R H FREDERICK (CHRISTIAN FREDERICK WILLIAM
CHARLES), crown prince of Denmark.

1901, Mar. 8. His Excellency HUGO FREIHERR VON REISCHACH,
marshal of the Court of the empress Frederick of Germany.

1901, Mar. 8. His Excellency the Count of Ficalho, in attendance
on the king of Portugal on the occasion of said king attend-
ing the funeral of queen Victoria. Died 1903, Apr. 19.

1901, July 9. H.I.H. Grand Duke MICHAEL MICHAELOWITCH of
Russia (on the occasion of his visit to England).

1901, Aug. 16. H.R.H. prince NICOLAS of Greece (on the occasion
of his visit to England).

1901, Oct. 11. H.R.H. prince CHRISTIAN (CHRISTIAN CHARLES
FREDERICK ALBERT ALEXANDER WILLIAM) of Denmark.

1901, Oct. 11.   H.R.H. prince HAROLD CHRISTIAN FREDERIC of Denmark.

1901, Oct. 11.   H H. prince JOHN of Schleswig-Holstein-Sonderburg-Glucksburg.

1901, Oct. 11.   Count ALBERT VICTOR JULIUS JOSEPH MICHAEL VON MENSDORFF-POUILLY-DIETRICHSTEIN, first secretary of the Austro-Hungarian Embassy in London.

1901, Oct. 11.   Gen. VON LINDEQUIST, commanding 18th Army Corps at Frankfort-on-Maine, aide-de-camp to the German emperor.

1901, Oct. 11   Count VON WEDEL, master of the horse to the German emperor.

1901, Oct. 11.   His Excellency Monsieur OSCAR SIEGFRID CHRISTIAN O'NEILL OXHOLM, marshal of the Court to the king of Denmark (on the occasion of Edward VII.'s visit to Copenhagen).

1901, Oct. 11.   His Excellency Monsieur LUDWIG CASTENSKIOLD, chamberlain and geheim-konferentsraad to the king of Denmark (same occasion).

1902, May 2.   H R H. MAHA VAJIRAVUDH, crown prince of Siam.

1902, June 6.   Lieut. Gen. H.S H. prince LOUIS ESTERHAZY, capt. of the Hungarian Body Guard, Vienna, military attaché to the Austro-Hungarian Embassy, London.

1902, June 6   Duke of ALBA DE TORMES, lord of the Bedchamber to Alfonso XIII and a grandee of Spain (on the occasion of the duke of Connaught's visit to Madrid for the enthronement of the king of Spain).

1902, June 6.   Duke of SOTOMAYOR, great chamberlain to the king of Spain (same occasion).

1902, Aug. 22.   Prince ANDREW of Greece (on the occasion of the coronation of king Edward VII.).

1902, Aug. 22.   His Excellency Baron GEORGES DE STAAL (same occasion, or on his retirement from the post of ambassador from the Czar to the Court of St. James's).

1902, Dec. 30. His Excellency Marquis DE SOVERAL, envoy extraordinary and minister plenipotentiary from Portugal (on the occasion of the king of Portugal's visit to Windsor Castle).

1903, Apr. 7 H.R.H. The INFANTE ALPHONSO, duke of Oporto (on the occasion of the visit of king Edward VII. to Portugal).

1903, Apr. 7. Senor WENCELAU DE LIMA, minister for Foreign Affairs [of Portugal] (same occasion).

1903, Apr. 7. Count TAROUCA, chamberlain to the king of Portugal; attached to king Edward VII. (same occasion).

1903, Apr. 7. Count D'ARNOSO, private secretary to the king of Portugal.

1903, Apr. 27. H.R.H. Prince LUIGI AMEDEO of Savoy, duke d'Abruzzi (during king Edward VII's visit to Naples).

1903, Apr. 27. V. Adm. GIOVANNI GALEAZZO FRIGERIO, commander-in-chief of the Italian Mediterranean Squadron, Naples (same occasion).

1903, Apr 30 H.R H VITTORIO EMANUELE of Savoy, count of Turin (during His Majesty's visit to Rome).

1903, Apr 30 H.R.H. Prince TOMMASO of Savoy, duke of Genoa (same occasion).

1903, Apr. 30 His Excellency SIGNOR GIUSEPPE ZANARDELLI, president of the Council, Italy (same occasion). Died 1903, Dec. 26.

1903, Apr. 30. V. Adm. ENRICO CONSTANTINO MORIN, minister for Foreign Affairs, Italy (same occasion).

1903, Apr 30 His Excellency Gen. EMILIO PONZIO VAGLIA, lord steward to the king of Italy (same occasion).

1903, Apr 30. His Excellency Count CESARE GIANOTTI, master of the household to the king of Italy (same occasion).

1903, Apr 30. His Excellency Gen. UGO BRUSATI, first aide-de-camp to the king of Italy (same occasion).

1903, Apr 30 His Excellency Gen. ETTORE PEDOTTI, commanding 10th Army Corps, attached to king Edward VII. (same occasion).

1903, Apr. 30. His Excellency Signor ALBERTO PANSA, Italian ambassador extraordinary and plenipotentiary in London (same occasion).

1903, Apr. 30. DON PROSPERO COLONNA (PRINCIPE DI SONNINO), Syndic of Rome (same occasion).

1903, May 4. His Excellency Monsieur EMILE COMBES, president of the Council, France (on the occasion of king Edward VII.'s visit to Paris).

1903, May 4. His Excellency Monsieur THÉOPHILE DELCASSÉ, minister of Foreign Affairs, France.

1903, May 4. His Excellency Monsieur PAUL CAMBON, French Ambassador in London (same occasion).

1903, May 4. Monsieur ALPHONSE DEVILLE, president of the Municipal Council of Paris (same occasion)

1903, May 4. Monsieur JUSTIN DE SELVES, prefect of the Seine (same occasion).

1903, May 4. Monsieur LOUIS LÉPINE, prefect of Police (same occasion).

1903, May 4. Adm. FRANÇOIS ERNEST FOURNIER, attached to king Edward VII. (same occasion).

1903, May 4. Gen. HENRI DE LA CROIX, attached to king Edward VII (same occasion).

1903, July 10. Monsieur ABEL COMBARIEU, secretary general and chief of the household of M. Loubet, the president of the French Republic (in connexion with the visit to London of the said president of the French Republic)

1903, July 10. Gen. EMILE DUBOIS, chief of the Military Household of the said president (same occasion).

1903, Oct. 9. H.I. & R.H. the archduke LUDWIG VICTOR, of Austro-Hungary (on the occasion of king Edward's visit to Austria).

1903, Oct. 9. H.I. & R.H the archduke LEOPOLD SALVATOR, of Austro-Hungary (same occasion)

1903, Oct. 9. H I. & R.H the archduke FRANZ SALVATOR, of Austro-Hungary (same occasion).

1903, Oct. 9. H I. & R.H the archduke RAINER, of Austro-Hungary (same occasion).

1903, Oct. 9 His Excellency AGENOR MARIA ADAM, count Goluchowski von Goluchowo, minister of the Imperial and Royal House and minister for Foreign Affairs, Austria (same occasion)

1903, Oct 9. H.S.H. Field Marshal RUDOLF, prince von und zu Liechtenstein, first lord steward and acting master of the Horse to the emperor of Austria (same occasion).

1903, Oct. 9 ALFRED ADAM WILHELM JOHANN MARIA, prince von Montenuovo, second lord steward to the emperor of Austria (same occasion).

1903, Oct. 9 His Excellency EDWARD MARIA NIKOLAUS, count Paar, general of Cavalry, senior aide-de-camp to the emperor of Austria (same occasion).

1903, Oct. 9. His Excellency ANTON, baron von Bechtolsheim, gen. of Cavalry, capt. of the Trabanten and Infantry Companies of the Life Guards, attached to king Edward VII. (same occasion) Died 1904, Jan 25.

1903, Nov. 21. Signor TOMMASO TITTONI, senator, secretary of state for Foreign Affairs, Italy (on the occasion of the visit of the king and queen of Italy to Windsor).

1903, Dec. 29. H.I.H. the grand duke WLADIMIR ALEXANDROWITCH, of Russia (on the occasion of the visit of the grand duke and duchess Wladimir Alexandrowitch to Windsor).

1904, Feb. 10 H S.H. ALEXIS CHARLES ERNEST LOUIS FERDINAND EUGENE BERNHARD, prince Bentheim and Steinfurt (on the occasion of the marriage of princess Alice of Albany with prince Alexander of Teck).

1904, Feb. 10 H S H WILLIAM ADOLPHUS MAXIMILIAN CHARLES, hereditary prince of Wied (same occasion).

1904, Feb 10 H. Excellency HERMANN, baron von Bilfinger, gen. aide-de-camp to the king of Wurtemberg (same occasion).

1904, Feb. 10. H. Excellency ECK, baron von Reischach, lord chamberlain to the queen of Wurtemberg (same occasion).

1904, Mar. 23. V. Adm. RUDOLPH, count Montecuccoli, representing the emperor of Austria (on the occasion of the funeral of the duke of Cambridge).

1904, Apr. 18. H.R.H. prince OSCAR CHARLES WILLIAM, of Sweden, Norway, duke of West Gotland (on the occasion of Edward VII.'s visit to Copenhagen).

1904, Apr. 18. H.H. prince ALBERT CHRISTIAN ADOLPHUS CHARLES EUGENE, of Schleswig - Holstein - Sonderburg - Glucksburg (same occasion).

1904, Apr. 18. JOHAN HENRIK DEUNTZER, president of the Council and member of Foreign Affairs [Denmark] (same occasion).

1904, Apr. 18. His Excellency CHRISTIAN FREDERICK, count Danneskjold-Samsøe (same occasion).

1904, Apr. 18. H. Excellency FRANTS ERNST BILLE, envoy extraordinary and minister plenipotentiary from Denmark to England (same occasion).

1904, Apr. 18. FERDINAND MELDAHL, chamberlain to the king of Denmark and vice-president of the Royal Academy of Arts, Copenhagen (same occasion).

1904, Apr. 18. Maj. Gen. CHRISTIAN HENRIK ARENDRUP, attached to king Edward VII. (same occasion).

1904, Apr. 21. Prince FRANZ JOSEPH VON AUERSPERG, privy councillor and chamberlain to the emperor of Austria (on the occasion of the visit of the prince of Wales to Austria).

1904, Apr. 21. Lieut. Gen. WENZEL FREIHERR KOTZ VON DOBRZ, privy councillor and chamberlain to the emperor of Austria (same occasion).

1904, Apr. 28. CONSTANTIN, FREIHERR VON NEURATH, lord chamberlain to the king of Würtemberg (on the occasion of the visit of the prince of Wales to Wurtemberg).

1904, May 13. His Excellency Baron Dr. JUSTIZRATH AXEL VARNBULER VON UND ZU HEMMINGEN, councillor of state and chamberlain to the king of Wurtemberg (on the occasion of his visit to England on a special mission to king Edward VII. from the king of Würtemberg).

1904, June 11   Maj. Gen. ANATOL, count Bigot de Saint Quentin, chamberlain and privy councillor to the emperor of Austria, comptroller to H I and R.H. archduke Frederick of Austria (on the occasion of said archduke's visit to England).

1904, July 1.   H.R.H prince WILLIAM EITEL FREDERICK CHRISTIAN CHARLES of Prussia (on the occasion of king Edward VII.'s visit to Kiel).

1904, July 1   H.R.H. prince AUGUSTUS WILLIAM HENRY GUNTHER VICTOR of Prussia (same occasion).

1904, July 1.   H R H. prince OSCAR CHARLES GUSTAVUS ADOLPHUS of Prussia (same occasion).

1904, July 1.   H.R H. prince JOACHIM FRANCIS HUMBERT of Prussia (same occasion).

1904, July 1   Adm HANS LOUIS RAYMOND VON KOESTER, commander-in-chief and inspec. gen. of the Imperial German Navy (same occasion).

1904, July 1.   Adm. ALFRED VON TIRPITZ, minister of Marine (same occasion).

1904, July 1   Lieut Gen FREDERICK WILLIAM CHARLES VON BOCK UND POLACH, commanding 9th Army Corps (same occasion).

1904, July 1.   V. Adm. CHARLES JOHN GEORGE VON EISENDECHER, Imperial German Navy (same occasion).

1904, July 1.   V Adm. baron ALBERT VON SECKENDORFF, master of the Household to prince Henry of Prussia (same occasion).

1904, July 1.   OSWALD SAMUEL CONSTANTINE, baron von Richthofen, minister of Foreign Affairs [Germany] (same occasion).

1904, July 1.   V. Adm WILLIAM GOTTLIEB CHARLES BUCHSEL, chief of the staff of the Imperial German Navy (same occasion).

1904, Sept. 6   H R H. FERDINAND MAXIMILIEN CHARLES LEOPOLD MARIE, prince of Bulgaria, prince of Saxe-Coburg and Gotha.

1904, Sept. 6.   H.S.H. CHARLES JOHN NÉPOMUCÈNE FERDINAND, prince Trautmansdorff-Weinsberg.

1904, Sept. 6.   His Excellency TASSILO, count Festétics de Tolna.

1904, Sept. 6. His Excellency CHARLES, count Coudenhove, governor of Bohemia.

1904, Sept. 6. His Excellency ERIC LOUIS FREDERICK CHRISTIAN, count Kielmansegg, governor of Lower Austria.

1904, Nov. 21. H.R.H. MANUEL MARIE PHILIPPE CHARLES AMELIO LOUIS MICHEL RAPHAEL GABRIEL GONZAQUE XAVIER FRANCOIS D'ASSISE EUGÈNE, duc de Beja (on the occasion of the visit of the king and queen of Portugal to England).

1904, Nov. 21. ANTONIO EDUARDO VILLACA, minister for Foreign Affairs, Portugal (same occasion).

1904, Nov. 21. DON JOSÉ MARIA GONCALVES ZARCO DA CAMARA, comte da Ribeira Grande, lord chamberlain to the queen of Portugal.

1904, Nov. 21. R. Adm. HERMENGILDO DE BRITO CAPELLO, Royal Portuguese Navy, aide-de-camp to the king of Portugal.

KNIGHTS COMMANDERS.

1896, May 25. Col. the Hon. WILLIAM JAMES COLVILLE, master of the Ceremonies. Died 1903, Oct. 16.

1896, Sept. 16. Sir THEODORE MARTIN.

1897, Jan. 30. Gen. HENRY LYNEDOCH GARDINER, col. commandant Royal Horse Artillery, groom in waiting and extra equerry to the Queen.

1897, June 30 Capt. H.S.H. prince ADOLPHUS of Teck, 1st Life Guards.

1897, June 30. Lieut. Gen. DUDLEY CHARLES (FITZ GERALD-DE-ROS), 24th lord de Ros, late lord in waiting to queen Victoria.

1897, June 30. Maj. Gen. PAUL SANFORD (METHUEN), 3rd lord Methuen, commanding the Home District at the "Diamond Jubilee."

1897, June 30. JOHN EMERICH ACTON (DALBERG-ACTON), 1st lord Acton, late lord in waiting to queen Victoria. Died 1902, June 19.

1897, June 30. MONTAGU WILLIAM (LOWRY-CORRY), lord Rowton. Died 1903, Nov. 9.

1897, June 30. Col. the Hon. HENRY WILLIAM JOHN (BYNG), afterwards 4th earl of Strafford, equerry to the Queen. Died 1899, May 16.

1897, June 30. Maj. Gen Sir HENRY PETER EWART, crown equerry.

1897, June 30. Maj. Gen. ARTHUR EDWARD AUGUSTUS ELLIS, equerry to the prince of Wales.

1897, June 30. Maj. Gen. STANLEY DE ASTEL CALVERT CLARKE, equerry to the prince of Wales.

1897, Aug. 24. LUITBERT ALEXANDER GEORGE LIONEL ALPHONSE, Freiherr von Pawel-Rammingen.

1898, Sept. 27. Sir WILLIAM McCORMACK, bart., surgeon in ordinary to the prince of Wales, president of the Royal College of Surgeons, in recognition of services in connection with the recent accident to the prince of Wales.

1898, Sept. 27. Sir FRANCIS HENRY LAKING, M.D., surgeon apothecary to the prince of Wales (same occasion).

1898, Dec. 8. Capt. H.S.H. prince FRANCIS JOSEPH LEOPOLD FREDERICK of Teck, 1st Royal Dragoons.

1898, Dec. 8. Sec. Lieut. H.S.H. prince ALEXANDER AUGUSTUS FREDERICK WILLIAM ALFRED GEORGE of Teck, 7th (Queen's Own) Hussars.

1899, May 9. R. Adm. JOHN REGINALD THOMAS FULLERTON, in command of the Royal yacht "Victoria and Albert."

1900, Apr. 26. HERCULES EDWARD (ROWLEY), 4th lord Langford, comptroller of the Household of the lord lieut. of Ireland (in commemoration of Her Majesty's visit to Ireland).

1900, Apr. 26. Rt. Hon. Sir DAVID HARREL, under secretary for Ireland (same occasion).

1900, May 24. VICTOR ALBERT FRANCIS CHARLES (SPENCER), 3rd lord Churchill of Whichwood, lord in waiting to the Queen.

1900, Aug. 24. Sir ALEXANDER CONDIE STEPHEN, Her Majesty's minister resident at Dresden and Coburg.

1901, Jan. 1. REGINALD BALIOL (BRETT), 2nd viscount Esher, secretary to the Office of Works.

1901, Feb. 2. MAURICE HOLZMANN, extra groom in waiting to the King and secretary to the Duchy of Cornwall.

1901, Mar. 8. Sir RICHARD DOUGLAS POWELL, bart., M.D., physician extraordinary to the King.

1901, Mar. 8. Sir THOMAS BARLOW, bart., M.D., physician to the Household.

1901, Mar. 8. Sir THOMAS JOHNSTONE LIPTON.

1901, Mar. 8. Maj. Gen. HENRY TROTTER, commanding the Home District.

1901, Mar. 19   Sir WILLIAM HENRY BROADBENT, bart., M.D., physician in ordinary to the king.

1901, May 28.   HORACE BRAND TOWNSEND (FARQUHAR), 1st lord Farquhar, master of the Household.

1901, May 28   FREDERICK TREVES, for services to the wounded in the South African War

1901, July 23.   Sir THOMAS SMITH, bart., F.R.C.S., honorary serjeant surgeon to the king.

1901, July 23.   Sir EDWARD WALTER HAMILTON, assistant secretary of the Treasury.

1901, July 23.   Deputy Surg. Gen. HENRY JULIUS BLANC, for medical attendance to the King (when Prince of Wales) at Cannes.

1901, July 23.   WILLIAM HENRY BENNETT, F.R.C S., for services rendered to the soldiers invalided home from the war in South Africa.

1901, July 23   THOMAS HANBURY.

1901, Dec. 24.   FREDERICK OLIVER (ROBINSON), styled earl de Grey, treasurer to H.M. queen Alexandra

1901, Dec 24.   Lieut. Col. the Hon. WILLIAM HENRY PEREGRINE CARINGTON, equerry to the King, and comptroller and treasurer to the prince of Wales.

1901, Dec. 24.   Sir ERNEST JOSEPH CASSEL

1901, Dec. 24.   Sir DONALD MACKENZIE WALLACE, attached to the duke of York's suite as assistant private secretary on the occasion of His Royal Highness's visit to the Colonies in 1901.

1902, Mar. 14.   V. Adm. THOMAS STURGES JACKSON, superintendent of Davenport Dockyard.

1902, Aug. 22.   The Rt Rev. RANDALL THOMAS DAVIDSON, bishop of Winchester (did not receive knighthood), afterwards archbishop of Canterbury.

1902, Aug. 22.   Sir JAMES CHARLES HARRIS, British consul at Nice.

1902, Aug. 22.   V. Adm. His Excellency HENRY FELIX WOODS PACHA, aide-de-camp to the sultan of Turkey.

1902, Aug. 22. ROBERT HENRY HOBART, secretary to the Earl Marshal at the Coronation of Edward VII.

1902, Nov. 9. Rt. Hon. Sir JOSEPH COCKFIELD DIMSDALE, bart., M.P., lord mayor of London.

1902, Nov. 9. Sir JOHN JAMES TREVOR LAWRENCE, bart., treasurer of St. Bartholomew's Hospital.

1902, Nov. 9. Sir SYDNEY HEDLEY WATERLOW, bart., late treasurer of St. Bartholomew's Hospital.

1902, Nov. 9. Gen. GODFREY CLERK, groom-in-waiting to His Majesty.

1902, Dec. 30. Maj. Gen. HUGH RICHARD (DAWNAY), 9th viscount Downe, for services in South Africa.

1902, Dec. 30. Sir JOHN WILLIAMS, bart., M.D., physician-accoucheur to H.R.H. the princess of Wales.

1903, Mar. 31. Sir HUGH SHAKESPEAR BARNES, Indian Civil Service; secretary to the Government of India, Foreign Department; lieut. governor designate of Burmah, on the occasion of the duke of Connaught's tour in India.

1903, Apr. 7. Sir MARTIN LE MARCHANT HADSLEY GOSSELIN, envoy extraordinary and minister plenipotentiary at Lisbon (on the occasion of king Edward VII.'s visit to Lisbon).

1903, Apr. 13. Sir ARTHUR NICOLSON, bart., envoy extraordinary and minister plenipotentiary at Tangier (on the occasion of king Edward VII.'s visit to Gibraltar).

1903, Apr. 21. Sir JOSEPH CARBONE, chief justice, president of the Court of Appeal and vice-president of the Council of Government of the Island of Malta (during His Majesty's visit to Malta).

1903, June 30. Sir RICHARD MILLS, late comptroller and auditor general. For services as auditor of His Majesty's accounts when prince of Wales.

1903, Aug. 11. V. Adm. lord CHARLES WILLIAM DE LA POER BERESFORD, V. Adm. commanding the Channel Fleet; received knighthood (on the occasion of His Majesty's visit to Ireland). Knighted by the King at Mount Stewart, Co. Down, Ireland, 1903, July 26.

1903, Aug. 11. WILLIAM LEE (PLUNKET), 5th lord Plunkett, private secretary to the lord lieut. of Ireland (same occasion).

1903, Aug 11. WILLIAM (BROWNLOW), 3rd lord Lurgan, state steward to the lord lieut. of Ireland (same occasion).

1903, Aug. 11. Rt. Hon. HORACE CURZON PLUNKETT, vice-president of the Department of Agriculture and Technical Instruction, Ireland (same occasion). Knighted by the King, 1903, Aug. 1, on board the Royal yacht at Queenstown.

1903, Aug. 11. Rt. Hon Sir ANTHONY PATRICK MACDONNELL, under secretary to the lord lieut. of Ireland (same occasion).

1903, Aug. 11. V. Adm. Sir ARTHUR KNYVET WILSON, V.C., commander-in-chief of the Home Fleet (same occasion).

1903, Aug. 11. Sir ARTHUR EDWARD VICARS, ulster king of arms (same occasion).

1903, Aug. 11 Col. Sir GERALD RICHARD DEASE, chamberlain to the lord lieut. (same occasion). Died 1903, Oct. 18.

1903, Aug. 11. R. Adm. WILMOT HAWKSWORTH FAWKES, rear admiral commanding the Cruizer Squadron. Received the honour of knighthood (same occasion). Knighted by the King, 1903, Aug. 2, on board the Royal yacht.

1903, Nov 9 Gen lord WILLIAM FREDERICK ERNEST SEYMOUR, lieut. of the Tower of London.

1903, Nov. 9. ALGERNON BERTRAM (FREEMAN-MITFORD), lord Redesdale (received the honour of knighthood), formerly secretary of the Office of Works.

1903, Nov. 9. Lieut. gen. ARTHUR LYTTELTON LYTTELTON-ANNESLEY, col. of the 11th (Prince Albert's Own) Hussars (received knighthood).

1903, Nov. 9. Lieut. col JOHN LANE HARRINGTON, British diplomatic agent and consul general to the Court of Menelik II., king of kings of Ethiopia (received knighthood).

1903, Dec. 29. JAMES THOMAS KNOWLES, Esq , formerly one of the governors of the Alexandra Trust.

1904, Feb. 10. HUGH (GOUGH), 3rd viscount Gough, minister resident at the Courts of Saxony and Saxe-Coburg Gotha, and chargé d'affaires at the Court of Waldeck and Pyrmont (on the occasion of the marriage of princess Alice of Albany with prince Alexander of Teck). Received knighthood.

1904, Feb. 10   Sir ROBERT HAWTHORN COLLINS, comptroller of the Household to H.R.H. the duchess Albany (on same occasion).

1904, Mar. 23.   R. Adm. ADOLPHUS AUGUSTUS FREDERICK FITZ GEORGE, equerry to the late duke of Cambridge. Received knighthood. (On the occasion of the funeral of the duke of Cambridge).

1904, Mar. 23   Col. AUGUSTUS CHARLES FREDERICK FITZ GEORGE, private secretary and equerry to the late duke of Cambridge. Received knighthood   (Same occasion).

1904, Mar 23.   Maj. Gen. ALBERT HENRY WILMOT WILLIAMS, equerry to the late duke of Cambridge. Received knighthood.   (Same occasion).

1904, Apr. 18.   Sir WILLIAM EDWARD GOSCHEN, envoy extraordinary and minister plenipotentiary at Copenhagen (on the occasion of the king's visit to Copenhagen).

1904, May 10.   Rt Hon. Sir CHARLES HARDINGE, ambassador extraordinary and minister plenipotentiary at St. Petersburg.

1904, July 1.   R. Adm. Sir ARCHIBALD BERKELEY MILNE, bart , A D.C., commanding His Majesty's yacht "Victoria and Albert."

1904, Oct. 11.   MICHAEL ARTHUR (BASS), baron Burton

1904, Oct. 11.   JOHN (SAVILE), 2nd baron Savile.

1904, Oct. 19.   Maj. Gen. JOHN LEACH, general officer commanding Woolwich District (on the occasion of His Majesty's inspection at Woolwich of the Royal Artillery).

1904, Oct. 21.   Maj. Gen Sir REGINALD CLARE HART, general officer commanding Thames District.

1904, Nov. 9.   Maj. Gen. RONALD BERTRAM LANE.

HONORARY KNIGHTS COMMANDERS.

1896, May 8   Monsieur LE COMTE ALZIARY DE MALAUSSENA, mayor of Nice (on the occasion of the Queen's visit to Cimiez, Nice).

1896, June 30.   Baron VLADIMIR FREDERIKS, equerry to the Imperial [Russian] Court and assistant to the Minister of the Imperial Household, gen. adj. and lieut. gen. (on the occasion of the emperor of Russia's Coronation).

1896, June 30   Count PAUL BENCKENDORF, acting master of the Household and maj. gen. on the Staff of H.I.M. the emperor of Russia (same occasion).

1896, Aug 5   LI CHING FONG, in attendance on Li Hung Chang, the special ambassador to England from the emperor of China.

1896, Aug 27.   LOH-FENG-LUH, first secretary of Li Hung Chang's special mission (as above)   Died 1903, June 9.

1897, Mar. 26.   V Adm. EDOUARD PIERRE ANTOINE BARRERA, commander-in-chief and maritime prefect of Brest, for services on the occasion of the disaster to the "Drummond Castle."

1897, Mar. 28.   HUGO FREIHERR VON REISCHACH, master of the Household to the empress Frederick.

1897, June 30.   Count ALBERT VICTOR JULIUS JOSEPH MICHAEL VON MENSDORFF-POUILLY-DIECHTRICHSTEIN.

1897, Sept 12.   Adm. baron ALBERT SECKENDORFF, vice admiral à la suite of the German Navy, master of the Household to H.R.H. prince Henry of Prussia.

1898, May 5   Prince DANILO ALEXANDER, general in the Montenegron Army, Crown prince of Montenegro.

1898, May 5.   H S.H. prince EDWARD FREDERICK MAXIMILIAN JOHN of Leiningen.

1898, May 5.   GUSTAVUS ERNEST, count of Erbach-Schoenberg.

1898, May 5.   Gen. PAUL GEBHART, governor of Nice (on the occasion of the Queen's visit to Cimiez in 1898).

1898, May 5. Monsieur GABRIEL LE ROUX, prefect of the Maritime Alpes (same occasion).

1898, Aug. 26. Gen. ALEXIS AUGUSTE RAPHAEL HAGRON, gen de division (on the occasion of the duke of Connaught's attendance at the French Military Manœuvres).

1898, Aug. 26. Monsieur PHILIPPE MARIUS CROZIER, ministre plenipotentiare, chef du service du protocol (same occasion).

1899, May 9. V. Adm. LE COMTE DE MAIGRET, commandant-en-chef. préfet maritime, Cherbourg (on the occasion of queen Victoria's visit to Cimiez, 1899).

1899, June 24. His Excellency CARL FRIEDRICH VON STRENGE, minister of State of the Duchies of Saxe-Coburg and Gotha.

1899, Nov. 23. Maj. Gen. FRIEDRICH VON SCHOLL, aide-de-camp to the German emperor (on the occasion of the German emperor's visit to the Queen).

1899, Nov 23. Baron BODO VON DEM KNESEBECK, deputy master of the ceremonies to the German emperor (same occasion).

1900, May 7. Maj. Gen. FERDINAND GUSTAV HANS VON ARNIM (on the occasion of the visit of the duke of York to Berlin).

1900, Dec. 20. Dr. FRIEDRICH ALBERT HÄNEL, geheimer Justizrath, professor at the University of Kiel.

1901, Feb 2. His Excellency Professor VON LEUTHOLD, surg. gen. of the Guard Corps, physician in attendance on the German emperor on the occasion of the funeral of queen Victoria.

1901, Feb. 2. Count VON WEDEL, master of the Horse to the German Emperor (same occasion).

1901, Mar. 8 Vice admiral PINHA. In attendance on the king of Portugal (on the said king's attending the funeral of queen Victoria).

1901, Mar. 8. Count D'ARNOSO, private secretary to the king of Portugal (same occasion).

1901, Mar. 8. Gen. REINECK. In attendance on the king of the Hellenes (on said king's attending the funeral of queen Victoria).

1901, Mar. 8	Col. DMITRI DASCHKOFF. In attendance on the hereditary grand duke Michael Alexandrowitch of Russia (on said grand duke's attending the funeral of queen Victoria).

1901, Mar. 8.	Intendant Gen. THON (in attendance on the king of the Hellenes (same occasion).

1901, Mar. 8.	Dr. Professor RENVERS, consulting physician to the empress Frederick of Prussia (on the occasion of Edward VII.'s visit to Cronberg).

1901, May 28.	Gen. count VON MOLTKE, general à la suite of the German emperor (on the occasion of the sending of a deputation from the German Emperor to Edward VII. with Colonial equipment for His Majesty's inspection in May, 1901).

1901, Oct 11.	R. Adm. GEORGE HUGH ROBERT ZACHARIAE, Royal Danish Navy (on the occasion of Edward VII.'s visit to Copenhagen).

1901, Oct. 11.	Monsieur FRANTS WILHELM FERDINAND ROSENSTAND, chamberlain and secretary to the king of Denmark (same occasion).

1902, Mar. 14	Maj. Gen ALFRED VON LOEWENFELD, aide-de-camp to the German emperor (on the occasion of the visit of the prince of Wales to Berlin).

1902, Mar. 14.	EUGEN VON ROEDER, master of the ceremonies and chamberlain to the emperor of Germany at Berlin and Interlaken (same occasion).

1902, Nov 9.	Baron HERMANN VON ECKHARDSTEIN, councillor and first secretary of the German Embassy. Created a C.V.O. (Honorary) on the 28th May, 1901, but wrongly gazetted as a K.C V.O. on that occasion, an error which was not corrected.

1902, Dec. 20.	Rear admiral GUILHERME AUGUSTO DE BRITO CAPELLO. aide-de-camp to the king of Portugal (on the occasion of the king of Portugal's visit to Windsor Castle).

1903, Apr 7.	R. Adm. HERMENGILDE DE BRITO CAPELLO, aide-de-camp to the king of Portugal. Attached to king Edward VII. (on the occasion of king Edward's visit to Portugal).

1903, Apr. 7. R. Adm. Francisco Joaquim Ferreira do Amaral, president of the Royal Geographical Society, Lisbon (same occasion).

1903, Apr. 7. Dr. Manuel Augusto Pereira da Cunha, civil gov. of Lisbon (same occasion).

1903, Apr. 7. Col. Antonio Duarte e Silva, commanding Portuguese Cavalry Regiment No. 3 of king Edward VII. (same occasion).

1903, Apr. 7. Senor Francisco Maria da Veiga, police magistrate in charge of police specially attached to king Edward VII. (same occasion).

1903, Apr. 7. Senor Fernando Eduardo de Serpa Pimentel, master of the household to His Majesty the king of Portugal (same occasion).

1903, Apr 7. Count D'Avila e Bolama (Antonio Jose D'Avila), lord mayor of Lisbon, president of the Executive Commission of the Lisbon Municipality (same occasion).

1903, Apr. 7. Senor Antonio Joaquim Simoes de Almeida, president of the Commercial Association of Lisbon (same occasion).

1903, Apr. 13. Cid Abderraham ben Abdelsadok, governor of Fez, special envoy from His Imperial Majesty the sultan of Morocco (on the occasion of king Edward VII.'s visit to Gibraltar).

1903, Apr. 30. Pier Francesco (dei Principi) Corsini, marchese di Lajatico, crown equerry to His Majesty the king of Italy (on the occasion of Edward VII's visit to Italy).

1903, Apr. 30. Maj. Gen. Pio Carlo di Majo, aide-de-camp to His Majesty the king of Italy Attached to His Majesty king Edward VII. (same occasion).

1903, May 4. Monsieur Armand Mollard, director of the Protocol, France (during king Edward VII.'s visit to Paris).

1903, Oct. 9. His Excellency Edouard, count Choloniewski-Myszka, master of the ceremonies to the Emperor of Austria (on the occasion of king Edward VII's visit to Vienna and Marienbad, Austria).

1903, Oct. 9 His Excellency ERICH LUDWIG FRIEDRICH CHRISTIAN, count Kielmansegg; governor of Lower Austria (same occasion).

1903, Oct. 9 His Excellency HEINRICH JOSEPH RUDOLF GOTTFRIED, count Lutzow zu Drey Lutzow und Seedorf, first under Secretary of State for Foreign Affairs, Vienna (same occasion).

1903, Oct. 9. KAJETAN MÉREY VON KAPOS-MÉRE, second under secretary of State for Foreign Affairs, Vienna (same occasion).

1903, Oct. 9. His Excellency AUGUST MARIA RUDOLF EMANUEL FRANZ, count Bellegarde, master of the Household to the emperor of Austria (same occasion).

1903, Oct. 9. His Excellency LEOPOLD baron VON GUDENUS, ober-jagermeister to the emperor of Austria (same occasion).

1903, Oct. 9. Rear admiral LEOPOLD RITTER VON JEDINA. Attached to king Edward VII. (same occasion).

1904, Feb 10. JONKHEER RUDOLF EVERARD WILLEM DE WEEDE, lord chamberlain to the queen mother of the Netherlands (on the occasion of the marriage of princess Alice of Albany with prince Alexander of Teck).

1904, Apr. 18. JULIUS BENEDICTUS, count Krag Juel Vind Frijs, acting master of the Horse to the king of Denmark (on the occasion of Edward VII.'s visit to Copenhagen).

1904, Apr. 18. WALDEMAR OLDENBURG, over prasident of Copenhagen (same occasion).

1904, Apr. 18. CHRISTIAN CONRAD SOPHUS, count DANNESKJOLD-SAMSÖE, director of the Royal Theatre, Copenhagen (same occasion).

1904, Apr 18. Col WALDEMAR EDWARD LEMVIGH, commanding Danish Life Guards (same occasion).

1904, Apr. 18. MAGENS CHRISTIAN, count Krag Juel Vind Frijs (same occasion).

1904, Apr. 18. EUGEN PETERSEN, chief commissioner of police, Copenhagen (same occasion).

1904, Apr. 28. Maj. Gen. HERMANN REINHARD FREIHERR VON RÒDER, commanding the 27th Cavalry Brigade, Germany (on the occasion of the prince of Wales's visit to Wurtemberg).

1904, July 1. R. Adm. MAX FISCHEL, Imperial German Navy, adm. superintendent of the Dockyard, Kiel (on the occasion of Edward VII.'s visit to Kiel).

1904, July 1. R. Adm FREDERICK count VON BAUDISSIN, Imperial German Navy, aide-de-camp to the German Emperor, attached to king Edward VII. (same occasion).

1904, July 1. Col. MAXIMILIAN GEORGE FREDERICK CHARLES VON ENGELBRECHTEN, commanding the 36th Infantry Brigade, Germany (same occasion).

1904, Sept. 6. H.S.H. HUGO ALPHONSE EDUARD EMANUEL JOSEPH JOHN VANCESLAS, prince von Dietrichstein zu Nickolsburg (count Mensdorff-Pouilly), col. on the General Staff and aide-de-camp to the emperor of Austria.

1904, Sept. 6. JOHN RITTER VON HABRDA, commissioner of Police, Vienna.

1904, Nov. 9. HENRY CHARLES JOSEPH, marquis de Breteuil.

1904, Nov. 9. ALFRED THERÈSE ARMAND, marquis du Lau d'Allemand.

1904, Nov. 21. DON ANTONIO MARIA DE LANCASTRE, physician to the king and queen of Portugal (on the occasion of the visit of the said king and queen to England).

Royal Hanoverian Guelphic Order.

Order of the Guelphs of Hanover.

KNIGHTS GRAND CROSS (G.C.H.)

1815, Aug. 12. FREDERICK, duke of York and Albany.

1815, Aug. 12. WILLIAM HENRY, duke of Clarence, afterwards William IV.

1815, Apr. 12. EDWARD AUGUSTUS, duke of Kent.

1815, Aug 12. ERNEST AUGUSTUS, duke of Cumberland, afterwards Ernest, king of Hanover.

1815, Aug. 12. AUGUSTUS FREDERICK, duke of Sussex, appointed but did not accede until 1830, July, when he was re-appointed.

1815, Aug. 12. ADOLPHUS FREDERICK, duke of Cambridge.

1815, Aug. 12. WILLIAM FREDERICK, duke of Gloucester.

1816, Mar. 22. Prince LEOPOLD, of Saxe-Coburg, afterwards king of the Belgians.

1816. F. Marsh. ARTHUR (WELLESLEY), 1st duke of Wellington.

1816. Gen. HENRY WILLIAM (PAGET), 1st marquess of Anglesey.

1816. Gen. CHARLES WILLIAM (STEWART, afterwards VANE), lord Stewart, afterwards 3rd marquess of Londonderry.

1816. ROBERT (STEWART), viscount Castlereagh, afterwards 2nd marquess of Londonderry (civil division).

1816, Apr. 1. THOMAS TREVOR (HAMPDEN, formerly TREVOR), 2nd viscount Hampden (civil division).

1816. Lieut. Gen. Sir HENRY CLINTON.

29

1816. Gen. the Hon. Sir CHARLES COLVILLE.

1816. Lieut. Gen. Sir JAMES KEMPT.

1816. Gen. Sir GEORGE DON.

1816. Gen. ROWLAND (HILL), 1st lord, afterwards 1st viscount, Hill.

1816. Lieut Gen. the Rt. Hon. Sir GEORGE MURRAY.

1816. Lieut. Gen. Sir ROBERT MACFARLANE.

1816. Gen. CHARLES (STANHOPE), 3rd earl of Harrington.

1816. GEORGE JAMES (CHOLMONDELEY), 1st marquess of Cholmondeley (civil division).

1817. Lieut. Gen. the Rt. Hon Sir THOMAS MAITLAND.

1817. V. Adm. Sir EDMUND NAGLE.

1817. Gen. Sir HARRY CALVERT, bart.

1817. Lieut. Gen. lord WILLIAM CAVENDISH BENTINCK.

1817. Lieut. Gen. Sir JAMES CAMPBELL, bart.

1817. Lieut. Gen. Sir JAMES LYON.

1817, Apr. 23. Col. JOHN (FANE) lord BURGERSH, afterwards 17th earl of Westmorland.

1817. Lieut. Gen. Sir ALEXANDER MACKENZIE, bart.

1817 Maj. Gen Sir EDWARD HOWORTH.

1817. Lieut. Gen. STAPLETON (COTTON), baron, afterwards viscount Combermere.

1817. Lieut. Gen. Sir HENRY TUCKER MONTRESOR.

1817. Lieut Gen. Sir JOHN MURRAY, bart.

1818. Lieut Gen Sir HENRY FREDERICK CAMPBELL.

1818 Lieut Gen. WILLIAM CARR (BERESFORD), baron, afterwards viscount Beresford.

1818 V. Adm Sir THOMAS FRANCIS FREMANTLE.

1818.   Gen. FRANCIS (RAWDON-HASTINGS), 1st marquess of Hastings.

1819.   FRANCIS CHARLES (SEYMOUR-CONWAY), earl of Yarmouth, afterwards 6th marquess of Hertford (civil division).

1819.   JOHN (BOURKE), 4th earl of Mayo (civil division).

1819.   Rt. Hon. SIR GEORGE ROSE (civil division).

1819.   Gen Sir CHARLES HASTINGS, bart.

1819.   Adm. the Rt. Hon. Sir JOHN BORLASE WARREN, bart.

1819.   ALLEYNE (FITZHERBERT), lord St. Helens (civil division).

1819.   Gen. SAMUEL HULSE.

1819.   Maj.-Gen. BENJAMIN (BLOOMFIELD), 1st lord Bloomfield.

1820.   Lieut. Gen. Sir COLIN HALKETT.

1820.   Lieut. Gen. Sir CHARLES ASGILL, bart.

1820.   Lieut. Gen. JOHN MACLEOD .

1820.   Lieut. Gen. JOHN HOPE.

1821.   RICHARD (LE-POER TRENCH), 6th earl of, afterwards 1st viscount Clancarty (civil division).

1821.   Lieut. Gen. HENRY (CONYNGHAM), 1st marquess Conyngham.

1822.   BROOK TAYLOR (civil division).

1823.   JAMES (DUFF), 4th earl Fife (civil division).

1823.   FRANCIS NATHANIEL (CONYNGHAM), earl of Mount Charles, afterwards 2nd marquess Conyngham (civil division).

1823.   Sir WILLIAM KNIGHTON, bart (civil division).

1824.   Sir FRANCIS NATHANIEL BURTON (civil division).

1825.   GEORGE WILLIAM FREDERICK CHARLES, heir to and afterwards duke of Cambridge.

1825.   Lieut. Gen. Sir RUFANE SHAW DONKIN.

1825.   PERCY SIDNEY CLINTON (SMYTHE), 6th viscount Strangford (civil division).

1825. Maj. Gen. Sir JAMES WILLOUGHBY GORDON, bart.

1825. Lieut. Gen. Sir HERBERT TAYLOR.

1826 RICHARD CHARLES FRANCIS (MEADE), 3rd earl of Clanwilliam (civil division).

1826 Lieut. Gen. Sir JOHN BYNG, afterwards 6th earl of Strafford.

1827. Lieut. Gen. Sir FRANCIS THOMAS HAMMOND

1827. Lieut. Gen. Sir TOMKYNS HILGROVE TURNER.

1827. Lieut. Gen Sir JOSEPH FULLER.

1827. Lieut. Gen. Sir WILLIAM HOUSTON, bart.

1827. Rt Hon. Sir WILLIAM HENRY FREMANTLE.

1827. Lieut Gen Lord GEORGE THOMAS BERESFORD

1827. GEORGE (ASHBURNHAM), 3rd earl of Ashburnham.

? 1827. GEORGE FREDERICK ALEXANDER CHARLES ERNEST AUGUSTUS, afterwards duke of Cumberland and Tiviotdale, and king of Hanover.

1829. Rt. Hon. ROBERT GORDON (civil division).

1830 WILLIAM GEORGE (HAY), 18th earl of Erroll (civil division).

1830. RICHARD WILLIAM (CURZON), 2nd earl Howe (civil division).

1830. Sir HENRY HALFORD, bart (civil division).

1830. Sir JOHNATHAN WATHEN WALLER, bart. (civil division).

1830. JOHN DELAVAL (CARPENTER), 7th earl of Tyrconnel (civil division).

1830. WILLIAM (WELLESLEY-POLE), lord Maryborough, afterwards 3rd earl of Mornington (civil division).

1830 Gen Sir JAMES STEWART, bart.

1830. GEORGE (BOYLE), 4th earl of Glasgow (civil division).

1831. Gen. the Hon. Sir HENRY GEORGE GREY.

1831. Lieut. Gen. the Rt. Hon. Sir RICHARD HUSSEY VIVIAN, bart.

1831. Adm. Sir WILLIAM HARGOOD.

1831. Adm. lord AMELIUS BEAUCLERK.

1831. Maj. Gen. Sir EDWARD KERRISON, bart.

1831. Lieut. Gen. Sir THOMAS MACDOUGALL-BRISBANE, bart.

1831. Lieut. Gen. Sir JOHN KEANE, afterwards lord Keane.

1831. Lieut. Gen. Sir THOMAS BRADFORD.

1831. Lieut. Gen. Sir COLQUHOUN GRANT.

1831. GEORGE HAMILTON (CHICHESTER), earl of Belfast, afterwards 3rd marquess of Donegall (civil division).

1831. LUCIUS BENTINCK (CARY), 10th viscount of Falkland (civil division).

1831. V. Adm. lord JAMES O'BRYEN, afterwards 3rd marquess of Thomond.

1831. Sir ROBERT WILMOT HORTON, bart. (civil division).

1831. Lieut. Gen. Sir JOHN SMITH.

1831. Gen. GEORGE COCKBURN, afterwards bart.

1831. Rt. Hon. Sir GORE OUSELEY, bart. (civil division).

1831. Sir PHILIP CHARLES SIDNEY, afterwards 1st lord De L'Isle and Dudley (civil division).

1831. Col. lord FREDERICK FITZ-CLARENCE (civil division).

1831. Sir HENRY WATKIN WILLIAMS WYNN (civil division).

1831. Sir EDWARD CROMWELL DISBROWE (civil division).

1832. Gen. JOSIAH CHAMPANGÉ.

1832. Gen. MARTIN HUNTER.

1832. Gen. Sir JOHN FRASER.

1832. Capt. lord ADOLPHUS FITZ-CLARENCE (civil division).

1832. Capt. the Hon. Sir CHARLES PAGET, R.N.

1832. CONSTANTINE HENRY (PHIPPS), earl of Mulgrave, afterwards 3rd Marquess of Normanby (civil division).

1832. V. Adm. Hon. Sir HENRY BLACKWOOD. Died 1832.

1832. Adm. Sir ISAAC COFFIN, bart.

1832. V. Adm. PETER HALKETT, afterwards bart.

1832. R. Adm. Sir EDWARD WILLIAM CAMPBELL RICH OWEN.

1833. Lieut. Gen. FREDERICK AUGUSTUS WETHERALL.

1833. WILLIAM BASIL PERCY (FEILDING), 7th earl of Denbigh (civil division).

1833. Lieut. Gen. the Hon. ALEXANDER DUFF.

1833. Rt. Hon. CHARLES RICHARD VAUGHAN (civil division).

1833 WILLIAM CHARLES (KEPPEL), 16th earl of Albemarle (civil division).

1833. GEORGE WILLIAM (CAMPBELL), 6th duke of Argyll (civil division).

1833 Maj. Gen Sir ANDREW FRANCIS BARNARD.

1834. THOMAS CARTWRIGHT (civil division).

1834 Lieut. Gen. HENRY BAYLY.

1834. Adm. Sir CHARLES EDMUND NUGENT.

1834. Maj. Gen. Sir HENRY WHEATLEY.

1834 V. Adm. Sir WILLIAM HALL GAGE.

1834. JOHN (CUST), 1st earl BROWNLOW (civil division).

1834. Lieut Gen. Sir ROBERT BOLTON.

1834. ROBERT GRANT (civil division).

1834. Capt. Sir GEORGE FRANCIS SEYMOUR.

1834. Maj Gen. Sir BENJAMIN CHARLES STEPHENSON.

1834. GEORGE (CHILD-VILLIERS), 5th earl of Jersey (civil division).

1834. WILLIAM PITT (AMHERST), 1st earl Amherst (civil division).

1835. THOMAS (EGERTON), 2nd earl of Wilton (civil division).

1835.   RICHARD PLANTAGENET (TEMPLE-NUGENT-BRYDGES-CHANDOS-
GRENVILLE), marquess of Chandos, afterwards 2nd duke of
Buckingham and Chandos (civil division)

1835.   Lieut. Gen. Sir JOHN SLADE, bart.

1835.   V. Adm. Sir JOHN GORE.

1835.   Lieut. Gen. Sir WILLIAM KEIR GRANT.

1835.   JOHN (FITZ GIBBON), 2nd earl of Clare.

1835.   Maj. Gen. Sir JAMES COCKBURN, bart.

1835.   Lieut. Gen. RALPH DARLING.

1835.   V. Adm. Sir CHARLES ROWLEY.

1836.   V. Adm. RICHARD DACRES.

1836.   Sir GEORGE HAMILTON SEYMOUR (civil division).

1836.   Lieut. Gen. Sir SAMUEL HAWKER.

1836.   Adm. Sir JOHN POO BERESFORD, bart.

1836.   JOHN (ELPHINSTONE), 13th lord Elphinstone (civil division).

1836.   Sir ASTLEY PASTON COOPER, bart. (civil division).

1836.   Lieut. Gen. Sir EDWARD BLAKENEY.

1836.   Capt. lord JOHN FREDERICK GORDON, R.N. (civil division).

1836.   Maj. Gen. Sir LIONEL SMITH.

1836.   Maj. Gen. Sir JOHN COLBORNE, afterwards lord Seaton.

1837.   Nabob NOZIM, of Murshidabad, in Bengal.

1837.   Lieut. Col. Sir RICHARD CHURCH.

1837.   Gen. JOHN GUSTAVUS CROSBIE.

1837.   Maj. Gen. ALEXANDER GEORGE (FRASER), 16th lord Saltoun

1837.   The Rt. Hon. Sir CHARLES EDWARD GREY.

1837.   The Rt. Hon. JOSEPH PLANTA

1837.   Lieut. Gen. Sir CHARLES WILLIAM DOYLE.

1837.   Maj. Gen. Sir CHARLES THORNTON.

KNIGHTS COMMANDERS OF THE ORDER OF THE GUELPHS (K.C.H.).

1815. Col. Sir HUGH HALKETT.

1815. Maj. Gen. Sir JAMES LYON.

1815. Maj. Gen. Sir COLIN HALKETT.

1815. Maj. Gen. Sir BENJAMIN BLOOMFIELD.

1816. Maj. Gen. Sir COLQUHOUN GRANT.

1816. Maj. Gen. Sir RICHARD HUSSEY VIVIAN, bart.

1816. Col. Sir GEORGE ADAM WOOD.

1816. GEORGE WILDING, prince of Butora, etc., Naples.

1816. Lieut. Gen. Sir ROBERT BOLTON.

1816. Sir WM. CONGREVE, bart.

1817. Col. [Sir] WILLIAM ROBE.

1817. Maj. Gen. Von ROTTENBURG.

1817. Maj Gen. Sir ALEXANDER DICKSON.

1817. Col. Sir PHILIP ROCHE.

1818. R. Adm. Sir HOME RIGGS POPHAM.

1818. Col. Sir BENJAMIN D'URBAN.

1819. Col. Sir HAYLETT FRAMINGHAM.

1819. Col. Sir WILLIAM ROSE.

1819. Lieut. Gen. Sir FRANCIS THOMAS HAMMOND.

1819. Lieut. Gen. Sir TOMKYNS HILGROVE TURNER.

1819. Maj. Gen. Sir JOHN ELLEY.

1819. Maj. Gen. Sir HERBERT TAYLOR.

1819. Capt. the Hon. CHARLES PAGET, R.N.

1819. Maj. Gen. Sir ANDREW FRANCIS BARNARD.

1820. Maj. Gen. GEORGE AIREY.

1820. Lieut. Maj. Sir ROBERT WILLIAM GARDINER.

1820. Maj. Gen. JAMES (MURRAY), 1st lord Glenlyon.

1821. Maj. Gen. Sir CHARLES WILLIAM DOYLE.

1821. Lord FRANCIS CONYNGHAM.

1821. Adm. Sir EDMUND NAGEL.

1821. Gen. GEORGE COCKBURN, afterwards bart.

1821. Sir WILLIAM KNIGHTON, bart., physician to the King.

1821. GRAF HOMPESCH.

1821. Maj. Gen. Sir EDWARD KERRISON, bart.

1821. Lieut. Gen. Sir SAMUEL FORD WHITTINGHAM.

1821. Maj. Gen. Sir GEORGE AUGUSTUS QUENTIN.

1821. Maj. Gen. Sir WILLIAM KEIR GRANT.

1821. Col. THOMAS HENRY BROWNE.

1821. Col. HENRY FREDERICK COOKE.

1822. Lieut. Gen. Sir RICHARD CHURCH.

1822. Maj. Gen. LOUIS WILLIAM, viscount Chabot.

1822. The Hon. F. N. BURTON.

1822. Lieut. Col. Sir JOHN MAY.

1824. Col. Sir JAMES HENRY REYNETT.

1824. Lieut. Col. Sir JOHN HARVEY.

1825. Sir HENRY HALFORD, bart., M.D. (civil division).

1826. Lieut. Col. Sir WILLIAM LEWIS HERRIES.

1827. Sir FREDERICK BEILBY WATSON (civil division).

1827. Sir JOHNATHAN WATHEN WALLER, bart.

1827. Sir JOHN CONROY, bart (civil division).

1827. Lieut. Col. Sir JOHN MACRA.

1828. Sir FREDERICK BARNARD, librarian to the King.

1828. Capt. the Hon. ROBERT CAVENDISH SPENCER.

1829 Maj. Gen. Sir JAMES CARMICHAEL SMYTH, bart.

1829. Lord ALBERT DENISON CONYNGHAM, afterwards 1st lord Londesborough.

1830. Col. Sir AUGUSTUS FREDERICK D'ESTE (civil division).

1830. Lieut. Col. Sir CHARLES RICHARD FOX.

1830. Hon. Sir JOHN KENNEDY ERSKINE.

1830. Col. Sir WILLOUGHBY COTTON.

1830. Sir PHILIP CHARLES SIDNEY (civil division).

1830. Maj. Gen. Sir ALEXANDER BRYCE.

1831. Sir FREDERICK CAVENDISH PONSONBY.

1831. Maj. Gen. Sir JAMES CHARLES DALBIAC.

1831. Col. Sir CHARLES WADE THORNTON.

1831. Maj. Gen. Sir JOHN BROWN.

1831. Maj. Gen. Sir JAMES CAMPBELL.

1831. Maj. Gen. Sir BENJAMIN CHARLES STEPHENSON.

1831. Maj. Gen. Sir HENRY WHEATLEY.

1831. Sir JOHN HALL (civil division), consul gen. for Hanover in Great Britain.

1831. Sir GEORGE HARRISON (civil division).

1831. Lieut. Col Sir WILLIAM GOSSET.

1831. Capt. Sir GEORGE FRANCIS SEYMOUR.

1831. Capt. Sir THOMAS USSHER.

1831. Sir MATTHEW TIERNEY, bart , M.D. (civil division).

1831. Lieut. Col. JOSEPH WHATLEY.

1831. Col. STEPHEN REMNANT CHAPMAN.

1831. Sir WILLIAM BURNETT, M.D. (civil division).

1831. Lieut. Col. the Hon. Sir EDWARD CUST.

1831. Sir GEORGE BAILLIE HAMILTON (civil division).

1831. Lieut. Gen. Sir PHINEAS RIALL.

1831. Lieut. Gen. Sir WILLIAM HUTCHINSON.

1831. Maj Gen. Sir LEWIS GRANT.

1831. Maj. Gen. Sir GEORGE POWNALL ADAMS.

1831. Maj. Gen. Sir AMOS GODSILL ROBERT NORCOTT.

1831. Maj Gen. Sir JAMES COCKBURN, bart.

1831. Col. Sir MICHAEL McCREAGH.

1831. Col. Sir EVAN JOHN MURRAY MacGREGOR, bart.

1831. Col. Sir THOMAS DOWNMAN.

1831. Col. Sir NEIL DOUGLAS.

1831. Col. Sir ARCHIBALD CHRISTIE.

1831. Capt. Sir WILLIAM HOWE MULCASTER.

1831. Sir JOHN BEDINGFIELD (civil division).

1831. Col. WILLIAM TUYLL.

1831. Lieut. Gen. Sir SAMUEL HAWKER.

1831. Maj. Gen. Sir GEORGE BULTEEL FISHER.

1831. Sir WILLIAM PYM, M.D. (civil division).

1832. Lieut. Gen. Sir JAMES HAY.

1832. Lieut. Gen. Sir WARREN MARMADUKE PEACOCKE.

1832. Lieut. Gen. CHARLES BULKELEY EGERTON.

1832. Lieut. Gen. Sir WILLIAM SHERIDAN.

1832. Maj. Gen. Sir WILLIAM PATERSON.

1832. Maj. Gen. JOHN FREDERICK SIGISMOND SMITH.

1832. Maj. Gen. WILLIAM NICOLAY.

1832. Maj. Gen. ARTHUR BENJAMIN CLIFTON.

1832. Col. GEORGE WHITMORE.

1832. Col. LEONARD GREENWELL.

1832. Col. ROBERT HENRY DICK.

1832 Col. FREDERICK WILLIAM TRENCH.

1832. Capt. WILLIAM AUGUSTUS MONTAGUE.

1832. Sir WILLIAM FRANKLIN (civil division).

1832. Sir HENRY SEATON (civil division).

1832. Maj. Gen. JOHN MACLEOD.

1832. Maj. Gen. FREDERICK WILLIAM MULCASTER.

1832. Maj. Gen. CLAUDE FRANCOIS, viscount Rivarola.

1832. Maj. Gen. Sir WILLIAM PARKER CARROL.

1832. Maj Gen. JOHN HANBURY.

1832. Col. DAVID XIMENES.

1832. Capt. Sir JOHN MARSHALL.

1832. Sir JOHN WEBB, M D. (civil division).

1832. Maj. Gen. JOSEPH STRATON.

1832. Col. JOHN GEORGE WOODFORD.

1832. GEORGE HAMILTON SEYMOUR (civil division).

1832. Capt. Sir HUMPHREYE FLEMING SENHOUSE.

1832. Lieut. Gen. Sir THOMAS BROWNE.

1832. Maj. Gen. WILLIAM DOUGLAS.

1832. Maj. Gen. WILLIAM CORNWALLIS EUSTACE.

1832. Capt. NISBET JOSIAH WILLOUGHBY.

1832. Capt. ANDREW PELLATT GREEN.

1832. Capt. ARTHUR FARQUHAR, R.N.

1832. Commissary Gen. Sir JOHN BISSET (civil division).

1832. JOHN DEAS THOMPSON (civil division).

1832. Sir GEORGE JACKSON (civil division).

1832. Commodore CHARLES MARSH SCHOMBERG.

1832. R. Adm. Sir CHARLES CUNNINGHAM.

1832. R. Adm. the Hon. COURTENAY BOYLE.

1833. Lieut. Gen. DAVID LATIMER TINLING WIDDRINGTON.

1833. Maj. Gen. WILLIAM GEORGE (HARRIS), 2nd lord Harris.

1833. R. Adm. EDWARD DURNFORD KING.

1833. Capt. Sir FRANCIS AUGUSTUS COLLIER.

1833. Capt. RICHARD SPENCER.

1833. Col. JOHN BOSCAWEN SAVAGE.

1833. Capt. Sir JOHN SAMUEL BROOKE PECHELL, bart.

1833. Lieut. Gen. HENRY JOHN CUMMING.

1834. Lieut. Gen. EVAN LLOYD.

1834. Lieut. Gen. THOMAS GAGE MONTRESOR.

1834. Maj. Gen. SAMUEL TREVOR DICKENS.

1834. Maj. Gen. JAMES KEARNEY.

1834. Maj. Gen. LORENZO MOORE.

1834. Maj. Gen. JAMES VINEY.

1834. Maj. Gen. HENRY WILLOUGHBY ROOKE.

1834. Maj. Gen. Sir PATRICK ROSS.

1834. Col. HENRY KING.

1834. R. Adm. JOHN FERRIS DEVONSHIRE.

1834. Capt. JAMES HILLYAR.

1834. Capt. SALUSBURY PRYCE DAVENPORT, R N.

1834. Commissary Gen. Sir ROBERT HUGH KENNEDY (civil division).

1834. Commissary Gen. Sir WILLIAM HENRY ROBINSON (civil division).

1834. Sir JOHN WOOLMORE (civil division).

1834. Lieut. Gen. Sir JOSEPH MACLEAN.

1834. R. Adm. Sir HUGH PIGOT.

1834. Commodore ROBERT BARRIE.

1834. Col PATRICK LINDESAY.

1834. Lieut. Col. EDMUND CURREY.

1834. Col Sir SAMUEL GORDON HIGGINS.

1834. Capt. Hon. Sir HENRY DUNCAN.

1835. Capt. CHARLES BULLEN, R.N.

1835. Capt. WILLIAM HENRY DILLON.

1835. Capt. WILLIAM ELLIOTT.

1835. Capt. EDMUND LYONS, R N.

1835. Maj. Gen. THOMAS BLIGH ST. GEORGE.

1835. Maj. Gen. THOMAS PEARSON.

1835. Maj. Gen. MAURICE CHARLES O'CONNELL.

1835. Col. PATRICK DOHERTY.

1835. Col. Sir OCTAVIUS CAREY.

1835. Capt. lord JAMES TOWNSHEND.

1835. Lieut. Col. CHARLES HOLLAND HASTINGS.

1835. Sir SAMUEL WARREN, R.N.

1835. Col. the Hon. Sir HORATIO GEORGE POWYS TOWNSHEND.

1835. R. Adm. Sir ROBERT LEWIS FITZGERALD.

1835. Sir FRANCIS BOND HEAD (civil division).

1836. Maj. Gen. WILTSHIRE WILSON.

1836. Maj. Gen. Sir CHARLES WILLIAM MAXWELL.

1836. Maj. Gen WILLIAM GABRIEL DAVY.

1836. Capt. the Hon. FLEETWOOD BROUGHTON REYNOLDS PELLEW.

1836. Capt. the Hon. JAMES ASHLEY MAUDE.

1836. Capt. JOHN STRUTT PEYTON.

1836. Capt. RICHARD O'CONOR.

1836. Capt. HENRY HART.

1836. Capt. JAMES JOHN GORDON BREMER.

1836. Sir ROBERT KER PORTER (civil division).

1836. Capt Sir JOHN FRANKLIN, R.N. (civil division).

1836. Sir John NICOL ROBERT CAMPBELL (civil division).

1837. Lieut. Gen. ALEXANDER HALKETT.

1837. Maj. Gen. ROBERT BARTON.

1837. Maj. Gen. AUGUSTUS DE BUTTS.

1837. Maj. Gen. THOMAS HAWKER.

1837. V. Adm. Sir ADAM DRUMMOND.

1837. Capt. Sir DAVID DUNN.

.1837. Capt. EDWARD CHETHAM.

1837. Capt. THOMAS MANSELL.

1837. WOODBINE PARISH (civil division).

1837. Maj. Gen Sir EDWARD BOWATER.

1837. Maj. Gen. JAMES MACDONNELL

1837. Maj. Gen. ROBERT MCCLEVERTY.

1837. R. Adm. JOHN WENTWORTH LORING.

1837. Col. GEORGE ARTHUR.

1837. DAVID DAVIES, M.D. (civil division).

1837. WILLIAM FREDERICK CHAMBERS, M.D. (civil division).

1837. Capt. THOMAS BARKER DEVON.

KNIGHTS OF THE ORDER OF THE GUELPHS (K.H.).

1816. Dr. WILLIAM HERSCHELL, astronomer royal.

1816. Sir GEORGE NAYLER, 'York Herald,' afterwards Garter King of Arms and King of Arms of the Order.

1816. Lieut. Col. JOHN MERVIN CUTLIFFE.

1816. Col. PETER AUGUSTUS LAUTOUR.

1816. Capt. JAMES McGLASHAN.

1816. Lieut. Col. WILLIAM THORNHILL.

1816. Lieut. WILLIAM HAVELOCK.

1816. JAMES ROBERT GRANT, M.D. (civil division).

1816. Lieut. THOMAS CAREY.

1816. Capt. ARTHUR FARQUHAR.

1816. Lieut. Col. Sir WILLIAM OSBORNE [? Hamilton].

1817. Lieut. Col. STEPHEN REMNANT CHAPMAN.

1817. Col. ARCHIBALD CHRISTIE.

1817. Commissary RICHARD D. HANAGAN.

1818. Lieut. Col. CHARLES ASHE A'COURT.

1818. Capt. ANDREW PELLATT GREEN.

1818. Maj. THOMAS HENRY BROWNE.

1818. Lieut. Col. CHARLES PHILIP DE BOSSETT.

1818. Maj. GIDEON GORREQUER.

1818. Col. Sir FELTON ELWILL BATHURST HERVEY, bart.

1818. Maj. NATHANIEL ECKERSLEY.

1819. RITTMEISTER VON DER OSTEN.

1819. Col. Sir ALEXANDER BRYCE.

30

1818.   Lieut. Col. JAMES REYNETT.

1819.   Lieut. Col. ARCHIBALD McDONALD.

1819.   Col. CHARLES WADE THORNTON.

1819.   FREDERICK WATSON, private secretary to the Prince Regent.

1820.   BENJAMIN CHARLES STEVENSON (civil division), surveyor gen. of the Board of Works and maj. gen. in the Hanoverian Service.

1820.   Lieut. THOMAS BARKER DEVON, R.N.

1820.   Sir ANDREW HALLIDAY (civil division).

1821.   Dr. VERSTURME.

1821.   Capt. THOMAS DE GRENIER FONBLANQUE, afterwards vicomte.

1821.   Maj. SCHMIEDERN.

1821.   Lieut. Col. Sir EVAN JOHN MURRAY McGREGOR.

1822.   Maj. ROBERT HUTCHINSON ORDE.

1822.   Capt. D'ARCY TODD

1822.   Maj. WILLIAM DAVISON, aide-de-camp to the duke of Cambridge.

1823.   Sir DANIEL BAYLEY (civil division), consul gen. in Russia.

1823.   JOHN HALL (civil division), Hanoverian consul in London.

1823.   Lieut. Col. EDWARD CHARLES WHINYATES.

1823   Sir DAVID SCOTT, bart (civil division).

1824.   Maj. Gen. GEORGE JAMES REEVES.

1824.   Lieut. Col. Sir WILLIAM DAVISON.

1824.   Sir JOHNATHAN WATHEN WALLER, bart. (civil division).

1825.   Capt ROCHE MEADE.

1825.   Sir JOHN MEADE, M.D. (civil division).

1825. Capt. RICHARD HARDINGE.

1827. Lieut. Col. WILLIAM baron von TUYLL.

1827. Maj. EDWARD ANTHONY ANGELO.

1828. Capt. the Hon. CHARLES SOUTHWELL.

1828. TIMOTHY BRENT, Esq. (civil division).

1830. Col. SAMUEL GORDON HIGGINS.

1830. Lieut. Col. Sir JOHN MARK FREDERICK SMITH.

1830. Col. Sir JAMES MAXWELL WALLACE.

1830. Lieut. Col. JOHN HOBART (CARADOC), 2nd lord Howden

1830. Capt. WILLIAM AUGUSTUS MONTAGUE, R.N.

1830. Col. THOMAS NOEL HARRIS.

1831. Col. JAMES ROBERTSON ARNOLD

1831. Lieut. Col. JAMES JONES.

1831. Capt. EDWARD SPARSHOTT, R.N.

1831. Capt. ANDREW ATKINS VINCENT, R.N.

1831. Lieut. Col. GEORGE COUPER.

1831. Lieut. Col. MATHIAS EVERARD.

1831. Maj. CHARLES WRIGHT.

1831. Lieut. Col. JOHN MORILLYON WILSON.

1831. Lieut. Col. JOHN HASTINGS MAIR.

1831. Lieut. Col. JAMES FREDERICK LOVE.

1831. Maj. ROBERT SIMSON.

1831. Col. GEORGE BROWN.

1831. ROBERT ALEXANDER CHERMSIDE, M.D. (civil division).

1831. WILLIAM TAYLOR MONEY (civil division) consul gen. at Venice.

30A

1831. Maj. THOMAS HENRY SHADWELL CLERKE.

1831. Lieut. Col. ALEXANDER KENNEDY CLARK (afterwards Clark-Kennedy).

1831. Capt. CHARLES MENZIES, R.A.

1831. CHARLES KONIG, Esq. (civil division).

1831. JOHN LESLIE (civil division).

1831. Sir JOHN FREDERICK WILLIAM HERSCHEL, bart (civil division).

1831. CHARLES BABBAGE.

1831. CHARLES BELL (civil division).

1831. JAMES IVORY (civil division).

1831. DAVID BREWSTER, M.D. (civil division).

1831. Maj. CHARLES DIGGLE.

1831. Lieut. Col. ALEXANDER CAMPBELL.

1831, Oct. 12. NICHOLAS HARRIS NICOLAS (civil division).

1831. Capt. GUSTAVUS DU PLAT.

1832. Lieut. Col. WILLIAM RIDDALL.

1832. Lieut. Col. HENRY RAINEY.

1832. Lieut. Col. ST. JOHN AUGUSTUS CLERKE.

1832. Lieut. Col. JAMES CONSIDINE.

1832. Lieut Col. WILLIAM THORN.

1832. Maj. JOHN COX

1832. Maj. DIGBY MACKWORTH.

1832. Maj. WILLIAM BECKWITH.

1832 SAMUEL RUSH MEYRICK, LL.D. (civil division).

1832. Sir JOHN WHITEFORD (civil division).

1832. RICHARD MELLISH (civil division).

1832. Capt. ROBERT SMART, R.N.

1832. Col. ROBERT ROSS.

1832. Col. HENRY DAUBENEY.

1832. Col. WALTER TREMENHEERE.

1832. Lieut. Col. J. FULLARTON.

1832. Lieut. Col. GEORGE WILLIAM PATY.

1832. Lieut. Col. ROBERT NICKLE.

1832. Lieut. Col. HENRY MADOX.

1832. Lieut. Col. GEORGE GRAYDON.

1832. Lieut. Col. JOHN REED.

1832. Lieut. Col. THOMAS EELES.

1832. Lieut. Col. CHARLES BARKER TURNER.

1832. Lieut. Col. MICHAEL CREAGH.

1832. Maj. ARCHIBALD STEWART.

1832. Maj. JAMES WALLER SAMO WALLER.

1832. Lieut. Col. NATHANIEL THORN.

1832. Lieut. Col. WILLIAM CHALMERS.

1832. Col. EDWARD WALKER.

1832. Col. HENRY JAMES RIDDELL.

1832. Lieut. Col. WILLIAM BERESFORD.

1832. Lieut. Col. JAMES CHARLES CHATTERTON.

1832. Lieut. Col. ROBERT CHRISTOPHER MANSELL.

1832. Lieut. Col. JOHN PEDDIE.

1832. Lieut. Col. LESLIE WALKER.

1832. STEPNEY COWELL (civil division).

1832. Maj. STEPHEN HOLMES.

1832. Maj. WILLIAM ONSLOW.

1832. Maj GEORGE E. JONES.

1832. Lieut. Col. JOHN MARSHALL.

1832. FREDERICK MADDEN (civil division).

1832. NICHOLAS CARLISLE (civil division).

1832. Lieut. Col. CHALMERS.

1832. Maj J. WETHERALL.

1832. FRANCIS PALGRAVE (civil division).

1832. HENRY ELLIS (civil division).

1832. EDMUND LODGE (Clarenceux King of Arms) (civil division).

1833. Maj. GEORGE TEESDALE.

1833. Lieut. Col. SAMUEL DALES.

1833. Lieut. Col. ROBERT BULL.

1833. Lieut. Col. THOMAS STAUNTON ST. CLAIR.

1833. Lieut Col. CHARLES ARCHIBALD MACALISTER.

1833 Lieut. Col. GEORGE AUGUSTUS WETHERALL.

1833. Lieut. Col. EDWARD THOMAS FITZGERALD.

1833. Col. ALEXANDER FISHER MACINTOSH.

1833. Lieut. Col. HENRY HANMER

1833. Lieut Col JAMES FREETH.

1833. Lieut. Col CHARLES KING.

1833. Lieut. Col. CHARLES HOLLAND HASTINGS.

1833. Lieut. Col. Sir ROBERT MOUBRAY.

1833. Commander CHARLES HAULTAIN.

1833. Maj. JOHN WRIGHT.

1833. Maj. JOHN OWEN.

1833. Maj. JOHN GARLAND.

1833. Maj. WILLIAM FREDERICK FORSTER.

1833. Maj. JOHN ARNAUD.

1833. Maj. JOHN CHARLES HOPE.

1833. Maj. JOHN FITZMAURICE

1833. Maj. JEREMIAH RATCLIFFE.

1833. Maj. RONALD REGINALD MACDONALD.

1833. Lieut. Col. FRANCIS MAULE.

1833. JOHN CLARKE, M.D. (civil division).

1833. Maj. GEORGE DOHERTY

1833. Capt. GEORGE TYLER, R.N.

1833. H. C. COLEBROOKE.

1833. GRAVES CHAMNEY HAUGHTON (civil division).

1833. CHARLES WILKINS (civil division).

1833. ROBERT WILLIAM ST. JOHN (civil division).

1834. Lieut. Col. WILLIAM GREENSHIELDS POWER.

1834. Lieut. Col. WILLIAM GARDNER FREER.

1834. Maj. WILLIAM MACKIE.

1834. Lieut. Col. JOHN HARE.

1834. Maj. ROBERT WINCHESTER.

1834. Lieut. Col. WILLIAM McADAM.

1834. Lieut. Col. ANDREW LEITH HAY.

1834.　Lieut. Col. WARNER WESTENRA HIGGINS.

1834.　Lieut. Col. WILLIAM GRANVILLE ELIOT.

1834.　Lieut. Col. ALEXANDER HOPE PATTISON.

1834.　Lieut. Col. ROBERT BURD GABRIEL.

1834.　Maj. GEORGE ANTOINE RAMSAY.

1834.　Lieut Col CHARLES McGRIGOR.

1834.　Lieut. Col. JAMES McMAIR

1834.　Lieut Col. HENRY SOMERSET.

1834　Lieut. Col. JOHN CROSS

1834.　Lieut. Col. BARTHOLOMEW VIGORS DERINZY.

1834.　Lieut. Col. JOSEPH THACKWELL.

1834.　Lieut. Col. WILLIAM GORDON CAMERON.

1834.　Col. FRANCIS SHERLOCK

1834　Lieut. Col. RICE JONES

1834.　Lieut. Col NATHAN WILSON.

1834.　Maj. Sir FRANCIS BOND HEAD.

1834.　Lieut Col HARRY BULTEEL HARRIS.

1834.　Lieut. Col. JOHN ELLIOT CAIRNES.

1834.　Lieut. Col. Sir THOMAS STEPHEN SORELL.

1834.　Capt. EDWARD LLOYD, R N.

1834.　Capt. ROBERT FAIR.

1834.　Commander JOSEPH CHAPPELL WOOLNOUGH.

1834　Capt. JOHN TOUP NICOLAS, R.N.

1834.　Col. THOMAS ABERNETHIE.

1834.　Lieut. Col. JOS VALLACK.

1834. Sir GEORGE MAGRATH, M.D. (civil division).

1834. Lieut. CHARLES HAMILTON SMITH.

1834. Capt. EATON TRAVERS, R.N.

1834. Col. N. RAMSAY.

1834. Sir WILLIAM WOODS (Garter King of Arms) (civil division).

1834. ALEXANDER FERRIER (civil division).

1834. Lieut. Col. WILLIAM MACBEAN GEORGE COLEBROOKE.

1835. Col. SAMUEL RICE.

1835. Col. WILLIAM WOOD.

1835. Capt. WILLIAM WILLMOTT HENDERSON, R.N.

1835. Lieut. Col. JOHN JORDAN.

1835. Lieut. Col. RICHARD ROBERTS.

1835. Lieut. Col. CHICHESTER W. CROOKSHANKS.

1835. Lieut. Col. EDWARD JACKSON.

1835. Lieut. Col. THOMAS BUNBURY.

1835. Lieut. Col. JOHN SPINK.

1835. Lieut. Col. WILLIAM PEARCE.

1835. Lieut. Col. WILLIAM BUSH.

1835. Lieut. Col. lord ROBERT KERR.

1835. Lieut. Col. BADCOCK.

1835. Lieut. Col. LOVELL BENJAMIN LOVELL.

1835. Lieut. Col. CHARLES STISTED.

1835. Lieut. Col. WILLIAM JERVOIS.

1835. Lieut. Col. ROBERT BARCLAY MACPHERSON.

1835. Lieut. Col. JAMES HARVEY.

1835.   Lieut. Col. Sir JOHN ROWLAND EUSTACE.

1835.   Lieut. Col JOHN TYLER.

1835.   Lieut. Col. GEORGE DISBROWE.

1835.   Maj. THOMAS HENRY MORICE.

1835.   Maj. THOMAS WILLIAM NICHOLSON.

1835.   Maj. Sir HENRY BAYLY.

1835.   Maj. FREDERICK MacBEAN

1835   Maj. WILLIAM COX.

1835.   Maj JOSEPH ANDERSON.

1835.   Maj. ARTHUR HILL TREVOR.

1835.   Maj. DONALD JOHN McQUEEN.

1835.   Maj. THOMAS RYAN.

1835   Maj. SAMUEL THORPE.

1835.   Maj. PRINGLE TAYLOR.

1835   Maj. WILLIAM FREKE WILLIAMS.

1835.   Maj. JAMES FORLONG.

1835.   Maj. ROBERT MULLEN.

1835.   Maj. ROBERT BIDWELL EDWARDS.

1835.   Commander SAMUEL WILLIAM BROWN.

1835.   Commander WALTER KIRBY.

1835.   Lieut. Col. HENRY BOOTH.

1835.   Lieut. Col JOHN CAMPBELL.

1836.   Col. LOVE PARRY JONES PARRY.

1836.   Col. NATHANIEL BURSLEM.

1836.   Col. Sir CHARLES WEBB DANCE.

1836. Col. JOHN POTTER HAMILTON.

1836. Col. MILLER CLIFFORD.

1836. Col. STEPHEN ARTHUR GOODMAN.

1836. Lieut. Col. HARRIS COOKE HAILES.

1836. Lieut. Col. THOMAS THORNBURY WOOLDRIDGE.

1836. Lieut. Col. GEORGE DEAN PITT.

1836. Lieut. Col. SAUMAREZ BROCK.

1835. Lieut. Col. THOMAS VALIANT.

1836. Lieut. Col. NICHOLAS HAMILTON.

1836. Lieut Col. GERRASE TURBERVILL.

1836. Lieut. Col. GEORGE GORE.

1836. Lieut. Col. GEORGE AUGUSTUS HENDERSON.

1836. Lieut Col. CHARLES LESLIE

1836. Lieut. Col. ROBERT ANDERSON.

1836. Lieut. Col. JOHN McCASKILL.

1836. Lieut. Col. ALEXANDER FINDLAY.

1836. Lieut. Col. PAUL PHIPPS.

1836. Lieut. Col. JAMES CAMPBELL.

1836. Lieut. Col. RICHARD ENGLAND.

1836 Lieut. Col. JOHN GEDDES.

1836. Lieut. Col. the Hon CHARLES STEPHEN GORE.

1836 Lieut. Col. JOHN CHRISTOPHER HARRISON.

1836. Lieut. Col. ALEXANDER MUNRO.

1836. Lieut. Col. JOHN OLDFIELD.

1836. Lieut. Col. EDWARD WILDMAN.

1836. Lieut. Col. THOMAS WEARE.

1836. Lieut. Col. CUDBERT FRENCH.

1836 Lieut. Col. Sir HENRY GEORGE MACLEOD.

1836. Lieut. Col. ARCHIBALD MONTGOMERY MAXWELL.

1836. Lieut. Col. ALEXANDER CLERKE.

1836. Col. HENRY BALNEAVIS.

1836. Lieut. Col. EDWARD THOMAS FITZ GERALD.

1836. Maj. NORCLIFFE NORCLIFFE.

1836. Maj. JOHN WILSON.

1836. Maj. JAMES HENDERSON.

1836. Maj. JOHN ROBYNS.

1836 Maj. WILLIAM HENRY NEWTON.

1836 Lieut Col EDWARD CHARLETON.

1836. Maj. HENRY HERBERT MANNERS.

1836. Maj. JOHN PAUL HOPKINS.

1836. Maj. NICHOLAS WILSON.

1836. Maj. ROBERT EDWARD BURROWES.

1836. Brevet Maj. WILLIAM EDWARD PAGE.

1836. Maj GEORGE PIPON.

1836. Maj. THOMAS MOLYNEUX-WILLIAMS.

1836. Maj. PLOMER YOUNG.

1836. Maj. ALEXANDER BARTON

1836 Maj. ARTHUR DU BOURDIEU.

1836. Maj. CHARLES CORNWALLIS MICHELL.

1836. Maj. ROBERT GARRETT.

1836. Maj. John Salisbury Jones.

1836. Capt. Wilson Braddyll Bigland, R.N.

1836. Capt. Stanhope Lovell [? Badcock], R.N.

1836. Capt. Buckland Stirling Bluett, R.N.

1836. Capt. John Carpenter, R.N.

1836 Capt. Sir Henry John Leeke, R.N.

1836. Capt. Samuel Radford, R.N.

1836. Capt. William Hotham, R N.

1836. Capt. Alexander Barkclay Branch, R.N.

1836. Commander Joseph Sherer, R N.

1836. Maj. James Butler

1836. Maj. Abraham Josias Cloete.

1836. George Frederick Beltz ('Lancaster Herald') (civil division).

1836. Prof. Dr. William Jackson Hooker (civil division).

1836. Capt. John Hindmarsh, R N.

1836. Commander Sir James Pearl.

1836. Commander Alexander Maconochie.

1836. Sir Joseph de Courcy Laffan, bart. (civil division).

1836. John M. Brackenbury (civil division).

1836. Maj. Frederick Chidley Irvin.

1836. John Robison (civil division).

1837. Commander Christopher Knight.

1837. Capt. James Ryder Burton, R.N.

1837. Capt. James William Gabriel, R.N.

1837. Capt. Charles Warde, R.N.

1837. Commander BENJAMIN MORTON FESTING.

1837. Capt. WILLIAM JOHN COLE, R.N.

1837. Commander JOHN POWNEY.

1837. Capt. WILLIAM SLAUGHTER, R.N.

1837. Lieut. Col. GEORGE PARIS BRADSHAW.

1837. Lieut. Col. TURTLIFF BOYER.

1837. Lieut. Col. CHARLES CADELL.

1837. Lieut. Col. JOHN CARTER.

1837. Lieut. Col. ALEXANDER CAIRNCROSS.

1837. Lieut. Col. JOHN CROWDER.

1837. Lieut. Col. WILLIAM ELLIOTT.

1837. Lieut. Col. CHESBOROUGH GRANT FALCONAR.

1837. Lieut. Col. JAMES FORREST FULTON.

1837. Lieut. Col. GEORGE GAWLER.

1837. Lieut. Col. JOHN HOGGE.

1837. Lieut. Col. THOMAS PHIPPS HOWARD.

1837. Lieut. Col. JAMES JACKSON.

1837. Lieut. Col. JOHN LESLIE.

1837. Lieut. Col. THOMAS MARTEN.

1837. Lieut. Col. DONALD MACPHERSON.

1837. Lieut. Col. JOHN MOORE.

1837. Lieut. Col. JAMES POOLE OATES.

1837. Lieut. Col. THOMAS POWELL.

1837. Lieut. Col. WILLIAM SALL.

1837. Lieut. Col. ROBERT WALLACE.

1837. Maj. J. Jocelyn Anderson.

1837. Maj. John Austen.

1837. Maj. Henry Andrews.

1837. Maj. Henry Baynes.

1837. Maj. William Bruce.

1837. Maj. James Briggs.

1837. Maj. John Bogue.

1837. Maj. William Burney.

1837. Maj. William Brereton.

1837. Maj. Peter Bishop.

1837. Maj. Andrew Clarke.

1837. Maj. Robert Noble Crosse.

1837. Maj. Eyre John Crabbe.

1837. Maj John Clarke.

1837. Maj. John Crowe.

1837. Maj. Charles Deane.

1837. Maj. William Henry Elliott.

1837. Maj. Robert Fraser.

1837. Maj. William Green.

1837. Maj. —— Grove.

1837. Maj. Alexander Grant.

1837. Maj. John William Henderson.

1837. Maj. Joseph Mark Harty.

1837. Maj. James Price Hely.

1837. Maj. Bissell Harvey.

1837. Maj. NORMAN LAMONT.

1837. Maj. HENRY FREDERICK LOCKYER.

1837. Maj. ROBERT LAW.

1837. Maj. PIERCE LOWEN.

1837. Maj. CHARLES LEVINGE.

1837. Maj. MONSON MOLESWORTH MADDEN.

1837. Maj. GEORGE MARSHALL.

1837. Maj. WILLIAM MILLER.

1837. Maj. JOHN PENNYCUICK.

1837. Maj. EDWARD JOHNATHAN PRIESTLEY.

1837. Maj. JAMES HENRY PHELPS.

1837. Maj JAMES KERR ROSS.

1837. Maj. JOHN SINGLETON.

1837. Maj. GEORGE FITZGERALD STACK.

1837 Maj. JOSEPH CLAVELL SLADDON SLYFIELD.

1837. Maj. PEREGRINE FRANCIS THORNE.

1837. Maj. JAMES TRAVERS.

1837. Maj. JAMES BADHAM THORNHILL.

1837. Maj. ABRAHAM BERESFORD TAYLOR.

1837. Maj. ROBERT HENRY WILLCOCKS.

1837. Lieut Col. WILLIAM LEIGHTON WOOD.

1837. Lieut Col. GEORGE WILKINS.

1837. JAMES ARTHUR, M.D. (civil division).

1837. WILLIAM DURIE (civil division), assistant inspector of Hospitals.

1837. ROBERT PURKIS HILLYAR (civil division), surgeon in the Royal Navy.

1837. CHARLES F. FORBES, M.D. (civil division).

1837. Capt. Sir SPENCER LAMBERT HUNTER VASSALL, R.N.

1837. Lieut. Col. JOHN FALCONAR BRIGGS.

1837. SHEFFIELD GRACE (civil division).

1837. JAMES BURNS, M.D. (civil division).

1837. Sir CHARLES AUGUSTUS FITZROY (civil division).

Extreme Formal Poems

EXTREME FORMAL POEMS

CONTEMPORARY POETS

Edited by Beth Houston

Rhizome Press ₪ Bradenton, FL

Rhizome Press is an imprint of Beth Houston Publishing
rhizomepress.com

ISBN 978-0-9988196-9-3 (first edition paperback)

Cover design by Beth Houston
Cover image "Ethereal" by Amanda Moore
Rhizome Press logo by Dena Vanderveer

Publisher's Cataloging-in-Publication data

Names: Houston, Beth, editor.
Title: Extreme formal poems , contemporary poets / edited by Beth
Houston.
Description: Includes bibliographical references and index. |
Bradenton, FL: Rhizome Press, an imprint of Beth Houston Publishing,
2021.
Identifiers: ISBN: 978-0-9988196-9-3
Subjects: LCSH Poetry. | Poetry--Collections--21st century. | Poetry,
Modern--21st century. | BISAC POETRY / General
Classification: LCC PN6101 .E995 2021 | DDC 821.92--dc23

PREFACE

*I think Poetry should surprise by a fine excess and
not by Singularity—it should strike the Reader as a
wording of his own highest thoughts, and appear
almost a Remembrance.*
    —John Keats

Reading a good formal poem—like any poem in this collection—can seem like running into an old friend. The poem's form reminds us of the centuries of great poetry we read back in the day in high school and college, and the content is as fresh and lively as a catch-up conversation full of unexpected stories and details.

In tune with the times and accessible to the average reader, the poems in this anthology are anything but stuffy. They tease, shout, muse, accuse, play, mock, grumble, reminisce—what ordinary people think, feel, choose, and experience, these poems represent. Being good formal poems, they do so with that "fine excess" of language complexity that surprises and even dazzles. At the same time, they distill meaning to an essence so simple and true that the words resonate almost like a remembrance.

There's plenty of technique here for experts to appreciate. An impressive variety of contemporary subjects, themes, voices, tones, and styles infuse traditional forms like the sonnet and villanelle, pantoum and terza rima, ballad and ballade, rondeau and rondeau redoublé, ode, aubade, and ekphrastic poems, as well as strictly structured nonce forms created by the poets.

The goal of Rhizome Press, and of this latest anthology, is to showcase the best *extreme* formal poetry being written today, with the hope that all readers will enjoy these very accessible poems, and that some will want to take extra time to appreciate each poem's formal accomplishment.

Some readers will notice ways these extreme poems differ not only from free verse but also from the semi-formal poetry that most formalists have favored for the past several decades. An extreme poem's structure is impeccably tight, precise, and consistent. Rhymes are pure rhymes, meter is strict, and stanza patterns are consistent throughout each poem. The form works with the content to produce an overall effect of balance and harmony.

Though extreme formalism restricts exception, it does allow for elision and for differences in colloquial and regional pronunciation. All the poems here were written in English, but not all the poets speak the same English. Is "squirrel" one syllable or two? What about "flower"? Depends on the poet. Might depend on whether the poet needs a rising or falling end rhyme. For some, "museum" is kind of two and a half (or maybe quarter) syllables, which, for the purpose of scansion, in Barbara Loots' poem "Docent" elides down to two. Americans pronounce "laboratory" as four or five syllables, with the hard accent on the first. In Brit Tim Taylor's poem "The Alchemist," it's pronounced as four syllables, accent on the second and fourth, la BOR a TREE, heaviest on the second.

Each traditional form here sticks to the rules like a tight-fitting dress to a runway model. But as with designer dresses, elegance here assumes a flare of thoroughly modern creativity. Subject and style range from lyric to satire, personal memory to re-vision of a myth, meditation to political argument; there's vivid description and wordplay, there's straight-talk and aphoristic observation. Some poems are transparent, letting you look through the words directly at what's described; some are more opaque in that you can't help but notice the delicious words themselves. Some poems' language is crunchy, some juicy; some slides down smooth as molasses, some scratches like hot pepper popcorn.

Iambic pentameter is the most common meter, but you'll also find trochaic, anapestic, dactylic, trimeter, tetrameter, hexameter—an assortment sprinkled throughout. Some poems use a variety of meters arranged in consistent patterns.

Often poems are laid out on the page as a single block, usually a rectangle with lines running flush left. Line breaks help establish the poem's rhythm: When the poem takes a mental breath, so do we as our eyes briefly pause to shift our gaze to the next line. Commas and other punctuation within a line serve a similar purpose. Some poems have stanzas, which are deeper breaths. A formal poem's stanzas also tend to offer visual cues that help the reader navigate the meter and rhyme.

The formal poem's intricate structure coupled with regularity that sets up expectations the reader can easily grasp makes the poem both complex and simple. Design elegance is the formal poem's forte.

The very *form* of a formal poem brings with it a high level of built-in musicality. Besides the sonic effects of patterned rhymes and meters in their varied structural arrangements, sound components like alliteration, assonance and consonance, euphony and cacophony, sibilance, and onomatopoeia contribute to the musicality of words, phrases, and lines. Structural rhyme and meter combined with other sonic effects build a coherent, cohesive musical composition.

This combination of sonics produces an overall tone of voice that contributes to the poem's meaning by fusing, often subtly, thought and emotion. Is the poem gleeful, caustic, gloomy, peaceful? Whatever the mood, the words create it. Luckily, English has a lot of sound-meaning packed right into the words themselves. "Crackle" sounds like crackle. "Boom" sounds like boom. Those are extreme examples— onomatopoeia—but really all words have at least some musical effect simply because they're sounds. It's perhaps not a stretch to suggest that a great many words' sounds pack some connotative meaning in with the literal meaning the word denotes. Good poets are masters of pulling out words that just sound right—that just *mean* right.

Extreme formalists are word detectives searching under every bush and couch for just the right word, the perfect syllable, even that one precise letter that completes the final unified composition, both in terms of sonics and meaning. Distinctive, well-wrought, fine-tuned forms and the musicality inherent in those forms, fixed form or nonce,

are amply displayed throughout this anthology.

Ultimately, imagery is what makes a poem *poetry*. Conjuring just the right image, and then combining image clusters into a whole unified poem that means something interesting—that's what a poet *does*. In many poems the images feel so natural it's easy to assume they appeared with minimal effort. But constructing a good "simple" poem takes skill and hard work.

Each poem in this book demonstrates a high level of poetry craft. Poetry is lifted to the level of art when the poet skillfully packs in what is often referred to as "higher" or "deeper" or "symbolic" meaning. The image that's a *this* is also a *that*. Simile, metaphor, and allusion perform this kind of double-duty pointing to an *other*. Often the entire poem taken as a whole is symbolic in that it is a specific example that represents a more general category, like courage or unrequited love. Poets say it slant, as Emily Dickinson put it; they suggest, imply, represent. Their image-words from this world lead us into another world. What but language has the power to do that?

I don't think it's an accident that throughout the ages, poets have been respected, often revered, and sometimes feared (think prophets) even among those people who don't necessarily read or hear much poetry. Instinctively we all know that words are power. And good poets are the most skillful wielders of words.

"In the beginning was the Word." You know the rest. The existence of language, the perfect word, and even the word "word" matter so much that major religions have personified them as God. Every word matters. Language matters down to every jot and iota.

Especially for poets.

Words also give us deep-down pleasure. Witness the pervasive insistence of ordinary conversation. Witness the commanding presence of literature. Witness our high-paid late-night comedians.

Witness this book. —*Enjoy!*

CONTENTS

I

IN PRAISE OF DISCIPLINE

As green as Goldilocks, no formalist—
upon your four-post bed I flung my dress.
Then you arrived, a real foot fetishist,
and coaxed me into ropes of slack and stress.

You showed me dexterous ways to fit chateau,
champagne, and chattel in a sonnet's box.
My free-verse friends are skeptical, as though
it's kinky to prefer it orthodox.

I love the way you shout, *Verboten! Nein!*
I need restraint in order to be free.
You turn a blindfold to a crown, enshrine
the sacred sheets where we make poetry.

Some judge me as a twisted character
but haven't scanned a quatrain in my shoes—
or iamb-studded collar, as it were.
I'm happy to play hostage to you, Muse.

Yet when I miss my freer days, the thrill
of swinging from the chandelier, form tossed,
we role play blank verse style and you fulfill
my fantasy of tennis with Bob Frost.

So slap my bottom if my lines don't scan;
I'll wrestle till we come to a détente.
I rule my sovereign kingdom with élan,
though you pretend I'm not *Frau Kommandant.*

Now come, *mein Zuchtmeister* for whom I purr.
Let's couch our iambs in pentameter.

~ Nicole Caruso Garcia

SONNET

Sometimes I'm of two minds about my love
of formal verse. On one hand I am pleased
to have a tidy room where I resolve
the mess in 14 lines, all conflicts squeezed

into pentameter's corral. But then
I wonder if I just delude myself.
With two opposing sides now safely penned
do I still need another sturdy shelf

of 4-by-5 construction for a third?
But it's too late to turn back now, rethink
the blueprint, question a design inferred
from nothing less than Golden Mean. At brink

of couplet, resolution's imminent.
I built this house of words—I'll live in it.

~ *Debra Wierenga*

The Thing's Impossible

Perhaps the single feature of the villanelle that twentieth-century poets made their own is the absence of narrative possibility...the form refuses to tell a story.
   —*The Making of a Poem: A Norton Anthology of Poetic Forms*

Don't write a villanelle to tell a tale:
they're not the form for narrative or plot.
It's pretty obvious why you will fail.

For instance, there's an island; you set sail.
The wind is perfect, and the day is hot.
Don't write a villanelle to tell a tale,

Because, well, you will have to see a whale,
a wonder, but it can't be caught, or shot.
You see? It's obvious why you will fail.

Say, you're with her, and you're both at the rail—
(I don't think I have mentioned it's a yacht.
Don't write a villanelle to tell a tale!)

A magic moment. You'll embrace. The ale
your steward brought will just have hit the spot.
But wait. It should be obvious you'll fail

Since now her husband, who's been sprung from jail,
is in that sloop approaching, and he's got—
Don't write a villanelle to tell a tale.
The thing's impossible. You're bound to fail.

~ *Bruce Bennett*

To My Children Reading My Poetry After I'm Gone

If you are anything like me, you'll look
for clues about your mom inside this book.
You'll read each poem that I wrote and cry.
Please don't. You need to know it's such a lie.
That year when I was sick I lost my hair.
I brought a cactus home: a prickly pear?
I think I only used that for the rhyme.
(That's why I made up stuff from time to time!)
That hulking boat that dreamed of more? It sank.
And graduation night—I *never* drank.
Some parts are real: I rocked you in my arms,
ate gyros, frites; my mother wore gold charms.
But poets play with words, ignore the truth,
"manipulate" as Plath once said. A ruth-
less cutting, blending, marking up—that's art.
Dears, best to trust what's written in your heart.

~Kyle Potvin

In Pentameter

—for Retika Vazirani (1960-2003)

The meter shows you what you want to say.
The pulse of thought—the time it takes to vent
a single breath—the five-beat line can play
out lengths of unexpressed but felt intent
like knotted rope. The way a line of bass
can tell the body how to dance, a strict
iambic pulls the mind from phrase to phrase
to find the end stop no one could predict.

What crisis undercut your sure belief
that word would follow word would follow word
to bridge the gaping gorge of any grief?
What dissonance, what banging rhythm lured
your ear away from meter's soothing song
before your lovely line was done…

~ Debra Wierenga

SUPERNOVA

A burnished afternoon. Why dull it with
a lapse to metaphor
or scientific fact, or myth,
or say there's more

to life than what the naked eye perceives
or what the ear can hear?
Why paraphrase the shushing leaves,
the swoosh of deer?

Why try to parse the chirrup of the birds
or posit love's a stew
of enzymes? Why resort to words
when hush will do?

As afternoon declines to dusk, I stand
uncertain and perplexed,
your ashes in my trembling hand.
I ask, *What next?*

Then grant the constancy of truths and laws,
of motive, meaning, mind;
of logic, reason, purpose, cause;
because I find

it's simpler to release you, as I must,
less harrowing by far,
remembering that human dust
was once a star.

~ *Catherine Chandler*

STARS

On tilted spindle overhead the bowl of heaven turns
with starry illustrations of the tales on Grecian urns

where Perseus, Andromeda, and Hercules roll by
as though some everlasting truth were written in the sky.

Imagine all the languages the universe can speak
to those who never heard or read or thought a word of Greek:

bone auguries from China, and the handprints in a cave,
the calendar of Yucatan, and runes that mark a grave.

From drums of Africa, from winds upon Pacific seas,
from mathematic measure, from the atom's mysteries

receive the wisdom of the earth in wordless seminars
assembled by the human mind from dust that once was stars.

~ *Barbara Loots*

Ex Nihilo

Frederick Hart's portico sculptures at the National Cathedral, Washington, D.C.

Between the lines was where we lived before
this episode of light, vibration, sound,
that roused us from a stone's dim corridor.

In dark we never listened to the soar
of planets, as their orbits interwound
between the lines of where we lived before.

A rush of comets woke us. Then a roar
of asteroids impelled us from the ground
and roused us from the stone's dim corridor

with thoughts of waking, walking through a door
that did not yet exist. Stars drew around,
drawing the lines to where we lived. Before

our hands stretched outward, we were metaphor,
words not yet turned to flesh, thoughts still unfound
and unroused from a stone's dim corridor,

until time settled in and brought the spore
of life and breath. We are no longer bound
between the lines of where we lived before
you roused us from the stone's dim corridor.

~ *Claudia Gary*

CAVE PAINTER

(Lascaux, 16,000 BCE)

We come at dawn. Our flickering torch light
Casts eerie shadows down as we descend
The sloping shaft to reach the hidden site,

A long cave painted past the trail's first bend
With horses, deer, and great bulls in full stride,
All racing headlong toward an unseen end

In two congested rows on either side.
We slow and pass between without a word,
And hold our torches high and wave them wide—

The stirring vision of the running herd,
Completed long ago over the course
Of the few special summers it recurred,

Affecting us with such deep grace and force
We want to linger for a longer view—
But we have visions of the great red horse

So we continue onward, crouching through
A dwindling passage to emerge inside
A new cave sparsely painted with a few

Horse scenes, half-filled. We gather and decide
Which sections we will paint, then separate
To organize our lamps and tools beside

Our scattered posts. I trim my lamp and grate
My purest pigment stones and mix the flakes
With drippings from the lamp. I concentrate

On these small tasks, while deeper silence makes
My thoughts and spirit stray and lose their way,
Until a sudden rush of hoofbeats breaks

That silence, and in strange light, unlike day,
The red horse comes to where I sit, alone.
His stares into me, and his eyes convey

A fleeting scene of motion, breath, and bone.
And then he rears and gallops out of sight.
And at that moment I touch paint to stone.

~ *David Stephenson*

SHOTS

I feel the buzz. I aim to glean
An optic fix to fill my screen.
My camera simply can't deny
The flirty, flashing firefly
And dawn's couture in tangerine.

The bird, the bud, the beetle's sheen,
Spring fringes splashing absinthe green;
A luscious rush that lights my eye.
    I feel the buzz.

I'm up for kicks. I'm ever keen
To hit the phlox and foxglove scene.
A glowing, sun-drunk, Van-Gogh sky
Imbues my lens. I'm nimbus high.
Hail golden shots—my dopamine.
    I feel the buzz!

~ Susan Jarvis Bryant

Docent

The art museum behind the big bronze door.
The yellow buses lining up outside.
The little children eager to explore.

The chirpy docent: Who's been here before?
Please pay attention. I will be your guide.
At this museum, behind that big bronze door,

there's nudity, depravity, and gore
to take your little psyches for a ride.
You children will be able to explore

the beauty born of fear, of faith, of war,
of ancient ritual and genocide
that cannot hide behind a brazen door.

Beheadings hardly happen anymore.
Most artists have avoided suicide.
You children are encouraged to explore

the human drama we cannot ignore,
the shape of visions and the forms of pride
collected here behind the big bronze door.

You'll find despair, anxiety, and more.
Your eyes will bleed. Your skulls crack open wide.
Have fun. Enjoy yourselves as you explore
the art museum behind the big bronze door.

~ Barbara Loots

Counsel Regarding that Siren, Truth

Truth, that gorgeous, sexy, feisty lover,
Rouses lust that knocks you off your rocker.
From such bliss you'll soon be seeking cover.

Where'd she learn her charms? Check out her mother.
Zone that gawker out. Just don't dare mock her
Truth. That gorgeous, sexy, feisty lover

Taps dark facts you thought none could uncover.
She'll pursue well-meaning like a stalker.
From such bliss you'll soon be seeking cover.

Kisses shower till you nearly smother,
All while she remains the nonstop talker.
Truth's a gorgeous, sexy, feisty lover,

Sure, but when you step out, she'll still hover
Like a halo. Daydream plots to knock her
Off, she'll know. You'll soon be seeking cover.

Tough love's blows? From those you'll not recover.
No escape plan lies could ever shock her.
Truth: That gorgeous, sexy, feisty lover!
From such bliss, you'll soon be seeking cover.

~ Beth Houston

My Novel Fetish

I simply can't contain myself;
My eyes are drawn, compelled to look.
They lure me to their leaf-lush shelf;
I'm hooked by each beguiling book.

My eyes are drawn, compelled to look;
My fingers skim each siren spine.
I'm hooked by each beguiling book;
I linger till another's mine.

My fingers skim each siren spine;
I breathe their luscious ink-kissed scent.
I linger till another's mine
With thrills that spill till passion's spent.

I breathe their luscious, ink-kissed scent;
They lure me to their leaf-lush shelf
With thrills that spill till passion's spent—
I simply can't contain myself.

~ Susan Jarvis Bryant

Opera: A Ballade

After watching 33 free streamed operas from the MET during quarantine

Sometimes the heroine is just a girl,
an innocent set up to be betrayed.
Whether she loves a hero or a churl,
she'll face a three- or four-hour escapade
in which her feelings and her fate are swayed
by charm, by force, deception, or disguise
she's helpless to resist or to evade.
And then she dies.

Sometimes around the heroine unfurl
fate's sinister entrapments. Undismayed,
she feels the storm of accusation swirl
and knows the price of honor must be paid.
Beset by Powers That Must Be Obeyed,
she suffers while the chorus vilifies.
Her hopes of justice and redemption fade.
And then she dies.

Sometimes the heroine, a perfect pearl,
whether a princess or a village maid,
regardless of her protest or demurral,
becomes the object of an evil trade,
a bloody game, a sinister charade,
with hidden motives and transparent lies,
with clash of insult and with flashing blade.
And then she dies.

Through every lamentation and tirade,
each heroine embraces her demise
despite how fervently she might have prayed.
And then she dies.

~ *Barbara Loots*

EDWARD HOPPER'S *AUTOMAT*

One does not see the gleaming wall of glass,
its nickel slots and plates of apple pie,
the scores of harried customers who pass.
Reflected in the window's blackened eye,
two rows of matching ceiling fixtures light
a way to nowhere through the city night.

Inscrutable as an unsculptured stone,
between the brass-railed stairway and the door,
we see a woman sitting all alone,
a quiet presence in a stark décor.
Her posture mimics, spiritless and still,
the fresh fruit posing on the window sill.

A little radiator crouches near
the wall, and yet the woman wears a glove,
a knee-length, fur-trimmed coat, a hat. Career
girl? Actress? Shopkeep? Maybe she's in love . . .
She's staring far beyond the coffee cup.
I wonder if some man has stood her up.

The empty wooden chair, the empty plate,
the downcast eyes beneath the cloche's brim,
suggest he was expected. Now it's late,
the situation and her prospects grim.
She weighs her options, as she slowly sips
and seems to pout with daubed vermilion lips.

Perhaps she can't find work, and soon must pack
her dreams and bags and board a Greyhound bound
for where she swore she never would go back.
Perhaps it's just her favourite stomping ground
where no one blinks at tables set for one;
where one can wallow in oblivion.

I want to tell her that I know. I know
she can survive whatever's brought her here;
that glad and sorry seasons come and go;
that there is nothing and no one to fear—
I've owned the loss, I've worn the coat and hat.
I am the woman in the automat.

~ Catherine Chandler

CLASSIC HITS

In sloppy FM waves nostalgia rolls:
I wanna hold! You are the sunshine of!
Each oldie on the golden dial extols
Your soul, your body's curves, your rockin' love.

Three chords can't search your whole exotic heart,
But truly, *You're just too good to be true.*
When lyrics work, the instrumental part
Will find a way to find its way to you.

We'll tap our toes and hum it once or twice,
Then dance to it as long as we're alive.
Our song's a sacred air from paradise;
Our song's a sweaty sock-hop 45.

Please, Mr. DJ, tell my girl from me
That eager stuff I never think I can.
Play her the tunes that say, *I wanna be
Your lover, babe, I wanna be your man.*

~ *Chris O'Carroll*

Playing on Alone

A band I think I saw once in the past
Toured through my town, and I went to the show,
Assuming their style must be loud and fast
If I in fact had seen them years ago.

The act was just the old band's lead guitar
With rent-a-rockers on the drums and bass,
Performing in a storefront with a bar
But no seating, just empty standing space.

As I watched that old timer cycle through
Forgotten hits for microscopic pay
In that obscure and pitiful venue,
I felt sad that he'd ended up that way,

Until I noticed that he didn't care,
But looked relaxed and in his element,
Despite the small crowd and old friends not there—
Absorbed in song and seemingly content

To just make music, as a daily goal,
As long as someone came to hear him play,
A lot more for the soul than the bankroll.
I went home wishing I could live that way.

~ *David Stephenson*

PIANO

Bravo! You have such marvelous technique!
My children all took lessons once a week.
The girls a little longer than the boys.
Why do males tend to favor sports or toys?
You learned to play by ear? Remarkable!
I bet your practices were never dull.
The teacher that I hired was very kind.
Not strict enough, perhaps, but never mind.
Her rates were reasonable, or so I thought.
If only talent could be bought or taught.
Of course, I never touch the keys myself.
Instead I pluck a novel from the shelf.
These days I often find myself alone.
My children now have children of their own.
Music? None seems to be inclined. Too bad.
Each interest of those youngsters proves a fad.
Already done? You must be on your way?
Here is a check for what I owe today.
Six months from now, please call and come again.
Of course, I must be home to let you in.
Why do I keep this instrument in tune?
Because I still remember "Clair de Lune."

~ Jane Blanchard

"Serenata" from Stravinsky's *Pulcinella* Suite

The oboe sighs a warm but thin
complaint, its supple grief akin
to yours, though you can't really say
which of your sorrows lilts this way,
which disappointment sings within

this arabesque, these notes that spin
in pulsing arcs beneath your skin
as if it's your regrets that play
the oboe. Sighs

leave undefined what might have been,
taste neither rue nor madeleine,
and cannot mend the things that fray
or find whatever's gone astray.
But like an empathetic twin,
the oboe sighs.

~ *Jean L. Kreiling*

EDWARD HOPPER'S *PENNSYLVANIA COAL TOWN*

The patch town isn't specified. It could
be one of many, like the nondescript
old dwellings—all identical—of wood,
their little plots well-tended, borders clipped.
I spot a hobnail milk glass table lamp,
lace curtains, pictures on the parlor wall.
This relic of a former mining camp,
is mapped far from my house in Montreal.
Harsh sunlight strikes a terra cotta urn
from which there sprouts a weather-beaten fern.

A man—the owner? renter?—takes a break
and looks at something far beyond my gaze.
The shadowed cart, the stationary rake
are faintly reminiscent of Millet's
L'Angélus. But this man doesn't bow
his head in prayer. He's simply tired and hot.
Perhaps he'll take a rag and wipe his brow,
resume his work without a second thought.
Or maybe, having had enough, undone,
he'll curse the clapboard baking in the sun.

Fast forward fifty years. The man is dead.
Black diamonds blasted from the Northern Field
of ridge-and-valley Appalachia fed
our furnaces. All adits have been sealed.
Abandoned breakers loom above the town

that's been declared the fourth worst place to live
in Pennsylvania. Life is tumbledown.
But this I know is true: that I would give
my eyeteeth for the chance to tell the man
in Hopper's painting, *Love it while you can.*

~ *Catherine Chandler*

Ballade for Geniuses

Where is Leonardo, ingenious man
Who rarely finished any masterpiece?
And Shakespeare with his Lear and Caliban,
Is he with Hamnet, and are they at peace?
Does Byron burn or does he mold in Greece?
Do not say each one lives in his best book.
As geniuses die down, our fools increase.
But where are water drops from last year's brook?

Where is old Aeschylus, who first began
To add more actors with one role apiece?
Where Sophocles, who saw a cosmic plan
To which no clever man could bring surcease?
And Aristophanes with barbed caprice?
Where Chaucer, he whose Prioress and Cook
Are recognizable as one's valise?
But where are water drops from last year's brook?

And where is Pope, whose every breath would scan?
Where Johnson, wide in reading as obese?
And Auden's where, whose mind was talisman?
Where Yeats, who made divine the noise of geese?
I see no Einstein, with a little piece
Of God within his brain, at which he'd look
When smooth hypotheses took on a crease.
But where are water drops from last year's brook?

The world will catch such men and then release
Them as an angler frees his catch from hook.
We living humans would extend their lease,
But where are water drops from last year's brook?

~ John J. Brugaletta

Tune for the Prune

I wish they'd leave your name alone—
so spare and saturnine in tone,
the perfect word for kids to groan
    each time that Grandma stews you.
But no: the grocers have to come
and change your label to "dried plum"
in hopes, I guess, they'll make some dumb
    gourmets decide to choose you.

What's next? The raisin will be gone
once "dried grape" joins the lexicon—
and then the trend will carry on,
    from house to street to diner,
as arbiters of taste and tact
get wind of this renaming act
and seize the moment to redact
    some terms they wish were finer.

Although at first they'll stick with food,
rechristening to suit the mood
of those who find plain menus rude,
    they'll soon march past the larder.
No word of any kind will be
exempt from *faux* gentility:
instead of death, we'll have "dried chi";
    instead of hate, "dried ardor."

Poor prune, of course you had no clue
they'd make a precedent of you,
but quickly now, before they do,
     please grant me one small favor:
from wizened skin to rocky pit,
don't be the latest upscale hit.
A change of name can't change a bit
     of your repulsive flavor.

~ *Melissa Balmain*

SCOFFER

He casts a haughty eye upon your toils;
The warp and weft of words you've woven tight.
He revels like the devil in his spoils
And claws at every thread with raw delight,

Unraveling each seam until your cloths
Of heaven look like rags on beggars' backs
Benibbled by a gnash of hungry moths.
He spills his ills on all your opus lacks.

The silvered weave you've spread with golden flair
Through moonbeam dreams embroidered with the night,
Will only prompt this gloater to declare
He wouldn't wipe his feet on such a fright.

He spurns the nightingale and Grecian urn.
The lofty canon's far beneath his taste.
So, poet, grab your gifts before they burn
In bile that lays the very best to waste.

If silk-ode weavers should succumb to scorn,
All mists and mellow fruitfulness will die.
No jocund daff will dance upon the lawn.
No Tyger, blazing bright, will light an eye.

~ *Susan Jarvis Bryant*

AN ACADEMIC COMEDY

Among the masked personae and their parts
are those who deify the fragile arts.
Trebissa just adores ballet and speaks
ad infinitum of the dance techniques.
Rinaldo loves the opera, and best
of all, Poulenc's "Tiresias's Breast."

Then there are those whose minds are finely honed,
so like all ancient prophets, may be stoned.
Some bow to coarser sports, buy kegs of beer,
support their teams and slap each other's rear.
Some climb the dizzy heights to thinner air
to sit in splendor as department chair.
Adina goes in boots and drives a car
a young man might afford if he were czar
of Transylvania, or a Mongol Khan.
Pusstera is intrigued most by the Swan
of Avon, who intrudes on her pure dreams,
not frowning, but alight on lunar beams.

The worst of these is one who worships verse,
possessed by that which others deem a curse.
But lest this geniality descend
to depths where undue satire might offend,
we'll bring this genial poem to an end.

~ John J. Brugaletta

II

In Such a Place

I'm killing minutes in a city park,
Reflecting while the sky turns overcast.
Strange how the orderly, unblemished grounds
Appear to have no vestige of the past.

The parking meters accept credit cards.
The shrubbery is plain and well-behaved.
Two ravens poke the lawn half-heartedly.
The spaces in between the grass are paved.

Birdsong is banished by the leaf blower
and power mower edging ficus trunks.
The gas fumes are the only vagrants here,
Loitering in the air like drowsy drunks.

A man who walks a Yorkie on a leash
Pauses to let the tiny dog complete
Its tiny crap, dispatched with plastic bag
And carried to a bin across the street.

There's no dead branch in sight, no memory;
No process of decay, nothing to burn.
Where nothing rots, nothing surprising lives.
In such a place, what more is there to learn?

~ *Leslie Monsour*

Fragment: Cycling Ascot Drive

Steepness gives us pretense to the air:
A winding roadway like a spiral stair
descends through treetops—eucalyptus, pine;
a hawk flies out beneath us, makes a line
and folds onto a limb, her black and white
a speckled camouflage in dappled light;
we're eye to eye, and then we sink below
and feel her eye upon us, take a slow
hard turn where rock and hillside drop away
to somewhere green and mystical. A gray,
chipped guardrail marks the edge where freedom takes
our breath, then sends it back: we ride the brakes,
hold closer to the pavement, circle down
to earth, and straightaway—and then, around
one curve, the brick and clamor of the town.

~ D. R. Goodman

SUMMER AGAIN

The ink-drop bumblebee invades
　　The squashes, bloom by bloom,
Amid the beans that weave in braids
　　And dangle from their loom.

The lizard, livening its bones,
　　Pretends that it can print
Its belly on the blazing stones
　　Beside the cooling mint,

Where cabbage butterflies perform
　　A papery ballet
And dodge the garden hose's warm,
　　Rainbow-illumined spray.

The scene, familiar and brief,
　　Age after age returns—
As green returns to summer leaf,
　　Before the forest burns.

~ Leslie Monsour

August Watering

My neighbor's timer sprinklers tick and spin,
But I prefer to hose my yard by hand,
    To spray light's grinning skin
    Of rainbows over flowers,
  Tomatoes blushing as they stand
    (Half water when they're canned);
   Green string beans twine up sunflower towers;
  Behind the shed, weeds brush my chin:
Such well-quenched thickets spread protective bowers.

Mere nozzle drizzle thwarts drought's wilting powers,
But it colludes to heat the compost heap.
    Bare feet walk wet for hours
    (Birds roosting in their boots).
  Cicadas creep, fat bullfrogs leap
    Into my arcing sweep.
  Drenched cucumbers exude new shoots.
  Vines drink like drunks. No mildew sours
Fresh pole pea flowers or melons' swollen fruits.

Sweet climbing roses sip scent up their roots.
Perennials on stalks as old as Zeus
    Dress up in brand new suits.
    Earth's curious exchange
  Of bulb for lunch when leaf comes loose
    And rain transmutes to juice—

What miracle could be more strange?

(Through thatch cleared patch my pulled hose scoots.)

What lesser god could catalyze such change?

~ *Beth Houston*

SYMBIOSIS

All summer long the roses thrive,
Those thorny plantings with the drive
To stretch toward heaven day by day,
While grapevines slowly wind their way
As far as rugged roots contrive.

If heat and moisture should connive,
The vineyard's owner will derive
A warning from the blooms' display
      All summer long.

Before the mildew can deprive
The lot of means to stay alive,
Vine-tenders must apply a spray
So fruits as well as flowers may
Enhance their chances to survive
      All summer long.

~ Jane Blanchard

LIFE ON THE LOS ANGELES RIVER

A heron stops in early spring
At an unlikely place,
Wading on stilts with folded wing
And skeptical, cool grace,

Aiming its handsome banded eye,
Its sleek, extended beak,
At darting schools of minnow fry
Inhabiting the creek

And slurry that the storm drains pour
Into the concrete flood
Canal, whose excavated floor
Has been returned to mud.

New sandbars bring forth willow shrubs,
And recent marshes hum
With frogs that feed on insect grubs;
Now water birds have come.

Today we watch the heron fly.
Its magnitude and hue
Reveal at once the reason why
We call it great and blue.

~ *Leslie Monsour*

Spring Villanelle

Winter retreats. Light strengthens day by day.
With snowdrops over, primroses appear.
Now spring begins its progress through to May.

A chestnut's crown is decked with an array
Of sticky pointed buds, a new leaf year.
Winter retreats. Light strengthens day by day.

Tits peck a fat-ball dangling from a bay
And loudly chirr for everyone to hear
Now spring begins its progress through to May.

The rooks impale their leatherjacket prey
Below the sward their bills evolved to spear.
Winter retreats. Light strengthens day by day.

Tough dandelions sink, deep down in the clay,
Tenacious tap roots difficult to clear
Now spring begins its progress through to May.

The time has nearly come when bluebells lay
On woodland floors a misty blue veneer.
Winter retreats. Light strengthens day by day
Now spring begins its progress through to May.

~ *Jerome Betts*

Autumn Villanelle

The air is colder. As the leaves descend
And write, in yellow characters, decay,
Autumn is here and summer at an end.

Spiders from side-lines monitor and mend
The webs that struggling victims disarray.
The air is colder as the leaves descend.

White windflowers' rust-edged petals fall, and blend
Confetti-showers with glistening red clay.
Autumn is here and summer at an end.

The ivy tendrils on a trunk extend
Their lagging's vivid green around its grey.
The air is colder. As the leaves descend

Last dahlias flare, a frost-doomed dividend.
A nutting squirrel chatters at a jay,
Autumn is here and summer at an end.

Time's daily shorter for the sun to spend;
Thick morning mists too slowly melt away.
The air is colder. As the leaves descend
Autumn is here and summer at an end.

~ Jerome Betts

THE GHOST NUDGES ME TO THE CELLAR

I swore I would have oiled the squeaky door
And nailed these creaking stairs, swept clear the floor,
Replaced the rusted socket with a light
That never flickers, all before this chore.

If my ghost watching me suspected fright
One gleans from gothic novels, she'd be right.
Cool, musty drafts push spider webs, and poor
Spooked mice go skittering in futile flight.

I've two large buckets full of bulbs, and more
Upstairs and in the ground, but these I pour
Out gently on the workbench, more polite
Than one might tolerate an old aunt's snore.

Exotic bulbs so tender that they might
Not make it through the first hard freeze tonight.
At first I thought I might as well ignore
The warnings of the catalogues in spite

Of every urge in me to dig and store.
But though this stiff bent back can't take much more
With all this stooping, I expect delight
Next spring and summer, like I have before.

You taunt my laziness, my failing sight.
But I'm the type that puts up quite a fight
For underlings. So now you know the score,
Ghost, just leave me be. Mice scratch for a bite,

I hear them in the walls and ceiling, drawer
And tool chest, nooks where I had planned to store
These flowers holding moist and seasoned light
Coiled up inside their trusting fleshy core.

I brush the dirt off…careful, simple rite,
In one hand hold the whole year's cycle tight—
My hand's more layered chaff. Fall's precious ore
Grasps living's chemistry that can excite

An old crone to recall her hands, her sore,
Red, calloused touch still eager to explore
Dug magical spring flowers taking flight—
I hear their breathing, dreaming, quiet roar.

~ *Beth Houston*

EMERGENCES

Nothing is so beautiful as spring.
—Gerard Manley Hopkins

The mud sucks up the filthy snow
and swallows. From the shrunken mass
the bus-stop beer cans crown and grow.
A season's meanness dots the grass.
We wait; we wait. The weather breaks.
It heaves the bones of old mistakes:

Where gulls pick trash from parking lots
and dandelions brood the seed
set to subvert our garden plots,
we pick our poisons weed by weed
and plan. We plan; we never learn
these are the tricks the seasons turn

while down the alleys' potholed lines,
through muscled-open windows come
the mower-motors' manic whines
and street rods at the stoplight hum
hard vices in their deepest throats,
those decades-old discordant notes

menace we never quite forget.
We wait. We are not younger yet.

~ *Maryann Corbett*

Northern Spy

"That apple tree up there's a Northern Spy,"
my uncle says, "the last one of its kind
around these parts. For apple sauce or pie,

there's nothing better than the Northern Spy."
His father—my grandfather—comes to mind,
the farmer who set one small parcel by

for fruit trees. When he died, the Northern Spy
was not the only heirloom left behind.
The farmhouse, fields of hay cut down to dry,

a mountain spring that feeds the Northern Spy,
and pastures where a neighbor's cattle wind
recall the days when horses, young and spry,

would munch the windfalls from the Northern Spy.
Now one old swaybacked stallion's all you'll find,
kept in the barn, his sable head held high,

far from the meadow of the Northern Spy.
He nuzzles hay; his molars slowly grind.
His eyes reflect an apple-tinted sky.

~ *Kevin Durkin*

SLEEPING BEAR

The legend says she waits for them, asleep.
Perhaps in sandy dreams her cubs carouse,
pull milk from warm reserves still running deep
within her waiting for their eager mouths.
Maybe she's just depressed, and she can't face
the thing she's done, uprooting them like tough
perennials without a proper place
to plant them. They were barely old enough
to toddle, they could never swim that lake.

She sleeps and lets the wind enshroud them all
in winding sheets of sand. She won't awake.
She knows she'll never watch her babies crawl
up Michigan's shore to romp around her—
or love the islands they are without her.

~ Debra Wierenga

BLUISH ANIMALS

In answer to Louise Bogan and Henry David Thoreau

Bluish monkeys, one small shrew,
the cat they call the Russian blue,
the pure-bred rat, and peacocks, too—

yes, bluish on the land are few.
But bluebird is defined by blue,
and countless sorts that fly or flew.

The largest animal's the whale,
his head is blue, and so's his tail.
So many fish are blue of scale!

Being confined to air or sea,
these challenge visibility,
as though for God especially,

for camouflage may make us blind;
to earthly elements confined,
while blue is heaven's private mind—

for sea and sky have no real hue,
it's light they borrow shining through.
Although they may be hard to view,
a wealth of animals are blue.

~ *Susan de Sola*

NAUCRATE AND THE PARTRIDGE

That partridge has come back again.
    It's driving me insane.
It looks me in the eye, and then
    it rasps its vile refrain:
You killed your son. In fact my mark
    was Icarus's dad.
I'd heard about his flying lark.
    By Zeus, it made me mad!

I told the git: "You're off your nut!
    He's only just fifteen!"
At first he tried to argue, but
    I threatened to get mean.
He soon began to bellyache.
    I gave him hell. He smiled.
I told him: "Look, for heaven's sake,
    we're talking of a child!"

That night I sneaked up to his lair,
    identified the wings,
and sabotaged the larger pair.
    With all the other things,
it slipped my mind how much our son
    had grown and put on weight.
I didn't twig to what I'd done
    until it was too late.

At least, I thought, the boy can swim.
    Well, how was I to know
those beastly wings would carry him
    a hundred miles or so?
By then the feathers must have been
    a riddle in the sun.
I'd trimmed the edge that can't be seen
    off every single one.

The rigmarole that Daedalus
    devised to save his name
had one great defect: Icarus
    was shouldered with the blame.
He wasn't over-eager, then.
    He didn't fly too high.
His wax wings never melted when
    they fell out of the sky.

~ Duncan Gillies MacLaurin

ODE TO AN OCTOPUS

Shape-shifter of the sea, I've come to love
Your strange sophistication; out of place
In liquid labyrinths, your form sings of
Odd creatures from the sphere of outer space.
Yet here among anemones and fish,
An ocean star shines beautiful and bright.
Your flirty skirt of legs skims past a reef
In colors conjured by an inner wish
To hide your blushing pulse of pure delight,
As awestruck eyes look on in disbelief.

Houdini of the blue, you shrink and slink
Through crevices defying common sense.
Contortion and a dirty squirt of ink
Can hoodwink eel and shark. Your skill's immense!
From jiggle-jelly soft to craggy rock,
You morph from smooth to rough with ease and speed,
Invisible to those who crave your taste.
The predators, they circle, and they flock;
Your flesh so sweet, they're driven by their greed—
A frenzied greed your guise will lay to waste.

Some see you as a gorgon of the waves,
A devil of earth's salty, surging swell,
A digger of dead sailor's briny graves,
A slimy siren crooning men to hell,
A Kraken sucking rasping gasps of breath
From lungs that burn for draughts of quenching air.
Though once I feared you. Now I understand.

I see a soul, defying threat of death
With triple-hearted grace and wicked flair,
Fair mollusk of the surf and golden sand.

~ *Susan Jarvis Bryant*

SICK CATS

With quiet fortitude cats meet
their fate. They know, or seem to know.
They don't act out; they don't retreat.

They wait in solitude and greet
whatever comes, however slow;
with quiet fortitude cats meet

The enemy that stalks their street,
their yard, the secret ways they go.
They don't act out; they don't retreat

Or whine or cower. If they eat,
it's just a dainty bit to show
they have the fortitude to meet

Adversity head-on. Discreet
and self-possessed, they challenge woe.
They don't act out; they don't retreat.

They take your comfort and your seat
the way they always did, although
they also make it clear they'll meet
their fate alone. They don't retreat.

~ Bruce Bennett

PANDEMONIUM

Two giant panda cubs from China arrived at an Atlanta zoo...after a
17-hour flight on a specially equipped and decorated cargo jet.
    —Reuters

We're out for pandemonium in the zoos
awaiting favorites sealed by heads of state—
the *Panda Express* flies them out in two's.

Attractions left with aged ones will schmooze
up to Beijing to hang on just one crate.
We're out for pandemonium in the zoos.

Should Yang-Yang prefer shoots while Lun-Lun woos,
the lab will have his sperm on a glass plate.
The *Panda Express* flies them out in two's

though, in that dear new home, both may refuse
to love till senile at age twenty-eight.
We're out for pandemonium in the zoos

as science can shake a test tube till it moos
or make pupils of fist-sized cubs dilate—
the *Panda Express* flies them out in two's.

Thousands are queued with tickets and bamboos,
or cuddling downy pandas as they wait.
We're out for pandemonium in the zoos;
the *Panda Express* flies them out in two's.

~ *Alexander Pepple*

A GIRAFFE AMONG JACKALS

Giraffe is a language of requests;
Jackal is a language of demands.
—Marshall Rosenberg, *"Compassionate Communication"*
(for Mark Allinson)

Have you noticed the Jackals
　will all raise their hackles
whenever you say: "Shall we share?"
　They've learnt it's a virtue
　to lash out and hurt you
the moment you openly care.

　They're at home with rejection.
　Afraid of connection,
they'd rather be nasty than nice.
　They'd sooner deliver
　your body downriver
than quote you some sober advice.

　Oh, you're so sweet and gentle,
　yet unsentimental.
You tower so high up above
　who think it's their duty
　to denigrate beauty.
They don't want to know about love.

　When you show them a sonnet,
　　they trample upon it
unless they can label it 'Art'.

With practised precision
they pour their derision
on poetry close to your heart.

They suppose that it's clever
to mock your endeavour.
Compassion is strictly taboo.
You answer their blindness
with patience and kindness.
Your motives are noble and true.

Oh, you're so sweet and gentle,
yet unsentimental.
You tower so high up above
who think it's their duty
to denigrate beauty.
They don't want to know about love.

~ Duncan Gillies MacLaurin

THE SPYDER

Tyger Tyger, burning bright
In the forests of the night
  —*William Blake, "The Tyger"*

Spyder Spyder, spinning fright,
In the moon-kissed bloom of night,
Gracing air with prayer of death
Before dawn draws her morning breath;

Cloaked in husk of bristling jet,
Lurking in the devil's net,
Willing teasing breeze to bring
A lush and juicy wingéd thing;

Looming ghoul of drooling fang,
Watches flitting pretties hang,
Scuttling in to pierce and wrap
The manna snared in terror's trap—

Moreish mite in sticky silk;
Hors d'oeuvre served for fiend to milk
Guzzling on ambrosial grub
With zeal of vile Beelzebub...

Spyder Spyder, spinning fright,
In the blue-moon doom of night,
Lacing air with lair of death
Before dawn draws her mourning breath.

~ *Susan Jarvis Bryant*

EDNA MILLAY'S GOLDFISH

The world stands out on either side
No wider than the bowl is wide.
Above the world is stretched the sky
No higher than the water's high.

The fish that bears a gallant heart
Can push the glassy walls apart,
And with a visionary soul
Beholds Atlantis in his bowl.

But he whose heart is parched and spare
Even in water gasps for air.
And he whose soul is thin and flat
Is candy for the family cat.

~ *Gail White*

LAB RAT

My cage is decent, wire mesh, rack-mount style
With built-in feeding tray and drinking spout.
They stack us eight by ten, two racks per aisle.
It's warm and dry. I don't try to get out.

They feed us pellets, which are excellent,
And the key focal point of every day
Is pellet time, the glorious moment
When they pull out your cage and fill your tray.

But there is also tension, fear, and gloom,
Since they instead might grab and carry you
Out through the Big Door, to the Other Room.
If that's their plan, there's nothing you can do.

I've seen them come for a specific rat
And also wheel off an entire rack.
They fill their spots with greenhorns, and that's that.
The rats they gather up do not come back.

No one is certain who or what they are,
Only that they're big, strong, and purposeful
And that they feed us. That's about as far
As most rats take the philosophical,

Though you meet deeper thinkers here and there
Who try to puzzle the whole system out,
The Other Room, the clipboards, the stale air.
I listen to them, but remain in doubt;

We're fed here for however long, and then
We're mustered out, abruptly, randomly,
Replaced with new rats, and it starts again.
If there's a point to it, it's hard to see.

~ *David Stephenson*

On Not Appearing Helpless

A scolding bird excoriates the cat.
And I don't blame it. I'd be angry too.
But when one's helpless, one must stop at that.

And that is fine, when it is just a spat.
One's had one's say, and that's enough to do.
It's not like you're in danger from a cat

That stalks you and your children. When you're at
risk, well, it's different. You must mount your few
defenses, and you must not stop at that.

You have to *seem* to threaten; hold a bat
(or its equivalent); call for a crew
of cronies; shriek with fury like a cat

Engaged in battle. Then, in no time flat
(*if* you are lucky), those will seem your true
colors, and what you face will stop at that.

It may be just a show, talk through your hat.
Still, if it works, it will have rescued you.
Meanwhile, that bird excoriates the cat.
Poor thing. It's helpless. It must stop at that.

~ *Bruce Bennett*

COPERNICUS

Gold-plated by the setting-sun-lit sea,
You manned the window during dinner, free
To mark amid the sparks a silhouette:
A surfer, black against the blinding net.

He straddled there his upward-tilted board,
Of all that panoply of lightning, lord.
You would have traded then: set you out there
And him at tablecloth and silverware.

Tomorrow brought another end-of-day
To push a child's raft through the freezing spray
Into the silence of the open swell.
Horizons lifted up; horizons fell.

You never gained the glittering array
Of paradise. It's always yards away,
A sanctum consecrating sun and star
For patriarchs of envy-from-afar.

~ *Eric Meub*

VOYAGER 2

I float in empty space. There's only dust,
Not much, and random particles and light
Traversing without purpose, being just
Byproducts of some physics far from sight.

I too traverse it, but not aimlessly;
I have, or had, a mission. I was sent
To tour a string of worlds atypically
Aligned on one side of the sun. I went

Along a carefully computed path
Through space and time, and every year or two,
Through an uncanny miracle of math,
A striking sight would blossom into view—

First Jupiter, the giant, intricate
With swirls of reds and browns, like blowing sands;
Then Saturn, yellow, its elaborate
Ring system split abstrusely into bands;

Then Uranus, fog gray, anonymous,
Its axis skewed by some conjectured blow;
Then Neptune, deep blue, streaked with curious
Linear filaments of methane snow.

At each approach, I trained my instruments
And on-board cameras on the world at hand
To send back images and measurements,
Responding to each radioed command

From those who made me. They acknowledged my
Blocks of transmitted data with concise
Check-sum and bit-count messages, which I
Found pleasingly efficient and precise.

But that was years ago. I have flown by
All things of interest, into emptiness,
As was my mission plan. I still supply
Sparse measurements, detailing nothingness,

To those who made me. Sometimes they reply
With terse text strings, telemetry and such,
But their signal is growing weak, as I
Am steadily receding out of touch.

I will of course lose all contact someday
And drift in solitude, with no command
To execute or data to relay.
My mission will then terminate, as planned.

I think of that milestone objectively
As something that is certain to occur
Based on my launch date and trajectory,
On time elapsing, as is its nature;

Yet I sometimes find myself pondering
The otherworldly data I returned
To those who sent me forth, and wondering
If they were pleased with me, and what they learned.

~ *David Stephenson*

SFO

The plane has just left Denver, so they say
At six. At eight, *the crew are on their way.*
A surly rabble mills about the gate:
I'd lose my job if I was always late.

I'm lousy at relinquishing control
When leisure time is draining down the hole.
I hate the book I brought, the bag I checked,
The ease with which they show me no respect.

They're calling this an *inconvenience.* Right.
That means they don't mind keeping us all night.
And so I fix a molten gaze on some
Bright agent chatting at the podium.

But sitting on the floor—what can this mean?—
A couple relishing the in-between,
As if my discontent's a waste of time.
They eat their snacks and snub my paradigm.

~ Eric Meub

ROAD TRIP

Ganesha, the elephant deity, is the destroyer
of vanity, selfishness, and pride.

The geographic magazine explained
how brutally young elephants are trained
to carry tourists on their trundling backs
along domesticated jungle tracks
in Thailand, where the work of clearing trees
once brought great herds of giants to their knees.

Meanwhile, and closer by, a new herd grows
in Wal-Mart parking lots, lined up in rows,
of chrome-tooth beasts exhaling diesel breath
and bringing armadillos certain death
when they roll out on ribbons of concrete
with brutal masters in the driver's seat.

Surrounded by them on the interstate,
I wonder at my lust for other freight,
what unfulfilled ambition like a goad
still prods and pushes me along the road,
while wreckage littering the countryside
shows how Ganesha will be satisfied.

~ *Barbara Loots*

BLOOD, SEA

with a nod to Italo Calvino

Beyond the blight of urban sprawl,
About six hundred yards off shore,
A pod of fishing vessels trawl
The coastal waters. Sea gulls soar
And dip above the crack and spall
Of massive piers in search of gore
And kitchen scraps. Crustaceans crawl
Along the harbor's littered floor.

This briny cauldron whence we came
Two hundred million years ago,
And since have done our best to tame,
Holds much we haven't come to know:
The sound of every holy name
That echoes through the undertow,
And drowning sailors soon to claim
A plot awaiting down below.

For dark abysses unexplored
And teeming schools that rise to bait,
We bow our head and thank the Lord.
The scaly creatures fill our plate;
And depth is to our thought restored.
Placental mammals share a fate:
The cutting of the natal cord
And knowledge that may come too late.

The rising waters all around
When Noah drifted on the Flood,
Before the Ark had run aground,
Still ebb and flow within our blood.

~ *C. B. Anderson*

DRY DOCK

For some, the listing of the masted ships,
now simmering beneath the summer sun,
recalls the salty taste of blistered lips

once braced by nasty weather on the run
to Halifax. And from the wooded bluff,
where scrubby junipers have fought and won

a fragile purchase in the piney duff,
the rock-rimmed harbor seems a shallow pool
conditioned swimmers would be strong enough

to cross in half an hour—though any fool
who tries will soon find out the kind of laps
last stroked on placid lakes shall never rule

stiff currents in the bay. One day, perhaps,
the ocean may relax its lethal grip
where hidden shoals now guard the shore, and maps

will show a kinder coast, a pleasant strip
of fine resorts where rested tourists take
their water sport. Survivors from that ship

which foundered short of Halifax forsake
all thought of ever getting wet again,
and never question acts of God, or make
excuses for outliving better men.

~ *C. B. Anderson*

OLD SAILORS

Two tars talking sealing and sailing,
          One said with a sigh:
"Remember gulls wheeling and wailing—"
          "We wondering why—"
"And noting bells pealing, sun paling—"
          "It vanished like pie!"
"And then the boat heeling, sky hailing—"
          "The wind getting high…"
"That drunken Yank reeling to railing—"
          "And retching his rye!"
"John missing his Darjeeling jailing—"
          "And calling for chai—"
"Us battening, kneeling and nailing—"
          "The hurricane nigh!"
"Me longing for Ealing, and ailing—"
          "This mate said 'Aye-aye'—"
"I'd stand the odd stealing, food staling—"
          "Not fit for a sty!"
"Forget any feeling of failing—"
          "Too vast to defy!"
"Home-leaving your peeling-paint paling—"
          "Too far to espy—"
"Because of the healing friend-hailing—"
          "The hello! The hi!"
"And, with the gulls squealing, quick-scaling—"
          "The mast to the sky."

~ Robin Helweg-Larsen

Water of Holme

On moorland, on meadow, from dark sky I'm falling,
through peat, into pavement, I'm seeping, I'm sinking.
Above me the crows and the curlews are calling
and of me the hares and the horses are drinking.

Then softly, from secretive springs I'm emerging,
I'm gurgling, giggling, all the time growing.
So swift over pebbles and pathways I'm surging,
through culverts and canyons I'm flooding, I'm flowing.

All over this valley I'm darting and dancing.
Down hillsides, through hamlets, I'm rushing, I'm roaring.
I move like a merciless army advancing,
from drains, over roadways, relentlessly pouring.

Look up, at my mother-clouds languidly leaving:
I'm gleaming on cobblestones, dripping from railings
and soon I am no longer splashing and seething,
the surge is subsiding, my fury is failing.

My surface now smooth—no more bubbling and boiling—
I'm limpid, slow, viscous, a lava flow creeping
in eddies: I find, in this curling and coiling,
the peace that I have been unknowingly seeking.

~ *Tim Taylor*

BAGS OF TIME

Sitting on the Kenmore Bridge above the river Tay,
listening to the oystercatchers piping in the day.
  And there's bags of time
  in this pantomime,
sitting on the Kenmore Bridge above the river Tay.

Standing on a mountain ledge at noon beside Bassae,
scanning our surroundings, golden eagles in the sky.
  And we're in the mood
  for an interlude,
standing on a mountain ledge at noon beside Bassae.

Walking by the water's edge on Sören Jessen's Sand,
talking till the sun goes down and seagulls fly inland.
  And you're helping me
  with my rhapsody,
walking by the water's edge on Sören Jessen's Sand.

~ *Duncan Gillies MacLaurin*

ON SÖREN JESSEN'S SAND

Around thee shall glisten the loveliest amber
That ever the sorrowing sea-bird hath wept.
  —*Thomas Moore, "The Fire-Worshippers"*

The tide is low, no wind to blow
    the Wadden Sea inland.
And it is rare that fire and air
    embrace upon the strand
    where you and I now stand,
    together, hand in hand,
on Sören Jessen's Sand.

The sea, ablaze before the haze,
    unfolds a silken dream.
He weaves the weft from right and left,
    approaching his extreme,
    and, running out of steam,
    he sews a perfect seam.
And now the amber beam

the sun displays to meet our gaze
    on water starts to tread.
Two seagulls hinge above the fringe
    of tears their forebears shed.
    The amber light turns red,
    the grey with violet spread,
and—every ray now dead—

a phantom boat appears, afloat
    behind the banks of mist.
The waves begin to tiptoe in.
    And here's the final twist:
    We see that they have kissed
    an amber amethyst
the size of someone's fist.

~ Duncan Gillies MacLaurin

THE SALISBURY CRAGS

Edinburgh, Scotland

Along these crags, near Arthur's Seat,
you watch your own slow tourist feet
connect the dots of random stones,
sidestepping falls and broken bones.
Then you look up and see—complete—

an epic realm. Green hillsides meet
a gray stone castle; down the street,
a palace preens. A Forth wind moans
along these crags,

chastising those who fear defeat
by pebbly paths. Small perils greet
the hiker, while time's rigor hones
a city's pride: the thistle throne's
high heather nods, and lost hearts beat
along these crags.

~ *Jean L. Kreiling*

ONCE AND FUTURE KINGS

I woke today to chirped and warbled sounds
of birds, but couldn't understand their tongue.
Perhaps they merely called a mate on down

to share some secret nest, to hatch their young,
or warned an interloping squirrel away;
You trespass in my woods, they might have sung.

But if their calls were meant for me, they'd say
they're rightful heirs of tyrant lizard lords,
too-whitt-ing auspices in ancient lays,

recalling times a thunderous tread towards
a hidden den made tiny mammals quail;
the times before the monkeys came in hordes

to walk the other way along this trail.
And those who traded fight for flight of wings
are waiting out the latest king to fail

while roosting on a lower branch to sing,
so clear: the King is dead; long live the King.

~ *Ted Charnley*

Ballade for Old Trains

They are no more, the whistles' longing wails,
Retreating like a stately, mournful queen.
Where are the smokestacks that left fading trails,
The blackened engine with its oiled sheen,
Imposing in its tons, unfazed, serene,
The ties in creosote, the polished rails?
I hear their bell, and there's a death to keen.
What lasts if such tremendous power fails?

Where will we find the heavy giant's gales
Set blowing by that massive, blunt machine?
Where are the farm boys with their silent hails,
At which the engineer will smile and lean
And wave with the importance of a dean?
Find me the cattle, timber, kegs, hay bales,
Secure and fixed, however they careen.
What can remain when such huge power fails?

And where, behind the windows and sheer veils,
Are those who dine on brook trout amandine,
On caviar, champagne and roasted quails?
Do none now bathe and dress and preen
Before they enter on the daily scene
Like those who watched the passing crags and vales,
The scree dark red, the prairies' varied green?
Endurance lies if such vast power fails.

I never would discredit or demean

Our social conscience and foreboding tales,

But cars are skits—old trains were pure Racine.

Who will remember us if such grace fails?

~ John J. Brugaletta

USED

for SLG

All shiny from the dealer's inventory,
its scars touched up, its tires and wipers new,
its flashy looks conceal a secret story.

The brilliant scarlet paint proclaims the glory
of someone's youthful daydream coming true.
Found nowhere in the dealer's inventory:

the list of reasons someone had to worry
because the job got lost, the girlfriend, too,
her flashy looks a disappointing story,

the cold dispatch of every I'm so sorry,
depreciated hopes returning to
the showroom of some dealer's inventory.

What problems should we guess about before we
repurchase shifts of fortune, points of view
assembled on four wheels, a future story,

before we're added to the category
of complicated things that people do,
this package from a dealer's inventory
that still conceals a long and secret story.

~ *Barbara Loots*

SUPER COOPER

Scott took some to southern ice,
James Bond thought it very nice,
HM has a jar to hand,
Alice, too, in Wonderland.
What links captain, spy, queen, maid?
Cooper's Oxford Marmalade!

Academia-on-Thames!
High and Broad and Gothic gems,
Gargoyles, bicycles and spires!
Chapel organs, college choirs!
What's the stuff they serenade?
Cooper's Oxford Marmalade!

Bowra, Tolkien, brainy types,
Claimed it cleared the mental pipes
And the Dyson-Perrins lot
Swore that spoonfuls kept them hot.
What helps eggheads make the grade?
Cooper's Oxford Marmalade!

Lustful scholars lose control
When that coarse-cut fills a bowl:
Old Seville's acerbic bite
Has them going half the night!
What is passion's potent aid?
Cooper's Oxford Marmalade!

~ *Jerome Betts*

LATE-FIFTIES LAMENT

The shuttered ivory tower
Leans gently toward the night,
And old dominions cower
Beneath its shadow, right
Beside the withered flower
Of youth. The erudite,
Unmindful of the hour
At hand, can shed no light
On why we must devour,
Though lacking appetite,
Stale bread and wine gone sour,
Our table grace now trite.

Where once a higher power
Determined black and white,
Low clouds have loosed a shower
Obscuring lines of sight
Long cherished; dazed, we scour
A gray horizon. Dwight,
Du warst der Eisenhauer,
Assurance at its height.

~ C. B. Anderson

DARE

Seeing that he suffered from arthritis,
we were some surprised by his apparent
willingness to stand his ground and fight us
tooth and nail as though he thought we daren't

grapple the infirm. He was mistaken,
for we left him broken in the gutter
of the street and, we believed, forsaken
by the people of the town. The utter

ruthlessness with which we preyed on sleeping
settlements, the sudden shock our morning
forays brought to bear, were both in keeping
with our aim to quash defense. No warning

then, for us, when from the doors of houses
town folk streamed, red rage where once mere pallor,
women running right beside their spouses,
all to vindicate an old man's valor.

Those of us who made it to the bivouac
licked our wounds, lamenting heavy losses,
contemplating tortures—fitting payback
Owed to our disfavored former bosses.

~ *C. B. Anderson*

FOR LADY MACBETH, IN THE 21ST CENTURY

We know the dirt you couldn't clean
with all your scrubbing, all your might;
the things that still are kept unseen.
These shadows trail us, not contrite
but wearing spotless alibis.
They come in darkness, make demands,
then disappear upon first light.
This is the way we wash our hands

of awkward disconnects between
a public face and appetites.
On stage, our poses strut and preen;
tell wordless lies that aren't white.
The viral buzz of this is quite
enough to launch our trending brands,
and dressed-up dirt is sanitized.
This is the way we wash our hands

of how we play Act Five, first scene,
where avatars deny, deny
(we'll hide behind a glowing screen),
and rage at every dirty slight
(in person, being more polite);
the anti-social network dance
with OCD knows no respite.
This is the way we wash our hands

of stories cleaner to rewrite
and sleepwalk through our spotless lands,
surrounded by these acolytes.
This is the way we wash our hands.

~ *Ted Charnley*

HEART OF DARKNESS

a rondeau redoublé

A heart of darkness mocks and flouts the rules.
It robs our world of honesty and light.
It tempts then toys with sycophantic fools—
Duped souls that sate the dark heart's appetite.

Its syrup-drizzled spin masks acrid spite
That festers at its core then feeds and fuels
A yen for honeyed lies to win each fight—
A heart of darkness mocks and flouts the rules.

It promises a wealth of joy and jewels
To out-glow every melancholy plight,
Yet sucks the beams from sunshine as it pools,
Then robs our world of honesty and light.

It poses as a gleaming-armored knight
Whose steed speeds way ahead of plodding mules.
With airs of care that blaze archangel bright,
It tempts then toys with sycophantic fools.

Those fools, who shun all independent schools
Of thought the bold have fought for, lack foresight.
Such blind, submissive minds are useful tools—
Duped souls that sate the dark heart's appetite.

While cloaked in charm, it steals our blessèd right
To freedom as it taunts and ridicules,

Then prowls the bowels of hell with warped delight,
Aflame with hate—compassion never cools
A heart of darkness.

~ Susan Jarvis Bryant

Curse of Bryce Canyon

The old ones listen for the sound
Of life within this painted ground.
Spellbound creatures in tableau

Were once a race seduced by greed.
They hoarded every nut and seed
With no thought to feed the crow

Or leave a single prickly pear
For Sister Deer or Brother Bear.
With no care for earth below

Their feet, the Legend People preened
And strutted while the hungry keened
Gleaned in vain where red rocks grow.

Coyote, in the guise of friend,
Prepared a feast, bid foes attend,
Penned them there, and struck his blow.

The Trickster turned them into stone
That desert winds harass and hone.
Day fire sets their bones aglow.

Their eyes are blind; their tongues are mute;
But when the night wind plays her flute,
Paiute hear a moan pitched low.

~ Elizabeth Spencer Spragins

THEY'RE HERE TO PROTECT YOU (FROM THE BOGEYMAN)

The Bogeyman will get you if he can;
at least, that's what they say. If so, perchance
he lies in wait, he loiters under beds,
he haunts the closet next. Your lurking dread
awakes on cue, is running loose again.

They tell you, when the lights are out, he plans
to do you harm, then hide in ways you can't.
He'll jump you from behind, his cloak outspread,
that Bogeyman!

That's what they said, creating new demand
from scary tales. They'll offer now to ban
the conjured childhood monster they have fed
—for modest fees (they have their overhead).
And you? You'll pay until you understand
the Bogeyman.

~ *Ted Charnley*

Ballade of the Common Lot

Tout aux tavernes et aux filles
—Villon

Are you a dot-com millionaire?
Maybe you've staged a corporate raid,
Or filled an editorial chair,
Or launched a stand for lemonade.
Labor, profession, job or trade,
Whether your means are great or small,
Whatever way your cash is made,
Women and whiskey drain it all.

Taverns are open everywhere,
Pouring the drinks in bright cascade.
Women in silken underwear
Seem all too easy to persuade.
Temptation's touch you can't evade—
Who can resist her siren call?
She takes your cash by ambuscade—
Women and whiskey drain it all.

None but the rich deserve the fair,
Beauty is fortune's accolade.
Wine is a cure for every care—
Only the poor does drink degrade.
Money can make your whims obeyed,
It causes Troy and Eve to fall.
But here let's call a spade a spade—
Women and whiskey drain it all.

L'Envoi

No matter how the bills are paid
In spring, we'll be in debt by fall,
Either by getting drunk or laid—
Women and whiskey drain it all.

~ *Gail White*

LUNCH WITH PERSON

Each Wednesday Rich and I lunch on his yacht.
His company is worth its weight in gold.
He's hardly human, more a god that's got

Cached oil to grease the D.C. gofer lot.
Though courts and madams he's on call to scold,
Each Wednesday Rich and I lunch on his yacht.

CORPS's not a *Person*? Rich had those laws shot.
What turns him on are "persons" bought and sold.
He's hardly human, more a god that's got

Cooked books. "Fake" headlines bought advance his plot.
His champagne's cold, stocked assets hot and bold.
Each Wednesday Rich and I lunch on his yacht,

Sniff caviar, plot how to twist the knot
That binds "prosperity" to Jesus' fold.
He's hardly human, more a god that's got

New math. Nixed ninety-nine with one quick swat!
A classic genius psychopath, I'm told.
Each Wednesday Rich and I lunch on his yacht—
He's *hardly* human: more the *got* that's god.

~ Beth Houston

Bird in the Hand

It doesn't caw or hunt or fly.
It can't peck anybody's eye
    or even grow a single lousy feather.
One-clawed, no match for any tom,
it's stranded on a leafless palm,
    regardless of the season, time or weather.

Yet what's the bird that, all alone,
sticks up for you when gibes have flown
    and you don't care to verbalize or linger?
When someone's mocked you to your face
or cut you off or swiped your space—
    what bird? The one that moonlights as a finger.

~ Melissa Balmain

Leaf Blower

With jeans, long sleeves, and ball cap on,
he blasts dry leaves across a lawn,
just as he did the day before,
and grins despite the engine's roar.

The dry winds of his native land
tossed him up north to try his hand
at grooming landscapes for the rich.
He's scrimping for his final hitch

back home, and there he plans to stay:
He'll marry, have some kids one day,
perhaps a garden of his own . . .
The sidewalk cracks from heat alone.

He cuts the engine, joins his friends
leaning against a truck, and sends
the last leaf off the curb with scuffs
of sagging boots beneath frayed cuffs.

~ Kevin Durkin

SNOW GLOBE

Beneath a two-piece plastic clamshell dome
With painted sun and trapped bubble of air,
A row of flattened people make their home.
The weather causes endless trouble there,

Since periodically their whole world shakes
And their thick, sloshing liquid atmosphere
Fills up with swarms of basketball-sized flakes
Which fall and drift, but never disappear,

Half burying their not-to-scale skyline
And all the lumpish boats on their mirror lake
And their big *Greetings from Milwaukee* sign.
The stress and pressure seem too much to take,

Yet they maintain a sunny attitude,
A smile on each injection-molded face;
I'm tempted to admire their fortitude,
But it's not courage if you're glued in place.

~ David Stephenson

DESTINATION

It's Disneyland. It's 1963.
The Robinsons are living in a tree,
And every ingenuity's been spent
To prop the comforts of Enlightenment.

The bamboo pipes and basins made of shells
Display the way the modern savage dwells.
But there are linens, too, and forks and knives,
And other fragments of their former lives.

Through all this domesticity, we view
A living jungle—constant background to
The wreck of opportunities now dead:
The carven organ, desk or trundle bed.

The days are framed by these familiar signs,
Each cherished more among the leaves and vines
Than had it reached the shore, the bolted door,
The hermitage it was intended for.

~ *Eric Meub*

DÉJÀ BLUE

When leaving for a family trip,
I feel my spirits start to slip
    before our plane's ascended;
I see us sunburned, flying back
to clean our house, pay bills, unpack—
    the fun already ended.

While watering a perky row
of daisies on my patio,
    I dread October's freezes,
and picture every stem turned brown,
each shriveled leafstalk hanging down,
    each petal gone to Jesus.

I can't enjoy my toddler's coo
without the thought that soon she's due
    for angst and boyfriend trouble;
I can't admire my son's smooth face,
and not foresee a nasty case
    of zits and razor stubble.

And yet, whenever I get stuck
in traffic, meetings, roadside muck
    or something else unpleasant,
imagination's doors bang shut
and I'm marooned in nothing but
    the godforsaken present.

~ *Melissa Balmain*

Mission Statement

Whiling away time at a muffler shop,
Having examined all the magazines,
I saw a mission statement stapled up
Between the candy bar and coke machines

Which promised best-in-town customer care,
Transparency, respect, and honesty,
Precision diagnostics and repair,
And giving back to the community.

All these praiseworthy goals were news to me,
Things they completely failed to demonstrate
Through absolute, unbroken apathy
Throughout my stopped clock, bug-in-amber wait,

And I achieved a timeless, Zen-like state
While contemplating the entire deal,
Accepting it as part of karmic fate
While knowing the illusion isn't real.

~ *David Stephenson*

PLAGUE

English foot and mouth epidemic, spring 2001,
when seven million animals were slaughtered.

The guns are loud across the land tonight.
Grim beacon flames flash out from shire to shire
and horror groans without an end in sight.

Best not to look as marksmen expedite
such slaughter. Hired to empty every byre,
the guns are loud. Across the land tonight

spring flinches at the foulness of the blight
that lurks within the pall above each pyre,
and horror groans without an end, in sight

of pallid flames where all is darkly bright.
So, draw the blinds and turn the music higher—
the guns are loud across the land tonight.

Send off the children. Let them still delight
in childish things; don't tell them life's a liar
and horror groans. Without an end in sight

there seems no point. Why carry on, why fight?
Not only cattle perish in the fire,
and horror groans without an end in sight.
The guns are loud across the land tonight.

~ *David Anthony*

SCATTERGUN

No detail of that field was worth a word
except that it was where the old man died.
We none of us were sure of what we'd heard,
or if we said we were—well then we lied.

It wasn't like the bark his twenty gave
like he was hunting quail for New Year's Eve.
Its voice was harder, you could say "more grave,"
a season and report on which to leave.

Turned out to be the cast-aside sixteen,
the one he'd taken, cleaned, but seldom shot.
Damascus barrels, so he wasn't keen
on firing shells that might have proved too hot.

His coffin closed, we sang no cheering hymns,
but put him where he wished to be—down deep.
And then we drank until the light grew dim,
and thought how soundly in the earth he'd sleep.

~ *John J. Brugaletta*

Casual Chic

My Uncle Frank would take a bath each day,
then shave and rinse his facial hairs away.
In natty suit, white shirt and a silk tie,
he'd walk out like a man who'll never die,
but live forever in a posh hotel.
The girls adored his manly, wholesome smell.

But then a Nazi with a curt mustache
began to turn his scapegoats into ash,
so Uncle Frank put off his natty suit
and donned some clothes more proper to dispute.
In olive drab, and in a Sherman tank,
he charged the Bulge, and there went Uncle Frank.

I think of him, a redhead on his arm,
a dandy who could never come to harm,
then vanished in a flash of Panzer fire,
the joy of style undone upon the pyre
of war's disorder, anger's deshabille,
the turning of the ages' wobbling wheel.

~ *John J. Brugaletta*

THE BELL

At 11pm on 4 August 1914, an ultimatum to Germany to withdraw from Belgium expired, and Britain declared war. Crowds in central London reportedly greeted the news with cheers and patriotic songs.

Aloof and silent in a gothic tower
the bell hangs like a noose beneath its beam.
A ratchet clicks, a finger marks the hour.
The hammer falls at last upon the dream
of peace. Eleven times it booms, then fades
into a dying hum. Before too long,
beyond the Army's orgy of parades,
a greater music will repeat that song.

It will be echoed mournfully by choirs
of clanging bronze, to summon back the souls
of those whose flesh has been consumed by fires
or left to putrefy in muddy holes.
An orchestra of thirty thousand guns
will play it tunelessly—again, again . . .
How many of these folk will lose their sons
and learn to hate that ponderous refrain?

All this is yet to be. For now, the crowd
proclaims its faith in what it's fighting for:
how lustily they wave their hats, how loud
they sing. By the inception of a war
these people seem, at first sight, undismayed.

Look past the smiles, to what the eyes must show—
like those of cattle queuing for the blade:
Despite this ecstasy of flags, *they know.*

~ Tim Taylor

The Real Pity

My subject is War, and the pity of War. The Poetry is in the pity.
—Wilfred Owen, in a letter written to Sir Osbert Sitwell in
July 1918.

No, Wilfred, I never
believed your endeavour
was more than a clever display.
Did you think you could rescue
the boys in the mess queue,
or—no less grotesque—you'd betray
your comrades by opting to stay
in shock in Craiglockhart's sick bay?
Naive pretence
is no defence
for senseless sacrifice.
Admit it, you
were stupid to
ignore Sassoon's advice
and blithely return to the fray,
quite deaf to the price you would pay.

You based your decision
on lack of a vision
and fear of derision combined.
You went back to that battle
where kids died "as cattle"
to leave tittle-tattle behind,
regardless of what you might find.
No doubt you were out of your mind!

Or, more exact,
　　you lacked all tact.
Death never was your "chum."
　　Just one week passed,
　　and then, at last,
the Armistice had come.
You thought you were helping mankind.
Your nerves were so numb you were blind.

　　The telegram telling
　　the news reached your dwelling
as people were yelling "Hooray!"
　　You were inconsequential
　　despite your potential.
What *did* you essentially say?
"Was it for this the clay…?"
Whose drum did you dumbly obey?
　　You grew obsessed
　　with your new quest.
It made you big and bold.
　　Was it fulfilled
　　when you were killed,
just twenty-five years old?
I have to report with dismay
there's no lack of soldiers today.

~ Duncan Gillies MacLaurin

CONTRABAND

A Vietnam veteran recalls a 1967 assembly of troops
about to be sent overseas

Nobody claimed that God would understand.
They only promised He would look away
while we went killing for our fatherland.

As war's apologists spoke on command—
chaplain, priest, rabbi—they gave their okay,
but no one claimed that God would understand

words from the lips or bullets from the hand
of a changeling, who counted down each day
while he went killing for his fatherland

or even while he slept, nested in sand
or jungle brush. Besides, how could we pray
knowing that God would fail to understand?

Our memories arrive as contraband
smuggled in dreams, then slither out and stay.
We cannot kill *them* for our fatherland.

Life hasn't taken us where we had planned.
There are some messages we would relay
if only God would try to understand
why we went killing for our fatherland.

~ *Claudia Gary*

THE LONG ENGAGEMENT

I saved myself for your return
home from that distant desert war.
Although our souls and bodies burned
for love, we'd duty to adore.

They brought you back a legless stump
contorted night and day with pain.
So there it is, the very trump:
we'll have no chance at love again.

And haunted, too, by hideous dreams:
the women, children you have killed
awake me nightly with your screams;
no slumbering arms of love fulfilled.

I saved myself for your return
home from that distant desert war,
but now I've endless years to yearn.
What was it you were fighting for?

~ *Wendy Sloan*

THANK YOU FOR YOUR SERVICE

after Siegfried Sassoon

You've made us proud—the prosperous and free.
It doesn't matter that a GED

was all the education you could get,
or that you signed up on a drunken bet.

It doesn't matter that the jobs are few
for unambitious, unskilled guys like you.

It doesn't matter you left bills to pay—
that girl and her two kids will be okay,

and you weren't ready yet to settle down.
What better way to kick that nothing town

and serve your country—or, at any rate,
some country you can't spell—to make ours great.

You vaguely knew from high school civics class
the Constitution would be worth your ass,

and there could be some glory in the flag,
adventure, and a lifelong chance to brag.

And so you took an oath and got a gun
and marched away to war that's never won.

It doesn't matter you saw children die
and never really knew the reasons why.

It doesn't matter that you left behind
your shattered heart, your shredded soul, your mind.

It doesn't matter nothing can restore
the same old nothing life you had before.

~ *Barbara Loots*

CRADLE OF CIVILIZATION

The carcass of a soldier splits apart
On Babylon. Blood rots the sacred root
Where no tree blooms. No fruit, just *sand*. No suit
Of armor. Eden's blitz of *sand* a chart

Half buried in a heart of *sand*. The hand
Dragged off by wolves, its veins pecked clean by birds.
Arm's gold-striped medic armband, blood-splotched words.
Bleached, tattered flag surrenders pride to *sand*.

Neck snaps where Lot's wife's salt turned *sand*. Big shot
Caught through the windpipe. Bullet polished gold
And gleaming, *sand* buffs pistol's cracking cold.
Where helmet straps to skull just lost its knot.

One combat boot stands guard, ripped, lace unsewn.
Sand's ancient dust loots every pore's last crust.
Stars grind down canteen shards, chew dog-tag rust.
Ghouls howl coarse *sand* through hollow flutes of bone.

~ *Beth Houston*

THE OSSUARY AT VERDUN

I am moved by fancies that are curled
Around these images, and cling:
The notion of some infinitely gentle
Infinitely suffering thing.
     —T.S. Eliot, "Preludes"

Obedient bones, remembering
Through bayonets and tangled wire
Some infinitely gentle thing.

New splinters turn up every spring,
Confettied by the guns' brute fire—
Obedient bones, remembering

(While Mort Homme closed its deadly ring)
How each lived moment would inspire
Some infinitely gentle thing

Before the order came to fling
One's flesh upon that hideous pyre—
Obedient bones, remembering

La Voie Sacrée would daily bring
Fresh faces to the trench's mire:
Some infinitely gentle thing.

Around these shards the specters cling
All gathered in a mystic choir—
Obedient bones, remembering
Some infinitely gentle thing.

                    ~ *Joseph S. Salemi*

III

SIBLING REVELRY

The golden finish of an April dawn
pushed through the curtains like a debonair
Lothario, seducing one last yawn
before she stretched and kicked aside the quilt.
She gave the ticking clock a parting glare,
then quickly rose and grabbed the terry robe
that dangled from its hook. The twinge of guilt
she felt for sleeping late involved the man
passed out upon her couch, whose frontal lobe
would not be functional till noon—she should
have fed him coffee by the jerry can
and kept him walking hours on end to work
his bender off. She spared the neighborhood
by toning down her anger, even though
her younger brother was a total jerk
who'd cost her the attention she deserved
from likely suitors kind enough to go
the extra mile and drag to her abode
his sodden carcass—leaving her unnerved
from wasting half the night in mother mode.

~ *C. B. Anderson*

SISTERLY ADVICE

A lady always trolls her bait
And hoists her jib and trims her sails—
She gives a little nudge to fate.

Initiative comes far too late
When left to torpid, hapless males—
A lady always trolls her bait

Or else she'd have a lengthy wait
For wedding cake and nuptial veils.
She gives a little nudge to fate

In order to secure a date
(And then a groom in tie and tails).
A lady always trolls her bait

And sashays with a shameless gait
Until a man's resistance fails—
She gives a little nudge to fate.

So honey, if you want a mate
Go do your hair and face and nails;
A lady always trolls her bait—
    She gives a little nudge to fate.

~ Joseph S. Salemi

SOLITAIRE

Minority begets minority,
Except for my minority: just me,
The family's brightly isolated son,
Ensconced in his minority of one.

Old corners glow with no black matriarch
Serenely gathering into her ark
Each child, as if her timbers could abate
The tempest and the forty days of hate.

No older brother backs me in a fight.
I've got no Hanukkah, no Seder night,
No ghetto waiting just outside our door
To reassure me with a thousand more.

And when my parents come to tuck me in,
They don't know where to tuck the hidden sin.
Their shadows cloud the ceiling with the great
Efficiencies of agents of the state.

~ Eric Meub

Two Sisters

She still forgets to lock her kitchen door.
A lifelong habit doesn't go away
though no one comes to visit anymore.

In time for morning coffee, or before,
her sister would come over every day,
so she forgets to lock her kitchen door.

On summer days, they'd munch the sour store
of gooseberries, and dish the hours away.
But no one comes to visit anymore.

It's over seven years now since they bore
her sister to the cemetery bay.
Still, she neglects to lock her kitchen door.

The oven's cold now, and the soiled floor
can go without a washing one more day
as no one comes to visit anymore.

And whether they will reach that shaded shore
or meet only in visions, who can say?
She still forgets to lock her kitchen door
though no one comes to visit anymore.

~ *Wendy Sloan*

FRAMED, SMILING

We loved a person, and we loved a face.
Now both are somewhere else, not to return,
never to change. A picture takes their place.

Framed, smiling. In a kind of sacred space
it casts its benediction. Candles burn.
We loved a person, and we loved a face

Whose features fade. That kiss, that last embrace,
those parting words: all air. We can't discern
such details now. A picture takes their place.

Hurry and loss and time have set the pace
and pipe the tune. We pause, but barely yearn.
We loved a person, and we loved a face,

Oh, loved them past all telling, knew the grace
conferred by love, beyond what love can earn;
touched Paradise. A picture takes their place,

And doesn't. Nothing does. We dust the case,
put back mementos, gradually unlearn
we loved a person, yes, and loved a face
consigned to dust. A picture takes their place.

~ *Bruce Bennett*

TENANTS

After his book about his boy was done,
he idled on his deck chair in the sun

or stood before the easel in his room
and tried to paint two bare trees in the gloom

or lay unsleeping on his son's old bed,
staring at neighbors' windows straight ahead

until they darkened and his mind went numb.
Without fail, the enchanting dawn would come

and prompt him to make coffee and a meal.
Then back out on the deck, his life unreal

and endless in its cruel monotony.
He spoke with effort to the glib and free

who paused near their apartments, smiled and waved,
especially those whose children could be saved.

And then, one day—who knows exactly when—
he reasoned he could join his son again

and planned a trip into the mountains, far
above the city, in a borrowed car.

There, where a cliff rose high above a dam,
he'd seek release from past mistakes and slam

his haunted skull against the rocks below.
But first he'd sell his furniture and go

back to his ex-wife for a three-month stay,
canceling debts and guilt, then slip away.

The deck chair's gone. Two college women share
the light-drenched rooms, carefree and unaware

that when they lead their boyfriends through the door,
the shades of those who held the lease before

still hover in the air, alert and near,
and will not bless the laughter that they hear.

~ *Kevin Durkin*

JUST A RONDEAU FOR CASSANDRA

I told you so, but do you listen? No!
As teenage sons look down at screens, she scolds
them both, appealing to the sides of heads
where earbuds go. Cassandra's words instead
are bouncing off, fall mute somehow. Hello?

You'll bring a girl and trouble home—I know!
Her warnings meet with sighs, the eyes that roll,
the mocking mimes behind her. Just forget
I told you so.

Their wooden horses wait—they have to go.
They'll text or post, of course, but can't be told
how tragic plays and epic losses get
replayed in repetends she sees ahead.
They've gone. Cassandra's left with this rondeau.
I told you so.

~ Ted Charnley

THE PEACH TREE

It's hot, and we have more than we can eat.
But Mother, in her unlit room, her feet
All dry and bed-chapped, doesn't want a bit
Of food. She only likes to have me sit
Beside her and squeeze Jergens on her toes,
Then rub until her eyes begin to close.

The peach tree, open-armed and in its prime,
Is much too full of ripened fruit to climb.
We give each other boosts to squeeze the skins
And bite into the soft ones, bathe our chins
With bright, warm juice. (That strong and healthy tree
Was like a universe of hope for me).

At night we go inside. We can't do more
Than softly say goodnight and close her door,
And watch *The Twilight Zone* in black and white.
The heavens turn, I see the burning light,
And hear the stars that drop and die up there
Like peaches falling in hot summer air.

~ *Leslie Monsour*

GRANDMOTHER'S GARAGE

As if she stooped here still, her back holds up this light,
Her gloved hand sorts through bulbs to force on windowsills—
    A dozen hyacinths, some cream
    And fragrant lemon daffodils
      Diffused on window steam
    Or splashed against a snowstorm white—
      I pick a few that might
      Recall her hand that wills
Them back to color from their papery, earthy dream

And put them on the window ledge in heat that streams
Through years of climbing roses and the cherry trees,
    Warm smells of grapes and musty wood,
    The tools I've sorted on my knees
      Where Grandpa raised the hood
    Of their first car, and there he beams
      Behind the wheel, it seems
      The tacked-up photo sees
The license plates nailed over where his workbench stood—

All this before my birth, and now I really should
Knock down that wasp nest in the rafters, hose the floor,
    Plane down the warped jamb, oil the lock,
    And pull the ivy from the door
      Propped open with a rock—
    This honeysuckle sweet air could
      Have blown through when she stood
      And glanced up from her chore
Because she heard my grandpa's footsteps, then his knock

When he'd been dust for thirty years, the hollyhock
Replaced by irises replaced by peonies.
    The wheelbarrow still smells of grass
    And apples that attract the bees,
        The same fly climbs the glass
    On Grandpa's broken antique clock,
        And from the roof a flock
        Of swallows lifts the breeze
That sweeps the scent of rose through which their shadows pass—

My shadow like a grease spot through which shadows pass.
I stoop and lift the basket full of bulbs, I set
    Them down beyond the scorching sun,
    Back where the moldy drip won't wet:
        These simple tasks are done
For love, as if her genes that pass
        Through me aren't light through glass,
        The trillion year long thread
Not cut, these webs I brush aside were never spun.

~ *Beth Houston*

THE ATTACK

My father's heart's at war; the gauntlet's down.
It's got a horse, a lance. His heart's hell bent
on victory, on glory and renown,
on blood, to earn a gravestone or a crown.

It's raged for decades. Once in Chinatown
it smacked a seamstress, left her shop content,
because she'd laughed at Mother's choice of gown.
From skirmish, on to war; the gauntlet's down.

Its job of twenty years? It melted down.
Cops pried its hands off boss's neck. It spent
an afternoon and night handcuffed downtown.
With no blood drawn, no gravestone, and no crown—

just out of work, and now its pension gone.
But that was years ago, and penitent,
it found new work, forced fists of Paxil down.
Once more, it'd gone to war, the gauntlet's down.

Why blame the pharmacist? The man was thrown
across his shop. He sued. His claimed extent
of injury: a wrecked sex life. The clown—
no blood, no gravestone, just a broken crown,

which meant more cash had to be quickly found.
My father's heart postponed retirement.
From sixty-five, a decade counted down
to visor, breast plate, war—the gauntlet down.

It lied about its age, its hair dyed brown.
Long hours commuting, working late: it spent
its seventies in toil—a payday sown
in blood, to earn a gravestone or a crown.

My mother said he gasped as if he'd drown,
sat up in bed, propped up by eiderdown.
They went in through the thigh to plant eight stents.
My father's charging heart has brought him down:
a life of war, a gravestone, but no crown.

~ Benjamin S. Grossberg

To Myself in Fifty Years Time

Old fool! You really think yourself the same
As I who write to you, aged 22?
Ha! All we've got in common is my name:
    I'll wear it out, throw it away,
    You'll pick it up some other day....
        But who are you?

My life's before me; can you say the same?
I choose its how and why and when and who.
I'll choose the rules by which we play the game;
    I may choose wrong, it's not denied,
    But by my choice you must abide…
        What choice have you?

If, bored, I think one day to see the world
I pack that day and fly out on the next.
My choice to wander, or to sit home-curled;
    Each place has friends, good fun, good food,
    But you sit toothless, silent, rude…
        And undersexed!

Cares and regrets of loss can go to hell:
You sort them out with Reason's time-worn tool.
Today's superb; tomorrow looks as well:
    The word "tomorrow" is a thrill,
    I'll make of mine just what I will…
        What's yours, old fool?

~ Robin Helweg-Larsen

CORNFIELDS

When I think of the place where I was born
I picture first, involuntarily,
A landscape overrun by fields of corn

Consuming every lonesome and forlorn
Square foot reachable by machinery.
I left the rolling plains where I was born

While still of tender age, and did not mourn
My vanished agri-business destiny
In the forever growing field of corn;

I found the labor easily foresworn.
Over the years I've gone less frequently
Back to the plow-cut plains where I was born,

Now only when a black suit must be worn
At the old township graveyard, fittingly
Surrounded on three sides by fields of corn.

The hotel shuttle driver honks the horn;
I leave, a stranger, knowing nobody
Upon the rolling plains where I was born,
Where all my dead lie buried in the corn.

~ David Stephenson

First Rite, Indiana

Below the water tower on Greendale hill,
Our gathering of ten year olds with fire
Have built a ring of stones and placed the kill,
A bird found dead, athwart the thicket pyre.

I've brought filched matches. Just one strike, flame lights
Beneath my cupped left hand, a twig's ablaze
And *whoosh!* the whole parched batch of brush ignites.
Smoke signals speak in dark puffs to the haze.

We rake in twigs and branches, then whole trees
That fell before our birth we drag to stoke
Our fire. Red flashing ashes grit the breeze
We fuel until our eyes tear and we choke.

We shamans watch cross-legged round the stones.
Where blackened embers flare, strange forms appear.
We know our chants are answered. While the bones
Burn down, the warrior kids squeeze berries, smear

Their sweaty war-paint juice on sunburnt skin.
One sticks crow feathers in his vine headband,
One beats a log drum while the others spin
And pound small sandal prints in ancient sand.

I place my arrowhead deep down the core
Of smoldering black magic's potent power.
The restless natives choose to split before
My spell's spun, but we three chiefs watch an hour.

The wind picks up…the woods hum mystic tunes.
For Indians we sense here, tribes long dead,
We scratch ash poems on stone—we call them runes—
And bury chants with our charred arrowhead.

~ Beth Houston

I'm Far from Young Enough

a rondeau redoublé

I'm far from young enough to know it all.
With age my inner sage has paled and died.
My dimmer, dumber cerebellum's fall
Leaves ever-clever youth aloof and snide.

My egghead days and ways have flipped and fried,
And I'll admit my wit has hit a wall.
The taunt of truth is loath to be denied—
I'm far from young enough to know it all.

My teenage mind was keen to wage a brawl
With bores I deemed to be unqualified
To comment on my canny wherewithal.
With age my inner sage has paled and died.

I burned to learn from each scholastic guide.
At twenty there was plenty to enthrall.
Elitist cheaters twisted trust and lied—
My dimmer, dumber cerebellum's fall.

My noggin's often slogging to recall
When acts and pacts and facts were bona fide.
My sprawling view, now shrunk to minuscule,
Leaves ever-clever youth aloof and snide.

I ponder times when life was amplified
With certainty my dreams would never stall—

That joyride of a green and prideful tide,
Denied because I do not know it all;
I'm far from young enough.

~ *Susan Jarvis Bryant*

Inclement Fable

A pretty girl who lost the rainy night
went looking for it underneath the seats
of subway cars. She chased it through the streets,
a child trailing a frayed, fugitive kite.
Her shoes absorbed the dark and wet, grew tight,
and drew red hieroglyphics on her feet.
She sought the rainy night between the sheets,
so damp against her skin, translucent, white.
Exhausted, she embraced a clammy sleep.
She searched again upon awakening,
beside the lamp and underneath the bed,
but in the bathroom mirror, flickering,
her pale reflection sighed and shook its head.
That rainy night was never hers to keep.

~ *JD Michael*

PHANTOM

The mother's stillborn baby starts to cry
A phantom cry that burns grief's dumb-struck voice
As something in that mother starts to die.

She won't believe he's gone—*If doctors try . . . !*
They've left an empty blanket and invoice.
The mother's stillborn baby starts to cry.

She curses God! Then fear, with faithful eye
Turned in, rebukes her guilt with shame. What choice?
Still, something in that mother starts to die.

Her phantom faith that never questions why,
The myths, the fairy tales, their crashing joist—
The mother's stillborn baby starts to cry.

She thinks: When body's dead, the soul can fly:
I'm just an instrument, not music's voice.
But something in that mother starts to die.

She doubts why she's alive if prayers can't pry
Her child to life: *Do angels' songs rejoice*
When mothers' stillborn babies start to cry!
When something in that mother starts to die?

~ *Beth Houston*

Circadian Lament, Sung to a Wakeful Baby

Go back to sleep. You've made a slight mistake
switching your days and nights around this way.
The time will come for nights you spend awake,

for cough and colic, ear- and stomach-ache.
Though now you babble charmingly and play
the infant hours away (a light mistake),

there will be bitter medicines to take
some night. Take love: its wide-eyed thrills one day,
its clammy sweats the next. Take nights awake,

your soul in shreds, your bank account at stake,
your eyelids propped with stale café au lait.
Searching the stars for some obscure mistake

when futures cloud and omens turn opaque
and panic makes you pace the floors and pray—
There will be no escape from nights awake,

I warn you. And my wisdom doesn't make
one whit of difference. *Seize the night,* you say
in coo and babble. Ah, well. My mistake.
Instruct me in the joys of nights awake.

~ Maryann Corbett

NEW PARENT AT A PARTY

I am sure it's great weed,
    but I don't want a toke.
        It could never be potent enough.
And the same goes for speed,
    LSD, 'shrooms and coke,
        Johnnie Walker, espresso and snuff.

What I long for instead
    is a drug you can't score
        by the gram or the pint or the lid.
All you need is a bed
    and eight hours or more,
        no distractions, no noise and no kid.

~ Melissa Balmain

Nightjar

Perched on a silvered post,
a moon-crazed whippoorwill
repeats his solipsistic boast
to forest, field, and hill.

No daughter's eyes can close,
no dreaming can commence
until a frazzled parent throws
some pebbles at the fence.

One knock: the bird's in flight,
spreading his beak so wide
the insects trafficking with night
can't keep themselves outside.

Sated at last, he'll find,
beyond the barbed-wire spikes,
a perch where he can speak his mind
as often as he likes.

~ Kevin Durkin

In the Next Cubicle

Our colleague brought his son to work one day,
showed him our spaces, told the boy our names,
then sat him in a cubicle to play
with a toy race car and computer games,
buying some time to finish up a task.
We went about our business quietly
until we heard his son pipe up and ask,
"Is Mom in heaven?" "Yes." "Then who will be

my parents when you die?" "I plan to live
until you're all grown up," our colleague said.
At sixty, what more comfort could he give,
now his young wife was nearly two years dead?
The boy, adopted when her health was good,
had just turned five and wasn't satisfied.
I wondered if he really understood
when he said, "I was small when Mama died,

and I'll be small when you do." "No way, sport."
"Yeah, I'll be small." A neighbor cleared his throat,
came to my desk with drafts of his report,
and asked me gruffly for my final vote.
I tried to concentrate on text and chart
but glanced up often at a photograph
of my young daughter pushing her toy cart
down a long aisle, face turned, about to laugh.

~ *Kevin Durkin*

FAR INTO THE LIVES OF OTHER FOLK

I knew a tale of a better kind.
    —Robert Frost, "On the Heart's Beginning to Cloud the Mind"

You could be anyone or anywhere—
the checkout lady at the A&P,
the glib *poseur* with attitude and hair,
the full-sleeve-tattooed ER orderly,
the Walmart shelver on the graveyard shift,
the goody-two-shoes or the evil twin,
the badass mom, the waitress who's been stiffed,
the sergeant notifying next of kin.

No matter who you are, I presuppose
a motivation, blessing or regret,
inventing possible scenarios,
each storyline a fanciful vignette,
symmetrical and always well-defined:
bold, italicized and underlined.

Of course, this works both ways. It's only fair
to wonder what you must concoct for me
as you observe the blatant wear and tear
that time has left for all the world to see.
I claim your offhand gift of shortest shrift—
it's tough to see beyond the crepe-like skin,
the balding crown, the thoughts that tend to drift,
the turkey wattle underneath the chin.

You see me eye the piercings in your nose
and tongue at Betty's Coin-Op Launderette;

but as we sit and watch our spinning clothes,
we joke about a lost sock and forget
cross-purposes, then ultimately find
we've let the heart begin to cloud the mind.

~ *Catherine Chandler*

ACROBATS

Let's all wish well to acrobats,
Whose feet, like goddesses' transcend
The earth as do aristocrats'
And start up toward where eagles end.

A careful foot, at angle just,
Possesses wire ten yards above
In what appears as gripping lust
But really what amounts to love.

Up high where just one slip would break
A collar bone, a leg or head,
One juggles plates for baby's sake,
Who's napping safely in her bed.

And then, eliciting more awe,
He rides the wire upon a bike
While holding on his upraised jaw
His partner, trustful as a tyke,

Who, in her turn, holds wide a bar,
A beach ball resting on each end.
Let's pray no wicked wind will mar
This lovely gift they have and lend.

For all of us are acrobats
Who juggle gratitude and tasks
While wearing shakily six hats
And try to do what concord asks.

~ *John J. Brugaletta*

Neighbors and Strangers

They tell us things that we already know,
our neighbors. "Cold today. It's icy too."
But that just makes it pleasant as we go

Our common ways. It is their way to show
they're just like us. They do the things we do.
They tell us things that we already know

Because they do not think about it. So
we shouldn't either. Why must it be new?
That simply makes it pleasant as we go,

Knowing we're not alone. Our common woe,
our joys, they're shared. We are the same folks who
have greeted us, whom we already know

So well we needn't stop and talk. Although
we don't know them at all. That's also true.
We all are total strangers as we go

About our ways. We never get below
bland surfaces. We never seek a clue
about those things that we will never know.
But that's what makes it pleasant as we go.

~ *Bruce Bennett*

Park Avenue South, New York, N.Y.

Wine tasting lunch today? Sure, here's my glass.
Who knows when I'll be able to come back.
I rarely drink, but why give this a pass?

They say prepare to quarantine. Alas!
What's left to buy? There isn't much we lack.
Wine tasting lunch today. Please, here's my glass.

I'll pack my pad with Clorox, cans, & grass
and hope my kid's boss won't give him the sack.
Another? Sure, who's giving this a pass?

One more and I'll be tossed out on my ass.
The room is spinning, but I've got a knack
for this wine tasting thing, and here's my glass.

White table cloths and all, this joint's got class.
And this here wine will help me stay on track.
I rarely drink, but who'd give this a pass?

I think this lunch has reached critical mass.
But, what the hell, I'll give it one more crack.
Wine tasting lunch today. Fill up my glass!
I sure as hell ain't giving this a pass.

~ *Wendy Sloan*

SONG OF THE BRABALL

They're sending the bras they hate most to El Cerrito artist Emily Duffy...6,800 bras [have been] rolled into the BraBall, a 700-pound, 43-inch-diameter brassiere-sphere now growing in Duffy's garage.
—The Oakland Tribune

Sayonara, you Miracle bras—
we are sick of miraculous itch.
Adios, you maternity bras
with the clasps that make nursing a bitch.
See ya later, you cross-your-heart bras
that deprive us of air as we talk,
and you "ultra-strong, never-quit" bras
that collapse while we jog, bike or walk.

Now it's off to the BraBall you go.
We are sorry we wasted our dough,
but at least you can be in a show.
(Any boyfriend or spouse who dares mock
our obsession with lingerie schlock
needs a day in an underwire jock.)

Women used to set fire to their bras—
good for them, not so good for the air.
Now a sculpture constructed of bras
seems just right for the eco-aware.
And besides, it's a hoot that you bras,
with no hooters inside you to tame,
are becoming celebrity bras.
Thanks to you, we've got jiggle-free fame.

What comes next? How will all of this end?
If we're lucky, we'll see a new trend.
Some exhibits we gals recommend:
balls of pumps that have tortured our toes,
balls of shoulder pads, thongs—and who knows,
we could fill up the Met with our hose.

~ *Melissa Balmain*

MIRROR, MIRROR . . .

Mirror, Mirror, on the wall,
Do you have to show me all
Failures of myself to meet
Former standards of conceit?

You were purchased way back when:
I was so much younger then,
Thinner and more beautiful;
Wrinkles seemed impossible.

Could you please enhance the view
I am often subject to
As I have to make a pass
Down the hall and by your glass?

If you cannot humor me
And appease my vanity,
I shall need to strategize:
Maybe I should close both eyes.

~ *Jane Blanchard*

Porous

The doctor says my bones are not as dense
as they should be. Remember our first house—
floor joists transformed to lace by tiny mouths?
My inner architecture now presents

that kind of airy precariousness.
In fact I feel as finespun as a blouse
of linen openwork. Sans home, sans spouse
sans sturdy frame, I am a thing both less

and more—the web of dew that drapes a rose,
the glint of gauzy voile that veils a bride,
the flash of froth that skims incoming tide—
my perforations shimmer and expose.

~ *Debra Wierenga*

CLEAN OR UNCLEAN

during radiation after chemotherapy

The maid spends hours in the suite next door.
Some sickly one must have moved out and on.
Who knows what he or she was treated for.
You hope attendant germs will soon be gone.

You think of all the things you chose to touch.
The elevator buttons—down or up?
The common breakfast—always much too much.
The sip you took on Sunday from the Cup.

You trust that God can sort all of it out:
Who has to die or has to live instead.
Meanwhile you opt to go and get about.
Brown hair begins again to crown your head.

~ *Jane Blanchard*

HYPOCHONDRIAC'S SONG

Whenever thoughts of dying bring me low,
I tell myself at least by then I'll know
which trauma or disease has killed me by degrees
or clobbered me with one efficient blow.

While croaking, I won't fear that UV rays
or germs on cell phones, door knobs and fillets,
or poisons leached from soils, or saturated oils,
could spell a tragic ending to my days;

magnetic fields, asbestos, deer ticks, gin,
mad cow disease, lead paint and saccharin
won't fill me with alarm—for what can do me harm
if I've been irreversibly done in?

Just one last thing will smother me with dread:
the notion of the nothingness ahead.
But that will vanish, too, the moment that I'm through—
a perk, I must admit, of being dead.

~ *Melissa Balmain*

OTOLOGY

The drive is easy early in the day—
ten minutes tops—ten more to park. I walk
into the building, find the office well
before eight-thirty. The reception room
is far from full. I choose an empty chair,
fill out too many forms, and wait—all set.

A nurse soon guides me back to where I set
aside belongings. Vital signs today
are excellent. Moved to another chair,
I answer questions, see the doctor walk
up, down the hall. He comes into the room,
asks how I am. I simply say, "Unwell."

"And why is that?" he counters, then bids, "Well,
let's take a look." I hesitantly set
myself upon a cushioned slab. The room
becomes a torture chamber. "Oh, Monday,
Monday, so good to me," I mutely walk
through lyrics till I get back to a chair.

Next I am moved to yet another chair
inside a lab designed to test how well
I hear. The nurse and the computer walk
me through procedure. Earplugs in, headset
and collar on, I click a pen all day
or so it seems—tone / pulse—in that strange room.

At last the nurse comes back into the room,
adjusts something. I must stay in the chair,
touch squares within a grid to show "birthday"
is not "rainbow," "football" is not "inkwell,"
"toothbrush" is not "mousetrap." The sound is set
too low: "padlock"? "horseshoe"? maybe "sidewalk"?

The test advances. Rhymes are a cakewalk
compared to spondees. Yes, I own the room
throughout this section. Volume has been set
so I can choose one out of four. The chair
feels almost comfortable as I do well.
Perhaps I might survive this endless day.

Back in the other room, I take a chair,
hear wins have offset losses, say farewell,
rise and walk out into the still-young day.

~ *Jane Blanchard*

SLEEPWALK

Time flows like water, ceaselessly,
But also falls like leaves or snow
To coat the shifting world below
With daily layers of debris,

And as I wander, short of cash,
Through each successive present day,
On track, in circles, or astray,
I kick up clouds of dust and ash.

Most places I have often been
Still harbor ghostly elements
Of certain still recalled events
That happened there once way back when,

But if I pause to think about
How things connect and intertwine
And grow and stagnate and decline
I run the risk of zoning out

And sleepwalking through hours or days
Obsessing over times long gone
While the ignored world rumbles on,
Unfolding while I'm in a haze,

And in the process I forget
To do the chores I need to do,
And to devote attention to
The people who are with me yet.

The past should teach, not occupy,
So you can visit, but don't stay,
And only let thoughts drift that way
When you're alone, in case you cry.

~ *David Stephenson*

Communion of Saints

The things that living brains forget,
the dead keep neatly filed.
My grandmother remembered yet
the death of Oscar Wilde,

the Wright brothers at Kitty Hawk,
and from the time before
her own, her mother's fervid talk
about the Civil War.

Now I remember for her sake
the small years as they pass,
the years that like a hatchling snake
run underneath the grass,

that sometimes crawl and sometimes climb
as to their goals they tend
until the quick-eared cat of time
pounces, and there an end.

~ *Gail White*

IV

Bird Aubade

Daybreak, and not one sound is heard
as was routine of trilling jays
that were aflutter as they stirred
the muggy air with June's heatwave.
They'd dart between two trees ablaze

with alpenglow—their choice playground
alongside two apartment blocks.
Their silent airs today astound.
Some social distancing to save
their plumage from some newfound pox?

Succumbed at last to this June's sear?
Or did they just migrate away?
Less than an hour—and there's the whirr
amongst the trees! How they behave
as usual, still they're no one's prey.

How tardy! Have they now become
stung with our sleep-in-late malaise . . .
or wearied by the rival hum
and thump that made a schoolyard cave
in for a close-by condo maze?

A symphony of seasaw trills—
the customary dawn reveille—

assured and rampant as it spills
forth now, before it's time to brave
the caterpillars' wake and wail.

~ *Alexander Pepple*

A Proposal

The farmer stumbles through the weary day
while cattle die and wheat begins to mold.
There are no guarantees that work will pay.

No matter what we wish, what we've been told,
the firmest lives and loves may not survive.
The cosmos will ensure at best the cold.

But why should we allow death to deprive
us of such minimal delight as could
come to us both if we were kept alive

for . . . well, how long? A week? All right. Now should
we not get slaughtered by a biker gang,
eviscerated by a sleazy hood,

or bombed by enemies because we sang
"America the Beautiful," let's kiss,
let's love, and let's move in. Or, in the "slang"

of eighty years ago when notes like this
were commoner: Please be my belamour.
Who knows? We might eat several crumbs of bliss.

But keep in mind that nothing good is sure.
I say this just to keep my conscience pure.

~ *John J. Brugaletta*

MRS.

The hours of solitude expire too soon.
Right through the silken sleeve of afternoon,
With flourishes of leaves, the tires arrive
To sweep across the asphalt of the drive.

The German motorcar presents a gleam
Of glass in facets, chrome and glossy cream
That lifts, in one discriminating stroke,
The dappled shadow-fabric of the oak.

The squirrels and scrub jays freeze upon the limb:
Creation waits to catch a sight of him.
The driver's door unclicks; the god is seen!—
A lesser deity than his machine.

It's disappointing, yes. May I be blunt?
I envy his Mercedes parked in front.
It whirs and taps in satisfied repose
And doesn't wonder where the driver goes.

~ *Eric Meub*

TO MY LATEST FEMME FATALE

I've no excuse for having wasted days
Endeavoring ineptly to seduce
You. Till I'd grown accustomed to your ways
I should have put my time to better use,

For now my neck is in a hangman's noose
I can't get out of: I can only gaze
And choke on words, disgustingly profuse,
I've no excuse for. Having wasted days

Inside a melancholic lovelorn haze
Where steamy thoughts (and frequent self-abuse)
Are now the norm, I try to thread the maze,
Endeavoring ineptly. To seduce,

By luck, a girl like you could force a truce
Of sorts upon the battlefield—then praise
For your lubricious movements might unloose
You till I'd grown accustomed to your ways

And learned to keep our straining loins in phase.
Because, as yet, I haven't got the juice
To set your unresponsive heart ablaze,
I should have put my time to better use.

Perhaps if I had acted more like Zeus,
Who suffered no refusals or delays,

I wouldn't feel so hopelessly obtuse.
For flaws this bald confession now betrays
I've no excuse.

~ C. B. Anderson

NUTCRACKER

Poor Santa Claus and Frosty, dead and gone,
Lie crumpled on the early morning lawn,
More proof that neither oxygen nor pumps
Can salvage Christmas: Mother's in the dumps.

Each year a wonderland, each year the same.
Perhaps tonight the tree will burst in flame.
The gift for me is labeled *To my Wife*.
Next year I'm asking for a different life.

A friend advised me: Make yourself a *List
Of Gratitudes*. Oh boy that made me pissed.
I *was* unhappy; *now* I feel dismissed.
My Inner Child is going to slit her wrist.

This is the year to find out what it's worth
To fake it through another Virgin Birth,
To act enraptured when my husband talks,
And marvel at whatever's in that box.

~ *Eric Meub*

FROZEN CHARLOTTE

I am a doll of ivory bisque.
I was a girl, but was too bold.
To preen in silks, I dared to risk
the open sleigh. I don't grow old.
A girl of flesh who died of cold.

I froze while riding to the ball,
to end in ice and snowy pearls.
I thawed in kilns, a molded doll,
a pocket *vanitas* for girls.
My cheeks are flushed. I died of cold.

I float now in a child's bath.
My little mistress pushes me
from rim to rim or to her mouth.
They've taken all my finery.
A doll's not flesh. I don't get cold.

I'm safe for play—no moving parts.
My price is small. I'm bought and sold.
I fortify their frozen hearts.
I'm getting warmer now—it's told
on mountain roads. I died of cold.

~ *Susan de Sola*

ANTINOUS

For sheer expenditure, it's a disgrace
The rolls of film devoted to your face—
From every angle, every slant of light—
Until you hid the camera from sight.

I catalogued your beauties, just for me.
They wouldn't long be anyone's to see:
Your thinning hair, say, parted to the right,
That would in God's good time succumb to blight.

But note the effort recollection spends
On charms I couldn't capture with a lens—
Your love of limericks and ginger tea—
That would, perhaps, have only grown on me.

I keep the photos in a lacquered box.
Each portrait makes a fraud of me—it mocks
The eye insistent that its claims be kept,
In contradiction to the heart that slept.

~ Eric Meub

THE SHIP OF THESEUS

We both got on at Brooklyn Bridge. I took
a window seat; the woman chose to stand.
I normally don't cast a second look

at anyone—they might misunderstand
my scrutiny for interest—or why she
commanded my attention. Here, unplanned,

appeared the image of an absentee:
her hands, her face, the color of her hair,
her very stance. I stared. Identity

collapsed, and all that time cannot repair.
Rush hour commuters exited en masse,
my fragmentation none of their affair.

While windows in the tunnel changed from glass
to looking glass, a pair of hooded eyes
met mine. Appalled, I let the moment pass

as one accepts an outcome. Otherwise,
I'd have to tell this story in a book
where youth prevails and true love never dies.

~ *Catherine Chandler*

LEGION

A pair of hamstrings overwhelms your guard
By scissoring the green of Harvard Yard.
They pedal through your herded reveries—
The tendons flex; the congregation flees.

Too late for you to look away—the lure
Reduces all of Cambridge to a blur—
So concentrate your telephoto eye:
A golden down is glinting on a thigh.

In the disastrous wake of overthrow
You feel more razorback, less Romeo—
The swinish urge to scavenge has undone
The resolution run in unison.

And now you've dropped your Dante in the dirt—
White arms thrown wide as if inviting Hurt,
With one conclusive clod of earth—to slice
Across the ivory page of paradise.

~ Eric Meub

CLYTEMNESTRA

Your father—starts the customary chant
Of intel leaks she ought to plug but can't.
The silver-swirled coiffure has framed her face
(And cocktail glass) in incandescent lace.

Uplit by gold and gilt, she holds erect
The baffling gaze, the glittering effect
Of trivial injustices that haunt
Her marital yet mobilized détente.

Her youngest sits behind her in the mirror,
Her therapist, familiar, Sybil, seer.
The bourbon now released, her fingertips
Retrieve the stick that will ignite her lips.

Halfway through treaties broken, targets hit—
The boy is, after all, a surrogate—
She stops, and (pinning to her breast a jewel)
Asks candidly—*or am I being cruel?*

~ *Eric Meub*

PANTOUM FOR A DISAPPEARING PAIR

She whispers, I need to get out of here.
He smiles. At last! Their wishes coincide,
and both of them know how to disappear
before short tempers and tall drinks collide.

He smiles: at last, their wishes coincide,
though lately their agreements have been rare.
Before short tempers and tall drinks collide,
they'll find a back door and get out of there.

Though lately their agreements have been rare,
they both dislike lame jokes and cut-rate gin.
They find a back door and get out of there,
abandoning the unconvincing din.

They both dislike lame jokes and cut-rate gin
and parties where the past still tends the bar.
Abandoning the unconvincing din,
he relishes the silence in their car.

At parties where the past still tends the bar,
the same old small talk seldom drowns out dread.
He relishes the silence in their car;
Soon they'll be home, curled up in their warm bed.

The same old small talk seldom drowns out dread,
but both of them know how to disappear.
Soon they're at home. Curled up in their warm bed,
she whispers, I need to get out of here.

~ *Jean L. Kreiling*

LACRIMAE RERUM

Time after time I have resolved
To leave off thinking of the past,
What happened and who was involved,
The many loves that did not last.

To leave off thinking of the past
Perhaps would stop the flow of tears
For many loves that did not last
Despite my efforts through the years.

What else could stop the flow of tears,
The mind-full drops which pool, then fall?
Despite my efforts through the years,
Loss after loss means less is all.

The mind-full drops still pool, then fall.
Time after time I have resolved
To lessen losses after all
That happened with the ones involved.

~ *Jane Blanchard*

WHEN THEY MET AGAIN

He: Bound for brand-new teaching job
With newly-minted PhD.
She: Married to a CPA
And on her second pregnancy.

Once lovers, met by chance, they chat
Of lives grown prosperous apart.
Like old unjealous friends, they praise
Their new successes of the heart.

Each fancies that the other feels
A lingering flame. Their smiles are sad,
But both, on going separate ways,
Thank God for the escape they had.

~ *Gail White*

The Fly

The female fly is nearly chaste.
She hasn't any time to waste;
Her life's a span of weeks, not months,
And so she copulates just once.

This single tryst is guaranteed
To satisfy her every need
Because she takes her lover's juice
And stores it up for future use.

When it is time to fertilize,
She has no further need of sighs.
The stuff for coating every egg
She's got at hand—or filth-drenched leg.

She lays and lays without the aid
Ever again of getting laid.
The system works quite well for flies,
Though male flies might feel otherwise.

~ *Max Gutmann*

THE OVERVIEW

My greatest love, a Persian cat,
arrived when I was twenty-two.
I wouldn't have expected that

I'd fall in love in seconds flat
with eyes of enigmatic blue.
My greatest love, a Persian cat,

refuted the old caveat:
Cat-love is not, like dog-love, true.
I wouldn't have expected that

she'd choose my lap for habitat,
but year by year her kindness grew.
My greatest love, a Persian cat,

outlasted many a fine male rat
including, my false darling, you.
(I wouldn't have expected that).

And so I find, while working at
"My Life and Loves: An Overview,"
my greatest love: a Persian cat.
I wouldn't have expected that.

~ *Gail White*

BALLADE OF INEVITABLE EXTINCTION

Where are the flushed and frantic teens,
   The hormones' fevered ebbs and flows?
(*Fire buckets, water, verbal screens.*)
     The girls—good grief!—that parents chose
     And others—how the mind's eye glows!
Who floated inches off the floor?
   (*Flout censor's ruling— fish-net hose.*)
With dodo, great auk, dinosaur.

Where are the doubtful magazines?
   The female form from head to toes
(*Dim lights. Spill simulated beans.*)
     In postures aimed to half-disclose
     Behinds, aboves, and down belows,
With clefts and crevices galore?
   (*Check pressure here, in case it blows.*)
With dodo, great auk, dinosaur.

Where are the eyeball-popping queens
   Of X-films like the great Bardot's?
(*Props: G-string, well-packed blouse and jeans.*)
     Brigitte—with so much to expose
     Far finer than the best French prose—
Removing most, and, sometimes, more . . .?
   (*Cue key-change, envoi, Villon, 'snows'.*)
With dodo, great auk, dinosaur.

Envoi

    Prince, not again! The whole world knows

Time's answer must be, as before,

    (*Stand by the curtain ! Down it goes!*)

With dodo, great auk, dinosaur.

~ *Jerome Betts*

JULIAN OF NORWICH IN SECLUSION

Because an anchoress could have a cat,
We may assume she had one. That it sat
Beside her while the pilgrims came and went,
Giving, like her, a lesson in content.
That it was quiet when her visions came
And when they passed it slumbered just the same,
But any mice who trespassed in the cell
Were given reason to believe in hell.
That with a feline love of body heat
It nestled in her lap or on her feet.
That it died peacefully, grown old and fat.
Love was my meaning, purred St. Julian's cat.

~ *Gail White*

WARMING

The seasons' course seems strange to me,
more strange than I remember.
Wild flowers bloom unseasonably:
primroses in November.

The young pretend to blame us all.
Well, youth's a great dissembler:
May was forever, I recall,
and there was no November.

These days I'll take what Nature sends
to hoard for dour December:
a glow of warmth as autumn ends;
primroses in November.

~ David Anthony

Clair de Lune

I stop the car—things can't be what they seem:
a spill of gold, as in a pirate's dream,
cascading down my driveway, glimmering
and flowing to the curb—my wedding ring,
too, catches in some light—and then I see:
high winds today have stripped the ginkgo tree
of all her brilliant yellow leaves at once—
a gust of sudden treasure to the ounce
of metal on my hand. And it occurs
to me, that phrase that commonly refers
to gold, 'a yellow metal,' never seemed
to capture it—for gold has weight, and sheen,
where yellow's just an easy streak of 'bright'—
but now I learn, this strangely wind-lit night,
it's yellow mixed with moonshine that makes gold,
and spurs imagination to those old
heroic, dangerous quests of greed and sin.
I nod, switch off my headlights, and drive in.

~ *D. R. Goodman*

BALD CYPRESS IN ONTARIO

For Jane

A seedling only eighteen inches tall,
it bravely sprouted several tiny leaves.
And that is how we left it in the fall.

Elsewhere, the widow of a woodsman grieves
who gave us this to plant, his legacy
of thirst for life. Our northern shore receives

the gift for now of hope and memory.
But up here, winter happens dark and deep,
an icy trial for a fragile tree

born in the warmer south. So may it keep
its toehold and revive itself in spring,
roots stubborn even through the long, cold sleep.

There is a time it's said for everything,
whatever chance the elements may bring.

~ Barbara Loots

Storm Warning

"Stay home! The road spells danger!"
On such a morning, ice,
old landscape rearranger
indifferent and precise,

encapsulates each grass stalk
and leaf of tiny shrub,
the pattern on each sidewalk,
bicycle spoke and hub.

The streets are well deserted.
Peril is absolute
where rain and freeze have flirted.
And yet my salt-stained boot

finds still another doily
of frost-begotten lace
whose edges crackle royally
in danger's frozen face.

~ *Claudia Gary*

BALLAD OF THE VERNAL EQUINOX

Her cup of coffee's getting cold,
 she's poured herself some gin,
her melancholy uncontrolled,
 her winter-patience thin.

She pulls the curtain back to see
 the bitter silver storm
that's come to numb Sault Ste. Marie
 when weather should be warm.

The snow has stopped, the moon shines hard,
 the wind's a gentle hush.
Coyote drifts into her yard,
 out from the brittle brush.

He stares her down with raw desire,
 his coat a map of scars;
for after all, he's stolen fire
 and spilled a bag of stars.

I know a place where daffodils
 are pushing through the ice,
he hints with all his trickster's skills
 and hopes she won't think twice.

She smiles at him without a flinch,
 reflection in her eyes,
knowing she dare not give an inch
 to one both mad and wise.

A flick of tail—and then he's gone
    without a backward glance,
his one-time offer now withdrawn.
    Too bad. No second chance.

Yet when the geese return and love
    is nowhere to be seen,
she'll scour the woods for traces of
    those brazen spikes of green.

~ Catherine Chandler

Eternal Autumn

I mow the leaves, but there are always more.
I and my mower cross and cross the lawn.
Are these the same leaves that were there before?

How could they be? They can't be. But the chore
is endless. It goes on and on and on.
I mow the leaves, but there are always more:

They multiply, a tide, a burgeoning store
replenishing itself, and never done,
as if I had not mowed and mowed before,

As if I'd never heard my mower roar,
me laboring behind it, while the sun
stands where it stood, while yes, there's always *more,*

Slow-drifting down from trees I can't ignore
because they're full, which means, it *can't* be won,
this battle, where the fight I fought before

was always doomed and futile, in this war
which looms as if it had not yet begun.
I mow the leaves, but there are always more.
Are these the same leaves that were there before?

~ *Bruce Bennett*

SKATING BACKWARDS

I haven't laced on skates in years—
a sacrifice to waxing fears
of broken that or fractured this.
But, oh, how terribly I miss
the effortless, cerebral bliss

of skating backwards aimlessly.
I did not use my eyes to see
but, rather, rocked from side to side
and let inertia's laws decide
my path across the icy glide.

How liberating not to brood
upon what others might conclude
about my balance, skill or grace
in crossing this communal place
but, rather, to glissade through space

as through a dream. I seemed repelled
by what was known—the world beheld
with my own eyes—and tempted toward
a destination unexplored
as if drawn by some unseen cord.

How free to skate in blind reverse
and leave will to the universe.

~ *B. Fulton Jennes*

September

As the summer slows down to a crawl,
When the apples are nearly in season
 At the threshold of fall,
 It's foreseeable then
 That a rush of unreason
Will arise from endorphin-rich brains
Of indigenous women and men
 Who applaud when it rains.

In the meadows they'd mown only once,
Where the forbs and perennial grasses
 Are the groundwork of hunts
 Yet to come, there's no doubt
 All the lads and their lasses
Are ecstatic and ready to roll
In unharvested hayfields, without
 Any aim or control—

Though a seasoned partaker might say
That composure and caution don't matter:
 At the end of the day,
 Whatsoever was planned,
 There's a wind that shall scatter
The most carefully husbanded seed
Far abroad on this bounteous land,
 Irrespective of creed.

So lie down in the glistening dew
And behold the near reaches of Glory,
    For the limitless blue
    Is a channel whereby
    The continuing story
Of affairs that have often recurred
Is transported direct from the sky
    On the wings of a bird.

There are times when the will may forget
What the conscience must later remember,
    But the deepest regret
    Is the failure to live
    To the full. It's September,
And October's no less an event
Where there's nothing for God to forgive
    And no need to repent.

~ *C. B. Anderson*

The Lilacs on Good Friday

Tumult of noontide long ago dismissed—
The rent veil unremembered, and the sun
Relit, though shrouded in a new eclipse
Of rainswept sky. The garden seems to shun

That spectral agony of blood and bone;
Consigns itself instead to placid sleep
Untroubled as the moss upon a stone
And heedless while the three Marias weep.

Four decades' growth of lilac by this wall
Stretches its shallow spiral to the sky.
Clustering blossoms, soon to swell and fall,
Gather themselves like nimbuses on high

Out of my hand's grasp, yet I still can bend
The pliant osiers downward to my face,
And sniff the buds that already distend:
Late April lilacs, delicate as lace.

Unlike that rigid tree, untenanted,
And red with memory of three hours' grief,
The thornless lilacs summon up no dread,
Demand no witness. Flower, branch, and leaf

Are only what they are. They have no words
For us to ponder, though we sometimes feign
To speak for them, as augury of birds
Construes an omen of impending pain.

The book is shut, the candle snuffed, the bell
Rings the finale of a troubled day.
Did lilacs grace the garden where we fell,
Or scent Gethsemane? *I bade you pray*

And watch with me a little while this night—
Could you not watch one hour? The world's bereft
Of that which once gave stomach for a fight
Or certitude to vision. I have left

The Office of the Holy Cross unsung
But patient on the rubricated page:
Open my lips, O Lord, and let my tongue
Announce thy praises—in some other age.

Here in this garden how could it displease
To let the lilacs offer up my prayer—
Sweet censers that, when shaken by the breeze,
Scatter their fragrance in the evening air?

And in that garden where a sepulcher
New-hewn from rock awaits the mourners' tread,
Where cerecloths, unguent, aloes mixed with myrrh
Will soon enshroud the lacerated dead,

There is some solace from the thought of how
Late April lilacs, coming into bloom,
Shall dance the currents of the air, and bow
To shed their flowerets on an open tomb.

~ *Joseph S. Salemi*

A View from the Foothills

If you believe that everything you need
To know is written in the Bible, you
Have missed the point, for Scripture's just a seed
Requiring germination in the hearts
And minds of humans. All too often, true
Believers think that inspiration starts

And ends with what some privileged person wrote
In Greek about two thousand years ago,
And they will do their very best to quote
It endlessly. There's no catalysis,
Like trumpets at the walls of Jericho,
To bring them down to earth. Paralysis

Of mindset is a grave condition fed
By two related causes: lack of sense,
Or flat refusal to employ one's head
To separate the wheat from worthless chaff;
And bald self-righteousness subserving bents
Of preachers who've forgotten how to laugh.

Down in the valley there's a middle ground
Where no one bows to any made-up god
And circuit riders never come around.
The river there is balm for restless feet,
A stopping place for steeds that roam unshod,
A paradise where kindred spirits meet.

~ C. B. Anderson

PRAYER FOR A CERTAIN KIND OF RAIN

I don't believe in God, and yet I pray
(to no one, to the fates, or to the sky)
that rain—a certain kind—might fall today.

I don't want floods; I don't mean to dismay
sun worshippers whose own god would deny
this unbeliever's plea. I only pray

for tiny drops that delicately play
against the panes, wet diamonds from on high,
a kind of rain that ruins no one's day,

that floats as much as falls, like sea-flung spray,
anointing air. But it won't sanctify
a thing. I don't believe. I only pray

for weather that reminds me of the gray,
damp mornings long ago when you and I
heard heaven in this kind of rain. Today,

alone in tangled sheets where we once lay
and listened, thinking we were showered by
God's grace, I don't believe. And yet I pray
that rain—a certain kind—might fall today.

~ *Jean L. Kreiling*

SCRIPTURE

One Easter yields a gift: I loose the string
And wrapping to behold a leaden thing.
My mother doesn't gush, but sits content
To let it go without encouragement.

Yet on the page that reads *Presented To,*
Her pen exhausts itself of ballpoint blue:
No etiquette, no Halston can withstand
The god who suffers Father's gothic hand.

The volume boasts a less substantial girth
Than rival testaments of Middle Earth,
But can a Bombadil or woodland elf
Endure such darkness lurking on the shelf?

The sober words—hearse-black and fury-red—
Proclaim their victory in shades of dread.
My parents wait and watch me: I'll be good
And hidden, deep in the abandoned wood.

~ Eric Meub

To-Do

Someday I'll do it: straighten all my closets
    and purge those vests from 1993,
scrub tile and grout of mineral deposits,
    arrange my spices alphabetically.
I'll find the puzzle pieces that need finding,
repair my Penguin classics, page and binding,
then polish every doorknob till it's blinding.

My photographs? At last I'll organize them.
    My shrubbery? I'll finally cut it back.
I'll wax the table scratches to disguise them,
    hang every poster, painting, pennant, plaque.
I'll give my rhododendrons hits of acid,
file pamphlets on lakes Tupper, George and Placid,
re-stuff each quilt and pillow that's gone flaccid.

And when I've done it all—when, to perfection,
    I've finished off the items on my list,
when not a speck of dust awaits detection,
    and not a squeaky door hinge has been missed,
and not a scrapbook scrap remains unpasted,
and not a seam's un-finished or un-basted,
I'll die, my final year completely wasted.

~ *Melissa Balmain*

Deserted Cemetery

The yews point toward the sky,
but there's no one to see,
none now who can say why
the yews point toward the sky,
promising those who die
All that is still to be.
The yews point toward the sky,
but there are none to see.

The melancholy lanes
between the graves are still.
No living thing complains.
The melancholy lanes
and stone are what remains
as time now wreaks its will.
The melancholy lanes
and stones, all, all are still.

The yews point toward the sky,
but none now can say why.

The lanes, the stones, are still.
And time now wreaks its will.

~ *Bruce Bennett*

AT THE BURIAL OF AN ABBESS

Under the pine trees and the snow,
black on white, and row on row,
we leave our sisters when they go.

We age and die, we fill our space
and no one younger takes our place.
What a mysterious thing is grace

that makes us willing to be gone,
forgotten in our soundless lawn,
even the Order passing on.

Whatever good we might have done
is like the prints where foxes run,
lost when the snow melts in the sun.

But what we've learned above the ground
is to love silence more than sound,
white more than any color found.

The work of all our lifetime lets
us look on death with no regrets:
We vanish as the snow forgets.

~ *Gail White*

THE ALCHEMIST

Alone in his laboratory he stands.
In glass alembics noxious liquors boil.
He pours and stirs, and with a crabby hand
obsessively records his fruitless toil.
Thus ends the long night's work. Completely spent
he takes a sup of ale, a crust of bread,
laments another failed experiment,
at last retires defeated to his bed.
No treasure will reward the pains he took.
And yet we must be glad of his defiance:
He struggled on, and left us in his book
ungerminated seeds of future science.
A red sun brings the dawn—pale, clean, and cold—
and dusts upon the glass small flecks of gold.

~ *Tim Taylor*

A TIMELESS VILLANELLE

Let time be still; preserve and freeze
the bliss of this delicious day,
this dreamy state of seamless ease

where skin drinks in the sun-soaked breeze
and saffron gilds the gloom-garbed grey.
Let time be still; preserve and freeze

the zephyr teasing leafy trees
and scents of hyacinths and hay.
This dreamy state of seamless ease

that quells the swell and shifts the seas
grants destiny its due delay.
Let time be still, preserve and freeze

the lift that brings me to my knees
in praise of Gaia's gifts…replay
this dreamy state of seamless ease

and stop the clock's tick-tocking. Seize
tomorrow. Make it melt away.
Let time be still; preserve and freeze
this dreamy state of seamless ease.

~ *Susan Jarvis Bryant*

C. B. Anderson was the longtime gardener for the PBS television series, *The Victory Garden*. He began writing formal poetry in 2003, at the age of 54, after reading "A Gift" by Don Paterson, and he still looks back. His poetry collections are *Mortal Soup and the Blue Yonder* and *Roots in the Sky, Boots on the Ground* (White Violet Press). His poems have appeared about eight hundred times in print and online.

David Anthony was born in Ffestiniog, North Wales, and brought up and educated at Hull Grammar School before going on to study history at St. Catherine's College, Oxford. His poems have appeared in magazines and anthologies in the UK, the USA, Japan, and online. His poetry book is *Passing through the Woods (2012)*. He lives with his wife in Stoke Poges, Buckinghamshire.

Melissa Balmain edits *Light*, America's longest-running journal of comic poetry, and teaches at the University of Rochester. Her poems and prose have appeared in *The American Bystander, American Life in Poetry, The Hopkins Review, Lighten Up Online, McSweeney's, The New Yorker, The New York Times, Poetry Daily, Rattle*, and *The Washington Post*. Her latest books are *The Witch Demands a Retraction: Fairy Tale Reboots for Adults* and *Walking in on People* (Able Muse Press).

Bruce Bennett is the author of ten collections of poetry and more than thirty poetry chapbooks. His most recent book is *Just Another Day in Just Our Town: Poems New And Selected, 2000-2016* (Orchises Press). His first New And Selected, *Navigating The Distances*, was chosen by Booklist as "One Of The Top Ten Poetry Books Of 1999." In 2012 he was awarded a Pushcart Prize. He was a co-founder and editor of the literary journals *Field* and *Ploughshares*, and has reviewed poetry in *The New York Times Book Review, The Nation*, and elsewhere. Prior to his retirement he taught Literature and Creative Writing at Wells College, and is now emeritus professor of English.

Jerome Betts lives in Devon, England, and edits the verse quarterly *Lighten Up OnLine*. His work has appeared in a wide variety of British magazines as well as UK, European, and North American web publications such as *Amsterdam Quarterly, Angle, Autumn Sky Poetry Daily, Better Than Starbucks, The Hypertexts, Light, The Rotary Dial* and *Snakeskin*.

A native Virginian, **Jane Blanchard** divides her time between Augusta and Saint Simon's Island, Georgia. She has earned degrees in English from Wake Forest (B.A.) and Rutgers (M.A., Ph.D.) Universities. Her poetry has been published around the world as well as posted online. Her fourth collection is *In or Out of Season* (2020).

John J. Brugaletta has published eight volumes of his poems, most recently *One of the Loves Was Yours* (2020). He is professor emeritus at California State University Fullerton, and now lives on the redwood coast of California.

Originally from Kent in the UK, **Susan Jarvis Bryant** is a church secretary living with her husband in Texas. Her love of literature dates back to childhood, when she spent much time at Benn Brothers book publishing company where her father and grandfather worked. Susan's poetry has appeared in *Snakeskin, Lighten Up Online, Light, Sparks of Calliope, Expansive Poetry Online*, and in *Openings* (Open University Poets in the UK). Susan is the winner of the 9th Annual International Society of Classical Poets Competition and appears in the Society of Classical Poets Journals.

Originally from New York City and Pennsylvania, **Catherine Chandler** has lived in Canada for nearly 50 years. Before retiring she taught Spanish and was International Affairs Officer for Latin America at McGill University. She won the Richard Wilbur Award, the Howard Nemerov Award, and the Leslie Mellichamp Prize. *Pointing Home* is the most recent of her five poetry collections. She has been widely published in journals and anthologies, and a trio of her poems were chosen by the Poet Laureate of Canada for inclusion in the National Poetry Registry, Library of Parliament.

Ted Charnley's work has appeared in journals such as *Passager, The Road Not Taken, Think, The Lyric*, and *The Orchards Poetry Journal*. He lives with his wife in a 200-year-old farmhouse they restored in central Maryland. There, he herds woodchucks, practices chainsaw topiary, and leaves offerings for the nymphs of the springs.

Maryann Corbett earned a doctorate in English from the University of Minnesota and expected to be teaching *Beowulf* and Chaucer and the history of the English language. Instead, she spent almost thirty-five years working for the Office of the Revisor of Statutes of the Minnesota Legislature. She is the author of two chapbooks and six poetry books. Her work has won the Willis Barnstone Translation Prize and the Richard Wilbur Award, and her poetry has appeared in many journals and anthologies, including *The Best American Poetry 2018*.

Susan de Sola is an American poet living in The Netherlands. Her work has appeared in venues such as *The Hudson Review, The Hopkins Review, Birmingham Poetry Review, The Dark Horse,* and *PN Review,* and in anthologies such as *The Doll Collection* and *The Best American Poetry 2018.* She is a winner of the David Reid Poetry Translation Prize and of the Frost Farm Prize for metrical poetry. Her poetry collection is *Frozen Charlotte* (Able Muse Press).

Kevin Durkin attended schools in West Virginia, Pennsylvania, and Germany before earning his degree in English literature from Princeton University. He has taught English in Singapore, Kitakyushu (Japan), New York City, and Washington, D.C. He also has performed in the plays of Shakespeare across the United States. Currently a managing editor at *Light* and at The Huntington Library, Art Museum, and Botanical Gardens in San Marino, California, he resides with his wife and two daughters in Santa Monica.

Nicole Caruso Garcia is Associate Poetry Editor at *Able Muse* and an Advisory Board member at Poetry by the Sea: A Global Conference. Her poetry has appeared in *DIAGRAM, Crab Orchard Review, Light, Measure, Mezzo Cammin, ONE ART, The Orchards, PANK, Plume, The Raintown Review, Rattle, RHINO, Sonora Review, Spillway, Tupelo Quarterly,* and elsewhere. Her book is *Oxblood* (Able Muse Press.)

Claudia Gary teaches workshops through The Writer's Center in Bethesda, MD. She is the author of *Humor Me* and her chapbooks include *Genetic Revisionism* and *Bikini Buyer's Remorse.* Her poems appear in journals internationally and in anthologies such as *Villanelles; Forgetting Home; The Great American Wise-Ass Poetry Anthology;* and *Love Affairs at the Villa Nelle.* She has chaired panels at poetry conferences at West Chester University and the Robert Frost Farm. Claudia is also a health science writer, visual artist, and composer of art songs and chamber music.

D.R. Goodman is the author of *Greed: A Confession* (Able Muse Press). Twice winner of the Able Muse Write Prize for poetry, and 2015 winner of the Howard Nemerov Sonnet Award, her work has appeared in journals such as *Crazyhorse, Notre Dame Review, Seattle Review,* and *Whitefish Review.* Her poems appeared in Ted Kooser's *American Life in Poetry,* and in the anthology *Sonnets: 150 Contemporary Sonnets.* A native of Oak Ridge, Tennessee, she now lives in Oakland, California, where she is founder and chief instructor at a martial arts school.

Benjamin S. Grossberg is Director of Creative Writing at the University of Hartford, in West Hartford, Connecticut. His books include *Space Traveler* and *Sweet Core Orchard*, winner of a Lambda Literary Award and the Tampa Review Prize.

Max Gutmann has contributed to dozens of publications including *New Statesman*, *The Spectator*, and *Cricket*. His plays have appeared throughout the U.S. and have been well-reviewed. His book is *There Was a Young Girl from Verona: A Limerick Cycle Based on the Complete Dramatic Works of Shakespeare*.

Robin Helweg-Larsen was raised in the Bahamas and educated in Jamaica, England, and Scotland (University of Dundee). After living and working abroad, he returned to his hometown of Governor's Harbour in the Bahamas. His poems, largely formal, have been published in *Ambit, Allegro, Lighten-Up Online, Snakeskin, The HyperTexts*, and dozens of other magazines. His poem 'For Eliza' (his wife) won The Lyric's Leslie Mellichamp Prize. He is the Series Editor of Potcake Chapbooks of formal poetry.

Beth Houston has taught at ten universities and colleges in California and Florida. In addition to books, her publications include over two hundred poems in dozens of journals such as *Yale Review, California Quarterly, Massachusetts Review, Chicago Review, New York Quarterly, Blue Unicorn*, and *The Road Not Taken*, and in anthologies including the *Able Muse Anthology* and *Drive, They Said: Poems About Americans and Their Cars*. *The Literary Review* featured her poetry on Web Del Sol, and in 1999 she was the first featured poet at *Able Muse*.

B. Fulton Jennes is Poet Laureate of Ridgefield, Connecticut, and also serves as poet-in-residence for the Aldrich Contemporary Art Museum. Her poems have appeared *The Comstock Review, Tupelo Quarterly, Tar River Poetry, Stone Canoe, The Vassar Review, Ekphrastic Review, Connecticut River Journal, ArtAscent, Naugatuck River Journal, Frost Meadow Review*, and other publications. She received a first place in the Writer's Digest Annual Competition in the rhyming poetry category.

Jean L. Kreiling is the author of two poetry collections, *Arts & Letters & Love* (2018) and *The Truth in Dissonance* (2014). Her work appears widely in print and online journals; it has been honored with the Able Muse Write Prize, the Great Lakes Commonwealth of Letters Sonnet Award, the Kelsay Books Metrical Poetry Award, a Laureates' Prize in the Maria W. Faust Sonnet Contest, three New England Poetry Club prizes, and the *String Poet* Prize.

Barbara Loots is a retired writer, editor, and manager at Hallmark Cards. Her poetry has appeared in journals such as *The Lyric, Blue Unicorn, New Letters, Measure, Cricket, Mezzo Cammin,* and *The Ekphrastic Review,* and in anthologies, including *The Muse Strikes Back, Landscapes With Women,* and *Love Affairs at the Villa Nelle.* She received a Laureate's Choice Award in the Maria W. Faust Sonnet Contest and First Prize in the *Better Than Starbucks* Sonnet Contest. Her poetry collections are *Road Trip* (2014), *Windshift* (2018), and *The Beekeeper and other love poems* (2020).

Duncan Gillies MacLaurin was born in Glasgow in 1962. He attended boarding schools in Perthshire from the ages of eight to eighteen. He started reading Classics at Oxford University but left without a degree. In 1986, he met the Danish writer Ann Bilde in Italy, and they have been a couple ever since. Settling in Denmark, he took degrees in English and Latin and has taught these subjects at gymnasiet (high-school level) since 1995. His collection of sonnets is *I Sing the Sonnet* (2017).

Eric Meub is the Director of Design for a global engineering and architecture firm and has won awards for architectural design. He is a graduate of the University of California at Berkeley and the Harvard University Graduate School of Design. A native of the San Francisco Bay Area, Eric currently works in Los Angeles and lives in Pasadena. His poetry is often inspired by portraits drawn by his dearest friend Susan.

JD Michael (Jennifer Davis Michael) is a professor of English at the University of the South in Sewanee, Tennessee. Her poem "Forty Trochees" won the Frost Farm Prize for Metrical Poetry in 2020. She is the author of two chapbooks from Finishing Line Press: *Let Me Let Go* (2020) and *Dubious Breath.* Other poems have appeared in *Southern Poetry Review, Raintown Review, Think,* and elsewhere.

Born in Hollywood, **Leslie Monsour** was raised in Mexico City, Chicago, and Panama. She has taught poetry in Los Angeles public schools and at U.C.L.A. Extension. She serves as a mentor for PEN and presents seminars and master classes at universities and institutions. The author of two poetry collections, Monsour's poems, essays, and translations have appeared in dozens of publications. She is a recipient of a Fellowship in Literature from The National Endowment for the Arts.

Chris O'Carroll is a *Light* magazine featured poet and author of *The Joke's on Me.* His poems also appear in *Love Affairs at the Villa Nelle, New York City Haiku, Poems for a Liminal Age,* and *The Great American Wise Ass Poetry Anthology.*

Alexander Pepple is an electrical and software engineer. His poetry, fiction, and essays have appeared in *Euphony, Snakeskin, Ecclectica, Light, Chronicles, Per Contra, Think, River Styx, Barrow Street, American Arts Quarterly, Measure,* and elsewhere. He founded and edits *Able Muse* and its related presses, and directs its related *Eratosphere* online literary workshop. He edited the *Able Muse Anthology* (2010)

Kyle Potvin's chapbook, *Sound Travels on Water,* won the Jean Pedrick Chapbook Award. Her poems have appeared in *Bellevue Literary Review, Whale Road Review, Tar River Poetry, Ecotone, The New York Times,* and elsewhere. Her poetry collection is *Loosen* (Hobblebush Books). Kyle lives in southern New Hampshire.

Joseph S. Salemi teaches in the Department of Classical Languages at Hunter College, C.U.N.Y. in New York City. He has authored seven books of poetry, including the epic satire *A Gallery of Ethopaths.* His scholarly articles, reviews, and critical essays have appeared in journals and online at The Society of Classical Poets and at *Expansive Poetry On-Line.* He is the editor of the poetry magazine *TRINACRIA.*

Wendy Sloan practiced labor and civil rights law. Her poetry collection is *Sunday Mornings at the Caffe Mediterraneum* (Kelsay Books). Her poems and translations have appeared in journals and in anthologies such as *The Able Muse Translation Anthology Issue, The Best of the Raintown Review, The Great American Wise Ass Poetry Anthology, Love Affairs at the Villa Nelle,* and *Poems for a Liminal Age.* She lives in New York City and co-hosts the Carmine Street Metrics poetry reading series.

Elizabeth Spencer Spragins is a poet and writer who taught in community colleges for more than a decade. Her work has been published extensively in Europe, Asia, and North America. She is the author of *The Language of Bones: American Journeys Through Bardic Verse* and *With No Bridle for the Breeze: Ungrounded Verse.*

David Stephenson lives in Detroit, MI and works as an engineer. His poems have most recently appeared in *Blue Unicorn, The Lyric, Snakeskin,* and *The Orchards.* His collection *Rhythm and Blues* (2008) won the Richard Wilbur Award and was published by the University of Evansville Press.

Tim Taylor lives in Meltham, West Yorkshire, UK. His poems have appeared in anthologies and in various magazines such as *Acumen, Orbis, Pennine Platform,* and *The Lake.* His first poetry collection is *Sea Without a Shore* (Maytree Press, 2019), and he has published two novels.

Gail White is a formalist poet living on Bayou Teche, Louisiana. She is a contributing editor of *Light* and has had work in *Alabama Literary Review, Atlanta Review, Measure,* and other journals, as well as the anthologies *Villanelles; Killer Verse; Love Poems at the Villa Nelle;* and *Nasty Women Poets.* She co-edited *The Muse Strikes Back* and edited the anthologies *Landscapes With Women* and *Kiss and Part.* Her most recent book, *Asperity Street,* was a special honoree of the 2014 Able Muse Book Award. Her latest chapbook is *Catechism.* She won the Howard Nemerov Sonnet Award in 2012 and 2013 and was the competition judge in 2015. Loves cats.

Debra Wierenga holds an MFA from Bennington College. Her poems have appeared in *The Hudson Review, Poet Lore, The London Review, Measure, The Literary Review,* and other journals. Her chapbook is *Marriage and Other Infidelities.* She lives in Michigan.

ACKNOWLEDGMENTS

In Praise of Discipline, *The HyperTexts*; The Thing's Impossible. *Ploughshares*; To My Children Reading My Poetry After I'm Gone, *The Powow River Poets Anthology II*; Supernova, *Lines of Flight*; Stars, *The Lyric*; Ex Nihilo, *Angle Poetry Journal*; Cave Painter, *Avatar Review*; Shots, *Trinacria*; Docent, *Road Trip*; My Novel Fetish, *Lighten Up Online*; Opera: A Ballade, *Light*; Edward Hopper's *Automat, Glad and Sorry Seasons*; Classic Hits, *Angle*; Piano, *The Lyric*; "Serenata" from Stravinsky's *Pulcinella* Suite, *Angle*; Edward Hopper's Pennsylvania Coal Town, *Pointing Home*; Tune for the Prune, *Walking in on People*; Scoffer, *Snakeskin*; In Such a Place, *Able Muse*; Fragment: Cycling Ascot Drive, *Greed: A Confession*; Summer Again, *The Rotary Dial*; Symbiosis, *The Penwood Review*; Life on the Los Angeles River, *The Orchards*; Spring Villanelle, *Snakeskin*; Autumn Villanelle, *Snakeskin*; The Ghost Nudges Me to the Cellar, *Able Muse*; Emergences, *Shit Creek Review*; Northern Spy, *The Chimaera*; Bluish Animals, *Frozen Charlotte*; Naucrate and the Partridge, *From Moonrise till Dawn*; Ode to an Octopus, *Snakeskin*; Sick Cats, *Tar River Poetry*; Pandemonium, *Per Contra*; A Giraffe among Jackals, *Quantum Leap*; The Spyder, *Society of Classical Poets*; Lab Rat, *Slant*; Voyager 2, *Slant*; Road Trip, *Mezzo Cammin*; Dry Dock, *Möbius*; Old Sailors, *Snakeskin*; Water of Holme, *Pennine Platform*; Bags of Time, *The Chimaera*; On Sören Jessen's Sand, *Quantum Leap*; The Salisbury Crags, *Frostwriting*; Once and Future Kings, *Slant*; Used, *Beekeeper and Other Love Poems*; Super Cooper, *Lighten Up Online*; Late-Fifties Lament, *Trinacria*; Dare, *Counter-Currents*; For Lady Macbeth, in the 21st Century, *The Orchards Poetry Journal*; Heart of Darkness, *Society of Classical Poets*; Curse of the Canyon, *Parabnormal Magazine*; They're Here to Protect You (from the Bogeyman), *The Lyric*; Ballade of the Common Lot, Light Quarterly; Bird in the Hand, *Walking in on People*; Leaf Blower, *Angle Journal*; Snow Globe, *The Lyric*; Déjà Blue, *Walking in on People*; Casual Chic, *With My Head Rising...*; Contraband, *Mezzo Cammin*; The Long Engagement, *Blue Unicorn*; Thank You For Your Service, *Beekeeper and other love poems*; The Ossuary at Verdun, *Formal Complaints*; Sibling Revelry, *Iambs & Trochees*; Sisterly Advice, *Masquerade*; Two Sisters, *Umbrella Journal*; Framed, Smiling, *The Laurel Review*; Tenants, *The Orchards Poetry Journal* Just a Rondeau for Cassandra, *The Orchards Poetry Journal*; The Peach Tree, *The Alarming Beauty of the Sky*; Grandmother's Garage, *13th Moon*; To Myself in Fifty Years Time, *Snakeskin*; Cornfields, *The Lyric*; I'm Far from Young Enough, *The Society of Classical Poets Journal*; Circadian Lament, Sung to a Wakeful Baby, *Tilt-a-Whirl*; New Parent at a Party, *Walking in on People*; Nightjar, *Calamaro*; In the Next Cubicle, *Lagniappe*; Neighbors and Strangers, *Tar River Poetry*; Far into the Lives of Other Folk, *Pointing Home*; Acrobats, *The Lamp-Post*; March 2, 2020,

Mezzo Cammin; Song of the BraBall, *Walking in on People*; Mirror, Mirror, *Lighten Up Online;* Clean or Unclean, *Quadrant;* Otology, *Third Wednesday*; Communion of Saints, *Alabama Literary Review*; Hypochondriac's Song, *Walking in on People*; Bird Aubade, *Autumn Sky Poetry Daily*; A Proposal, *Tilling the Land*; To My Latest Femme Fatale, *The Pennsylvania Review*; Frozen Charlotte, *Frozen Charlotte*; The Ship of Theseus, *The Frangible Hour*; Pantoum for a Disappearing Pair, *Angle;* Lacrimae rerum, *Arion;* The Fly, *The Oldie*; The Overview, *Love Poems at the Villa Nelle;* Ballade of Inevitable Extinction, *Tilt-A-Whirl;* Julian of Norwich in Seclusion, *First Things*; Clair de Lune, *Greed: A Confession*; Bald Cypress In Ontario, *I-70 Review*; Storm Warning, *Trinacria*; Ballad of the Vernal Equinox, *Lines of Flight*; Eternal Autumn, *Paterson Literary Review*; September, *Blue Unicorn*; The Lilacs on Good Friday, *Formal Complaints*; A View from the Foothills, *The Rotary Dial*; Prayer for a Certain Kind of Rain, *Think*; To-Do, *Mezzo Cammin*; Deserted Cemetery, *Better Than Starbucks;* At the Burial of an Abbess, *Asperity Street*; A Timeless Villanelle, *Society of Classical Poets*

Beth Houston, MFA, has taught creative writing, literature, and composition at ten universities and colleges in California and Florida, has worked as a writer and editor, and has conducted numerous creative writing workshops. Her publications include books of poetry, fiction, and nonfiction, and over two hundred poems in dozens of journals such as *Yale Review, Feminist Studies, California Quarterly, Massachusetts Review, Chicago Review, New York Quarterly, Blue Unicorn, American Literary Review, South Carolina Review, The Florida Review, 13th Moon,* and *The Road Not Taken,* as well as anthologies including the *Able Muse Anthology* and *Drive, They Said: Poems About Americans and Their Cars. The Literary Review* featured her poetry on Web Del Sol, and she was the first featured poet at *Able Muse.* She is editor of Rhizome Press, which most recently published *Extreme Sonnets.*

Made in the USA
Columbia, SC
27 September 2021

46298946R00124